OECD ENVIRONMENTAL DATA

DONNÉES OCDE SUR L'ENVIRONNEMENT

COMPENDIUM 1995

ORGANISATION FOR ECONOMIC CO-OPERATION AND DEVELOPMENT
ORGANISATION DE COOPÉRATION ET DE DÉVELOPPEMENT ÉCONOMIQUES

ORGANISATION FOR ECONOMIC CO-OPERATION AND DEVELOPMENT

ORGANISATION DE COOPÉRATION ET DE DÉVELOPPEMENT ÉCONOMIQUES

Pursuant to Article 1 of the Convention signed in Paris on 14th December 1960, and which came into force on 30th September 1961, the Organisation for Economic Co-operation and Development (OECD) shall promote policies designed:

— to achieve the highest sustainable economic growth and employment and a rising standard of living in Member countries, while maintaining financial stability, and thus to contribute to the development of the world economy;

— to contribute to sound economic expansion in Member as well as non-member countries in the process of economic development; and

— to contribute to the expansion of world trade on a multilateral, non-discriminatory basis in accordance with international obligations.

The original Member countries of the OECD are Austria, Belgium, Canada, Denmark, France, Germany, Greece, Iceland, Ireland, Italy, Luxembourg, the Netherlands, Norway, Portugal, Spain, Sweden, Switzerland, Turkey, the United Kingdom and the United States. The following countries became Members subsequently through accession at the dates indicated hereafter: Japan (28th April 1964), Finland (28th January 1969), Australia (7th June 1971), New Zealand (29th May 1973) and Mexico (18th May 1994). The Commission of the European Communities takes part in the work of the OECD (Article 13 of the OECD Convention).

En vertu de l'article 1ᵉʳ de la Convention signée le 14 décembre 1960, à Paris, et entrée en vigueur le 30 septembre 1961, l'Organisation de Coopération et de Développement Économiques (OCDE) a pour objectif de promouvoir des politiques visant :

— à réaliser la plus forte expansion de l'économie et de l'emploi et une progression du niveau de vie dans les pays Membres, tout en maintenant la stabilité financière, et à contribuer ainsi au développement de l'économie mondiale ;

— à contribuer à une saine expansion économique dans les pays Membres, ainsi que les pays non membres, en voie de développement économique ;

— à contribuer à l'expansion du commerce mondial sur une base multilatérale et non discriminatoire conformément aux obligations internationales.

Les pays Membres originaires de l'OCDE sont : l'Allemagne, l'Autriche, la Belgique, le Canada, le Danemark, l'Espagne, les États-Unis, la France, la Grèce, l'Irlande, l'Islande, l'Italie, le Luxembourg, la Norvège, les Pays-Bas, le Portugal, le Royaume-Uni, la Suède, la Suisse et la Turquie. Les pays suivants sont ultérieurement devenus Membres par adhésion aux dates indiquées ci-après : le Japon (28 avril 1964), la Finlande (28 janvier 1969), l'Australie (7 juin 1971), la Nouvelle-Zélande (29 mai 1973) et le Mexique (18 mai 1994). La Commission des Communautés européennes participe aux travaux de l'OCDE (article 13 de la Convention de l'OCDE).

FOREWORD

The Organisation for Economic Co-operation and Development, in carrying out its task of promoting economic development in Member countries, is concerned with the qualitative and quantitative aspects of economic growth. The OECD's programme of work relating to environmental matters emphasises the importance of sustainable development.

In the Recommendations adopted on 31 January 1991 by the OECD Council, and approved by Environment Ministers, Member country governments agreed to ensure the development of objective, reliable and comparable environmental statistics and information at international level. The OECD Environmental Data Compendium, published every two years, responds to this objective.

The Group on the State of the Environment contributed, with data and expert advice, to the elaboration of the present document, which is published on the responsibility of the Secretary-General of the OECD.

AVANT - PROPOS

L'Organisation de Coopération et de Développement Économiques, dans son effort pour promouvoir le développement économique des pays Membres, se préoccupe à la fois des aspects qualitatifs et quantitatifs de la croissance économique. Le programme de travail de l'OCDE concernant l'environnement met l'accent sur l'importance du développement durable.

Dans la Recommandation adoptée le 31 janvier 1991 par le Conseil de l'OCDE et approuvée par les ministres de l'Environnement, les gouvernements des États Membres ont convenu d'assurer l'obtention au niveau international, d'informations et de statistiques objectives, fiables et comparables sur l'environnement. Le Compendium OCDE de données sur l'environnement, publié tous les deux ans, répond à cet objectif.

Le Groupe sur l'État de l'environnement a contribué, au moyen de données, de son expertise et de ses conseils, à l'élaboration de ce document qui est publié sous la responsabilité du Secrétaire général de l'OCDE.

TABLE OF CONTENTS

TABLE DES MATIÈRES

1. Introduction

1. Introduction

PART I. THE STATE OF THE ENVIRONMENT

2. Air
3. Inland Waters
4. Land
5. Forest
6. Wildlife
7. Waste

PARTIE I. L'ÉTAT DE L'ENVIRONNEMENT

2. Air
3. Eaux intérieures
4. Sols
5. Forêts
6. Faune et flore
7. Déchets

PART II. PRESSURES ON THE ENVIRONMENT

8. Energy
9. Transport
10. Industry
11. Agriculture

PARTIE II. LES PRESSIONS SUR L'ENVIRONNEMENT

8. Énergie
9. Transports
10. Industrie
11. Agriculture

PART III. MANAGING THE ENVIRONMENT

12. General Data

PARTIE III. GÉRER L'ENVIRONNEMENT

12. Données générales

Annex 1 : References
Annex 2 : Abbreviations

Annexe 1 : Références
Annexe 2 : Abréviations

List of the Members of the Group on the State of the Environment

Liste des Membres du Groupe sur l'État de l'Environnement

INTRODUCTION

I Background

Environmental information and reporting are important activities of the governments of OECD Member countries. They are a way of responding to public demands for environmental information, and they assist in the implementation, development and harmonisation of environmental policies. They also help to incorporate environmental concerns in decision making, to promote sustainable development at national and international level and to evaluate national environmental performances.

On the occasion of the ministerial meeting of the OECD Environment Committee held in Paris in 1991, the governments of the Member countries agreed to ensure through appropriate co-ordination the development of objective, reliable and comparable environmental statistics and information at international level.

II The Compendium

The Compendium of Environmental Data is a regular OECD publication that appears every two years. It aims at presenting the best internationally available data in the environment and related areas. The Compendium has been published since 1985.

The 1995 Compendium includes updated, revised and new data and has an expanded geographical coverage. It supplements other OECD work on environmental indicators and the OECD environmental performance reviews.

III Data

Most of the information included in this Compendium consists of data collected by means of the joint OECD/Eurostat questionnaire, initially developed by the OECD Group on the State of the Environment. This questionnaire was revised in 1990/91 within the framework of joint OECD/Eurostat meetings with the participation of the UN Economic Commission for Europe in Geneva.

In executing the task of data collection and treatment, the co-operation of statistical services and administrations within Member countries has been invaluable and this Compendium would not exist without it. Our sincere thanks are therefore extended to all concerned. Supplementary data have been drawn from international sources, within the OECD itself and other international organisations. Data received up to 30 June 1995 were taken into account.

No attempt has been made to suggest interpretations in presenting the data. This is a deliberate choice. The data take on their full meaning only when interpreted by readers familiar with the subject.

Generally, data relating to the environment are relatively recent. Therefore, definitions and classifications used, difficulties of comparability and gaps in information are indicated whenever necessary in the introductions to the various sections of the Compendium and in texts and notes attached to tables.

IV   Geographical Coverage

Data presented in this publication cover OECD Member countries and those central and eastern European countries co-operating with the OECD through the Partners in Transition (PIT) Programme. Where possible, regional and world totals are displayed in tables.

The Member countries of the OECD are Canada, Mexico, the United States, Japan, Australia, New Zealand, Austria, Belgium, Denmark, Finland, France, Germany, Greece, Iceland, Ireland, Italy, Luxembourg, the Netherlands, Norway, Portugal, Spain, Sweden, Switzerland, Turkey and the United Kingdom. The Commission of the European Communities also takes part in the work of the OECD.

"Germany" refers to the country after unification — i.e. it includes eastern and western Germany. Where possible, regional totals (OECD Europe, European Union, OECD) have been calculated with Germany as a whole. Totals including western Germany only are marked with an asterisk. Totals excluding Mexico are marked with two asterisks.

The countries in the PIT Programme are the Czech Republic, Hungary, Poland and the Slovak Republic. As most of the data in the Compendium relate to years before 1993, an effort has been made to show figures both for the Czech Republic and Slovak Republic and for the former ČSFR.

V   Compendium Organisation

Figure 1 presents the conceptual framework within which the OECD core set of environmental data is organised.

Sections 2 to 7 of this Compendium relate to the state of the environment itself, including direct pressures on the environment (i.e. emissions of pollutants, use of water resources), and sections 8 to 11 relate to activities generating pressures on the environment: energy, transport, industry, agriculture. The last part includes general information and a list of international Conventions concerning the environment.

Figure 1

Framework of the OECD core set of environmental data

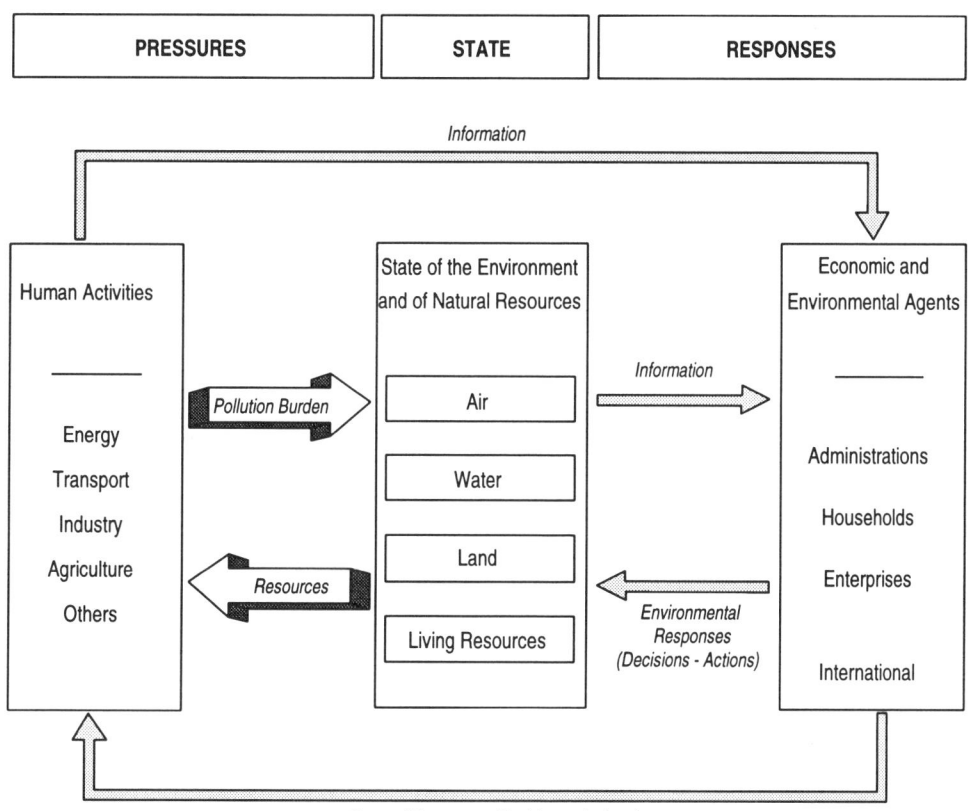

INTRODUCTION

I   Le contexte

Faire rapport sur l'état de l'environnement et produire des informations sur l'environnement sont des activités importantes des gouvernements des pays Membres de l'OCDE. C'est une façon de répondre aux demandes d'information sur l'environnement qui émanent du public et d'aider à mettre en oeuvre, à élaborer et à harmoniser les politiques d'environnement. Cela aide aussi à intégrer les préoccupations relatives à l'environnement dans la prise de décision, à promouvoir le développement durable aux niveaux national et international, et à évaluer les performances environnementales des pays.

Les Gouvernements des pays Membres ont convenu à l'occasion de la réunion ministérielle du Comité de l'Environnement de l'OCDE à Paris en 1991 d'assurer par une coordination appropriée l'obtention, au niveau international, d'informations et de statistiques sur l'environnement qui soient objectives, fiables et comparables.

II   Le compendium

Le compendium de données sur l'environnement est une publication régulière de l'OCDE qui paraît tous les deux ans. Elle vise à présenter les meilleures données de base disponibles au niveau international en matière d'environnement et de sujets connexes. Le compendium est publié depuis 1985.

Le compendium 1995 inclut des données mises à jour, révisées et nouvelles, et couvre un champ géographique plus large. Il complète d'autres travaux de l'OCDE sur les indicateurs d'environnement et les examens des performances environnementales.

III   Les données

La plus large part des informations contenues dans ce compendium sont des données recueillies au moyen du questionnaire conjoint OCDE/Eurostat, initialement élaboré par le Groupe de l'OCDE sur l'État de l'Environnement. Ce questionnaire a été révisé en 1990/1991 dans le cadre de réunions conjointes OCDE, Eurostat, avec la participation de la Commission Economique pour l'Europe des Nations Unies de Genève.

Dans l'effort de collecte et de traitement des données, la coopération des services statistiques et des administrations concernés des pays Membres a été précieuse et sans elle ce compendium n'existerait pas. Qu'ils soient sincèrement remerciés ici. Des données complémentaires ont été collectées de sources internationales, de l'OCDE même, et d'autres organisations internationales. Les chiffres ont été pris en compte jusqu'au 30 juin 1995.

Les données sont présentées sans interprétation. Cela est délibéré. Elles prennent tout leur sens lorsqu'elles sont interprétées par des utilisateurs habitués à ces sujets.

En général, les données concernant l'environnement sont relativement récentes. Aussi, les définitions et classifications utilisées, les difficultés de comparabilité et les lacunes sont-elles mentionnées quand cela est nécessaire dans les introductions aux diverses sections du compendium, et les textes et notes accompagnant les tableaux.

IV   Couverture géographique

Les données présentées dans cette publication couvrent les pays Membres de l'OCDE et les pays de l'Europe centrale et orientale qui coopèrent avec l'OCDE dans le cadre du programme "Partenaires pour la transition". Le monde et les régions du monde sont présentés à chaque fois que cela est possible.

Les pays Membres de l'OCDE sont le Canada, le Mexique, les États-Unis, le Japon, l'Australie, la Nouvelle-Zélande, l'Autriche, la Belgique, le Danemark, la Finlande, la France, l'Allemagne, la Grèce, l'Islande, l'Irlande, l'Italie, le Luxembourg, les Pays-Bas, la Norvège, le Portugal, l'Espagne, la Suède, la Suisse, la Turquie et le Royaume-Uni. La Commission des Communautés Européennes participe aussi aux travaux de l'OCDE.

Le terme "Allemagne" concerne ici le pays après la réunification, c.à.d. la partie occidentale et la partie orientale. Dans les tableaux le calcul des totaux régionaux (OCDE Europe, Union Européenne, et OCDE) prend en compte l'Allemagne dans son ensemble à chaque fois que cela est possible. Les totaux qui incluent l'Allemagne occidentale seulement sont marqués d'un astérisque. Les totaux qui excluent le Mexique sont marqués de deux astérisques.

Les pays participant au programme "Partenaires pour la transition" sont la Hongrie, la Pologne, la République Slovaque et la République Tchèque. Comme les données présentées dans le compendium couvrent les années avant 1993, un effort a été fait afin d'inclure à la fois les chiffres pour la République Slovaque, la République Tchèque et l'ex-République Fédérative Tchèque et Slovaque (RFTS).

V   Organisation du compendium

La figure 1 présente le cadre conceptuel selon lequel est organisé le corps central de données de l'OCDE sur l'environnement.

Les sections 2 à 7 du compendium concernent l'état de l'environnement lui-même, y compris les pressions directes qui s'excercent sur lui (p. ex. émissions de polluants, utilisation des ressources en eau) et les sections 8 à 11 concernent des activités générant des pressions sur l'environnement : le secteur de l'énergie, les transports, l'industrie, l'agriculture. La dernière partie comprend des données générales et une liste des conventions internationale concernant l'environnement.

Figure 1

Structure du corps central de l'OCDE de données sur l'environnement

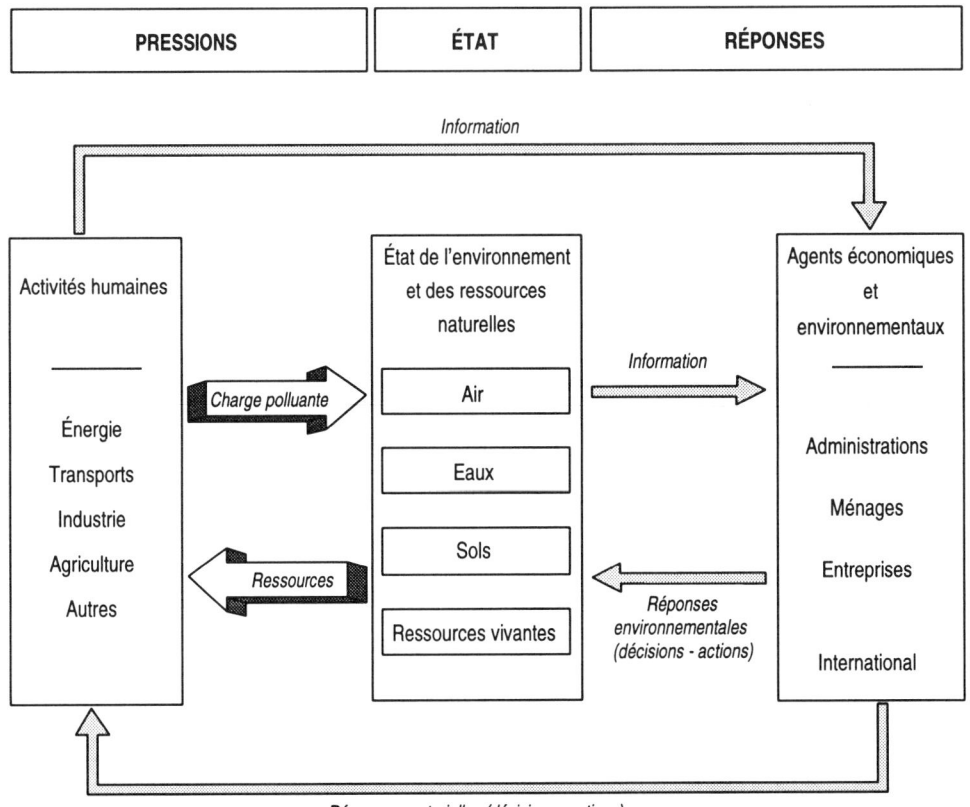

2. AIR

2. AIR

INTRODUCTION

This section contains quantitative information regarding air as a natural resource, emission estimates of various air pollutants and concentration data describing ambient air quality.

The tables provide selected information on:

a) traditional air pollutants:

> ▸ emission data are based upon the best available engineering estimates for a given period; they concern man-made emissions of sulphur oxides (SO_x), particulate matter (Part.), nitrogen oxides (NO_x), carbon monoxide (CO) and volatile organic compounds (VOC);

> ▸ ambient levels represent measured concentrations; they concern sulphur dioxide (SO_2), nitrogen dioxide (NO_2) and suspended particulates;

b) international and global air pollution:

> ▸ acid precipitation;
> ▸ carbon dioxide (CO_2) and other greenhouse gases (e.g. methane, CFCs).

The share of human activities as a source in global emissions of traditional air pollutants varies depending on the type of pollutant; most SO_x emissions are man-made whereas CO and NO_x emissions are mainly of natural origin.

Several important environmental concerns related to ambient air quality are not covered, such as pollution by toxic metals, organic compounds and fibres. International conventions related to air pollution are presented in the section on general data.

INTRODUCTION

La présente section contient des informations quantitatives concernant l'atmosphère en tant que ressource naturelle, des estimations sur les émissions de différents polluants atmosphériques et des données sur leurs niveaux de concentration respectifs permettant de donner une description de la qualité de l'air ambiant.

Les tableaux présentent des informations sélectionnées sur :

a) les polluants atmosphériques traditionnels :

   ▸ les données relatives aux émissions sont basées sur les meilleures estimations d'ingénieur disponibles pour une période de temps donnée ; elles concernent les émissions anthropiques d'oxydes de soufre (SO_x), de particules (Part.), d'oxydes d'azote (NO_x), de monoxyde de carbone (CO) et de composés organiques volatils (COV) ;

   ▸ les données relatives à la qualité de l'air ambiant sont des concentrations mesurées ; elles concernent le dioxyde de soufre (SO_2), le dioxyde d'azote (NO_2) et les particules en suspension ;

b) la pollution atmosphérique à l'échelle internationale et globale :

   ▸ les précipitations acides ;
   ▸ le dioxyde de carbone (CO_2) et d'autres gaz à effet de serre (p.ex. méthane, CFCs).

La part que prennent les activités humaines dans l'émission globale des polluants classiques est plus ou moins grande suivant le type de polluant ; la presque totalité des émissions de SO_x est d'origine anthropique alors que pour le CO et les NO_x les sources sont principalement naturelles.

Certains sujets de préoccupation importants relatifs à l'air ambiant ne sont pas abordés, tels que la pollution par des éléments toxiques, comme les métaux, les composés organiques et les fibres. Les conventions internationales, concernant la pollution de l'air sont présentées dans la section sur les données générales.

The following table shows total man-made emissions of traditional air pollutants for the most recent year available: SO_x and NO_x (given as quantities of SO_2 and NO_2), CO, particulates and VOCs.

Traditional air pollutants play a major role in local and regional air pollution and affect human health and the environment more generally.

The reader should note that the definitions of sources as well as the measurement methods may vary from country to country. Caution should be exercised when interpreting this table. Attention should also be given to the footnotes of related tables on air emission trends by source.

Le tableau suivant montre les émissions totales dues aux activités humaines de SO_x et de NO_x (exprimées en quantités de SO_2 et de NO_2), CO, particules et COV.

Les polluants atmosphériques traditionnels jouent un rôle important dans la pollution de l'air locale et régionale et affectent la santé humaine et l'environnement en général.

Le lecteur devra noter que les définitions des sources de pollution ainsi que les méthodes de mesure peuvent varier d'un pays à l'autre. Il convient d'être prudent dans l'interprétation de ce tableau et de tenir compte des notes associées aux tableaux sur l'évolution des émissions atmosphériques par source.

TOTAL EMISSIONS OF TRADITIONAL AIR POLLUTANTS, early 1990s (a)
ÉMISSIONS TOTALES DE POLLUANTS TRADITIONNELS, début des années 90 (a)

1000 tonnes

		Sulphur oxides/ Oxydes de soufre (SOx)	Nitrogen Oxides/ Oxydes d'azote (NOx)	Carbon Monoxide/ Monoxyde de carbone (CO)	Particulates/ Particules	Volatile Organic Compounds/ Composés organiques volatils (b)
Canada	*	3030	1939	10781	1855	2014
Mexico/Mexique	*	1100	462	234	354	231
USA/Etats-Unis		19518	21072	83960	7080	20287
Japan/Japon	*	876	1476	2320	177	..
Australia/Australie	*	93	279	2454	..	582
New Zealand/Nouvelle Zélande		..	146	..	..	..
Austria/Autriche		71	182	1326	38	388
Belgium/Belgique	*	420	300	272	..	139
Denmark/Danemark	*	158	267	695	..	95
Finland/Finlande		139	268	556	..	209
France		1221	1519	9759	228	2286
Germany/Allemagne		3896	2904	9245	1336	2765
w.Germany/Allemagne occ.		875	2426	6577	430	2073
Greece/Grèce		510	338	1480	..	243
Iceland/Islande	*	9	23	30	..	7
Ireland/Irlande		187	128	454	105	97
Italy/Italie		1682	2041	9268	524	2396
Luxembourg	*	10	22	..	..	20
Netherlands/Pays-Bas	*	164	545	899	52	411
Norway/Norvège		36	229	805	21	284
Portugal	*	286	216	1086	..	207
Spain/Espagne	*	2205	1247	4950	33	1118
Sweden/Suède	*	101	399	1500	..	502
Switzerland/Suisse	*	58	150	358	20	263
Turkey/Turquie	*	750	512	..	..	..
UK/Royaume-Uni		3188	2347	5641	444	2338
Czech Rep./Rép. Tchèque		1538	698	1045	501	205
Slovak Rep./Rép. Slovaque		374	224	313	226	107
Hungary/Hongrie		827	183	836	160	136
Poland/Pologne		2725	1120	2109	1517	777
North America/Amérique du Nord	*	24000	24000	94200	..	..
OECD/OCDE Europe	*	15900	13600	49700	..	..
EU/UE 15	*	14200	12700	47500	..	..
OECD/OCDE	*	42000	39500	149200	..	..

Notes:
a) Man-made emissions. Data refer to 1993 or to the most recent year from 1990 on, except as noted. For detailed footnotes, please refer to the tables on air emission trends by source.
b) Emissions of non methane VOCs.
CAN) CO: 1985 data. VOC: total VOCs.
MEX) Partial data. SOx: power stations only. Other: stationary sources only.
JAP) SOx, Part.: 1989 data. CO: road transport only.
AUS) 1985 data. National estimates based on capital city figures.
BEL) CO, VOC: Wallon region only.
DNK) VOC: mobile sources only.
ISL) CO: excludes industrial processes.
LUX) NOX, VOC: 1985 data. VOC: total VOCs.
NLD) VOC: includes CH4 from fuel combustion.
PRT) VOC: 1989 data.
SPA) Part.: Road transport only.
SWE) CO: Secretariat estimate for 1988. VOC: total VOCs.
CHE) VOC: total VOCs.
TUR) SOx: partial data; stationary sources only.
TOT) Rounded figures; include Secretariat estimates.

Notes:
a) Emissions anthropiques. 1993 ou la dernière année disponible depuis 1990, sauf indication contraire. Pour les notes détaillées, veuillez consulter les tableaux sur l'évolution des émissions atmosphériques par source.
b) Emissions de COV autres que le méthane.
CAN) CO: données 1985. COV: COV totaux.
MEX) Données partielles. SOx: centrales électriques uniquement. Autres polluants: sources fixes uniquement.
JAP) SOx, Part.: données 1989. CO: transports routiers uniquement.
AUS) Données 1985. Estimations nationales fondées sur des chiffres pour la capitale.
BEL) CO, COV: Wallonie uniquement.
DNK) COV: sources mobiles seulement.
ISL) CO: exclut les procédés industriels.
LUX) NOx, COV: données 1985. COV: COV totaux.
NLD) COV: incluent le CH4 issu des combustions.
PRT) COV: données 1989.
SPA) Part.: transports routiers seulement.
SWE) CO: estimation du Secrétariat pour 1988. COV: COV totaux.
CHE) COV: COV totaux.
TUR) SOx: données partielles; sources fixes uniquement.
TOT) Chiffres arrondis; incluent des estimations du Secrétariat.

Source: OECD/OCDE

The following tables provide information on trends in man-made emissions of SO_x and NO_x (given as quantities of SO_2 and NO_2) for selected countries. The figures refer to the major categories of emission sources for these pollutants: mobile sources (motor vehicles, etc.) and stationary sources, which include power stations, fuel combustion (industrial, domestic, etc.); and industrial processes (pollutants emitted in manufacturing). Total emissions also include such miscellaneous sources as waste incineration and agricultural burning.

Sulphur oxides exert a pressure on human health; they also contribute to acid deposition and thus have negative effects on aquatic ecosystems and buildings and may have negative effects on crops and forests.

Man-made NO_x emissions mainly stem from the burning of fossil fuels at high temperatures. Nitrogen oxides play an important role in the production of photochemical oxidants and of smog, and contribute, together with SO_x, to acid precipitation. They are of concern because of their negative effects both on human health and on the environment.

The reader should note that the definitions of sources as well as the measurement methods may vary from country to country. When interpreting these tables, attention should also be given to the footnotes.

Les tableaux suivants montrent l'évolution des émissions de SO_x et de NO_x dues aux activités humaines (exprimées en quantités de SO_2 et de NO_2), pour des pays sélectionnés. Les données portent sur les grandes catégories d'émetteurs de ces polluants : sources mobiles (véhicules à moteur, etc.), et sources fixes qui comprennent les centrales de production d'énergie, l'utilisation de combustibles (industrie, ménages, etc.), et les procédés industriels (émissions liées à la fabrication de produits à partir de matières premières). Les émissions totales incluent également d'autres sources telles que l'incinération des déchets et les brûlis agricoles.

Les oxydes de soufre mettent en danger la santé humaine, participent aux dépôts acides et ont ainsi des effets néfastes sur les écosystèmes aquatiques et les bâtiments. Ils peuvent également avoir des effets négatifs sur les cultures et les forêts.

Les émissions de NO_x par les activités humaines proviennent principalement de la combustion à haute température de combustibles fossiles. Les oxydes d'azote jouent un rôle important dans la formation d'oxydants photochimiques et de smog et contribuent ensemble avec les SO_x aux précipitations acides. Ils sont préoccupants en raison de leurs effets néfastes pour la santé des hommes et pour l'environnement.

Le lecteur devra noter que les définitions des sources de pollution ainsi que les méthodes de mesure peuvent varier d'un pays à l'autre. Dans l'interprétation de ces tableaux, il convient de tenir compte des notes en bas de page.

EMISSIONS OF SOx, by source, 1980-1993
ÉMISSIONS DE SOx, par source, 1980-1993

1 000 tonnes

	1980	1981	1982	1983	1984	1985	1986	1987	1988	1989	1990	1991	1992	1993
Canada *														
Mobile s./S. mobiles	137	123	118	120	116	95	95	95	95	95	95	95	..	..
Road/Routier	..	..	..	..	..	..	..	..	..	..	..	..	..	..
Other/Autres	..	..	..	..	..	..	..	..	..	..	..	..	..	..
Stationary s./S. fixes	4506	4168	3494	3505	3839	3597	3532	3667	3743	3600	3228	3211	..	..
Power st./C. éléctr.	768	790	849	821	870	736	755	810	814	824	677	641	..	..
Combustion	608	485	426	349	312	300	300	300	300	300	300	300	..	..
Industrial/Industrielle	..	..	..	..	..	..	..	..	..	..	..	..	..	..
Other/Autres	..	..	..	..	..	..	..	..	..	..	..	..	..	..
Ind. proc./Proc. ind.	3127	2890	2216	2332	2654	2561	2477	2557	2629	2476	2251	2270	..	..
Miscellaneous/Divers	3	3	3	3	3	2	..	4	..	..	..	..	..	..
Total	4643	4291	3612	3625	3955	3692	3627	3762	3838	3695	3323	3306	3030	..
USA/Etats-Unis *														
Mobile s./S. mobiles	897	895	834	793	825	842	715	812	862	874	915	947	958	721
Road/Routier	415	447	441	438	460	521	510	595	632	638	674	698	712	469
Other/Autres	482	448	392	354	365	320	205	218	230	235	241	248	245	252
Stationary s./S. fixes	22882	21617	20378	19826	20642	20377	19676	19707	20086	20169	19786	19713	19664	18797
Power st./C. éléctr.	15861	14681	14216	14017	14536	14736	14244	14256	14506	14713	14398	14319	14371	13781
Combustion	3558	3370	3310	2923	3130	3399	3381	3384	3421	3364	3360	3400	3337	3213
Industrial/Industrielle	2677	2618	2533	2289	2470	2875	2827	2783	2822	2799	2818	2848	2803	2669
Other/Autres	881	752	777	634	660	524	554	601	599	565	542	552	534	544
Ind. proc./Proc. ind.	3423	3528	2819	2854	2945	2207	2015	2031	2122	2055	1991	1957	1919	1760
Miscellaneous/Divers	40	38	33	32	31	35	36	36	37	37	37	37	37	44
Total	23779	22512	21212	20619	21467	21219	20391	20519	20948	21043	20701	20660	20622	19518
Japan/Japon *														
Mobile s./S. mobiles	..	..	..	..	..	..	..	..	..	..	..	..	..	..
Road/Routier	119	..	..	131	..	..	151	..	..	199	..	..	..	..
Other/Autres	..	..	..	..	..	..	..	..	..	..	..	..	..	..
Stationary s./S. fixes	1158	1041	957	918	854	795	684	..	..	677	718	..	..	..
Power st./C. éléctr.	347	324	290	279	238	201	173	..	..	192	..	..	..	..
Combustion	791	697	647	610	597	561	493	..	..	459	..	..	..	..
Industrial/Industrielle *	736	651	598	566	554	525	467	..	..	425	..	..	..	..
Other/Autres	55	46	49	44	43	36	26	..	..	34	..	..	..	..
Ind. proc./Proc. ind. *	..	..	..	..	..	..	..	..	..	..	..	..	..	..
Miscellaneous/Divers	20	20	20	29	19	33	18	..	..	26	..	..	..	..
Total	1277	..	..	1049	..	..	835	..	..	876	..	..	..	..
Austria/Autriche *														
Mobile s./S. mobiles	14	..	..	15	..	12	..	5	6	6	7	7	7	8
Road/Routier	14	..	..	..	..	10	..	5	5	6	6	..	7	..
Other/Autres	..	..	..	..	..	..	..	5	5	6	6	..	..	..
Stationary s./S. fixes	383	..	..	227	..	182	..	147	116	87	83	77	69	63
Power st./C. éléctr.	90	..	..	55	..	50	..	25	15	17	16	16	16	18
Combustion	235	..	..	125	..	94	..	90	80	52	53	47	51	45
Industrial/Industrielle *	168	..	..	..	..	55	..	52	50	36	47	..	35	29
Other/Autres	67	..	..	..	..	39	..	37	30	24	22	..	16	16
Ind. proc./Proc. ind. *	56	..	..	47	..	38	..	32	21	19	15	14	..	..
Miscellaneous/Divers *	1.4	..	..	..	..	..	..	..	..	..	..	..	0.5	0.4
Total	397	..	..	242	..	195	..	152	122	93	90	84	76	71
Belgium/Belgique *														
Mobile s./S. mobiles	5	..	5	..	5	5	6	6	7	5	5	5	6	..
Road/Routier	..	..	..	..	..	5	5	6	7	5	5	5	5	..
Other/Autres	..	..	..	..	..	0.50	0.51	0.48	0.47	0.28	0.31	0.41	0.31	..
Stationary s./S. fixes	176	..	142	..	118	112	101	95	94	89	89	92	88	..
Power st./C. éléctr.	83	..	65	..	42	32	23	23	22	22	22	21	18	..
Combustion	..	..	..	..	..	75	73	66	67	60	61	65	65	..
Industrial/Industrielle *	72	..	59	..	59	56	54	49	51	49	50	54	54	..
Other/Autres	21	..	18	..	17	19	20	18	16	11	11	12	11	..
Ind. proc./Proc. ind. *	..	..	..	..	..	5	4	5	5	6	5	5	5	..
Miscellaneous/Divers	..	..	..	..	..	0.18	0.18	0.22	0.23	0.24	0.43	0.44	0.43	..
Total	181	..	147	..	123	117	107	101	101	94	94	97	94	..

Notes: see page 23 / voir page 23

... / ...

EMISSIONS OF SOx, by source, 1980-1993
ÉMISSIONS DE SOx, par source, 1980-1993

1 000 tonnes

	1980	1981	1982	1983	1984	1985	1986	1987	1988	1989	1990	1991	1992	1993
Denmark/Danemark														
Mobile s./S. mobiles	21	21	24	22	24	27	22	22	21	21	19	21	16	14
Road/Routier	7	7	8	8	10	11	7	7	7	5	5	5	3	2
Other/Autres	14	14	16	14	14	16	15	15	14	16	14	16	13	12
Stationary s./S. fixes	427	341	345	290	270	312	260	228	220	170	164	222	174	144
Power st./C. éléctr.	216	155	179	137	120	167	168	150	157	127	119	175	130	100
Combustion	204	178	160	146	144	138	86	73	60	40	37	41	37	36
Industrial/Industrielle	92	78	65	63	65	61	45	38	34	24	23	26	24	24
Other/Autres	112	100	95	83	79	77	41	35	26	16	14	15	13	12
Ind. proc./Proc. ind.	7	8	6	7	6	7	6	5	3	3	8	6	7	8
Miscellaneous/Divers	..	..	..	..	..	..	..	..	..	..	..	..	..	..
Total	448	362	369	312	294	339	282	250	241	191	183	243	190	158
Finland/Finlande *														
Mobile s./S. mobiles	10	11	8	6	6	8	8	6	5	4	4	5	5	..
Road/Routier	..	..	..	..	..	..	..	..	..	..	..	3	3	..
Other/Autres	..	..	..	..	..	..	..	..	..	..	..	2	2	..
Stationary s./S. fixes	574	523	476	366	362	377	327	321	295	240	256	184	134	..
Power st./C. éléctr. *	..	..	..	..	..	..	..	..	..	..	..	56	38	..
Combustion *	330	304	286	186	192	207	175	170	146	126	157	83	55	..
Industrial/Industrielle	..	..	..	..	..	..	..	..	..	..	..	60	36	..
Other/Autres	..	..	..	..	..	..	..	..	..	..	..	23	19	..
Ind. proc./Proc. ind.	245	219	190	180	170	170	152	151	149	114	99	44	42	..
Miscellaneous/Divers	..	..	..	..	..	..	..	..	..	..	..	..	..	..
Total	584	534	484	372	368	382	331	328	302	244	260	189	139	..
France *														
Mobile s./S. mobiles	126	92	93	95	98	107	114	120	130	139	145	152	155	..
Road/Routier	..	..	..	..	..	..	..	..	..	..	..	..	..	..
Other/Autres	..	..	..	..	..	..	..	..	..	..	..	..	..	..
Stationary s./S. fixes	3222	2425	2332	1979	1717	1344	1217	1141	1016	1142	1055	1162	1066	..
Power st./C. éléctr.	1222	887	874	666	508	408	309	271	231	379	313	403	330	..
Combustion	1488	1124	1045	956	877	631	605	575	482	454	440	454	431	..
Industrial/Industrielle *	1065	805	734	655	583	369	342	334	267	267	259	256	250	..
Other/Autres	423	319	311	301	294	262	263	241	215	187	181	198	181	..
Ind. proc./Proc. ind.	302	267	258	235	218	194	190	188	191	181	179	182	182	..
Miscellaneous/Divers *	210	148	155	122	115	111	113	107	113	127	123	123	123	..
Total	3348	2517	2425	2074	1815	1451	1331	1261	1146	1281	1200	1314	1221	..
Germany/Allemagne *														
Mobile s./S. mobiles	..	..	..	..	..	..	..	..	..	..	99	88	96	..
Road/Routier	..	..	..	..	..	..	..	..	..	..	66	63	75	..
Other/Autres	..	..	..	..	..	..	..	..	..	..	33	25	21	..
Stationary s./S. fixes	..	..	..	..	..	..	..	..	..	..	5534	4342	3800	..
Power st./C. éléctr.	..	..	..	..	..	..	..	..	..	..	4060	3316	2913	..
Combustion	..	..	..	..	..	..	..	..	..	..	..	..	..	..
Industrial/Industrielle *	..	..	..	..	..	..	..	..	..	..	881	616	541	..
Other/Autres	..	..	..	..	..	..	..	..	..	..	593	410	346	..
Ind. proc./Proc. ind. *	..	..	..	..	..	..	..	..	..	..	..	..	..	..
Miscellaneous/Divers	..	..	..	..	..	..	..	..	..	..	..	..	..	..
Total	..	..	..	..	..	..	..	..	..	..	5633	4430	3896	..
w. Germany/All. occ.														
Mobile s./S. mobiles	89	87	85	85	79	68	72	71	59	56	55	54	55	..
Road/Routier	67	65	64	65	61	52	56	56	46	42	40	40	41	..
Other/Autres	22	22	21	20	18	16	16	15	13	14	15	14	14	..
Stationary s./S. fixes	3077	2923	2758	2581	2499	2301	2158	1836	1159	883	823	842	820	..
Power st./C. éléctr.	1879	1856	1769	1678	1625	1506	1398	1154	530	334	295	316	313	..
Combustion	1088	960	889	815	779	699	665	589	538	459	443	445	427	..
Industrial/Industrielle	750	682	626	572	528	467	428	396	369	323	309	295	281	..
Other/Autres	338	278	263	243	251	232	237	193	169	136	134	150	146	..
Ind. proc./Proc. ind.	110	107	100	88	95	96	95	93	91	90	85	81	80	..
Miscellaneous/Divers	..	..	..	..	..	..	..	..	..	..	..	..	..	..
Total	3166	3010	2843	2666	2578	2369	2230	1907	1218	939	878	896	875	..

Notes: see page 23 / voir page 23

... / ...

EMISSIONS OF SOx, by source, 1980-1993
EMISSIONS DE SOx, par source, 1980-1993

1 000 tonnes

	1980	1981	1982	1983	1984	1985	1986	1987	1988	1989	1990	1991	1992	1993
Iceland/Islande *														
Mobile s./S. mobiles	0.5	..	..	..	..	1.4	1.7	1.6	1.8	2.0	2.3	2.8	2.9	3.1
Road/Routier	0.1	..	..	..	..	0.1	0.1	0.1	0.1	0.1	0.2	0.2	0.2	0.2
Other/Autres	0.4	..	..	..	..	1.3	1.6	1.5	1.6	1.9	2.1	2.6	2.7	2.9
Stationary s./S. fixes	8.1	..	..	..	..	5.2	5.2	5.0	5.6	5.3	5.8	4.4	5.0	5.5
Power st./C. éléctr. *	0.04	..	..	..	..	..	..	..	..	..	0.01	0.01	0.01	0.01
Combustion	..	..	..	..	..	4.0	3.9	3.5	4.2	3.9	2.3	2.0	2.6	2.7
Industrial/Industrielle	0.8	..	..	..	..	3.7	3.7	3.4	3.9	3.6	2.1	1.8	2.4	2.5
Other/Autres		..	..	..	..	0.3	0.2	0.2	0.3	0.3	0.2	0.2	0.2	0.2
Ind. proc./Proc. ind.	1.6	..	..	..	..	1.2	1.4	1.5	1.4	1.4	3.0	2.3	2.3	2.7
Miscellaneous/Divers	5.6	..	..	..	..	..	..	..	..	..	0.5	0.1	0.1	0.1
Total	8.6	..	..	..	..	6.6	7.0	6.7	7.3	7.3	8.1	7.2	7.9	8.6
Ireland/Irlande														
Mobile s./S. mobiles	5	5	4	5	4	4	7	7	7	..	5	..	..	..
Road/Routier	..	..	..	..	..	..	..	..	..	..	..	..	..	..
Other/Autres	..	..	..	..	..	..	..	..	..	..	..	..	..	..
Stationary s./S. fixes	217	184	151	135	125	130	156	166	146	..	181	..	..	..
Power st./C. éléctr.	101	73	53	44	45	39	80	95	71	..	103	..	..	..
Combustion	113	111	98	91	80	89	74	69	72	..	77	..	..	..
Industrial/Industrielle	79	..	..	..	..	49	35	40	44	..	41	..	..	..
Other/Autres	35	..	..	..	..	40	39	29	28	..	36	..	..	..
Ind. proc./Proc. ind.	..	..	..	..	..	..	..	..	..	..	..	..	..	..
Miscellaneous/Divers	2	..	..	..	..	2	2	2	2	..	1	..	..	..
Total	222	189	155	140	129	135	163	173	152	..	187	..	..	..
Italy/Italie *														
Mobile s./S. mobiles	154	..	..	..	119	124	134	132	137	140	151	..	..	..
Road/Routier	..	..	..	..	..	75	83	86	93	100	103	..	..	..
Other/Autres	..	..	..	..	..	49	51	46	44	40	48	..	..	..
Stationary s./S. fixes	3057	..	..	..	2121	2120	2124	2142	2079	1860	1531	..	..	..
Power st./C. éléctr.	1511	..	..	..	1154	1001	1071	1170	1110	965	767	..	..	..
Combustion	1546	..	..	..	967	747	684	600	604	538	655	..	..	..
Industrial/Industrielle	..	..	..	..	..	554	510	435	462	437	573	..	..	..
Other/Autres	..	..	..	..	..	193	174	165	142	101	82	..	..	..
Ind. proc./Proc. ind. *	..	..	..	..	..	177	176	180	178	180	105	..	..	..
Miscellaneous/Divers	..	..	..	..	..	195	193	192	187	177	4	..	..	..
Total	3211	..	..	2233	2240	2244	2257	2274	2216	2001	1682	..	..	..
Netherlands/Pays-Bas *														
Mobile s./S. mobiles	38	33	33	31	30	29	31	31	31	29	29	30	31	31
Road/Routier	15	12	12	12	11	11	13	15	15	12	13	14	14	14
Other/Autres	22	21	21	19	19	18	17	16	15	17	17	17	17	17
Stationary s./S. fixes	451	430	370	291	269	232	232	231	216	179	174	165	139	134
Power st./C. éléctr.	194	208	145	91	70	62	64	62	63	43	45	35	29	27
Combustion	178	149	153	130	128	108	108	114	104	92	91	93	77	73
Industrial/Industrielle	157	128	135	115	113	96	96	102	95	84	83	86	68	64
Other/Autres	21	21	18	15	13	12	12	12	9	8	8	7	9	9
Ind. proc./Proc. ind.	79	74	73	70	73	62	61	56	49	44	38	37	33	34
Miscellaneous/Divers	..	..	..	..	..	..	..	..	..	..	..	..	..	..
Total	489	463	403	323	299	261	263	262	247	208	204	195	170	164
Norway/Norvège *														
Mobile s./S. mobiles	16	17	17	18	17	19	19	19	16	13	11	10	9	9
Road/Routier	5	5	5	4	4	4	5	5	4	4	4	3	3	4
Other/Autres *	11	12	12	13	12	14	14	14	12	10	8	7	5	5
Stationary s./S. fixes	124	110	93	85	78	79	72	55	51	45	42	35	29	27
Power st./C. éléctr. *	..	..	..	..	..	0.3	0.4	0.6	0.5	0.9	0.7	0.8	0.8	0.7
Combustion *	65	59	43	34	28	31	28	23	20	14	11	9	8	6
Industrial/Industrielle	..	..	..	..	..	24	21	17	15	10	8	7	6	5
Other/Autres	..	..	..	..	..	7	6	6	5	4	4	2	2	1
Ind. proc./Proc. ind.	59	51	50	51	50	47	44	31	30	31	31	26	20	21
Miscellaneous/Divers	..	..	..	..	..	0	0	0	0	0	0	0	0	0
Total	141	127	110	103	95	97	91	74	67	59	54	45	37	36

Notes: see page 23 / voir page 23.   ... / ...

EMISSIONS OF SOx, by source, 1980-1993
EMISSIONS DE SOx, par source, 1980-1993

1 000 tonnes

	1980	1981	1982	1983	1984	1985	1986	1987	1988	1989	1990	1991	1992	1993
Portugal *														
Mobile s./S. mobiles	11	..	..	12	..	7	7	9	9	..	17	..	..	..
Road/Routier	7	..	..	..	..	..	..	..	..	..	14	..	..	..
Other/Autres *	4	..	..	..	..	..	..	..	..	..	3	..	..	..
Stationary s./S. fixes	255	..	..	293	..	192	227	210	196	..	269	..	..	..
Power st./C. éléctr.	92	..	..	107	..	85	120	83	72	..	175	..	..	..
Combustion	88	..	..	109	..	84	86	107	103	..	58	..	..	..
Industrial/Industrielle	88	..	..	..	..	83	85	106	102	..	54	..	..	..
Other/Autres	..	..	..	..	..	1	1	1	1	..	4	..	..	..
Ind. proc./Proc. ind.	76	..	..	77	..	23	22	20	21	..	36	..	..	..
Miscellaneous/Divers	..	..	..	..	..	..	..	..	..	..	0	..	..	..
Total	266	..	..	305	..	199	234	218	205	..	286	..	..	..
Spain/Espagne *														
Mobile s./S. mobiles	..	..	..	..	..	..	..	..	..	..	86	..	..	..
Road/Routier	57	..	..	..	..	67	73	52	61	..	69	..	..	..
Other/Autres	..	..	..	..	..	..	..	..	..	..	17	..	..	..
Stationary s./S. fixes	..	..	..	..	..	2124	..	..	..	..	2119	..	..	..
Power st./C. éléctr.	1728	..	..	..	..	1635	1404	1367	..	..	1463	..	..	..
Combustion	..	..	..	..	..	329	..	..	..	..	576	..	..	..
Industrial/Industrielle	..	..	..	..	..	263	..	..	..	..	478	..	..	..
Other/Autres	56	..	..	..	..	66	61	58	64	..	98	..	..	..
Ind. proc./Proc. ind.	..	..	..	..	..	160	168	168	..	..	38	..	..	..
Miscellaneous/Divers	..	..	..	..	..	..	..	..	..	..	42	..	..	..
Total	..	..	..	..	..	2191	..	..	..	..	2205	..	..	..
Sweden/Suède														
Mobile s./S. mobiles	44	..	..	39	..	39	..	40	..	40	37	27	25	24
Road/Routier	11	..	..	8	..	8	..	8	..	8	8	4	3	2
Other/Autres	32	..	..	31	..	31	..	32	..	32	29	23	22	22
Stationary s./S. fixes	464	..	..	266	..	227	..	188	..	120	99	85	78	77
Power st./C. éléctr.	101	..	..	52	..	64	..	45	..	18	16	15	14	13
Combustion	227	..	..	118	..	95	..	77	..	52	38	27	21	24
Industrial/Industrielle	143	..	..	73	..	53	..	45	..	32	22	18	13	16
Other/Autres	84	..	..	45	..	42	..	32	..	20	16	9	8	8
Ind. proc./Proc. ind.	137	..	..	96	..	68	..	66	..	50	45	43	43	40
Miscellaneous/Divers	..	..	..	..	..	..	..	..	..	..	..	..	..	..
Total	507	..	..	305	..	266	..	228	..	160	136	112	103	101
Switzerland/Suisse														
Mobile s./S. mobiles	6	..	..	..	5	..	..	..	5	5	5	5	4	3
Road/Routier	..	..	..	..	..	..	..	..	..	..	..	..	..	..
Other/Autres	..	..	..	..	..	..	..	..	..	..	..	..	..	..
Stationary s./S. fixes	120	..	..	..	90	..	..	..	67	63	58	56	56	55
Power st./C. éléctr.	2	..	..	..	1	..	..	..	1	1	1	1	..	..
Combustion	88	..	..	..	56	..	..	..	46	44	42	41	..	..
Industrial/Industrielle	56	..	..	..	33	..	..	..	29	28	27	26	..	..
Other/Autres	32	..	..	..	23	..	..	..	17	16	15	15	..	..
Ind. proc./Proc. ind.	30	..	..	..	33	..	..	..	16	14	12	11	..	..
Miscellaneous/Divers	..	..	..	..	..	..	..	..	4	4	3	4	..	..
Total	126	..	..	..	95	..	..	..	72	68	63	61	60	58
UK/Royaume-Uni														
Mobile s./S. mobiles	117	117	116	101	106	102	103	96	105	115	113	112	118	114
Road/Routier	42	53	49	42	43	45	50	46	54	61	63	58	62	59
Other/Autres	75	64	67	59	63	57	53	50	51	54	50	54	56	55
Stationary s./S. fixes	4786	4326	4099	3765	3618	3628	3798	3803	3719	3610	3641	3453	3376	3075
Power st./C. éléctr.	3007	2847	2748	2631	2589	2627	2722	2830	2728	2640	2722	2534	2428	2089
Combustion	1739	1444	1320	1102	997	970	1047	946	963	943	895	896	929	968
Industrial/Industrielle	1295	1039	933	752	681	632	706	661	716	722	690	690	734	757
Other/Autres	444	405	387	350	316	338	341	285	247	221	205	206	195	211
Ind. proc./Proc. ind.	40	35	31	32	32	31	29	27	28	27	24	23	19	18
Miscellaneous/Divers	0	0	0	0	0	0	0	0	0	0	0	0	0	0
Total	4903	4441	4216	3865	3724	3729	3901	3900	3825	3725	3754	3564	3494	3188

Notes: see page 23 / voir page 23.

... / ...

EMISSIONS OF SOx, by source, 1980-1993
EMISSIONS DE SOx, par source, 1980-1993

1 000 tonnes

	1980	1981	1982	1983	1984	1985	1986	1987	1988	1989	1990	1991	1992	1993
Hungary/Hongrie														
Mobile s./S. mobiles	49	..	..	..	..	21	19	18	19	16	16	13	13	..
Road/Routier	..	..	..	..	..	..	..	..	..	..	..	..	..	..
Other/Autres	..	..	..	..	..	..	..	..	..	..	..	..	..	..
Stationary s./S. fixes	1584	..	..	..	..	1383	1343	1268	1199	1086	994	900	814	..
Power st./C. éléctr.	688	..	..	..	..	526	547	549	475	449	435	421	456	..
Combustion	523	..	..	..	..	471	453	383	379	329	290	220	193	..
Industrial/Industrielle	485	..	..	..	..	442	426	355	354	304	268	204	182	..
Other/Autres	38	..	..	..	..	29	27	27	26	25	22	16	11	..
Ind. proc./Proc. ind.	37	..	..	..	..	46	45	44	44	35	18	16	10	..
Miscellaneous/Divers	336	..	..	..	..	340	298	292	301	273	251	243	155	..
Total	1633	..	..	..	1460	1403	1362	1285	1218	1102	1010	913	827	..
Poland/Pologne														
Mobile s./S. mobiles	62	..	..	..	..	62	..	64	64	65	54	..	..	50
Road/Routier	..	..	..	..	..	..	..	..	..	..	..	..	..	..
Other/Autres	..	..	..	..	..	..	..	..	..	..	..	..	..	..
Stationary s./S. fixes	4038	..	..	..	..	4238	4194	4136	4116	3845	3156	2905	2730	2675
Power st./C. éléctr.	..	..	..	..	..	..	2270	2050	2020	2020	1570	1480	1310	1290
Combustion	..	..	..	..	..	..	1414	1696	1716	1475	1316	1190	1170	1150
Industrial/Industrielle	..	..	..	..	..	..	590	730	720	670	500	430	420	400
Other/Autres	..	..	..	..	..	..	824	966	996	805	816	760	750	750
Ind. proc./Proc. ind.	..	..	..	..	..	..	510	390	380	350	270	235	250	235
Miscellaneous/Divers	..	..	..	..	..	..	..	..	..	..	..	..	..	..
Total	4100	..	..	..	..	4300	..	4200	4180	3910	3210	..	..	2725

Notes (SOx emissions):
CAN) SO$_2$ only.
USA) Break in time series in 1993.
JPN) 1990 data are provisional. Industrial combustion includes industrial processes.
AUT) SO$_2$ only. Break in time series in 1992. 1992-93 data for industrial combustion include industrial processes. Miscellaneous: Secretariat estimates.
BEL) Data refer to Wallonia only. 1980-84 industrial combustion data include industrial processes.
FIN) Break in time series in 1991. 1980-90 industrial combustion data include power stations.
FRA) Industrial combustion includes agriculture. Miscellaneous data refer to emissions from energy transformation.
DEU) 1992 data are provisional. Industrial combustion includes industrial processes.
GRC) Data are CORINAIR project estimates and not official national figures.
ISL) The estimation methodology changed in 1990. The 1993 figure for power stations is provisional.
ITA) The estimation methodology changed in 1985. Through 1984, industrial processes are excluded.
NLD) The estimation methodology changed in 1992.
NOR) Ocean transport and national aircraft abroad are excluded. From 1980 to 1984 combustion includes power stations.
PRT) SO$_2$ only. Break in time series in 1990. Other mobile sources: air transport only.
ESP) Break in time series in 1985 and 1990 (CORINAIR 85 and 90).

Notes (émissions de SOx):
CAN) SO$_2$ seulement.
USA) Rupture de série en 1993.
JPN) Les données 1990 sont provisoires. La combustion industrielle inclut les procédés industriels.
AUT) SO$_2$ seulement. Rupture de série en 1992. Les chiffres 1992 et 1993 pour la combustion industrielle incluent les procédés industriels. Divers: estimations du Secrétariat.
BEL) Données relatives à la Wallonie seulement. Les données 1980-84 relatives à la combustion industrielle incluent les procédés industriels.
FIN) Rupture de série en 1991. Les données 1980-90 relatives à la combustion industrielle incluent les centrales électriques.
FRA) La combustion industrielle inclut l'agriculture. Divers: émissions dues à la transformation d'énergie.
DEU) Les données 1992 sont provisoires. La combustion industrielle inclut les procédés industriels.
GRC) Les données sont des estimations de CORINAIR et ne représentent pas les chiffres officiels.
ISL) La méthode d'estimation a été changée en 1990. Le chiffre 1993 pour les centrales électriques est provisoire.
ITA) Rupture de série en 1985 due à un changement de méthode d'estimation. Jusqu'en 1984, les procédés industriels sont exclus.
NLD) 1992: changement de méthode d'estimation.
NOR) Les transports en mer et les avions nationaux à l'étranger sont exclus. Combustion: les données 1980-84 incluent les centrales électriques.
PRT) SO$_2$ seulement. Rupture de série en 1990. Les données relatives aux autres sources mobiles concernent les transports aériens seulement.
ESP) Rupture de série en 1985 et 1990 (CORINAIR 85 et 90).

Source: OECD/OCDE

EMISSIONS OF NOx, by source, 1980-1993
ÉMISSIONS DE NOx, par source, 1980-1993

1 000 tonnes

	1980	1981	1982	1983	1984	1985	1986	1987	1988	1989	1990	1991	1992	1993
Canada														
Mobile s./S. mobiles	1297	1271	1254	1269	1233	1223	1209	1249	1276	1249	1218	1180	..	..
Road/Routier	..	..	..	..	..	791	779	803	798	772	747	708	..	..
Other/Autres	..	..	..	..	..	431	431	446	478	477	471	472	..	..
Stationary s./S. fixes	662	636	643	615	638	760	724	788	841	870	781	796	..	..
Power st./C. éléctr.	238	220	237	229	252	300	254	296	322	343	265	280	..	..
Combustion	358	350	340	320	320	336	341	353	375	382	376	384	..	..
Industrial/Industrielle	..	..	..	..	..	265	271	287	303	306	301	306	..	..
Other/Autres	..	..	..	..	..	71	70	66	72	76	75	78	..	..
Ind. proc./Proc. ind.	48	48	48	48	48	101	103	110	113	114	111	107	..	..
Miscellaneous/Divers	18	18	18	18	18	25	26	30	31	31	28	26	..	..
Total	1959	1907	1897	1884	1871	1984	1934	2037	2117	2120	1999	1976	1939	..
USA/Etats-Unis *														
Mobile s./S. mobiles	10368	10376	9946	9510	9511	9718	9329	9608	9801	9578	9670	9511	9371	9639
Road/Routier	7897	7962	7667	7345	7209	7360	6925	7138	7237	6988	7091	6999	6783	6831
Other/Autres	2471	2414	2279	2165	2302	2358	2403	2470	2564	2590	2579	2512	2587	2808
Stationary s./S. fixes	11101	10939	10625	10457	11015	10620	10886	11086	11639	11721	11703	11729	11630	11601
Power st./C. éléctr.	6372	6399	6147	6278	6593	6057	6268	6466	6831	6901	6828	6787	6775	7072
Combustion	3897	3750	3824	3454	3706	3746	3602	3633	3792	3815	3871	3945	3861	3568
Industrial/Industrielle	3225	3125	3193	2866	3098	3107	2973	2989	3123	3153	3207	3269	3196	2908
Other/Autres	672	625	631	588	608	639	629	644	669	662	664	676	665	660
Ind. proc./Proc. ind.	506	498	410	411	444	622	819	791	817	808	809	804	798	724
Miscellaneous/Divers	326	291	243	313	272	196	197	197	199	197	195	193	195	237
Total	21469	21315	20571	19967	20526	20338	20214	20694	21440	21299	21373	21240	21001	21240
Japan/Japon *														
Mobile s./S. mobiles	..	..	..	..	..	..	..	..	..	..	..	..	..	..
Road/Routier	803	750	701	670	643	623	622	631	651	662	650	..	..	..
Other/Autres	..	..	..	..	..	..	..	..	..	..	..	..	..	..
Stationary s./S. fixes	819	763	717	721	722	699	662	..	..	777	826	..	..	..
Power st./C. éléctr.	234	226	209	211	201	187	172	..	..	200	..	..	..	..
Combustion	..	..	..	..	..	..	..	..	..	..	..	..	..	..
Industrial/Industrielle *	542	497	460	465	478	463	438	..	..	516	..	..	..	..
Other/Autres	15	12	19	13	13	13	14	..	..	17	..	..	..	..
Ind. proc./Proc. ind. *	..	..	..	..	..	..	..	..	..	..	..	..	..	..
Miscellaneous/Divers	28	28	29	32	30	36	38	..	..	44	..	..	..	..
Total	1622	1513	1418	1391	1365	1322	1284	..	..	1439	1476	..	..	..
Austria/Autriche *														
Mobile s./S. mobiles	142	..	..	150	..	155	..	155	154	153	152	148	130	119
Road/Routier	141	..	..	..	..	149	..	149	148	..	145	..	..	..
Other/Autres	1	..	..	..	..	2	..	2	3	..	3	..	..	..
Stationary s./S. fixes	104	..	..	91	..	90	..	79	72	68	70	68	71	63
Power st./C. éléctr.	20	..	..	20	..	23	..	15	12	12	12	12	12	9
Combustion	48	..	..	42	..	40	..	43	36	32	34	33	52	47
Industrial/Industrielle *	37	..	..	..	..	30	..	30	30	..	25	..	40	35
Other/Autres	11	..	..	..	..	9	..	12	10	..	10	..	12	12
Ind. proc./Proc. ind. *	30	..	..	28	..	27	..	21	20	24	23	23	..	..
Miscellaneous/Divers *	6	..	..	..	..	..	..	..	..	..	..	..	7	7
Total	246	..	..	241	..	245	..	234	226	221	221	216	201	182
Belgium/Belgique *														
Mobile s./S. mobiles	79	..	78	..	77	79	84	87	92	96	98	98	97	..
Road/Routier	..	..	..	..	..	76	80	84	89	93	95	95	94	..
Other/Autres	..	..	..	..	..	3.3	3.3	3.1	3.1	2.7	3.0	3.0	2.9	..
Stationary s./S. fixes	89	..	75	..	69	68	63	66	67	71	74	74	76	..
Power st./C. éléctr.	..	..	..	..	..	14	10	10	9	12	12	14	14	..
Combustion	..	..	..	..	..	53	52	55	56	57	59	58	61	..
Industrial/Industrielle *	55	..	47	..	46	46	45	48	50	51	53	52	55	..
Other/Autres	8	..	7	..	6	7	7	7	7	6	6	7	6	..
Ind. proc./Proc. ind. *	..	..	..	..	..	1.08	0.99	0.89	1.31	1.44	1.38	1.10	0.57	..
Miscellaneous/Divers	..	..	..	..	..	0.22	0.22	0.27	0.27	0.29	0.52	0.53	0.52	..
Total	168	..	153	..	146	147	146	153	158	166	172	172	173	..

Notes: see page 29 / voir page 29

... / ...

EMISSIONS OF NOx, by source, 1980-1993
ÉMISSIONS DE NOx, par source, 1980-1993

1 000 tonnes

	1980	1981	1982	1983	1984	1985	1986	1987	1988	1989	1990	1991	1992	1993
Denmark/Danemark														
Mobile s./S. mobiles	131	125	131	133	141	146	144	151	152	156	158	154	153	148
Road/Routier	79	75	78	81	89	91	97	96	97	98	101	95	94	91
Other/Autres	52	50	53	52	52	55	57	55	55	58	57	59	59	57
Stationary s./S. fixes	142	114	127	120	124	148	159	153	143	120	112	157	115	119
Power st./C. éléctr.	102	77	93	87	89	110	122	118	110	89	83	124	82	86
Combustion	37	34	31	30	31	33	32	30	27	25	24	26	25	26
Industrial/Industrielle	17	15	13	13	14	14	14	13	13	12	12	13	13	13
Other/Autres	20	19	18	17	17	19	18	17	14	13	12	13	12	13
Ind. proc./Proc. ind.	3	3	3	3	4	5	5	5	6	6	5	7	8	7
Miscellaneous/Divers	..	..	..	..	..	..	..	..	..	..	..	..	..	..
Total	273	239	258	253	265	294	313	304	295	276	270	311	268	267
Finland/Finlande *														
Mobile s./S. mobiles	137	140	143	146	148	152	158	164	171	175	182	179	176	..
Road/Routier	..	..	..	..	..	..	..	..	..	..	..	149	148	..
Other/Autres	..	..	..	..	..	..	..	..	..	..	..	31	28	..
Stationary s./S. fixes	127	108	102	94	85	100	98	106	105	109	108	104	92	..
Power st./C. éléctr.	..	..	..	..	..	82	80	88	87	91	91	53	41	..
Combustion	..	..	..	69	..	..	..	..	..	..	..	51	50	..
Industrial/Industrielle	..	..	..	..	..	..	..	..	..	..	..	38	38	..
Other/Autres	..	..	..	..	..	..	..	..	..	..	..	13	12	..
Ind. proc./Proc. ind.	18	18	18	18	18	18	18	18	18	18	17	1	1	..
Miscellaneous/Divers	..	..	..	..	..	..	..	..	..	..	..	..	..	..
Total	264	248	245	236	233	252	256	270	276	284	290	284	268	..
France *														
Mobile s./S. mobiles	..	..	..	..	..	..	..	..	..	..	..	..	..	
Road/Routier	860	868	880	900	915	910	950	980	1040	1057	1060	1088	1088	..
Other/Autres	..	..	..	..	..	..	..	..	..	..	..	..	..	
Stationary s./S. fixes	786	677	654	597	555	490	446	428	407	431	427	447	431	..
Power st./C. éléctr.	287	225	238	203	160	134	100	89	81	112	105	128	111	..
Combustion	302	267	248	232	232	196	190	184	169	164	157	155	154	..
Industrial/Industrielle *	207	177	162	149	147	111	103	101	89	87	81	75	75	..
Other/Autres	95	90	86	83	85	85	87	83	80	77	76	80	79	..
Ind. proc./Proc. ind.	170	163	149	143	146	144	140	139	141	141	143	143	145	..
Miscellaneous/Divers	27	23	20	18	16	16	15	16	17	14	21	21	21	..
Total *	1646	1545	1534	1497	1470	1400	1396	1408	1447	1488	1487	1535	1519	..
Germany/Allemagne *														
Mobile s./S. mobiles	..	..	..	..	..	..	..	..	..	..	1986	1949	1953	
Road/Routier	..	..	..	..	..	..	..	..	..	..	1656	1638	1641	
Other/Autres	..	..	..	..	..	..	..	..	..	..	330	311	312	
Stationary s./S. fixes	..	..	..	..	..	..	..	..	..	..	1047	985	951	
Power st./C. éléctr.	..	..	..	..	..	..	..	..	..	..	609	572	526	
Combustion	..	..	..	..	..	..	..	..	..	..	..	..	..	
Industrial/Industrielle *	..	..	..	..	..	..	..	..	..	..	319	280	277	
Other/Autres	..	..	..	..	..	..	..	..	..	..	119	133	148	
Ind. proc./Proc. ind. *	..	..	..	..	..	..	..	..	..	..	..	..	..	
Miscellaneous/Divers	..	..	..	..	..	..	..	..	..	..	..	..	..	..
Total	..	..	..	..	..	..	..	..	..	..	3033	2934	2904	..
w. Germany/All. occ.														
Mobile s./S. mobiles	1587	1550	1576	1611	1675	1711	1779	1790	1794	1766	1769	1739	1737	..
Road/Routier	1364	1318	1342	1374	1450	1481	1543	1564	1565	1523	1519	1498	1491	..
Other/Autres	223	232	234	237	225	230	236	226	229	243	250	241	246	..
Stationary s./S. fixes	1339	1292	1241	1251	1248	1197	1160	1071	983	851	691	721	689	..
Power st./C. éléctr.	800	800	789	813	808	762	730	661	588	484	335	352	316	..
Combustion	496	455	422	408	411	409	404	387	373	343	340	355	361	..
Industrial/Industrielle	353	326	299	285	278	271	261	253	253	241	231	230	225	..
Other/Autres	143	128	123	123	132	137	143	133	121	106	109	125	136	..
Ind. proc./Proc. ind.	43	38	30	30	30	27	26	24	21	20	16	14	12	..
Miscellaneous/Divers	..	..	..	..	..	..	..	..	..	..	..	..	..	
Total	2926	2842	2817	2862	2923	2908	2939	2861	2777	2617	2460	2460	2426	..

Notes: see page 29 / voir page 29.   ... / ...

EMISSIONS OF NOx, by source, 1980-1993
ÉMISSIONS DE NOx, par source, 1980-1993

1 000 tonnes

	1980	1981	1982	1983	1984	1985	1986	1987	1988	1989	1990	1991	1992	1993
Greece/Grèce *														
Mobile s./S. mobiles	137	..	..	..	..	..	..	..	..	..	217	..	..	..
Road/Routier	..	..	..	..	..	120	..	..	..	..	141	..	..	..
Other/Autres	..	..	..	..	..	..	..	..	..	..	76	..	..	..
Stationary s./S. fixes	80	..	..	..	..	188	..	..	..	..	121	..	..	..
Power st./C. éléctr.	..	..	..	..	..	146	..	..	..	..	65	..	..	..
Combustion	..	..	..	..	..	10	..	..	..	..	49	..	..	..
Industrial/Industrielle	..	..	..	..	..	8	..	..	..	..	46	..	..	..
Other/Autres	..	..	..	..	..	2	..	..	..	..	4	..	..	..
Ind. proc./Proc. ind.	..	..	..	..	..	28	..	..	..	..	4	..	..	..
Miscellaneous/Divers *	..	..	..	..	..	4	..	..	..	..	4	..	..	..
Total	217	..	..	..	..	308	..	..	..	..	338	..	..	..
Iceland/Islande *														
Mobile s./S. mobiles	12	..	..	..	..	20	22	25	25	27	23	21	21	22
Road/Routier	1.7	..	..	..	..	2.1	2.1	2.6	2.6	2.6	3.6	3.6	3.7	3.7
Other/Autres	10	..	..	..	..	17	20	22	22	24	19	17	18	18
Stationary s./S. fixes	1.8	..	..	..	..	1.3	1.4	1.2	1.4	1.4	1.0	1.0	0.9	0.9
Power st./C. éléctr.	0.03	..	..	..	..	..	..	..	..	..	..	..	..	..
Combustion	..	..	..	..	..	..	..	..	..	..	0.5	0.4	0.2	0.3
Industrial/Industrielle *	0.6	..	..	..	..	1.3	1.3	1.2	1.3	1.4	0.3	0.3	0.2	0.3
Other/Autres	1.1	..	..	..	..	0.04	0.07	0.07	0.07	0.08	..	..	..	..
Ind. proc./Proc. ind. *	..	..	..	..	..	..	..	..	..	..	0.6	0.6	0.5	0.5
Miscellaneous/Divers	..	..	..	..	..	..	..	..	..	..	0.1	0.1	0.1	0.1
Total	14	..	..	..	..	21	23	26	26	28	24	22	22	23
Ireland/Irlande *														
Mobile s./S. mobiles	35	21	20	19	18	42	52	54	61	..	60	..	..	..
Road/Routier	..	..	..	..	..	..	..	..	..	..	..	..	..	..
Other/Autres	..	..	..	..	..	..	..	..	..	..	..	..	..	..
Stationary s./S. fixes	39	43	44	44	43	49	48	61	62	..	68	..	..	..
Power st./C. éléctr.	21	29	29	29	32	29	28	41	42	..	46	..	..	..
Combustion	12	14	15	15	11	15	14	14	14	..	17	..	..	..
Industrial/Industrielle	8	..	..	..	..	8	7	9	6	..	10	..	..	..
Other/Autres	4	..	..	..	..	7	7	6	9	..	7	..	..	..
Ind. proc./Proc. ind.	..	..	..	..	..	..	..	..	..	..	..	..	..	..
Miscellaneous/Divers	5	..	..	..	..	5	5	6	6	..	5	..	..	..
Total	73	68	68	67	66	91	100	115	122	..	128	..	..	..
Italy/Italie *														
Mobile s./S. mobiles *	753	..	..	..	779	907	970	992	1058	1137	1224	..	..	..
Road/Routier	..	..	..	..	..	858	919	943	1010	1089	946	..	..	..
Other/Autres	..	..	..	..	..	48	51	49	48	47	278	..	..	..
Stationary s./S. fixes *	832	..	..	..	750	830	832	909	921	896	817	..	..	..
Power st./C. éléctr.	403	..	..	..	399	378	383	442	441	400	407	..	..	..
Combustion	..	..	..	..	..	265	264	276	290	299	362	..	..	..
Industrial/Industrielle	..	..	..	..	..	200	199	211	227	242	303	..	..	..
Other/Autres	..	..	..	..	..	65	65	65	63	57	59	..	..	..
Ind. proc./Proc. ind.	..	..	..	..	..	154	149	155	154	161	12	..	..	..
Miscellaneous/Divers	..	..	..	..	..	34	36	35	35	36	35	..	..	..
Total	1585	..	..	..	1529	1736	1802	1901	1979	2033	2041	..	..	..
Netherlands/Pays-Bas *														
Mobile s./S. mobiles	344	339	336	335	337	337	344	349	363	363	352	353	351	338
Road/Routier	269	266	263	262	264	262	269	274	286	283	273	274	272	259
Other/Autres	75	73	73	73	73	75	75	75	77	80	79	78	79	79
Stationary s./S. fixes	239	238	227	222	236	239	243	250	238	227	228	223	217	208
Power st./C. éléctr.	83	85	81	78	81	80	87	83	87	77	73	68	68	64
Combustion	126	122	116	114	124	127	125	137	123	123	125	131	130	125
Industrial/Industrielle	77	75	70	68	74	74	72	83	82	82	83	85	78	77
Other/Autres	49	47	46	46	50	53	53	54	41	41	42	46	52	48
Ind. proc./Proc. ind.	29	28	28	28	29	29	29	28	28	26	24	21	16	16
Miscellaneous/Divers	2	2	2	2	2	2	2	2	2	2	2	2	2	2
Total	584	577	563	556	573	578	588	599	601	590	575	575	566	545

Notes: see page 29 / voir page 29. ... / ...

EMISSIONS OF NOx, by source, 1980-1993
ÉMISSIONS DE NOx, par source, 1980-1993

1 000 tonnes

	1980	1981	1982	1983	1984	1985	1986	1987	1988	1989	1990	1991	1992	1993
Norway/Norvège *														
Mobile s./S. mobiles	140	138	142	150	166	174	189	192	183	185	182	176	176	182
Road/Routier	59	60	62	64	68	75	82	88	88	87	83	80	79	81
Other/Autres *	81	79	81	86	98	100	107	105	95	98	98	97	97	102
Stationary s./S. fixes	44	39	40	38	37	40	40	45	46	47	48	44	44	47
Power st./C. éléctr. *	..	..	..	..	..	0.4	0.8	1.1	0.9	1.3	1.1	1.1	1.3	1.0
Combustion *	35	30	31	29	27	28	29	33	34	35	37	35	36	38
Industrial/Industrielle	..	..	..	..	..	25	25	28	31	32	35	32	33	36
Other/Autres	..	..	..	..	..	3	4	4	3	3	3	2	2	2
Ind. proc./Proc. ind.	9	9	9	9	10	12	10	10	11	11	10	8	7	7
Miscellaneous/Divers	..	..	..	..	..	0	0	0	0	0	0	0	0	0
Total	184	177	183	188	204	215	229	237	229	232	230	221	220	229
Portugal *														
Mobile s./S. mobiles	106	..	..	120	..	57	62	71	77	..	131	..	..	..
Road/Routier	75	..	..	..	..	..	..	..	..	..	107	..	..	..
Other/Autres *	31	..	..	..	..	..	..	..	..	..	24	..	..	..
Stationary s./S. fixes	59	..	..	72	..	39	48	45	45	..	85	..	..	..
Power st./C. éléctr.	19	..	..	28	..	14	21	16	16	..	50	..	..	..
Combustion	13	..	..	16	..	13	14	16	15	..	27	..	..	..
Industrial/Industrielle	13	..	..	..	..	13	14	16	15	..	24	..	..	..
Other/Autres	..	..	..	..	..	..	..	..	..	..	3	..	..	..
Ind. proc./Proc. ind.	27	..	..	28	..	12	13	13	15	..	8	..	..	..
Miscellaneous/Divers	..	..	..	..	..	..	..	..	..	..	0	..	..	..
Total	165	..	..	192	..	96	110	116	122	..	216	..	..	..
Spain/Espagne *														
Mobile s./S. mobiles	..	..	..	..	..	..	..	..	..	..	758	..	..	..
Road/Routier	407	..	..	..	..	454	484	521	577	..	512	..	..	..
Other/Autres	..	..	..	..	..	..	..	..	..	..	246	..	..	..
Stationary s./S. fixes	..	..	..	..	..	395	..	..	..	..	489	..	..	..
Power st./C. éléctr.	258	..	..	..	..	258	253	253	..	..	249	..	..	..
Combustion	..	..	..	..	..	56	..	..	..	..	190	..	..	..
Industrial/Industrielle	..	..	..	..	..	40	..	..	..	..	169	..	..	..
Other/Autres	12	..	..	..	..	16	17	18	18	..	21	..	..	..
Ind. proc./Proc. ind.	..	..	..	..	..	81	80	83	..	..	15	..	..	..
Miscellaneous/Divers	..	..	..	..	..	..	..	..	..	..	35	..	..	..
Total	..	..	..	..	..	849	..	..	..	..	1247	..	..	..
Sweden/Suède														
Mobile s./S. mobiles	319	..	..	..	..	..	..	342	344	339	337	334	335	328
Road/Routier	183	..	..	..	..	..	..	195	196	190	184	180	178	171
Other/Autres	136	..	..	..	..	..	..	147	148	149	153	154	157	157
Stationary s./S. fixes	135	..	..	..	..	..	..	96	88	79	74	75	67	71
Power st./C. éléctr.	26	..	..	..	..	..	..	27	23	17	16	16	14	14
Combustion	70	..	..	..	..	..	..	45	42	39	36	36	30	31
Industrial/Industrielle	42	..	..	..	..	..	..	28	27	26	23	23	18	20
Other/Autres	28	..	..	..	..	..	..	17	15	13	13	13	12	11
Ind. proc./Proc. ind.	38	..	..	..	..	..	..	23	23	23	22	24	24	26
Miscellaneous/Divers	..	..	..	..	..	..	..	..	..	..	..	..	..	..
Total	454	..	..	..	..	..	..	438	432	418	411	410	402	399
Switzerland/Suisse														
Mobile s./S. mobiles	138	..	..	..	158	..	..	..	136	130	125	117	106	96
Road/Routier	..	..	..	..	..	..	..	..	..	..	..	..	..	..
Other/Autres	..	..	..	..	..	..	..	..	..	..	..	..	..	..
Stationary s./S. fixes	58	..	..	..	56	..	..	..	58	59	59	58	56	54
Power st./C. éléctr.	1	..	..	..	1	..	..	..	1	1	1	1	..	..
Combustion	27	..	..	..	25	..	..	..	26	26	26	26	..	..
Industrial/Industrielle	19	..	..	..	16	..	..	..	17	17	17	17	..	..
Other/Autres	9	..	..	..	9	..	..	..	9	9	9	9	..	..
Ind. proc./Proc. ind.	31	..	..	..	31	..	..	..	28	29	29	28	..	..
Miscellaneous/Divers	..	..	..	..	..	..	..	..	4	4	4	4	..	..
Total	196	..	..	..	214	..	..	..	194	189	184	175	161	150

Notes: see page 29 / voir page 29.

... / ...

EMISSIONS OF NOx, by source, 1980-1993
ÉMISSIONS DE NOx, par source, 1980-1993

1 000 tonnes

	1980	1981	1982	1983	1984	1985	1986	1987	1988	1989	1990	1991	1992	1993
Turkey/Turquie														
Mobile s./S. mobiles	..	..	..	..	..	..	..	..	..	236	..	..	..	..
Road/Routier	..	..	..	..	..	..	..	..	..	..	..	..	..	..
Other/Autres	..	..	..	..	..	..	..	..	..	..	..	..	..	..
Stationary s./S. fixes	..	..	..	..	..	..	..	..	..	275	..	..	..	..
Power st./C. éléctr.	..	..	..	..	..	..	..	..	..	87	..	..	..	..
Combustion	..	..	..	..	..	..	..	..	..	106	..	..	..	..
Industrial/Industrielle	..	..	..	..	..	..	..	..	..	68	..	..	..	..
Other/Autres	..	..	..	..	..	..	..	..	..	39	..	..	..	..
Ind. proc./Proc. ind.	..	..	..	..	..	..	..	..	..	..	..	..	..	..
Miscellaneous/Divers	..	..	..	..	..	..	..	..	..	81	..	..	..	..
Total	..	..	..	..	..	..	..	..	..	512	..	..	..	..
UK/Royaume-Uni														
Mobile s./S. mobiles	1022	1011	1046	1076	1151	1178	1226	1332	1429	1530	1497	1487	1415	1308
Road/Routier	850	859	882	918	982	1014	1070	1186	1276	1364	1336	1319	1245	1144
Other/Autres	172	152	164	158	169	164	156	146	153	166	161	168	170	164
Stationary s./S. fixes	1372	1321	1270	1256	1165	1243	1281	1298	1276	1224	1184	1145	1127	1037
Power st./C. éléctr.	877	838	797	786	707	771	805	825	799	767	776	674	661	570
Combustion	428	409	395	386	370	381	383	375	380	358	305	365	357	356
Industrial/Industrielle	293	275	262	252	238	240	238	236	246	232	177	226	222	221
Other/Autres	135	134	133	134	132	141	145	139	134	126	128	139	135	135
Ind. proc./Proc. ind.	67	74	78	84	88	91	93	98	97	99	103	106	109	111
Miscellaneous/Divers	0	0	0	0	0	0	0	0	0	0	0	0	0	0
Total	2395	2334	2318	2331	2315	2420	2508	2630	2706	2754	2731	2632	2544	2347
Hungary/Hongrie														
Mobile s./S. mobiles	111	..	..	..	..	111	115	118	119	117	116	98	94	..
Road/Routier	..	..	..	..	..	..	..	..	..	..	..	..	..	..
Other/Autres	..	..	..	..	..	..	..	..	..	..	..	..	..	..
Stationary s./S. fixes	162	..	..	..	..	152	149	147	139	130	122	105	89	..
Power st./C. éléctr.	73	..	..	..	..	65	66	63	55	50	48	39	41	..
Combustion	40	..	..	..	..	35	34	34	33	30	27	22	18	..
Industrial/Industrielle	30	..	..	..	..	26	26	25	25	23	20	17	15	..
Other/Autres	10	..	..	..	..	9	8	8	8	8	7	5	3	..
Ind. proc./Proc. ind.	23	..	..	..	..	23	23	23	23	23	21	19	10	..
Miscellaneous/Divers	25	..	..	..	..	29	26	28	28	27	26	25	20	..
Total	273	..	..	..	..	263	264	265	258	246	238	203	183	..
Poland/Pologne														
Mobile s./S. mobiles	463	..	..	..	..	460	460	360	490	480	480	395	400	420
Road/Routier	..	..	..	..	..	..	..	..	..	..	..	..	..	..
Other/Autres	..	..	..	..	..	..	..	..	..	..	..	..	..	..
Stationary s./S. fixes	..	..	..	..	..	1040	1040	1170	1060	1000	800	810	730	700
Power st./C. éléctr.	..	..	..	..	..	..	560	..	470	470	370	395	370	380
Combustion	..	..	..	..	..	..	370	..	310	270	230	240	215	200
Industrial/Industrielle	..	..	..	..	..	..	170	..	180	170	130	140	115	70
Other/Autres	..	..	..	..	..	..	200	..	130	100	100	100	100	130
Ind. proc./Proc. ind.	..	..	..	..	..	..	110	..	280	260	200	175	145	120
Miscellaneous/Divers	..	..	..	..	..	..	..	..	..	..	..	..	..	..
Total	..	..	..	..	..	1500	1500	1530	1550	1480	1280	1205	1130	1120

Notes: see next page / voir page suivante.

Source: OECD/OCDE

Notes (NOx emissions):

USA) Break in time series in 1993.
JPN) Industrial combustion includes industrial processes. 1990 data are provisional.
AUT) Break in time series in 1992. 1992-93 data for industrial combustion include industrial processes. Miscellaneous: Secretariat estimates.
BEL) Data refer to Wallonia only. 1980-84 industrial combustion data include industrial processes.
FIN) Break in time series in 1991.
FRA) Industrial combustion includes agriculture. Total emissions: Some agriculture-related emissions are excluded, e.g. from fertiliser and slurry, which are estimated at 700kt/y. Mobile sources other than road transport are excluded.
DEU) 1992 data are provisional. Industrial combustion includes industrial processes.
GRC) Miscellaneous includes emissions from waste and nature.
ISL) The estimation methodology changed in 1990. 1993 data for industrial combustion and industrial processes are provisional. 1980-89 data for industrial combustion include industrial processes.
IRL) 1981-84 data are based on a different methodology.
ITA) The estimation methodology changed in 1985. Through 1984, industrial processes are excluded.
NLD) The estimation methodology changed in 1992.
NOR) Ocean transport and national aircraft abroad are excluded. 1980-84 data for combustion include power stations.
PRT) Other mobile sources refer to air transport only. Break in time series in 1990.
ESP) Break in time series in 1990 (CORINAIR 90).

Source: OECD/OCDE

Notes (émissions de NOx):

USA) Rupture de série en 1993.
JPN) Les données relatives à la combustion industrielle incluent les procédés industriels. Les données 1990 sont provisoires.
AUT) Rupture de série en 1992. Les chiffres 1992-93 pour la combustion industrielle incluent les procédés industriels. Divers: estimations du Secrétariat.
BEL) Données relatives à la Wallonie seulement. Les données 1980-84 relatives à la combustion industrielle incluent les procédés industriels.
FIN) Rupture de série en 1991.
FRA) La combustion industrielle inclut l'agriculture. Les émissions totales excluent certaines émissions à caractère agricole (e.g. engrais, lisier) estimées à 700 kt/an. Les sources mobiles autres que le transport routier sont exclues.
DEU) Les données 1992 sont provisoires. La combustion industrielle inclut les procédés industriels.
GRC) Divers: émissions naturelles et des déchets.
ISL) La méthode d'estimation a été changée en 1990. Les données 1993 relatives à la combustion industrielle et aux procédés industriels sont provisoires. 1980-1989: les données relatives à la combustion industrielle incluent les procédés industriels.
IRL) Les données comprises entre 1981 et 1984 sont fondées sur une méthodologie différente.
ITA) Rupture de série en 1985 due à un changement de méthode d'estimation. Jusqu'en 1984, les procédés industriels sont exclus.
NLD) Changement de méthode d'estimation en 1992.
NOR) Les transports en mer et les avions nationaux à l'étranger son exclus. Les données 1980-84 relatives à la combustion incluent les centrales électriques.
PRT) Les données relatives aux autres sources mobiles concernent les transports aériens seulement. Rupture de série en 1990.
ESP) Rupture de série en 1990 (CORINAIR 90).

The following tables show man-made emissions of particulate matter, CO and VOCs for selected countries, presented by source (mobile sources, stationary sources and total) and over time.

▸ Particulate matter contributes significantly to visibility reduction and, as a carrier of toxic metals and other toxic substances, exerts pressures on human health.

▸ CO can cause adverse health effects, in particular because it interferes with the absorption of oxygen by red blood cells.

▸ VOCs are considered, along with NO_x, to be the main precursors of photochemical air pollution.

The interpretation of this table should take into account differences among countries in the definition of emission sources and in measurement methods.

Dans les tableaux suivants les émissions anthropiques de particules, de CO et des COV sont présentées par source (sources mobiles, sources fixes et total) et dans le temps.

▸ Les particules contribuent considérablement à la réduction de la visibilité et, en tant que supports à des métaux toxiques et autres substances toxiques, elles mettent en danger la santé humaine.

▸ Le CO peut avoir des effets néfastes pour la santé, en particulier parce qu'il perturbe l'absorption de l'oxygène par les globules rouges.

▸ Les COV sont avec les NO_x les principaux précurseurs de la pollution photochimique de l'atmosphère.

Dans l'interprétation de ce tableau, il faut tenir compte des définitions des sources d'émission et des méthodes de mesure qui diffèrent selon les pays.

EMISSIONS OF PARTICULATES, by source, 1980-1993
ÉMISSIONS DE PARTICULES, par source, 1980-1993

1 000 tonnes

	1980	1981	1982	1983	1984	1985	1986	1987	1988	1989	1990	1991	1992	1993
Canada														
Mobile s./S. mobiles	98	..	..	..	..	111	..	..	..	..	118	..	..	..
Stationary s./S. fixes	1809	..	..	..	..	1598	..	..	..	..	1736	..	..	..
Total	1907	..	..	..	..	1709	..	..	..	..	1855	..	..	..
Mexico/Mexique														
Mobile s./S. mobiles	..	..	..	..	..	..	..	..	..	..	..	..	..	..
Stationary s./S. fixes	..	..	..	..	..	..	..	..	..	..	..	..	..	354
Total	..	..	..	..	..	..	..	..	..	..	..	..	..	..
USA/Etats-Unis *														
Mobile s./S. mobiles	1308	1327	1295	1278	1305	1379	1356	1388	1477	1519	1539	1565	1568	..
Stationary s./S. fixes	7684	7187	6310	6453	6739	6433	5912	5991	6423	6022	5807	5417	5512	..
Total	8992	8514	7605	7731	8044	7812	7268	7379	7901	7541	7345	6982	7080	..
Japan/Japon *														
Mobile s./S. mobiles	..	..	..	41	..	..	52	..	..	69	..	..	..	..
Stationary s./S. fixes *	..	..	..	133	..	..	100	..	..	108	..	..	..	..
Total *	..	..	..	174	..	..	152	..	..	177	..	..	..	..
Austria/Autriche *														
Mobile s./S. mobiles *	12	..	..	12	..	12	12	12	12	13	13	13	..	..
Stationary s./S. fixes	67	..	..	58	..	46	30	33	28	26	26	25	..	..
Total	79	..	..	70	..	58	42	45	40	39	39	38	..	..
France *														
Mobile s./S. mobiles *	40	41	42	43	45	46	51	57	64	67	74	75	76	..
Stationary s./S. fixes *	395	340	327	298	279	249	219	202	189	174	160	156	152	..
Total	435	381	369	341	324	295	270	259	253	241	234	231	228	..
Germany/Allemagne *														
Mobile s./S. mobiles	..	..	..	..	..	..	..	..	..	..	100	102	103	..
Stationary s./S. fixes	..	..	..	..	..	..	..	..	..	..	2296	1679	1233	..
Total	..	..	..	..	..	..	..	..	..	..	2396	1781	1336	..
w. Germany/All. occ.														
Mobile s./S. mobiles	63	65	66	67	64	62	66	66	66	68	70	71	72	..
Stationary s./S. fixes	628	589	542	520	521	504	462	432	411	380	366	364	358	..
Total	691	654	608	587	585	566	528	498	477	448	436	435	430	..
Ireland/Irlande														
Mobile s./S. mobiles	8	9	8	8	8	10	9	9	9	..	10	..	..	..
Stationary s./S. fixes	86	88	90	92	104	107	93	97	91	..	95	..	..	..
Total	94	97	98	100	112	117	102	106	100	..	105	..	..	..
Italy/Italie *														
Mobile s./S. mobiles *	170	..	..	..	..	147	162	172	185	199	225			
Stationary s./S. fixes *	263	..	..	..	209	298	278	296	306	302	299			
Total *	433	..	..	..	412	445	440	468	491	501	524	..	..	..
Netherlands/Pays-Bas *														
Mobile s./S. mobiles	27	26	25	24	24	23	23	22	23	22	22	22	22	22
Stationary s./S. fixes	116	113	101	86	80	74	66	63	62	58	55	54	30	30
Total	143	139	126	110	103	97	89	85	85	80	77	76	53	52
Norway/Norvège														
Mobile s./S. mobiles	6	6	7	7	8	8	9	9	8	7	7	7	8	8
Stationary s./S. fixes	19	16	13	13	13	13	14	14	13	15	15	14	13	13
Total	25	22	20	20	21	21	23	23	21	22	22	21	21	21
Spain/Espagne *														
Mobile s./S. mobiles *	19	..	..	..	..	23	24	26	31	..	33	..	..	..
Stationary s./S. fixes	..	..	..	..	..	..	..	..	..	..	..	..	..	..
Total	..	..	..	..	..	..	..	..	..	..	..	..	..	..
Switzerland/Suisse														
Mobile s./S. mobiles	1	..	..	..	1	..	..	..	1	1	1	..	..	1
Stationary s./S. fixes	27	..	..	..	21	..	..	..	20	20	19	..	..	18
Total	28	..	..	..	22	..	..	..	21	21	20	..	..	20

Notes: see next page / voir page suivante

... / ...

EMISSIONS OF PARTICULATES, by source, 1980-1993
ÉMISSIONS DE PARTICULES, par source, 1980-1993

1 000 tonnes

	1980	1981	1982	1983	1984	1985	1986	1987	1988	1989	1990	1991	1992	1993
UK/Royaume-Uni *														
Mobile s./S. mobiles	124	117	122	129	140	146	159	171	188	202	210	212	220	232
Stationary s./S. fixes	436	413	407	382	334	399	415	357	304	277	250	255	238	212
Total	560	530	529	511	474	545	574	528	492	479	460	467	458	444
CSFR/RFTS														
Mobile s./S. mobiles	..	..	..	..	..	..	..	..	..	..	..	..	..	..
Stationary s./S. fixes	..	..	..	..	..	..	..	..	..	..	..	..	..	..
Total	1350	..	..	..	..	1372	1352	1299	1145	991	940	..	..	..
Czech Rep./Rép. Tchèque														
Mobile s./S. mobiles	..	..	..	..	..	..	..	..	..	..	..	..	..	..
Stationary s./S. fixes	..	..	..	..	..	..	..	..	..	..	..	..	..	..
Total	..	..	..	..	..	1015	988	951	840	673	631	592	501	..
Slovak Rep./Rép. Slovaque														
Mobile s./S. mobiles	..	..	..	..	..	..	..	..	..	..	..	..	..	..
Stationary s./S. fixes	..	..	..	..	..	..	..	..	..	..	..	..	..	..
Total	..	..	..	..	..	358	364	349	304	317	308	226	..	..
Hungary/Hongrie														
Mobile s./S. mobiles	19	..	..	..	..	11	6	6	12	6	6	11	10	..
Stationary s./S. fixes	557	..	..	..	..	481	458	406	396	270	199	187	150	..
Total	577	..	..	..	..	492	464	412	408	276	205	198	160	..
Poland/Pologne *														
Mobile s./S. mobiles	24	..	..	..	..	23	..	25	..	25	25	20	20	22
Stationary s./S. fixes *	2338	1901	1860	1731	1711	1787	1821	1803	2650	2400	1950	1680	1580	1495
Total	..	..	..	..	..	..	..	..	..	2425	1975	1700	1600	1517

Notes (emissions of particulates):

USA) Data refer to total suspended particulates.
JPN) Stationary sources and total emissions exclude industrial processes.
AUT) Mobile sources: road transport only.
FRA) Data for stationary sources include agriculture. Mobile sources: road transport only.
DEU) 1992 data are provisional.
ITA) The methodology for mobile sources changed in 1985. 1980-84 data for stationary sources and total emissions exclude industrial processes.
NLD) The estimation methodology changed in 1992.
ESP) Mobile sources: road transport only.
UKD) Data refer to black smoke.
POL) 1980-87 data for stationary sources refer to major emission sources only.

Notes (émissions de particules):

USA) Les données se réfèrent à toutes les particules en suspension.
JPN) Sources fixes et total: les émissions des procédés industriels sont exclus.
AUT) Sources mobiles: transports routiers uniquement.
FRA) Les données relatives aux sources fixes incluent l'agriculture. Sources mobiles: transports routiers uniquement.
DEU) Les données 1992 sont provisoires.
ITA) La méthodologie pour les sources mobiles a été changée en 1985. Les données 1980-84 relatives aux sources fixes et émissions totales excluent les émissions des procédés industriels.
NLD) Changement de méthode d'estimation en 1992.
ESP) Sources mobiles: transports routiers uniquement.
UKD) Les données concernent les fumées noires.
POL) Les données 1980-87 pour les sources fixes se réfèrent aux principales sources uniquement.

Source: OECD/OCDE

EMISSIONS OF CO, by source, 1980-1993
ÉMISSIONS DE CO, par source, 1980-1993

1 000 tonnes

	1980	1981	1982	1983	1984	1985	1986	1987	1988	1989	1990	1991	1992	1993
Canada														
Mobile s./S. mobiles	7757	7704	7412	7464	7136	7164	..	..	..	..	..	..	..	..
Stationary s./S. fixes	2516	..	..	..	..	3617	..	..	..	..	..	..	..	..
Total	10273	..	..	..	..	10781	..	..	..	..	..	..	..	..
Mexico/Mexique														
Mobile s./S. mobiles	..	..	..	..	..	..	..	..	..	..	..	..	..	..
Stationary s./S. fixes	..	..	..	..	..	..	..	..	..	..	..	..	..	234
Total	..	..	..	..	..	..	..	..	..	..	..	..	..	..
USA/Etats-Unis *														
Mobile s./S. mobiles	94447	90622	87100	84293	82572	81025	78137	73422	73046	68152	67534	66283	63474	68467
Stationary s./S. fixes	22585	20962	18269	20907	19917	16861	17023	16664	16828	16575	16273	15984	15619	15492
Total	117032	111583	105369	105200	102489	97885	95159	90086	89874	84727	83807	82266	79092	83960
Japan/Japon *														
Mobile s./S. mobiles *	3782	3437	3137	2901	2713	2511	2468	2434	2440	2430	2320	..	..	..
Stationary s./S. fixes	..	..	..	..	..	..	..	..	..	..	..	..	..	..
Total	..	..	..	..	..	..	..	..	..	..	..	..	..	..
Australia/Australie *														
Mobile s./S. mobiles	..	..	..	..	..	2160	..	..	..	..	..	..	..	..
Stationary s./S. fixes	..	..	..	..	..	294	..	..	..	..	..	..	..	..
Total	..	..	..	..	..	2454	..	..	..	..	..	..	..	..
Austria/Autriche *														
Mobile s./S. mobiles	754	..	..	687	..	638	629	575	534	489	444	412	348	292
Stationary s./S. fixes *	882	..	..	874	..	1010	496	1110	1044	1116	1129	1091	1066	1034
Total *	1636	..	..	1561	..	1648	1125	1685	1578	1605	1573	1503	1414	1326
Belgium/Belgique *														
Mobile s./S. mobiles	..	..	..	..	..	..	..	..	..	..	..	220	213	207
Stationary s./S. fixes	..	..	..	..	..	..	..	..	..	..	..	153	60	64
Total	..	..	..	..	..	..	..	..	..	..	..	373	273	272
Denmark/Danemark														
Mobile s./S. mobiles	505	476	472	485	506	518	547	548	557	557	575	562	529	489
Stationary s./S. fixes	130	161	175	179	182	183	191	194	188	181	183	197	203	206
Total	635	637	647	664	688	701	738	742	745	738	758	759	732	695
Finland/Finlande *														
Mobile s./S. mobiles	..	..	..	..	..	..	..	..	..	..	439	..	..	..
Stationary s./S. fixes	..	..	..	..	..	..	..	..	..	..	120	..	..	..
Total	660	..	..	..	..	..	..	..	..	..	556	..	..	..
France *														
Mobile s./S. mobiles *	8100	8000	7800	7650	7500	7400	7200	7100	6900	6700	7324	7235	6881	6376
Stationary s./S. fixes	1216	1146	1058	998	1029	999	956	936	921	975	3411	3362	3387	3383
Total	9316	9146	8858	8648	8529	8399	8156	8036	7821	7875	10735	10597	10268	9759
Germany/Allemagne *														
Mobile s./S. mobiles	..	..	..	..	..	..	..	..	..	..	6345	5919	5640	..
Stationary s./S. fixes	..	..	..	..	..	..	..	..	..	..	4564	3685	3605	..
Total	..	..	..	..	..	..	..	..	..	..	10909	9604	9245	..
w. Germany/All. occ.														
Mobile s./S. mobiles	8820	7771	7354	6899	6770	6357	6413	6233	5987	5604	5233	4802	4512	..
Stationary s./S. fixes	3193	3001	2620	2394	2577	2582	2415	2238	2189	2158	2043	2095	2065	..
Total	12013	10772	9974	9293	9347	8939	8828	8471	8176	7762	7276	6897	6577	..
Greece/Grèce														
Mobile s./S. mobiles	..	..	..	..	..	..	..	..	..	..	1059	..	..	..
Stationary s./S. fixes	..	..	..	..	..	..	..	..	..	..	421	..	..	..
Total	..	..	..	..	..	..	..	..	..	..	1480	..	..	..
Iceland/Islande *														
Mobile s./S. mobiles	28.8	..	..	..	..	32.5	34.3	40.9	40.8	40.7	29.9	29.4	29.8	29.5
Stationary s./S. fixes *	0.3	..	..	..	..	0.3	0.4	0.3	0.4	0.6	1.4	1.2	1.3	0.9
Total	29.1	..	..	..	..	32.8	34.7	41.2	41.2	41.3	31.3	30.6	31.1	30.4

Notes: see page 37 / voir page 37.

... / ...

EMISSIONS OF CO, by source, 1980-1993
ÉMISSIONS DE CO, par source, 1980-1993

1 000 tonnes

	1980	1981	1982	1983	1984	1985	1986	1987	1988	1989	1990	1991	1992	1993
Ireland/Irlande														
Mobile s./S. mobiles	420	421	408	384	366	355	337	337	317	..	341	..	..	..
Stationary s./S. fixes	77	79	85	88	98	101	107	105	102	..	113	..	..	..
Total	497	500	493	472	464	456	444	442	419	..	454	..	..	..
Italy/Italie *														
Mobile s./S. mobiles	4990	..	..	..	4920	5305	5304	5173	5096	5043	6254	..	..	..
Stationary s./S. fixes	497	..	..	..	506	1614	1517	1571	1572	1547	3014	..	..	..
Total	5487	..	..	..	5426	6919	6821	6744	6668	6590	9268	..	..	..
Netherlands/Pays-Bas *														
Mobile s./S. mobiles	1154	1055	1041	1035	1029	951	910	853	846	796	707	634	619	579
Stationary s./S. fixes	462	449	419	405	414	441	428	425	418	416	400	396	328	320
Total	1616	1504	1460	1440	1443	1392	1338	1278	1265	1212	1108	1029	947	899
Norway/Norvège														
Mobile s./S. mobiles	729	719	752	752	770	784	828	830	813	760	743	708	682	640
Stationary s./S. fixes	157	154	142	145	156	178	178	184	184	195	198	173	167	166
Total	886	873	894	897	926	962	1007	1014	997	955	941	881	849	805
Portugal *														
Mobile s./S. mobiles	511	..	..	249	..	..	..	..	..	..	626	..	..	..
Stationary s./S. fixes	22	..	..	18	..	..	..	..	..	..	460	..	..	..
Total	533	..	..	267	..	..	..	..	..	..	1086	..	..	..
Spain/Espagne *														
Mobile s./S. mobiles *	2828	..	..	..	..	2769	2822	2856	2966	..	2721	..	..	..
Stationary s./S. fixes	..	..	..	..	..	..	..	..	..	..	2229	..	..	..
Total	..	..	..	..	..	..	..	..	..	..	4950	..	..	..
Sweden/Suède *														
Mobile s./S. mobiles *	1430	..	1434	..	..	1200	..	..	1350	..	..	..	..	..
Stationary s./S. fixes	20	..	320	..	..	..	..	..	..	..	..	..	..	..
Total *	1450	..	1754	..	..	..	..	..	1500	..	..	..	..	..
Switzerland/Suisse														
Mobile s./S. mobiles	538	..	..	456	..	..	..	..	332	301	271	247	223	199
Stationary s./S. fixes	173	..	..	165	..	..	..	..	162	161	160	159	159	159
Total	711	..	..	621	..	..	..	..	494	462	431	406	382	358
UK/Royaume-Uni														
Mobile s./S. mobiles	3990	4070	4210	4229	4428	4535	4779	5109	5495	5911	5884	5909	5679	5163
Stationary s./S. fixes	905	871	863	836	743	869	862	806	740	692	653	676	638	478
Total	4895	4941	5073	5065	5171	5404	5641	5915	6235	6603	6537	6585	6317	5641
CSFR/RFTS														
Mobile s./S. mobiles	..	..	..	..	..	..	..	..	..	..	..	..	..	..
Stationary s./S. fixes	..	..	..	..	..	..	..	..	..	..	..	..	..	..
Total	..	..	..	..	..	1239	1085	1083	1090	1496	1291	..	..	..
Czech Rep./Rép. Tchèque														
Mobile s./S. mobiles	..	..	..	..	..	..	..	..	..	..	..	..	..	..
Stationary s./S. fixes	..	..	..	..	..	..	..	..	..	..	..	..	..	..
Total	..	..	..	..	..	899	740	738	737	885	888	1102	1045	..
Slovak Rep./Rép. Slovaque *														
Mobile s./S. mobiles	..	..	..	..	..	..	..	..	..	..	..	..	..	..
Stationary s./S. fixes	..	..	..	..	..	..	..	..	..	..	..	..	..	..
Total	..	..	..	..	..	339	345	345	353	544	403	313	..	..
Hungary/Hongrie *														
Mobile s./S. mobiles	309	..	..	..	..	270	284	299	308	328	323	487	490	..
Stationary s./S. fixes	1019	..	..	..	..	661	669	618	656	559	444	426	346	..
Total	1328	..	..	..	..	931	953	917	964	887	767	913	836	..
Poland/Pologne *														
Mobile s./S. mobiles	1457	..	..	..	..	1192	..	1250	1250	1380	1418	1470	1512	1576
Stationary s./S. fixes *	1946	1700	1496	1610	1486	1353	1496	1456	1368	1335	1106	793	675	533
Total	3403	..	..	..	..	2545	..	2706	2618	2715	2524	2263	2187	2109

Notes: see page 37 / voir page 37

EMISSIONS OF VOC (a), by source, 1980-1993
ÉMISSIONS DE COV (a), par source, 1980-1993

1 000 tonnes

	1980	1981	1982	1983	1984	1985	1986	1987	1988	1989	1990	1991	1992	1993
Canada *														
Mobile s./S. mobiles	1026	1045	1015	1008	960	908	905	922	915	863	816	748	..	..
Stationary s./S. fixes	1073	..	..	..	..	1198	1214	1239	1266	1278	1270	1266	..	..
Total	2099	..	..	..	..	2107	2120	2161	2181	2141	2086	2014	..	..
Mexico/Mexique														
Mobile s./S. mobiles	..	..	..	..	..	..	..	..	..	..	..	..	..	..
Stationary s./S. fixes	..	..	..	..	..	..	..	..	..	..	..	..	..	231
Total	..	..	..	..	..	..	..	..	..	..	..	..	..	..
USA/Etats-Unis *														
Mobile s./S. mobiles	12070	11762	11454	11072	10868	10650	10248	9510	9353	8463	8253	8048	7462	7538
Stationary s./S. fixes	13649	12282	11102	11980	12844	12041	12749	12920	13345	13227	13224	13184	13154	12750
Total	25719	24044	22556	23053	23712	22691	22997	22430	22698	21690	21477	21232	20617	20287
Australia/Australie *														
Mobile s./S. mobiles	..	..	..	..	..	271	..	..	..	..	..	..	..	..
Stationary s./S. fixes	..	..	..	..	..	311	..	..	..	..	..	..	..	..
Total	..	..	..	..	..	582	..	..	..	..	..	..	..	..
Austria/Autriche *														
Mobile s./S. mobiles	138	..	..	145	..	149	..	148	142	136	131	129	114	105
Stationary s./S. fixes *	236	..	..	246	..	263	..	291	290	297	299	292	301	283
Total *	374	..	..	391	..	412	..	439	432	433	430	421	415	388
Belgium/Belgique *														
Mobile s./S. mobiles	..	..	..	..	..	..	..	..	..	..	89	..	..	..
Stationary s./S. fixes	..	..	..	..	..	..	..	..	..	..	50	..	..	..
Total	..	..	..	..	..	..	..	..	..	..	139	..	..	..
Denmark/Danemark														
Mobile s./S. mobiles	100	94	93	96	99	102	107	108	109	109	111	108	103	95
Stationary s./S. fixes	..	..	..	..	..	..	..	..	..	..	..	..	..	..
Total	..	..	..	..	..	..	..	..	..	..	..	..	..	..
Finland/Finlande *														
Mobile s./S. mobiles	80	..	..	..	..	85	..	103	104	..	86	..	..	..
Stationary s./S. fixes *	80	..	..	..	..	96	..	103	104	..	123	..	..	..
Total	163	..	..	..	..	181	..	206	208	..	209	..	..	..
France *														
Mobile s./S. mobiles	..	..	..	..	..	..	..	..	..	..	1292	1272	1251	1166
Stationary s./S. fixes	..	..	..	..	..	..	..	..	..	..	1110	1089	1081	1120
Total	..	..	..	..	..	..	..	..	..	..	2402	2361	2332	2286
Germany/Allemagne *														
Mobile s./S. mobiles	..	..	..	..	..	..	..	..	..	..	1324	1251	1204	..
Stationary s./S. fixes	..	..	..	..	..	..	..	..	..	..	1642	1597	1561	..
Total	..	..	..	..	..	..	..	..	..	..	2966	2848	2765	..
w. Germany/All. occ.														
Mobile s./S. mobiles	1093	1037	1047	1053	1068	1055	1061	1035	998	928	876	796	752	..
Stationary s./S. fixes	1520	1497	1491	1470	1466	1454	1439	1423	1402	1387	1362	1343	1321	..
Total	2613	2534	2538	2523	2534	2509	2500	2458	2400	2315	2238	2139	2073	..
Greece/Grèce *														
Mobile s./S. mobiles *	62	..	..	..	..	115	..	..	..	..	138	..	..	..
Stationary s./S. fixes *	68	..	..	..	..	58	..	..	..	..	105	..	..	..
Total *	130	..	..	..	..	173	..	..	..	..	243	..	..	..
Iceland/Islande *														
Mobile s./S. mobiles	4.4	..	..	..	..	4.9	5.2	6.3	6.2	6.3	3.9	3.9	3.9	..
Stationary s./S. fixes *	1.0	..	..	..	..	1.0	2.0	2.0	1.0	2.0	2.3	3.3	2.9	..
Total	5.4	..	..	..	..	5.9	7.2	8.3	7.2	8.3	6.2	7.2	6.8	..
Ireland/Irlande														
Mobile s./S. mobiles	72	38	36	34	32	58	61	65	66	..	62	..	..	..
Stationary s./S. fixes	29	25	27	28	32	33	37	36	35	..	35	..	..	..
Total	101	63	63	62	64	91	97	101	101	..	97	..	..	..

Notes: see page 37 / voir page 37.

... / ...

EMISSIONS OF VOC (a), by source, 1980-1993
ÉMISSIONS DE COV (a), par source, 1980-1993

1 000 tonnes

	1980	1981	1982	1983	1984	1985	1986	1987	1988	1989	1990	1991	1992	1993
Italy/Italie *														
Mobile s./S. mobiles *	599	..	..	..	629	827	859	866	883	907	1085	..	..	..
Stationary s./S. fixes	97	..	..	..	95	944	939	999	996	1005	1312	..	..	..
Total	696	..	..	..	724	1771	1798	1865	1879	1912	2396	..	..	..
Netherlands/Pays-Bas *														
Mobile s./S. mobiles	262	249	247	248	248	235	229	222	224	215	201	182	177	168
Stationary s./S. fixes	333	321	311	292	281	281	275	278	271	271	237	237	250	243
Total	595	570	558	540	529	516	505	500	495	486	439	419	427	411
Norway/Norvège														
Mobile s./S. mobiles	84	84	96	96	102	98	103	107	105	105	102	99	96	95
Stationary s./S. fixes	90	103	101	115	122	136	147	146	144	164	164	167	183	189
Total	174	186	197	211	224	234	251	253	248	268	266	266	279	284
Portugal *														
Mobile s./S. mobiles	51	..	..	56	..	53	59	58	62	87	..	..	..	..
Stationary s./S. fixes	41	..	..	51	..	81	86	90	94	120	..	..	..	..
Total	92	..	..	107	..	134	145	149	156	207	..	..	..	..
Spain/Espagne *														
Mobile s./S. mobiles *	404	..	..	..	..	407	442	472	513	..	488	..	..	..
Stationary s./S. fixes *	356	..	..	..	..	378	374	378	391	..	630	..	..	..
Total	760	..	..	..	..	785	816	850	904	..	1118	..	..	..
Sweden/Suède *														
Mobile s./S. mobiles	..	..	..	..	..	..	..	..	225	..	200	..	186	..
Stationary s./S. fixes	..	..	..	..	..	..	..	..	361	..	331	..	316	..
Total	..	..	..	..	..	..	..	..	586	..	531	..	502	..
Switzerland/Suisse *														
Mobile s./S. mobiles	92	..	..	..	90	..	..	..	73	68	64	59	53	48
Stationary s./S. fixes	219	..	..	..	249	..	..	..	238	236	233	231	221	215
Total	311	..	..	..	339	..	..	..	311	304	297	290	274	263
UK/Royaume-Uni														
Mobile s./S. mobiles	866	867	888	890	923	934	976	1027	1089	1142	1119	1096	1035	938
Stationary s./S. fixes	1411	1408	1413	1414	1404	1429	1440	1437	1429	1428	1425	1430	1428	1400
Total	2277	2275	2301	2304	2327	2363	2416	2464	2518	2570	2544	2526	2463	2338
CSFR/RFTS														
Mobile s./S. mobiles	..	..	..	..	..	..	..	..	..	..	..	..	..	..
Stationary s./S. fixes	..	..	..	..	..	..	..	..	..	..	..	..	..	..
Total	..	..	..	..	..	197	203	202	202	320	304	..	..	..
Czech Rep./Rép. Tchèque														
Mobile s./S. mobiles	..	..	..	..	..	..	..	..	..	..	..	..	..	..
Stationary s./S. fixes	..	..	..	..	..	..	..	..	..	..	..	..	..	..
Total	..	..	..	..	..	136	140	139	139	228	225	227	205	..
Slovak Rep./Rép. Slovaque														
Mobile s./S. mobiles	..	..	..	..	..	..	..	..	..	..	..	..	..	..
Stationary s./S. fixes	..	..	..	..	..	..	..	..	..	..	..	..	..	..
Total	..	..	..	..	..	61	63	62	64	67	79	..	107	..
Hungary/Hongrie *														
Mobile s./S. mobiles	..	..	..	..	..	..	..	..	..	91	..	..	73	68
Stationary s./S. fixes	..	..	..	..	..	..	..	..	..	114	..	..	71	68
Total *	215	..	..	..	..	232	..	228	205	205	205	144	136	..
Poland/Pologne														
Mobile s./S. mobiles	371	350	320	339	337	330	348	345	347	390	401	345	369	320
Stationary s./S. fixes	771	733	735	763	783	821	828	835	832	793	589	451	410	457
Total	1142	1083	1055	1102	1120	1151	1176	1180	1179	1183	990	796	779	777

Notes: see next page / voir page suivante.

Source: OECD/OCDE

Notes (CO emissions):
USA) Break in time series in 1993.
JPN) Mobile sources: road transport only.
AUS) National figures based on capital city data.
AUT) 1980, 1985 and 1992 data for stationary sources and total emissions are Secretariat estimates.
BEL) Data refer to Wallonia only. Change in estimation methodology in 1991.
FIN) 1990 data are from CORINAIR 90.
FRA) 1991-93 data are provisional. 1991-93 data for mobile sources include 1990 data for air and sea traffic. The estimation methodology changed in 1990.
DEU) 1992 data are provisional.
ISL) Emissions from industrial processes are excluded. The estimation methodology changed in 1990. 1993 figure for stationary sources is provisional.
ITA) The estimation methodology changed in 1985. Through 1984, industrial processes are excluded.
NLD) Change in estimation methodology in 1992.
PRT) 1980-85 data are Secretariat estimates.
ESP) Break in time series in 1990 (CORINAIR 90). 1980-88 data for mobile sources refer to road transport only.
SWE) Mobile sources: road transport only. 1988 figure for total emissions is a Secretariat estimate.
SLO) 1991 data are Secretariat estimates.
HUN) 1980-90 data are estimates.
POL) Stationary sources: data refer to major emission sources only.

Source: OECD/OCDE

Notes (émissions de CO):
USA) Rupture de série en 1993.
JPN) Sources mobiles: transports routiers uniquement.
AUS) Données nationales fondées sur des données relatives à la capitale.
AUT) Les données 1980, 1985 et 1992 relatives aux sources fixes et aux émissions totales sont des estimations du Secrétariat.
BEL) Données relatives à la Wallonie uniquement. Changement de méthode d'estimation en 1991.
FIN) Les données 1990 sont de CORINAIR 90.
FRA) Les données 1991-93 sont provisoires. Les données 1991-93 pour les sources mobiles comprennent des chiffres 1990 pour les transports maritimes et aériens. La méthode d'estimation a été changée en 1990.
DEU) Les données 1992 sont provisoires.
ISL) Les émissions des procédés industriels sont exclus. La méthode d'estimation a été changée en 1990. Le chiffre 1993 pour les sources fixes est provisoire.
ITA) Rupture de série en 1985 due à un changement de méthode d'estimation. Jusqu'en 1984, les procédé industriels sont exclus.
NLD) 1992: changement de méthode d'estimation.
PRT) Les données 1980-85 sont des estimations du Secrétariat.
ESP) Rupture de série en 1990 (CORINAIR 90). Les données 1980-88 relatives aux sources mobiles concernent les transports routiers uniquement.
SWE) Sources mobiles: transports routiers uniquement. Le chiffre 1988 pour les émissions totales est une estimation du Secrétariat.
SLO) Les données 1991 sont des estimations du Secrétariat.
HUN) Les données 1980-90 sont des estimations.
POL) Sources fixes: se réfèrent aux principales sources uniquement.

Notes (VOC emissions):
a) Anthropogenic emissions of VOC other than methane (CH_4).
CAN) Total VOCs.
USA) Break in time series in 1993.
AUS) National figures based on capital city data.
AUT) Stationary sources and total emissions include Secretariat estimates.
BEL) 1990 data are for Wallonia only.
FIN) 1990 data are from CORINAIR 90. Stationary sources: 1990 excludes non-industrial fuel combustion.
FRA) 1991-93 data are provisional. 1990 data are from CORINAIR 90. 1991-93 data are from CORINAIR/UNECE-EMEP. Mobile sources 1991-93: use the same air and sea traffic data as 1990.
DEU) 1992 data are provisional.
GRC) Break in time series between 1980 and 1985. 1985 data are from CORINAIR 85 and 1990 data are from CORINAIR 90. 1985-1990 data for mobile sources refer to road transport only. Stationary sources exclude emissions from the extraction and distribution of fossil fuels.
ISL) Not all stationary sources are included; totals are primarily from the use of solvents. 1990-92 data for stationary sources are provisional. Solvents included in stationary sources refer to white spirit only. The estimation methodology changed in 1990.
ITA) The methodology for mobile sources changed in 1985. For mobile and stationary sources, data up to 1984 are based only on emissions from fuel combustion and include CH_4; from 1985, other processes are taken into account.
LUX) Total VOCs.
NLD) Includes CH_4 emissions from mobile and stationary fuel combustion. Change in the estimation methodology in 1992.
PRT) 1983 data are Secretariat estimates. From 1986, data include emissions from sludge treatment.
ESP) 1980-88 data for mobile sources refer to road transport only. Break in time series in 1990 (CORINAIR 90). Stationary sources: 1980-89 exclude industrial combustion; 1980 excludes industrial processes.
SWE) Total VOCs.
CHE) Total VOCs.
HUN) 1980-90 data are estimates.

Source: OECD/OCDE

Notes (émissions de COV):
a) Émissions anthropiques de COV autres que le méthane (CH_4).
CAN) COV totaux.
USA) Rupture de série en 1993.
AUS) Données nationales fondées sur des données relatives à la capitale.
AUT) Sources fixes et émissions totales: estimations du Secrétariat.
BEL) Les données 1990 concernent la Wallonie seulement.
FIN) Les données 1990 sont de CORINAIR 90. Le chiffre 1990 pour les sources fixes exclut la combustion non industrielle.
FRA) Données 1991-93: provisoires. Données 1990: CORINAIR 90. Données 1991-93: CORINAIR/UNECE-EMEP. Sources mobiles 1991-93: comprennent les chiffres 1990 pour les transports maritimes et aériens.
DEU) Les données 1992 sont provisoires.
GRC) Rupture de série entre 1980 et 1985. Les données 1985 sont de CORINAIR 85 et les données 1990 sont de CORINAIR 90. Sources mobiles: les données 1985, 1990 concernent les transports routiers uniquement. Sources fixes: Les données excluent les émissions dues à l'estraction et à la distribution des combustibles solides.
ISL) Toutes les sources ne sont pas comprises. Total: émissions que proviennent principalment de l'utilisation des solvants. Les données 1990-92 pour les sources fixes sont provisoires. Les solvants compris dans les sources fixes se rapportent au white spirit seulement. La méthode d'estimation a été changée en 1990.
ITA) La méthodologie pour les sources mobiles a été changée en 1985. Les données 1980-84 relatives aux sources mobiles et fixes ne comprennent que les émissions issues de la combustion et incluent le méthane; depuis 1985, les autres procédés sont pris en compte.
LUX) COV totaux.
NLD) Inclut les émissions mobiles et fixes de CH_4 dues à la combustion. Changement de méthode d'estimation en 1992.
PRT) Les données 1983 sont des estimations du Secrétariat. Depuis 1986, les données incluent les émissions issues du traitement des boues.
ESP) Sources mobiles: les données 1980-88 concernent les transports routiers uniquement. Rupture de série en 1990 (CORINAIR 90). Sources fixes: les données 1980-89 excluent la combustion industrielle; 1980 exclut les procédés industriels.
SWE) COV totaux.
CHE) COV totaux.
HUN) Les données 1980-90 sont des estimations.

The following table presents trends in emissions of CO_2 from energy use. Emission estimates are based on data for total primary energy supply (excluding international marine bunkers) and refer to fossil fuel combustion. Flaring of natural gas is excluded. Calculations have been made according to the methodology developed by the Intergovernmental Panel on Climate change (IPCC).

Combustion emissions contribute to the increase of atmospheric CO_2 concentrations and thus to global atmospheric problems: CO_2 is the gas that contributes the largest share to the greenhouse effect, with its potential effects on climate, sea level and world agriculture.

When interpreting these data, it should be kept in mind that they are provisional OECD estimates based on the same emission coefficients for all countries, and that they do not include CO_2 emissions from other human activities (e.g. cement production). See also footnotes below table.

Le tableau suivant présente les tendances en matière d'émissions de CO_2 dues à l'utilisation de l'énergie. Les émissions ont été estimées sur la base des approvisionnements totaux en énergie primaire (non compris les soutages marins internationaux) et concernent la combustion de combustibles fossiles. Le brûlage du gaz naturel est exclus. Les calculs ont été faits selon la méthologie elaboré par le Groupe d'experts intergouvernemental sur l'évolution des climats (GIEC).

Les émissions de combustion contribuent à l'augmentation des concentrations de CO_2 dans l'atmosphère et ainsi aux problèmes atmosphériques mondiaux : le CO_2 est le gaz qui contribue pour la plus grande part à l'effet de serre, avec des répercussions potentielles sur le climat, le niveau de la mer et l'agriculture mondiale.

En interprétant ces données il faut tenir compte du fait que ce sont des estimations provisoires de l'OCDE, utilisant les mêmes coefficients d'émissions pour tous les pays, et qu'elles ne comprennent pas les émissions de CO_2 provenant d'autres activités humaines telles que la production de ciment. Voir également les notes en bas du tableau.

CO$_2$ EMISSIONS FROM ENERGY USE (a), 1980-1993
ÉMISSIONS DE CO$_2$ DUES A L'UTILISATION D'ÉNERGIE (a), 1980-1993

million tonnes/millions de tonnes

	\multicolumn{14}{c}{Emissions / Émissions (a)}	Marine bunkers/ Soutages marins (b)
	1980	1981	1982	1983	1984	1985	1986	1987	1988	1989	1990	1991	1992	1993	1993 (c)
Canada	435	420	406	391	411	405	403	418	437	455	432	427	439	443	1.8
Mexico/Mexique	244	258	268	251	268	273	263	277	279	298	308	323	328	323	1.2
USA/Etats-Unis	4 770	4 627	4 400	4 400	4 556	4 621	4 594	4 769	4 943	5 020	4 895	4 885	4 948	5 095	102.0
Japan/Japon	920	899	871	870	932	913	911	899	990	1 020	1 068	1 089	1 101	1 091	20.9
Australia/Australie	215	215	225	215	223	225	227	240	242	261	268	268	271	283	2.1
N.Zealand/N.Zélande	18	17	19	19	20	23	22	23	24	26	25	26	28	28	0.9
Austria/Autriche	59	56	53	53	56	56	56	57	54	56	59	64	57	57	0.0
Belgium/Belgique	127	118	113	103	104	105	106	107	108	110	109	118	117	113	13.7
Denmark/Danemark	63	54	56	52	54	63	63	62	58	52	53	63	57	59	4.3
Finland/Finlande	59	47	45	43	43	52	54	61	54	55	53	55	51	55	1.7
France	487	438	423	406	392	388	371	373	361	379	379	398	374	368	7.7
Germany/Allemagne	1 085	1 048	1 005	1 001	1 024	1 034	1 035	1 030	1 023	999	983	951	911	897	7.0
Greece/Grèce	49	48	49	52	54	59	56	61	66	72	73	73	75	74	9.9
Iceland/Islande	2	2	2	2	2	2	2	2	2	2	3	2	2	2	0.1
Ireland/Irlande	27	27	26	27	27	28	30	31	31	31	33	33	33	34	0.2
Italy/Italie	377	368	358	356	359	363	366	385	389	407	412	418	416	408	7.7
Luxembourg	12	10	10	9	10	10	10	9	10	10	11	11	11	12	0.0
Netherlands/Pays-Bas	159	157	135	140	148	149	153	156	157	158	160	168	166	171	37.0
Norway/Norvège	31	29	27	28	29	30	34	32	29	33	32	32	31	32	1.6
Portugal	26	26	28	29	28	27	30	31	33	41	42	43	47	46	1.6
Spain/Espagne	197	201	197	199	191	191	190	191	196	214	217	226	235	223	10.8
Sweden/Suède	73	70	63	59	57	62	62	58	60	56	53	52	51	52	2.9
Switzerland/Suisse	42	40	38	41	41	42	44	42	42	41	44	45	45	43	0.1
Turkey/Turquie	73	73	79	85	90	99	108	130	116	126	138	141	144	150	0.3
UK/Royaume-Uni	594	570	561	553	536	568	579	589	585	572	584	592	570	558	7.7
Former CSFR/Ex-RFTS	254	253	254	254	261	257	257	256	238	229	221	199	179	..	0.0
Hungary/Hongrie	87	84	83	84	86	84	82	83	79	71	69	67	63	..	0.0
Poland/Pologne	449	412	413	420	446	459	465	481	450	430	352	349	339	..	0.9
North America/Amérique N.	5 449	5 305	5 073	5 041	5 235	5 300	5 260	5 464	5 659	5 773	5 634	5 635	5 715	5 861	105.0
OECD/OCDE Europe	3 543	3 381	3 269	3 237	3 243	3 328	3 349	3 408	3 373	3 415	3 439	3 485	3 396	3 353	114.0
EU/UE-15	3 394	3 238	3 123	3 081	3 082	3 156	3 160	3 202	3 184	3 214	3 222	3 265	3 174	3 126	111.9
OECD/OCDE	10 145	9 818	9 457	9 383	9 653	9 788	9 768	10 034	10 289	10 495	10 434	10 503	10 510	10 616	242.9
Non-OECD/Non OCDE Europe	1 166	1 119	1 126	1 147	1 190	1 202	1 220	1 242	1 195	1 153	1 028	931	856	..	4.7
Africa/Afrique	434	478	513	545	565	577	583	617	631	648	666	670	675	..	20.8
Asia/Asie	903	946	965	1 030	1 067	1 145	1 233	1 295	1 411	1 509	1 619	1 718	1 848	..	68.9
P.Rep.China/Rép.Pop.Chine	1 482	1 463	1 524	1 603	1 741	1 871	1 984	2 115	2 248	2 337	2 374	2 485	2 563	..	0.0
Former USSR/Ex-URSS	3 315	3 332	3 390	3 405	3 450	3 525	3 595	3 714	3 786	3 765	3 660	3 613	3 299	..	14.2
Latin America/Amérique Latine	806	807	823	797	819	830	855	904	912	938	976	984	1 014	..	22.2
Middle East/Moyen Orient	364	398	416	462	518	554	583	611	628	646	682	654	713	..	47.3
Total Non-OECD/non OCDE	8 232	8 293	8 497	8 746	9 089	9 436	9 795	10 225	10 537	10 704	10 704	10 737	10 650	..	176.9
World/Monde	18 347	18 076	17 916	18 088	18 703	19 185	19 524	20 223	20 797	21 170	21 109	21 207	21 141	..	408.8

Notes:
a) Anthropogenic CO$_2$ emissions from energy use only. Oil held in international marine bunkers is excluded and presented separately. Oil and gas for non-energy purposes, and the use of biomass fuels are excluded. Peat is included.
b) International marine bunkers represent quantities delivered to sea-going ships of all flags, including warships and fishing vessels. Quantities are assigned to the country in which these bunkers are situated.
c) Non OECD countries: 1992 data.

Source: IEA-OECD / AIE-OCDE

Notes :
a) Emissions anthropiques de CO2 issues de l'utilisation de l'énergie. Le pétrole détenu dans les soutages marins internationaux est exclu et est présenté séparément. Le pétrole et le gaz utilisés à des fins non énergétiques, et la biomasse ne sont pas inclus. La tourbe est incluse.
b) Les soutages marins sont les quantités livrées aux navires (y compris les navires de guerre et les bateaux de pêche), quel que soit leur pavillon. Les quantités sont attribuées aux pays où se situent ces soutages.
c) Pays non OCDE: données 1992.

The following table shows changes in energy-related emissions of CO_2 by source: mobile sources, bunkers, industry, energy transformation, and other.

See preceding table for definitions. See also footnotes below table.

Le tableau suivant présente les variations des émissions de CO_2 dues à l'énergie, par source : sources mobiles, soutages marins, industrie, transformation de l'énergie et autres.

Voir le tableau précédent pour les définitions. Voir également les notes en bas du tableau.

CO$_2$ EMISSIONS BY SOURCE (a), 1980-1993 (b)
ÉMISSIONS DE CO$_2$ PAR SOURCE (a), 1980-1993 (b)

	Mobile sources/ Sources mobiles		Bunkers/ Soutages		Energy transformation/ Transformation de l'énergie (c)		Industry Industrie (d)		Others/ Autres (e)	
	1980	1993	1980	1993	1980	1993	1980	1993	1980	1993
Canada	129.6	129.9	4.7	1.8	98.9	124.5	106.0	93.6	89.6	86.0
Mexico/Mexique	69.9	103.8	0.9	1.2	61.4	94.0	58.1	75.7	33.8	43.9
USA/Etats-Unis	1 251.4	1 489.8	89.3	102.0	1 749.1	2 128.4	928.7	694.3	697.9	625.1
Japan/Japon	160.3	244.1	36.9	20.9	318.8	383.8	307.3	296.9	126.0	149.1
Australia/Australie	51.7	68.0	3.5	2.1	108.8	143.3	42.1	46.6	11.1	12.9
N.Zealand/N.Zélande	7.3	11.0	1.1	0.9	3.0	5.8	4.5	5.8	2.8	2.2
Austria/Autriche	13.0	17.7	0.0	0.0	11.2	12.1	17.6	11.9	16.1	13.1
Belgium/Belgique	17.2	25.2	7.6	13.7	35.3	24.9	40.8	31.1	33.4	29.3
Denmark/Danemark	10.7	13.3	1.3	4.3	26.5	30.9	8.1	5.0	18.8	9.3
Finland/Finlande	8.9	12.1	1.9	1.7	19.9	19.2	14.0	14.5	11.5	7.8
France	94.9	133.2	12.6	7.7	126.7	41.3	134.5	86.2	119.5	101.5
Germany/Allemagne	137.8	184.6	11.1	7.0	429.7	370.2	254.5	152.7	252.9	199.6
Greece/Grèce	11.9	19.5	2.7	9.9	19.7	37.8	10.1	9.2	5.9	7.9
Iceland/Islande	0.6	0.8	0.0	0.1	0.0	0.0	0.5	0.4	0.7	0.9
Ireland/Irlande	5.2	6.9	0.2	0.2	8.6	12.6	5.7	4.5	7.2	8.6
Italy/Italie	73.6	109.6	13.2	7.7	120.2	131.9	98.6	84.6	81.3	78.3
Luxembourg	1.5	3.9	0.0	0.0	0.1	0.2	9.1	6.0	1.5	1.5
Netherlands/Pays-Bas	25.4	34.5	29.6	37.0	46.7	55.1	37.9	34.7	46.3	42.0
Norway/Norvège	9.3	13.7	0.9	1.6	3.2	7.7	10.9	6.0	5.5	2.4
Portugal	7.7	13.5	1.4	1.6	6.7	18.9	8.0	9.2	2.8	4.0
Spain/Espagne	48.1	73.9	5.1	10.8	70.6	75.4	54.5	45.3	19.9	23.4
Sweden/Suède	17.3	21.3	2.7	2.9	10.2	9.2	21.4	12.0	26.6	9.8
Switzerland/Suisse	12.5	17.7	0.0	0.1	1.5	1.2	8.7	4.7	19.3	21.1
Turkey/Turquie	16.8	33.4	0.0	0.3	15.0	43.7	22.9	38.7	17.4	30.5
UK/Royaume-Uni	98.9	139.0	7.6	7.7	259.0	203.1	107.1	81.8	119.8	117.2
Former CSFR/Ex-RFTS	16.0	6.0	0.0	0.0	131.6	101.6	60.8	30.1	40.5	41.8
Hungary/Hongrie	10.2	10.1	0.0	0.0	34.8	25.8	17.5	8.0	24.8	17.9
Poland/Pologne	33.7	25.6	2.7	0.9	243.5	204.6	76.6	46.6	93.3	65.6
North America/Amérique N.	1 450.9	1 723.5	94.9	105.0	1 909.4	2 346.9	1 092.7	863.5	821.3	754.9
Australia/Australie-NZ	59.0	79.1	4.6	3.0	111.8	149.0	46.6	52.4	13.8	15.1
OECD/OCDE Europe	611.3	873.8	97.7	114.0	1 210.6	1 095.2	865.0	638.4	806.3	707.9
UE/EU-15	572.1	808.1	96.9	111.9	1 190.8	1 042.7	822.1	588.8	763.4	653.0
OECD/OCDE	2 281.4	2 920.5	234.2	242.9	3 550.6	3 974.9	2 311.6	1 851.2	1 767.4	1 627.0
Non-OECD/Non OCDE Europe	89.7	77.6	3.3	4.7	532.1	504.5	294.0	131.1	223.7	154.1
Africa/Afrique	105.5	131.4	16.8	20.8	192.7	361.9	118.7	135.2	39.5	72.4
Asia/Asie	188.9	407.1	22.8	68.9	260.4	698.1	340.4	616.5	122.9	195.6
P.Rep.China/Rép.Pop.Chine	83.1	152.6	0.0	0.0	396.4	836.2	691.4	1 080.9	320.9	491.1
Former USSR/Ex-URSS	362.1	276.0	14.2	14.2	1 329.6	1 448.2	1 126.4	128.6	597.4	1 456.6
Latin America/Amérique Latine	288.0	366.9	22.9	22.2	206.9	267.0	225.3	267.5	101.4	128.9
Middle East/Moyen Orient	124.8	182.8	34.9	47.3	121.0	274.0	106.5	122.0	49.4	187.7
Total Non OECD/non OCDE	1 171.3	1 490.5	113.9	176.9	2 976.1	4 290.3	2 844.2	2 406.0	1 421.7	2 640.4
World/Monde	3 452.7	4 411.0	348.1	419.9	6 526.7	8 265.2	5 155.8	4 257.2	3 189.1	4 267.4

Notes:
a) Anthropogenic CO2 emissions from energy use only. Oil held in international marine bunkers is presented separately. Quantities are assigned to the countries in which bunker deliveries were made. Oil and gas for non-energy purposes, and the use of biomass fuels are excluded. Peat is included.
b) Non OECD countries: 1992 data.
c) Electricity and heat plants, refineries.
d) Refineries excluded.
e) Agriculture, commerce, residential sector.

Notes :
a) Emissions anthropiques de CO2 issues de l'utilisation de l'énergie. Le pétrole détenu dans les soutages marins internationaux est présenté séparément. Les quantités sont attribuées aux pays auxquels sont délivrés ces soutages. Le pétrole et le gaz utilisés à des fins non énergétiques et la biomasse ne sont pas inclus. La tourbe est incluse.
b) Pays non OCDE : données 1992.
c) Centrales électriques, raffineries.
d) Non compris les raffineries.
e) Agriculture, commerce, résidentiel.

Source: OECD-IEA/OCDE-AIE

The following table presents man-made emissions of greenhouse gases for the latest year available. Data refer to total emissions of CO_2 (emissions from energy use and industrial processes, i.e. cement production), CH_4 (methane emissions from solid waste, livestock, mining of hard coal and lignite, rice paddies, agriculture and leaks from natural gas pipelines), CFCs (based on consumption of CFCs) and nitrous oxide (N_2O).

The addition of man-made greenhouse gases to the earth-atmosphere system disturbs the balance of its radiative energy budget, leading to a potential increase in the temperature of the earth's surface and related potential effects on climate, sea level rise and world agriculture. CO_2, CFCs and CH_4 account for a major proportion of the global warming potential.

When interpreting these data, it should be kept in mind that these are preliminary estimates of amounts of greenhouse gases emitted and that these are gross emissions.

Le tableau suivant présente les émissions anthropiques de gaz à effet de serre pour la dernière année disponible. Les données concernent les émissions totales de CO_2 (émissions provenant de l'utilisation de l'énergie et des procédés industriels, *i.e.* production du ciment), de CH_4 (émissions de méthane provenant des déchets solides, du bétail, de l'exploitation minière de charbon et de lignite, des rizières, et des fuites des conduites de gaz naturel), des CFC (émissions basées sur la consommation de CFCs) et d'oxyde nitreux (N_2O).

L'addition humaine de gaz à effet de serre au système terre-atmosphère perturbe l'équilibre de son budget d'énergie radiative intensifiant ainsi l'augmentation potentielle de la température à la surface de la terre et d'autres effets qui y sont liés (impacts sur le climat, sur l'augmentation du niveau de la mer et sur l'agriculture mondiale). Ensemble, les CFC, le CH_4 et le CO_2 sont responsables d'une majeure partie du potentiel de réchauffement.

En interprétant ces informations, il faut tenir compte du fait qu'il s'agit d'évaluations préliminaires des quantités de gaz à effet de serre émis et que ce sont des émissions brutes.

EMISSIONS OF GREENHOUSE GASES, early 1990s (a)
ÉMISSIONS DE GAZ À EFFET DE SERRE, début des années 90 (a)

1 000 tonnes

| | | CH₄ | CFCs (b) | N₂O | CO₂ emissions/Émissions de CO₂ | | |
					from energy use/ de l'utilisation d'énergie (c)	from ind. processes/ des procédés industriels (d)	Total CO2
Canada		2 153	5	92	443 260	16 130	459 390
Mexico/Mexique		2 400	10	..	323 420	13 304	336 724
USA/Etats-Unis		29 000	60	428	5 094 560	34 174	5 128 734
Japan/Japon		1 380	47	48	1 090 660	55 700	1 146 360
Australia/Australie	*	4 500	3.4	..	282 920	3 363	286 283
N.Zealand/N.Zélande	*	2 087	0.8	12-48	27 730	2 490	30 220
Austria/Autriche		608	6	4	57 000	5 580	62 580
Belgium/Belgique	*	179	3	27	113 200	3 582	116 782
Denmark/Danemark		396	2	23	59 190	2 000	61 190
Finland/Finlande		249	0.8	21	55 130	1 200	56 330
France	*	3 850	24	223	368 140	48 000	416 140
Germany/Allemagne	*	6 164	15	223	896 740	25 000	921 740
Greece/Grèce	*	342	3	14	74 430	5 890	80 320
Iceland/Islande		21	0.06	-	2 360	403	2 763
Ireland/Irlande	*	723	1	..	33 510	850	34 360
Italy/Italie	*	3 637	17	116	407 700	27 581	435 281
Luxembourg	*	7	-	..	11 540	275	11 815
Netherlands/Pays-Bas		1 160	33	41	170 850	8 100	178 950
Norway/Norvège		294	0.22	12	31 590	6 900	38 490
Portugal	*	254	3	..	45 900	4 000	49 900
Spain/Espagne		2 142	12.5	..	222 770	35 264	258 034
Sweden/Suède		490	0.7	11	51 760	3 680	55 440
Switzerland/Suisse	*	230	1.6	10	43 220	6 075	49 295
Turkey/Turquie		1 253	4	..	150 060	11 933	161 993
UK/Royaume-Uni	*	4 173	17	78	558 370	5 981	564 351
CSFR/RFTS	e)	710	3	..	178 810	4 136	182 946
Hungary/Hongrie	*	581	1.7	..	62 980	1 345	64 325
Poland/Pologne	*	2 700	2.88	..	339 380	3 830	343 210
North America/Amérique N.	f)	33 600	74	..	5 861 240	63 600	5 924 840
OECD/OCDE Europe	f)	26 200	143	..	3 353 460	202 300	3 555 760
EU/UE-15	f)	24 400	137	..	3 126 230	177 000	3 303 230
OECD/OCDE	f)	67 800	269	..	10 616 010	327 500	10 943 510
Non-OECD/Non-OCDE Europe	e)	13 300	14	..	856 390	24 715	881 105
Africa/Afrique	e)	16 000	12	..	674 690	25 138	699 828
Asia+Middle East/Asie+Moy.Orient	e)	75 300	27	..	2 561 600	101 733	2 663 333
P.Rep.China/Rép.Pop.Chine	e)	40 000	8	..	2 562 870	123 411	2 686 281
Former USSR/Ex-URSS	e)	28 000	44	..	3 298 710	63 288	3 361 998
Latin America/Amérique Latine	f)	20 400	36	..	1 014 190	18 884	1 033 074
Total Non-OECD/Non-OCDE	f)	193 000	140	..	10 649 510	357 200	11 006 710
World/Monde	f)	260 800	410	..	21 141 070	684 700	21 825 770

Notes :
a) 1993 or latest available year from 1990 on, except as noted.
b) Total apparent consumption of CFCs controlled by the Montreal Protocol.
c) 1993 IEA-OECD data, excluding international marine bunkers. Italics: 1992.
d) All emissions from industrial processes, except those from fuel combustion. Some figures, from WRI, include estimates of emissions from cement production based on world data for cement manufacturing and on IPCC emission factors.
e) CH₄, CFCs and CO₂ from ind. processes: 1991 WRI estimates.
f) Rounded figures, which include WRI estimates.
AUS) CH₄ and CO₂ from ind. processes: 1991 WRI estimates.
NZL) CH₄: upper value estimate.
BEL) CFCs: 1991 WRI estimates.
FRA) CH₄: provisional 1993 data.
DEU) CO₂ from ind. processes: provisional data.
GRC) CFCs: 1991 WRI estimates.
IRL) CH₄: 1989 data. CFCs: 1991 WRI estimate.
ITA) CFCs: 1991 WRI estimates.
LUX) CH₄, CFCs and CO₂ from ind. proc.: 1989 WRI estimates.
PRT) CFCs: 1991 WRI estimates.
CHE) CO₂ from ind. proc.: 1990 data including fuel combustion.
UKD) CFCs and CO₂ from ind. processes: WRI 1991 estimates.
HUN) CO₂ from ind. processes: WRI 1991 estimate.
POL) CH₄: 1988 data.

Notes :
a) 1993 ou la dernière année disponible depuis 1990, sauf indication contraire.
b) Consommation apparente totale de CFCs contrôlés par le protocole de Montréal.
c) Données AIE-OCDE 1993, excluent les soutages marins internationaux. Italiques: 1992.
d) Toutes les émissions des procédés ind. sauf les émissions de combustion. Certains chiffres, provenant du WRI, sont des estimations d'émissions provenant de la production de ciment. Ils se fondent sur la production mondiale de ciment, et sur les facteurs d'émission IPCC.
e) CH₄, CFCs et CO₂ des procédés ind.: estimations du WRI pour 1991.
f) Chiffres arrondis. Incluent des estimations du WRI.
AUS) CH₄ et CO₂ des procédés ind. estimation du WRI pour 1991.
NZL) CH₄: valeur supérieure de la fourchette d'estimation.
BEL) CFCs: estimation du WRI pour 1991.
FRA) CH₄: données 1993 provisoires.
DEU) CO₂ des procédés ind.: données provisoires.
GRC) CFCs: estimation du WRI pour 1991.
IRL) CH₄: données 1989. CFCs: estimation du WRI pour 1991.
ITA) CFCs: estimations du WRI pour 1991.
LUX) CH₄, CFCs et CO₂ des procédés ind.: estimations 1989 du WRI.
PRT) CFCs: estimations du WRI pour 1991.
CHE) CO₂ des procédés ind.: données 1990 incluant la combustion.
UKD) CFCs et CO₂ des procédés ind.: estimations du WRI pour 1991.
HUN) CO₂ des procédés ind.: estimations du WRI pour 1991.
POL) CH₄: données 1988.

Source: OECD/OCDE, WRI

The next set of tables provides trends in concentrations of SO_2, NO_2 and suspended particulates at national level and for selected cities. Whenever possible, concentrations from background stations are provided in addition to the urban concentrations. Composite averages of the annual mean concentrations presented as values relative to a base year are calculated over the number of sites for each year. In addition, the measurement method and the number of stations (which varies significantly from city to city) are provided.

These data give an indication of trends in ambient air quality at national level and in cities. The national trend is defined as the trend in the urban areas, where the monitors are typically located in areas of high concentration. With respect to city trends, the following two factors place a restriction on the examination of this information if generalisations are to be made to an entire city:

i)   often only one site is available for trend purposes;

ii)   in some cities the number of trend sites will change significantly from one year to the next. In general, one site is not sufficient when trying to assess citywide trends. While no firm rule exists, five or more sites are recommended as a minimum number from which to derive such trend information, assuming a distribution of sites that represents multiple areas of a city.

In general the reader should be extremely cautious when interpreting these tables, especially because of the large differences in the number of monitoring sites used in the calculation of citywide averages. In many cases a comparison between two or more cities does not seem to be advisable. Further, this variation in the number of sites may also introduce a bias of some kind on the trend within an individual city. Finally, it should be borne in mind that sometimes monitoring is carried out only at sites where there is a severe problem, leading to a bias towards higher concentrations. For additional explanations the reader is referred to footnotes.

Le groupe de tableaux suivant présente l'évolution des concentrations de SO_2, NO_2, et de particules en suspension au niveau national et pour des villes sélectionnées. Chaque fois que cela est possible, les concentrations de stations de référence représentant la pollution de fond sont fournies en sus des concentrations observées dans les villes. Les moyennes composées des concentrations moyennes annuelles sont calculées sur une année sur l'ensemble des sites d'une même ville, et sont présentées en valeurs relatives par rapport à une année de base. Les méthodes de mesure et le nombre des stations de mesure (qui varient beaucoup d'une ville à l'autre) sont également indiqués.

Ces données fournissent une indication sur l'évolution de la qualité de l'air ambiant au niveau national et dans les villes. L'évolution nationale est définie comme étant l'évolution dans les zones urbaines où les stations de surveillance sont habituellement situées dans des zones à concentration élevée. En ce qui concerne l'évolution dans les villes, les données ne peuvent pas être généralisées pour une ville dans son ensemble, et leur analyse est limitée par les deux facteurs suivants :

i)   les tendances sont parfois calculées à partir de chiffres disponibles pour un seul site ;

ii)   dans certaines villes, le nombre de sites utilisés pour le calcul des tendances change beaucoup d'une année à l'autre. En général, un seul site ne suffit pas pour aboutir à des tendances significatives sur l'ensemble d'une ville. Bien qu'il n'existe aucune règle stricte, cinq sites ou plus semblent être un minimum recommandable pour le calcul de telles tendances, en faisant l'hypothèse que la répartition des sites recouvre les diverses zones de la ville.

En règle générale, le lecteur devrait être extrêmement prudent lors de l'interprétation de ces tableaux, en particulier parce qu'il existe de grandes différences dans le nombre de sites de surveillance utilisés pour calculer les moyennes de concentration pour les villes. Dans de nombreux cas, il ne semble pas recommandable de comparer deux villes ou plus. Ces différences dans le nombre de sites risquent également d'introduire un biais dans l'évolution relative à une seule ville. Enfin, on gardera à l'esprit que la surveillance de la qualité de l'air n'est parfois mise en oeuvre que pour des sites où se posent des problèmes graves, conduisant ainsi à une distorsion vers les niveaux élevés de concentration de polluants de l'air. Pour tout détail complémentaire, le lecteur se reportera aux notes de bas de page.

CONCENTRATIONS OF SO$_2$, selected cities, 1980-1993
CONCENTRATIONS EN SO$_2$, villes sélectionnées, 1980-1993

Cat. (a)	City or area/ Ville ou région	Measurement method/ Méthode de mesure	No. Stn.	1985 base reference/ année de base (ug/m3)	Index (1985=100) 1980	1981	1982	1983	1984	1985	1986	1987	1988	1989	1990	1991	1992	1993
Canada		*																
N	National *	Coul./P.fluor.c	58-65	16	163	132	132	99	115	100	100	81	100	100	100	75	81	..
A	MONTREAL	UV Fluor.	7	14 (1988)	..	..	..	..	..	..	..	..	100	136	107	71	86	..
B	HAMILTON	UV Fluor.	3	25 (1988)	..	..	..	..	..	..	..	..	100	124	96	96	88	..
C	VANCOUVER	UV Fluor.	4	16 (1988)	..	..	..	..	..	..	..	..	100	94	125	81	75	..
B.G.	DORSET	Coul./P.fluor.c	1	3	..	..	..	..	..	100	100	100	100	..	192	..	..	..
Mexico/Mexique																		
A	MEXICO, D.F.	..	5	163 (1988)	..	..	..	..	..	..	..	..	100	88	95	103	88	39
USA/Etats-Unis		*																
N	National *	Pulsed fluor. c.	234	25	120	113	107	104	107	100	99	96	98	95	88	87	81	80
A	NEW YORK	Pulsed fluor. c.	15	34	111	113	105	98	105	100	92	94	100	95	84	83	75	67
A	LOS ANGELES	Pulsed fluor. c.	6	16	116	115	116	103	121	100	87	77	76	57	46	46	43	40
B	STEUBENVILLE	Pulsed fluor. c.	2	52	120	109	109	103	111	100	106	108	111	122	116	103	88	..
C	DENVER	Pulsed fluor. c.	2	16	142	158	132	153	126	100	99	107	106	91	91	102	109	99
B.G.	DUNN CO.	Pulsed fluor. c.	1	4	69	82	133	100	92	100	95	77	79	82	79	77	79	87
Japan/Japon		*																
N	National	Conduct. c.	23	17	118	118	118	100	100	100	100	100	100	100	100	100	82	..
A	TOKYO	Conduct. c.	20	29	176	159	159	107	100	100	90	90	79	90	100	100	79	..
B	KAWASAKI	Conduct. c.	7	26	142	142	119	112	112	100	100	100	100	112	112	100	88	..
C	KANAZAWA	Conduct. c.	8	17	135	118	118	118	118	100	82	82	82	82	82	82	82	..
B.G.	..	Conduct. c.	8	11	127	127	127	127	127	100	127	127	127	127	127	127	100	..
Australia/Australie		*																
A	MELBOURNE *	UV Fluor.	3-5	11	..	..	..	25	125	100	100	125	150	150	325	399	..	..
B	WOLLONGONG	Pulsed fluor.	2	20	75	95	85	100	100	100	60	60	65	85	75	70	96	..
B	PORT KEMBLA	Pulsed fluor.	1	20	50	85	65	50	45	100	60	70	70	80	110	95	238	..
N. Zealand/N. Zélande		*																
A	AUCKLAND	Acidimetry	1	3 (1986)	719	491	247	228	138	..	100	78	94	63	59	63	147	134
A	CHRISTCHURCH *	Fluorescence	3-1	19	167	135	132	128	108	100	131	..	..	14	29	26	32	5
Austria/Autriche		*																
A	WIEN	Pulsed fluor.	18	46	150	124	113	91	85	100	85	80	50	48	41	50	33	..
B	LINZ	Pulsed fluor.	7	28 (1986)	114	114	93	86	..	..	100	..	54	39	32	39	36	..
Belgium/Belgique		*																
N	National	UV Fluor.	5	46	109	115	93	102	122	100	93	65	61	..	57	54	57	52
A	BRUXELLES	UV Fluor.	8-6	39	110	118	82	90	115	100	95	67	69	..	69	64	62	56
B	ANTWERPEN	UV Fluor.	12-8	42	150	157	121	133	124	100	100	74	74	..	76	76	79	76
C	LIEGE	UV Fluor.	7-3	43	130	107	84	79	107	100	86	56	51	..	53	53	44	42
B.G.	SIG.D.BOT.-Liège	UV Fluor.	1	20	40	90	75	55	95	100	90	60	50	..	55	65	60	55
Denmark/Danemark		*																
A	KØBENHAVN *	KOM Imp. F.	6-1	21 (1988)	148	86	110	119	124	124	90	..	100	96	82	89	67	57
C	ÅLBORG	KOM Imp. F.	1	23	..	..	91	87	109	100	74	61	61	52	52	52	31	29
B.G.	TANGE	KOM Imp. F.	1	6	177	123	145	100	129	100	97	85	71	52	58	61	53	50
Finland/Finlande		*																
A	HELSINKI	UV Fluor.	3-2	28	..	105	78	87	89	100	82	82	75	54	46	43	25	29
B	TAMPERE	Thorin	2	37	166	158	164	110	93	100	79	64	29	16	21	19	..	..
C	TURKU	Fluorescence	1-3	32	..	256	..	..	..	100	84	122	84	39	49	31	20	19
B.G.	SODANKYLA *	Ion Chrom.	1	4	140	116	70	70	86	100	93	93	70	47	60	64	33	32
France		*																
N	National	Acidimetry	124	42 (1986)	..	..	..	..	..	100	102	82	89	81	74	64	..	
A	PARIS	Acidimetry	4-13	54	165	131	126	113	106	100	93	87	67	81	71	76	56	48
B	ROUEN	Acidimetry	10-13	37	189	132	130	111	105	100	100	105	100	95	78	78	65	46
C	NANTES	Acidimetry	10-11	15	200	140	173	147	107	100	93	73	67	80	80	87	73	47
B.G.	DONON	Acidimetry	1	5 (1989)	..	..	..	..	..	..	..	..	..	100	100	140	120	100
Germany/Allemagne		*																
A	BERLIN *	..	15-34	67	134	115	122	100	99	100	97	113	76	91	72	69	48	36
B	GELSENKIRCHEN	..	1	87	109	95	90	84	85	100	84	75	45	41	33	38	34	31
B	LEIPZIG	..	1	377	59	54	56	52	79	100	77	77	52	55	28	36	25	22
C	FRANKFURT	..	1	61	116	123	118	93	84	100	90	103	56	44	34	38	30	..
B.G.	DEUSELBACH	..	1	18	100	94	94	83	94	100	89	78	33	56	39	44	33	28

Notes: see page 48 / voir page 48.

... / ...

CONCENTRATIONS OF SO$_2$, selected cities, 1980-1993
CONCENTRATIONS EN SO$_2$, villes sélectionnées, 1980-1993

Cat. (a)	City or area/ Ville ou région	Measurement method/ Méthode de mesure	No. Stn.	1985 base reference/ année de base (ug/m3)	1980	1981	1982	1983	1984	1985	1986	1987	1988	1989	1990	1991	1992	1993
Greece/Grèce *																		
A	ATHENS *	Pulsed fluor.	5	27	..	..	..	..	..	100	134	127	151	186	149	171	187	147
Iceland/Islande																		
A	REYKJAVIK	UV Fluor.	1	4 (1990)	..	..	..	..	..	..	..	..	..	..	100	79	55	..
B.G.	..	..	1	1	..	..	..	..	..	100	88	43	115	68	55	23	18	15
Ireland/Irlande																		
A	DUBLIN	..	13	33	142	206	133	152	..	100	142	106	85	76	79	..	..	..
B	CORK	..	6	16	169	..	..	..	..	100	219	150	119	81	81	..	..	..
B.G.	AGHADA	..	1	7 (1987)	171	..	..	..	..	..	..	100	114	71	29	..	..	..
Italy/Italie *																		
A	MILANO *	UV p. fluor. c.	5	91	214	203	150	135	122	100	111	73	105	72	51	62	39	34
Luxembourg *																		
N	National	UV Fluor.	3	22 (1988)	..	..	..	..	..	..	..	..	100	145	127	150	141	123
A	LUXEMBOURG	UV Fluor.	2	27 (1988)	..	..	..	..	..	..	..	..	100	135	119	135	122	111
B	ESCH	UV Fluor.	1	12 (1988)	..	..	..	..	..	..	..	..	100	192	175	225	225	167
B.G.	VIANDEN	UV Fluor.	2	9 (1988)	..	..	..	..	..	..	..	..	100	156	144	200	167	122
Netherlands/Pays Bas *																		
N	National	UV Fluor.	8	29 (1986)	110	123	95	94	..	..	100	70	58	57	58	..	..	..
A	AMSTERDAM	UV Fluor.	10	16	159	163	135	124	124	100	86	86	89	70	63	..	..	..
B	RIJNMOND-Rott.	UV Fluor.	10	34	132	133	117	110	113	100	..	87	87	72	72	..	..	..
C	DEN HAAG	..	1	19 (1987)	158	..	..	..	..	..	..	100	89	84	84	..	..	..
B.G.	..	UV Fluor.	8	16	117	139	97	106	119	100	111	70	65	56	62	..	..	..
Norway/Norvège *																		
N	National	Thorin/H$_2$O$_2$	35-26	15	139	125	101	99	103	100	93	78	65	61	60	56	55	43
A	OSLO *	Thorin/H$_2$O$_2$	2	15	237	210	135	103	108	100	83	85	..	..	48	52	55	55
B	PORSGRUNN	Thorin/H$_2$O$_2$	1	12	96	125	58	75	112	100	100	125	67	83	41	38	21	..
C	KRISTIANSAND	Thorin/H$_2$O$_2$	1	9	128	116	133	161	139	100	111	111	100	73	66	56	44	33
B.G.	..	Ion Chrom.	6	1	92	126	55	92	112	100	123	115	108	54	69	62	46	46
Portugal *																		
A	LISBOA *	UV Fluor.	11	31	142	110	110	113	103	100	87	100	139	97	65	145	84	129
B	BARREIRO/SEIXAL *	UV Fluor.	5	83	331	214	123	130	123	100	105	107	..	89	83	30	36	14
C	PORTO *	Acid./UV fluor.	8	27	177	225	181	140	97	100	113	147	241	323	301	331	241	..
B.G	SINES	..	..	3 (1987)	..	..	..	..	..	..	..	100	133	167	233	167	267	200
Spain/Espagne *																		
A	MADRID *	UV Fluor.	14-10	87 (1987)	..	..	..	..	..	..	..	100	105	..	64	70	54	45
B	BILBAO *	Thorin	7-5	52 (1986)	..	..	..	..	..	..	100	119	119	102	96	115	73	40
C	SANTANDER *	Thorin	4-1	14 (1986)	..	..	..	..	..	..	100	86	114	93	186	214	221	..
Sweden/Suède *																		
A	GOTEBORG	UV fluor/Ion.c.	2-3	16	136	181	119	94	131	100	106	119	75	69	56	44	31	38
B	STOCKHOLM *	UV Fluor. c.	2	30	220	203	147	83	103	100	100	77	70	40	30	23	20	20
C	SUNDSVALL *	UV Fluor. c.	1	22 (1986)	164	136	95	127	91	..	100	109	59	59	18	18	14	23
B.G.	RORVIK	Colorimetry	1	8	121	87	111	74	84	100	92	76	74	71	47	45	32	32
Switzerland/Suisse																		
A	ZURICH	UV Fluor. c.	1	50	..	86	98	96	92	100	76	60	54	46	36	38	32	26
B	BASEL	UV Fluor. c.	1	36	106	83	106	100	86	100	92	44	47	50	39	36	31	25
C	DUEBENDORF	UV Fluor. c.	1	35	89	77	89	71	74	100	71	80	51	49	34	37	29	23
B.G.	PAYERNE	UV Fluor. c.	1	10	110	120	90	80	60	100	90	80	60	50	40	40	30	30
Turkey/Turquie																		
A	ANKARA	Conduct.	6-10	132	158	166	195	117	106	100	93	119	197	117	129	95	..	55
B	ISTANBUL	Gas Bubbler	6-15	125	..	..	..	..	..	100	146	132	148	168	193	227	198	163
C	ESKISEHIR	Gas Bubbler	1-2	129	..	..	..	..	..	100	95	119	111	132	133	140	149	129
UK/Royaume-Uni *																		
N	National	Acid. Titr. c.	143	37	132	137	111	108	104	100	97	96	89	89	..	..	..	..
A	LONDON	Acid. Titr. c.	11	42	167	162	145	117	119	100	107	93	93	88	93	76	67	..
B	NEWCASTLE	Acid. Titr. c.	1	40	173	165	188	100	100	100	95	148	90	90	75	78	78	..
C	BRISTOL	Acid. Titr. c.	1	61	105	108	69	85	87	100	64	48	28	39	33	33	33	..
B.G.	LITTLE HORKESLEY	Acid. Titr. c.	1	32	88	69	56	63	84	100	53	34	31	25	22	22	16	..

Notes: see page 48 / voir page 48.

.../...

CONCENTRATIONS OF SO$_2$, selected cities, 1980-1993
CONCENTRATIONS EN SO$_2$, villes sélectionnées, 1980-1993

Cat. (a)	City or area/ Ville ou région	Measurement method/ Méthode de mesure	No. Stn.	1985 base reference/ année de base (ug/m3)	1980	1981	1982	1983	1984	1985	1986	1987	1988	1989	1990	1991	1992	1993
Czech Rep./Rép. Tchèque																		
A	PRAHA	Coulometric c.	29	86	86	..	..	..	..	100	81	91	50	76	52	73	..	..
B	OSTRAVA	..	23	77	83	..	..	..	..	100	70	81	68	70	57	64	..	..
C	HRADEC KRALOVE	Coulometric c.	3	51	108	..	..	..	..	100	45	76	75	94	65	63	..	..
B.G.	SVRATOUCH	Coulometric c.	1	21	..	..	96	71	69	100	..	86	90	97	119	143	..	..
Slovak Rep./Rép.Slovaque *																		
N	National *	..	..	53	115	..	..	..	..	100	92	79	60	77	55	58	..	..
A	BRATISLAVA	West, Gaeke	7	44	86	..	..	..	..	100	95	95	64	61	48	48	..	..
B	PRIEVIDZA-District	West, Gaeke	4	65	131	169	123	92	92	100	105	112	85	65	49	51	..	..
C	KOSICE	West, Gaeke	9	30	103	..	..	..	..	100	107	100	97	100	83	90	..	..
B.G.	CHOPOCK *	..	1	5	124	98	90	80	89	100	92	60	57	69	78	80	..	..
Hungary/Hongrie																		
A	BUDAPEST	Pararosanilin	36	12 (1992)	..	..	..	..	..	..	..	..	..	..	..	..	100	174
B.G.	K-PUSZTA	UV Fluor.	1	25	100	46	43	34	46	100	60	87	40	32	21	35	13	14
Poland/Pologne																		
N	National	Colorimetry	305	34 (1990)	..	..	..	..	..	..	..	..	..	..	100	97	79	82
A	LODZ	Colorimetry	19	48	96	81	85	79	94	100	88	90	67	65	54	67	50	54
B	CHORZOW	Colorimetry	1	104	..	77	82	80	87	100	136	87	128	79	60	62	99	95
C	WARSZAWA	Colorimetry	8	54	87	96	85	76	59	100	54	50	43	44	35	37	28	37
B.G.	SUWALKI	Thorin	4	12	71	53	56	56	61	100	95	89	79	44	50	73	31	34

Notes:
a) Categories: N- country network, national trend; A- city in which a notable portion (5-10%) of national population is concentrated; B- industrial city in which a significant number of inhabitants are considered to be exposed to the worst level of pollution in 1980; C- city with residential and service functions and intermediate pollution level; B.G.- selected station(s), representing background pollution.
CAN) Measurement temperature: -15.6°. National trend: comparable over ten years only.
USA) National trend: urban and suburban sites only.
JPN) Fiscal year, commencing 1 April. Operating temperature 20°C.
AUS) Melbourne: Number of monitoring stations increased during series.
NZL) Christchurch: change in measurement method in 1989. Reduction in number of monitoring sites from three to one in 1989.
BEL) Fiscal year, commencing 1 April. Urban areas: 1991 data refer to a smaller number of stations.
DNK) Köbenhavn (Copenhagen): break in the time series in 1987.
FIN) Sodankyla: number of measurements per year ranges from 24 to 36; measurement network was renewed in 1989.
FRA) Weighted averages of specific monitoring stations. National: urban sites only.
DEU) Data referring to one station only represent intermediate pollution level. Berlin: number of monitoring stations and data up to 1992 refer to West Berlin; 1993: Berlin as a whole (45 stations).
GRC) Athens: four monitoring sites in 1985 and 1992.
ITA) Milano: four monitoring sites in 1988 and six in 1991.
LUX) 1988 data refer to the sampling period July-December.
NLD) Fiscal year, commencing 1 April.
NOR) Fiscal year, commencing 1 April. Data referring to one station only represent intermediate pollution level. National: stations gradually reduced from 1980 to 1990. Oslo: mean pollution level of St. Olavs plass and Bryn skole.
PRT) Lisboa 1989-93: different stations. Barreiro/Seixal 1980, 1991-93: different stations. Porto: break in time series in 1988.
ESP) The number of monitoring stations differs from year to year. Madrid and Bilbao: data refer to city centre.
SWE) Monitoring period from October to March, except for B.G. Stockholm: change of one station in 1988. Sundsvall: data refer to city centre. Change in measurement method in 1990.
UKD) Fiscal year, commencing 1 April. Measurement method follows British Standard 1747 Part 3. Data referring to one station only represent intermediate pollution level.
SLO) National data: arithmetic mean of nine regions. Chopock: change in measurement method in 1987.

Notes:
a) Catégories : N - réseau du pays, évolution nationale; A - ville englobant une part notable (5 à 10%) de la population nationale; B - ville industrielle où un nombre notable d'habitants sont exposés aux niveaux les plus élevés de pollution en 1980; C - ville à dominante résidentielle et de service et d'un niveau moyen de pollution; B.G. - station(s) sélectionnée(s) pour être représentative(s) de la pollution de fond.
CAN) Mesures faites à -15.6°. Evolution nationale: données comparables sur dix ans seulement.
USA) Evolution nationale: sites urbains et suburbains uniquement.
JPN) Année fiscale, commençant le 1er avril. Température de fonctionnement de 20°C.
AUS) Melbourne: le nombre de stations de mesures a augmenté au cours du temps.
NZL) Christchurch: changement de méthode de mesure en 1989. Réduction du nombre de stations de mesures de trois à un en 1989.
BEL) Année fiscale, commençant le 1er avril. Zones urbaines: les données 1991 se réfèrent à un nombre inférieur de stations.
DNK) Köbenhavn (Copenhague): rupture de série en 1987.
FIN) Sodankyla: nombre de mesures annuelles variant de 24 à 36; réseau de stations renouvelé en 1989.
FRA) Moyennes pondérées de stations de mesures spécifiques. National: sites urbains uniquement.
DEU) Les données provenant d'une seule station représentent un niveau de pollution intermédiaire. Berlin: nombre de stations et données jusqu'en 1992 se réfèrent à Berlin ouest uniquement à partir de 1993, Berlin, 45 stations.
GRC) Athènes: quatre stations de mesures en 1985 et 1992.
ITA) Milano: quatre stations de mesures en 1988, six en 1991.
LUX) Les données 1988 couvrent la période de mesure juillet-décembre.
NLD) Année fiscale, commençant le 1er avril.
NOR) Année fiscale, commençant le 1er avril. Les données provenant d'une seule station représentent un niveau de pollution intermédiaire. National: le nombre de stations a été progressivement réduit entre 1980 et 1990. Oslo: niveau de pollution moyen des stations St. Olavs plass et Bryn skole.
PRT) Lisboa: Les données 1991-93 proviennent d'autres stations. Barreiro/Seixal: Les données 1980, 1991-93 proviennent d'autres stations. Porto: rupture de série en 1988.
ESP) Le nombre de stations de mesures varie d'une année sur l'autre. Madrid et Bilbao: les données concernent le centre ville.
SWE) Période de surveillance d'octobre à mars, excepté pour B.G. Stockholm: changement d'une des stations en 1988. Sundsvall: les données concernent le centre ville. Changement de méthode de mesure en 1990.
UKD) Année fiscale, commençant le 1er avril. Méthode de mesure selon la norme britannique 1747 Partie 3. Les données provenant d'une seule station représentent un niveau de pollution intermédiaire.
SLO) Les données nationales se réfèrent à la moyenne arithmétique de neuf régions. Chopock: changement de méthode de mesure en 1987.

Source: OECD/OCDE

CONCENTRATIONS OF NO$_2$, selected cities, 1980-1993
CONCENTRATIONS EN NO$_2$, villes sélectionnées, 1980-1993

Cat. (a)	City or area/ Ville ou région	Measurement method/ Méthode de mesure	No. Stn.	1985 base reference/ année de base (ug/m3)	1980	1981	1982	1983	1984	1985	1986	1987	1988	1989	1990	1991	1992	1993
Canada		*																
N	National	* Chem.	34-47	41	115	106	106	101	110	100	100	95	98	105	98	90	83	..
A	MONTREAL	Chem.	3	48 (1988)	..	..	..	..	..	..	..	..	100	108	108	98	73	..
B	HAMILTON	Chem.	2	46 (1988)	..	..	..	..	..	..	..	..	100	100	83	89	80	..
C	VANCOUVER	Chem.	3	51 (1988)	..	..	..	..	..	..	..	..	100	94	92	94	92	..
B.G.	DORSET	Chem.	1	11	..	..	..	..	166	100	66	34	34	..	35	..	..	..
Mexico/Mexique																		
B	MEXICO, D.F.	..	5	228 (1986)	..	..	..	..	..	100	60	72	71	74	69	73	69	
USA/Etats-Unis		*																
N	National	* Chem.	83	46	106	104	102	100	101	100	101	100	102	98	93	94	89	86
A	LOS ANGELES	Chem.	12	86	110	110	106	100	98	100	99	92	101	99	90	92	85	80
A	NEW YORK	Chem.	3	53	107	105	114	115	107	100	103	114	112	101	101	102	97	100
B	CHICAGO	Chem.	1	67	93	93	106	97	95	100	90	89	91	98	88	92	86	86
C	WASHINGTON	Chem.	5	56	97	97	94	95	98	100	102	97	92	85	93	90	87	88
B.G.	MERCER CO.	Chem.	4	7	99	103	91	86	87	100	120	96	91	90	96	93	97	97
Japan/Japon		*																
N	National	Saltzman	23	27	100	100	100	100	100	100	100	107	107	107	107	115	107	..
A	TOKYO	Saltzman	20	62	116	106	110	106	103	100	100	110	113	113	113	119	113	..
B	KAWASAKI	Saltzman	7	62	85	85	82	106	110	100	106	110	110	110	113	119	116	..
C	KANAZAWA	Saltzman	7	25	160	100	100	100	100	100	92	100	100	108	100	108	108	..
B.G.	..	Saltzman	8	14	100	100	100	100	100	100	100	114	100	114	114	129	114	..
Australia/Australie																		
C	CANBERRA	Chem.	1	68	..	..	..	..	..	100	97	115	61	103	97	112	..	..
N. Zealand/N. Zélande																		
A	AUCKLAND	Chem.	1	24 (1987)	..	..	..	..	..	..	..	100	102	80	110	47	95	64
A	CHRISTCHURCH	Chem.	1	13 (1989)	..	..	..	..	..	..	..	..	100	114	90	135	94	
Austria/Autriche																		
A	WIEN	Chem.	18	42 (1988)	..	..	..	..	..	..	..	100	107	95	88	83	..	
B	LINZ	Chem.	7	44 (1988)	..	..	..	..	..	..	..	100	98	98	91	84	..	
Belgium/Belgique		*																
N	National	Chem. c.	5	54	98	96	100	98	111	100	89	89	98	..	94	85	78	63
A	BRUXELLES	Chem. c.	4-5	52	121	100	96	119	100	100	98	88	94	..	94	87	77	63
B	ANTWERPEN	Chem. c.	2	46	104	109	104	100	117	100	96	89	109	..	100	85	93	91
C	LIEGE	Chem. c.	1	51	82	80	98	92	112	100	96	84	98	..	94	94	76	75
B.G.	SIG.D.BOT.-Liège	Chem. c.	1	45	189	100	73	136	102	100	100	84	84	..	36	44	42	31
Denmark/Danemark		*																
A	KÖBENHAVN	* Chem.	3-1	58 (1988)	..	..	138	122	97	110	102	..	100	96	84	90	90	76
C	ÅLBORG	Chem.	1	40	..	..	78	103	105	100	105	98	125	113	93	103	95	98
Finland/Finlande																		
A	HELSINKI	Chem. c.	2	56 (1987)	..	..	..	..	..	..	..	100	75	75	81	77	79	76
B	OULU	Chem.	1-2	12	..	..	..	..	92	100	125	175	225	167	167	229	238	229
France		*																
N	National	* Chem.	14	51 (1987)	..	..	..	..	..	..	..	100	90	114	108	102	102	..
A	PARIS	Chem.	2-6	68	..	..	..	..	..	100	93	69	74	87	82	82	81	84
B	ROUEN	Chem.	1-6	79	..	..	..	..	..	100	104	70	52	61	44	44	56	48
C	NANTES	Chem.	1-4	17 (1986)	..	..	..	..	..	..	100	171	271	294	294	271	265	247
B.G.	DONON	Chem.	1	12	..	..	..	..	..	100	58	25	42	67	67	83	67	75
Germany/Allemagne		*																
A	BERLIN	* ..	5-20	42	83	79	95	86	90	100	90	110	107	102	76	81	71	74
B	GELSENKIRCHEN	..	1	56	155	..	109	91	88	100	114	125	114	93	79	86	80	..
B	LEIPZIG	..	1	30	80	203	90	97	90	100	133	187	120	137	97	..	110	..
C	FRANKFURT	..	1	43	126	121	116	160	121	100	105	119	123	128	130	121	109	..
B.G.	DEUSELBACH	..	1	14	93	93	86	86	93	100	86	93	79	114	93	107	93	64

Notes: see page 51 / voir page 51.

... / ...

CONCENTRATIONS OF NO$_2$, selected cities, 1980-1993
CONCENTRATIONS EN NO$_2$, villes sélectionnées, 1980-1993

Cat. (a)	City or area/ Ville ou région	Measurement method/ Méthode de mesure	No. Stn.	1985 base reference/ année de base (ug/m3)	Index (1985=100)													
					1980	1981	1982	1983	1984	1985	1986	1987	1988	1989	1990	1991	1992	1993
Greece/Grèce	*																	
A	ATHENS *	Chem.	5	56	..	..	..	..	..	100	108	107	122	136	115	116	114	100
Iceland/Islande																		
A	REYKJAVIK	Chem.	1	15 (1990)	..	..	..	..	..	..	..	..	..	..	100	114	118	..
Italy/Italie	*																	
B	MILANO *	Chem. c.	3	212	..	81	94	108	89	100	101	148	119	140	127	117	117	..
Luxembourg	*																	
N	National	Chem.	2-3	34 (1988)	..	..	..	..	..	..	..	..	100	141	150	153	129	121
A	LUXEMBOURG *	Chem.	1	37 (1988)	..	..	..	..	..	..	..	..	100	154	181	170	138	127
B	ESCH/ALZETTE	Chem.	1	31 (1988)	..	..	..	..	..	..	..	..	100	126	116	123	100	103
B.G.	VIANDEN	Chem.	2	11 (1988)	..	..	..	..	..	..	..	..	100	173	164	155	118	100
Netherlands/Pays Bas	*																	
N	National	Chem. c.	5	42	102	107	98	109	111	100	108	108	112	109	103	..	..	..
A	AMSTERDAM	Chem. c.	5	45	88	96	100	95	89	100	113	124	124	128	128	..	..	..
B	RIJNMOND-Rott.	Chem. c.	3	43	94	111	107	120	104	100	119	108	128	108	122	..	..	..
C	DEN HAAG	Chem. c.	1	41	107	..	..	..	..	100	110	110	110	110	115	..	..	..
B.G.	..	Chem. c.	4	26	86	107	89	94	103	100	94	86	85	85	92	..	..	..
Norway/Norvège	*																	
N	National	TGS abs. sol.	8	59 (1986)	..	..	..	..	..	..	100	94	98	82	97	82	84	97
A	OSLO *	TGS abs. sol.	1	64 (1987)	..	..	..	..	..	..	..	100	111	97	93	77	80	84
B	DRAMMEN *	TGS abs. sol.	1	73 (1986)	..	..	..	..	..	..	100	93	102	89	100	89	89	103
C	BERGEN	TGS abs. sol.	1	51 (1986)	..	..	..	..	..	..	100	94	86	93	116	96	92	125
B.G.	..	TGS abs. sol.	6	2 (1989)	..	..	..	..	..	..	..	..	..	100	100	84	68	63
Portugal	*																	
A	LISBOA *	Chem.	..	27 (1986)	104	111	111	126	104	..	100	44	96	122	122	115	119	148
B	BARREIRO/SEIX.	Chem.	..	17	..	..	106	71	82	100	..	..	..	..	..	94	..	129
B.G.	SINES	Chem.	..	3 (1988)	..	..	..	..	..	..	..	..	100	67	100	200	300	133
Spain/Espagne	*																	
A	MADRID *	Chem.	6-12	92 (1990)	..	..	..	..	..	..	..	..	..	..	100	86	87	79
B	VALLADOLID	Chem.	6-7	70 (1991)	..	..	..	..	..	..	..	..	..	..	..	100	77	60
Sweden/Suède	*																	
A	GOTEBORG	Chem. c.	1-2	43	116	161	65	63	79	100	95	67	81	63	77	79	70	61
B	STOCKHOLM *	Chem. c.	2	45	..	77	96	91	99	100	89	82	49	53	64	67	42	47
C	SUNDSVALL *	DOAS	5-1	38 (1986)	..	..	137	116	..	..	100	97	100	116	84	84	89	..
B.G.	RORVIK	..	1	8	..	..	120	99	99	100	94	92	92	88	87	98	99	86
Switzerland/Suisse																		
A	ZURICH	Chem. c.	1	60	..	98	100	97	92	100	97	98	96	96	82	80	75	68
B	BASEL	Chem. c.	1	47	..	68	113	115	94	100	81	77	87	95	87	77	66	66
C	DUEBENDORF	Chem. c.	1	51	100	100	102	106	98	100	92	78	76	88	82	76	65	65
B.G.	PAYERNE	Chem. c.	1	21	..	..	..	..	..	100	110	105	95	105	86	110	90	86
Turkey/Turquie																		
C	ESKISEHIR	Saltzman	1	25 (1989)	..	..	..	..	..	..	..	..	..	100	88	32	32	20
UK/Royaume-Uni																		
A	LONDON	Chem. c.	1	61	107	108	133	120	133	100	110	121	110	117	113	134	123	..
C	STEVENAGE	Chem. c.	1	48	71	71	79	79	88	100	83	108	96	100	100	96	88	..
Czech Rep./Rép. Tchèque																		
A	PRAHA	..	19	77	..	..	..	..	..	100	96	91	61	91	96	81	..	..
B	OSTRAVA	..	10	64	..	..	..	..	..	100	119	95	84	111	106	83	..	..
C	HRADEC KRALOVE	..	3	65	..	..	..	..	..	100	80	74	89	88	85	95	..	..
B.G.	SVRATOUCH	..	1	11 (1986)	..	..	..	..	..	..	100	111	88	82	50	66	..	..
Slovak Rep./Rép. Slovaque																		
A	BRATISLAVA	Saltzman	7	25	..	..	72	104	96	100	104	112	100	104	116	108	..	..
B	PRIEVIDZA-District	Saltzman	2	17	..	..	..	..	..	100	153	135	135	88	94	124	..	..
B.G.	CHOPOCK	..	1	3	..	..	213	132	116	100	104	117	119	101	119	148	..	..

Notes: see next page / voir page suivante.

CONCENTRATIONS OF NO$_2$, selected cities, 1980-1993
CONCENTRATIONS EN NO$_2$, villes sélectionnées, 1980-1993

Cat. (a)	City or area/ Ville ou région	Measurement method/ Méthode de mesure	No. Stn.	1985 base reference/ année de base (ug/m3)	Index (1985=100)													
					1980	1981	1982	1983	1984	1985	1986	1987	1988	1989	1990	1991	1992	1993
Hungary/Hongrie																		
A	BUDAPEST	Saltzman	36	48 (1992)	..	..	..	..	..	..	..	..	..	..	..	..	100	107
B.G.	K-PUSZTA	Saltzman	1	10	70	70	61	76	92	100	98	93	99	85	89	74	15	12
Poland/Pologne																		
N	National	Saltzman	167	33 (1990)	..	..	..	..	..	..	..	..	..	..	100	97	91	94
A	LODZ	Saltzman	4	53	91	92	94	91	96	100	96	113	98	108	100	85	68	72
B	CHORZOW	Saltzman	6-1	138	..	46	64	123	94	100	78	83	101	87	92	67	80	49
C	WARSZAWA	Saltzman	1-3	67	..	..	..	78	99	100	75	73	106	124	97	78	73	84
B.G.	SUWALKI	Griess	4	15	..	..	..	..	..	100	67	86	64	69	64	78	84	47

Notes:
a) Categories: N - country network, national trend; A - city in which a notable portion (5-10%) of the national population is concentrated; B - industrial city in which a significant number of inhabitants are considered to be exposed to the worst level of pollution in 1980; C - city with residential and service functions and with intermediate pollution level; B.G. - selected station(s), representing the background concentration.
CAN) Measurement temperature: -15.6°. National trend: comparable over ten years only.
USA) National trend: urban and suburban sites only.
JPN) Fiscal year, commencing 1 April. Operating temperature 20°C.
BEL) Fiscal year, commencing 1 April.
DNK) Köbenhavn (Copenhagen): break in time series in 1987.
FRA) National trend: urban sites only.
DEU) Data referring to one station only represent intermediate pollution level. Berlin: number of monitoring stations and data up to 1992 refer to West Berlin; 1993 figure refers to Berlin as a whole.
GRC) Athens: four monitoring sites in 1989.
ITA) Milano: annual 98th percentile of average hourly concentrations.
LUX) 1988 data refer to the sampling period July-December. Luxembourg: data refer to city centre.
NLD) Fiscal year, commencing 1 April.
NOR) Monitoring period from October to March, except for B.G. Oslo: Data refer to St. Olavs plass. Drammen: Heavy traffic area.
PRT) Lisboa: break in time series between 1980 and 1981. 1981-84 data refer to one station representing medium concentration level.
ESP) Madrid: data refer to city centre. The number of monitoring stations differs from year to year.
SWE) Monitoring period from October to March, except for B.G. Stockholm: Change of one station in 1988. Sundsvall: Data refer to city centre. Change in measurement method in 1990.

Notes:
a) Catégories: N - réseau du pays, évolution nationale ; A - ville englobant une part notable (5 à 10%) de la population nationale ; B - ville industrielle où un nombre notable d'habitants sont exposés aux niveaux les plus élevé de pollution en 1980; C - ville à dominante résidentielle et de service et d'un niveau moyen de pollution; B.G. - station(s) sélectionnée(s) pour être représentative(s) de la pollution de fond.
CAN) Mesures faites à -15.6°. Evolution nationale: données comparables sur dix ans seulement.
USA) Evolution nationale: sites urbains et suburbains uniquement.
JPN) Année fiscale, commençant le 1er avril. Température de fonctionnement de 20°C.
BEL) Année fiscale, commençant le 1er avril.
DNK) Köbenhavn (Copenhague): rupture de série en 1987.
FRA) Evolution nationale: sites urbains uniquement.
DEU) Les données provenant d'une seule station représentent un niveau de pollution intermédiaire. Berlin: nombre de stations et données jusqu'en 1992 se réfèrent à Berlin ouest uniquement; 1993: Berlin.
GRC) Athènes: quatre stations de mesures en 1989.
ITA) Milano: 98e percentile annuel des concentrations horaires moyennes.
LUX) Les données 1988 couvrent la période de mesure juillet-décembre. Luxembourg: les données concernent le centre ville.
NLD) Année fiscale, commençant le 1er avril.
NOR) Période de surveillance d'octobre à mars, excepté pour B.G. Oslo: les données se réfèrant à St. Olavs plass. Drammen: concernent une zone de traffic intense.
PRT) Lisboa: rupture de série entre 1980 et 1981. Les données 1981-84 proviennent d'une seule station représentant la concentration moyenne.
ESP) Madrid: les données concernent le centre ville. Le nombre de stations de mesures varie d'une année sur l'autre.
SWE) Période de surveillance d'octobre à mars, excepté pour B.G. Stockholm: changement d'une des stations en 1988. Sundsvall: les données concernent le centre ville. Changement de méthode de mesure en 1990.

Source: OECD/OCDE

CONCENTRATIONS OF PARTICULATES, selected cities, 1980-1993
CONCENTRATIONS EN PARTICULES, villes sélectionnées, 1980-1993

Cat. (a)	City or area/ Ville ou région	Measurement method/ Méthode de mesure	No. Stn.	1985 base reference/année de base (ug/m3)	1980	1981	1982	1983	1984	1985	1986	1987	1988	1989	1990	1991	1992	1993
Canada																		
N	National *	..	85	43	156	136	120	111	107	100	100	112	102	102	91	91	84	..
A	MONTREAL	Gravimetry	6	46 (1988)	..	..	..	..	..	..	..	..	100	102	80	83	83	..
B	HAMILTON	Gravimetry	2	81 (1988)	..	..	..	..	..	..	..	..	100	99	89	83	70	..
C	VANCOUVER	Gravimetry	8	35 (1988)	..	..	..	..	..	..	..	..	100	100	91	94	91	..
Mexico/Mexique																		
B	MEXICO, D.F.	..	5	619	86	89	87	85	93	100	95	68	73	94	127	148	89	71
USA/Etats-Unis *																		
N	National	EPA Hi-Vol S.	241	34 (1988)	..	..	..	..	..	..	..	..	100	99	90	90	82	79
A	LOS ANGELES	EPA Hi-Vol S.	13	58 (1988)	..	..	..	..	..	..	..	..	100	100	88	87	73	70
A	NEW YORK	EPA Hi-Vol S.	14	31 (1988)	..	..	..	..	..	..	..	..	100	97	96	99	81	78
B	STEUBENVILLE	EPA Hi-Vol S.	5	43 (1988)	..	..	..	..	..	..	..	..	100	104	92	97	88	..
C	DENVER	EPA Hi-Vol S.	6	35 (1988)	..	..	..	..	..	..	..	..	100	100	86	85	87	102
B.G.	Fargo Moorhead, ND	EPA Hi-Vol S.	1	21 (1988)	..	..	..	..	..	..	..	..	100	98	101	89	100	84
Japan/Japon *																		
N	National	B-ray absorp.	40	37	116	116	111	97	111	100	111	111	105	105	111	108	..	..
A	TOKYO	L.Scatt/B-ray	7	53	91	98	96	89	98	100	109	111	94	104	102	111	..	..
B	KAWASAKI	L.Scatt/B-ray	7	44	..	..	114	109	107	100	111	120	109	105	111	120	..	..
C	KANAZAWA	L.Scatt/B-ray	2	20	125	115	130	115	105	100	125	135	130	125	120	125	..	..
B.G.	..	B-ray absorp.	1	30	127	90	117	103	117	100	87	113	87	100	100	107	..	..
Australia/Australie																		
A	SYDNEY	EPA Hi-Vol S.	1	39	93	67	70	95	83	100	..	..	..	..	..	..	71	..
A	MELBOURNE	EPA Hi-Vol S.	1	44	..	..	..	..	..	100	94	103	99	98	98	95	..	..
B	WOLLONGONG	EPA Hi-Vol S.	1	7	69	72	79	79	79	100	117	78	74	88	76	..	..	..
C	CANBERRA	EPA Hi-Vol S.	1	53	..	158	157	160	113	100	96	100	83	74	74	58	53	51
N. Zealand/N. Zélande *																		
A	AUCKLAND *	Hi-Vol/Grav.	4-6	32	118	118	129	105	94	100	103	98	101	87	77	79	73	76
A	CHRISTCHURCH *	Hi-Vol/Grav.	4-3	53	117	110	115	101	84	100	92	88	92	70	54	62	77	77
C	HAMILTON	Hi-Vol/Grav.	1	43	..	..	..	..	75	100	79	69	60	59	50	47	47	49
Austria/Autriche *																		
A	WIEN	B-ray absorp.	12-16	52 (1988)	..	..	..	..	..	..	..	..	100	90	..	88	79	..
B	LINZ	B-ray absorp.	9-7	56 (1986)	138	120	146	136	..	..	100	..	88	98	93	105	82	..
Belgium/Belgique *																		
N	National	Nephelometry	5	103	102	108	87	98	108	100	82	71	81	..	79	70	68	63
A	BRUXELLES *	Nephelometry	3	92	170	182	103	112	121	100	102	85	96	..	101	90	85	86
B	ANTWERP	Nephelometry	2	98	105	109	102	97	134	100	91	72	80	..	83	74	77	79
C	LIEGE	Nephelometry	2	84	113	108	108	113	113	100	95	88	96	..	92	99	80	71
B.G.	SIG.D.BOT.-Liege	Nephelometry	1	99	80	88	93	86	160	100	85	72	87	..	80	86	69	60
Denmark/Danemark *																		
A	KÖBENHAVN	Gravimetry	3-1	64	..	..	89	81	97	100	89	..	123	117	103	108	116	109
C	ÅLBORG	Gravimetry	1	98	..	..	84	73	93	100	94	82	79	80	72	73	60	65
Finland/Finlande *																		
A	HELSINKI	EPA Hi-Vol S.	4-3	83 (1986)	103	89	93	97	97	..	100	93	101	94	84	76	81	76
B	TAMPERE	Hi-Vol S.	1	126 (1987)	100	118	100	..	..	..	..	100	91	90	72	99	87	93
B	OULU *	TEOM	1-3	28	107	107	107	..	89	100	86	96	89	71	75	79	68	71
C	TURKU *	Hi-Vol S.	1	100	..	..	..	..	112	100	100	110	96	92	89	84	89	69
B.G.	SODANKYLA *	Low-Vol S. nc.	1	6	133	117	100	83	150	100	100	133	117	83	93	..	..	..
France *																		
N	National *	Cont.	40	29 (1986)	..	..	..	..	..	..	100	97	83	100	97	97	86	..
A	PARIS	Cont.	8-13	49	104	102	96	94	96	100	94	94	59	69	63	80	67	43
B	ROUEN *	Cont.	4-5	25	100	108	108	84	68	100	72	120	108	116	128	112	104	68
C	NANTES	Cont.	8-12	19	74	79	58	84	74	100	95	95	..	..	..	137	111	89

Notes: see page 55 / voir page 55.

... / ...

CONCENTRATIONS OF PARTICULATES, selected cities, 1980-1993
CONCENTRATIONS EN PARTICULES, villes sélectionnées, 1980-1993

Cat. (a)	City or area/ Ville ou région	Measurement method/ Méthode de mesure	No. Stn.	1985 base reference/année de base (ug/m3)	1980	1981	1982	1983	1984	1985	1986	1987	1988	1989	1990	1991	1992	1993
Germany/Allemagne		*																
A	BERLIN	* ..	34	124	79	61	69	89	97	100	101	77	73	77	56	56	49	13
B	GELSENKIRCHEN	..	1	76	134	..	134	87	95	100	97	118	88	109	82	91	79	..
B	LEIPZIG	..	1	113 (1989)	..	..	..	..	..	..	..	..	..	100	87	71	58	..
C	FRANKFURT	..	1	68	107	104	106	96	..	100	85	104	90	74	66	72	69	..
B.G.	DEUSELBACH	..	1	38	108	100	124	105	103	100	100	92	68	82	82	76	53	45
Greece/Grèce		*																
A	ATHENS	* Black Smoke	6	95	..	..	..	..	..	100	87	92	73	56	51	42	50	67
Iceland/Islande		*																
A	REYKJAVIK	* Grav./Radio.	1	33 (1987)	..	..	..	..	..	..	..	100	106	79	72	83	..	..
Ireland/Irlande		*																
A	DUBLIN	OECD B. S.	13	45	76	..	..	..	..	100	131	118	118	96	58	..	..	..
B	CORK	OECD B. S.	6	33	67	..	..	..	..	100	91	130	139	91	124	..	..	..
B.G.	AGHADA, Cork	OECD B. S.	1	10 (1987)	..	..	..	..	..	..	..	100	50	30	50	..	..	..
Italy/Italie																		
B	MILANO	B-ray absorp.	3	133	99	119	103	97	78	100	109	110	102	74	58	84	74	58
Luxembourg		*																
N	National	Reflectometry	2	55 (1988)	..	..	..	..	..	..	..	..	100	102	71	80	73	73
A	LUXEMBOURG	Reflectometry	1	58 (1988)	..	..	..	..	..	..	..	..	100	112	72	69	67	74
B	ESCH/ALZETTE	Reflectometry	1	52 (1988)	..	..	..	..	..	..	..	..	100	90	67	90	77	69
Netherlands/Pays Bas		*																
A	AMSTERDAM	EPA Hi-Vol S.	5	64	103	104	98	99	101	100	83	70	67	64	63	..	..	..
B	RIJNMOND-Rott.	EPA Hi-Vol S.	2	62	103	103	94	93	102	100	87	80	81	82	82	..	..	..
Norway/Norvège		*																
N	National	* Light reflect.	35-28	23	104	99	84	87	99	100	89	81	91	78	80	60	60	78
A	OSLO	* Light reflect.	2	28	105	113	112	118	113	100	95	96	..	..	94	..	68	53
B	PORSGRUNN	* Light reflect.	1	18	169	135	111	123	137	100	111	80	126	89	103	100	94	..
C	KRISTIANSAND	* Light reflect.	1	16	116	103	88	..	106	100	103	109	88	91	81	75	69	59
Portugal		*																
A	LISBOA	* B.S./B ray a.	11	165	141	127	119	116	93	100	72	107	122	..	..	..	55	..
B	BARREIRO/SEIX.	Hi-Vol/Grav.	5	188 (1986)	14	..	..	..	..	..	100	90	91	68	44	46	48	46
C	PORTO	Black Smoke	8	23	214	241	227	230	101	100	107	98	..	58	67	80	67	..
B.G.	SINES	..	..	6 (1987)	..	..	..	..	..	..	100	450	383	550	567	767	..	..
Spain/Espagne		*																
A	MADRID	* B ray absorp.	13-10	56 (1987)	..	..	..	..	..	..	..	100	109	..	73	73	75	..
B	BILBAO	Black Smoke	7-5	67 (1986)	..	..	..	..	..	..	100	119	121	116	96	78	67	61
C	SANTANDER	Black Smoke	4-1	40 (1986)	..	..	..	..	..	..	100	90	100	118	103	70	30	..
Sweden/Suède		*																
A	GOTEBORG	Reflectometry	1-2	10	100	180	120	90	100	100	70	90	80	70	100	100	80	70
B	STOCKHOLM	Reflectometry	2	16	94	131	100	106	119	100	131	106	131	75	56	44	38	38
B.G.	RORVIK	Reflectometry	1	5	142	76	130	72	108	100	100	100	100	80	80	80	40	60
Switzerland/Suisse		*																
A	ZURICH	Hi-Vol/Grav.	1	50	..	92	100	98	102	100	100	92	76	90	76	82	74	72
B	BASEL	Hi-Vol/Grav.	1	50	..	..	104	94	88	100	110	86	76	89	76	82	70	66
C	DUEBENDORF	Hi-Vol/Grav.	1	52	..	81	90	92	88	100	100	88	75	90	71	79	69	63
B.G.	PAYERNE	Hi-Vol/Grav.	1	45	73	78	82	89	87	100	100	89	71	82	76	76	69	67
Turkey/Turquie		*																
A	ANKARA	B ray absorp.	6-10	57	147	153	223	154	98	100	174	193	216	179	181	146	..	140
B	ISTANBUL	OECD B. S.	6-10	41	..	..	..	..	..	100	115	198	249	285	288	320	224	212
C	ESKISEHIR	OECD B. S.	1-2	46	..	..	..	..	..	100	106	120	122	133	94	80	109	91

Notes: see page 55 / voir page 55.

... / ...

CONCENTRATIONS OF PARTICULATES, selected cities, 1980-1993
CONCENTRATIONS EN PARTICULES, villes sélectionnées, 1980-1993

Cat. (a)	City or area/ Ville ou région	Measurement method/ Méthode de mesure	No. Stn.	1985 base reference/année de base (ug/m3)	Index (1985=100)													
					1980	1981	1982	1983	1984	1985	1986	1987	1988	1989	1990	1991	1992	1993
UK/Royaume-Uni		*																
N	National	Black Smoke	143	15	124	149	110	116	100	100	99	95	88	86	..	..	..	..
A	LONDON	Black Smoke	11	15	140	160	133	133	120	100	100	107	127	99	107	113	93	..
B	NEWCASTLE	Black Smoke	1	22	127	136	114	114	95	100	86	109	91	95	100	95	86	..
C	BRISTOL	Black Smoke	1	18	100	100	83	122	122	100	78	67	61	61	50	50	39	..
B.G.	LITTLE HORKESLEY	Black Smoke	1	8	113	125	100	113	113	100	88	100	113	75	88	..	..	..
Czech Rep./Rép. Tchèque																		
A	PRAHA	..	12	137	130	..	..	..	..	100	81	87	55	66	50	58	..	..
B	OSTRAVA	..	11	133	104	..	..	..	..	100	95	88	68	82	75	73	..	..
C	HRADEC KRALOVE	..	3	84	36	..	..	..	..	100	92	94	75	85	64	76	..	..
Slovak Rep./Rép. Slovaque																		
A	BRATISLAVA	Gravimetry	7	53	170	..	..	..	..	100	128	187	160	183	175	125	..	..
B	PRIEVIDZA-District	Gravimetry	4	78	103	103	128	77	90	100	90	81	77	87	63	74	..	..
C	KOSICE	Gravimetry	6	60	150	150	167	133	117	100	100	103	93	120	95	73	..	..
B.G.	CHOPOCK	..	1	16	..	..	..	..	..	100	100	131	119	138	88	116	..	..
Hungary/Hongrie		*																
A	BUDAPEST	Hi-Vol/Grav.	1	235 (1992)	..	..	..	..	..	..	..	..	..	..	..	..	100	107
B	MISKOLC	Hi-Vol/Grav.	4	377 (1992)	..	..	..	..	..	..	..	..	..	..	..	..	100	50
C	SZEKESFEHERVAR	Hi-Vol/Grav.	1	251 (1992)	..	..	..	..	..	..	..	..	..	..	..	..	100	95
Poland/Pologne		*																
N	National	Black Smoke	284	44 (1990)	..	..	..	..	..	..	..	..	..	..	100	107	89	82
A	LODZ	Black Smoke	19	74	73	58	70	65	73	100	81	85	65	50	45	61	54	54
B	CHORZOW	* TSP	1	287	..	113	108	91	102	100	92	90	78	78	83	76	70	57
C	WARZAWA	Black Smoke	8	75	64	51	83	57	59	100	81	79	65	63	67	67	57	51

Notes: see next page / voir page suivante.

Source: OECD/OCDE

Notes:

a) Categories: N - country network, national trend; A - city in which a notable portion (5-10%) of the national population is concentrated; B - industrial city in which a significant number of inhabitants are considered to be exposed to the worst level of pollution in 1980; C - city with residential and service functions and with intermediate pollution level; B.G. - selected station(s), representing the background concentration.

CAN) National trend: comparable over ten years only.
USA) Particulates smaller than 10 µm (standard adopted in 1987).
JPN) Fiscal year, commencing 1 April. Particulates smaller than 10 µm.
NZL) Particulates smaller than 50 µm. Auckland: monitoring sites increased from four to five in 1982 and from five to six in 1993. Christchurch: monitoring sites reduced from four to three in 1989.
BEL) Fiscal year, commencing 1 April. Brussels, 1991: lower number of stations.
DNK) Particulates smaller than 25 µm.
FIN) Oulu, 1980-90 PM5; 1991-93 PM10. Turku: particulates smaller than 40 µm. Sodankyla: monitoring terminated after 1990.
FRA) Data refer to black smoke. National: urban sites only. Rouen: change in estimation methodology in 1993.
DEU) Data referring to one station only represent intermediate pollution level. Berlin: number of monitoring stations and data up to 1992 refer to West Berlin; 1993 figure refers to Berlin as a whole.
GRC) Athens: five monitoring sites from 1985 to 1987 and four in 1993.
ISL) Measurement station located near a busy street corner.
IRL) Black smoke.
LUX) 1988 data refer to the sampling period July-December.
NLD) Fiscal year, commencing 1 April. Sampling is 24 hours every three days.
NOR) National, Porsgrunn and Kristiansand: measurement months are February, May, August, November; particulates smaller than 20 µm. National: stations gradually reduced since 1980. Oslo: mean pollution level of St. Olavs plass and Bryn skole stations.
PRT) Lisboa: 1992 data are from different stations. Barreiro/Seixal: 1989-93 data refer to different stations.
ESP) The number of monitoring stations differs from year to year except for Torrelavega. Madrid: data refer to city centre.
SWE) Monitoring period from October to March, except for B.G. Data refer to particulates smaller than 6 µm.
TUR) Beta-ray absorption method since 1987.1
UKD) Fiscal year, commencing 1 April. Measurement method follows British Standard 1747. Data referring to one station only represent intermediate pollution level.
HUN) Measuring stations are 5-10 metres away from the road in busy areas. Sampling is made during rush hours (six hours every second week).
POL) Particulates smaller than 10 µm. Chorzow: refers to total suspended particulates.

Source: OECD/OCDE

Notes:

a) Catégories: N - réseau du pays, évolution nationale; A - ville englobant une part notable (5 à 10%) de la population nationale; B - ville industrielle où un nombre notable d'habitants sont exposés aux niveaux les plus élevé de pollution en 1980; C - ville à dominante résidentielle et de service et d'un niveau moyen de pollution; B.G. - station(s) sélectionnées pour être représentative(s) de la pollution de fond.

CAN) Evolution nationale: données comparables sur dix ans seulement.
USA) Particules inférieures à 10 µm (norme adoptée en 1987).
JPN) Année fiscale, commençant le 1er avril. Particules inférieures à 10 µm.
NZL) Particules inférieures à 50 µm. Auckland: modifications du nombre de stations de mesures de quatre à cinq en 1982, de cinq à six en 1993. Christchurch: réduction du nombre de stations de mesures de quatre à trois en 1989.
BEL) Année fiscale, commençant le 1er avril. Bruxelles, 1991: nombre inférieur de stations.
DNK) Particules inférieures à 25 µm.
FIN) Oulu, 1980-90: particules inférieures à 5 µm; 1991-93: particules inférieures à 10 µm. Turku: particules inférieures à 40 µm. Sodankyla: mesures interrompues en 1990.
FRA) Fumées noires. National: sites urbains uniquement. Rouen: la méthode d'estimation a été changée en 1993.
DEU) Les données provenant d'une seule station représentent un niveau de pollution intermédiaire. Berlin, nombre de stations et données jusqu'en 1992: Berlin ouest uniquement; 1993: Berlin.
GRC) Athènes: cinq stations de mesures entre 1985 et 1987, quatre en 1993.
ISL) Station de mesure située près d'un carrefour à circulation intense.
IRL) Fumées noires.
LUX) Les données 1988 couvrent la période de mesure juillet-décembre.
NLD) Année fiscale, commençant le 1er avril. Prélèvement sur 24 heures tous les tois jours.
NOR) National, Porsgrunn et Kristiansand: mesures effectuées en février, mai, août et novembre; particules inférieures à 20 µm. Réseau national: le nombre de stations a été progressivement réduit depuis 1980. Oslo: niveau de pollution moyen des stations St. Olavs plass et Bryn skole.
PRT) Barreiro/Seixal: les données 1989-93 proviennent d'une autre station. Lisboa: les données 1992 proviennent de stations différentes.
ESP) Le nombre de stations de mesures varie d'une année sur l'autre sauf pour Torrelavega. Madrid: les données concernent le centre ville.
SWE) Période de surveillance d'octobre à mars, excepté pour B.G. Particules inférieures à 6 µm.
TUR) Méthode d'absorption de rayons béta depuis 1987.
UKD) Année fiscale, commençant le 1er avril. Méthode de mesure selon la norme britannique 1747. Les données provenant d'une seule station représentent un niveau de pollution intermédiaire.
HUN) Stations de mesures éloignées de 5 à 10 metres d'une rue a circulation intense. Les mesures sont effectuées aux heures de pointes (six heures toutes les deux semaines).
POL) Particules inférieures à 10 µm. Chorzow: particules en suspension totales.

The following table shows concentrations in acid precipitation for selected areas. Trend figures for pH, SO_4^- and NO_3^- are presented as well as the number of measurement stations.

Sulphur and nitrogen oxides can undergo chemical transformation in the atmosphere, forming acids and acid salts and returning to the earth as acid precipitation. Therefore, SO_4^- and NO_3^- are characteristic indicators concerning this issue, while pH values are a direct indicator of acidity in rainwater.

The interpretation of this table should take into account differences in the methods of measurement and in the calculation of mean concentrations as reflected in the footnotes.

Le tableau suivant montre les concentrations des précipitations acides pour des zones sélectionnées. L'évolution du pH et de la concentration en SO_4^- et en NO_3^- est présentée ainsi que le nombre de postes de mesures.

Les oxydes de soufre et d'azote peuvent subir des transformations chimiques dans l'atmosphère, constituer des acides et des sels acides et retomber sur le sol sous forme de précipitations acides. C'est pourquoi le SO_4^- et le NO_3^- sont des indicateurs caractéristiques de ce problème. Le pH est un indicateur direct de l'acidité de l'eau de pluie.

Dans l'interprétation de ce tableau, il faut tenir compte des différences dans les méthodes de mesure et dans le calcul des concentrations moyennes telles qu'elles sont reflétées dans les notes de bas de page.

CONCENTRATIONS IN ACID PRECIPITATION, selected areas, 1980-1993
CONCENTRATIONS DES PRÉCIPITATIONS ACIDES, régions sélectionnées, 1980-1993

Countries and regions/ Pays et régions	No. Stn.	pH						SO_4^{2-} (mg/l)						NO_3^- (mg/l)					
		1980	1985	1990	1991	1992	1993	1980	1985	1990	1991	1992	1993	1980	1985	1990	1991	1992	1993
Canada *																			
Great Lakes	4	4.40	4.23	4.34	4.32	4.33	4.30	3.61	2.65	2.36	2.52	2.12	2.07	2.59	2.24	1.87	2.17	1.91	2.09
Low. Can. Shield	4	4.40	4.29	4.46	4.48	4.45	4.41	2.26	2.20	1.71	1.53	1.48	1.35	1.26	1.74	1.46	1.37	1.24	1.39
East coast	4	4.40	4.50	4.68	4.65	4.62	4.70	2.18	1.17	0.87	0.98	0.98	0.71	0.97	0.76	0.62	0.62	0.66	0.53
B.G. ..	6	5.10	5.00	5.06	4.95	4.88	4.90	1.30	0.60	0.71	0.71	0.80	0.61	0.76	0.54	0.66	0.63	0.64	0.60
USA/Etats-Unis																			
Great Lakes	23	4.45	4.54	..	..	..	..	2.65	2.09	..	..	..	..	1.60	1.33	..	..	..	..
Japan/Japon *																			
National	23	..	..	4.70	..	..	..	..	..	1.94	..	..	..	..	..	1.04	..	..	..
Tokyo	1	..	5.00	4.60	..	..	..	..	2.30	3.70	..	..	..	..	1.20	2.99	..	..	..
B.G. ..	1	..	..	4.70	..	..	..	..	..	1.28	..	..	..	..	..	1.21	..	..	..
N.Zealand/N.Zélande *																			
Wellington	1	5.12	5.36	..	5.14	4.98	..	4.47	3.14	1.58	1.71	1.48	..	0.24	0.11	0.11	0.17	0.17	..
Lauder	1	..	5.76	5.56	5.29	5.52	5.44	..	1.94	0.31	0.21	0.18	0.14	..	0.15	0.14	0.13	0.15	0.09
Austria/Autriche *																			
Illmitz	1	4.47	..	5.30	..	..	..	6.03	..	4.26	..	..	..	2.83	..	2.75	..	..	..
Belgium/Belgique *																			
Bruxelles	1	..	5.26	5.12	..	..	..	..	6.51	5.70	..	..	..	..	3.10	3.76	..	..	..
Offagne	1	5.96	5.61	4.47	..	..	..	5.13	4.62	3.51	..	..	..	5.30	2.92	2.57	..	..	..
Denmark/Danemark																			
Tange	1	4.43	4.48	4.41	4.53	4.98	5.21	1.87	1.70	1.60	1.80	1.21	1.52	0.70	0.88	0.77	0.89	0.74	0.83
Finland/Finlande *																			
Uto, Ahtari, Virolahti	3	4.63	4.46	4.54	4.56	4.57	4.60	4.12	3.67	2.51	2.74	2.60	2.05	..	2.56	2.08	1.91	2.05	1.64
France																			
National	13	..	..	5.07	4.89	5.01	5.11	..	..	2.01	2.07	1.86	1.65	..	..	1.33	2.12	1.33	1.33
Revin	1	..	..	4.98	4.91	4.79	4.92	..	..	1.98	1.86	2.28	1.53	..	..	1.73	1.73	1.49	1.46
Donon	1	..	..	5.00	4.72	4.91	5.03	..	..	1.50	1.62	1.53	1.53	..	..	1.33	1.55	1.33	1.37
Abbeville	1	..	..	4.81	4.69	4.88	4.84	..	..	2.46	2.70	2.73	2.04	..	..	1.42	1.64	1.82	1.73
Germany/Allemagne																			
Deuselbach	1	..	4.36	4.64	4.55	4.62	4.79	..	3.33	2.18	2.43	2.19	1.84	..	2.49	1.90	2.49	2.22	1.83
Greece/Grèce																			
Patission	1	..	..	4.70	5.19	..	..	..	..	7.70	7.10	..	..	..	..	2.83	1.33	..	..
B.G. ..	1	..	..	4.86	4.70	..	..	..	..	9.20	5.20	..	..	..	..	2.30	1.37	..	..
Iceland/Islande *																			
B.G. ..	1	4.92	5.41	5.41	5.15	5.34	5.09	3.30	4.44	2.85	2.82	2.70	2.64	..	..	..	0.18	0.18	0.18
Italy/Italie *																			
Pallanza	1	4.20	4.25	4.25	4.24	4.34	4.31	5.24	3.36	3.22	3.27	2.79	4.09	2.98	2.42	3.60	3.10	2.85	2.91
L.Toggia	1	..	5.06	4.84	4.92	5.51	5.44	..	1.78	0.91	1.15	0.95	1.55	..	0.81	0.93	0.93	0.87	0.93
Milano Brera	1	..	..	4.26	4.80	4.62	4.69	..	..	5.09	7.06	5.04	3.53	..	..	3.72	4.40	3.29	2.92
Petralia	1	..	..	5.79	6.30	6.79	..	..	..	3.41	4.29	3.55	..	..	..	1.30	2.21	2.23	..
Netherl./Pays-Bas *																			
National	9	4.46	4.71	4.70	..	..	..	6.16	5.43	4.70	..	..	..	3.08	2.81	2.50	..	..	..
Rijnmond	4	4.34	4.76	4.60	..	..	..	7.65	7.16	11.06	..	..	..	..	3.34	2.01	..	..	..
Limburg	6	5.04	5.02	5.00	..	..	..	8.06	7.29	6.40	..	..	..	4.24	3.44	4.10	..	..	..
Norway/Norvège *																			
Birkenes	1	4.16	4.24	4.37	4.33	4.37	4.37	3.69	2.94	2.13	2.25	2.22	2.31	2.52	2.57	2.08	2.53	2.30	2.26
Skreadalen	1	4.54	4.48	4.61	4.61	4.70	4.81	1.44	1.77	1.17	1.23	1.11	0.87	0.93	1.42	1.02	1.20	1.06	1.11
Treungen	1	4.23	4.33	4.37	4.42	4.44	4.46	2.64	2.04	1.89	1.77	1.80	1.77	1.64	1.73	1.86	1.86	1.77	1.42
B.G. ..	11	4.42	4.50	4.61	4.63	4.67	4.68	1.98	1.65	1.22	1.19	1.13	1.22	1.27	1.39	1.11	1.24	1.13	1.22
Portugal *																			
Braganca	1	6.22	5.30	5.60	5.80	5.80	5.50	1.60	1.00	0.74	..	0.54	0.35	0.21	0.30	0.17	..	0.16	0.22
Sines	..	..	..	5.60	5.80	6.10	5.45	..	..	0.82	..	1.07	0.65	..	..	0.33	..	0.24	0.14

Notes: see next page / voir page suivante.

... / ...

CONCENTRATIONS IN ACID PRECIPITATION, selected areas, 1980-1993
CONCENTRATIONS DES PRÉCIPITATIONS ACIDES, régions sélectionnées, 1980-1993

Countries and regions/ Pays et régions	No. Stn.	pH 1980	1985	1990	1991	1992	1993	SO4²⁻ (mg/l) 1980	1985	1990	1991	1992	1993	NO3⁻ (mg/l) 1980	1985	1990	1991	1992	1993
Spain/Espagne *																			
Logroño	1	..	..	6.26	6.29	6.58	6.44	..	..	1.77	1.26	1.35	1.57	..	..	0.76	0.45	0.53	0.73
Roquetas	1	..	..	6.42	6.97	7.22	6.64	..	..	1.54	2.75	2.23	2.77	..	..	0.94	0.90	0.90	2.46
San Pablo	1	..	..	6.18	6.53	6.42	6.46	..	..	1.18	0.86	1.02	0.85	..	..	0.56	0.32	0.34	0.36
Sweden/Suède																			
Rorvik	1	4.20	4.20	4.30	4.30	4.30	4.20	4.14	4.29	3.75	3.36	2.49	3.03	3.03	3.49	2.79	3.10	2.70	2.66
Goteborg	1	..	4.40	4.43	4.45	4.45	4.88	..	10.60	5.30	6.90	6.70	7.30	..	6.50	4.60	4.40	4.10	4.70
Switzerland/Suisse																			
Duebendorf	1	..	4.39	4.62	4.33	4.56	4.71	..	2.76	1.86	2.46	1.80	1.86	..	1.77	1.68	2.35	1.68	1.72
Payerne	1	..	4.75	4.93	4.79	5.27	5.09	..	2.22	1.92	2.10	1.20	1.68	..	1.55	1.59	1.95	1.24	1.64
Turkey/Turquie																			
Cubuk	1	..	..	..	..	..	5.16	..	..	..	..	..	1.32	..	..	..	..	..	0.48
Antalya	1	..	..	..	..	4.57	4.16	..	..	..	..	7.73	5.01	..	..	..	..	4.25	5.53
UK/Royaume-Uni																			
Inverpolly	1	4.70	5.30	4.90	4.82	4.83	..	1.30	0.91	0.54	0.69	0.57	..	0.37	0.56	0.44	0.58	0.45	..
Eskdalemuir	1	4.24	4.72	4.71	4.70	4.68	..	2.50	1.49	1.22	1.26	1.23	..	1.24	0.93	0.87	0.93	0.78	..
Czech Rep./Rép.Tchèque																			
Praha-Libus	1	..	..	4.89	4.44	..	..	..	..	6.48	7.57	..	..	..	..	4.18	5.24	..	..
Hradec Kralove	1	..	4.24	4.26	4.45	..	..	..	6.69	5.95	4.62	..	..	..	3.84	3.90	2.70	..	..
Svratouch	1	4.28	4.28	4.42	4.32	..	..	5.67	6.48	4.47	4.59	..	..	3.18	4.12	2.69	2.80	..	..
Slovak Rep./Rép. Slovaque																			
Bratislava	1	4.19	4.44	4.90	5.67	..	..	13.29	9.06	8.13	12.36	..	..	3.78	3.92	4.05	3.92	..	..
Chopock	1	4.18	4.30	4.43	4.66	..	..	5.58	5.52	5.97	4.71	..	..	1.85	2.24	2.60	1.94	..	..
Hungary/Hongrie																			
B.G. K-Puszta	1	5.09	5.11	4.97	4.69	4.63	4.98	5.93	7.55	3.84	1.71	1.23	4.93	2.44	2.49	2.87	2.36	2.37	2.46
Poland/Pologne *																			
Sudety	1	..	3.89	4.20	4.31	4.23	4.26	..	10.48	7.79	5.21	5.21	6.20	..	5.18	5.58	3.36	3.36	3.72
Suwalki	1	4.45	4.53	4.27	4.77	4.57	4.64	5.36	5.54	4.67	4.52	3.80	3.32	2.39	2.67	2.48	2.66	2.52	2.08

Notes:
CAN) All monitoring sites are in eastern Canada's areas of high acid deposition. Sampling protocols for all constituents were upgraded in 1984.
JPN) Sampling protocols for all constituents were upgraded in 1984. 1980 data refer to 1979.
NZL) Wellington: monitoring terminated on April 1992. SO4²⁻ reduction largely due to increased sensitivity of analysis method.
AUT) Measurement station is used in the EMEP monitoring network and is in an area where the influence of local sources is as small as possible; data are averages referring to the sampling periods October-March and April-September. 1990 data refer to 1988.
BEL) SO4²⁻ and NO3⁻ data originally expressed in mgS/l and mgN/l; data weighted by amount of rainfall.
FIN) Mean values weighted by amount of rainfall.
ISL) Measurement station is used in the EMEP monitoring network and is in an area where the influence of local sources is as small as possible; data are averages referring to the sampling periods October-March and April-September.
ITA) Pallanza, subalpine station in northern Italy; L. Toggia, remote alpine station; Milano Brera, urban station in Po Valley; Petralia, rural station in southern Italy.
NLD) Data refer to the sampling period April-March. National: 1990 data refer to January-December. Rijnmond: 1990 data refer to 1989.
NOR) All values are precipitation weighted means and the SO4²⁻ values are corrected for sea-salt. All single monitoring sites are background (rural) stations. B.G.: Precipitation weighted mean calculated for 11 Norwegian background stations.
PRT) Measurement stations are used in the EMEP monitoring network and are in an area where the influence of local sources is as small as possible; data are averages referring to the sampling periods October-March and April-September.
ESP) Data from BAPMON-EMEP network.
POL) Sudety: south-west mountainous region. Suwalki: north-east region. Data from WMO/BAPMON and EMEP networks.

Notes:
CAN) Tous les sites de surveillance sont situés dans l'est du Canada dans des zones de dépôts acides élevés. Les protocoles d'échantillonnage ont été revisés pour tous les constituants en 1984.
JPN) Les protocoles d'échantillonnage ont été revisés pour tous les constituants en 1984. Les données 1980 sont de 1979.
NZL) Wellington: mesures arrêtées en Avril 1992. SO4²⁻: la réduction fait suite à une modification de la méthode d'analyse.
AUT) La station de mesure fait partie du réseau de surveillance EMEP et se situe dans une région où l'influence des sources locales est la plus faible possible; les données sont des moyennes basées sur les périodes de mesure octobre-mars et avril-septembre. Données 1990: 1988.
BEL) Données SO4²⁻ et NO3⁻ exprimées à l'origine en mgS/l et mgN/l; données pondérées par la quantité de pluie.
FIN) Moyennes pondérées par la quantité de pluie.
ISL) La station de mesure fait partie du réseau de surveillance EMEP et se situe dans une région où l'influence des sources locales est la plus faible possible; les données sont des moyennes basées sur les périodes de mesure octobre-mars et avril-septembre.
ITA) Pallanza, station subalpine dans le nord de l'Italie; L. Toggia, station alpine; Milano Brera, station urbaine dans la vallée du Pô; Petralia, station rurale dans le sud de l'Italie.
NLD) Les données couvrent la période de mesure avril-mars. National: les données pour 1990 couvrent la période janvier-décembre. Rijnmond, données 1990 : 1989.
NOR) Moyennes pondérées par la quantité de pluie. SO4²⁻ : valeurs corrigées du sel marin. Les stations uniques sont des stations de fond rurales. BG : moyenne pondérée calculée sur 11 stations de fond.
PRT) La station de mesure fait partie du réseau de surveillance EMEP et se situe dans une région où l'influence des sources locales est la plus faible possible ; les données sont des moyennes basées sur les périodes de mesure octobre-mars et avril-septembre.
ESP) Les données sont des chiffres du réseau BAPMON-EMEP.
POL) Sudety: région montagneuse du sud-ouest. Suwalki: région nord-est. Les données sont des chiffres des réseaux WMO/BAPMON et EMEP.

Source: OECD/OCDE, EMEP

3. INLAND WATERS

3. EAUX INTÉRIEURES

INTRODUCTION

Inland water resources are one of the four components of the natural environment, with air, land and living resources.

The tables presented in this section give information concerning:

a)   the use of inland water resources:

      ►   available freshwater resources and water abstractions from ground and surface waters, particularly for public water supplies, irrigation, industrial uses and the cooling of electric power plants;

b)   the state of inland water resources:

      ►   pollution of rivers;

      ►   pollution of lakes;

c)   the management of inland water resources:

      ►   waste water treatment facilities.

It should be noted that a number of important topics are not covered by these data, including pollution discharged to inland waters, drinking water quality, performance of water treatment plants, the state of groundwater stocks, and other uses of water such as recreation and leisure activities, transport and wildlife related uses. Irrigation data are given in the section on agriculture. International conventions related to water pollution are presented in the section on general data.

INTRODUCTION

Les ressources en eaux intérieures font référence à l'une des quatre composantes de l'environnement naturel à côté de l'air, des sols et des matières vivantes.

Les tableaux présentés dans cette section fournissent des informations concernant :

a)   l'utilisation des ressources en eaux intérieures :

    ►   les ressources en eau douces disponibles et les prélèvements d'eau de surface et d'eau souterraine, en particulier pour l'alimentation en eau des ménages, l'irrigation, les usages industriels et le refroidissement des centrales électriques ;

b)   l'état des ressources en eaux intérieures :

    ►   la pollution des rivières ;

    ►   la pollution des lacs ;

c)   la gestion des ressources en eaux intérieures :

    ►   les équipements de traitement des eaux usées.

On doit noter que plusieurs thèmes importants ne sont pas couverts par ces données, tels que les rejets de polluants dans les eaux intérieures, la qualité des eaux potables, l'état de fonctionnement des stations de traitement des eaux, l'état des eaux souterraines, les autres usages de l'eau, tels que les activités de récréation et de loisir, les transports et les usages liés à la faune et à la flore sauvages. Les données sur l'irrigation se trouvent dans la section sur l'agriculture. Les conventions internationales concernant la pollution de l'eau sont présentées dans la section sur les données générales.

The following table presents long term annual averages of renewable freshwater resources and their various flows (precipitation, evapotranspiration, inflows from neighbouring countries, outflows to neighbouring countries or to the sea). The "renewable resources" total aggregates the quantity of water received from precipitation net of evapotranspiration, and from inflowing rivers.

Freshwater resources, particularly their renewable component (i.e. available for abstraction), are essential to the development of human life and economic activities.

When interpreting this table, it should be borne in mind that the definitions and estimation methods may vary considerably among countries.

Le tableau suivant présente les moyennes annuelles à long terme des ressources en eau douce renouvelables, de même que les différents flux d'eau constituant la ressource (précipitations, évapotranspiration, apports d'eau des pays voisins, évacuation d'eau vers les pays voisins ou vers la mer). Les "ressources renouvelables" comprennent la quantité d'eau des précipitations moins l'évapotranspiration, plus la quantité d'eau importée par les rivières de pays voisins.

Les ressources en eau douce et plus particulièrement leur composante renouvelable (donc disponible pour prélèvement) sont essentielles au développement de la vie humaine et des activités économiques.

Lors de l'interprétation de ce tableau, on gardera à l'esprit que les définitions et les méthodes d'évaluation peuvent varier considérablement d'un pays à l'autre.

ESTIMATES OF RENEWABLE FRESHWATER RESOURCES, long term annual average
ESTIMATION DES RESSOURCES EN EAUX DOUCES RENOUVELABLES, moyenne annuelle à long terme

billion/milliards

		Precipitation/ Précipitation (1)	Evapo-transpiration (2)	Internal Resources/ Ressources internes (1-2)	Inflow/ Apport (a) (3)	Total renewable/ Total renouvelable (1-2)+(3)	Outflow/ Evacuation (a)
Canada		4930	2190	2740	52	2792	..
Mexico/Mexique	*	1532	1120	412	2	414	352
USA/Etats-Unis		6440	3980	2460	18	2478	
Japan/Japon		661	226	435	-	435	..
Australia/Australie		3252	2900	352	-	352	350
N.Zealand/N.Zélande		537	210	327	-	327	326
Austria/Autriche		98	43	55	29	84	84
Denmark/Danemark		21	9	12	..	..	
Finland/Finlande		222	115	107	3	110	110
France		450	270	180	18	198	150
Germany/Allemagne		274	179	95	69	164	..
Greece/Grèce		112	65	47	14	61	45
Iceland/Islande		200	30	170	-	170	170
Ireland/Irlande	*	77	30	47	3	50	40
Italy/Italie		296	129	167	8	175	155
Luxembourg		2	1	1	4	5	..
Netherlands/Pays-Bas		30	20	11	80	91	86
Norway/Norvège		458	76	382	10	392	392
Portugal		82	45	37	35	72	68
Spain/Espagne		340	224	116	1	117	..
Sweden/Suède		328	150	178	-	178	178
Switzerland/Suisse	*	60	20	40	13	53	54
Turkey/Turquie		501	274	227	7	234	186
UK/Royaume-Uni	*	143	67	76	-	76	..
Former CSFR/ex-RFTS	*	86	62	28	68	96	30
Czech Rep./Rép. Tchèque	*	49	37	13	..	..	..
Slovak Rep./Rép. Slovaque	*	37	22	15	..	..	..
Hungary/Hongrie		58	52	6	114	120	120
Poland/Pologne		193	138	55	8	63	63
North America/Amérique Nord	*	12900	7300	5600	..	..	..
OECD/OCDE Europe	*	3700	1700	1900	..	..	..
EU/UE-15	*	2500	1300	1100	..	..	..
OECD/OCDE	*	21000	12400	8700	..	..	..

Notes:
a)   Inflow: water flows from neighbouring countries. Outflow: water flows to other countries and to the sea; Underground flows of surface waters are included.
MEX)   Inflow: excluding inflow from Guatemala.
IRL)   Data include Secreteriat estimates.
CHE)   Difference between total renewable resources and outflow due to inclusion of glaciers melting (-250 million m3/year).
UKD)   England and Wales only. Precipitation: average based on 1961-90. Evapotranspiration: actual amounts.
CSFR)   Data include Secreteriat estimates.
CZE)   Data include Secreteriat estimates.
SLO)   Data include Secreteriat estimates.
Totals)   Rounded figures.

Notes :
a)   Apport : écoulements d'eau importés des pays voisins. Evacuation : écoulements d'eau exportés vers des pays voisins ou vers la mer. L'écoulement souterrain des eaux de surface est inclus.
MEX)   Apport : excluant les apports provenant du Guatemala.
IRL)   Les données comprennent des estimations du Secrétariat.
CHE)   La différence entre les ressources renouvelables et l'évacuation est due à l'inclusion de la fonte des glaciers (-250 millions m3/an).
UKD)   Angleterre et Pays de Galles uniquement. Précipitation : moyenne pour la période 1961-90. Évapotranspiration : quantités réelles.
CSFR)   Les données comprennent des estimations du Secrétariat.
CZE)   Les données comprennent des estimations du Secrétariat.
SLO)   Les données comprennent des estimations du Secrétariat.
Totaux)   Chiffres arrondis.

Source: OECD/OCDE, World Resources Institute, BRGM

Table 1B shows total, surface and groundwater abstractions by country. Water abstractions refer to water taken from ground or surface water sources and conveyed to the place of use. If the water is returned to a surface water source, abstraction of the same water by the downstream user is counted again in compiling total withdrawal. Table 1C shows total water abstraction by major uses and by country.

Water abstraction is a major pressure on freshwater resources, particularly from public water supplies, irrigation, industrial processes and cooling of electric power plants. It has significant implications for issues of quantity and quality of water resources.

When interpreting these tables, it should be borne in mind that the definitions employed by Member countries may vary considerably, as mentioned in the notes. The irrigation table in the agriculture section provides additional information.

Le tableau 1B présente les prélèvements totaux d'eau, les prélèvements d'eau de surface et d'eau souterraine par pays. Le prélèvement d'eau correspond à l'eau retirée des sources de surface ou souterraines et transportée à son lieu d'usage. Si cette eau est par la suite retournée dans une source d'eau de surface, le prélèvement de la même eau par un utilisateur situé en aval est compté à nouveau dans l'évaluation du prélèvement total. Le tableau 1C présente le prélèvement total d'eau par usages majeurs et par pays.

Les prélèvements d'eau exercent une pression majeure sur les ressources en eaux intérieures, en particulier à cause des réseaux publics d'eau, de l'irrigation, des processus industriels et du refroidissement des centrales électriques. Ces prélèvements jouent un rôle important dans la quantité et la qualité des ressources en eau.

Lors de l'interprétation de ces tableaux, on gardera à l'esprit que les définitions employées par les pays Membres peuvent différer considérablement, ainsi que l'indiquent les notes. Le tableau irrigation dans la section agriculture donne des informations supplémentaires.

FRESHWATER ABSTRACTIONS BY SOURCE, 1980, 1985, 1990, 1993
PRÉLÈVEMENTS D'EAUX DOUCES PAR SOURCE, 1980, 1985, 1990, 1993

million m³

		Total abstractions/ Prélèvement total				Surface water/ Eau de surface				Groundwater/ Eau souterraine			
		1980	1985	1990	1993 a)	1980	1985	1990	1993 a)	1980	1985	1990	1993 a)
Canada	*	37594	42383	43888	45096	36733	41486	42936	44059	861	897	952	1037
Mexico/Mexique		57251	..	..	77620	40696	..	..	51995	16555	..	..	25625
USA/Etats-Unis		517720	467335	468620	..	402750	366095	358790		114970	101240	109830	..
Japan/Japon		88200	89200	90800	..	75450	76300	77700	..	12750	12900	13100	..
Australia/Australie	*	10900	14600	..	..	..	..	..	..	..	..	..	..
N.Zealand/N.Zélande	*	1200	1900	..	2000	..	..	..	..	..	..	..	..
Austria/Autriche	*	2190	2120	..	2360	1055	..	1005	930	1135	1115	..	1430
Denmark/Danemark	*	1205	..	1200	..	..	..	..	..	..	..	..	
Finland/Finlande	*	3700	4000	2347	2203	3510	3680	2087	1875	190	320	240	239
France	*	35104	34898	37733	..	29400	28725	31523	..	5704	6173	6210	..
Germany/Allemagne	*	42206	41216	58852	46272	35344	34225	51125	38506	6862	6991	7727	7766
Iceland/Islande		100	103	..	164	5	8	..	14	95	95	..	150
Italy/Italie	*	56200	52000	56200	..	..	40000	..	..	..	12000	..	..
Luxembourg	*	..	..	261	..	..	..	217	..	..	..	43	..
Netherl./Pays-Bas	*	9197	9302	..	7806	8190	8231	..	6757	1007	1071	..	1049
Norway/Norvège	*	..	2025	..	..	..	1620	..	..	..	405	..	..
Portugal	*	..	..	7288	..	..	..	4233	..	..	..	3065	..
Spain/Espagne	*	39920	46250	45845	30750	34800	40840	41719	25150	5120	5410	4126	5600
Sweden/Suède		4106	2937	2968	2957	3511	2320	2361	2345	595	617	607	612
Switzerland/Suisse		1104	1143	1162	1192	181	190	221	212	922	953	941	980
Turkey/Turquie	*	16200	19400	31800	33500	11800	14100	25200	26000	4400	5300	6600	7500
UK/Royaume-Uni	*	13912	12947	14237	11791	11422	10426	11528	9439	2491	2521	2709	2352
Former CSFR/ex-RFTS		5573	5537	5786	..	4196	4169	4189	..	1377	1368	1597	..
Czech R./R.Tchèque		3559	3531	3647	2740	2839	2834	2799	2210	720	697	848	530
Slovak R./R.Slov.		2014	2006	2139	1776	1357	1335	1390	..	657	671	749	..
Hungary/Hongrie		4805	6267	6263	6813	3551	4880	5236	5830	1254	1386	1027	983
Poland/Pologne		14184	15453	14248	12278	11899	13076	11928	10225	2285	2377	2320	2053
N.America/Amér.N.	*	612600	574800	586000	591300	..	..	..	..	..	..	..	..
OECD/OCDE Europe	*	248200	253600	282700	261500	..	..	..	..	..	..	..	..
EU/UE-15	*	228800	231000	247300	224400	..	..	..	..	..	..	..	..
OECD/OCDE	*	961000	934100	976000	960300	..	..	..	..	..	..	..	..

Notes: see page 67 / voir page 67.

Source: OECD/OCDE

FRESHWATER ABSTRACTIONS BY MAJOR USE, 1980, 1985 and early 1990s
PRELEVEMENT D'EAUX DOUCES PAR USAGE MAJEUR, 1980, 1985 et début des années 1990

Per cent/pour cent

		Public Water Supply/ Réseau public			Irrigation			Industry no Cooling/ Industrie sauf refroidissement			Electrical cooling/ Refroidissement production électricité		
		1980	1985	early 1990s/ début des années 1990 b)	1980	1985	early 1990s/ début des années 1990 b)	1980	1985	early 1990s/ début des années 1990 b)	1980	1985	early 1990s/ début des années 1990 b)
Canada	*	11.3	11.1	11.3	7.4	7.0	7.1	8.6	8.9	7.9	39.9	56.9	59.7
Mexico/Mexique		7.1	..	10.5	51.5	..	..	10.1	..	9.6	..	..	0.3
USA/Etats-Unis	*	9.1	10.8	11.4	38.7	40.5	40.2	10.4	6.6	5.7	40.4	38.7	38.6
Japan/Japon	*	15.5	16.9	18.3	65.3	65.0	64.0	18.7	17.5	17.2	..	..	..
N.Zeal./N.Zélande	*	..	..	9.2	..	..	55.0	..	..	13.0	..	..	..
Austria/Autriche	*	22.8	24.8	33.3	2.3	2.6	8.5	25.1	23.6	20.7	47.9	47.2	37.5
Denmark/Danemark	*	..	..	52.1	..	..	30.4	..	..	18.8	..	..	..
Finland/Finlande	*	10.5	10.2	18.9	..	0.5	0.9	..	..	64.6	..	..	14.1
France	*	15.5	16.9	16.1	..	..	..	15.8	14.6	11.8	56.3	55.6	59.0
Germany/Allemagne	*	12.0	12.4	14.1	0.4	0.5	..	6.8	5.8	23.7	60.4	62.0	62.2
Iceland/Islande	*	84.0	84.5	50.0	..	..	..	10.0	9.7	6.1	..	..	..
Italy/Italie	*	14.2	14.1	..	57.3	..	..	14.2	..	..	12.5	..	..
Luxembourg	*	..	..	95.0	..	..	0.3	..	..	4.7	..	..	..
Netherl./Pays-Bas	*	11.2	11.9	16.4	..	..	..	1.9	2.0	2.5	65.4	70.4	65.9
Norway/Norvège	*	..	26.6	..	..	3.4	..	..	..	..	..	..	..
Portugal		..	..	7.9	..	..	52.6	..	..	3.3	..	..	36.8
Spain/Espagne	*	11.8	11.6	15.9	65.7	65.7	55.3	..	..	6.2	22.5	22.7	14.8
Sweden/Suède	*	23.3	33.1	32.7	1.6	2.0	3.2	..	35.2	34.4	..	0.9	0.9
Switzerl./Suisse	*	54.9	61.2	66.7	..	..	..	27.7	22.0	19.2	..	..	..
Turkey/Turquie	*	..	14.4	8.3	..	73.7	84.3	..	11.9	1.7	..	..	2.8
UK/Royaume-Uni	*	38.3	47.1	51.8	0.2	0.3	0.5	13.4	8.1	4.1	27.2	19.2	4.4
Former CSFR/ex-RFTS		25.9	29.3	28.6	2.5	3.2	7.0	36.3	34.4	31.6	32.6	30.4	26.6
Czech R./R.Tchèque		29.4	32.9	41.4	1.5	1.6	2.2	30.9	30.0	23.7	35.0	32.6	32.1
Slovak R./R.Slovaque		19.7	22.9	17.3	4.2	6.1	13.1	45.8	42.1	35.6	28.5	26.7	22.1
Hungary/Hongrie		16.7	14.8	13.8	7.0	4.6	3.3	8.6	5.5	4.1	49.7	60.0	69.7
Poland/Pologne		19.2	18.9	22.4	2.0	3.4	2.4	12.9	10.6	7.4	50.7	53.1	53.6

Notes: see next page / voir page suivante.

Source: OECD/OCDE

Notes: (3.1B)

a) Data prior to 1991 have not been considered.
CAN) 1980 and 1990: 1981 and 1989 data.
AUS) 1980: 1977 data adjusted for an average climatic year. 1985: fiscal year 1983/84.
NZL) 1980: composite total based on 1975 agricult. withdrawal (except irrigation) and industry (no cooling), and 1980 public supply. 1985: estimate excluding irrigation, and industr. and electrical cooling. Early 1990s: estimate excluding industr. and electr. cooling.
AUT) Surface water: excluding agriculture, irrigation and industry except cooling. Groundwater: excluding industry and electrical cooling.
DNK) 1980: 1977 data.
FIN) Excluding agriculture except irrigation. 1990 and early 1990s: including 1985 data for irrigation.
FRA) 1980 and 1990: 1981 and 1988 data.
DEU) Early 1990s: excluding agriculture. 1980 and 1985: 1979 and 1983 data for western Germany only.
ITA) Excluding agriculture except irrigation. 1980: including 1973 estimates for industriel cooling. 1990: 1987 data.
LUX) Excluding agriculture.
NLD) Excluding agriculture and irrigation. 1980 and 1985: 1981 and 1986 data.
NOR) 1985: 1983 data, including 1978 data for industry.
PRT) 1990: 1989 data.
ESP) Excluding agriculture except irrigation. Groundwater: excluding industry. 1990: 1989 data.
TUR) 1980: excluding agriculture except irrigation. 1980 and 1985: excluding electrical cooling.
UKD) England and Wales only. Irrigation: spray irrigation only.
Totals) Rounded figures, including Secretariat estimates. OECD and EU until 1985: western Germany only.

Source: OECD/OCDE

Notes: (3.1B)

a) Les données antérieures à 1991 nont pas été prises en compte.
CAN) 1980 et 1990 : données 1981 et 1989.
AUS) 1980 : données 1977 ajustées pour une année climatique moyenne. 1985 : année fiscale 1983/84.
NZL) 1980 : total composite de données 1975 pour les prélèvements agricoles autres que l'irrigation et pour l'industrie hors refroidissement, de données 1980 pour les réseaux publics. 1985 : estimation excluant l'irrigation et le refroidissement industriel et des centrales électriques. Début des années 1990: estimations excluant le refroidissement industriel et des centrales électriques.
AUT) Eau de surface : exclut l'agriculture, l'irrigation et l'industrie (hors refroidissement). Eau souterraine : exclut l'industrie et le refroidissement des centrales électriques.
DNK) 1980 : données 1977.
FIN) Exclut les prélèvements agricoles autres que l'irrigation. 1990 et début des années. 1990 : inclut des données 1985 pour l'irrigation.
FRA) 1980 et 1990 : données 1981 et 1988.
DEU) Début des années 90 : exclut les prélèvements agricoles. 1980 et 1985 : données 1979 et 1983 pour l'Allemagne occidentale seulement.
ITA) Exclut les prélèvements agricoles autres que l'irrigation. 1980 : inclut des estimations 1973 pour le refroidissement industriel. 1990 : données 1987.
LUX) Exclut les prélèvements agricoles.
NLD) Exclut l'agriculture et l'irrigation. 1980 et 1985 : données 1981 et 1986.
NOR) 1985 : données 1983, incluant des données de 1978 pour l'industrie.
PRT) 1990 : données 1989.
ESP) Exclut les prélèvements agricoles autres que l'irrigation. Eau souterraine: exclut l'industrie. 1990 : données 1989.
TUR) 1980 : exclut les prélèvements agricoles autres que l'irrigation. 1985 : exclut le refroidissement des centrales électriques.
UKD) Angleterre et Pays de Galles seulement. Irrigation : irrigation d'aspersion seulement.
Totaux) Chiffres arrondis, incluant des estimations du Secrétariat. OCDE et UE jusqu'en 1985 : Allemagne occidentale uniquement.

Notes: (3.1C)

a) Withdrawal from the four sectors does not necessarily add up to 100%, since "other agricultural uses than irrigation", "industrial cooling" and "other uses" are not covered in this table.
b) Latest data prior to 1989 have not been considered.
CAN) 1980: 1981 data.
USA) Industry: includes cooling.
JPN) Industry: includes industrial and electrical cooling.
NZL) Early 1990s: % based on 1993 estimate excluding industrial electrical cooling.
AUT) Irrigation and industry no cooling: groundwater only. Electrical cooling: surface water only. Early 1990s: irrigation includes other agricultural abstractions.
DNK) Industry: includes industial and electrical cooling.
FIN) Early 1990s: % based on total including 1985 data for irrigation and excluding agriculture.
FRA) 1980: 1981 data. Industry: includes industr. cooling. Early 1990s: 1988 data.
DEU) % based on totals excluding agriculture. Industry: includes industr. cooling. 1980 and 1985: 1979 and 1983 data, including western Germany only. Industry: includes industr. cooling and mining and quarrying.
ISL) Industry: includes industr. cooling. After 1985 fish farming became a major user of abstracted water, which explains the change in the relative contribution of other sectors.
ITA) % based on totals excluding agriculture except irrigation. 1985: 1987 data.
LUX) % based on totals excluding agriculture.
NLD) % based on totals excluding agriculture and irrigation. 1980 and 1985: 1981 and 1986 data.
NOR) 1985: 1983 data including 1978 data for industry. Industry: includes industrial and electrical cooling.
ESP) % based on totals excluding agriculture except irrigation. Industry: surface water only; includes industial cooling.
SWE) % based on totals excluding agriculture except irrigation. Irrigation: 1980 data refer to 1976; since 1985 data are estimations for dry year. Industry: since 1985, data refer to 1983 and to manufacturing industry. Rough estimate is used to remove industry cooling (40% of total). Electrical cooling: since 1985 data refer to 1983.
CHE) Industry: data refer to total industry (ISIC 10-45 rev. 3).
TUR) 1985: data exclude electr. cooling. Industry no cooling: 1985 data include cooling.
UKD) England and Wales only. Irrigation: spray irrigation only. Early 1990s: 1993 data.

Source: OECD/OCDE

Notes : (3.1C)

a) La somme des prélèvements pour les quatre secteurs n'est pas nécessairement égale à 100% : les "usages agricoles autres que l'irrigation", les "eaux de refroidissement industriels" et les "autres usages" ne sont pas présentés ici.
b) Les données antérieures à 1989 n'ont pas été prises en compte.
CAN) 1980 : données 1981.
USA) Industrie : inclut le refroidissement.
JPN) Industrie : inclut le refroidissement industriel et des centrales électriques.
NZL) Début des années 90 : % fondés sur des estimations 1993 excluant le refroidissement industriel et des centrales électriques.
AUT) Irrigation et industrie hors refroidissement : eau souterraine uniquement. Centrales électriques : eau de surface uniquement. Début des années 90 : l'irrigation inclut d'autres prélèvements agricoles.
DNK) Industrie : inclut le refroidissement industriel et des centrales électriques.
FIN) Début des années 1990 : % fondés sur un total incluant des données 1985 pour l'irrigation et excluant l'agriculture.
FRA) 1980 : données 1981. Industrie : inclut le refroidissement industriel. Début des années 1990 : données 1988.
DEU) % fondés sur des totaux excluant les prélèvements agricoles. Industrie : inclut le refroidissement industriel. 1980 et 1985 : données 1979 et 1983 pour l'Allemagne occidentale seulement. Industrie : inclut le refroidissement industriel et les mines et carrières.
ISL) Industrie : inclut le refroidissement industriel. Après 1985 l'importance des prélèvements par la pisciculture explique le changement dans la contribution relative des autres secteurs.
ITA) % fondés sur des totaux excluant les prélèvements agricoles autres que l'irrigation. 1985 : données 1987.
LUX) % fondés sur des totaux excluant les prélèvements agricoles.
NLD) % fondés sur des totaux excluant l'agriculture et l'irrigation. 1980 et 1985 : données 1981 et 1986.
NOR) 1985 : données 1983 incluant des données 1978 pour l'industrie. Industrie : inclut le refroidissement industriel et des centrales électriques.
ESP) % fondés sur des totaux excluant les prélèvements agricoles autres que l'irrigation. Industrie : eau de surface uniquement ; inclut le refroidissement industriel.
SWE) % fondés sur des totaux excluant les prélèvements agricoles autres que l'irrigation. Irrigation : les données 1980 sont de 1976 ; depuis 1985 ; estimations pour une année sèche. Industrie : depuis 1985, les données se rapportent à 1983 et à l'industrie manufacturière. Le refroidissement industriel a été retiré en utilisant des estimations grossières (40% du total). Refroidissement électrique : depuis 1985 les données sont de 1983.
CHE) Industrie : industrie totale (CITI 10-45 rév. 3).
TUR) 1985 : exclut le refroidissement des centrales électriques. Industrie sauf refroidissement : les données 1985 incluent le refroidissement.
UKD) Angleterre et Pays de Galles seulement. Irrigation : irrigation d'aspersion seulement. Début des années 1990: données 1993.

Table 2A shows the percentage of national population connected to public sewage networks and related treatment facilities.

Table 2B shows the percentage of national population served by waste water treatment plants, and the degree of treatment (primary treatment only, secondary treatment and tertiary treatment). "Served" here means actually connected to a waste water treatment plant through a public sewage network.

Table 2C shows amounts of sludge generated in public sewage treatment plants, and related disposal methods, for the latest year available.

These indicators provide information on the level of equipment installed by countries to manage and abate water pollution.

The interpretation of these tables should take into account some variations in countries' definitions, as reflected in footnotes. Primary treatment otherwise refers to the physical and mechanical removal of 20 to 30 per cent or more of the biological oxygen demand (BOD), secondary treatment to the biological removal of 80 to 90 per cent or more of BOD, and tertiary treatment to the chemical or biological/chemical removal of 95 per cent or more of BOD.

Le tableau 2A présente les pourcentages de population nationale raccordée à un réseau d'assainissement public et à des installations de traitement.

Le tableau 2B présente les pourcentages de population nationale desservie par une station de traitement des eaux usées, et le degré de traitement (primaire seulement, secondaire et tertiaire). "Desservi" signifie connecté à une station de traitement des eaux usées à travers un réseau public d'assainissement.

Le tableau 2C présente les quantités de boues d'épuration produites dans les stations d'épuration publiques et les méthodes d'élimination utilisées pour la dernière année disponible.

Ces indicateurs fournissent des informations concernant le niveau d'équipement existant dans les pays pour gérer et lutter contre la pollution de l'eau.

L'interprétation de ces tableaux doit prendre en compte les différences de définition entre les pays telles que les notes le précisent. En l'absence de notes, un traitement primaire signifie une réduction par des moyens physiques et mécaniques de 20 à 30 pour cent de la demande biologique en oxygène (DBO), un traitement secondaire une réduction par des moyens biologiques de 80 à 90 pour cent de la DBO et un traitement tertiaire une réduction par des moyens chimiques ou biologiques/chimiques de 95 pour cent et plus de la DBO.

POPULATION CONNECTED TO SEWERAGE, latest year available (a)
POPULATION RACCORDÉE AUX RÉSEAUX D'ASSAINISSEMENT, dernière année disponible (a)

% of national Population

| | | Population connected to public sewerage / population raccordée aux réseaux d'assainissement publics | | | | Population not connected to public sewerage/ population non raccordée à un réseau d'assain. |
| | Total | *of which:* served by a sewage treatment plant (STP)/ *dont:* desservie par une station d'épuration des eaux usées (STEP) | | | *of which:* not served by a STP/ *dont:* non desservie par une STEP (d) | |
		Public treatment/ traitement public (b)	Other treatment/ autre traitement (c)			public (e)
Canada	75.0	63.0	-		12.0	25.0
Mexico/Mexique	..	21.8	..		..	..
USA/Etats-Unis	..	70.8	..		..	..
Japan/Japon	..	50.1	..		..	..
Austria/Autriche	..	72.0	..		..	..
Denmark/Danemark *	..	98.0	..		..	..
Finland/Finlande	77.3	77.0	-		0.3	22.7
France *	77.6	68.3	-		9.3	22.4
Germany/Allemagne	90.2	85.6	3.0		1.5	9.8
w.Germany/All. occ.	93.9	92.0	1.3		0.6	6.1
Greece/Grèce	50.6	11.4	-		39.2	49.4
Iceland/Islande	100.0	2.0	4.0		94.0	0.0
Netherlands/Pays-Bas	95.3	93.3	-		2.0	4.7
Norway/Norvège	77.0	57.0	-		20.0	23.0
Portugal	55.3	20.9	-		34.4	44.7
Spain/Espagne	72.5	59.1	-		13.4	27.5
Sweden/Suède	95.0	95.0	-		-	5.0
Switzerland/Suisse	91.0	91.0	-		0.0	9.0
Turkey/Turquie	22.0	6.3	-		15.7	78.0
UK/Royaume-Uni *	96.4	87.4	-		9.0	3.6
Czech Rep./Rep. Tchèque	65.3	50.6	-		14.7	34.7

Notes: (3.2A)
a) Data refer to early 1990s unless noted otherwise.
b) National population served by public sewage treatment. Includes primary, secondary and tertiary treatment. (See Tab.3.2B for further details.)
c) Population connected to public sewerage, and served by waste water treatment in non-public treatment plants, e.g. industrial waste water plants.
d) Population connected to public sewage network but not served by any sewage treatment.
e) May include individual private treatment facilities (e.g. septic tanks).
DNK) 1989 data.
FRA) 1987 data.
UKD) Great Britain only.

Source: OECD/OCDE

Notes : (3.2A)
a) Les données se rapportent au début des années 1990 sauf indication contraire.
b) Population nationale desservie par un traitement public des eaux usées. Inclut les traitements primaire, secondaire et tertiaire. (Voir tab. 3.2B pour plus de détails.)
c) Population raccordée aux réseaux d'assainissement publics, et desservie par un traitement d'eaux usées dans une station d'épuration qui n'est pas publique, p. ex. une station d'épuration industrielle.
d) Population raccordée au réseau d'assainissement public, mais ne bénéficiant pas d'un traitement des eaux usées.
e) Peut inclure les installations de traitement individuelles et privées (p. ex. fosses septiques).
DNK) Données 1989.
FRA) Données 1987.
UKD) Grande-Bretagne uniquement.

POPULATION SERVED BY WASTE WATER TREATMENT PLANTS (a), 1980, 1985, 1990, 1993
POPULATION DESSERVIE PAR UNE STATION D'ÉPURATION DES EAUX USÉES (a), 1980, 1985, 1990, 1993

% Population

		Primary treatment only / traitement primaire uniquement (b)				Secondary treatment / traitement secondaire (c)				Tertiary treatment / traitement tertiaire (d)				Total served / Total desservi			
		1980	1985	1990	1993 (e)	1980	1985	1990	1993 (e)	1980	1985	1990	1993 (e)	1980	1985	1990	1993 (e)
Canada	*	14.0	13.0	15.0	15.0	25.0	23.0	21.0	20.0	25.0	27.0	24.0	28.0	64.0	63.0	60.0	63.0
Mexico/Mexique		..	..	..	2.6	..	..	..	19.2	..	..	..	..	..	..	..	21.8
USA/Etats-Unis	*	15.9	14.2	10.8	8.4	27.1	29.8	31.7	32.2	22.8	27.4	29.2	29.8	65.8	71.5	71.6	70.8
Japan/Japon	*	..	..	..	..	30.0	36.0	44.1	50.1	..	..	..	..	30.0	36.0	44.1	50.1
N.Zealand/N.Zélande		10.0	8.0	..	..	49.0	80.0	..	..	-	..	..	..	59.0	88.0	..	..
Austria/Autriche		10.0	7.0	5.0	2.0	25.0	53.0	60.0	42.0	3.0	5.0	7.0	28.0	38.0	65.0	72.0	72.0
Denmark/Danemark	*	..	18.0	8.0	..	..	66.0	69.0	..	..	7.0	21.0	..	..	91.0	98.0	..
Finland/Finlande	*	2.0	0.1	-	..	15.0	10.0	0.1	10.0	48.0	62.0	76.0	67.0	65.0	72.1	76.1	77.0
France	*	..	..	7.5	..	..	..	..	..	..	..	..	..	61.5	64.0	68.3	..
Germany/Allemagne	*	10.2	7.5	..	6.5	64.7	70.5	..	31.5	5.0	6.7	..	47.6	79.8	84.0	..	85.6
Greece/Grèce		-	0.7	..	0.7	0.5	9.3	..	10.7	-	..	..	..	0.5	10.0	..	11.4
Iceland/Islande		..	..	2.0	2.0	-	..	..	..	..	..	..	..	..	..	2.0	2.0
Italy/Italie	*	..	..	..	..	..	..	..	..	..	..	..	..	30.0	..	60.7	..
Luxembourg		16.0	14.0	5.0	3.2	65.0	69.0	86.0	82.2	-	..	..	5.0	81.0	83.0	91.0	90.4
Netherlands/Pays-Bas	*	7.0	8.0	1.0	0.5	56.0	72.0	84.0	83.5	9.0	7.0	8.0	9.3	73.0	87.0	93.0	93.3
Norway/Norvège		7.0	8.0	13.0	..	1.0	1.0	1.0	..	26.0	33.0	43.0	..	34.0	42.0	57.0	..
Portugal	*	..	..	9.4	..	..	..	11.4	..	..	..	0.1	..	2.3	3.5	20.9	..
Spain/Espagne		8.8	13.2	6.2	15.0	9.1	15.8	41.0	40.1	..	..	0.9	4.0	17.9	29.0	48.0	59.1
Sweden/Suède	*	1.0	1.0	1.0	..	20.0	11.0	9.0	7.0	61.0	82.0	85.0	88.0	82.0	94.0	94.0	95.0
Switzerland/Suisse		-	-	-	..	..	36.0	..	27.0	..	48.0	..	64.0	73.0	84.0	90.0	91.0
Turkey/Turquie		0.1	0.1	1.1	1.3	..	0.2	1.1	4.6	..	..	..	0.5	0.1	0.3	2.2	6.3
UK/Royaume-Uni	*	6.0	6.0	8.0	13.6	51.0	52.0	65.0	61.5	25.0	25.0	14.0	12.3	82.0	83.0	87.0	87.4
Former CSFR/ex-RFTS		..	..	..	..	38.4	43.8	..	47.0	..	..	..	..	41.7	47.9	52.3	52.1
Czech Rep./R. Tchèque		..	..	..	..	..	47.5	..	49.6	..	..	..	..	..	47.5	50.3	50.6
Slovak Rep./R. Slovaque		..	..	..	..	27.3	36.4	41.7	..	..	..	..	..	27.3	36.4	41.7	..
Hungary/Hongrie		7.0	8.0	9.0	..	12.0	17.0	22.0	..	..	..	..	..	19.0	25.0	31.0	..
Poland/Pologne		..	..	..	10.8	..	..	..	26.5	..	..	..	..	..	..	34.4	37.3
N. America/Amérique N.	*	..	..	..	..	..	..	..	..	..	..	..	..	66	71	70	70
OECD/OCDE Europe	*	..	..	..	..	..	..	..	..	..	..	..	..	48	54	61	63
EU/UE-15	*	..	..	..	..	..	..	..	..	..	..	..	..	54	62	70	71
OECD/OCDE	*	..	..	..	..	..	..	..	..	..	..	..	..	51	57	62	63

Notes: (3.2B)
a) National population connected to public sewage treatment. Population connected to public sewage network without treatment is excluded.
b) Physical and mechanical processes which result in decanted effluents and separate sludge (sedimentation, flotation, etc.).
c) Biological treatment technologies (processes employing anaerobic or aerobic micro-organisms).
d) Advanced treatment technologies (chemical processes).
e) Data refer to 1993 or to the most recent year. Data prior to 1991 have not been taken into account.
CAN) 1980 and 1985: 1981 and 1986 data. Secondary treatment usually includes private treatment and waste stabilisation ponds. Tertiary treatment refers to secondary treatment with phosphorus removal.
USA) Data refer to 1982, 1984, 1988 and 1992 data. 1988 data are estimates. Primary: may include ocean outfalls and some biological treatment. Tertiary: include 2-3% of non-discharge treatment e.g. lagoons, evaporation ponds. Exclude rural areas served by Onsite Disposal Systems.
JPN) 1985 and 1990: 1984 and 1987 data. Secondary treatment may include data for primary treatment and some tertiary treatment.
DNK) 1985 and 1990: 1986 and 1989 data.
FIN) Secondary: 50-80% removal of BOD; tertiary: 70-90% removal of BOD.
FRA) 1980 and 1985: Secretariat estimates. 1990: 1987 data.
DEU) 1980 and 1985 data refer to 1979 and 1983 and to western Germany only. Recent data are estimates.
ITA) 1990: 1987 data.
NLD) 1980: 1981 data. Tertiary includes dephosphatation and/or desinfection.
PRT) 1980 and 1985: 1981 and 1984 data.
SWE) Primary: removal of sediments. Secondary: chemical or biological treatment. Tertiary: chemical and biological plus complementary treatment.
UKD) Great Britain only. Primary: removal of gross solids. Secondary: removal of organic material or bacteria under aerobic conditions. Tertiary: removal of suspended solids following secondary treatment.
Totals) Secretariat estimates. N. America, OECD: does not include Mexico. OECD and EU until 1990: western Germany only.
Source: OECD/OCDE

Notes : (3.2B)
a) Population nationale connectée au traitement public des eaux usées. La population connectée au réseau d'assainissement public sans traitement, est exclue.
b) Procédés physiques et mécaniques par lesquels on obtient des effluents décantés d'une part et de la boue d'autre part (sédimentation, flottation, etc.).
c) Techniques d'épuration biologique (procédés faisant appel aux micro-organismes aérobies ou anaérobies).
d) Techniques avancées de traitement (procédés chimiques).
e) 1993 ou l'année la plus récente; les données antérieures à 1991 n'ont pas été prises en compte.
CAN) 1980 et 1985 : données 1981 et 1986. Secondaire: inclut normalement le traitement privé et comprend les bassins de stabilisation. Tertiaire : traitement secondaire avec élimination du phosphore.
USA) Données pour 1982, 1984, 1988 et 1992. 1988 : estimations. Primaire: peut inclure des rejets en mer et une part de traitement biologique. Tertiaire: inclut 2-3% de traitement d'eaux non rejetées p.ex. lagunage ou étangs d'évaporation. Exclut les zones rurales desservies par des systèmes d'épuration indépendants.
JPN) 1985 et 1990 : données 1984 et 1987. Secondaire: peut inclure des données concernant le traitement primaire et une part de traitement tertiaire.
DNK) 1985 et 1990 : données 1986 et 1989.
FIN) Secondaire : élimination de 50-80% de la DBO ; 70-90% pour le tertiaire.
FRA) 1980 et 1985 : estimations du Secrétariat. 1990 : données 1987.
DEU) Début des années 1990 : estimations. 1980 et 1985 : données 1979 et 1983, pour l'Allemagne occidentale uniquement.
ITA) 1990 : données 1987.
NLD) 1980 : données 1981. Tertiaire : inclut la déphosphatation et/ou la désinfection.
PRT) 1980 et 1985 : données de 1981 et 1984.
SWE) Primaire : élimination des sédiments. Secondaire : traitement chimique ou biologique. Tertiaire : traitement chimique et biologique et traitement complémentaire.
UKD) Grande-Bretagne uniquement. Primaire : élimination des éléments solides. Secondaire : élimination aérobie des matières organiques ou bactériennes. Tertiaire : élimination des matières en suspension à la suite du traitement secondaire.
Totaux) Estimations du Secrétariat. Amérique du Nord, OCDE : n'inclut pas le Mexique. OCDE et UE jusqu'en 1990 : Allemagne occidentale uniquement.

SEWAGE SLUDGE PRODUCTION AND DISPOSAL (a), latest year available
PRODUCTION ET ÉLIMINATION DE BOUES D'ÉPURATION (a), dernière année disponible

		Year/ année	Total (dry weight/poids sec) (1 000 tonnes)	Disposal methods/ méthodes d'élimination (%)			
				Agricultural use/ usage agricole	Landfill/ mise en décharge	Incineration/ incinération	Other/ autres b)
Canada	*	1992	500	42	18	40	-
USA/États-Unis		1986	11454	..	..	..	-
Japan/Japon	*	1992	171450	14	42	-	43
Australia/lie	*	1992	60000	..	..	..	-
Austria/Autriche	*	1992	165	22	41	37	-
Belgium/Belgique		1988	687	..	..	..	-
Denmark/Danemark	*	1992	192	45	55	-	-
Finland/Finlande	*	1992	219	16	21	-	32
France		1992	866	58	24	18	-
Germany/Allemagne		1991	2956	28	42	9	-
w.Germany/Allemagne occ.		1991	2630	28	43	10	-
Ireland/Irlande		1985	570	..	..	..	-
Italy/Italie	*	1991	3428	..	..	..	-
Luxembourg		1992	10	..	..	..	-
Netherlands/Pays-Bas	*	1992	583	21	53	6	19
Norway/Norvège		1992	87	61	27	-	6
Portugal		1991	8	..	..	..	-
Spain/Espagne		1992	694	21	26	5	24
Sweden/Suède	*	1990	221	23	74	-	2
Switzerland/Suisse	*	1990	411	27	..	..	37
UK/Royaume-Uni	*	1993	1024	49	10	8	32
Former CSFR/ex-RFTS		1987	3791	..	..	..	-
Czech Rep./Rép. Tchèque		1987	2750	..	..	..	-
Slovak Rep./Rép. Slovaque		1987	1041	..	..	..	-
Hungary/Hongrie		1987	30000	..	..	-	-

Notes:
a)   Sludge produced in public sewage treatment plants.
b)   Composting, dumping at sea and other methods.
CAN) Percentages refer to early 1980s.
JPN) Percentages refer to early 1980s. Other: sea dumping (35%) and other methods (8%).
AUS) Queensland only.
AUT) Sludge treated by municipalities only.
DNK) Percentages refer to 1982.
FIN)   Other: composting (34%) and storage (12%).
ITA)   May include liquid waste.
NLD) Includes sludge from public and other treatment (private treatment, e.g. industrial waste water treatment). Other: composting (12%) and other methods.
SWE) Agricultural use includes other recovery use. Other: composting.
CHE) Other: includes composting, landfill and incineration.
UKD) Other: includes dumping at sea (26%) as well as beneficial uses for land reclamation and forestry, and soil and compost products.

Source: OECD/OCDE

Notes :
a)   Boues produites dans les stations d'épuration publiques.
b)   Compostage, rejets en mer et autres méthodes.
CAN) Les pourcentages concernent le début des années 80.
JPN) Les pourcentages concernent le début des années 90. Autres : Rejet en mer (35%) et autres méthodes (8%).
AUS) Queensland seulement.
AUT) Boues traitées par les municipalités seulement.
DNK) Les pourcentages concernent 1982.
FIN)   Autres : compostage (34%) et stockage (12%).
ITA)   Peut inclure des déchets liquides.
NLD) Inclut boues issues du traitement public et d'autres types de traitement (traitement privé, p.ex. stations d'épuration industrielles). Autres : compostage (12%) et autres méthodes.
SWE) Usage agricole inclut d'autres méthodes de récupération. Autres: compostage.
CHE) Autres : inclut le compostage, la mise en décharge et l'incinération.
UKD) Autres : inclut le rejet en mer (26%) et les utilisations bénéfiques pour la récupération des terres, la sylviculture, les sols et les produits de compostage.

The following tables show water quality of selected rivers. Water quality is measured in terms of annual mean concentrations of dissolved oxygen and BOD; of nitrates, phosphorus and ammonium. The rivers selected are main rivers draining large watersheds in the countries chosen; the measurement locations are at the mouths or downstream frontiers of the rivers. Data are given for selected years, as well as for the average of the last three years available.

These parameters provide information concerning the state and trends of pollution by organic matter and nutrients.

In reading the data, one should compare trends rather than absolute values, since measurement methods vary by country, as reflected in the footnotes.

Les tableaux suivants concernent la qualité de l'eau de rivières sélectionnées. La qualité de l'eau est exprimée en valeurs moyennes annuelles de la concentration en oxygène dissous et de la DBO ; en nitrates, en phosphore et en ammonium. Les rivières sélectionnées sont des rivières principales drainant de larges bassins versants dans les pays sélectionnés ; les mesures ont été effectuées à l'embouchure ou à la frontière aval des rivières. Les données sont relatives à des années sélectionnées ainsi qu'à la moyenne des 3 dernières années disponibles.

Ces paramètres fournissent des informations relatives à l'état et à l'évolution de la pollution par les matières organiques et les substances nutritives.

Lors de la lecture de ces données, on devrait comparer les tendances plutôt que les valeurs absolues parce que les méthodes de mesure varient d'un pays à l'autre, ainsi que l'indiquent les notes.

WATER QUALITY OF SELECTED RIVERS (a), annual mean concentrations, 1980-1993
QUALITÉ DES EAUX DE RIVIÈRES SÉLECTIONNÉES (a), concentrations annuelles moyennes, 1980-1993

mg O2/ litre

Country	River		1980	1985	1986	1987	1988	1989	1990	1991	1992	1993	Average last 3 years/ moyenne 3 dernières années (b)
								DO/ OD					
Canada	Saskatchewan		10.8	10.8	10.4	10.3	..	10.4	10.0	..	..	..	
Mexico/Mexique	Bravo		9.2	8.4	8.5	7.5	..	7.9	7.0	8.1	8.8	8.6	8.5
	Lerma Santiago	*	2.9	2.5	2.9	3.0	..	..	2.4	..	3.2	4.0	3.2
	Pánuco		..	3.9	..	..	4.4	..	5.4	4.2	4.3	..	4.6
	Grijalva Usumacinta		5.9	7.5	6.8	6.4	5.5	6.5	6.9	6.4	7.4	6.0	6.6
USA/Etats-Unis	Delaware		11.7	11.7	11.5	12.4	11.2	10.9	9.1	11.1	11.6	9.9	10.9
	Mississippi		8.4	8.6	8.5	8.9	9.1	8.7	9.1	9.2	9.3	8.9	9.1
Japan/Japon	Ishikari		10.0	10.0	10.0	11.0	11.0	10.0	10.0	11.0	11.0	11.0	11.0
	Yodo		9.1	8.7	8.5	8.0	8.8	8.5	9.0	9.1	9.2	9.4	9.2
	Tama		6.3	7.5	7.2	6.8	7.6	7.6	7.4	7.3	8.0	7.8	7.7
	Chikugo		9.4	9.7	10.0	9.7	9.7	9.6	9.9	9.9	9.9	9.9	9.9
Austria/Autriche	Donau	*	9.6	10.5	10.4	10.2	10.6	10.4	10.3	10.9	10.6	10.7	10.7
	Inn	*	10.5	10.2	12.1	12.3	11.8	11.5	11.0	..	11.9	11.1	11.3
Denmark/Danemark	Gudenå		9.6	11.0	11.3	10.3	10.0	9.9	10.7	..	..	..	10.2
	Suså	*	8.7	8.7	..	..	..	10.6	10.0	10.0	11.2	11.0	10.7
Finland/Finlande	Torniojoki		11.0	11.3	12.1	12.1	11.0	11.7	11.8	12.1	11.1	11.6	11.6
	Kymijoki		9.9	10.7	10.4	10.6	11.1	10.8	10.9	10.7	11.8	11.0	11.2
	Kokemäenjoki		9.5	10.1	10.9	11.5	11.6	11.4	11.8	10.2	10.9	10.5	10.5
France	Loire		11.8	12.1	10.7	11.7	..	..	..	..	12.0	12.3	..
Germany/Allemagne	Rhein		9.0	9.3	9.7	9.8	10.1	9.6	10.1	9.4	9.5	..	9.7
	Elbe		9.1	9.1	9.2	9.1	8.7	8.2	8.9	10.8	10.9	..	10.2
	Weser		8.7	8.6	8.8	9.6	9.2	9.0	8.8	9.1	9.5	..	9.1
	Donau		10.6	10.5	..	..	..	10.7	10.9	11.2	..	..	10.9
Greece/Grèce	Strimonas	*	9.5	8.6	9.5	10.4	11.5	11.2	10.9	11.1	10.5	10.4	10.7
	Axios	*	8.2	8.9	9.0	10.3	10.6	11.2	10.6	11.1	11.4	10.9	11.1
	Aliakmonas	*	10.0	9.9	10.4	11.3	11.9	11.3	11.9	11.2	11.4	11.1	11.2
Ireland/Irlande	Boyne		..	10.0	10.1	9.4	10.2	9.2	10.3	10.6	..	..	10.0
	Barrow		..	10.5	10.5	10.5	11.0	10.9	11.0	11.1	..	..	11.0
Italy/Italie	Po	*	7.7	8.6	8.7	8.8	6.1	7.8	8.7	..	..	..	7.5
	Adige		..	..	..	9.2	11.2	..	10.5	..	..	..	
	Arno		..	..	..	..	..	5.5	10.5	8.0	7.7	..	8.7
Luxembourg	Moselle		9.3	9.7	..	..	..	9.1	9.1	9.3	7.8	8.9	8.7
	Sûre		10.2	10.6	9.7	10.1	9.8	10.7	9.9	12.1	12.3	10.8	11.7
	Wiltz		10.2	11.0	..	..	..	10.4	10.3	9.0	10.6	10.6	10.1
Netherlands/Pays-Bas	Maas-Keizersveer		10.1	9.7	10.0	10.1	9.8	9.1	9.6	10.0	10.1	..	9.9
	Rijn/Maas Delta		10.4	10.3	10.7	10.0	10.4	10.7	10.6	10.9	11.0	..	10.8
	Rijn-Maassluis		8.1	9.3	9.2	9.5	9.5	9.2	9.1	9.4	9.8	..	9.4
	Rijn-Lobith		8.0	8.0	8.8	8.9	9.3	9.2	9.8	10.2	9.6	..	9.9
	IJssel-Kampen		8.2	8.3	8.8	8.8	8.4	8.2	9.4	9.2	9.1	..	9.2
Portugal	Tejo	*	9.2	7.8	..	8.2	8.7	8.5	9.3	7.2	7.6	..	8.0
	Minho	*	9.1	10.1	9.9	10.0	10.1	9.7	9.5	9.2	9.6	..	9.4
	Douro		..	9.9	9.8	9.3	9.8	9.9	9.5	9.5	9.7	..	9.6
	Guadiana	*	8.5	9.4	9.8	9.0	8.1	9.2	9.5	8.4	7.7	..	8.5
Spain/Espagne	Guadalquivir		3.1	5.7	4.6	4.8	4.4	3.2	2.5	3.9	2.9	3.8	3.5
	Duero		7.6	7.3	6.6	6.8	7.4	6.3	7.1	7.9	7.2	7.0	7.4
	Ebro		9.8	8.6	9.7	9.4	9.4	8.7	9.1	9.2	9.4	8.9	9.2
	Guadiana		8.0	3.9	2.4	5.2	5.5	5.5	6.0	7.4	6.8	8.1	7.4
Switzerland/Suisse	Rhin		10.3	10.5	11.6	10.7	10.3	10.2	10.7	10.7	10.8	10.9	10.8
	Aare		10.1	10.4	10.5	10.6	10.1	10.1	10.4	10.6	10.6	10.7	10.6
	Limmat	*	9.1	9.7	10.0	10.0	9.7	..	..	10.0	10.0	10.3	10.1
	Rhône		10.7	11.2	11.3	11.1	11.0	11.3	11.6	11.3	11.2	11.2	11.2
Turkey/Turquie	Porsuk		9.3	9.4	9.2	9.3	10.0	9.9	9.2	9.5	9.5	10.0	9.7
	Sakarya		9.6	8.9	9.4	9.1	9.5	9.5	9.7	9.5	9.2	9.1	9.3
	Gediz		9.2	8.6	7.0	8.6	6.6	6.5	3.8	5.5	5.1	5.5	5.4
UK/Royaume-Uni	Thames		9.9	10.0	10.9	9.8	10.8	8.1	9.2	10.1	9.5	9.7	9.8
	Severn		10.4	10.8	11.7	10.3	10.5	10.5	10.7	11.1	10.4	11.1	10.9
	Clyde		9.4	9.1	9.1	9.7	9.0	8.6	10.0	9.0	9.9	9.6	9.5
	Mersey		6.1	6.2	6.8	7.5	7.9	7.6	6.0	6.8	7.3	6.4	6.8
Czech Rep./Rép.Tchèque	Labe		8.2	7.8	..	..	..	7.3	7.7	..	..	..	..
	Odra		8.6	8.3	..	..	..	7.3	6.4	..	..	..	..
Hungary/Hongrie	Duna		10.6	10.6	10.0	10.3	10.3	10.0	9.8	10.3	9.7	9.7	9.9
	Drava		10.6	10.0	9.7	9.8	10.0	9.9	10.3	10.3	10.7	10.9	10.6
	Tisza		11.3	12.0	11.6	12.5	12.0	12.1	11.6	11.7	11.9	12.4	12.0
Poland	Wisla		9.5	11.4	..	..	..	..	10.2	10.1	10.2	10.7	10.3
	Odra		9.8	9.0	..	..	..	..	10.2	10.6	10.8	11.1	10.8
	Nysa Luzycka		10.0	9.0	..	..	..	..	9.5	9.9	10.4	9.3	9.9

Notes: *see page 75 / voir page 75.*

Source: OECD/OCDE

WATER QUALITY OF SELECTED RIVERS (a), annual mean concentrations, 1980-1993
QUALITÉ DES EAUX DE RIVIÈRES SÉLECTIONNÉES (a), concentrations annuelles moyennes, 1980-1993

mg O₂/ litre

			1980	1985	1986	1987	1988	1989	1990	1991	1992	1993	Average last 3 years/ moyenne 3 dernières années (b)
								BOD/ DBO					
Mexico/Mexique	Bravo		3.1	2.2	2.3	3.2	..	3.3	3.6	3.2	3.1	3.6	3.3
	Lerma Santiago	*	14.3	13.5	..	18.0	..	..	13.5	..	15.3	16.1	15.0
	Pánuco		..	1.7	..	..	1.3	..	1.4	1.2	0.7		1.1
	Grijalva Usumacinta		4.3	1.5	4.1	1.7	1.7	1.8	2.2	2.3	3.0	3.7	3.0
USA/Etats-Unis	Delaware		2.0	2.1	2.0	1.9	2.5	2.0	1.1	1.0	1.4	1.3	1.2
	Mississippi		1.9	1.2	1.5	1.4	1.6	1.4	1.9	1.4	1.9	1.8	1.7
Japan/Japon	Ishikari		1.5	1.5	1.3	1.1	1.5	1.3	1.2	1.4	1.2	1.3	1.3
	Yodo		3.3	3.4	3.7	3.6	3.3	3.0	2.5	2.0	2.1	2.2	2.1
	Tama		6.7	4.7	5.6	6.7	5.4	4.2	4.6	4.7	4.1	3.7	4.2
	Chikugo		1.9	2.2	2.3	2.0	1.6	1.8	1.7	1.5	1.6	1.0	1.4
N. Zealand/N. Zélande	Waikato	*	..	..	..	..	..	1.2	1.2	1.2	1.2	1.2	..
	Manawatu	*	..	..	..	..	..	2.1	2.1	1.9	1.9	1.9	..
	Mataura	*	..	..	..	..	..	1.2	1.2	0.9	0.9	0.9	..
Austria/Autriche	Donau		3.3	..	..	5.4	3.8	4.0	3.8	3.5	3.8	3.3	3.5
	Inn		2.2	..	..	2.5	2.8	2.0	1.4	..	3.0	2.0	2.1
Denmark/Danemark	Gudenå		3.7	3.4	3.2	3.3	2.1	3.5	2.8	2.4	2.4	2.4	2.4
	Skjernå		8.1	5.5	4.2	2.5	2.4	2.8	2.3	2.3	..	2.0	2.2
	Suså		1.4	2.6	2.1	2.1	2.8	..	..	..	..	2.7	..
France	Loire		6.6	7.8	6.4	6.4	..	..	..	..	6.6	7.5	..
Germany/Allemagne	Rhein		4.0	3.8	3.7	2.6	2.9	3.0	3.3	3.1	..	..	3.1
	Elbe	*	7.5	9.5	7.3	5.4	9.6	11.7	9.6	9.1	7.8	..	8.8
	Weser	*	5.0	3.0	2.6	2.8	3.4	3.1	3.3	3.8	3.2	..	3.4
	Donau		3.1	3.2	3.3	2.5	2.6	2.5	2.8	3.1	..	..	2.8
Ireland/Irlande	Boyne		..	1.7	1.9	1.7	1.5	1.6	1.7	1.2	..	..	1.5
	Barrow		..	1.7	2.6	2.0	1.9	1.9	1.7	1.7	..	..	1.8
Italy/Italie	Po	*	6.1	4.6	6.9	6.3	8.3	4.3	3.6	2.9	3.4	..	3.3
	Adige		..	..	..	..	..	3.4	6.7	7.6	4.3	..	6.2
Luxembourg	Moselle		4.2	3.6	..	..	..	3.7	4.3	3.2	3.7	5.2	4.0
	Sûre		4.1	3.1	3.7	3.2	3.5	4.2	3.3	1.0	7.3	5.4	4.6
	Wiltz		3.2	2.5	..	..	..	4.5	4.6	6.8	7.8	3.5	6.0
Netherlands/Pays-Bas	Maas-Keizersveer	*	3.3	1.6	1.7	1.5	1.3	1.7	1.2	2.3	1.3	..	1.6
	Rijn/Maas Delta	*	1.6	1.3	1.6	1.5	1.2	2.0	1.5	..	..	..	1.6
	Rijn-Maassluis	*	2.2	1.5	1.5	1.9	1.4	1.2	1.5	1.2	1.5	..	1.4
	Rijn-Lobith	*	3.2	2.3	2.3	2.0	2.8	2.8	2.8	2.8	2.0	..	2.5
	IJssel-Kampen	*	4.0	2.1	2.0	1.6	1.3	2.3	2.2	2.9	1.7	..	2.3
Norway/Norvège	Skienselva		3.5	..	..	..	..	2.6	0.6	3.6	1.9	0.4	2.0
Portugal	Tejo		3.7	1.7	..	1.5	1.7	2.2	1.7	2.1	2.2	..	2.0
	Minho	*	2.7	2.9	2.1	1.3	1.6	1.6	1.4	1.7	1.5	..	1.5
	Douro		..	3.4	2.2	3.4	1.7	1.9	1.6	1.4	1.8	2.3	1.8
	Guadiana	*	8.0	2.3	3.0	2.5	3.0	3.1	6.5	5.9	5.9	4.9	5.6
Spain/Espagne	Guadalquivir		11.8	8.8	11.0	8.4	8.3	17.2	13.2	12.1	21.2	13.4	15.6
	Duero		2.1	2.7	2.9	3.3	2.9	3.1	3.0	2.4	2.0	2.5	2.3
	Ebro		3.3	4.3	4.4	3.1	2.6	4.0	2.3	4.6	7.1	6.8	6.2
	Guadiana		2.7	1.6	0.5	2.1	2.5	3.0	2.3	3.0	5.8	6.5	5.1
Turkey/Turquie	Porsuk		1.8	2.0	1.6	1.1	1.6	1.2	1.1	1.4	1.4	1.2	1.3
	Sakarya		2.0	3.6	2.7	2.0	3.4	3.4	2.7	2.3	2.8	4.2	3.1
	Gediz		2.4	2.3	4.4	4.8	6.6	2.3	10.6	14.3	21.9	12.5	16.2
UK/Royaume-Uni	Thames	*	2.7	2.4	3.6	2.6	2.7	2.4	2.9	3.1	2.4	2.4	2.6
	Severn	*	2.6	1.7	2.5	2.3	2.3	2.5	2.8	2.6	1.9	2.2	2.2
	Clyde	*	4.1	3.2	4.0	3.5	3.2	3.2	3.5	4.3	4.5	3.9	4.2
	Mersey	*	5.1	5.0	5.5	4.7	4.8	5.6	4.4	3.8	3.5	3.6	3.6
Czech Rep./Rép.Tchèque	Labe		8.2	6.6	..	..	..	6.0	6.8	..	..	..	..
	Odra		12.0	10.0	..	..	..	10.0	5.9	..	..	..	..
Hungary/Hongrie	Duna		4.7	4.9	4.4	4.5	4.0	3.4	3.1	3.3	2.4	2.6	2.8
	Drava		5.0	3.8	3.7	3.6	3.4	4.3	3.4	3.5	3.7	3.3	3.5
	Tisza		2.9	1.9	1.9	2.8	3.5	2.3	1.5	2.1	2.2	2.0	2.1
Poland	Wisla		3.7	5.6	..	..	..	5.9	6.0	5.2	5.4	4.6	5.1
	Odra		5.9	4.6	..	..	..	7.1	7.0	6.1	6.7	6.2	6.3
	Nysa Luzycka		6.5	7.6	..	..	..	..	6.3	6.4	6.5	5.2	6.0

Notes: see next page / voir page suivante.

Source: OECD/OCDE

Notes (DO):
a)   Measured at the mouth or downstream frontier of river.
b)   Average over the last three years available: data prior to 1988 have not been taken into account.
MEX) Lerma Santiago: 1980 refer to 1981.
AUT) 1985 data refer to 1984.
DNK) Suså: 1980 and 1985 data refer to 1982 and 1983.
GRE) 1980 data refer to 1982.
ITA)   Po: until 1988 data refer to Ponte Polesella (76 km from the mouth);since 1989 data refer to Pontelagoscuro (91 km from the mouth).
PRT) Tejo: 1980 data refer to 1981. Minho: Since 1987, data are from another station. Guadiana: 1980 data refer to 1982.
CHE) Limmat-Baden: 1980 data refer to 1979.

Source: OECD/OCDE

Notes (OD):
a)   Mesuré à l'embouchure ou à la frontière aval de la rivière.
b)   Moyenne sur les trois dernières années disponibles: les données antérieures à 1988 n'ont pas été prises en compte.
MEX) Lerma Santiago: les données 1980 sont de 1981.
AUT) Les données 1985 sont de 1984.
DNK) Suså: les données 1980 et 1985 sont de 1982 and 1983.
GRE) Les données 1980 sont de 1982.
ITA)   Po: jusqu'en 1988 les données concernent Ponte Polesella (à 76 km de l'embouchure); depuis 1989 elles concernent Pontelagoscuro (à 91 km de l'embouchure).
PRT) Tejo: les données 1980 sont de 1981. Minho: depuis 1987, les données proviennent d'une autre station. Guadiana: les données 1980 sont de 1982.
CHE) Limmat-Baden: les données 1980 sont de 1979.

Notes (BOD):
a)   Measured at the mouth or downstream frontier of river.
b)   Average over the last three years available: data prior to 1988 have not been taken into account.
MEX) Lerma: 1980 and 1985 data refer to 1981 and 1983.
NZL) 1989-90 and 1991-93 figures are medians of 1989-90, and 1989-93.
DEU) Elbe: 1988-92- BOD (20°, 7d); 1980 data refer 1981. Weser: 1990-92-BOD (20°,7d).
ITA)   Po: until 1988 data refer to Ponte Polesella (76 km from the mouth); since 1989 data refer to Pontelagoscuro (91 km from the mouth).
NLD) Rijn-Lobith 1989, Rijn/Maas Delta 1990, Issel- Kampen1992, Rijn-Maassluis 1989-92 and Maas-Keizersveer 1990 and 1992: averages include limit of detection values.
PRT) Minho: since 1987, data are from another station. Guadiana: 1980 data referto 1984.
UKD) When the parameter is unmeasurable (quantity is too small), limit of detection values are used when calculating annual averages. Actual averages may therefore be lower. Clyde: 1980 data refer to 1982.

Source: OECD/OCDE

Notes (DBO):
a)   Mesuré à l'embouchure ou à la frontière aval de la rivière.
b)   Moyenne sur les trois dernières années disponibles: les données antérieures 1988 n'ont pas été prises en compte.
MEX) Lerma: les données 1980 et 1985 sont de 1981 et 1983.
NZL) Les chiffres 1989-90 et 1991-93 représentent les médianes des années1989-90 et 1991-93.
DEU) Elbe: 1988-92 - DBO (20°, 7j); les données 1980 sont de 1981. Weser:1990-92 - DBO (20°, 7j).
ITA)   Po: jusqu'en 1988 les données concernent Ponte Polesella (à 76 km de l'embouchure); depuis 1989 elles concernent Pontelagoscuro (à 91 km de l'embouchure).NLD) Rijn-Lobith 1989, Rijn/Maas Delta 1990, Issel- Kampen 1992, Rijn-Maassluis 1989-92 et Maas-Keizersveer 1990 et 1992: les moyennes incluent des seuils de détection.
PRT) Minho: depuis 1987, les données proviennent d'une autre station. Guadiana: les données 1980 sont de 1982.
UKD) Quand le paramètre n'est pas mesurable (concentrations tropfaibles) les seuils de détection sont utilisées dans le calcul des moyenne annuelles. Les moyennes reélles peuvent donc être inférieures à ces chiffres. Clyde: les données 1980 sont de 1982.

WATER QUALITY OF SELECTED RIVERS (a), annual mean concentrations, 1980-1993
QUALITÉ DES EAUX DE RIVIÈRES SÉLECTIONNÉES (a), concentrations annuelles moyennes, 1980-1993

mgN/litre

			Nitrates (b)										Average last 3 years/ moyenne 3 dernières années (c)
			1980	1985	1986	1987	1988	1989	1990	1991	1992	1993	
Canada	St. Lawrence	*	0.160	0.200	0.230	0.190	0.270	0.420	..	..	..	..	
	Fraser	*	0.086	0.100	0.097	0.081	0.103	..	0.140	0.120	..	..	0.121
	Saskatchewan	*	0.100	0.160	0.070	..	..	0.110	0.120				
Mexico/Mexique	Bravo		3.400	0.115	0.259	0.337	0.219	0.121	0.168	0.340	0.225	0.156	0.240
	Lerma Santiago		0.670	1.320	1.470	1.340	1.300	0.330	0.260	1.130	1.680	..	1.023
	Pánuco	*	0.750	0.100	0.390	0.780	0.710	0.630	0.520	0.480	0.610	..	0.537
	Grijalva Usumacinta		..	..	0.626	0.841	0.621	..	0.189	0.417	0.110	0.082	0.203
USA/Etats-Unis	Delaware	*	0.960	1.100	0.950	1.200	..	..	..	0.900	0.880	0.770	0.850
	Mississippi		1.330	1.200	1.700	1.300	1.100	0.900	1.020	1.550	1.500	1.700	1.583
Australia/Australie	Murray-Darling	*	0.010	0.010	0.010	0.010	0.020	0.030	0.030	0.020	0.010	..	..
N. Zealand/N. Zélande	Waikato	*	..	..	..	..	..	0.392	0.392	0.340	0.340	0.340	..
	Manawatu	*	..	..	..	..	..	0.490	0.490	0.460	0.460	0.460	..
	Mataura	*	..	..	..	..	..	0.543	0.543	0.755	0.755	0.755	..
Austria/Autriche	Donau		2.393	2.348	2.506	3.003	2.552	2.439	2.520	2.546	2.500	2.230	2.425
	Inn		0.632	0.745	0.858	0.994	1.060	1.153	1.000	..	0.600	0.600	0.733
Denmark/Danemark	Gudenå	*	1.698	1.733	1.410	1.273	1.745	1.254	1.690	1.692	1.667	1.996	1.785
	Skjernå	*	2.675	2.597	2.798	2.648	3.343	2.860	2.941	2.858	3.638	3.103	3.200
	Suså	*	4.950	4.602	5.242	4.206	5.020	3.720	5.150	4.940	4.610	5.951	5.167
Finland/Finlande	Kokemäenjoki		0.349	0.419	0.608	0.554	0.573	0.530	1.040	..	..	..	0.714
France	Loire	*	1.989	2.215	2.938	2.480	..	..	..	..	3.100	4.020	..
Germany/Allemagne	Rhein	*	3.590	4.200	3.900	3.700	3.700	4.100	3.900	3.800	3.600	..	3.767
	Elbe	*	3.780	3.010	3.990	4.750	4.460	4.020	4.420	4.010	4.510	..	4.313
	Weser		3.070	5.720	5.810	5.450	5.220	4.500	5.020	4.750	5.330	..	5.033
	Donau	*	2.200	2.450	..	..	..	2.160	2.390	2.450	..	..	2.333
Greece/Grèce	Strimonas	*	0.957	1.095	1.224	1.106	1.707	1.422	1.058	1.409	1.390	1.100	1.300
	Axios	*	0.982	1.524	1.800	1.734	1.745	1.628	1.942	1.892	1.937	2.080	1.970
	Aliakmonas	*	0.434	0.208	0.580	0.585	0.273	0.337	0.191	0.824	0.303	0.479	0.535
Ireland/Irlande	Boyne		..	3.014	2.226	2.233	2.032	2.028	2.673	3.238	..	..	2.646
	Barrow		..	2.642	4.252	3.574	3.150	3.325	3.500	4.000	..	..	3.608
Italy/Italie	Po	*	1.630	2.393	2.619	2.610	1.648	1.806	2.281	2.221	2.280	..	2.261
	Adige		0.940	..	..	1.577	1.825	1.335	..	1.340	0.208	..	0.961
	Arno		..	..	..	..	..	..	5.150	2.300	3.170	..	3.540
Luxembourg	Moselle		2.667	..	..	..	..	2.444	2.956	2.867	3.616	3.616	3.366
	Sûre		4.667	5.645	5.419	4.968	4.742	4.667	4.000	4.222	4.520	4.520	4.421
	Wiltz		4.578	3.333	..	..	..	4.222	5.333	4.000	4.972	3.842	4.271
Netherlands/Pays-Bas	Maas-Keizersveer	*	3.770	4.280	4.200	4.200	3.860	4.400	4.220	4.300	4.380	..	4.300
	Rijn/Maas Delta		..	3.800	3.900	3.800	3.630	3.700	3.400	3.377	3.556	..	3.444
	Rijn-Maassluis	*	3.840	4.160	4.080	4.100	3.640	4.043	3.713	3.716	3.611	..	3.680
	Rijn-Lobith	*	3.950	4.530	4.340	4.110	3.810	4.630	4.220	3.897	3.971	..	4.029
	IJssel-Kampen		4.300	4.800	4.700	4.500	4.000	4.700	4.400	4.390	4.312	..	4.367
Norway/Norvège	Skienselva	*	0.350	0.340	..	0.302	0.248	0.204	0.199	0.280	0.200	0.212	0.231
Portugal	Tejo	*	0.840	1.120	..	0.670	2.062	0.535	1.125	1.280	0.700	..	1.035
	Minho		..	..	..	..	..	..	0.506	0.966	0.736	..	0.736
	Douro		..	..	..	..	..	..	0.913	0.766	0.736	0.874	0.792
	Guadiana		..	..	..	0.510	0.928	0.359	1.104	0.368	0.299	0.902	0.523
Spain/Espagne	Guadalquivir	*	2.210	3.291	3.183	3.360	3.473	..	..	4.347	2.999	1.971	3.106
	Duero	*	1.840	1.027	0.964	1.445	1.079	..	..	1.240	1.050	1.129	1.140
	Ebro	*	1.231	2.461	2.473	1.856	2.150	2.506	2.190	2.777	2.739	2.581	2.699
	Guadiana	*	1.174	1.664	1.181	1.971	1.678	1.445	2.145	1.265	1.023	0.826	1.038
Sweden/Suède	Dalälven		0.136	0.106	0.115	0.129	0.149	0.127	0.103	0.041	0.133	0.096	0.090
	Råne älv		0.034	0.052	0.046	0.050	0.053	0.039	0.039	0.048	0.036	0.036	0.040
	Mörrumsån		0.170	0.245	0.224	0.177	0.230	0.167	0.188	0.215	0.206	0.199	0.207
	Rönneån		1.487	1.308	1.355	1.242	1.430	1.313	1.450	1.402	1.500	1.356	1.419
Switzerland/Suisse	Rhin		1.340	1.500	1.780	1.760	1.730	1.670	1.780	1.770	1.800	1.670	1.747
	Aare		1.400	1.750	2.000	2.010	2.050	2.000	1.960	2.030	1.970	1.930	1.977
	Limmat		0.905	1.110	1.370	1.300	1.270	1.270	1.410	1.350	1.400	1.290	1.347
	Rhône		0.500	0.540	0.460	0.580	0.600	0.560	0.600	0.570	0.590	0.550	0.570
Turkey/Turquie	Porsuk		1.630	1.560	1.330	1.470	1.320	1.290	1.300	1.460	1.240	1.320	1.340
	Sakarya		1.080	0.820	1.140	1.190	0.840	0.990	1.210	0.980	1.060	1.140	1.060
	Gediz		1.490	0.980	1.180	..	..	0.500	1.870	1.070	0.170	0.980	0.740

Notes: see page 77 / voir page 77.

... / ...

WATER QUALITY OF SELECTED RIVERS (a), annual mean concentrations, 1980-1993
QUALITÉ DES EAUX DE RIVIÈRES SÉLECTIONNÉES (a), concentrations annuelles moyennes, 1980-1993

mgN/litre

			Nitrates (b)										Average last 3 years/ moyenne 3 dernières années (c)
			1980	1985	1986	1987	1988	1989	1990	1991	1992	1993	
UK/Royaume-Uni	Thames	*	6.894	7.985	6.860	6.852	6.693	6.948	7.668	8.172	7.940	7.192	7.768
	Severn	*	5.804	6.328	6.612	6.534	5.715	6.151	6.032	6.279	6.098	6.096	6.158
	Clyde	*	1.855	2.156	2.139	1.833	1.653	2.131	2.100	2.353	1.724	1.424	1.834
	Mersey	*	2.287	3.117	3.208	2.948	2.710	2.815	2.754	3.272	3.158	3.308	3.246
Czech Rep./Rép.Tchèque	Labe		4.290	4.740	..	..	..	5.640	5.240	..	..	..	..
	Odra		4.520	4.290				3.160	3.070				..
Hungary/Hongrie	Duna		2.097	2.167	2.231	2.264	2.210	2.131	2.341	2.427	2.102	2.079	2.203
	Drava		0.974	1.191	1.209	1.290	1.121	1.225	1.229	1.345	1.300	1.243	1.296
	Tisza		0.949	1.261	1.003	1.119	1.035	1.012	1.030	1.064	1.092	1.139	1.098
Poland	Wisla		0.768	1.694	..	..	..	0.713	1.420	1.430	1.910	1.552	1.631
	Odra		2.032	2.642	..	..	..	1.760	1.740	1.920	2.230	2.162	2.104
	Nysa Luzycka		1.174	3.071	..	..	..	..	2.450	2.900	3.210	3.230	3.113

Notes: (3.3C Nitrates)
a) Measured at the mouth or downstream frontier of river.
b) Data refer to total concentrations unless otherwise specified.
c) Average over the last three years available: data prior to 1988 have not been taken into account.
CAN) $NO_2 + NO_3$.
MEX) Pánuco: 1980 data refer to 1981.
USA) Delaware: 1985 data refer to 1984.
AUS) Data refer to fiscal year. Murray-Darling: data refer to medians and to $NO_3 + NO_2$.
NZL) 1989-90 and 1991-93 figures are medians of 1989-90 and 1989-93, and refer to NO_3-N.
AUT) 1985 data refer to 1984.
DNK) Data refer to $NO_2 + NO_3$. 1985 data refer to 1984.
FRA) Dissolved concentrations.
DEU) Rhein, Elbe, Donau: dissolved concentrations.
GRE) 1980 data refer to 1982.
ITA) Po: until 1988 data refer to Ponte Polesella (76 km from the mouth); since 1989 data refer to Pontelagoscuro (91 km from the mouth).
NLD) Maas-Keizersveer, Rijn-Maassluis, Rijn-Lobith: dissolved concentrations.
NOR) 1985 data refer to 1983.
PRT) Tejo: 1980 data refer to 1981.
ESP) Dissolved concentrations.
UKD) When a parameter is unmeasurable (quantity too small) limit of detection values are used when calculating annual averages. Actual averages may therefore be lower. Clyde: 1980 data refer to 1982.

Source: OECD/OCDE

Notes: (3.3C Nitrates)
a) Mesuré à l'embouchure ou à la frontière aval de la rivière.
b) Les données représentent des concentrations totales sauf indication contraire.
c) Moyenne sur les trois dernières années disponibles: les données antérieures à 1988 n'ont pas été prises en compte.
CAN) $NO_2 + NO_3$.
MEX) Pánuco: les données 1980 sont de 1981.
USA) Delaware: les données 1985 sont de 1984.
AUS) Les données représentent l'année fiscale. Murray-Darling: médianes concernant $NO_3 + NO_2$.
NZL) Les chiffres 1989-90 et 1991-93 sont les médianes des années 1989-90 et 1989-93, et concernent NO_3-N.
AUT) Les données 1985 sont de 1984.
DNK) Les données concernent $NO_3 + NO_2$. Les données 1984 sont de 1984.
FRA) Concentrations en matières dissoutes.
DEU) Rhein, Elbe, Donau: concentrations en matières dissoutes.
GRE) Les données 1980 sont de 1982.
ITA) Po: jusqu'en 1988 les données concernent Ponte Polesella (à 76 km de l'embouchure); depuis 1989 elles concernent Pontelagoscuro (à 91 km de l'embouchure)
NLD) Maas-Keizersveer, Rijn-Maasluis, Rijn-Lobith: concentrations en matières dissoutes.
NOR) Les données 1985 sont de 1983.
PRT) Tejo: les données 1980 sont de 1981.
ESP) Concentrations en matières dissoutes.
UKD) Quand un paramètre n'est pas mesurable (concentrations trop faibles) les seuils de détection sont utilisés dans le calcul des moyennes annuelles. Les moyennes réelles peuvent donc être inférieures à ces chiffres. Clyde: les données 1980 sont de 1982.

WATER QUALITY OF SELECTED RIVERS (a), annual mean concentrations, 1980-1993
QUALITÉ DES EAUX DE RIVIÈRES SÉLECTIONNÉES (a), concentrations annuelles moyennes, 1980-1993

mgP/ litre

			Phosphorus/ Phosphore										Average last 3 years/ moyenne 3 dernières années (b)
			1980	1985	1986	1987	1988	1989	1990	1991	1992	1993	
Canada	St. Lawrence	*	0.082	0.041	0.018	0.021	0.019	..	0.020	0.020	..	..	0.020
	Fraser		0.126	0.081	..	..	..	..	0.035	0.170	..	..	..
	Saskatchewan		0.064	0.073	0.069	0.043	..	0.043	0.032	..	..	..	..
Mexico/Mexique	Bravo	*	0.020	0.160	0.150	0.280	..	0.600	0.370	..	0.190	..	0.387
	Lerma Santiago	*	1.072	1.408	1.317	..	1.550	..	5.217	0.390	..	0.547	2.051
	Pánuco	*	..	0.010	0.029	0.054	0.081	0.062	0.046	0.043	0.018	0.031	0.031
	Grijalva Usumacinta	*	..	..	0.020	..	1.110	..	0.284	0.028	0.261	0.092	0.127
USA/Etats-Unis	Delaware		0.100	0.140	0.060	0.100	0.080	0.090	0.110	0.070	0.100	0.100	0.090
	Mississippi		0.230	0.100	0.240	0.280	0.200	0.210	0.170	0.170	0.250	0.200	0.207
Australia/Australie	Murray-Darling	*	0.064	0.132	0.117	0.074	0.144	0.165	0.165	0.108	0.085	..	0.119
	Derwent	*	..	..	..	..	..	..	..	..	..	0.006	..
N. Zealand/N. Zélande	Waikato	*	..	..	..	..	..	0.059	0.059	0.060	0.060	0.060	..
	Manawatu	*	..	..	..	..	..	0.130	0.130	0.120	0.120	0.120	..
	Mataura	*	..	..	..	..	..	0.037	0.037	0.035	0.035	0.035	..
Austria/Autriche	Donau	*	0.280	0.290	0.250	0.200	0.199	0.180	0.148	0.141	0.140	0.113	0.131
	Inn	*	0.150	0.080	0.160	0.140	0.139	0.124	0.125	..	0.080	0.116	0.107
Denmark/Danemark	Gudenå		0.158	0.155	0.161	0.169	0.133	0.119	0.139	0.108	0.132	0.114	0.118
	Skjernå		0.138	0.126	0.133	0.115	0.117	0.099	0.079	0.080	0.072	0.071	0.074
	Suså		0.348	0.362	0.364	0.403	0.277	0.364	0.356	0.255	0.259	0.176	0.230
Finland/Finlande	Torniojoki		0.060	0.010	0.010	0.040	0.022	0.028	0.025	0.024	0.024	..	0.024
	Kymijoki		0.030	0.030	0.030	0.030	0.013	0.027	0.024	0.023	0.017	0.020	0.020
	Kokemäenjoki		0.054	0.059	0.053	0.079	0.059	0.055	0.065	0.054	0.043	0.054	0.050
France	Loire		0.069	0.036	0.095	0.069	..	..	..	..	0.440	0.400	..
Germany/Allemagne	Rhein		0.360	0.480	0.380	0.230	0.250	0.260	0.220	0.150	0.170	..	0.180
	Elbe		0.380	0.630	0.470	0.340	0.390	0.470	0.400	0.330	0.350	..	0.360
	Weser		0.710	0.750	0.620	0.430	0.410	0.410	1.360	0.280	0.240	..	0.627
	Donau		0.180	0.210	..	..	..	0.130	0.130	0.160	..	..	0.140
Greece/Grèce	Strimonas	*	0.140	0.120	0.100	0.118	0.160	0.160	0.110	0.096	0.130	0.128	0.118
	Axios	*	0.330	0.610	0.490	0.543	0.930	0.500	1.030	0.541	0.658	0.990	0.730
	Aliakmonas	*	0.020	0.030	0.010	0.020	0.020	0.010	0.013	0.016	0.015	0.012	0.014
Ireland/Irlande	Boyne		..	0.089	0.110	0.110	0.100	0.082	0.123	0.087	..	..	0.097
	Barrow		..	0.108	0.120	0.130	0.130	0.127	0.193	0.137	..	..	0.152
Italy/Italie	Po	*	0.280	0.260	0.340	0.250	0.180	0.220	0.210	0.074	0.140	..	0.141
	Adige		0.180	..	..	0.150	0.184	0.443	0.120	0.050	0.059	..	0.076
	Arno		..	..	..	..	0.150	0.380	0.700	0.140	0.290	..	0.377
Luxembourg	Moselle		0.370	0.550	..	..	..	0.700	0.770	0.570	0.724	0.550	0.615
	Sûre		0.490	0.550	0.650	0.370	0.390	0.490	0.800	0.540	0.720	0.310	0.523
	Wiltz		..	..	..	..	..	..	1.000	..	2.100	1.000	1.367
Netherlands/Pays-Bas	Maas-Keizersveer		0.500	0.480	0.420	0.390	0.380	0.372	0.308	0.302	0.289	..	0.300
	Rijn/Maas Delta		0.360	0.340	0.310	0.250	0.230	0.227	0.192	0.160	0.176	..	0.176
	Rijn-Maassluis		0.650	0.550	0.520	0.380	0.510	0.435	0.355	0.296	0.257	..	0.303
	Rijn-Lobith		0.660	0.620	0.520	0.370	0.340	0.340	0.300	0.270	0.240	..	0.270
	IJssel-Kampen		0.640	0.630	0.550	0.390	0.360	0.390	0.320	0.283	0.242	..	0.282
Norway/Norvège	Skienselva	*	0.012	0.010	..	0.009	0.015	0.010	0.008	0.013	0.006	0.007	0.009
	Glomma	*	0.020	0.017	0.049	0.025	0.024	0.023	0.064	0.023	0.021	0.018	0.021
	Drammenselva	*	0.013	0.008	0.007	0.008	0.007	0.007	0.006	0.008	0.011	0.007	0.009
Portugal	Tejo	*	0.300	0.190	0.170	0.290	0.220	0.240	0.170	0.200	0.290	..	0.220
	Douro		..	..	..	..	..	..	0.080	0.080	0.080	..	0.080
	Guadiana		..	..	..	0.100	0.490	..	0.200	0.210	..	0.242	0.217
Spain/Espagne	Guadalquivir		0.865	0.717	0.763	0.802	0.855	..	..	0.393	0.430	0.440	0.421
	Duero		0.694	0.353	0.611	0.923	0.663	..	..	..	0.230	0.320	0.404
	Ebro		0.330	0.790	0.815	0.810	0.508	..	..	..	0.230	0.250	0.329
	Guadiana		0.487	0.838	0.266	0.436	0.403	..	..	..	0.580	0.430	0.471
Sweden/Suède	Dalälven		0.023	0.016	0.017	0.016	0.017	0.017	0.017	0.021	0.015	0.017	0.018
	Råne älv		0.025	0.017	0.017	0.016	0.017	0.018	0.017	0.018	0.015	0.019	0.017
	Mörrumsån		0.024	0.018	0.018	0.023	0.020	0.018	0.024	0.025	0.021	0.019	0.022
	Rönneån		0.084	0.058	0.071	0.068	0.059	0.059	0.054	0.046	0.044	0.050	0.047
Switzerland/Suisse	Rhin		0.165	0.140	0.132	0.094	0.095	0.080	0.090	0.090	0.084	0.069	0.081
	Aare		0.113	0.118	0.126	0.096	0.080	0.083	0.096	0.080	0.091	0.073	0.081
	Limmat		0.131	0.148	0.134	0.094	0.077	0.056	0.079	0.086	0.060	0.055	0.067
	Rhône		0.102	0.127	0.172	0.201	0.106	0.093	0.159	0.170	0.134	0.141	0.148

Notes: see page 79 / voir page 79.

... / ...

WATER QUALITY OF SELECTED RIVERS (a), annual mean concentrations, 1980-1993
QUALITÉ DES EAUX DE RIVIÈRES SÉLECTIONNÉES (a), concentrations annuelles moyennes, 1980-1993

mgP/ litre

			1980	1985	1986	1987	1988	1989	1990	1991	1992	1993	Average last 3 years/ moyenne 3 dernières années (b)
							Phosphorus/ Phosphore						
Turkey/Turquie	Porsuk	*	0.100	0.040	0.050	0.060	0.080	0.025	0.050	0.050	0.070	0.055	0.058
	Sakarya	*	0.110	0.150	0.140	0.170	0.240	0.310	0.210	0.290	0.290	0.280	0.287
	Gediz	*	0.710	0.420	0.940	..	0.650	1.400	0.610	0.290	0.950	0.370	0.537
UK/Royaume-Uni	Thames	*	1.160	1.320	1.312	1.335	1.387	3.330	2.639	1.573	1.238	0.964	1.258
	Severn	*	0.535	0.710	0.854	0.724	0.814	1.154	1.152	0.840	0.569	0.725	0.711
	Clyde	*	0.497	0.319	0.489	0.377	0.331	0.446	0.412	0.439	0.432	0.316	0.396
	Mersey	*	0.783	1.362	1.394	1.052	1.048	1.466	1.406	1.463	1.023	0.946	1.144
Czech Rep./Rép.Tchèque	Labe		..	0.960	..	..	..	1.100	1.220	..	..	..	..
Hungary/Hongrie	Duna		..	0.280	0.290	..	..	0.250	0.250	0.250	0.210	0.160	0.207
	Drava		..	..	0.250	0.420	0.380	0.200	0.240	0.230	0.130	0.080	0.147
	Tisza	*	0.042	0.029	0.020	0.046	0.029	0.029	0.033	0.042	0.039	0.026	0.036
Poland	Wisla		0.106	0.200	..	..	..	0.200	0.210	0.210	0.210	0.256	0.225
	Odra		0.600	0.480	..	..	..	0.550	0.570	0.490	0.400	0.412	0.434
	Bug		0.360	0.210	..	..	..	..	0.208	0.219	0.250	0.190	0.220
	Nysa Luzycka		0.100	0.600	..	..	..	0.397	0.317	0.310	0.300		0.309

Notes: (3.3D Phosphorus)
a) Measured at the mouth or downstream frontier of river.
b) Average over the last three years available: data prior to 1988 have not been taken into account.
CAN) St. Lawrence 1990 and 1991: estimates.
MEX) Orthophosphate concentrations.
AUS) Fiscal year. Murray-Darling: median values.
NZL) 1989-90 and 1991-93 figures are medians of 1989-90 and 1989-93.
AUT) 1985 data refer to 1984.
GRE) 1980 data refer to 1982.
ITA) Po: until 1988 data refer to Ponte Polesella (76 km from the mouth); since 1989 data refer to Pontelagoscuro (91 km from the mouth).
NOR) Skienselva and Glomma: 1985 data refer to 1983. Drammenselva 1980: median value.
PRT) Tejo: 1980 data refer to 1981.
TUR) Orthophosphate concentrations. Gediz: 1980 data refer to 1981.
UKD) Orthophosphate concentrations. When a parameter is unmeasurable (quantity too small), limit of detection values are used when calculating annual averages. Actual averages may therefore be lower.
HUN) Tisza: orthophosphate concentrations.

Source: OECD/OCDE

Notes: (3.3D Phosphore)
a) Mesuré à l'embouchure ou à la frontière aval de la rivière.
b) Moyenne sur les trois dernières années disponibles : les données antérieures à 1988 n'ont pas été prises en compte.
CAN) St. Lawrence 1990 et 1991 : estimations.
MEX) Concentrations en orthophosphate.
AUS) Année fiscale. Murray-Darling : valeurs médianes.
NZL) 1989-90 et 1991-93: médianes des années 1989-90 et 1989-93.
AUT) Les données 1985 sont de 1984.
GRE) Les données 1980 sont de 1982.
ITA) Po : jusqu'en 1988 les données concernent Ponte Polesella (à 76 km de l'embouchure) ; depuis 1989, elles concernent Pontelagoscuro (à 91 km de l'embouchure).
NOR) Skienselva et Glomma 1985: données 1983. Drammenselva 1980 : valeur médiane.
PRT) Tejo : les données 1980 sont de 1981.
TUR) Concentrations en orthophosphate. Gediz : les données 1980 sont de 81.
UKD) Concentrations en orthophosphate. Quand un paramètre n'est pas mesurable (concentrations trop faibles) les seuils de détection sont utilisées dans le calcul des moyennes annuelles. Les moyennes réelles peuvent donc être inférieures à ces chiffres.
HUN) Tisza : concentrations en orthophosphate.

WATER QUALITY OF SELECTED RIVERS (a), annual mean concentrations, 1980-1993
QUALITÉ DES EAUX DE RIVIÈRES SÉLECTIONNÉES (a), concentrations annuelles moyennes, 1980-1993

mgN/litre

			Ammonium (b)										Average last 3 years/ moyenne 3 dernières années (c)
			1980	1985	1986	1987	1988	1989	1990	1991	1992	1993	
Canada	Saskatchewan	*	0.100	0.080	0.070	0.080	..	0.039	0.043	..	..	..	..
Mexico/Mexique	Bravo		0.082	..	0.605	1.369	0.411	0.650	0.604	1.568	0.435	0.651	0.885
	Lerma Santiago		0.883	0.443	1.863	..	0.630	..	11.980	0.395	0.590	1.300	0.762
	Grijalva Usumacinta		0.061	..	0.063	0.065	0.070	0.029	0.020	0.004	0.002	0.001	0.002
USA/Etats-Unis	Delaware	*	0.050	0.090	0.060	0.140	0.040	0.060	0.030	0.040	0.060	0.050	0.050
	Mississippi	*	0.080	0.040	0.060	0.030	0.040	0.040	0.020	0.020	0.040	0.030	0.030
Australia/Australie	Derwent	*	..	..	..	..	..	..	..	..	..	13.300	..
N. Zealand/N. Zélande	Waikato	*	..	..	..	..	..	0.029	0.029	0.024	0.024	0.024	..
	Manawatu	*	..	..	..	..	..	0.065	0.065	0.049	0.049	0.049	..
	Mataura	*	..	..	..	..	..	0.026	0.026	0.027	0.027	0.027	..
Austria/Autriche	Donau	*	0.260	0.220	0.300	0.310	0.290	0.290	0.216	0.238	0.210	0.150	0.199
	Inn	*	0.100	0.230	0.300	0.390	0.140	0.323	0.290	..	0.180	0.210	0.227
Denmark/Danemark	Gudenå		0.118	0.130	0.154	0.163	0.068	0.138	0.103	0.141	0.050	0.056	0.082
	Skjernå		0.146	0.274	0.252	0.170	0.158	0.125	0.106	0.116	0.105	0.121	0.114
	Suså		0.075	0.368	0.144	0.103	0.096	0.059	0.083	0.079	0.079	0.054	0.071
Finland/Finlande	Torniojoki	*	0.023	0.029	0.014	0.016	0.021	0.014	0.011	0.014	0.020	0.011	0.015
	Kokemäenjoki		0.116	0.149	0.131	0.175	0.099	0.093	0.083	0.103	0.056	0.068	0.076
France	Loire	*	0.070	0.100	0.130	0.110	..	..	..	..	0.180	0.170	..
Germany/Allemagne	Rhein	*	0.590	0.520	0.480	0.350	0.240	0.260	0.230	0.240	0.240	..	0.237
	Elbe	*	1.230	3.010	2.150	1.300	1.220	1.930	1.140	0.640	0.360	..	0.713
	Weser		0.520	0.360	0.330	0.300	0.200	0.170	0.190	0.170	0.140	..	0.167
	Donau	*	0.160	0.220	..	..	..	0.150	0.180	0.210	..	..	0.180
Greece/Grèce	Strimonas	*	0.109	0.086	0.054	0.046	0.023	0.031	0.026	0.018	0.044	0.080	0.047
	Axios	*	0.054	0.070	0.093	0.134	0.039	0.039	0.046	0.034	0.498	0.160	0.231
	Aliakmonas	*	0.171	0.047	0.031	0.031	0.023	0.062	0.084	0.020	0.023	0.034	0.026
Ireland/Irlande	Boyne		..	0.050	0.090	0.090	0.060	0.032	0.053	0.065	..	..	0.050
	Barrow		..	0.110	0.150	0.110	0.070	0.073	0.068	0.061	..	..	0.067
Italy/Italie	Po	*	0.180	0.260	0.400	0.372	0.070	0.269	0.320	0.242	0.158	..	0.240
	Adige	*	1.400	0.090	..	0.070	0.100	0.077	0.110	0.170	0.128	..	0.136
	Arno		..	..	..	..	..	1.799	0.770	1.110	0.809	..	0.896
Luxembourg	Moselle		0.400	0.800	..	..	..	0.400	0.400	0.500	0.205	0.407	0.371
	Sûre	*	0.300	0.900	0.358	0.163	0.117	0.300	0.100	0.140	0.100	0.100	0.113
	Wiltz	*	0.100	0.500	..	..	..	0.100	0.100	0.200	0.130	0.100	0.143
Netherlands/Pays-Bas	Rijn-Maassluis	*	0.670	0.560	0.540	0.520	..	0.300	0.310	..	..	..	..
	Rijn-Lobith	*	0.809	0.818	0.720	0.560	0.346	0.341	0.397	0.410	0.310	..	0.372
	IJssel-Kampen		0.638	0.607	0.593	0.461	0.280	0.305	0.271	..	..	..	0.285
Norway/Norvège	Skienselva		0.002	..	..	0.020	0.051	0.013	0.051	0.053	0.020	0.023	0.032
Portugal	Tejo		..	..	..	..	..	..	..	0.030	0.480	0.470	0.327
	Minho	*	0.110	0.070	0.070	0.070	0.040	0.031	0.187	0.187	0.109	..	0.161
	Douro	*	..	0.090	0.100	0.070	0.040	0.023	0.068	0.109	0.047	0.030	0.062
	Guadiana	*	0.290	0.130	0.091	0.091	0.148	0.086	0.211	0.080	0.226	0.117	0.141
Spain/Espagne	Guadalquivir	*	0.937	0.915	1.019	0.742	1.060	..	..	1.157	1.252	1.276	1.228
	Duero	*	0.185	0.225	0.373	0.278	0.270	..	..	0.290	0.373	0.638	0.434
	Ebro	*	0.315	0.135	0.270	0.091	0.110	0.190	0.100	0.390	0.288	0.334	0.337
	Guadiana	*	0.062	0.016	0.190	0.150	0.040	0.124	0.116	0.047	0.148	0.342	0.179
Sweden/Suède	Dalälven		0.025	0.012	0.018	0.015	0.017	0.018	0.014	0.023	0.023	0.020	0.022
	Råne älv		0.019	0.013	0.013	0.012	0.008	0.013	0.015	0.013	0.012	0.012	0.012
	Mörrumsån		0.028	0.032	0.028	0.022	0.022	0.012	0.021	0.021	0.014	0.025	0.020
	Rönneån		0.088	0.092	0.095	0.131	0.053	0.070	0.054	0.051	0.044	0.059	0.051
Switzerland/Suisse	Rhin		0.090	0.130	0.140	0.140	0.110	0.140	0.150	0.120	..	..	0.137
Turkey/Turquie	Porsuk		0.700	0.270	0.240	0.250	0.200	0.160	0.170	0.100	0.120	0.100	0.107
	Sakarya		0.460	0.350	0.460	0.390	0.200	0.160	0.330	0.280	0.280	0.340	0.300
	Gediz		0.170	0.080	0.150	0.110	0.120	0.630	0.420	0.050	0.050		0.033
UK/Royaume-Uni	Thames	*	0.277	0.290	0.282	0.350	0.254	0.422	0.449	0.373	0.313	0.402	0.362
	Severn	*	0.141	0.224	0.298	0.219	0.220	0.293	0.205	0.144	0.121	0.120	0.128
	Clyde	*	0.973	1.236	1.521	1.217	0.661	0.943	0.548	0.683	0.469	0.901	0.684
	Mersey	*	4.521	4.554	4.692	4.131	3.651	4.314	4.096	4.894	2.967	2.869	3.577
Czech Rep./Rép.Tchèque	Labe		1.870	2.260	..	..	..	1.400	1.950	..	..	..	..
	Odra		4.200	5.060	..	..	..	4.670	5.720	..	..	..	..
Hungary/Hongrie	Duna		0.404	0.474	0.357	0.365	0.272	0.249	0.210	0.210	0.256	0.194	0.220
	Drava		0.225	0.233	0.264	0.241	0.155	0.179	0.218	0.163	0.225	0.194	0.194
	Tisza		0.295	0.590	0.699	0.280	0.256	0.412	0.210	0.163	0.241	0.194	0.199
Poland	Wisla		0.880	1.090	..	..	..	0.726	0.670	0.600	0.620	0.487	0.569
	Odra		0.890	1.040	..	..	..	0.446	0.430	0.490	0.360	0.346	0.399
	Nysa Luzycka		0.580	0.820	..	..	..	..	0.570	0.840	0.610	0.740	0.730

Notes: see next page / voir page suivante.

Notes: (3.3E Ammonium)
a)   Measured at mouth or downstream frontier of river.
b)   Data refer to total concentrations unless otherwise specified.
c)   Average over the last three years available: data prior to 1988 have not been taken into account.
CAN) Dissolved concentrations. 1980 data refer to 1981.
USA) Dissolved concentrations.
AUS) Data refer to fiscal year.
NZL) 1989-90 and 1991-93 figures are medians of 1989-90, and 1989-93, and refer to NH$_4$-N.
AUT) 1985 data refer to 1984.
FIN) Tornionjoki: 1980 data refer to 1981.
FRA) Dissolved concentrations.
DEU) Dissolved concentrations, except for the Weser.
GRE) 1980 data refer to 1982. Strimonas: 1988 data include limit of detection values.
ITA) Adige: 1988 average includes limit of detection values. 1985: 1984 data. Po: until 1988 data refer to Ponte Polesella (76 km from the mouth); since 1989 data refer to Pontelagoscuro (91 km from the mouth).
LUX) Wiltz: 1993 average includes limit of detection values. Sûre-Wasserbillig: 1992 and 1993 averages include limit of detection values.
NLD) Rijn-Maassluis, Rijn-Lobith: dissolved concentrations.
PRT) Minho: since 1987 data refer to a different station; 1980 data refer to 1981. Douro: 1990 average includes limit of detection values. Guadiana: 1990 and 1991 averages include limit of detection values; 1980 data refer to 1982.
ESP) Dissolved concentrations.
UKD) When a parameter is unmeasurable (quantity too small), limit of detection values are used when calculating annual averages. Actual averages may therefore be lower.

Notes: (3.3E Ammonium)
a)   Mesuré à l'embouchure ou à la frontière aval de la rivière.
b)   Les données représentent des concentrations totales sauf indication contraire.
c)   Moyenne sur les trois dernières années disponibles: les données antérieures à 1988 n'ont pas été prises en compte.
CAN) Concentrations en matières dissoutes; les données 1980 sont de 1981.
USA) Concentrations en matières dissoutes.
AUS) Les données représentent l'année fiscale.
NZL) Les données 1989-90 et 1991-93 réprésentent les médianes des années 1989-90, et 1989-93, et concernent NH$_4$-N.
AUT) Les données 1985 sont de 1984.
FIN) Tornionjoki: les données 1980 sont de 1981.
FRA) Concentrations en matières dissoutes.
DEU) Concentrations en matières dissoutes sauf pour la Weser.
GRE) Les données 1980 sont de 1982. Strimonas: le chiffre 1988 inclut des seuils de détection.
ITA) Adige: la moyenne 1988 inclut des seuils de détection. 1985: données de 1984. Po: jusqu'en 1988 les données concernent Ponte Polesella (à 76 km de l'embouchure); depuis 1989 elles concernent Pontelagoscuro (à 91 km de l'embouchure).
LUX) Wiltz: la moyenne 1993 inclut des seuils de détection. Sûre-Wasserbillig: les moyennes 1992 et 1993 incluent des seuils de détection.
NLD) Rijn-Maassluis, Rijn-Lobith: concentrations en matières dissoutes.
PRT) Minho: depuis 1987 les données proviennent d'une autre station; les données 1980 sont de 1981. Douro: le chiffre 1990 inclut des seuils de détection. Guadiana: les chiffres 1990 et 1991 incluent des seuils de détection; les données 1980 sont de 1982.
ESP) Concentrations en matières dissoutes.
UKD) Quand un paramètre n'est pas mesurable (concentrations trop faibles) les seuils de détection sont utilisés dans le calcul des moyennes. Les moyennes réelles peuvent donc être inférieures à ces chiffres.

Source: OECD/OCDE

The following tables show water quality of selected rivers. Water quality is measured in terms of annual mean concentrations of lead, cadmium, chromium and copper. The rivers selected are main rivers draining large watersheds in the countries chosen; the measurement locations are at the mouths or downstream frontiers of the rivers. Data are given for selected years, as well as for the average of the last three years available.

These parameters provide information concerning the state and trends of pollution by heavy metals and other metals.

In reading the data, one should compare trends rather than absolute values, since measurement methods vary by country, as reflected in the footnotes.

Les tableaux suivants concernent la qualité de l'eau de rivières sélectionnées. La qualité de l'eau est exprimée en valeurs moyennes annuelles de la concentration en plomb, en cadmium, en chrome et en cuivre. Les rivières sélectionnées sont des rivières principales drainant de larges bassins versants dans les pays sélectionnés ; les mesures ont été effectuées à l'embouchure ou à la frontière aval des rivières. Les données sont relatives à des années sélectionnées ainsi qu'à la moyenne des 3 dernières années disponibles.

Ces paramètres fournissent des informations relatives à l'état et à l'évolution de la pollution par les métaux lourds et les autres métaux.

Lors de la lecture de ces données, on devrait comparer les tendances plutôt que les valeurs absolues parce que les méthodes de mesure varient d'un pays à l'autre, ainsi que l'indiquent les notes.

WATER QUALITY OF SELECTED RIVERS (a), annual mean concentrations, 1980-1993
QUALITÉ DES EAUX DE RIVIÈRES SÉLECTIONNÉES (a), concentrations annuelles moyennes, 1980-1993

μg/ litre

			Lead/ Plomb (b)										
			1980	1985	1986	1987	1988	1989	1990	1991	1992	1993	Average last 3 years/ moyenne 3 dernières années (c)
Canada	Fraser		..	1.00	..	..	..		0.40	2.70	..	..	1.03
	Saskatchewan		4.00	1.00	1.90	1.20	1.00	1.00	1.00	..	..		1.00
USA/Etats-Unis	Delaware	*	1.30	2.80	3.00	5.00	5.00	4.00	1.00	1.00	1.00	1.00	1.00
	Mississippi	*	0.42	4.90	5.00	5.00	5.20	3.50	1.00	1.00	24.60	6.50	10.70
Japan/Japon	Ishikari	*	50.00	50.00	..	..	50.00	50.00	50.00	..	..	..	50.00
	Yodo	*	50.00	50.00	..	..	50.00	50.00	50.00	..	..	..	50.00
	Tama	*	50.00	50.00	..	..	50.00	50.00	50.00	..	..	..	50.00
	Chikugo	*	50.00	50.00	..	..	50.00	50.00	50.00	..	..	..	50.00
Australia/Australie	Murray-Darling	*	5.00	5.00	5.50	9.50	10.00	3.50	3.00	2.00	2.50	..	2.50
Austria/Autriche	Donau	*	4.00	3.00	2.00	..	..	..		2.00	2.00	0.70	1.57
	Inn	*	1.00	8.00	..	..	3.00	3.00	4.00	..	1.00	1.30	2.10
Finland/Finlande	Torniojoki	*	0.95	0.26	0.32	..	0.10	0.54	0.28	0.57	0.50	0.47	0.51
	Kymijoki	*	0.43	0.39	0.40	0.17	0.12	0.10	0.50	0.80	..	..	0.47
	Kokemäenjoki	*	0.40	0.90	1.03	0.45	0.24	0.70	1.00	1.10	1.00	0.69	0.93
Germany/Allemagne	Rhein			..	11.90	10.00	6.90	2.80	2.50	5.70	4.80	..	4.33
	Elbe	*			..	..	1.00	1.00	1.00	1.00	1.00	..	1.00
	Weser		5.40	6.40	6.40	5.00	5.00	5.00	5.00	5.00	3.20	..	4.40
	Donau	*	..	2.60	..	..	..	3.30	4.20	2.80	..	..	3.43
Luxembourg	Moselle	*	..	1.00	..	..	..	1.80	2.00	1.00	..	2.00	1.67
	Wiltz	*	..	0.50	..	..	..	0.30	0.30	0.30	0.30	0.02	0.21
Netherlands/Pays-Bas	Maas-Keizerveer		12.00	3.60	5.60	8.30	3.30	4.93	2.37	..	..	..	3.53
	Rijn/Maas Delta	*	..	1.40	1.60	2.30	1.90	1.20	2.40	1.90	1.70	..	2.00
	Rijn-Maassluis		11.00	1.90	2.60	2.50	3.00	2.89	3.26	2.70	2.90	..	2.95
	Rijn-Lobith		14.70	4.20	6.00	4.00	3.40	4.90	5.10	4.70	4.00	..	4.60
	IJssel-Kampen		9.30	4.70	5.40	5.50	2.80	5.60	4.40	..	..	..	4.27
Portugal	Tejo	*	50.00	..	..	..	21.00	11.00	13.00	30.00	30.00	..	24.33
Spain/Espagne	Guadalquivir	*	12.70	10.00	13.00	12.80	8.50	..	..	16.70	8.00	6.00	10.23
	Ebro	*	5.00	..	..	..	..	..	..	0.01	9.00	14.00	7.67
Sweden/Suède	Dalälven	*	..	..	0.69	0.95	0.97	1.83	1.30	0.22	0.16	0.22	0.20
	Mörrumsån	*	..	..	0.28	0.36	0.44	0.35	0.26	0.14	0.13	0.07	0.11
Switzerland/Suisse	Rhin		1.70	0.80	1.00	..	..	..	..	1.00	1.50	0.70	1.07
	Aare	*	3.38	2.13	..	..	2.70	2.70	..	1.00	1.40	0.50	0.97
	Limmat		..	..	..	..	..	3.00	..	..	1.20	0.50	1.57
	Rhône		3.38	3.50	4.52	7.80	5.80	6.90	7.00	3.70	5.80	5.30	4.93
Turkey/Turquie	Porsuk		..	48.00	48.00	28.00	23.00	..	..	18.00	21.00	12.00	17.00
	Sakarya		..	29.50	70.20	21.50	20.00	22.00	23.00	20.00	20.00	13.00	17.67
	Gediz		..	..	..	..	..	26.00	..	..	14.80	..	
UK/Royaume-Uni	Thames	*	10.00	9.40	7.40	6.10	4.00	2.70	3.60	6.10	5.30	5.20	5.53
	Severn	*	40.40	4.40	5.10	5.40	3.30	4.00	7.50	4.90	3.80	3.20	3.97
	Clyde	*	18.20	8.40	7.60	4.70	5.40	3.00	8.30	4.60	3.60	8.60	5.60
	Mersey	*	15.20	10.70	10.50	10.80	9.10	11.60	8.60	8.00	6.80	5.80	6.87
Poland	Wisla		7.00	6.00	..	..	..	5.00	6.00	7.00	5.00	14.39	8.80
	Odra		..	..	..	..	..	9.02	10.00	11.00	7.00	4.70	7.57
	Nysa Luzycka		..	..	..	..	..	10.71	7.52	8.30	9.10		8.31

Notes: (3.3F Lead)
a) Measured at the mouth or downstream frontier of river.
b) Data refer to total concentrations unless otherwise specified.
c) Average over the last 3 years available: data prior to 1988 have not been taken into account.
USA) Dissolved concentrations. Delaware 1988: upper limits.
JPN) Data represent limit of detection values; actual data are lower.
AUS) Data refer to fiscal year and represents median values.
AUT) 1985: 1984 data. Donau 1980, 1986 and Inn 1984: limit of detection values.
FIN) Torniojoki and Kymijoki: include limit of detection values. Kokemäenjoki: 1980 data refer to 1981.
DEU) Elbe: dissolved concentrations; 1988-89 and 1991-92: include limit of detection values. Donau 1991: include limit of detection values; 1980: 1982 data. Weser 1988-91: include limit of detection values.
LUX) Moselle 1991,1993 and Wiltz 1985, 1989-92: include limit of detection values.
NLD) Rijn/Maas Delta: 1992 include limit of detection values.
PRT) 1988 and 1991-92: include limit of detection values.
ESP) Dissolved concentrations.
SWE) Dissolved concentrations based on analysis of unfiltered samples.
CHE) Aare-Brugg: 1985 data refer to 1983.
UKD) When a parameter is unmeasurable (quantity too small), the limit of detection values are used when calculating averages; actual averages may be lower.

Notes : (3.3F Plomb)
a) Mesuré à l'embouchure ou à la frontière aval de la rivière.
b) Les données représentent des concentrations totales sauf indication contraire.
c) Moyenne sur les trois dernières années disponibles : les données antérieures à 1988 n'ont pas été prises en compte.
USA) Concentrations en matières dissoutes. Delaware 1988: seuils supérieurs.
JPN) Seuils de détection; les valeurs réelles sont inférieures.
AUS) Les données représentent l'année fiscale et des valeurs médianes.
AUT) 1985: données 1984. Donau 1980, 1986 et Inn 1984 : seuils de détection.
FIN) Torniojoki et Kymijoki : incluent des seuils de détection. Kokemäenjoki 1980: données 1981.
DEU) Elbe : concentrations en matières dissoutes ; 1988-89 et 1991-92: incluent des seuils de détection. Donau 1991: inclut des seuils de détection ; 1980: données 1982. Weser 1988-91: inclut des seuils de détection.
LUX) Moselle 1991, 1993 et Wiltz 1985, 89-92: incluent des seuils de détection.
NLD) Rijn/Maas Delta 1992: inclut des seuils de détection.
PRT) Tejo 1988, 1991 et 1992: incluent des seuils de détection.
ESP) Concentrations en matières dissoutes.
SWE) Concentrations en matières dissoutes basées sur l'analyse d'échantillons non filtrés.
CHE) Aare-Brugg : les données 1985 sont de 1983.
UKD) Quand un paramètre n'est pas mesurable (concentrations trop faibles) les seuils de détection sont utilisés dans le calcul des moyennes. Les moyennes réelles peuvent donc être inférieures à ces chiffres.

Source: OECD/OCDE

WATER QUALITY OF SELECTED RIVERS (a), annual mean concentrations, 1980-1993
QUALITÉ DES EAUX DE RIVIÈRES SÉLECTIONNÉES (a), concentrations annuelles moyennes, 1980-1993

µg/litre

			Cadmium (b)										Average last 3 years/ moyenne 3 dernières années (c)
			1980	1985	1986	1987	1988	1989	1990	1991	1992	1993	
Canada	St. Lawrence	*	1.00	1.00	0.10	0.10	0.10	0.20	0.20	..	..	..	0.17
	Fraser	*	..	1.00	..	..	..	..	0.20	0.50	..	..	..
	Saskatchewan		..	1.00	6.00	1.00	0.10	0.10	0.10	..	..	..	0.10
USA/Etats-Unis	Delaware	*	3.50	1.00	1.00	1.00	1.00	1.00	1.00	1.00	1.00	1.00	1.00
	Mississippi	*	1.40	1.00	1.10	1.20	1.30	1.00	1.00	1.00	1.10	1.00	1.03
Japan/Japon	Ishikari	*	5.00	5.00	..	..	5.00	5.00	5.00	..	..	..	5.00
	Yodo	*	5.00	5.00	..	..	5.00	5.00	5.00	..	..	..	5.00
	Tama	*	5.00	5.00	..	..	5.00	5.00	5.00	..	..	..	5.00
	Chikugo	*	5.00	5.00	..	..	5.00	5.00	5.00	..	..	..	5.00
Australia/Australie	Murray-Darling	*	1.00	1.00	1.00	1.00	-	-	-	-	-	..	-
Austria/Autriche	Donau	*	0.20	0.10	0.10	0.10	..	..	..	0.10	0.10	0.10	0.10
	Inn	*	0.10	0.10	0.10	0.10	0.10	0.10	0.10	..	0.10	0.20	0.13
Finland/Finlande	Torniojoki	*	0.01	0.10	..	..	0.10	0.09	0.05	0.06	0.05	..	0.05
	Kymijoki	*	0.10	0.10	..	..	..	..	0.25	0.15	..	..	..
	Kokemäenjoki		0.10	0.10	..	..	0.10	..	0.50	0.20	0.05	..	0.25
France	Loire		-	-	-	-	..	..	..	..	0.83	..	..
Germany/Allemagne	Rhein	*	1.40	0.30	0.30	0.30	0.30	0.30	0.10	0.10	0.10	..	0.10
	Elbe	*	..	..	..	..	0.20	0.20	0.10	0.10	0.10	..	0.10
	Weser	*	0.50	0.60	0.50	0.40	0.30	0.30	0.30	0.30	0.20	..	0.27
	Donau	*	0.20	0.10	..	..	0.30	0.30	0.30	0.30	..	..	0.30
Greece/Grèce	Strimonas	*	-	..	0.10	0.20	..	..	0.20	0.10	0.10	0.20	0.13
	Axios	*	0.01	..	-	0.20	0.50	..	0.40	0.10	0.20	0.20	0.17
	Aliakmonas	*	-	..	0.10	0.10	..	..	0.20	..	0.20	0.20	0.20
Ireland/Irlande	Boyne	*	..	0.20	0.20	0.20	0.20	0.20	0.20	0.20	..	..	0.20
	Barrow	*	..	0.20	0.20	0.20	0.20	0.20	0.20	0.20	..	..	0.20
Italy/Italie	Po	*	0.05	0.12	0.03	0.04	..	..	..	0.50	..	..	..
	Adige	*	0.03	2.80	..	..	..	..	..	1.00	1.00	..	..
	Arno	*	0.04	..	..	..	..	..	..	-	0.54	..	..
Luxembourg	Moselle	*	4.10	2.00	..	..	..	1.30	0.10	0.10	..	0.10	0.10
	Sûre	*	4.00	4.00	0.30	0.10	0.10	1.00	..	..	..	..	..
	Wiltz	*	..	0.05	..	..	..	0.01	0.01	0.02	0.001	0.001	0.01
Netherlands/Pays-Bas	Maas-Keizersveer		1.50	0.21	0.35	0.59	0.63	0.34	0.18	0.23	0.22	..	0.21
	Rijn/Maas Delta		0.70	0.04	0.40	0.10	0.09	0.06	0.10	0.07	0.06	..	0.08
	Rijn-Maassluis		0.90	0.26	0.22	0.10	0.28	0.16	0.11	0.10	0.08	..	0.10
	Rijn-Lobith		1.58	0.14	0.14	0.10	0.10	0.12	0.11	0.10	0.07	..	0.09
	IJssel-Kampen		1.30	0.10	0.10	0.10	0.10	0.20	0.10	..	..	..	0.13
Portugal	Tejo	*	10.00	..	..	..	8.30	3.20	5.00	5.00	5.00	..	5.00
	Guadiana		..	..	..	..	1.60	1.50	1.90	..	..	..	1.13
Spain/Espagne	Guadalquivir	*	-	0.60	0.70	-	-	..	..	0.30	0.50	2.30	1.03
	Duero	*	-	-	-	0.20	-	..	..	-	-	0.40	0.13
	Guadiana	*	0.10	..	..	..	-	..	..	-	-	-	-
Sweden/Suède	Dalälven	*	..	0.06	0.03	0.03	0.03	0.03	0.02	0.02	0.02	0.02	0.02
	Mörrumsån	*	..	0.02	0.01	0.01	0.01	0.01	0.01	0.01	0.01	0.01	0.01
Switzerland/Suisse	Rhin		0.14	0.02	0.02	0.02	0.03	0.09	0.12	0.08	0.03	0.02	0.04
Turkey/Turquie	Porsuk	*	..	..	..	..	..	..	..	5.00	5.00	5.00	5.00
	Sakarya	*	..	..	..	..	5.00	5.00	..	5.00	5.00	5.00	5.00
UK/Royaume-Uni	Thames	*	1.00	0.80	0.50	0.51	0.40	0.20	0.10	0.30	0.50	0.50	0.43
	Severn	*	10.00	0.20	0.30	0.20	0.20	0.40	0.50	0.40	0.20	0.10	0.23
	Clyde	*	1.10	0.80	0.60	0.50	0.50	0.50	0.20	0.20	0.40	0.30	0.30
	Mersey	*	0.80	0.20	0.30	0.20	0.30	0.20	0.30	0.30	0.30	0.10	0.23
Hungary/Hongrie	Duna		..	..	..	..	..	1.00	..	1.00	..	..	..
	Drava		..	..	..	..	..	..	1.20	0.50	0.40	0.20	0.37
Poland	Wisla		1.00	2.00	..	..	..	0.25	0.40	0.70	0.80	1.03	0.84
	Odra		..	..	..	..	..	1.26	1.50	1.40	1.10	0.45	0.98
	Nysa Luzycka		..	..	..	..	..	1.36	..	..	..	0.20	0.52

Notes: see next page / voir page suivante.

NOTES: (3.3G Cadmium)
a) Measured at the mouth or downstream frontier of river.
b) Data refer to total concentrations unless otherwise specified.
c) Average over the three last years available: data prior to 1988 have not taken into account.
CAN) St. Lawrence and Fraser: include limit of detection values. St. Lawrence 1980: 1981 data.
USA) Dissolved concentrations. Delaware 1982-89, 1992-93 and Mississippi 1980, 1989-93: include limit of detection values.
JPN) Data represent upper limits.
AUS) Data refer to fiscal year and median values.
AUT) 1985 data refer to 1984. Donau 1980: figure is approximate; Donau 1986-87, 1991, 1993 and Inn 1984, 1986, 1988-90: upper limits.
FIN) Tornionjoki and Kymijoki: upper limits; 1985 data refer to 1984.
DEU) Rhine 1985-91: upper limits. Elbe: dissolved concentrations; 1990-92: upper limits. Weser 1988-92 and Donau 1980, 1989-91: upper limits.
GRE) 1980 data refer to 1982. Aliakmonas 1990, 1992, Strimonas and Axios 1990-92: include limit of detection values.
IRL) Data represent upper limits.
ITA) Adige 1987-88, 1991-92: upper limits; 1985: 1984 data. Arno: dissolved concentrations. Po: until 1988 data refer to Ponte Polesella (76 km from the mouth); since 1989 data refer to Pontelagoscuro (91 km from the mouth); 1991: upper limit.
LUX) Moselle: 1980, 1985, 1989-91, 1993: upper limits. Sûre/Wasserbillig: 1980, 1985, 1989 data: upper limits. Wiltz: 1985, 1989-93 data: upper limits.
PRT) Tejo: 1990 and 1991 data represent upper limits.
ESP) Dissolved concentrations. Guadiana: 1980 data refer to 1981.
SWE) Dissolved concentrations based on analysis of unfiltered samples.
TUR) Sakarya: 1984 and 1991 data represent upper limits. Porsuk: 1991 and 1993 data represent upper limits.
UKD) When a parameter is unmeasurable (quantity too small), limit of detection values are used when calculating averages. Actual averages may be lower.

Source: OECD/OCDE

NOTES : (3.3G Cadmium)
a) Mesuré à l'embouchure ou à la frontière aval de la rivière.
b) Les données représentent des concentrations totales sauf indication contraire.
c) Moyenne sur les trois dernières années disponibles : les données antérieures à 1988 n'ont pas été prises en compte.
CAN) St.Lawrence et Fraser: incluent des seuils de détection. St.Lawrence 1980: données 1981.
USA) Concentrations en matières dissoutes. Delaware 1982-89 et 1992-93: incluent des seuils de détection. Mississippi 1980 et 1989-93: incluent des seuils de détection.
JPN) Limites supérieures.
AUS) Les données représentent l'année fiscale et des valeurs médianes.
AUT) 1985: données 1984. Donau 1980: données approximatives. 1986-87 et 1993 : limites supérieures. Inn 1984, 1986 et 1988-90: limites supérieures.
FIN) Tornionjoki et Kymijoki: limites supérieures; 1985: données 1984.
DEU) Rhine 1985-91: limites supérieures. Elbe: concentrations en matières dissoutes ; 1990-92: limites supérieures. Weser 1989-92 et Donau 1980, 1989-91: limites supérieures.
GRE) 1980: données 1982. Aliakmonas 1990 et 1992: incluent des seuils de détection. Strimonas et Axios 1990-92: incluent des seuils de détection.
IRL) Limites supérieures.
ITA) Adige 1987-88 et 1991-92: limites supérieures ; les données 1985 sont de 1984. Arno: concentrations en matières dissoutes. Po : jusqu'en 1988 les données concernent Ponte Polesella (à 76 km de l'embouchure) ; depuis 1989 elles concernent Pontelagoscuro (à 91 km de l'embouchure) ; le chiffre 1991 représente une limite supérieure.
LUX) Moselle 1980, 1985, 1989-91, 1993, Sûre/Wasserbillig 1980, 1985, 1989 et Wiltz 1985, 1989-93: limites supérieures.
PRT) Tejo 1990 et 1991: limites supérieures.
ESP) Concentrations en matières dissoutes. Guadiana 1980: données 1981.
SWE) Concentrations en matières dissoutes basées sur l'analyse d'échantillons non filtrés.
TUR) Sakarya 1984, 1991 et Porsuk 1991, 1993: limites supérieures.
UKD) Quand un paramètre n'est pas mesurable (concentrations trop faibles) les seuils de detection sont utilisés dans le calcul des moyennes. Les moyennes réelles peuvent donc être inférieures.

WATER QUALITY OF SELECTED RIVERS (a), annual mean concentrations, 1980-1993
QUALITÉ DES EAUX DE RIVIÈRES SÉLECTIONNÉES (a), concentrations annuelles moyennes, 1980-1993

µg/ litre

			1980	1985	1986	1987	1988	1989	1990	1991	1992	1993	Average last 3 years/ moyenne 3 dernières années (c)
							Chromium/ Chrome (b)						
Canada	St. Lawrence		..	1.50	..	1.00	..	2.00	2.80	..	..	..	..
	Fraser		..	..	..	..	..	..	3.10	7.50	..	..	..
	Saskatchewan		..	1.00	1.00	1.00	0.10	1.00	4.80	..	..		1.93
USA/Etats-Unis	Delaware	*	10.00	1.30	1.00	1.00	1.00	3.00	2.00	1.00	1.00	1.00	1.00
	Mississippi	*	2.50	1.00	1.00	1.30	1.00	1.00	1.00	1.80	5.70	4.20	3.90
Australia/Australie	Murray-Darling	*	2.00	5.00	5.00	8.50	6.00	5.00	5.00	5.00	5.00	..	5.00
Austria/Autriche	Donau	*	1.00	2.00	..	..	..	..	..	2.00	1.00	2.00	1.67
	Inn	*	2.00	1.00	..	..	0.10	0.40	0.30	..	2.00	4.00	2.10
Finland/Finlande	Torniojoki	*	1.50	0.72	0.70	..	0.60	0.50	0.31	0.77	0.65	0.68	0.70
	Kymijoki	*	0.50	0.50	2.10	..	..	..	..	11.70	..	..	..
	Kokemäenjoki		3.00	8.00	3.40	3.15	2.43	1.94	3.40	2.60	1.40	1.57	1.86
Germany/Allemagne	Rhein		..	..	11.00	8.90	8.00	4.20	4.50	3.60	2.30	..	3.47
	Elbe	*	..	..	..	..	1.00	1.70	1.00	1.40	1.00	..	1.13
	Weser	*	4.30	6.00	5.20	5.00	5.00	5.00	5.00	5.00	2.00	..	4.00
	Donau	*	..	1.70	..	..	..	2.00	2.00	2.00	..	..	2.00
Luxembourg	Moselle	*	..	1.80	..	..	..	1.40	3.30	3.00	..	6.80	4.37
	Wiltz	*	0.01	0.10	..	..	..	0.06	0.09	0.09	0.07	0.01	0.06
Netherlands/Pays-Bas	Maas-Keizersveer		7.00	3.00	6.90	7.30	4.20	4.53	2.12	..	..	..	3.62
	Rijn/Maas Delta		..	3.00	2.00	3.30	3.20	1.60	2.60	1.80	1.50	..	1.97
	Rijn-Maassluis		19.00	5.26	5.80	4.50	10.90	4.88	3.29	3.30	3.20	..	3.26
	Rijn-Lobith		19.40	7.60	9.40	7.50	8.30	6.50	6.20	4.90	4.30	..	5.13
	IJssel-Kampen		14.30	7.30	7.70	7.10	6.70	7.80	5.20	..	..	..	6.57
Portugal	Tejo	*	10.00	..	..	..	7.70	10.00	15.00	5.00	10.00	..	10.00
Spain/Espagne	Guadalquivir	*	10.00	..	..	..	..	..	..	..	..	0.50	..
	Duero	*	-	-	-	-	..	..	..	-	-	5.00	1.67
	Ebro	*	-	-	-	..	-	-	-	-	3.00	0.80	1.27
	Guadiana	*	-	0.50	..	..	-	-	-	-	-	-	-
Switzerland/Suisse	Rhin	*	2.00	0.80	0.80	0.80	0.70	0.40	0.70	0.90	0.70	0.50	0.70
Turkey/Turquie	Porsuk		..	..	28.00	29.00	6.50	..	..	5.00	19.00	5.00	9.67
	Sakarya		15.00	37.00	45.00	21.00	13.00	14.00	11.00	6.00	24.00	8.00	12.67
	Gediz		..	..	..	..	..	90.00	..	..	33.70	..	..
UK/Royaume-Uni	Thames	*	10.70	10.00	9.00	10.00	8.30	5.00	5.00	8.50	10.00	10.00	9.50
	Severn	*	30.00	11.20	10.40	6.30	3.10	2.10	2.10	2.00	1.20	1.40	1.53
	Clyde		24.70	20.90	31.60	29.90	23.90	31.10	26.10	22.00	19.30	20.40	20.57
	Mersey		20.00	12.40	14.40	12.50	9.60	10.70	10.70	8.70	5.50	6.00	6.73
Czech Rep./Rép.Tchèque	Labe		..	..	..	..	..	30.00	10.00	..	..	..	..
Hungary/Hongrie	Duna		..	..	..	..	..	2.70	9.90	6.40	..	..	6.33
	Drava		..	..	..	..	..	..	6.00	2.70	4.80	3.00	3.50
Poland	Wisla		..	..	..	..	..	1.25	1.17	4.62	1.50	1.23	2.45
	Odra		..	..	..	..	..	2.49	2.70	3.90	1.36	2.29	2.52
	Nysa Luzycka		..	..	..	..	..	..	8.13	7.26	8.60	7.80	7.89

Notes: (3.3H Chromium)
a) Measured at the mouth or downstream frontier of river.
b) Data refer to total concentrations unless otherwise specified.
c) Average over the last three years available: data prior to 1988 have not been taken into account.
USA) Dissolved concentrations. Delaware 1980-82, 1986-88 and Mississippi 1985, 1988-89: include limit of detection values.
AUS) Data refer to fiscal year and median values.
AUT) 1985 data refer to 1984.
FIN) Torniojoki: include limit of detection values. Kymijoki 1985: 1984 data.
DEU) Elbe: dissolved concentrations; 1990-93 data include limit of detection values. Weser 1985-91 and Donau 1985, 1989-91: include limit of detection values; 1980 data refer to 1982.
LUX) Moselle 1991 and Wiltz 1985 and 1989-92: include limit of detection values.
PRT) 1990-92 data include limit of detection values.
ESP) Dissolved concentrations. Guadiana: 1985 data refer to 1983.
CHE) Rhin 1993: includes limits of detection values.
UKD) When a parameter is unmeasurable (quantity too small), limit of detection values are used when calculating averages. Actual averages may be lower.

Notes : (3.3H Chrome)
a) Mesuré à l'embouchure ou à la frontière aval de la rivière.
b) Les données représentent des concentrations totales sauf indication contraire.
c) Moyenne sur les trois dernières années disponibles : les données antérieures à 1988 n'ont pas été prises en compte.
USA) Concentrations en matières dissoutes. Delaware 1980-82, 1986-88 et Mississippi 1985, 1988-89: incluent des seuils de détection.
AUS) Les données concernent l'année fiscale et des valeurs médianes.
AUT) Les données 1985 sont de 1984.
FIN) Torniojoki: inclut des seuils de détection. Kymijoki 1985: données 1984.
DEU) Elbe: matières dissoutes ; 1990-93: incluent des seuils de détection. Weser 1985-91 et Donau 1985, 1989-91: incluent des seuils de détection. Donau 1980: données 1982.
LUX) Moselle 1991 et Wiltz 1985, 1989-92: incluent des seuils de détection.
PRT) 1990-92: incluent des seuils de détection.
ESP) Concentrations en matières dissoutes. Guadiana : les données 1985 sont de 1983.
CHE) Rhin 1993: inclut des seuils de détection.
UKD) Quand un paramètre n'est pas mesurable (concentrations trop faibles) les seuils de détection sont utilisés dans le calcul des moyennes. Les moyennes réelles peuvent donc être inférieures à ces chiffres.

Source: OECD/OCDE

WATER QUALITY OF SELECTED RIVERS (a), annual mean concentrations, 1980-1993
QUALITÉ DES EAUX DE RIVIÈRES SÉLECTIONNÉES (a), concentrations annuelles moyennes, 1980-1993

µg/ litre

			1980	1985	1986	1987	1988	1989	1990	1991	1992	1993	Average last 3 years/ moyenne 3 dernières années (c)
							Copper/ Cuivre (b)						
Canada	Fraser		..	4.80	..	..	..	2.60	6.90	..	..	..	..
	Saskatchewan	*	6.00	8.90	3.10	6.30	4.60	1.70	2.60	..	..	..	2.97
Mexico/Mexique	Pánuco		..	..	..	..	..	0.10	0.10	..	0.05	0.06	0.07
USA/Etats-Unis	Delaware	*	3.30	4.30	6.00	3.80	3.30	2.80	2.30	2.50	4.00	3.00	3.17
	Mississippi	*	4.10	5.70	5.90	5.60	5.50	5.50	5.30	3.80	19.10	12.30	11.73
Australia/Australie	Murray-Darling	*	5.00	5.00	5.50	5.50	8.00	9.90	9.00	5.00	5.00		6.33
Austria/Autriche	Donau		4.00	2.00	..	..	..	..	..	3.00	3.00	2.00	2.67
	Inn		8.00	2.00			2.00	2.00	2.00	..	2.50	4.00	2.83
Finland/Finlande	Torniojoki		3.20	0.72	1.40	..	0.75	1.01	0.82	2.00	0.79	1.01	1.27
	Kymijoki	*	1.20	..	3.50					1.50			
	Kokemäenjoki		5.20	5.30	5.40	2.80	19.17	31.16	5.36	17.50	14.60	3.66	11.92
Germany/Allemagne	Rhein		..	..	10.80	8.00	11.00	8.20	7.90	7.70	5.70	..	7.10
	Elbe	*					4.30	3.40	4.30	5.20	5.00	..	4.83
	Weser		16.20	6.10	9.10	6.90	6.80	4.90	4.60	7.20	4.20	..	5.33
	Donau	*	..	4.10	..	..	..	4.40	4.70	4.40	..	..	4.50
Luxembourg	Moselle	*	..	2.40	..	..	..	6.00	6.00	5.00	..	3.90	4.97
	Wiltz	*	0.01	0.05				0.01	0.03	0.00	0.00	0.01	0.00
Netherlands/Pays-Bas	Maas-Keizersveer		12.00	3.50	6.20	6.20	4.70	4.00	3.13	5.00	5.30	..	4.48
	Rijn/Maas Delta		..	3.60	4.50	3.50	4.20	2.90	3.20	3.50	3.70	..	3.47
	Rijn-Maassluis		12.00	4.85	5.90	4.10	6.90	4.64	4.91	4.80	4.80	..	4.84
	Rijn-Lobith		14.10	5.90	6.60	5.30	5.10	6.00	5.70	6.50	5.80	..	6.00
	IJssel-Kampen		9.30	5.10	6.10	4.90	4.10	5.10	5.00	8.00	6.30	..	6.43
Portugal	Tejo	*				..	2.00	6.00	6.00	3.00	5.00	..	4.67
Spain/Espagne	Guadalquivir	*	2.70	0.90	0.90	-	14.50	..	..	4.20	8.00	5.00	5.73
	Duero	*	0.80	2.50	-	-	7.50	..	..			-	..
	Ebro	*	-		-	-			0.01	0.01	14.00	10.00	8.00
Sweden/Suède	Dalälven	*	..	6.30	2.80	10.10	3.80	3.30	1.90	2.10	1.50	3.20	2.27
	Råne älv	*	..	1.30	0.60	0.70	0.70	0.70	0.70	0.60	0.90	0.80	0.77
	Mörrumsån	*	..	1.50	1.20	1.30	1.10	1.20	1.40	1.00	0.90	1.00	0.97
	Rönneån	*	..	2.80	2.00	2.10	1.70	1.40	1.60	1.70	1.30	1.40	1.47
Switzerland/Suisse	Rhin		4.20	2.76	2.60	2.50	2.20	2.20	2.70	1.90	1.70	1.30	1.63
	Aare	*	3.48	3.82				1.90	2.90	1.90	1.80		2.20
	Rhône		3.48	4.70	5.60	7.30	6.60	3.40	2.20	2.30	3.00	3.30	2.87
Turkey/Turquie	Porsuk		..	..	29.00	36.00	11.50	..	..	9.00	7.00	12.00	9.33
	Sakarya		5.00	32.50	40.10	21.60	14.00	18.00	18.00	12.00	15.00	13.00	13.33
UK/Royaume-Uni	Thames	*	10.00	10.50	11.20	11.00	8.30	5.40	8.40	7.90	6.70	6.20	6.93
	Severn	*	20.80	12.00	11.20	8.50	5.80	6.00	9.60	5.50	4.80	5.30	5.20
	Clyde	*	10.20	5.80	5.60	4.20	4.20	2.70	5.40	3.10	3.50	5.60	4.07
	Mersey	*	18.60	9.10	10.10	9.20	9.10	10.90	7.60	8.30	8.50	8.10	8.30
Hungary/Hongrie	Duna		..	..	..	..	..	5.00	10.60	10.00	..	..	8.53
	Drava		..	..	..	..	..	..	12.20	10.30	5.40	6.30	7.33
Poland	Wisla		..	..	..	..	..	6.30	7.00	6.00	7.00	3.18	5.39
	Odra		..	..	..	..	..	8.70	9.00	10.00	9.00	8.87	9.29
	Nysa Luzycka		..	..	..	..	..	..	14.35	11.32	9.60	9.10	10.01

Notes: (3.3I Copper)
a) Measured at the mouth or downstream frontier of river.
b) Data refer to total concentrations unless otherwise specified.
c) Average over the last three years available: data prior to 1988 have not been taken into account.
CAN) Saskatchewan: 1980 data refer to 1979.
USA) Dissolved concentrations.
AUS) Data refer to fiscal year and median values.
AUT) 1980 data include limit of detection values; 1985 data refer to 1984.
FIN) Kymijoki: 1985 data refer to 1984.
DEU) Elbe: dissolved concentrations. Donau: 1980 data refer to 1982.
LUX) Moselle: 1991 and 1993 data refer to upper limits. Wiltz: 1985 and 1989-92 data refer to upper limits.
PRT) 1988, 1990 and 1992 data include limit of detection values.
ESP) Dissolved concentrations.
SWE) Dissolved concentrations based on analysis of unfiltered samples. 1980 data refer to 1982.
CHE) Aare-Brugg: 1985 data refer to 1983.
UKD) When a parameter is unmeasurable (quantity too small), limit of detection values are used when calculating averages. Actual averages may therefore be lower.

Notes: (3.3I Cuivre)
a) Mesuré à l'embouchure ou à la frontière aval de la rivière.
b) Les données représentent des concentrations totales sauf indication contraire.
c) Moyenne sur les trois dernières années disponibles : les données antérieures à 1988 n'ont pas été prises en compte.
CAN) Saskatchewan : les données 1980 sont de 1979.
USA) Concentrations en matières dissoutes.
AUS) Les données représentent l'année fiscale et des valeurs médianes.
AUT) Le chiffre 1980 inclut des seuils de détection ; le chiffre 1985 est de 1984.
FIN) Kymijoki : les données 1985 sont de 1984.
DEU) Elbe : concentrations en matières dissoutes. Donau : le chiffre 1980 est de 1982.
LUX) Moselle : les données 1991 et 1993 incluent des seuils de détection. Wiltz : les données 1985 et 1989-92 incluent des seuils de détection.
PRT) Les données 1988, 1990 et 1992 incluent des seuils de détection.
ESP) Concentrations en matières dissoutes.
SWE) Concentrations en matières dissoutes basées sur l'analyse d'échantillons non filtrés. Les données 1980 sont de 1982.
CHE) Aare-Brugg : les données 1985 sont de 1983.
UKD) Quand un paramètre n'est pas mesurable (concentrations trop faibles) les seuils de détection sont utilisés dans le calcul des moyennes. Les valeurs moyennes réelles peuvent donc être inférieures.

Source: OECD/OCDE

The following tables show trends in annual mean concentrations of phosphorus and nitrogen in selected lakes.

These parameters concern nutrient concentrations and related degrees of eutrophication of lakes and reservoirs.

The interpretation of these tables should take into account variations in the methods of sampling (e.g. sampling location and number of measurements at different sampling locations and in different years).

Les tableaux suivants présentent les évolutions des concentrations moyennes annuelles en phosphore et en azote dans des lacs sélectionnés.

Ces paramètres concernent les concentrations en matières nutritives et les niveaux associés d'eutrophisation des lacs et réservoirs.

L'interprétation de ces tableaux doit prendre en compte les différences dans les modes d'échantillonnage telles que sélection des points de mesure, nombre de mesures aux différents points sélectionnés et années retenues.

WATER QUALITY OF SELECTED LAKES, annual mean concentrations, 1980-1993
QUALITÉ DES EAUX DE LACS SÉLECTIONNÉES, concentrations annuelles moyennes, 1980-1993

mgP/litre

			1980	1985	1986	1987	1988	1989	1990	1991	1992	1993	Average last 3 years/ moyenne 3 dernières années (a)
Canada	Ontario	*	0.015	0.011	0.010	0.010	0.010	0.010	0.010	0.009	0.009	0.010	0.009
	Huron	*	0.005	0.004	0.005	0.006	0.005	0.004	0.005	0.005	..	0.005	0.005
	Superior	*	..	0.003	0.003	0.004	..	0.003	0.003	0.003	0.003	..	0.003
Mexico/Mexique	Chapala	*	0.280	0.730	0.380	0.340	0.420	0.390	0.240	0.280	0.270	..	0.263
	Pátzcuaro	*	..	0.025	0.150	0.001	..	..	..	..	0.130	..	..
	Almoloya	*	0.590	2.800	0.400	..	..	..	..	..	2.730	..	..
Japan/Japon	Biwa (North)		0.010	0.009	0.010	0.008	0.010	0.010	0.009	0.010	0.009	0.009	0.009
	Biwa (South)		0.027	0.027	0.024	0.022	0.024	0.022	0.025	0.023	0.024	0.002	0.016
	Kasumigaura		0.080	0.060	0.060	0.070	0.060	0.070	0.066	0.076	0.082	0.097	0.085
N. Zealand/N. Zélande	Pupuke	*	..	..	..	0.018	..	..	..	..	..	0.011	..
Austria/Autriche	Mondsee	*	0.025	0.011	0.014	0.010	0.009	0.010	0.009	0.009	0.009	0.009	0.009
	Ossiachersee	*	0.012	0.013	0.011	0.009	0.011	0.014	0.014	0.011	0.010	0.011	0.011
	Wallersee	*	0.030	0.027	0.025	0.022	..	0.029	0.027	0.023	0.028	0.021	0.024
	Zeller-See	*	0.018	0.015	0.010	0.010	0.001	0.011	0.011	0.005	0.014	0.017	0.012
Denmark/Danemark	Dons Norreso		..	..	..	..	..	0.239	0.222	0.187	0.161	0.157	0.168
	Arreso		..	..	..	..	..	0.457	0.519	0.413	0.433	0.552	0.466
	Fureso		..	..	..	..	..	0.129	0.169	0.265	0.275	0.307	0.282
Finland/Finlande	Pääjärvi		0.010	0.014	0.014	0.014	0.018	0.017	0.013	0.012	0.014	0.014	0.013
	Päijänne		0.009	0.008	0.008	0.009	0.008	0.007	0.007	0.007	0.007	0.007	0.007
	Yli-Kitka		0.006	0.007	..	..	0.007	0.007	0.008	0.008	0.007	0.006	0.007
France	Parentis-Biscarrosse		..	..	..	..	..	0.164	0.084	0.266	0.143	0.098	0.169
Germany/Allemagne	Bodensee		0.079	0.062	0.059	0.052	0.042	0.040	0.036	0.032	0.030	0.026	0.029
Greece/Grèce	Mikri Prespa		..	0.019	0.031	0.019	0.018	..	..	0.013	0.026	..	0.019
	Vegoritis	*	..	0.080	0.012	0.075	0.047	0.008	..	0.035	0.020	..	0.021
	Petron		..	0.057	0.129	0.084	..	0.079	..	0.049	0.029	..	0.052
	Megali Prespa	*	..	0.015	0.013	0.008	0.010	0.013	..	0.013	0.010	..	0.012
Italy/Italie	Maggiore		0.036	0.019	0.021	0.018	0.016	0.014	0.015	0.016	0.011	0.010	0.012
	Como		0.078	0.052	0.057	0.064	0.052	0.047	0.047	0.053	0.052	0.046	0.050
	Garda		0.020	0.011	0.008	0.013	0.012	0.013	0.015	0.014	0.018	0.016	0.016
	Orta		0.004	0.006	0.006	0.004	0.006	0.004	0.004	0.005	0.005	0.003	0.004
Luxembourg	Esch/Sûre	*	..	0.030	..	..	..	0.060	0.050	..	..	0.030	0.047
	Weiswampach		0.600	0.600	..	..	..	0.600	0.600	0.300	0.300	0.250	0.283
Netherlands/Pays Bas	Issel		0.350	0.300	0.250	0.210	0.240	0.210	0.180	..	..	..	0.210
Norway/Norvège	Mjoesa		0.009	0.007	0.008	0.009	0.010	0.011	0.007	0.007	0.005	0.005	0.005
	Randsfjorden		0.004	..	..	..	0.006	0.005	0.004	0.005	0.003	0.004	0.004
	Tyrifjorden		0.007	0.008	0.006	..	..	..	0.006	0.005	..	0.004	0.005
Portugal	Castelo de Bode	*	0.150	0.110	..	0.020	..	..	0.010	-	-	..	0.003
Spain/Espagne	Alcántara	*	0.428	0.141	0.383	0.399	0.251	..	..	..	0.390	0.930	0.524
Sweden/Suède	Mälaren		0.034	0.031	0.024	0.023	0.030	0.024	0.025	0.028	0.020	0.022	0.023
	Vänern		0.012	0.008	0.007	0.008	0.008	0.008	0.009	0.009	0.008	0.008	0.008
	Vättern		0.009	0.006	0.005	0.005	0.006	0.006	0.007	0.006	0.007	0.007	0.007
	Hjälmaren		0.047	0.042	0.050	0.039	0.050	0.042	0.040	0.046	0.043	0.048	0.046
Switzerland/Suisse	Léman		0.083	0.073	0.072	0.068	0.062	0.058	0.055	0.052	0.050	0.049	0.050
	Constance		0.083	0.066	0.063	0.058	0.046	0.042	0.039	0.033	0.032	0.030	0.032
Turkey/Turquie	Kurtbogazi	*	0.110	0.200	0.040	0.190	0.090	0.060	0.050	0.030	0.020	0.050	0.033
	Sapanca	*	0.030	0.030	0.030	0.030	0.030	0.060	0.030	0.040	0.020	0.040	0.033
	Altinapa	*	0.020	0.150	0.130	1.060	0.570	0.150	0.110	0.130	0.050	0.090	0.090
UK/Royaume Uni	Neagh		0.108	0.115	0.108	0.094	0.090	0.106	0.096	0.100	0.100	0.112	0.104
	Lomond	*	0.009	0.009	0.008	0.005	0.003	0.015	0.019	0.019	0.023	0.015	0.019
	Bewl Water		..	0.023	0.075	..	0.080	0.081	..	..	0.090	0.133	0.101
Hungary	Fertö		..	0.140	0.150	0.090	..	0.170	..	..	..	..	..
	Balaton		0.010	0.020	0.030	0.030	0.020	0.020	0.030	0.030	0.030	0.030	0.030

Notes: see page 91 / voir page 91.

Source: OECD/OCDE

WATER QUALITY OF SELECTED LAKES (a), annual mean concentrations, 1980-1993
QUALITÉ DES EAUX DE LACS SÉLECTIONNÉS (a), concentrations annuelles moyennes, 1980-1993

mgN/litre

			Total Nitrogen/Azote total										Average last 3 years/ moyenne 3 dernières années (a)
			1980	1985	1986	1987	1988	1989	1990	1991	1992	1993	
Canada	Ontario	*	0.31	0.34	0.36	0.38	0.37	0.39	0.39	0.40	0.38	0.37	0.39
	Huron	*	0.28	..	0.33	0.33	0.33	0.33	0.34	0.37	0.34	0.33	0.36
	Superior	*	..	0.34	0.34	0.34	0.34	0.34	0.34	0.33	0.34	0.34	0.35
Mexico/Mexique	Chapala	*	0.21	0.59	0.16	0.18	0.28	0.19	0.15	0.36	0.18	..	0.23
	Pátzcuaro	*	..	..	..	..	2.40	2.99	3.03	2.18	..	..	2.73
	Almoloya	*	..	..	..	..	10.28	7.70	..	12.46	..	..	10.15
	Centenario	*	..	0.05	0.05	0.05	0.08	0.35	0.26	0.23	0.05	..	0.18
Japan/Japon	Biwa (North)		0.29	0.27	0.27	0.24	0.29	0.29	0.28	0.31	0.30	0.32	0.31
	Biwa (South)		0.41	0.41	0.37	0.34	0.41	0.39	0.40	0.39	0.41	0.39	0.40
	Kasumigaura		1.00	1.20	1.30	1.10	1.20	1.20	1.10	1.40	1.10	1.20	1.23
N. Zealand/N. Zélande	Pupuke	*	..	..	..	0.47	..	..	..	..	..	0.26	..
Denmark/Danemark	Dons Norreso		..	..	..	..	..	5.27	4.93	5.06	4.96	5.32	5.12
	Arreso		..	..	..	..	..	3.01	3.55	3.34	3.73	4.60	3.89
	Fureso		..	..	..	..	..	0.97	0.97	0.93	0.90	0.87	0.90
Finland/Finlande	Pääjärvi		1.19	1.10	1.03	1.04	1.20	1.23	1.28	1.17	1.50	1.27	1.31
	Päijänne		0.46	0.51	0.50	0.51	0.53	0.60	0.56	0.51	0.50	0.51	0.51
	Yli-Kitka		0.19	0.26	0.22	0.24	0.26	0.21	0.21	0.20	0.22	0.26	0.23
France	Parentis-Biscarrosse		..	..	..	..	..	1.70	0.86	1.26	0.84	1.00	1.04
	Reservoir Marne	*	1.62	1.22	0.97	1.10	1.68	1.72	1.18	0.23	0.80	0.73	0.59
	Reservoir Seine	*	2.12	0.95	1.43	1.52	1.52	1.70	1.02	0.52	0.88	0.53	0.64
Germany/Allemagne	Bodensee	*	0.88	0.92	0.94	1.01	0.97	0.97	0.96	0.98	0.98	1.00	0.99
Greece/Grèce	Mikri Prespa	*	..	..	..	0.05	0.05	..	..	0.16	0.10	..	0.10
	Petron	*	..	..	..	0.08	..	0.10	..	0.10	0.10	..	0.10
	Megali Prespa	*	..	..	..	0.05	0.05	0.05	..	0.05	0.10	..	0.07
Italy/Italie	Maggiore	*	0.91	0.90	0.89	0.95	0.87	0.85	0.99	0.87	0.98	0.95	0.93
	Como		..	0.96	0.88	0.93	..	0.92	0.96	0.98	0.96	0.92	0.95
	Garda		..	0.43	0.51	0.39	..	..	0.41	0.41	0.41	0.43	0.42
	Orta		9.90	7.66	7.15	6.45	5.07	4.90	4.71	4.44	4.35	3.48	4.09
Luxembourg	Esch/Sûre		..	..	..	..	..	..	2.95	..	2.19	2.95	2.70
	Weiswampach		..	..	..	..	..	..	2.03	2.23	1.94	1.85	2.00
	Remerschen		..	..	..	..	..	..	0.54	0.45	0.24	0.24	0.31
Netherlands/Pays Bas	Issel		4.39	4.14	4.24	4.45	3.95	..	3.96	..	..	..	..
Norway/Norvège	Mjoesa		0.50	0.43	0.46	0.54	0.52	0.43	0.38	0.44	0.45	0.46	0.45
	Randsfjorden		0.51	..	..	..	0.46	0.56	0.58	0.56	0.50	0.52	0.52
	Tyrifjorden		0.38	0.50	0.41	..	..	..	0.39	0.40	..	0.45	0.41
Portugal	Castelo de Bode	*	..	..	..	0.24	..	0.18	0.60	0.09	0.27	..	0.32
Sweden/Suède	Mälaren		0.71	0.86	0.80	0.70	0.79	0.69	0.61	0.63	0.60	0.54	0.59
	Vänern		0.84	0.86	0.87	0.81	0.84	0.83	0.81	0.84	0.81	0.80	0.81
	Vättern		0.63	0.68	0.73	0.70	0.68	0.73	0.73	0.73	0.69	0.69	0.70
	Hjälmaren		0.76	0.84	0.74	0.72	0.92	0.74	0.76	0.68	0.76	0.76	0.73
Switzerland/Suisse	Léman		0.66	0.73	0.72	0.71	0.71	0.71	0.69	0.66	0.69	0.63	0.66
	Constance	*	0.90	0.92	0.93	0.94	1.00	0.97	0.96	0.98	0.98	1.07	1.01
Turkey/Turquie	Kurtbogazi	*	0.43	0.36	0.36	0.66	0.21	0.28	..	..	0.20	0.13	0.20
	Sapanca	*	0.94	0.62	0.62	0.81	0.31	0.37	..	..	0.19	0.17	0.24
	Altinapa	*	1.55	0.55	0.71	0.96	1.09	1.81	..	..	1.76	2.07	1.88
UK/Royaume Uni	Neagh	*	0.48	0.48	0.34	0.30	0.63	0.26	0.77	0.58	0.38	0.41	0.46
	Lomond	*	0.30	0.29	0.27	0.23	0.21	0.16	0.13	0.20	0.36	0.15	0.24
	Bewl Water		0.91	0.77	0.97	1.33	0.78	0.80	1.12	1.81	1.46	1.40	1.56
Hungary/Hongrie	Fertö		..	1.82	2.08	2.33	..	1.37	..	2.12	..	..	..
	Balaton		0.93	0.78	0.74	0.62	0.62	0.70	0.82	0.48	0.63	0.80	0.64

Notes: see next page / voir page suivante.

Source: OECD/OCDE

Notes: (3.4A)
a)   Average over the last three years available: data prior to 1988 have not been taken into account.
CAN) Spring means.
MEX) Orthophosphates. Almoloya: 1980 data refer to 1981.
NZL) 1987 and 1993 data are medians of 1984-90 and 1992-93.
AUT) 1985: 1984 data. Zeller-See 1986-88: include limit of detection valuets.
GRE) Vegoritis: 1985 data refer to a six-month average. Megali Prespa: 1992 data include limit of detection values.
LUX) Esch/Sûre 1993: include limit of detection values.
PRT) Dam lake 1980, 1995: 1981 and 1985 data.
ESP) 1980 data refer to 1977. 1992-93 data refer to orthophosphates.
TUR) Orthophosphates.
KD) Lomond: 1980-88 data refer to ortophosphates.

Source: OECD/OCDE

Notes : (3.4A)
a)   Moyenne sur les trois dernières années disponibles : les données antérieures à 1988 n'ont pas été prises en compte.
CAN) Moyennes printanières.
MEX) Orthophosphates. Almoloya 1980: données 1981.
NZL) Les données 1987 et 1993 sont les médianes des années 1984-90 et 1992-93.
AUT) 1985 données 1984. Zeller-See 1986-88: incluent des seuils de détection.
GRE) Vegoritis 1985: moyenne sur six mois. Megali Prespa 1992: inclut des seuils de détection.
LUX) Esch/Sûre 1993: inclut des seuils de détection.
PRT) Lac de barrage 1980: données 1981.
ESP) Les données 1980 sont de 1977 ; les données 1992-93 concernent les orthophosphates.
TUR) Orthophosphates.
UKD) Lomond : les données 1980-88 concernent les orthophospates.

Notes: (3.4B)
a)   Average over the last three years available: data prior to 1988 have not been taken into account.
CAN) Spring means of NO_3+NO_2.
MEX) Nitrates only.
NZL) 1987 and 1993: medians of 1984-90 and 1992-93.
FRA) Réservoirs Marne and Seine: Kjeldahl nitrogen; 1980: 1981 data.
DEU) Total inorganic nitrogen ($NH_4+NO_3+NO_2$).
GRE) Nitrates only. Mikri Prespa, Megali Prespa 1992 and Petron 1989, 1991-92: limit of detection values.
ITA) Maggiore: total inorganic nitrogen ($NH_4+NO_3+NO_2$). Average of monthly samples taken at deepest point; 1980 data refer to 1981.
PRT) Castelo de Bode: dam lake.
CHE) Constance: 1985 data refer to 1984.
TUR) Total inorganic nitrogen ($NH_4+NO_3+NO_2$).
UKD) Neagh and Lomond: nitrates (NO_3) only.

Source: OECD/OCDE

Notes : (3.4B)
a)   Moyenne sur les trois dernières années disponibles : les données antérieures a 1988 n'ont pas été prises en compte.
CAN) Moyennes printanières de NO_3+NO_2.
MEX) Nitrates uniquement.
NZL) 1987 et 1993 : médianes des années 1984-90 et 1992-93.
FRA) Réservoirs Marne et Seine : azote Kjeldahl ; les données 1980 sont de 1981.
DEU) Azote total minéral ($NH_4+NO_3+NO_2$).
GRE) Nitrates seulement. Mikri Prespa, Megali Prespa : les données 1992 représentent des seuils de détection. Petron : les données 1989 et 1991-92 représentent des seuils de détection.
ITA) Maggiore: azote total minéral ($NH_4+NO_3+NO_2$). Moyenne des échantillons prélevés chaque mois au point le plus profond du lac ; les données 1980 sont de 1981.
PRT) Castelo de Bode : lac de barrage.
CHE) Constance : les données 1985 sont de 1984.
TUR) Azote total minéral ($NH_4+NO_3+NO_2$).
UKD) Neagh et Lomond : nitrates (NO_3) seulement.

4. LAND

4. SOLS

INTRODUCTION

Land resources are one of the four components of the natural environment: water, air, land and living resources. In this context land is both:

- a physical "milieu" necessary for the development of natural vegetation as well as cultivated vegetation;

- a resource for human activities.

The tables presented in this section give information concerning:

- land use state and changes (e.g. agricultural land, forest land);

- management of natural areas: national parks and natural areas with similar levels of protection.

A number of important topics are not covered by these data, including wetlands, land degradation by the loss of farmland to urban use; land degradation through erosion and desertification; and soil pollution (acidification by acid precipitation, excessive use of fertilizers and pesticides, improper hazardous waste dumping, sludge spreading). The reader may refer to tables in the sections on forest, agriculture, and wildlife for data concerning related topics.

INTRODUCTION

La ressource sol constitue l'un des quatres domaines de l'environnement naturel : eau, air, sol, ressources vivantes. Dans ce contexte les sols représentent à la fois :

- ▸ un milieu physique nécessaire au développement de la végétation naturelle et de la production agricole ;

- ▸ une ressource pour les activités humaines.

Les tableaux présentés dans cette section fournissent des informations concernant :

- ▸ l'état et l'évolution de l'utilisation des sols (e.g. sols agricoles, sols forestiers) ;

- ▸ la gestion des espaces naturels : parcs nationaux et zones naturelles de protection similaire.

Plusieurs thèmes importants ne sont pas couverts par ces données, tels que les zones humides, la dégradation des sols par la perte de terres agricoles pour des usages urbains ; la dégradation des sols par l'érosion et la désertification, la pollution des sols (acidification des sols par les pluies acides, utilisation excessive d'engrais et de pesticides, pollution due aux dépôts inadaptés de déchets dangereux, épandage de boues). Le lecteur peut également consulter les tableaux des sections sur la forêt, l'agriculture, la faune et la flore.

The following table shows the structure of land use in selected countries in broad categories.

Arable area includes land used for cereals, pulses, root crops, industrial crops (e.g. textile crops, tobacco, oilseeds), vegetables, flowers, ornamental plants, etc. Land under permanent crop includes that used for orchards, vineyards, olive growing, hardy nursery stocks, etc. "Arable and crop land" is defined as the sum of arable area and land under permanent crop. "Other areas" include built-up land, desert, tundra, ice, dunes and mountains. Areas under inland water bodies (rivers and lakes) are excluded.

The definitions used in different countries may show variations, particularly for "permanent grassland". The comparability of data is therefore not satisfactory.

See Table 4.1B, for changes in land use for the same categories.

Le tableau suivant présente la structure de l'utilisation des sols des divers pays par grande catégorie.

Les terres arables comprennent les plantations telles que céréales, légumes secs, plantes sarclées, plantes industrielles (textiles, tabacs, oléagineux...), légumes, fleurs et plantes ornementales, etc. Les cultures permanentes comprennent les vergers, les vignes, les oliveraies, les pépinières, etc. Les "terres arables et cultures permanentes" sont définies comme la somme des superficies des terres arables et des cultures permanentes. La catégorie "autres" comprend les terrains bâtis, les déserts, la toundra, les glaces, les dunes et les montagnes. Les superficies occupées par les eaux intérieures (c'est-à-dire cours d'eau et lacs) sont exclues.

Les définitions employées peuvent varier selon les pays, en particulier en ce qui concerne les superficies toujours en herbe. La comparabilité des données n'est donc pas satisfaisante.

Voir également le tableau 4.1B qui présente l'évolution de l'utilisation des sols pour les mêmes catégories.

LAND USE (a), 1993
UTILISATION DES SOLS (a), 1993

		Arable and Permanent Crop Land/ Terres arables et cultures permanentes		Permanent Grassland/ Superficies toujours en herbe		Forest and other wooded land/ Forêts et autres terres boisées		Other Areas/ Autres Terres		Land Area/ Superficie des terres b)
		km²	%	km²	%	km²	%	km²	%	km²
Canada		414 290	4.5	263 250	2.9	4 161 750	45.1	4 381 680	47.5	9 220 970
Mexico/Mexique		247 300	13.0	744 990	39.0	487 000	25.5	429 400	22.5	1 908 690
USA/Etats-Unis	*	1 877 760	19.6	2 391 720	25.0	2 981 360	31.1	2 322 270	24.3	9 573 110
Japan/Japon		44 630	11.9	6 610	1.8	252 120	67.0	73 160	19.4	376 520
Australia/Australie	*	464 860	6.1	4 138 000	53.9	1 491 750	19.4	1 587 690	20.7	7 682 300
N.Zealand/N.Zélande	*	4 100	1.5	135 200	50.6	75 400	28.2	52 320	19.6	267 020
Austria/Autriche		14 980	18.1	19 540	23.6	38 780	46.9	9 430	11.4	82 730
Belgium/Belgique		7 170	23.7	6 050	20.0	6 120	20.2	10 920	36.1	30 250
Denmark/Danemark	*	25 420	59.9	1 970	4.6	4 450	10.5	10 590	25.0	42 430
Finland/Finlande		25 800	8.5	1 060	0.3	232 670	76.4	45 080	14.8	304 610
France		194 390	35.4	107 640	19.6	152 400	27.7	94 760	17.3	549 190
Germany/Allemagne	*	117 070	33.5	52 430	15.0	104 330	29.9	75 440	21.6	349 270
w. Germany/Allemagne occ.		75 340	30.9	42 940	17.6	74 100	30.4	51 740	21.2	244 120
Greece/Grèce	*	34 940	27.1	52 500	40.7	26 200	20.3	15 260	11.8	128 900
Iceland/Islande	*	1 400	1.4	17 600	18.0	1 400	1.4	77 600	79.2	98 000
Ireland/Irlande		9 230	13.4	46 900	68.1	3 960	5.7	8 800	12.8	68 890
Italy/Italie		118 600	40.3	48 780	16.6	67 700	23.0	58 980	20.1	294 060
Luxembourg		670	26.0	820	31.9	880	34.2	210	8.2	2 570
Netherlands/Pays-Bas		9 550	28.1	10 510	31.0	3 500	10.3	10 380	30.6	33 940
Norway/Norvège		8 900	2.9	1 230	0.4	119 200	38.9	177 470	57.8	306 800
Portugal	*	31 600	34.5	8 400	9.2	32 290	35.3	19 260	21.0	91 550
Spain/Espagne		196 560	39.4	103 000	20.6	161 370	32.3	38 510	7.7	499 440
Sweden/Suède	*	29 880	7.3	5 760	1.4	281 000	68.3	94 980	23.1	411 620
Switzerland/Suisse		4 670	11.8	11 140	28.2	12 520	31.6	11 230	28.4	39 560
Turkey/Turquie		275 750	35.8	85 190	11.1	201 990	26.2	206 700	26.9	769 630
UK/Royaume-Uni	*	65 950	27.4	106 860	44.4	24 380	10.1	43 750	18.2	240 940
CSFR/RFTS		49 060	39.1	17 080	13.6	46 200	36.9	13 020	10.4	125 360
Czech Rep./Rép. Tchèque		32 930	42.6	8 730	11.3	26 290	34.0	9 330	12.1	77 280
Slovak Rep./ Rép. Slovaque		16 130	33.5	8 350	17.4	19 910	41.4	3 690	7.7	48 080
Hungary/Hongrie		49 730	53.9	11 570	12.5	17 640	19.1	13 400	14.5	92 340
Poland/Pologne		146 680	48.2	40 470	13.3	87 850	28.9	29 420	9.7	304 420
North America/Amérique N.		2 539 350	12.3	3 399 960	16.4	7 630 110	36.9	7 133 350	34.5	20 702 770
Australia/ie-NZ.		468 960	5.9	4 273 200	53.8	1 567 150	19.7	1 640 010	20.6	7 949 320
OECD/OCDE Europe		1 172 530	27.0	687 370	15.8	1 475 140	34.0	1 009 350	23.2	4 344 380
EU/UE - 15		881 810	28.2	572 210	18.3	1 140 020	36.4	536 350	17.1	3 130 390
OECD/OCDE		4 225 460	12.7	8 367 140	25.1	10 924 520	32.7	9 855 870	29.5	33 372 990
World/Monde		14 475 090	11.0	33 617 330	25.6	41 798 080	31.9	41 270 140	31.5	131 160 640

Notes:
a) Include Secretariat estimates. All figures are rounded to the nearest 10 km².
b) Excludes area under inland water bodies (i.e. major rivers and lakes).
USA) Forest land with annual production > 20 cubic feet per acre.
AUS) Arable and permanent crop land includes about 300 000 km². Permanent grassland refer to native pastures and include fallow and unused land.
NZL) Data excludes outlying islands.
DNK) Arable and permanent crops, permanent grassland: based on holdings with agricultural land of at least 5 hectares and less than 5 hectares whose production exceeds a fixed minimum.
DEU) Agricultural land: includes land on holdings of 1 hectare and above, and on holdings of less than 1 hectare whose production market values exceeds a fixed minimum.
GRC) Forest and other wooded land: according to 1992 national inventory: 65 130 km².
ISL) Forest and other wooded land: land outside agricultural areas.
PRT) Arable and permanent crops: include about 8 000 km² of temporary crops grown in association with permanent crops and forests.
SWE) Arable and permanent crops: holdings of 2 hectares and above; forest and other wooded area: land with annual production greater than 1 m³ per hectare.
UKD) Arable and permanent crops: include fallow land. Permanent grassland: includes set-aside land.

Notes:
a) Y compris des estimations du Secrétariat. Tous les chiffres sont arrondis à 10 km² près.
b) Exclut la superficie des eaux intérieures (c.à.d. les principaux cours d'eau et lacs).
USA) Forêts de production annuelle supérieure à 20 pieds cube par acre.
AUS) Les données sur les terres arables comprennent environ 300 000 km² d'herbages cultivés. Les superficies toujours en herbe comprennent les pâturages indigènes ainsi que les jachères et les terres non utilisées.
NZL) Les données excluent les îles isolées.
DNK) Terres arables, cultures permanentes et superficies toujours en herbe: exploitations d'au moins 5 hectares et exploitations de moins 5 hectares dont la production dépasse un minimum fixé.
DEU) Terres agricoles: terres des exploitations d'au moins 1 hectare, et des exploitations de moins de 1 hectare dont la production a une valeur marchande qui dépasse un minimum donné.
GRC) Forêts et autres terres boisées: selon l'inventaire national 1992: 65 130 km².
ISL) Forêts et autres terres boisées: excluent les superficies agricoles.
PRT) Terres arables et cultures permanentes: comprennent environ 8 000 km² de cultures temporaires associées à des cultures permanentes ou à des forêts.
SWE) Terres arables et cultures permanentes: exploitations de 2 hectares et plus. Superficie forestière de production annuelle supérieure à 1 m³ par hectare.
UKD) Terre arables et cultures permanentes: incluent les terres en jachère; superficies toujours en herbe: incluent les terres en friche.

Source: FAO, OECD, national statistical yearbooks/ FAO, OCDE, annuaires statistiques nationaux

The following table shows changes in land use in selected countries in broad categories.

Definitions of the variables shown in this table are similar to those of the preceding table.

Because statistics relating to changes from one type of land use to another are not available, only net changes are shown here. Changes of definition over time within a single country can sometimes alter the validity of trend series.

Le tableau suivant présente l'évolution de l'utilisation des sols dans divers pays par grandes catégories.

Les définitions des variables présentées dans ce tableau sont identiques à celles du tableau précédent.

En l'absence de statistiques relatives aux changements d'utilisation des sols d'une catégorie à une autre, seules les évolutions nettes sont présentées ici. La validité de certaines séries temporelles peut quelquefois être altérée par des changements de définition à l'intérieur d'un même pays.

CHANGES IN LAND USE, 1970-1993
ÉVOLUTION DE L'UTILISATION DES SOLS, 1970-1993

Index (1970=100)

	Arable and Crop Land/ Terres arables et cultures permanentes			Permanent Grassland/ Superficies toujours en herbe			Forest and other wooded land/ Forêts et autres terres boisées		
	1980	1985	1993	1980	1985	1993	1980	1985	1993
Canada *	100	105	107	100	84	88	98	102	94
Mexico/Mexique	106	107	107	100	100	100	89	87	91
USA/Etats-Unis	100	100	99	97	99	98	97	97	97
Japan/Japon	89	86	81	203	217	231	100	100	100
Australia/Australie	108	115	111	100	97	91	106	106	108
N. Zealand/N. Zélande	78	88	71	112	109	107	99	100	105
Austria/Austrie	97	91	89	92	90	88	102	105	105
Belgium/Belgique	91	89	84	84	86	81	103	101	101
Denmark/Danemark *	99	98	95	84	74	66	105	104	94
Finland/Finlande	96	90	97	109	88	71	104	104	104
France	102	104	105	91	87	76	106	108	109
Germany/Allemagne	97	97	91	86	83	75	101	101	102
w. Germany/Allemagne occ.	93	92	93	86	83	78	103	103	104
Greece/Grèce	100	101	89	100	100	100	100	100	100
Iceland/Islande	110	113	116	94	94	94	106	109	112
Ireland/Irlande	80	75	67	108	109	109	142	153	162
Italy/Italie *	83	81	79	98	95	93	103	104	110
Luxembourg *	89	85	101	103	101	118	99	105	107
Netherl./Pays-Bas	101	106	110	87	85	79	110	112	117
Norway/Norvège *	104	108	112	78	63	78	105	105	105
Portugal	102	102	102	100	100	100	105	109	114
Spain/Espagne	100	99	96	93	89	89	110	110	114
Sweden/Suède	98	96	98	83	81	81	101	103	104
Switzerl./Suisse	107	107	101	91	90	79	107	112	112
Turkey/Turquie	104	101	101	90	82	79	100	100	100
UK/Royaume-Uni	97	98	92	99	97	99	122	132	141
CSFR/RFTS	97	97	92	96	93	97	103	103	104
Hungary/Hongrie	95	95	89	101	97	90	106	107	107
Poland/Pologne	98	97	96	96	96	96	102	103	102
N.America/Amérique du Nord	101	101	101	98	98	98	97	99	99
OECD/OCDE Europe	98	97	95	94	90	87	105	106	108
EU/UE-15	97	96	94	94	92	89	104	105	107
OECD/OCDE	100	101	100	99	97	94	99	101	102
World/Monde	103	104	104	102	104	106	101	101	98

Notes:
CAN) Forest and other wooded land: numerical differences between successive national inventories do not necessarily reflect real changes. 1980 and 1985 data refer to 1981 and 1986. 1993 data refer to an average on the period 1987-91 and include inventory figure for forest lands whose area was previously overestimated.
DNK) Change in wooded land due to change in definition. 1979, 1980, 1993: 1965, 1976 and 1990 data. The limit for including the area of agricultural land from a holding has been changed several times since 1970. Comparisons between the years should be considered with caution.
ITA) Since 1986 some agricultural land has been reclassified as forest land. Since 1985 mediterrean maquis included in mixed forest.
LUX) Forest inventory methodology has changed between 1985 and 1993.
NOR) Change in forest area: data include Secretariat estimates.

Source: FAO, OECD/OCDE

Notes:
CAN) Forêts et autres terres boisées: les différences entre les inventaires nationaux successifs ne reflètent pas nécessairement des changements réels; elles proviennent de l'amélioration de la couverture et des procédures de l'inventaire. Les données 1980 et 1985 se réfèrent à 1981 et 1986. Les données 1993 se rapportent à une moyenne sur la période 1987-1991 et montrent une surestimation des superficies boisées pour les années précédentes.
DNK) L'évolution des superficies boisées est due à un changement de définition. 1970, 1980, 1993: données 1965, 1976 et 1990. Les critères d'inclusion des terres agricoles des exploitations ont été changés plusieurs fois depuis 1970. Les comparaisons doivent être effectuées avec précaution.
ITA) Depuis 1986 certaines superficies agricoles ont été reclassées comme forêts. Depuis 1985, le maquis méditerranéen est compris dans les forêts mixtes.
LUX) Changement de méthodologie d'inventaire forestier entre 1985 et 1993.
NOR) Evolution des terres forestières: les données comprennent des estimations du Secrétariat.

The following table provides a summary of the number and extent of protected areas by country. The broadest definition of "protected area" is one in which some restrictions are enforced on the activities allowed. This may range from a restriction on building to limited access by humans to a given area. More precisely, the category includes scientific reserves, national parks, natural monuments, nature reserves and protected landscapes.

Protected areas change over time: new areas are created, boundaries of existing areas are revised and some sites may be destroyed through industrial development, shifting agriculture or natural disasters. Actual protection levels and related trends are difficult to evaluate as they are not only a matter of the number and area of protected sites but also a question of the effectiveness of management and of the achievement of protection objectives.

When interpreting this table, it should be borne in mind that the definitions, although harmonised by the IUCN, may still vary among countries. See also the last table in this section, and related tables in the wildlife section.

Le tableau suivant fournit un résumé du nombre et de l'étendue des zones protégées par pays. La définition la plus large d'une "zone protégée" est qu'il y a certaines restrictions concernant les activités autorisées. Les restrictions peuvent aller de l'interdiction de construire à l'interdiction d'accéder à une zone donnée. Ce tableau inclut plus précisément les réserves scientifiques, les parcs nationaux, les monuments naturels, les réserves naturelles et les paysages protégés.

Les zones protégées évoluent rapidement: de nouvelles zones sont créées, les limites des zones existantes sont modifiées tandis que d'autres zones sont détruites par le développement industriel, l'agriculture ou les catastrophes naturelles. Il reste difficile d'évaluer les niveaux de protection réels et leur évolution: ce n'est pas simplement le nombre de sites et leur superficie qui compte, mais plutôt l'efficacité de leur gestion et le respect des objectifs fixés.

Lors de l'interprétation de ce tableau, on doit garder à l'esprit que les définitions, bien qu'harmonisées par l'UICN, peuvent varier selon les pays. Voir également le dernier tableau de cette section et les tableaux sur le même sujet de la section sur la faune et la flore.

MAJOR PROTECTED AREAS (a), 1993
PRINCIPALES ZONES PROTÉGÉES (a), 1993

		Protected areas/Zones protégées		Percentage of national territory/ Pourcentage du territoire national (%)	Protected area per 1000 inhabitants/ Superficie protégée pour 1 000 habitants (ha/1000 cap.)
		Number of sites/ Nombre de zones (b)	Total size/ Superficie totale (km²)		
Canada	*	640	892 749	8.9	3 104.9
Mexico/Mexique	*	65	97 287	5.0	106.7
USA/Etats-Unis	*	1 466	1 041 069	10.6	403.7
Japan/Japon		80	27 582	7.3	22.1
Australia/Australie	*	891	591 655	7.7	3 350.8
N.Zealand/N.Zélande		205	61 476	22.8	1 766.6
Austria/Autriche		170	20 055	23.9	251.0
Belgium/Belgique		3	771	2.5	7.6
Denmark/Danemark	*	113	13 888	32.2	267.6
Finland/Finlande	*	82	27 286	8.1	538.6
France	*	83	53 591	9.7	92.9
Germany/Allemagne		504	91 957	25.8	113.3
Greece/Grèce		24	2 231	1.7	21.5
Iceland/Islande	*	22	9 159	8.8	3 495.9
Ireland/Irlande		12	468	0.7	13.2
Italy/Italie		172	22 748	7.6	39.9
Luxembourg		1	360	13.9	91.1
Netherlands/Pays-Bas	*	77	3 808	10.2	24.9
Norway/Norvège	*	113	55 365	17.1	1 284.0
Portugal	*	25	5 826	6.3	58.9
Spain/Espagne	*	215	42 456	8.4	108.6
Sweden/Suède		214	29 890	6.6	342.9
Switzerland/Suisse		109	7 307	17.7	105.3
Turkey/Turquie	*	44	8 194	1.1	13.8
UK/Royaume-Uni		146	49 666	20.3	85.3
Czech Rep./Rép. Tchèque		34	10 668	13.5	103.6
Slovak. Rep./Rép. Slovaque		40	10 155	20.7	191.1
Hungary/Hongrie		53	5 740	6.2	55.8
Poland/Pologne		111	30 636	9.8	79.7
OECD/OCDE		5 476	3 156 847	9.1	327.3
World/Monde		9 832	9 263 496	6.9	167.1

Notes:
a) IUCN management categories I-V. National classifications may differ. Includes only areas greater than 10 km² except for islands.
b) Number of sites for which the size is known.
CAN) Total size: national figures.
MEX) There are 82 national protected areas under the National System of Natural Protected Areas (SINAP), with a total size of 97 277 km².
USA) Including Alaska: 113 protected areas totalling 915 397 km². Excluding American Samoa, Minor Outlying Islands, Puerto Rico and Virgin Islands.
AUS) Excludes the Great Barrier Reef Marine Park (cat.V).
DNK) Excluding Greenland: two protected areas totalling 982 500 km².
FIN) According to national classification, there are 135 protected areas of a total size 27 721 km².
FRA) Excluding non metropolitan areas.
ISL) According to national classification, there are 72 protected areas.
NLD) Excluding the Netherlands Antilles.
NOR) Including Svalbard, Jan Mayen and Bouvet islands: seven protected areas totalling 34 985 km².
PRT) Includes Azores and Madeira Islands. According to the national classification, there are 66 protected areas totalling 6 446 km² (mainland and islands).
ESP) Includes Baleares and Canary Islands.
TUR) According to national classification there are 103 protected areas.

Notes:
a) Catégories I-V de l'UICN. Les classifications nationales peuvent être différentes. Chaque zone a une superficie supérieure à 10 km²; limite non appliquée aux îles.
b) Nombre de sites pour lesquels la superficie est connue.
CAN) Superficie totale: chiffres nationaux.
MEX) Il y a 82 zones protégées selon le système national des sites naturels protégés sur une superficie totale de 97 277 km².
USA) Y compris l'Alaska: 113 zones protégées, d'une superficie totale de 915 397 km². Exclut les Samoa, les îles Mineures, Puerto Rico et les îles Vierges américaines.
AUS) Ne comprend pas le Parc marin du Récif de la Grande-Barrière (cat.V).
DNK) Ne comprend pas le Groenland: deux zones protégées, d'une superficie totale de 982 500 km².
FIN) Selon la classification nationale il y a 135 zones protégées d'une superficie totale de 27 721 km².
FRA) Ne comprend pas les zones non métropolitaines.
ISL) Selon la classification nationale il y a 72 zones protégées.
NLD) Ne comprend pas les Antilles Néerlandaises.
NOR) Y compris les îles de Svalbard, Jan Mayen et Bouvet: sept zones protégées d'une superficie totale de 34 985 km².
PRT) Inclut les îles des Açores et de Madère. Selon la classification nationale il y a 66 zones protégées, d'une superficie totale de 6 446 km² (continent et îles).
ESP) Inclut les îles Baléares et Canaries.
TUR) Selon la classification nationale il y a 103 zones protégées.

Source: IUCN, OECD/UICN, OCDE

The next table shows the number of national parks (and equivalent reserves) and their total size for selected countries. It further indicates, for each country, the percentage of the total territory concerned as well as the protected area per thousand inhabitants in square kilometres.

As in the preceding table, the IUCN classification system for protected areas serves as the basis for the definition of national parks. This definition may vary significantly from country-specific classifications in which the term "national park" may be used in a much broader sense. The reader is also referred to tables in the wildlife section.

Le tableau suivant présente le nombre et la superficie des parcs nationaux (et réserves équivalentes) dans divers pays. Il indique également le pourcentage affecté par rapport à la superficie totale des pays de même que la superficie protégée pour 1 000 habitants en kilomètres carrés.

Comme pour le tableau précédent, la classification UICN des zones protégées a servi de base à la définition du terme "parc national". Cette définition peut varier de façon significative par rapport à la classification nationale des différents pays qui peut utiliser ce terme dans un sens beaucoup plus large. Le lecteur peut également consulter les tableaux de la section sur la faune et la flore.

NATIONAL PARKS (a), 1993
PARCS NATIONAUX (a), 1993

		National parks/ Parcs nationaux		Percentage of national territory/ Pourcentage du territoire national (%)	Protected area per 1 000 inhabitants/ Superficie protégée pour 1 000 habitants (ha/1 000 cap.)
		Number of sites/ Nombre de zones	Total size/ Superficie totale (km²)		
Canada	*	251	366 169	3.7	1 273.5
Mexico/Mexique	*	33	15 978	0.8	17.5
USA/Etats-Unis	*	174	219 952	2.2	85.3
Japan/Japon	*	15	12 991	3.4	10.4
Australia/Australie		415	278 492	3.6	1 577.2
N.Zealand/N.Zélande		30	42 146	15.6	1 211.1
Austria/Autriche		1	760	0.9	9.5
Belgium/Belgique		-	-	-	-
Denmark/Danemark	*	-	-	-	-
Finland/Finlande	*	22	3 940	1.2	77.8
France	*	5	2 613	0.5	4.5
Germany/Allemagne		1	131	-	0.2
Greece/Grèce		8	604	0.5	5.8
Iceland/Islande		3	1 801	1.7	687.4
Ireland/Irlande		5	368	0.5	10.3
Italy/Italie		11	4 719	1.6	8.3
Luxembourg		-	-	-	-
Netherlands/Pays-Bas	*	4	136	0.4	0.9
Norway/Norvège	*	20	23 281	7.2	539.9
Portugal		1	211	0.2	2.1
Spain/Espagne		10	1 325	0.3	3.4
Sweden/Suède		15	4 950	1.1	56.8
Switzerland/Suisse		-	-	-	-
Turkey/Turquie	*	19	3 960	0.5	6.7
UK/Royaume-Uni		-	-	-	-
Czech. Rep./ Rép. Tchèque		2	748	0.9	7.3
Slovak. Rep./ Rèp. Slovaque		5	1 997	4.1	37.6
Hungary/Hongrie		5	1 591	1.7	15.5
Poland/Pologne		15	1 483	0.5	3.9
OECD/OCDE		1 043	984 527	2.8	102.1
World/Monde		2 041	3 767 842	2.8	68.0

Notes:
a) IUCN category II: national parks and equivalent reserves.
CAN) Total size: national figures.
MEX) According to national classification there are 44 national parks (6 881 km²).
USA) Including Alaska: 27 national parks and equivalent reserves totalling 151 924 m². Excluding American Samoa and Virgin Islands.
JPN) According to national classification, there are 28 national parks (20 488 km²).
DNK) Excluding Northeast Greenland National Park (972 000 km²).
FIN) According to national classification there are 30 national parks (7 223 km²).
FRA) Excluding non metropolitan areas.
NLD) Excluding two areas (77.6 km²) in the Netherlands Antilles.
NOR) Including Svalbard and Jan Mayan islands: three national parks (9 500 km²).
TUR) According to national classification there are 27 national parks.

Notes:
a) Catégorie II de l'UICN: parcs nationaux et réserves équivalentes.
CAN) Superficie totale: chiffres nationaux.
MEX) Selon la classification nationale il y a 44 parcs nationaux (6 881 km²).
USA) Y compris l'Alaska: 27 parcs nationaux et réserves équivalentes, d'une superficie totale de 151 924 km². Exclut les Samoa et les îles Vierges américaines.
JPN) Selon la classification nationale il y a 28 parcs nationaux (20 488 km²).
DNK) Ne comprend pas le parc national du nord-est du Groenland (972 000 km²).
FIN) Selon la classification nationale il y a 30 parcs nationaux (7 223 km²).
FRA) Ne comprend pas les zones non métropolitaines.
NLD) Ne comprend pas deux zones (77.6 km²) situées dans les Antilles Néerlandaises.
NOR) Y compris les îles Svalbard et Jan Mayan: trois parcs nationaux (9 500 km²).
TUR) Selon la classification nationale, il y a 27 parcs nationaux.

Source: IUCN/UICN, OECD/OCDE

5. FOREST

5. FORÊTS

INTRODUCTION

Forests are a renewable living resource. They have the following functions:

- ▸ an economic function (e.g. forest industry, trade in forest products);

- ▸ an environmental function (e.g. regulation of the water cycle, soil protection, habitat for animals and plants, role in the carbon cycle);

- ▸ a social function (e.g. recreational and touristic value, collective heritage).

Tables presented in this section provide information concerning:

a) the state of forest resources:

- ▸ area of forest and other wooded land;

- ▸ volume of standing wood;

- ▸ forest depletion and growth;

- ▸ forest ownership;

- ▸ damage caused by forest fire;

b) economic exploitation of forest resources:

- ▸ production of roundwood and different forest industry products;

- ▸ international trade in forest industry products;

- ▸ trade in tropical wood.

Some important issues are not covered by these data; these include ecological stability of the forest environment and forest damage and its major causes (droughts, storms, insect attacks, introduction of exotic species, air pollution, acidification, etc.) The reader may want to refer to the sections on air and land.

INTRODUCTION

Les ressources forestières font partie des ressources vivantes renouvelables. Elles ont à la fois :

- ► une fonction économique (e.g. industrie du bois, commerce de produits forestiers) ;

- ► une fonction environnementale (e.g. régularisation du cycle de l'eau, protection des sols, habitat d'espèces animales et végétales, rôle dans le cycle du carbone) ;

- ► une fonction sociale (e.g. activités récréatives et touristiques, patrimoine collectif).

Les tableaux présentés dans cette section fournissent des informations sur :

a) l'état des ressources forestières :

- ► étendue des forêts et des terrains boisés ;

- ► volume de bois sur pied ;

- ► diminution et accroissement des ressources forestières ;

- ► propriété des terrains forestiers ;

- ► dommages dus aux incendies de forêt ;

b) l'exploitation économique des ressources forestières :

- ► production de bois rond et de différentes catégories de produits de l'industrie du bois ;

- ► commerce international des produits forestiers;

- ► commerce de bois tropicaux.

Plusieurs thèmes importants ne sont pas couverts par ces données. Il s'agit notamment de la stabilité écologique de l'environnement forestier, des dommages qu'il subit et des facteurs qui risquent de les provoquer (sécheresses, tempêtes, attaques d'insectes, introduction d'espèces exotiques, pollution de l'air, acidification, etc.). Le lecteur peut également consulter les sections sur l'air et sur la ressource sol.

The following table shows trends in the wooded area in selected countries. Absolute figures are in square kilometres; relative figures present wooded area per capita. The percentage of the total land area covered by forest is also provided. The definition of wooded area includes land under coniferous, non-coniferous and mixed forest as well as other wooded land according to FAO specifications.

The extent of wooded area provides important information about countries' endowment in forest resources, whether these resources are seen in an economic or an environmental perspective.

In interpreting this table it should be borne in mind that definitions may vary among countries.

Le tableau suivant montre les tendances concernant la superficie boisée dans les pays sélectionnés. Les données absolues sont exprimées en kilomètres carrés et les données relatives présentent la superficie boisée par habitant. Le pourcentage de la superficie totale couverte de forêts ou d'autres terres boisées est également donnée. La définition de la superficie boisée comprend les forêts de conifères, de feuillus et les forêts mixtes, de même que d'autres terres boisées, en accord avec les spécifications de la FAO.

L'étendue de la superficie boisée donne des informations importantes sur le patrimoine des pays en ressources forestières, que ces ressources soient considérées d'un point de vue économique ou environnemental.

Pour la bonne interprétation de ce tableau, il faut tenir compte du fait que les définitions peuvent varier d'un pays à l'autre.

WOODED AREA (a), 1980-1993
SUPERFICIE BOISÉE (a), 1980-1993

		Wooded Area (a)/ Superficie boisée (a) (km²)			km² per 1000 inhabitants/ km² pour 1000 habitants			% of land area/ % de la superficie des terres		
		1980	1985	1993	1980	1985	1993	1980	1985	1993
Canada	*	4 358 930	4 533 000	4 161 750	177.2	174.7	144.7	47.3	49.2	45.1
Mexico/Mexique		478 400	470 000	487 000	6.9	6.0	5.3	25.1	24.6	25.5
USA/Etats-Unis	*	3 000 660	2 988 900	2 981 360	13.2	12.5	11.6	31.3	31.2	31.1
Japan/Japon	*	252 790	252 550	252 120	2.2	2.1	2.0	67.1	67.1	67.0
Australia/Australie		1 458 840	1 460 000	1 491 750	99.3	92.5	84.5	19.0	19.0	19.4
N.Zealand/N.Zélande		70 920	71 800	75 400	22.6	21.9	21.7	26.6	26.9	28.2
Austria/Autriche	*	37 540	38 570	38 780	5.0	5.1	4.9	45.4	46.6	46.9
Belgium/Belgique		6 200	6 110	6 120	0.6	0.6	0.6	20.5	20.2	20.2
Denmark/Danemark	*	4 930	4 930	4 450	1.0	1.0	0.9	11.6	11.6	10.5
Finland/Finlande		233 210	232 220	232 670	48.8	47.4	45.9	76.6	76.2	76.4
France		148 630	151 270	152 400	2.8	2.7	2.6	27.1	27.5	27.7
Germany/Allemagne	*	102 750	103 380	104 330	1.3	1.3	1.3	29.3	29.6	29.9
w.Germany/All. occ.		73 180	73 600	74 100	1.2	1.2	1.1	30.1	30.1	30.4
Greece/Grèce	*	26 190	26 200	26 200	2.7	2.6	2.5	20.3	20.3	20.3
Iceland/Islande	*	1 330	1 360	1 400	5.8	5.7	5.3	1.4	1.4	1.4
Ireland/Irlande		3 470	3 750	3 960	1.0	1.1	1.1	5.0	5.4	5.7
Italy/Italie	*	63 550	64 140	67 700	1.1	1.1	1.2	21.6	21.8	23.0
Luxembourg	*	820	870	880	2.2	2.4	2.2	31.9	33.7	34.4
Netherlands/Pays-Bas		3 290	3 350	3 500	0.2	0.2	0.2	9.7	9.9	10.3
Norway/Norvège		119 200	119 200	119 200	29.2	28.7	27.6	38.9	38.9	38.9
Portugal		29 760	31 020	32 290	3.0	3.1	3.3	32.5	33.9	35.3
Spain/Espagne		155 980	156 140	161 370	4.2	4.1	4.1	31.2	31.3	32.3
Sweden/Suède	*	274 000	279 000	281 000	33.0	33.4	32.2	66.6	67.8	68.3
Switzerland/Suisse		12 000	12 520	12 520	1.9	1.9	1.8	30.3	31.7	31.7
Turkey/Turquie		201 990	201 990	201 990	4.5	4.0	3.4	26.2	26.2	26.2
UK/Royaume-Uni		21 020	22 800	24 380	0.4	0.4	0.4	8.7	9.5	10.1
Former CSFR/Ex-RFTS		45 780	45 860	46 200	3.0	3.0	3.0	36.5	36.6	36.9
Czech Rep./R.Tchèque		..	..	26 290	..	..	2.6	..	..	34.0
Slovak Rep./R.Slovaque		..	19 780	19 910	..	3.0	3.8	..	..	41.4
Hungary/Hongrie		17 480	17 520	17 640	1.6	1.7	1.7	18.9	19.0	19.1
Poland/Pologne		87 540	88 360	87 850	2.5	2.4	2.3	28.7	29.0	28.9
North America/Amérique N.	*	7 467 990	7 621 900	7 630 110	23.2	22.2	20.2	36.1	36.8	36.9
Australia/Australie-NZ		1 529 760	1 531 800	1 567 150	85.8	80.4	74.1	19.2	19.3	19.7
OECD/OCDE Europe		1 445 860	1 468 820	1 475 140	3.5	3.5	3.3	33.3	33.6	34.0
EU/UE - 15		1 111 340	1 123 750	1 140 020	3.1	3.1	3.1	35.5	35.9	36.4
OECD/OCDE	*	10 696 400	10 865 100	10 924 520	12.3	12.0	11.3	32.1	32.6	32.7
World/Monde		43 448 070	43 469 110	41 798 080	9.8	9.0	7.5	33.2	33.2	31.9

Notes:
a) Include Secretariat estimates. Data rounded to the nearest 10km².
CAN) Numerical differences between successive national inventories do not necessarily reflect real changes. 1980 and 1985 data refer to 1981 and 1986. 1993: average on the period 1987-91; include inventory figure for forest lands whose area was previously overestimated.
USA) Forest land with annual production > 20 cubic feet per acre.
JPN) 1980, 1985 and 1993 data refer to 1981, 1986 and 1991.
AUT) 1980, 1985 and 1993 data refer to 1971-80, 1981-85 and 1986-90. Exploitable forests only.
DNK) Change in definition in wooded area. Comparison should be done with caution. 1980 and 1993 data refer to 1976 and 1990.
DEU) Forest and woodland on holdings of 1 hectare and above, and on holdings of less than 1 hectare whose production market value exceeds a fixed minimum.
GRC) According to 1992 national inventory: 65 130 km².
ISL) Data refer to land outside agricultural areas.
ITA) Since 1986 some agricultural land has been reclassified as forest land. Since 1985 mediterraean maquis included in mixed forest.
LUX) Forest inventory methodology changed between 1985 and 1993.
SWE) Forest land with annual production greater than 1 m³ per hectare. 1980 and 1985 data refer to 1978-82 and 1983-1987 respectively.
TOT) Data include Secretariat estimates.

Notes :
a) Inclut des estimations du Sécretariat. Chiffres arrondis à 10 km² pres.
CAN) Les différences entre les inventaires nationaux successifs ne reflètent pas nécessairement des changements réels; elles proviennent de l'amélioration de la couverture et des procédures de l'inventaire. 1980 et 1985: données 1981 et 1986. 1993: moyenne sur la période 1987-1991; montre une surestimation des superficies boisées pour les années précédentes.
USA) Forêts de production annuelle supérieure à 20 pieds cube par acre.
JPN) Les données 1980, 1985 et 1993 sont de 1981, 1986 et 1991.
AUT) Les données 1980, 1985 et 1993 se rapportent aux périodes 1971-80, 1981-85 et 1986-90. Forêts exploitables uniquement.
DNK) Changement de définition de la superficie boisée. Les comparaisons doivent être effectuées avec précautions. 1980, 1993: données 1976 et 1990.
DEU) Les données se rapportent aux forêts et terrains boisés des exploitations d'au moins 1 hectare, et des exploitations de moins de 1 hectare dont la production a une valeur marchande qui dépasse un minimum donné.
GRC) Selon l'inventaire national 1992: 65 130 km².
ISL) Les données excluent les superficies agricoles.
ITA) Depuis 1986 certaines superficies agricoles ont été reclassées comme forêts. Depuis 1985, le maquis méditerranéen est compris dans les forêts mixtes.
LUX) Changement de méthodologie d'inventaire entre 1985 et 1993.
SWE) Superficie forestière de production annuelle supérieure à 1 m³ par hectare. Les données 1980 et 1985 se rapportent aux périodes 1978-82, et 1983-87 respectivement.
TOT) Les données comprennent des estimations du Secrétariat.

Sources: FAO, OECD, national statistical yearbooks/FAO, OCDE, annuaires statistiques nationaux

The following table provides information on trends in forest cover and the share of softwood, hardwood, man-made softwood and man-made hardwood in the total forest cover. Forest is defined as land with a forest cover, i.e. with trees whose crowns cover more than 20 per cent of the area, and not used primarily for purposes other than forestry. This excludes isolated tree groups (smaller than 0.5 ha), city parks and gardens, which do not meet the conditions of forests as described above. Softwood forests are those in which 75 per cent or more of the volume is of coniferous species classified botanically as Gymnospermae. Hardwood forests are those in which 75 per cent or more of the volume is of non-coniferous species classified botanically as Angiospermae. The term "man-made" is applicable to forest crop either artificially sown or planted.

The extent and type of forest cover are important for economic and environmental reasons.

When interpreting this table it should be borne in mind that definitions may vary among countries.

Le tableau suivant donne des informations sur les tendances concernant le couvert forestier et la proportion de résineux et de feuillus, naturels et plantés par l'homme en pourcentage du couvert forestier total. Le terme de "forêt" se rapporte aux terrains comportant un couvert forestier, c'est-à-dire dont plus de 20 pour cent de la superficie est couverte par les cimes d'arbres qui ne sont pas essentiellement utilisés à des fins autres que la sylviculture. Ceci exclut les groupes d'arbres isolés (inférieurs à 0.5 ha) et les parcs et jardins des villes qui ne répondent pas aux conditions décrites plus haut. Les forêts de résineux sont celles dont au moins 75 pour cent du volume est constitué par des conifères entrant dans la catégorie botanique des Gymnospermes. Les forêts de feuillus sont celles dont au moins 75 pour cent du volume sont constitués d'espèces non-conifères entrant dans la catégorie botanique des Angiospermes. Le qualificatif de "plantées par l'homme" s'applique aux peuplements forestiers obtenus artificiellement par semis ou plantation.

L'étendue et le type du couvert forestier jouent un rôle important pour des raisons économiques et environnementales.

Pour la bonne interprétation de ce tableau, il faut tenir compte du fait que les définitions peuvent varier d'un pays à l'autre.

FOREST COVER, 1980-1992
COUVERT FORESTIER, 1980-1992

		Forest/Forêt (km²)				Softwood/Résineux (%)				Hardwood/Feuillus (%)		
		1980	1985	1990	1992	1980	1985	1990	1992	1980	1985	1990	1992
Canada	*	1 959 660	2 180 000	..	2 279 690	64	63	..	64	13	14	..	15
Mexico/Mexique		478 000	470 000	486 950	487 000	..	..	..	..	..	..	..	..
USA/Etats-Unis	*	3 000 660	2 988 900	2 980 850	2 981 360	45	46	49	50	51	50	47	46
Japan/Japon	*	238 890	238 860	238 510	..	48	49	49	..	41	42	42	..
Australia/lie		416 500	..	446 900	421 300	..	..	6	12	88	..	94	88
N.Zealand/N.Zélande	*	70 920	71 800	73 500	75 400	..	..	..	..	45	45	..	..
Austria/Autriche	*	37 540	38 570	38 780	38 780	61	61	70	70	16	19	30	30
Belgium/Belgique	*	6 200	6 110	6 120	6 120	..	..	..	49	..	..	..	51
Denmark/Danemark	*	4 060	..	..	4 170	55	..	60	..	28	..	32	..
Finland/Finlande	*	197 380	200 650	201 980	201 480	88	75	76	79	8	5	5	5
France	*	137 100	138 600	139 860	140 060	34	29	29	30	67	61	61	61
Germany/Allemagne	*	..	..	103 220	101 490	..	..	49	44	..	..	16	13
w.Germany/All.occ.	*	73 180	73 600	73 400	..	69	69	..	..	31	31	..	..
Greece/Grèce	*	25 810	25 120	..	33 600	40	38	..	42	60	62	..	58
Iceland/Islande		..	..	250	250	..	..	..	..	..	..	..	..
Ireland/Irlande	*	3 470	3 750	3 960	3 960	82	83	86	..	6	6	4	..
Italy/Italie	*	63 550	64 140	67 600	67 720	21	21	21	21	73	72	68	68
Luxembourg	*	810	840	850	850	34	37	36	36	66	63	64	64
Netherl./Pays-Bas	*	2 940	3 000	3 050	3 070	54	53	52	52	37	37	38	38
Norway/Norvège	*	66 600	66 600	72 270	72 270	67	68	64	64	14	13	17	17
Portugal		26 270	27 550	28 670	..	53	49	43	..	47	51	57	..
Spain/Espagne		83 790	..	83 880	..	..	..	45	..	..	..	51	..
Sweden/Suède	*	244 130	248 790	..	250 980	87	86	..	86	6	6	..	7
Switzerl./Suisse	*	9 940	10 380	10 550	10 570	..	49	..	..	..	19	..	..
Turkey/Turquie	*	201 990	201 990	201 990	201 990	42	42	42	42	53	53	53	53
UK/Royaume-Uni	*	19 300	21 100	22 000	22 400	74	72	72	73	26	28	28	27
Former CSFR/Ex-RFTS	*	43 840	44 110	45 050	..	64	64	62	..	33	34	33	..
Czech Rep./R. Tchèque		..	25 780	25 830	..	..	78	78	..	..	19	21	..
Slovak Rep./R. Slovaque		..	18 330	19 700	..	..	44	44	..	..	56	54	..
Hungary/Hongrie	*	16 100	16 480	16 950	17 090	14	15	16	15	86	85	84	85
Poland/Pologne		86 220	86 540	86 940	87 180	80	80	78	78	20	20	22	22

Notes:
CAN) Data refer to 1981, 1986 and 1991.
MEX) Wooded area.
USA) Wooded area.
JPN) Forest includes also bamboo forest and treeless area after clear-cuts. Data on forest types are available only for forests under District Plans, therefore their sum is not equal to total forest land.
NZL) Wooded area.
AUT) Wooded area 1992: exploitable forests only. Softwood and hardwood include mixedwood.
BEL) Wooded area.
DNK) 1980 data refer to 1976.
FIN) Softwood and hardwood 1980: include mixed wood. Forest cover includes treeless regeneration areas (4423 km² in 1992).
FRA) 1992 data refer to 1991.
DEU) 1990, 1992 data refer to production forest only. W. Germany 1980 and 1985: wooded area.
GRC) 1980 and 1985: closed forests. 1992: new inventory.
IRL) Wooded area. 1990 data on softwood and hardwood refer to 1989.
ITA) Wooded area. Since 1986 some agricultural land has been reclassified as forest land. Since 1985 mediterranean maquis included in mixed forest.
LUX) Since 1985 softwood and harwood include mixed wood.
NLD) 1980 data refer to 1979.
NOR) Forest land with production higher than 1 m³ per hectare.
SWE) Data refer to periods 1978-82, 1983-87 and 1988-92. Forest land with production higher than 1 m³ per hectare. Data include subalpine woodland and forest and wooded areas within national parks, nature reserves and certain military areas.
CHE) Softwood and hardwood include some mixed wood.
TUR) Data refer to wooded area.
UKD) Softwood and hardwood include some mixed wood.
CSFR) Due to different sources, the sum of the two republics differs from total CSFR.
HUN) Softwood and hardwood include mixed wood and some wooded areas.

Notes :
CAN) Les données sont de 1981, 1986 et 1991.
MEX) Superficie boisée.
USA) Superficie boisée.
JPN) Y compris les forêts de bambous et les zones dépourvues d'arbres suite à des coupes à blanc. Les données concernant les types de couvert forestier sont disponibles seulement pour les forêts faisant partie du plan de district, leur somme diffère donc du total.
NZL) Superficie boisée.
AUT) Superficie boisée. Les données 1992 concernent les forêts exploitables uniquement. Les résineux et les feuillus comprennent quelques forêts mixtes.
BEL) Superficie boisée.
DNK) Les données 1980 sont de 1976.
FIN) Résineux et de feuillus 1990: incluent les forêts mixtes. Le couvert forestier inclut des zones de regénération dépourvues d'arbres (4423 km² en 1992).
FRA) Les données 1992 sont de 1991.
DEU) 1990 et 1992: forêts de production seulement. Allemagne occidentale 1980 et 1985: superficie boisée.
GRC) 1980 et 1985: forêts denses. 1992: nouvel inventaire.
IRL) Superficie boisée. Résineux et feuillus 1990: données 1989.
ITA) Superficie boisée. Depuis 1986 certaines superficies agricoles ont été reclassées comme forêts. Depuis 1985 le maquis méditerranéen est compris dans les forêts mixtes.
LUX) Depuis 1985 les forêts mixtes sont comprises dans les résineux et les feuillus.
NLD) Les données 1980 sont de 1979.
NOR) Superficie forestière de production supérieure à 1 m³ par hectare.
SWE) Les données concernent les périodes 1978-82, 1983-87 et 1988-92. Superficie forestière de production supérieure à 1 m³ par hectare. Les données portent sur la superficie boisée subalpine et les forêts et terrains boisés inclus dans les parcs nationaux, réserves naturelles, et certaines zones militaires.
CHE) Résineux et aux feuillus: comprennent quelques forêts mixtes.
TUR) Superficie boisée.
UKD) Résineux et feuillus: comprennent quelques forêts mixtes.
CSFR) La somme des deux républiques diffère du total RFTS en raison de sources différentes.
HUN) Résineux et feuillus: incluent les forêts mixtes et quelques superficies boisées.

Source: OECD/OCDE

This table presents figures on the timber volume (volume of standing wood) in forest, on roundwood production and on production of fuel wood and charcoal. Data are provided for the year given or for the nearest year available. Timber volumes are expressed in cubic metres measured. With respect to the term "forest" the definition given in the previous table is applicable. "Roundwood" refers to wood in rough and comprises all wood obtained from removals, i.e. the quantities removed from forests and from trees outside forests, including wood recovered (e.g. natural and felling losses). It also includes the estimated roundwood equivalent of charcoal, chips and wood residue.

In interpreting this table, it should be borne in mind that definitions vary among countries.

Ce tableau fournit des données sur le volume de bois sur pied en forêt, la production de bois rond et la production de bois de chauffe et de charbon de bois. Les chiffres sont donnés pour l'année indiquée ou l'année la plus proche. Les volumes de bois sont exprimés en m³. En ce qui concerne le terme de "forêt", la définition donnée pour le tableau précédent est applicable. Le terme de "bois rond" désigne le bois brut et comprend tout le bois provenant des quantités enlevées en forêt ou provenant des arbres poussant hors forêt, y compris le bois de récupération (par exemple chablis, mortalité). Il comprend en outre l'équivalent estimé en bois rond du charbon de bois, des plaquettes et des résidus de bois.

L'interprétation de ce tableau doit également tenir compte du fait que les définitions peuvent varier d'un pays à l'autre.

VOLUME OF STANDING WOOD, PRODUCTION OF ROUNDWOOD, FUELWOOD AND CHARCOAL, early 1990s
VOLUME DE BOIS SUR PIED, PRODUCTION DE BOIS ROND, DE BOIS DE CHAUFFE ET DE CHARBON DE BOIS, début des années 90

1 000 m³

	Volume of Standing Wood in Forest/ (a) Volume de bois sur pied en forêt (a)	Roundwood Production/ Production de bois rond (b)	Production of Fuelwood and Charcoal/ Production de bois de chauffe et de charbon de bois (b)
Canada	26 043 035	179 967	6 834
Mexico/Mexique	1 773 357	23 285	15 769
USA/Etats-Unis *	21 997 276	495 800	93 300
Japan/Japon *	3 137 581	32 570	361
Australia/Australie	1 419 522	20 531	2 898
N. Zealand/N. Zélande *	256 000	15 948	50
Austria/Autriche *	972 000	12 857	3 149
Belgium/Belgique *	120 000	4 240	550
Denmark/Danemark *	55 200	2 192	532
Finland/Finlande *	1 848 000	39 644	4 161
France	1 912 442	44 069	10 454
Germany/Allemagne	2 814 696	36 156	3 795
Greece/Grèce	138 107	2 779	1 519
Iceland/Islande	-	-	-
Ireland/Irlande	32 800	1 756	50
Italy/Italie	490 000	9 860	4 902
Luxembourg *	..	4 240	550
Netherlands/Pays-Bas	47 500	1 403	167
Norway/Norvège	693 000	10 134	934
Portugal	184 778	11 584	598
Spain/Espagne *	470 000	14 796	1 990
Sweden/Suède *	2 752 000	62 954	4 424
Switzerland/Suisse	365 128	4 553	845
Turkey/Turquie	813 082	15 350	9 750
UK/Royaume-Uni	250 000	6 195	255
Czech Rep./R. Tchèque	617 822	10 306	1 006
Slovak Rep./R. Slovaque	..	5 250	490
Hungary/Hongrie	298 000	4 660	2 339
Poland/Pologne *	1 495 500	18 822	2 860
N. America/Amérique N.	49 961 844	682 859	118 391
Australia/Australie - NZ	1 675 522	36 479	2 942
OECD/OCDE Europe	13 958 733	280 522	48 075
EU/UE - 15	12 087 523	250 485	36 546
OECD/OCDE	68 585 504	1 048 623	167 287
World/Monde	..	3 404 413	1 875 856

Notes:
a)   1992 or latest year available.
b)   1993. Includes FAO estimates.
USA) Standing wood: under bark. Productive unreserved forest land only.
JPN) Standing wood: bamboo stand excluded.
NZL) Standing wood: natural forests excluded.
AUT) Standing wood: data refer to 1990.
BEL) Production: Belgium and Luxembourg.
DNK) Standing wood: data refer to 1990.
LUX) Production: Belgium and Luxembourg.
FIN) Standing wood: data refer to forest and wooded land.
ESP) Production of fuelwood and charcoal: fuelwood only.
SWE) Standing wood: data refer to 1988-92.
POL) Standing wood: data include estimates.

Source: FAO, OECD/FAO, OCDE

NOTES :
a)   1993 ou année la plus récente.
b)   1993. Comprend des estimations de la FAO.
USA) Bois sur pied: sans écorce. Forêts de production non protégées uniquement.
JPN) Bois sur pied: bois de bambou exclu.
NZL) Bois sur pied: Ne concerne pas les forêts naturelles.
AUT) Bois sur pied: les données 1990.
BEL) Production : Belgique et Luxembourg.
DNK) Bois sur pied: les données 1990.
LUX) Production : Belgique et Luxembourg.
FIN) Production : les données se rapportent aux forêts et aux superficies boisées.
ESP) Bois de chauffe et de charbon de bois : bois de chauffe uniquement.
SWE) Bois sur pied: les données se rapportent à la période 1988-92.
POL) Bois sur pied: les données incluent des estimations.

The next table gives accounts of forest depletion and growth volumes and changes over time, and intensity of use of forest resources. Forest depletion concerns removals by harvesting or by losses caused by natural phenomena such as epidemics, fire, windfall and flooding. Forest growth is measured or estimated as gross annual growth based on ecological and meteorological conditions. Depletion and growth volumes are given as overbark values.

Forest depletion and growth describe balances or imbalances in different types of forests. The intensity of use of forest resources reflects various forest management methods and their sustainability.

When interpreting this table it should be borne in mind that definitions and estimation methods vary among countries.

Le tableau suivant rend compte de la diminution et de l'accroissement des ressources forestières en volume au cours du temps, et de l'intensité de l'exploitation forestière. La diminution concerne le déboisement dû aux récoltes ou aux pertes causées par les phénomènes naturels comme épidémies, incendies, bris de vent ou inondations. L'accroissement est mesuré ou estimé comme accroissement annuel brut basé sur les conditions écologiques et météorologiques. Les volumes de diminution et d'accroissement sont donnés en volumes avec écorce.

La diminution et l'accroissement des ressources forestières décrivent l'équilibre ou le déséquilibre dans les différents types de forêts. L'intensité de l'exploitation forestière rend compte des différents méthodes de gestion forestière et de la durabilité de ces méthodes.

Pour la bonne interprétation de ce tableau, il faut tenir compte du fait que les définitions et les méthodes d'estimation varient d'un pays à l'autre.

FOREST DEPLETION AND GROWTH, 1980-early 1990s [a]
DIMINUTION ET ACCROISSEMENT DES RESSOURCES FORESTIÈRES, 1980-début des années 90 [a]

		Annual depletion / Diminution annuelle (1 000 m³)									Annual growth/ Accroissement annuel (1000 m³)			Intensity of use/ Intensité d'exploitation Harvest/Annual growth récolte/croissance annuelle		
		Harvest/Récoltes			Natural Losses/ Pertes naturelles			Total [b]								
		1980	1985	early 1990s/ début des années 90	1980	1985	early 1990s/ début des années 90	1980	1985	early 1990s/ début des années 90	1980	1985	early 1990s/ début des années 90	1980	1985	early 1990s/ début des années 90
Canada	*	156000	169000	162000	..	..	..	..	..	..	228000	203000	253000	0.68	0.83	0.64
Mexico/Mexique		9048	9946	7682							38795	..	33910	0.23	..	0.23
USA/Etats Unis	*	412225	431947	456626	117233	120739	153468	529458	552686	610094	732452	737716	758996	0.56	0.59	0.60
Japan/Japon	*	42932	42067	34445	2100	1286	1126	45032	43353	35571	..	115500	106000	..	0.36	0.32
Australia/lie		..	16907	16551	..	..	..	..	..	..	..	42000	..	..	0.40	..
N.Zeal./N.Zél.	*	9911	9626	14416	..	..	..	..	..	..	..	17556	21000	..	0.55	0.69
Austria/Austriche	*	12732	11626	12249	..	..	..	..	..	..	19581	..	20400	0.65	..	0.60
Belgium/Belgique	*	..	3480	1730	..	..	239	..	..	1969	..	3380	3500	..	1.03	0.49
Denmark/Danemark	*	2139	2248	2018	..	..	..	..	..	..	2851	..	3200	0.75	..	0.63
Finland/Finlande		58503	53906	47886	1197	1294	1269	59700	55200	49155	62800	68380	76132	0.93	0.79	0.63
France	*	43300	45600	54500	..	..	..	..	..	..	64500	74700	76500	0.67	0.61	0.71
Germany/Allemagne	*	..	..	42000	..	..	..	..	..	..	..	..	61000	..	..	0.69
w.Germany/All.occ.	*	30327	31219	31819	..	616	353	..	45769	35348	..	42000	..	..	0.74	..
Greece/Grèce		2825	2651	2242	..	..	305	..	..	2547	4000	4278	4117	0.71	0.62	0.54
Ireland/Irlande	*	527	953	..	7	53	..	534	1006	..	2370	2710	..	0.22	0.35	..
Italy/Italie		7712	9383	8357	200	250	250	7912	9633	8607	12080	11667	..	0.64	0.80	..
Luxembourg	*	325	326	801	..	140	80	..	466	881	..	661	660	..	0.49	0.72
Netherl./Pays-Bas		..	1500	1300	..	..	..	..	..	..	..	..	2520	..	..	0.52
Norway/Norvège		10451	11183	12649	1284	1363	1592	11735	12546	14241	18836	19890	23133	0.55	0.56	0.55
Portugal		9976	11035	13515	4790	4177	5143	14765	15212	18658	10131	11762	12131	0.98	0.94	1.11
Spain/Espagne	*	7661	9512	15439	..	..	2250	..	..	17689	16674	24000	30000	0.46	0.40	0.51
Sweden/Suède		68000	61400	62100	3000	1700	2000	71000	63100	64100	83900	95200	98500	0.81	0.64	0.63
Switzerland/Suisse		4384	4116	4483	200	200	200	4584	4316	4683	6200	6200	6000	0.71	0.66	0.75
Turkey/Turquie	*	23243	18124	16820	..	..	..	..	..	..	22135	22135	22135	1.05	0.82	0.76
UK/Royaume-Uni	*	4660	5300	7000	..	..	..	4660	5300	7000	11500	..	15000	0.41	..	0.47
Czech R./R.Tchèq.		7140	2741	3852	9379	14148	12376	16519	16889	16228	17120	17121	17047	0.42	0.16	0.23
Slovak R./R.Slov.		..	..	..	..	..	..	..	..	..	..	..	..	..	..	..
Hungary/Hongrie	*	6078	6677	5865	1465	1669	1550	7543	8346	7415	10794	11105	11002	0.56	0.60	0.53
Poland/Pologne		15100	11460	20638	3600	3600	5200	18700	15060	25838	39470	38610	45120	0.38	0.30	0.46

Notes:
a) Data refer to 1992 or to the most recent year.
b) Salvaged volumes included.
CAN) Growth: refers to Canada's definition of "allowable annual cut".
USA) Under bark volumes. Data refer to 1976 and 1986. Concerns timberland with an annual production greater than 20 cubic feet per acre (about 66% of total forest land). Growth: excludes natural forests.
JPN) Losses: damage by Pine tree nematoda. Growth: national forest. Intensity of use, early 1990s: based on data for 1992 and 1990 respectively.
NZL) Includes planted production forests only. Growth of natural forests is considered to be near zero with a growth rate equal to mortality. Harvest from natural forests i less than 3 percent on NZL harvest. Intensity of use, early 1990s: based on data for 1992 and 1990 respectively.
AUT) Growth: early 1990s data are Secretariat estimates.
BEL) Walloon region only.
DNK) 1980 data are Secretariat estimates for 1980-85. Growth: expected mean annual volume increment for 1990-2000.
FRA) Depletion: includes fuelwood and charcoal. Production forest only.
DEU) Growth and harvest: UNECE/FAO estimates for 1989.
wDEU) Data refer to all harvested and sold hard- and softwood.1985 lost volumes refer to 1983-84. Depletion 1985: include losses from the storm in November 1984 (12.3 m³). Growth and intensity of use 1980: Secretariat estimates for 1980-85. 1985 data refer to 1986.
IRL) Losses: salvaged volumes only.
LUX) Harvest early 1990s: includes volumes salvaged from the storm in winter 89/90. Intensity of use, early 1990s: based on 1989 harvest.
ESP) Growth and intensity of use 1985: Secretariat estimates for 1980-85.
SWE) Data refer to 1971-80, 1981-85 and 1986-90.
TUR) Losses: exclude salvaged volumes.
UKD) Harvest: includes salvaged volumes.
HUN) Harvest: includes salvaged volumes.

Notes :
a) Les données concernent 1992 ou l'année la plus récente.
b) Les volumes récupérés sont inclus.
CAN) Croissance : définition canadienne de "quantité annuelle exploitable".
USA) Volumes sans écorce. Les données sont de 1976 et 1986. Se rapporte aux forêts de production annuelle supérieure à 20 pieds cube par acre (~66% des superficies forestières totales). Croissance : exclut les forêts naturelles.
JPN) Pertes : dommages causés aux Pins nematoda dans la forêt privée. Croissance annuelle : forêt nationale. Intensité d'exploitation, début des années 1990: fondée sur les chiffres 1992 et 1990 respectivement.
NZL) Inclut les forêts de production seulement. La croissance des forêts naturelles est considéré proche de zéro avec des taux de croissance et de mortalité égaux. Les récoltes des forêts naturelles sont inférieures à 3 pour cent du volume total récolté en NZL. Intensité d'exploitation, début des années 1990: fondée sur les chiffres 1992 et 1990 respectivement.
AUT) Croissance, début des années 90 : estimation du Secrétariat.
BEL) Région wallonne uniquement.
DNK) 1980 : estimations du Secrétariat pour 1980-85. Croissance : augmentation moyenne annuelle prévue pour la période 1990-2000.
FRA) Diminution : prend en compte le bois de chauffe et le charbon de bois. Forêts de production uniquement.
DEU) Croissance et intensité de l'exploitation : estimations CEENU/FAO pour 1989.
wDEU) Les données concernent les résineux et les feuillus récoltés et vendus. Pertes 1985 données 1983-84. Diminution 1985 comprend les pertes de la catastrophe de novembre 1984 (12.3 m³). Croissance et intensité de l'exploitation : estimations du Secrétariat pour la période 1980-85. Les données 1985 sont de 1986.
IRL) Pertes : volumes récupérés seulement.
LUX) Récoltes début des années 90 : incluent du chablis récupéré de la tempête de l'hiver 89/90. Intensité d'exploitation, début des années 1990: fondée sur les récoltes 1989.
ESP) Croissance et intensité d'exploitation 1985 : estimations du Secrétariat pour 1980-85.
SWE) Les données sont de 1971-80, 1981-85 et 1986-90.
TUR) Pertes : ne comprennent pas les volumes récuperés.
UKD) Récoltes : comprennent les volumes récuperés.
HUN) Récoltes : comprennent les volumes récuperés.

Source: OECD/OCDE

The following table provides information on the production of industrial roundwood and the amounts used in the production of some major forest industry products. Industrial roundwood means roundwood produced for use in forest industries. The term production is synonymous with the term final harvesting. For exact definitions of the categories used in this table, the reader is referred to the FAO Yearbook of Forest Products.

Timber is largely used as a raw material in forest industries that process sawn wood and sleepers, wood-based panels, wood pulp, and paper and paperboard.

Le tableau suivant donne des informations sur la production de bois rond industriel et sur les quantités employées dans la production de quelques principaux produits de l'industrie du bois. Le terme de bois rond industriel se rapporte à la production de bois rond destinée à l'industrie du bois. Le terme de production est synonyme du terme récoltes définitives. Pour les définitions exactes des catégories utilisées dans ce tableau, le lecteur peut se référer à l'annuaire FAO des produits forestiers.

Le bois est utilisé en grande partie comme matériel brut dans les industries du bois qui fabriquent des sciages et traverses, des panneaux à base de bois, de la pâte de bois et des papiers et cartons.

PRODUCTION OF INDUSTRIAL ROUNDWOOD AND FOREST INDUSTRY PRODUCTS, 1993
PRODUCTION DE BOIS ROND INDUSTRIEL ET DE PRODUITS DE L'INDUSTRIE DU BOIS, 1993

	Industrial Roundwood/ Bois rond industriel		Sawnwood & Sleepers/ Sciages et traverses		Wood based panels/ Panneaux à base de bois		Wood Pulp/ Pâte de bois		Paper & Paperboard/ Papiers et cartons	
	1000 m³	% world/ % monde	1000 m³	% world/ % monde	1000 m³	% world/ % monde	1000 tonnes	% world/ % monde	1000 tonnes	% world/ % monde
Canada	173 133	11.33	59 774	13.82	7 497	5.63	23 658	15.53	17 557	6.92
Mexico/Mexique	7 516	0.49	2 696	0.62	645	0.48	491	0.32	2 763	1.09
USA/Etats-Unis	402 500	26.33	106 167	24.55	31 568	23.73	58 310	38.28	77 250	30.46
Japan/Japon	32 209	2.11	26 260	6.07	7 863	5.91	10 590	6.95	27 764	10.95
Australia/Australie	17 633	1.15	3 185	0.74	961	0.72	996	0.65	2 012	0.79
N.Zealand/N.Zél.	15 898	1.04	2 773	0.64	862	0.65	1 373	0.90	836	0.33
Austria/Autriche	9 708	0.64	6 786	1.57	1 862	1.40	1 491	0.98	3 301	1.30
Belgium/Belgique *	3 690	0.24	1 184	0.27	2 511	1.89	310	0.20	1 147	0.45
Denmark/Danemark	1 660	0.11	583	0.13	331	0.25	109	0.07	317	0.13
Finland/Finlande	35 483	2.32	8 367	1.93	1 203	0.90	9 430	6.19	9 990	3.94
France	33 615	2.20	9 080	2.10	3 450	2.59	2 658	1.75	7 824	3.09
Germany/Allemagne	32 361	2.12	13 066	3.02	9 430	7.09	2 107	1.38	13 034	5.14
Greece/Grèce	1 260	0.08	337	0.08	363	0.27	25	0.02	750	0.30
Iceland/Islande	-	-	-	-	-	-	-	-	-	-
Ireland/Irlande	1 706	0.11	665	0.15	246	0.18	0	0.00	36	0.01
Italy/Italie	4 958	0.32	1 717	0.40	3 420	2.57	432	0.28	6 019	2.37
Luxembourg *	..	..	..	..	..	..	..	..	..	..
Netherl./Pays-Bas	1 236	0.08	371	0.09	99	0.07	119	0.08	2 855	1.13
Norway/Norvège	9 200	0.60	2 362	0.55	559	0.42	2 167	1.42	1 968	0.78
Portugal	10 986	0.72	1 494	0.35	1 000	0.75	1 518	1.00	876	0.35
Spain/Espagne	12 806	0.84	2 721	0.63	2 378	1.79	1 349	0.89	3 348	1.32
Sweden/Suède	58 530	3.83	12 738	2.95	817	0.61	10 272	6.74	8 781	3.46
Switzerland/Suisse	3 708	0.24	1 410	0.33	877	0.66	260	0.17	1 332	0.53
Turkey/Turquie	5 600	0.37	5 580	1.29	1 110	0.83	339	0.22	1 013	0.40
UK/Royaume-Uni	5 940	0.39	2 078	0.48	2 057	1.55	554	0.36	5 243	2.07
Czech Rep./R. Tchèque	9 300	0.61	2 650	0.61	745	0.56	734	0.48	624	0.25
Slovak Rep./R. Slovaque	4 760	0.31	80	0.02	..		..		..	..
Hungary/Hongrie	2 321	0.15	548	0.13	411	0.31	5	0.00	292	0.12
Poland/Pologne	15 962	1.04	4 180	0.97	1 797	1.35	780	0.51	1 171	0.46
N. America/Amérique N.	583 149	38.15	168 637	39.00	39 710	29.85	82 459	54.14	97 570	38.48
Australia/lie - NZ	33 531	2.19	5 958	1.38	1 823	1.37	2 369	1.56	2 848	1.12
OECD/OCDE-Europe	232 447	15.21	70 539	16.31	31 713	23.84	33 140	21.76	67 834	26.75
EU/UE - 15	213 939	14.00	61 187	14.15	29 167	21.92	30 374	19.94	63 521	25.05
Developed c./p. développés	1 099 278	71.92	318 885	73.75	91 700	68.92	137 033	89.97	201 737	79.55
Developing c./p. en développ¹	429 280	28.08	113 525	26.25	41 348	31.08	15 283	10.03	51 849	20.45
OECD/OCDE	881 336	57.66	271 394	62.76	81 109	60.96	128 558	84.40	196 016	77.30
World/Monde	1 528 558	100.00	432 410	100.00	133 049	100.00	152 316	100.00	253 586	100.00

Notes:
BEL) Belgium and Luxembourg.
LUX) Belgium and Luxembourg.

Notes:
BEL) Belgique et Luxembourg.
LUX) Belgique et Luxembourg.

Source: FAO

The next table shows imports and exports of forest industry products. Both absolute values and per capita figures are presented. Figures for exports represent average "free on board" (f.o.b.) values and those for imports average "cost, insurance, freight" (c.i.f.) values. This explains the difference between world exports and imports. For the definitions of imports and exports, the reader should refer to the FAO Yearbook of Forest Products.

Le tableau suivant montre les importations et exportations des produits de l'industrie du bois. Il présente les données absolues de même que les données relatives par habitant. Il s'agit de valeurs moyennes f.o.b. (franco de bord) pour les exportations et de valeurs moyennes c.a.f. (coût, assurance, fret) pour les importations. Ceci explique la différence entre les exportations et les importations mondiales. Pour les définitions des importations et exportations, le lecteur peut se référer à l'annuaire FAO des produits forestiers.

TRADE IN FOREST INDUSTRY PRODUCTS, 1993
COMMERCE DE PRODUITS DE L'INDUSTRIE DU BOIS, 1993

	Importations	Exports/ Exportation	Exp-Imp Balance	Imports/ Importations	Exports/ Exportation	Exp-Imp Balance
		Million US$ (a)			US$ per capita/$US par habitant	
Canada	2 082	19 295	17 213	72	671	599
Mexico/Mexique	1 187	276	-911	13	3	-10
USA/Etats-Unis	16 873	13 401	-3472	65	52	-13
Japan/Japon	16 767	1 684	-15083	134	14	-121
Australia/Australie	1 216	468	-748	69	27	-42
N.Zealand/N.Zél.	273	1 310	1 037	78	376	298
Austria/Autriche	1 471	2 813	1 342	184	352	168
Belgium/Belgique *	2 993	1 742	-1251	286	166	-119
Denmark/Danemark	1 108	231	-877	214	45	-169
Finland/Finlande	475	7 411	6 936	94	1 463	1 369
France	4 962	3 997	-965	86	69	-17
Germany/Allemagne	9 502	5 751	-3751	117	71	-46
Greece/Grèce	402	47	-355	39	5	-34
Iceland/Islande	54	-	-54	206	..	-206
Ireland/Irlande	487	109	-378	137	31	-106
Italy/Italie	5 545	2 008	-3537	97	35	-62
Luxembourg *	..	..	..	..	..	..
Netherl./Pays-Bas	4 250	1 921	-2329	278	126	-152
Norway/Norvège	642	1268	626	149	294	145
Portugal	528	734	206	53	74	21
Spain/Espagne	2 479	1 032	-1447	63	26	-37
Sweden/Suède	845	7 483	6 638	97	858	761
Switzerland/Suisse	1 926	1 240	-686	278	179	-99
Turkey/Turquie	834	38	-796	14	1	-13
UK/Royaume-Uni	8 192	1 932	-6260	141	33	-108
Czech Rep./R. Tchèque	168	351	183	16	34	18
Slovak Rep./R. Slovaque	32	108	76	6	20	14
Hungary/Hongrie	280	136	-144	27	13	-14
Poland/Pologne	260	388	128	7	10	3
N. America/Amérique N.	20 142	32 972	12 830	53	87	34
Australia/Australie-NZ	1 489	1 778	289	70	84	14
OECD/OCDE-Europe	46 695	39 757	-6938	106	90	-16
EU/UE - 15	43 239	37 211	-6028	117	101	-16
Developed countries/pays développés	85 325	80 232	-5093	67	63	-4
Developing countries/pays en développement	21 417	19 386	-2031	5	5	0
OECD/OCDE	85 093	76 191	-8902	88	79	-9
World/Monde	106 742	99 618	-7124	19	18	-1

Notes:
a)   At current exchange rates.
BEL) Belgium and Luxembourg.
LUX) Belgium and Luxembourg.

Source : FAO

Notes:
a)   Aux taux de change courants.
BEL) Belgique et Luxembourg.
LUX) Belgique et Luxembourg.

The following table provides a breakdown of the trade in roundwood and forest industry products by product category. Figures are expressed in US$. They present average f.o.b. values for exports and average c.i.f. values for imports. Definitions for import and export, as well as for the product categories, are based on the FAO Yearbook of Forest Products.

In comparison with the table on overall trade in forest products, this breakdown by main forest industry sector allows a more detailed analysis of the structure and importance of forest industries in OECD Member countries and world regions.

Le tableau suivant montre le détail du commerce de bois rond et des produits de l'industrie du bois par catégorie de produit. Les données sont exprimées en $EU. Elles représentent les valeurs moyennes f.o.b. pour les exportations et les valeurs moyennes c.a.f. pour les importations. Les définitions concernant les importations et les exportations de même que les catégories de produits proviennent de l'annuaire FAO des produits forestiers.

En comparaison avec le tableau sur le commerce global de produits forestiers, cette division en secteurs principaux de l'industrie du bois permet une analyse plus détaillée de la structure et de l'importance des industries du bois dans les pays de l'OCDE et les régions du monde.

TRADE IN ROUNDWOOD AND FOREST INDUSTRY PRODUCTS, 1993
COMMERCE DE BOIS ROND ET DE PRODUITS DE L'INDUSTRIE DU BOIS, 1993

1000 US$ (a)

	Industrial Roundwood/ Bois rond industriel		Sawnwood & Sleepers/ Sciages et traverses		Wood based panels/ Panneaux à base de bois		Wood pulp/ Pâte de bois		Paper & Paperboard/ Papiers et cartons	
	Imp.	Exp.	Imp.	Exp.	Imp.	Exp.	Imp.	Exp.	Imp.	Exp.
Canada	220030	260384	402325	7377804	239639	916039	138266	3602220	1075408	7115666
Mexico/Mexique	11937	20201	264519	187635	154104	13941	233186	-	520969	47286
USA/Etats-Unis	133837	3071542	5411296	2601501	1667662	926425	1991036	2398868	7643044	4306903
Japan/Japon	7282368	9190	4280576	15052	2370159	34375	1451490	2959	1303792	1621106
Australia/Australie	1046	301575	333241	15808	81154	33382	93409	475	706044	116320
N.Zealand/N.Zél.	1367	479059	23473	274101	5502	160615	6284	203679	236236	186806
Austria/Autriche	272952	70337	239083	748422	156714	374587	205820	80515	577098	1536336
Belgium/Belgique *	130770	73459	684207	100392	360987	408494	342201	29449	1463348	1128254
Denmark/Danemark	17716	17454	316182	56302	148420	40811	24766	14855	597567	100479
Finland/Finlande	209958	71482	42241	1087883	21212	443345	63102	540638	136035	5264772
France	263640	254424	600592	371717	423503	474078	822336	175715	2827184	2705137
Germany/Allemagne	220483	329126	1535302	328973	1156107	668593	1576934	101678	4949761	4296329
Greece/Grèce	7001	10468	73703	3440	46390	10769	27951	-	246305	22225
Iceland/Islande	619	-	17139	190	10118	59	33	85	26099	38
Ireland/Irlande	7538	19471	52216	22427	47523	44160	12855	361	366340	21904
Italy/Italie	511764	3701	1606238	182366	358377	325673	1046778	14394	1997357	1481215
Luxembourg *	..	..	..	..	..	..	..	..	..	..
Netherl./Pays-Bas	70065	38469	1052724	235687	636132	143139	320835	34913	2159331	1465011
Norway/Norvège	80490	34598	148817	158605	75328	48474	26294	219900	302757	805956
Portugal	96829	19255	61465	56674	49276	137285	25969	343851	293966	170869
Spain/Espagne	143238	4865	446509	43156	152874	205330	243137	158254	1488957	598862
Sweden/Suède	262039	54792	69915	1847118	141434	79803	62217	1115568	302234	4383611
Switzerland/Suisse	48055	97610	191268	36907	201618	151534	169902	39579	1305284	912775
Turkey/Turquie	269466	214	28090	8596	43791	4924	94915	163	389672	24046
UK/Royaume-Uni	83289	12328	1671902	19548	926802	92917	892738	10668	4585786	1793355
Czech Rep./R. Tchèque	6642	71883	5915	107176	22613	30942	30260	60058	102606	74488
Slovak Rep./R. Slovaque	354	21716	679	25529	6820	10446	277	..	24098	47088
Hungary/Hongrie	18363	52250	78090	41372	10344	14832	12337	1253	159622	12969
Poland/Pologne	736	38639	9025	185198	20200	55739	12951	18122	215961	77128
N. America/Amérique N.	365804	3352127	6078140	10166940	2061405	1856405	2362488	6001088	9239421	11469855
Australia/Iie - NZ	2413	780634	356714	289909	86656	193997	99693	204154	942280	303126
OECD/OCDE-Europe	2695912	1112053	8837593	5308403	4956606	3653975	5958783	2880586	24015081	26711174
EU/UE - 15	2297282	979631	8452279	5104105	4625751	3448984	5667639	2620859	21991269	24968359
Developed c./p. dével.	10148968	6543408	19560688	16735048	9485107	6105514	9744919	9661624	36043808	40887584
Developing c./p. en dével.	2717760	3506205	3302969	4217019	3591731	6867419	2302098	1349268	9387001	3294898
OECD/OCDE	10346497	5254004	19553023	15780304	9474826	5738752	9872454	9088787	35500574	40105261
World/Monde	12866728	10049613	22863648	20952064	13076838	12972933	12047017	11010892	45430809	44182482

Notes:
a)   At 1993 exchange rates.
BEL) Belgium and Luxembourg.
LUX) Belgium and Luxembourg.

Notes:
a)   Taux de change 1993.
BEL) Belgique et Luxembourg.
LUX) Belgique et Luxembourg.

Source: FAO

The following table gives information on the share of different regions in the total trade (import/export) in industrial roundwood and forest industry products. Forest industry product categories are the same as in the previous table. The table also indicates the evolution of trade over the last decade in each region.

This table gives an overall view of the world trade in forest industry products.

Le tableau suivant donne des informations sur la part que prennent les régions mondiales dans le commerce total (importations/exportations) du bois rond industriel et des produits de l'industrie du bois. Les catégories de produits de l'industrie du bois présentées ici sont les mêmes que celles du tableau précédent. Le tableau indique également l'évolution du commerce dans chaque région durant la dernière décennie.

Ce tableau donne un aperçu global du commerce mondial des produits de l'industrie du bois.

TRADE IN FOREST INDUSTRY PRODUCTS, by world region, 1980-1993
COMMERCE DE PRODUITS DE L'INDUSTRIE DU BOIS, par région du monde, 1980-1993

Forest Industry Products/ Produits de l'industrie du bois			Share of world total/part du total mondial (%)			World total/ Total mondial million US$ (a)
			OECD/ OCDE	Developed economies/ Économies développées	Developing economies/ Économies en développement	
Industrial Roundwood/ Bois rond industriel	Imports/ importations	1980	80.9	83.6	16.4	12 316
		1990	83.3	84.0	16.0	11 270
		1993	80.4	78.9	21.1	12 867
	Exports/ exportations	1980	39.6	52.5	47.5	8 679
		1990	54.6	65.8	34.2	9 429
		1993	52.3	65.1	34.9	10 050
Sawnwood and Sleepers/ Sciages et traverses	Imports/ importations	1980	83.9	86.3	13.7	13 969
		1990	83.4	84.3	15.7	20 429
		1993	85.5	85.6	14.4	22 864
	Exports/ exportations	1980	67.3	82.0	18.0	12 342
		1990	74.4	83.6	16.4	17 310
		1993	75.3	79.9	20.1	20 952
Wood based Panels/ Panneaux à base de bois	Imports/ importations	1980	77.4	80.9	19.1	5 237
		1990	74.4	76.7	23.3	11 012
		1993	72.5	72.5	27.5	13 077
	Exports/ exportations	1980	58.6	67.8	32.2	5 161
		1990	51.6	56.5	43.5	10 170
		1993	44.2	47.1	52.9	12 973
Wood Pulp/ Pâte de bois	Imports/ importations	1980	84.0	89.2	10.8	9 777
		1990	84.2	86.3	13.7	17 321
		1993	81.9	80.9	19.1	12 047
	Exports/ exportations	1980	83.8	93.1	6.9	7 838
		1990	87.1	92.2	7.8	15 794
		1993	82.5	87.7	12.3	11 011
Paper and Paperboard/ Papiers et cartons	Imports/ importations	1980	74.5	78.7	21.3	20 846
		1990	80.5	82.5	17.5	49 349
		1993	78.1	79.3	20.7	45 431
	Exports/ exportations	1980	93.1	97.1	2.9	21 613
		1990	92.4	94.7	5.3	45 886
		1993	90.8	92.5	7.5	44 182

Notes:
a)   Current exchange rates.

Notes:
a)   Taux de change courants.

Source: FAO

The following table presents the average c.i.f. value of cork and wood imports by OECD countries from tropical countries for the latest available year. Data are expressed at current prices and exchange rates and given by region of origin, per capita and in per cent of total cork and wood imports.

Harvesting of wood from tropical forests and the export of part of this harvest to OECD countries is one of many causes of tropical deforestation. It not only affects the environment of the tropical countries concerned but also plays an important role in reducing the world's genetic resources and in increasing CO_2 concentration and its potential impact on the climate.

When interpreting this information, it should be kept in mind that definitions and classifications are those of official trade statistics and that comparisons among countries need to be subject to caution.

Le tableau suivant présente la valeur moyenne c.a.f. des importations par les pays de l'OCDE de liège et de bois en provenance des pays tropicaux pour la dernière année disponible. Les données sont exprimées aux prix et taux de change courants et présentées par région d'origine, par habitant et en pourcentage des importations totales de liège et de bois.

La récolte de bois provenant des forêts tropicales et l'exportation d'une partie de ce bois vers les pays de l'OCDE est une des nombreuses raisons de la déforestation tropicale. Elle a non seulement un impact sur les pays tropicaux concernés, mais elle contribue également de façon importante à réduire les ressources génétiques mondiales et à augmenter la concentration en CO_2 et son impact potentiel sur le climat.

En interprétant ces données il faut tenir compte du fait que les définitions et les classifications sont celles utilisées par les statistiques officielles sur le commerce, et que les comparaisons entre pays doivent être faites avec prudence.

TRADE IN TROPICAL WOOD (a), OECD countries, 1992
COMMERCE DE BOIS TROPICAUX (a), pays de l'OCDE, 1992

Imports of cork and wood from tropical countries (a):/
Importations de liège et de bois en provenance des pays tropicaux (a):

	Africa/ Afrique (1000 US$)	Latin America/ Amérique Latine (1000 US$)	Far East/ Extrême Orient (1000 US$)	Oceania/ Océanie (1000 US$)	Total		
					(1000 US$)	per capita/ par habitant (US$/cap.)	% of total imports of wood and cork/ % des importations totales de liège et de bois
Canada	88	4773	10853	-	15714	0.6	2.3
USA/Etats-Unis	6690	277299	97004	25	381018	1.5	8.9
Japan/Japon	35149	6949	2251385	209880	2503363	20.1	27.3
Australia/Australie	76	1859	109453	4908	116296	6.6	30.7
N.Zealand/N.Zélande	130	9	4646	1790	6575	1.9	34.3
Austria/Autriche	3894	266	7817	13	11990	1.5	1.9
Belgium/Belgique *	23661	6645	84906	2	115214	11.0	15.1
Denmark/Danemark	1981	2157	12440	-	16578	3.2	3.3
Finland/Finlande	3880	7683	2918	-	14481	2.9	4.4
France	260109	30805	104135	10	395059	6.9	38.3
w.Germany/Allemagne occ.	117698	9949	176988	82	304717	4.7	13.4
Greece/Grèce	35463	104	540	-	36107	3.5	18.3
Iceland/Islande	21	256	209	-	486	1.9	2.3
Ireland/Irlande	23034	4279	2996	-	30309	8.5	24.3
Italy/Italie	243068	40028	151185	4	434285	7.6	16.6
Luxembourg *	..	..	..	..	..	..	..
Netherlands/Pays-Bas	50989	10950	217532	-	279471	18.4	27.2
Norway/Norvège	11863	3206	4925	-	19994	4.7	7.3
Portugal	140538	14703	2038	498	157777	16.0	58.2
Spain/Espagne	177796	35416	19225	-	232437	6.0	28.3
Sweden/Suède	1701	5119	3296	62	10178	1.2	2.6
Switzerland/Suisse	4061	87	1421	2	5571	0.8	2.2
Turkey/Turquie	32841	472	955	-	34268	0.6	22.7
UK/Royaume-Uni	30675	49379	140654	321	221029	3.8	12.2
North America/Amérique N.	6778	282072	124345	19	396732	1.4	8.0
OECD/OCDE Europe *	1163273	221504	934180	994	2319951	5.5	17.2
EU/UE - 15 *	1114487	217483	926670	992	2259632	6.4	17.7
OECD/OCDE *	1205406	512393	3407521	217597	5342917	6.3	19.1

Notes:
a)   Imports of wood and cork from countries located between the Tropic of Cancer and the Tropic of Capricorn.
BEL)   Data for Belgium include Luxembourg.
LUX)   Data for Belgium include Luxembourg.
Totals)   Includes western Germany only.

Notes :
a)   Importations de liège et de bois en provenance des pays situés entre le Tropique du Cancer et le Tropique du Capricorne.
BEL)   Les données pour la Belgique incluent le Luxembourg.
LUX)   Les données pour la Belgique incluent le Luxembourg.
Totaux)   Inclut l'Allemagne occidentale uniquement.

Source: OECD/OCDE

The following table provides information on the percentage of the forest land area owned publicly and privately within selected countries. These two main types of ownership are subdivided into:

▶ national government ownership vs. regional/local government and other public ownership;

▶ industry ownership vs. other private ownership (including farms).

Forest ownership influences the management of the forest both as an economic and as an environmental resource.

The interpretation of this table should take into account differences among countries in definitions, as mentioned in the footnotes.

Le tableau suivant fournit des renseignements sur le pourcentage des terres forestières appartenant à des propriétaires publics et privés dans des pays sélectionnés. Ces deux principaux types de propriété sont subdivisés respectivement en :

▶ propriété gouvernementale nationale, régionale, locale et autres propriétés publiques ;

▶ propriété industrielle et autres types de propriété privée (y compris les propriétés rurales).

Le type de propriété de la forêt joue un rôle important dans la gestion de la forêt, qu'elle soit considérée comme ressource économique ou environnementale.

Pour la bonne interprétation de ce tableau, il faut tenir compte des différences de définition qui existent entre certains pays ; elles sont mentionnées dans les notes en bas de page.

FOREST OWNERSHIP, early 1990s (a)
PROPRIÉTÉ FORESTIÈRE, début des années 1990 (a)

% of area covered/% de superficie couverte

		Public/Publique			Private/Privé		
		National/ Nationale	Other/ Autres	Total	Forestry Industry/ Industries forestières	Other/ Autres	Total
Canada	*	27	67	94	5	1	6
Mexico/Mexique		5	80	85	..	..	15
USA/Etats Unis	*	34	9	43	10	48	57
Japan/Japon		31	11	42	-	..	58
Australia/Australie		72	-	72	..	..	28
N. Zealand/N. Zélande		75	-	75	6	19	25
Austria/Autriche	*	15	3	18	..	..	82
Belgium/Belgique		12	36	48	-	..	52
Denmark/Danemark		26	5	31	-	69	69
Finland/Finlande		25	3	28	8	64	72
France		12	17	29	..	..	71
Germany/Allemagne		34	20	54	..	..	46
Greece/Grèce		65	12	77	..	..	23
Ireland/Irlande		83	1	84	..	..	16
Italy/Italie	*	7	33	40	..	..	60
Luxembourg		11	35	46	-	54	54
Netherlands/Pays Bas		31	17	48	-	52	52
Norway/Norvège		9	3	12	4	84	88
Portugal		3	6	9	8	83	91
Spain/Espagne		8	31	39	4	57	61
Sweden/Suède	*	22	9	31	22	47	69
Switzerland/Suisse		1	72	73	-	27	27
Turkey/Turquie		100	-	100	-	-	-
UK/Royaume-Uni	*	41	-	41	..	..	59
Former CSFR/Ex-RFTS		97	3	100	-	-	-
Hungary/Hongrie		68	31	99	-	-	1
Poland/Pologne		80	3	83	-	17	17

Notes:
a)   1992 or most recent year.
CAN)   Data refer to wooded areas.
USA)   "National" refers to federally owned public lands. "Other" includes non-federal public lands (state, county, municipal).
AUT)   Data refer to 1986-90.
ITA)   "National" includes regions.
SWE)   Data refer to 1988-92.
UKD)   "Private" includes public woodlands not managed by the Forestry Commission or by the Northern Forest Service.

Source: OECD, FAO/OCDE, FAO

Notes:
a)   1992 ou l'année la plus récente.
CAN)   Les données concernent la superficie boisée.
USA)   "Nationale" se réfère à les forêts publiques fédérales. "Autres" inclut les forêts publiques non fédérales (état, comtés, municipalités).
AUT)   Les données concernent la période 1986-90.
ITA)   "Nationale" comprend les régions.
SWE)   Les données concernent la période 1988-92.
UKD)   "Privé" comprend les superficies boisées publiques qui ne sont pas gérées par la "Forestry Commission" ou par le "Northern Forest Service".

The next table gives information on the area of forest and other wooded land burned by wildfires in selected countries. Wildfires are caused by arson, negligence, lightning and other causes.

Although wildfires can have an ecologically beneficial effect, generally, they are one of the worst causes of forest damage. They are especially dangerous in areas with a hot dry climate. Fire fighting can be extremely difficult, so damage may cover large areas. Furthermore, wildfires contribute to emissions of greenhouse gases.

Forest fires occur on forest land, other wooded land and brush land. Not all countries separate these three land categories in their fire statistics and therefore great caution should be used in comparing the information from different countries. Furthermore, the methods of evaluating related losses may vary among countries. Some differences in definitions are reflected in footnotes, which should be borne in mind when interpreting this table.

Le tableau suivant donne des informations sur la superficie de terres forestières et autres terres boisées brûlées par des incendies dans des pays sélectionnés. Les causes des incendies de forêt sont multiples : incendies volontaires, négligence, foudre, etc.

Même si les incendies de forêt peuvent dans certains cas avoir des effets bénéfiques du point de vue écologique, ils sont une des causes de dégâts les plus graves pour la forêt. Le danger qu'ils représentent est particulièrement important dans les zones à climat sec et chaud. En plus la lutte contre l'incendie peut être extrêmement difficile de sorte que les dégâts peuvent couvrir des superficies importantes. D'autre part, les incendies de forêt contribuent aux émissions de gaz à effet de serre.

Les incendies de forêt touchent les terres forestières, les autres terrains boisés et les terres couvertes de broussailles. Comme tous les pays ne font pas la distinction entre ces trois catégories dans leurs statistiques sur les incendies, les données des différents pays doivent être comparées avec grande prudence. De plus, les méthodes d'évaluation des pertes relatives aux incendies de forêt peuvent varier d'un pays à l'autre. Les notes en bas de page indiquent quelques différences au niveau des définitions utilisées et doivent être prises en compte pour la bonne interprétation du tableau.

BURNED AREA OF FORESTS AND OTHER WOODED LAND, 1980-1993
SUPERFICIE DE FORÊTS ET DE TERRES BOISÉES BRÛLÉES, 1980-1993

hectares

		Burned area/Superficie brûlée									
		1980	1985	1986	1987	1988	1989	1990	1991	1992	1993
Canada		4822150	757260	950123	1085629	1336070	7559570	930900	1574500	868400	..
Mexico/Mexique		110709	152224	290815	287347	518265	507471	80400	269266	44401	235020
USA/Etats-Unis	*	1254080	2125529	1291448	2017058	2994227	1320972	2207600	1298700	..	..
Japan/Japon		5307	4924	4893	4890	3176	2117	1300	2700	2300	..
Australia//Australie	*	..	..	..	..	..	..	500	1900	1400	..
Austria/Autriche	*	63	83	99	53	87	52	200	50	100	..
Belgium/Belgique	*	67	16	29	..	8	24	19	54	17	107
Denmark/Danemark		..	1	6	..	..	..	..	..	..	..
Finland/Finlande		774	238	367	153	289	516	433	227	1081	..
France	*	22176	57400	51800	11000	6701	75566	70000	10100	..	..
Germany/Allemagne	*	2160	708	759	785	748	747	947	919	3266	1492
w.Germany/All. occ.		1545	242	293	319	282	281	482	349	373	320
e.Germany/All.or.	*	615	466	466	466	466	466	466	570	2893	1172
Greece/Grèce		..	92471	21166	37271	88347	36040	33733	18239	56688	47927
Ireland/Irlande	*	1212	356	713	840	840	840	840	..	..	..
Italy/Italie		46221	75806	26694	48484	59206	44653	96157	24530	40549	104385
Luxembourg		5	4	2	2	-	-	10	4	1	..
Netherlands/Pays-Bas		153	14	15	27	26	22	40	..	..	..
Norway/Norvège	*	105	31	63	35	209	170	87	530	1370	224
Portugal	*	44260	146255	99522	76268	22435	126235	78056	121815	30171	23812
Spain/Espagne		265954	484476	264887	146662	137734	426468	202825	224706	104592	89267
Sweden/Suède		..	..	..	..	..	..	..	..	3500	..
Switzerland/Suisse	*	643	213	63	312	183	213	1102	148	52	..
Turkey/Turquie		10248	26006	11037	10746	17032	12348	13000	7590	12310	..
UK/Royaume-Uni	*	1349	1411	304	157	400	100	300	100	100	..
Former CSFR/Ex-RFTS		163	170	727	265	387	250	976	..	..	..
Hungary/Hongrie		92	770	1810	1349	1349	1349	1349	..	..	..
Poland/Pologne	*	1842	1659	3382	1454	3063	5086	5029	2100	33300	..

Notes:
USA) Data refer to affected areas, not necessarily destroyed; they include other burned land.
AUS) Data refer to pine plantations only: most eucalypts are fire adapted.
AUT) Data include other burned land.
BEL) Break in time series in 1982. From 1991: Wallonia only.
FRA) Data include subforest land (scrubland, garrigues, sandy moors).
DEU) Data include other burned land. Data from 1982 are estimates.
IRL) Data include estimates. State forests only.
NOR) Forest land with annual production greater than 1 m³ per hectare.
PRT) 1980-89 data include other burned land.
CHE) Data include other burned land and estimates. Break in time series in 1982.
UKD) Up to 1984 state forests only.
POL) Data include estimates and refer to national forests only (i.e 80% of total forest land).

Notes:
USA) Les données concernent les zones touchées, mais pas forcément détruites. Elles comprennent aussi d'autres terres brûlées.
AUS) Plantations de pin uniquement; la plupart des eucalyptus sont adaptés au feu.
AUT) Les données comprennent aussi d'autres terres brûlées.
BEL) Rupture de série en 1982. A partir de 1991, Wallonie seulement.
FRA) Inclut les forêts et les zones subforestières (maquis, garrigues, landes).
DEU) Inclut aussi d'autres terres brûlées. A partir de 1982: estimations.
IRL) Les données incluent des estimations. Forêts d'état uniquement.
NOR) Superficies forestières de production supérieure à 1 m³ par hectare.
PRT) Les données 1980-89 comprennent d'autres terres brûlées.
CHE) Inclut d'autres terres brûlées et des estimations. Rupture de série en 1982.
UKD) Jusqu'en 1984 forêts d'état uniquement.
POL) Les données incluent des estimations et se rapportent aux forêts nationales uniquement (c.à.d. 80% de la superficie des forêts).

Source: UNECE, FAO, OECD/CEENU, FAO, OCDE

6. WILDLIFE

6. FAUNE ET FLORE

INTRODUCTION

Wildlife encompasses all non-human living organisms and the ecosystems of which they are a part. As a resource for human activities, wildlife plays an essential role for material needs, in maintaining life-support systems and for the quality of life. The question of the preservation of wildlife and the importance of biodiversity have met with specific interest in international forums recently (e.g. Convention on Biological Diversity).

The tables presented in this section give information concerning:

a) the state of wildlife resources:

   ▸ mammals, birds and fish species;

   ▸ reptiles, amphibians and invertebrate species;

   ▸ vascular plants as well as of mosses, lichens, fungi and algae;

b) the uses of wildlife resources and related pressures from human activities:

   ▸ fish production;

   ▸ catches of fish and other aquatic animals and products;

c) the management of wildlife resources:

   ▸ biosphere reserves;

   ▸ major protected areas;

   ▸ wetlands of international importance.

It should be noted that a number of important topics are not covered, either because data on the state of wildlife are lacking or because a large part of scientific and administrative knowledge is based on information that cannot be quantified. The reader will, however, find other data concerning wildlife habitats in the section on land (e.g. wetlands, national parks, major protected areas) and in the section on forest. International conventions related to wildlife are presented in the section on general data.

INTRODUCTION

La faune et la flore comprennent l'ensemble des organismes vivants autres qu'humains ainsi que les écosystèmes dont ils font partie. En tant que ressource pour les activités humaines, elles jouent un rôle essentiel dans la satisfaction des besoins matériels, dans le maintien des mécanismes de la vie et de la qualité de la vie. La question de la préservation de la faune et de la flore ainsi que l'importance de la biodiversité ont rencontré une attention particulière dans les récents forums internationaux (p. ex. la convention sur la Biodiversité).

Les tableaux présentés dans cette section fournissent des informations relatives à :

a) l'état des ressources de la faune et de la flore :

- ▸ l'état des espèces de mammifères, d'oiseaux et de poissons ;

- ▸ l'état des espèces de reptiles, d'amphibiens et d'invertébrés ;

- ▸ l'état des plantes vasculaires, ainsi que des mousses, lichens et autres champignons et algues ;

b) l'utilisation des ressources de la faune et de la flore et les pressions liées aux activités humaines :

- ▸ la production de poisson ;

- ▸ les captures de poissons et d'autres animaux et produits aquatiques ;

c) la gestion des ressources de la faune et de la flore :

- ▸ les réserves de la biosphère ;

- ▸ les principales zones protégées par type ;

- ▸ les zones humides d'importance internationale.

On doit noter qu'un certain nombre de thèmes importants ne sont pas couverts par ces données, soit parce que les données sur l'état de la faune et de la flore sont inexistantes, soit parce qu'une part importante de la connaissance scientifique et administrative est composée d'informations qui ne peuvent pas être quantifiées. Le lecteur trouvera cependant des données concernant les habitats de la faune et de la flore dans les sections sur la ressource sol (p. ex. zones humides, parcs nationaux, principales zones protégées) et sur la forêt. Les conventions internationales concernant la faune et la flore sont présentées dans la section sur les données générales.

The following tables show numbers of known species, threatened species and species with decreasing population, with the aim of indicating the state of:

- ▸ mammals, birds and fish;

- ▸ reptiles, amphibians and invertebrates;

- ▸ vascular plants, mosses, lichens, fungi and algae.

The "threatened" category refers to the number of species considered "endangered" and "vulnerable". Species considered "endangered" are species in danger of extinction and whose survival is unlikely if the causal factors continue operating. Species considered "vulnerable" are species believed likely to move into the "endangered" category in the near future if the causal factors continue operating. The "decreasing" category refers to the number of species for which the population size has been found to be decreasing.

Over the past two decades, a body of scientific information has been developed in response to the recognition of the importance of species diversity by international, national and non-governmental organisations.

When interpreting these tables, it should be borne in mind that:

- ▸ the number of species known does not always accurately reflect the number of species in existence;

- ▸ the definitions are applied with varying degrees of rigour in Member countries, although international organisations such as the IUCN and the OECD are promoting standardisation;

- ▸ more generally, accurate, comprehensive and comparable time-series data on wildlife populations still need to be fully developed to pinpoint all species in danger of global extinction, and to determine precisely which human activities exert the greatest pressure on species populations.

Les tableaux suivants fournissent le nombre d'espèces connues, le nombre d'espèces menacées, et le nombre d'espèces dont la population décroît, afin de décrire :

- ► l'état des mammifères, des oiseaux et des poissons ;

- ► l'état des reptiles, des amphibiens et des invertébrés ;

- ► l'état des plantes vasculaires, des mousses, des lichens, champignons et algues.

La catégorie "menacée" est la somme du nombre d'espèces considérées comme "en danger" et "vulnérables". Sont considérées comme "en danger", les espèces menacées d'extinction et dont la survie est improbable si les causes de cette menace persistent. Sont considérées comme "vulnérables", les espèces dont on pense qu'elles risquent d'appartenir bientôt à la catégorie "en danger" si les cause des menaces qui pèsent sur elles persistent. La catégorie "décroissant" fait référence au nombre d'espèces pour lesquelles on a observé une diminution de la taille de leur population.

Ces vingt dernières années, un ensemble d'informations scientifiques ont été développées en réponse à la reconnaissance de l'importance de la diversité des espèces par les organisations internationales, nationales et non-gouvernementales.

Lors de l'interprétation de ces tableaux, on doit se rappeler que :

- ► le nombre des espèces connues ne représente pas toujours avec précision le nombre des espèces existantes ;

- ► les définitions sont appliquées avec des degrés variables de rigueur dans les pays Membres, bien que des organismes internationaux tels que l'UICN et l'OCDE s'efforcent de promouvoir une meilleure standardisation ;

- ► plus généralement, des séries temporelles précises, d'ensemble et comparables sur les populations de la faune et de la flore sont encore largement à développer afin d'indiquer clairement toutes les espèces en danger d'extinction globale, et de déterminer précisément celles des activités humaines qui exercent les plus fortes pressions sur les populations de ces espèces.

STATE OF MAMMALS, BIRDS AND FISH, early 1990s
L'ÉTAT DES MAMMIFERES, DES OISEAUX ET DES POISSONS, début des années 90

		Mammals/Mammifères				Birds/Oiseaux				Fish/Poissons			
	Species known/ Espèces connues	threatened/ menacées (a)		decreasing/ décroissantes		Species known/ Espèces connues	threatened/ menacées (a)		decreasing/ décroissantes		Species known/ Espèces connues	threatened/ menacées (a)		decreasing/ décroissantes	
		Number/ Nombre	%	Number/ Nombre	%		Number/ Nombre	%	Number/ Nombre	%		Number/ Nombre	%	Number/ Nombre	%
Canada	* 193	15	7.8	..	..	514	23	4.5	..	..	1066	47	4.4	11	1.0
Mexico/Mexique	* 449	143	31.8	9	0.8	1150	339	29.5	10	0.9	4000	140	3.5	11	0.3
USA/Etats-Unis	* 466	49	10.5	..	..	1090	79	7.2	..	..	2640	64	2.4	..	..
Japan/Japon	* 188	14	7.4	C	C	665	54	8.1	C	C	200	..	..	..	..
Australia/Australie	348	48	13.8	..	..	850	50	5.9	..	..	3600	13	0.4	..	..
New Zealand/N. Zélande	* 5	5	100.0	..	..	149	44	29.5	..	..	27	10	37.0	..	..
Austria/Autriche	* 88	33	37.5	19	21.6	228	64	28.1	30	13.2	73	31	42.5	D	D
Belgium/Belgique	* 65	14	21.5	14	21.5	169	49	29.0	52	30.8	182	B	B	B	B
Denmark/Danemark	* 50	12	24.0	2	4.0	170	22	12.9	16	9.4	33	6	18.2	..	
Finland/Finlande	59	7	11.9	3	5.1	234	16	6.8	12	5.1	60	7	11.7	2	3.3
France	* 113	24	21.2	15	13.3	354	52	14.7	51	14.4	426	27	6.3	31	7.3
Germany	* 100	51	51.0	D	D	273	120	44.0	D	D	70	49	70.0	D	D
Greece/Grèce	* 116	43	37.1	18	4.4	407	48	11.8	52	12.8	111	41	36.9	9	8.1
Iceland/Islande	* 4	-	-	-	-	75	10	13.3	6	8.0	5	-	-	..	..
Ireland/Irlande	31	5	16.1	1	3.2	146	36	24.7	..	..	..	..	..	..	..
Italy/Italie	* 118	38	32.2	..	..	473	146	30.9	..	..	85	..	..	..	..
Luxembourg	* 62	33	53.2	..	..	280	54	19.3	..	..	34	13	38.2	..	..
Netherlands/Pays-Bas	* 67	30	44.8	20	30.0	172	56	32.6	41	23.8	46	20	43.5	..	..
Norway/Norvège	* 50	4	8.0	-	-	222	23	10.4	11	5.0	191	-	-	-	-
Portugal	* 99	17	17.2	17	17.2	312	109	34.9	..	..	43	8	18.6	12	27.9
Spain/Espagne	* 119	20	16.8	..	..	327	38	11.6	..	..	68	16	23.5	..	..
Sweden/Suède	66	12	18.2	12	18.2	244	19	7.8	62	25.4	140	6	4.3	35	25.0
Switzerland/Suisse	* 83	22	26.5	B	B	204	83	40.7	40	19.6	65	12	18.5	B	B
Turkey/Turquie	128	13	10.2	4	3.1	449	39	8.7	5	1.1	439	17	3.9	..	..
UK/Royaume-Uni	* 42	19	45.2	..	..	520	117	22.5	..	..	41	5	12.2	..	..
Czech Rep./R. Tchèque	87	26	29.9	..	..	220	62	28.2	..	..	65	4	6.2	..	..
Slovak Rep./R. Slovaque	43	28	65.1	21	48.8	235	68	28.9	63	26.8	61	15	24.6	12	19.7
Hungary/Hongrie	* 83	58	69.9	..	..	361	340	94.2	..	..	81	28	34.6	29	35.8
Poland/Pologne	93	6	6.5	14	15.1	360	27	7.5	50	13.9	117	3	2.6	..	..

Notes: see next page/voir page suivante.

Source: OECD/OCDE

Notes: (6.1A)
Capital letters in the table refer to estimates of the number of species in each category: A = few species; B = some species; C = several species; D = a large part of species; E = a major part of species.
a) "Threatened" refers to the sum of the number of species in the "endangered" and "vulnerable" categories.
CAN) Fish: marine and euryhaline fish, and 181 freshwater species.
MEX) "Threatened" refers to official Mexican standard. Decreasing mammals: extinct. Birds: resident and migratory species.
USA) Including Pacific and Caribbean Islands.
JPN) Birds: includes species that are occasionally present. Fish: marine and brackish water species.
NZL) "Threatened" refers to indigenous species only (many species have been introduced, most of them classed as noxious). Mammals: land-breeding mammals only; data refer to two species of bats and three species of pinnipeds, all of which are threatened; cetaceans are excluded (their population status is often uncertain). Fish: freshwater only.
AUT) Threatened mammals: includes extinct and/or vanished species. Birds: breeding species on national territory only. Fish: freshwater only.
BEL) Threatened and decreasing fish species numbers are estimates.
DNK) Fish: freshwater only. Decreasing includes only taxa that have declined by at least 50 per cent since the 1960s.
FRA) Fish: marine and freshwater species.
DEU) Data include exctinct species; fish: freshwater only.
GRC) Fish: freshwater only; no marine species are threatened. Data refer to 1993.
ISL) Birds: breeding species only. About 335 species have been recorded one or more times on national territory. Fish: freshwater only.
ITA) Fish: freshwater only.
LUX) Fish: freshwater only.
NLD) Birds: breeding species only; threatened species include two extinct species. Fish: freshwater only.
NOR) Mammals: terrestrial species only; the status of the 26 known species of marine mammals is uncertain. Birds: breeding species on national territory.
PRT) Fish: freshwater only.
ESP) Fish: freshwater only.
CHE) The number of species refers to all species ever observed, even if now extinct; includes introduced and migratory species. Birds: all breeding species on national territory. Fish: all Pisces and the Cyclostomata species; includes seven extinct species.
UKD) Data refer to Great Britain only. Mammals: terrestrial and marine native species; "threatened" refers to national standard. Birds: "species known" refers to the total recorded; these include 219 species regularly breeding on national territory and 54 common passage migrants and winter visitors. Fish: freshwater fish, including that leave the sea to breed in fresh water (e.g. salmon).
HUN) "Threatened" refers to protected and highly protected species.

Source: OECD/OCDE

Notes : (6.1A)
Les lettres placées dans le tableau font référence à des estimations du nombre d'espèces dans chaque catégorie : A = peu d'espèces ; B = quelques espèces ; C = plusieurs espèces ; D = une part importante des espèces ; E = la plupart des espèces.
a) La catégorie "menacée" fait référence à la somme du nombre d'espèces des "catégories en danger" et "vulnérables".
CAN) Poissons: espèces marines et euryhalines, et 181 espèces d'eau douce.
MEX) Espèces menacées: selon la norme officielle Mexicaine. Espèces décroissantes de mammifères: espèces disparues. Oiseaux: espèces résidentes et migratoires.
USA) Y compris les îles du Pacifique et des Caraïbes.
JPN) Oiseaux: incluent les espèces présentes occasionnellement. Poissons: espèces marines et d'eau saumâtre.
NZL) Espèces menacées: espèces indigènes seulement (un grand nombre d'espèces ont été introduites, la plupart étant classées comme nocives). Mammifères: espèces terrestres seulement ; il s'agit de deux espèces de chauve-souris et de trois espèces de palmipèdes qui sont toutes menacées; les cétacés sont exclus (l'état de leurs populations est souvent incertain). Poissons: esp. d'eau douce seulement.
AUT) Mammifères menacés: comprennent les espèces déjà disparues. Oiseaux: espèces nichant sur le territoire national seulement. Poissons: esp. d'eau douce seulement.
BEL) Poissons menacés et décroissants: estimations.
DNK) Poissons: esp. d'eau douce seulement. "Décroissantes" ne concernent que les taxa qui ont diminué d'au moins 50 pour cent depuis les années 60.
FRA) Poissons: espèces marines et d'eau douce.
DEU) Y compris les espèces disparues. Poissons: esp. d'eau douce seulement.
GRC) Poissons: esp. d'eau douce seulement ; il n'existe pas d'espèces marines menacées en Grèce. Données 1993.
ISL) Oiseaux: espèces nichant sur le territoire national seulement. Environ 335 espèces ont été enregistrées une ou plusieurs fois sur le territoire national. Poissons: esp. d'eau douce seulement.
ITA) Poissons: esp. d'eau douce seulement.
LUX) Poissons: esp. d'eau douce seulement.
NLD) Oiseaux: espèces nichant sur le territoire national seulement ; espèces menacées: incluent 2 espèces disparues. Poissons: esp. d'eau douce seulement.
NOR) Mammifères: espèces terrestres uniquement ; il y a 26 espèces connues de mammifères marins dont le statut est incertain. Oiseaux: espèces nichant sur le territoire national.
PRT) Poissons: esp. d'eau douce seulement.
ESP) Poissons: esp. d'eau douce seulement.
CHE) Nombre d'espèces: toutes les espèces observées, même si elles ont disparues, y compris celles introduites et migratoires. Oiseaux: toutes les espèces nichant sur le territoire national. Poissons: toutes les espèces de poisson et de cyclostomates; inclut sept espèces éteintes.
UKD) Grande-Bretagne uniquement. Mammifères: espèces indigènes terrestres et marines ; espèces menacées: définies selon la norme nationale. Oiseaux: nombre total enregistré, incluant 219 espèces nichant regulièrement sur le territoire national et 54 espèces courantes de migration de passage et d'hiver. Poissons: esp. d'eau douce seulement, mais incluant les espèces marines qui se reproduisent dans l'eau douce (e.g. saumon).
HUN) Espèces menacées: espèces protégées et hautement protégées.

STATE OF REPTILES, AMPHIBIANS AND INVERTEBRATES, early 1990s
L'ÉTAT DES REPTILES, DES AMPHIBIENS ET DES INVERTÉBRÉS, début des années 90

	Reptiles					Amphibians/Amphibiens					Invertebrates/Invertébrés				
	Species known/ Espèces connues	threatened/ menacées (a)		decreasing/ décroissantes		Species known/ Espèces connues	threatened/ menacées (a)		decreasing/ décroissantes		Species known/ Espèces connues	threatened/ menacées (a)		decreasing/ décroissantes	
		Number/ Nombre	%	Number/ Nombre	%		Number/ Nombre	%	Number/ Nombre	%		Number/ Nombre	%	Number/ Nombre	%
Canada *	43	30	69.8	43	100.0	42	10	23.8	42	100.0	34880	..	..	..	..
Mexico/Mexique *	717	476	66.4	1	0.1	284	199	70.1	..	..	250442	51	0.0	..	..
USA/Etats-Unis *	368	26	7.1	..	..	222	8	3.6	..	..	..	..	..	..	..
Japan/Japon *	87	3	3.4	C	C	59	6	10.2	C	C	33776	125	0.1	C	C
Australia/Australie *	700	21	3.0	..	..	180	9	5.0	..	..	92000	..	..	..	..
New Zealand/N.Zélande *	45	22	48.9	..	..	3	3	100.0	..	..	2205	24	0.1	..	..
Austria/Autriche *	14	14	100.0	11	78.6	19	18	94.7	15	78.9	6	4	66.7	3	50.0
Belgium/Belgique *	8	6	75.0	6	75.0	17	17	100.0	11	64.7	42000	..	..	C	C
Denmark/Danemark *	5	-	-	1	20.0	14	4	28.6	9	64.3	3760	498	13.2	228	6.1
Finland/Finlande	5	1	20.0	..	..	5	1	20.0	..	..	18499	148	0.8	139	0.8
France	37	6	16.2	9	24.3	31	11	35.5	9	29.0	42600	71	0.2	..	..
Germany *	13	10	76.9	E	E	19	13	68.4	E	E	..	..	..	D	D
Greece/Grèce	58	3	5.2	..	..	16	-	-	7	43.8	..	..	..	..	..
Iceland/Islande *	-	-	-	-	-	-	-	-	-	-	1245	7	0.6	..	..
Ireland/Irlande	1			-	-	3	1	33.3	-	-	..	..	..	..	..
Italy/Italie *	58	13	22.4	..	..	38	8	21.1	..	..	56500	2435	4.3	..	..
Luxembourg	7	6	85.7	6	85.7	15	13	86.7	13	86.7	30000	..	..	..	..
Netherlands/Pays-Bas	7	7	100.0	5	71.0	16	10	62.5	7	43.0	27700	..	..	..	..
Norway/Norvège *	5	1	20.0	..	..	5	2	40.0	..	..	15120	59	0.4	..	..
Portugal	34	3	8.8	-	-	18	-	-	-	-	..	..	..	..	..
Spain/Espagne	55	10	18.2	..	..	25	2	8.0	..	..	25000	391	1.6	..	..
Sweden/Suède *	7	-	-	2	28.6	13	6	46.2	5	38.5	23400	711	3.0	1,810	7.7
Switzerland/Suisse *	15	11	73.3	D	D	20	16	80.0	B	B	45400	15713	34.6	D	D
Turkey/Turquie	106	5	4.7	5	4.7	21	1	4.8	1	4.8	..	..	..	..	..
UK/Royaume-Uni *	6	2	33.3	..	..	6	2	33.3	..	..	22770	998	4.4	..	..
Czech Rep./R. Tchèque	13	8	61.5	..	..	20	13	65.0	..	..	27000	94	0.3	..	..
Slovak Rep./R. Slovaque	12	10	83.3	9	75.0	17	12	70.6	10	58.8	..	157	..	67	..
Hungary/Hongrie *	16	16	100.0	16	100.0	16	16	100.0	16	100.0	41460	>382	>0.9	9	0.0
Poland/Pologne	9	2	22.2	3	33.3	18	-	-	3	16.7	26347	..	..	..	..

Notes:
Capital letters in the table refer to estimates of the number of species in each category: A = few species; B = some species; C = several species; D = a large part of species; E = a major part of species.
a) "Threatened" refers to the sum of the number of species in the "endangered" and "vulnerable" categories.
CAN) All reptiles and amphibians are declining due to urbanisation and agriculture. Invertebrates have been greatly threatened by the introduction of the zebra mussel into the Great Lakes; mortality in the native bivalves is often 90-99%, but threatened or declining invertebrates species are still unknown.
MEX) "Threatened": official Mexican standard. Decreasing reptiles: extinct species.
USA) Including Pacific and Caribbean islands.
JPN) Invertebrates: Insecta and Crustacea freshwater species only.
AUS) Invertebrates: estimates. The number of known insects is 54 000.
NZL) Indigenous species only (many species have been introduced, most of them classed as noxious). Invertebrates: all species, including introduced ones.
AUT) Invertebrates: decapod crayfish species only. Estimated number of invertebrate species is 30 000.
BEL) Invertebrates: estimates.
DNK) Invertebrates: selected insect species only. Decreasing species: only taxa that have declined by at least 50 per cent since the 1960s.
ISL) Invertebrates: insect species only.
ITA) Invertebrates: include 39 000 species of insects.
NOR) Invertebrates: Insecta and freshwater molluscs. In addition 2 050 species of Crustacea and 700 of marine Mollusca are known.
SWE) Invertebrates include species in marine habitats not yet registered in an official Red List; estimates
CHE) Invertebrates: estimates.
UKD) Invertebrates: estimates. Great Britain only. Reptiles: non marine species only. Threatened reptiles and amphibians: national standard. Threatened invertebrates: include 232 endangered and 165 vulnerable species unpublished.
HUN) "Threatened" reptiles and amphibians: protected and highly protected species.
Source: OECD/OCDE

Notes:
Les lettres placées dans le tableau font référence à des estimations du nombre d'espèces dans chaque catégorie:
A = peu d'espèces ; B = quelques espèces ; C = plusieurs espèces ; D = une part importante d'espèces ; E = la plupart des espèces.
a) La catégorie "menacée" fait référence à la somme du nombre d'espèces des catégories "en danger" et "vulnérable".
CAN) Tous les reptiles et amphibiens sont en déclin, en partie à cause de l'urbanisation et de l'agriculture. Les invertébrés ont été grandement menacés par l'introduction de la moule zebra dans les Grands Lacs. La mortalité des bivalves indigènes est souvent de 90-99%, mais, le nombre d'espèces menacées ou en déclin reste inconnu.
MEX) "Menacées": norme officielle Mexicaine. Reptiles espèces décroissantes: esp. diparues.
USA) Y compris les îles du Pacifique et des Caraïbes.
JPN) Invertébrés: les insectes et crustacés d'eau douce uniquement.
AUS) Invertébrés: données estimées. 54 000 espèces d'insectes sont connues.
NZL) Espèces indigènes seulement (un grand nombre d'espèces ont été introduites, la plupart étant classées comme nocives). Invertébrés: toutes les espèces, incluant celles introduites.
AUT) Invertébrés: les données ne concernent que les espèces d'écrevisses décapodes. On estime qu'il y a environ 30 000 espèces d'invertébrés au total.
BEL) Invertébrés: données estimées.
DNK) Invertébrés: ne concernent qu'un nombre sélectionné d'insectes. Espèces décroissantes ne concernent que les taxa qui ont diminué d'au moins 50 pour cent depuis les années 60.
ISL) Invertébrés: ne concernent que les insectes.
ITA) Invertébrés: comprennent 39 000 espèces d'insectes.
NOR) Invertébrés: données incluent les insectes et les mollusques d'eau douce ; 2 050 espèces de crustacés et 700 espèces de mollusques marins sont connues.
SWE) Invertébrés: comprennent des esp. marines, pas encore sur une liste rouge officielle; estimations.
CHE) Invertébrés: données estimées.
UKD) Grande-Bretagne seulement. Invertébrés: données estimées. Reptiles: espèces non marines seulement. Reptiles et amphibiens menacés: norme nationale. Invertébrés meancés: incluent 232 espèces en danger et 165 espèces vulnérables, non publiées.
HUN) Reptiles et amphibiens menacés: espèces protégées et hautement protégées.

STATE OF VASCULAR PLANTS, MOSSES, LICHENS, FUNGI AND ALGAE, early 1990s
L'ÉTAT DES PLANTES VASCULAIRES, MOUSSES, LICHENS, CHAMPIGNONS ET ALGUES, début des années 90

		Vascular plants/Plantes vasculaires					Mosses/ Mousses	Lichens	Fungi/ Champignons	Algae/ Algues
		Species known/ Espèces connues	threatened/ menacées (a) Number/ Nombre	%	decreasing/ décroissantes Number/ Nombre	%	Species known/ Espèces connues	Species known/ Espèces connues	Species known/ Espèces connues	Species known/ Espèces connues
Canada	*	3,300	83	2.5	27	0.8	970	2,200	4,000	4,300
Mexico/Mexique	*	30,000	902	3	..		1,200	..	10,172	2,661
USA/Etats-Unis	*	22,200	118	0.5			..	..	..	..
apan/Japon	*	7,301	824	11.3	D	D	1,800	1,000	16,000	1,850
Australia/Australie		22,000	886	4.0	..	..	3,500	2,000	10-20000	28,000
New Zealand/N. Zélande	*	2,200	200-300	9-14			1,050	1,200	3,500	1,100
Austria/Autriche		2,900	209	7.2	701	24.2	1,000	..	..	..
Belgium/Belgique		1,415	340	24.0	459	32.4	662	..	4,200	5,000
Denmark/Danemark	*	1,200	117	9.8	..		900	900	3,000	450
Finland/Finlande		1,305	88	6.7	50	3.8	840	1,500	3,000	7-10000
France		4,762	142	3.0	261	5.5	2,000	3,000	5-10000	4,500
w.Germany/Allem.occ.	*	3,001	850	28.3	..		1,000	1,850	4,385	34
Greece/Grèce	*	6,000	114	1.9	16	0.3	..	..	..	..
Iceland/Islande	*	483	13	2.7	8	1.7	560	550	300	250
Ireland/Irlande		..	..	..	..		..	..	..	..
Italy/Italie		5,820	261	4.5	14	0.2	3,000	3,000	10,000	6,200
Luxembourg		1,200	153	12.8	366	30.5	468	1,000	1,000	600
Netherlands/Pays-Bas		1,448	110	7.6	..	..	560	633	3,395	..
Norway/Norvège	*	1,310	87	6.6	..	..	1,032	1,800	5,000	..
Portugal		3,095	255	8.2	7	0.2	625	800	2,500	..
Spain/Espagne		8,000	485	6.1	600	7.5	475	3,500	12,000	31
Sweden/Suède		2,000	210	10.5	309	15.5	1,000	2,000	3,000	4,000
Switzerland/Suisse	*	2,696	579	21.5	141	5.2	1,030	1,500	5,000	..
Turkey/Turquie		8,575	494	5.8	..	..	750	..	..	..
UK/Royaume-Uni	*	2,300	144	6.3	..	..	1,000	1,700	> 20 000	15-20 000 000
Czech Rep./R. Tchèque		2,500	507	20.3	240	9.6	..	..	..	..
Slovak Rep./R. Slovaque	*	2,500	893	35.7	893	35.7	..	..	..	..
Hungary/Hongrie		2,411	480	19.9	..	..	589	ca. 1 000	ca. 2 000	ca. 3 000 000
Poland/Pologne		2,800	196	7.0	..	..	900	1,600	4,000	>10 000

Notes:
Capital letters in the table refer to estimates of the number of species in each category: A = few species; B = some species; C = several species; D = a large part of species; E = a major part of species.
a) "Threatened" refers to the sum of the number of species in the "endangered" and "vulnerable" categories.
CAN) Data for fungi and algae are estimated.
MEX) "Threatened" refers to official Mexican standard.
USA) Including Pacific and Caribbean islands.
JPN) Mosses, lichens, fungi and algae number are rounded.
NZL) Vascular plants: indigenous species only (many of species have been introduced, most of them being classed as noxious).
DNK) Known species of vascular plants: indigeneous species only. Non-vascular plants: estimates.
DEU) Western Germany only except for vascular plants and fungi. Vascular plants: may include exctinct species.
GRC) Vascular plants, threatened: includes eight extinct species.
ISL) Decreasing vascular plants: include wetland species not yet on the Red List.
NOR) Vascular plants: native species only.
CHE) Data for lichen are estimated.
UKD) Great Britain only. Mosses: approximate figure; includes liverworts. Algae: including marine and microscopic species. Vascular plants, species known: includes 800 microspecies.
SLO) Vascular plants: trees only.

Notes:
Les lettres placées dans le tableau font référence à des estimations du nombre d'espèces dans chaque catégorie: A = peu d'espèces ; B = quelques espèces ; C = plusieurs espèces ; D = une part importante d'espèces ; E = la plupart des espèces.
a) La catégorie "menacée" fait référence à la somme du nombre d'espèces des catégories "en danger" et "vulnérable".
CAN) Champignons et algues: données estimées.
MEX) Espèces menacées: selon la norme officielle Mexicaine.
USA) Y compris les Iles du Pacifique et des Caraïbes.
JPN) Plantes non-vasculaires: chiffres arrondis.
NZL) Plantes vasculaires: espèces indigènes seulement (un grand nombre d'espèces ont été introduites, la plupart étant classées comme nocives).
DNK) Espèces connues de plantes vasculaires: espèces indigènes uniquement. Plantes non-vasculaires: données estimées.
DEU) Allemagne occidentale sauf pour les plantes vasculaires et champignons. Plantes vasculaires: peuvent inclure des espèces disparues.
GRC) Plantes vasculaires, menacées: incluent huit espèces disparues.
ISL) Espèces en déclin: comprennent certaines espèces de plantes vasculaires des zones humides pas encore sur la Liste Rouge.
NOR) Plantes vasculaires: espèces indigènes uniquement.
CHE) Lichens: données estimées.
UKD) Grande-Bretagne uniquement. Mousses: chiffre approximatif ; inclut les hépatiques trilobées. Algues: inclut les espèces marines et microscopiques. Espèces connues de plantes vasculaires: inclut 800 micro espèces.
SLO) Plantes vasculaires: arbres uniquement.

Source: OECD/OCDE

Table 2.A includes information by country on catches of fish, crustaceans, molluscs, whales, seals, other aquatic animals and products and aquatic plants. Table 2B presents trends in total fish catches.

Fish and other aquatic animals and products provide an important resource for humans and for human activities. The question of sustainable use of this natural resource has become important after several cases of overfishing.

Table 2C shows fish production in OECD countries. Fish production includes fish, crustaceans, molluscs, etc.

Although fish production accounts for only a small percentage of the economic activity in OECD countries, it remains an important source of food in all of them. Not all fish production is consumed domestically and about 30 per cent of the catch is used for animal feed. Therefore, this statistic indicates the weight concerned and the economic importance of fishing, not the value of fish as a source of nutrition.

When interpreting these tables, it should be borne in mind that the definitions employed may vary according to countries, as mentioned in the footnotes.

Le tableau 2.A présente des informations sur les captures de poissons, de crustacés, de mollusques, de baleines, de phoques, d'autres animaux et produits aquatiques, et des plantes aquatiques, par pays. Le tableau 2B présente les tendances des captures totales de poisson.

Le poisson et les autres animaux et produits aquatiques constituent une ressource importante pour l'homme et l'activité humaine. En raison de plusieurs cas de surpêche l'utilisation soutenue de cette ressource naturelle est devenue une question importante.

Le tableau 2C présente la production de poisson dans les pays de l'OCDE. La production de poisson inclut les poissons, les crustacés, les mollusques, etc.

Bien que la production de poisson représente seulement un faible pourcentage de l'activité économique des pays de l'OCDE, elle demeure une source importante de nourriture dans tous ces pays. Les ménages ne consomment pas la totalité de la production de poisson et environ 30 pour cent des prises sont utilisés pour la nourriture des animaux. C'est pourquoi ces données statistiques indiquent le poids concerné et l'importance économique de la pêche, et non la valeur des poissons comme source de nourriture.

Dans l'interprétation de ces tableaux, on se rappellera que les définitions utilisés peuvent varier selon les pays ainsi que l'indiquent les notes en bas de page.

CATCHES OF FISH AND OTHER AQUATIC ANIMALS AND PRODUCTS, 1992
CAPTURES DE POISSONS ET D'AUTRES ANIMAUX ET PRODUITS AQUATIQUES, 1992

	Fish / Poissons			Crustaceans/ Crustacés	Molluscs/ Mollusques	Whales/ Baleines (a)	Seals/ Phoques (b)	Aquatic animal products/ Produits d'animaux aquatiques (c)	Aquatic plants/ Plantes aquatiques
	Freshwater/ d'eau douce	Diadromous/ Diadromes	Marine/ Marins						
	tonnes	tonnes	tonnes	tonnes	tonnes	number	number	kg	tonnes
Canada	33568	109563	848640	123022	136225	1	56700	-	22929
Mexico/Mexique	165111	2852	896625	81315	100589	-	-	2550	61590
USA/Etats-Unis	250303	372671	3622610	506639	819416	1618	1676	48495	83773
Japan/Japon	49560	304879	6210288	184259	1557081	14728	1261	88290	788131
Australia/Australie	2000	6512	129351	46670	49367	17	-	200000	16108
N. Zealand/N. Zélande	500	4365	556226	4098	113230	22	-	-	-
Austria/Autriche	1700	2400	-	-	-	-	-	-	-
Belgium/Belgique	300	546	34379	1495	636	-	-	-	-
Denmark/Danemark	411	44190	1796939	14253	139232	119	-	-	-
Finland/Finlande	2570	24165	73588	-	-	-	42	-	-
France	8526	45991	476431	20667	247831	475	-	16500	81893
Germany/Allemagne	21669	26639	193249	11815	51396	8	-	-	-
Greece/Grèce	8983	3118	129586	4849	25154	-	-	4800	-
Iceland/Islande	-	3870	1511768	49140	12429	-	-	-	8529
Ireland/Irlande	-	11453	227720	9593	26563	-	-	-	-
Italy/Italie	10071	43377	250429	32957	219042	-	-	9500	5000
Luxembourg	-	-	-	-	-	-	-	-	-
Netherlands/Pays-Bas	744	2126	372191	10125	52818	95	-	-	-
Norway/Norvège	-	135040	2356462	50379	7249	95	14076	-	189294
Portugal	15	18247	257375	1322	33914	-	-	-	5000
Spain/Espagne	5400	2658	982047	35342	288964	-	-	4400	7700
Sweden/Suède	1874	10419	297903	3115	1384	-	-	-	-
Switzerland/Suisse	1632	2268	-	-	-	-	-	-	-
Turkey/Turquie	23381	11183	378155	3660	35691	-	-	600	-
UK/Royaume-Uni	50	53414	679902	42648	63896	-	15	1500000	6399
Former CSFR/Ex-RFTS	23146	989	-	-	-	-	-	-	-
Hungary/Hongrie	28973	461	-	2	-	-	-	-	-
Poland/Pologne	48232	6149	416525	8607	26234	-	-	-	-
N. America/Amérique N.	448982	485086	5367875	710976	1056230	1619	58376	51045	168292
Australia/Australie-NZ	2500	10877	685577	50768	162597	39	-	200000	16108
OECD/OCDE Europe	87326	441104	10018124	291360	1206199	792	14133	1535800	303815
EU/UE - 15	62313	288743	5771739	188181	1150830	697	57	1535200	105992
OECD/OCDE	588368	1241946	22281864	1237363	3982107	17178	73770	1875135	1276346
World/Monde	13071252	3001933	67196443	5395435	8885001	34425	166100	10834893	6178886

Notes
a) Blue whales, fin whales, sperm whales, pilot whales, white whales, etc.
b) Eared seals, hair seals and walruses.
c) Pearls, shells, corals and sponges.
DNK) Excludes Greenland and Faroe Islands.

Source: FAO

Notes
a) Baleines bleues, rorquals communs,cachalots, globicéphales, dauphins blancs, etc.
b) Otaries, phoques et morses.
c) Perles, coquilles, coraux et éponges.
DNK) Exclut le Groenland et les iles Feroe.

TOTAL FISH CATCHES (a), 1980-1993
CAPTURES TOTALES DE POISSON (a), 1980-1993

1 000 tonnes

	1980	1981	1982	1983	1984	1985	1986	1987	1988	1989	1990	1991	1992	1993
Canada	1347	1417	1403	1349	1284	1453	1513	1568	1612	1575	1626	1544	1276	1172
Mexico/Mexique	1223	1541	1315	1065	1108	1226	1316	1419	1373	1470	1401	1453	1248	1201
USA/Etats-Unis	3653	3793	4024	4319	4988	4948	5183	5989	5953	5775	5868	5486	5588	5939
Japan/Japon	10401	10651	10749	11255	12022	11409	11976	11858	11966	11173	10354	9301	8502	8128
Australia/Australie	132	146	166	169	169	161	180	205	213	182	220	237	234	218
N.Zealand/N.Zélande	215	236	250	282	218	214	218	247	292	334	372	417	503	470
Austria/Autriche	4	4	5	5	5	5	5	5	5	5	5	5	4	5
Belgium/Belgique	46	49	48	49	48	45	39	40	42	40	42	40	37	36
Denmark/Danemark	2028	1852	1927	1870	1851	1797	1850	1708	1974	1929	1518	1793	1996	1534
Finland/Finlande	118	110	119	130	171	172	157	156	165	155	140	127	149	152
France	788	775	756	804	787	833	874	849	889	851	864	817	817	830
Germany/Allemagne	542	575	550	543	553	427	415	399	394	412	391	303	307	316
Greece/Grèce	105	102	105	100	108	115	125	135	127	140	146	157	179	200
Iceland/Islande	1515	1442	789	839	1535	1680	1659	1633	1758	1502	1508	1050	1577	1718
Ireland/Irlande	149	190	212	203	210	231	232	251	258	202	236	262	273	305
Italy/Italie	507	515	547	552	580	591	571	565	580	551	525	561	557	552
Luxembourg	-	-	-	-	-	-	-	-	-	-	-	-	-	-
Netherlands/Pays-Bas	340	434	505	506	432	504	455	447	400	453	460	444	439	487
Norway/Norvège	2409	2552	2501	2836	2466	2119	1915	1949	1840	1908	1745	2168	2547	2562
Portugal	271	261	255	250	302	317	409	390	346	332	322	326	300	274
Spain/Espagne	1315	1356	1474	1413	1441	1483	1489	1526	1593	1560	1400	1320	1330	1290
Sweden/Suède	241	265	264	269	275	240	215	215	251	258	260	245	315	348
Switzerland/Suisse	4	4	3	4	4	5	5	5	4	4	4	5	4	3
Turkey/Turquie	427	470	503	557	567	578	583	628	674	456	385	365	454	551
UK/Royaume-Uni	835	871	903	840	836	891	851	945	937	824	771	820	827	898
former CSFR/ex-RFTS	16	17	18	20	20	20	21	21	21	22	23	22	24	-
Hungary/Hongrie	34	39	42	44	39	37	36	37	38	36	34	29	29	23
Poland/Pologne	641	630	608	735	719	683	645	671	655	565	473	457	506	423
North America/Amérique N.	6223	6751	6742	6733	7380	7627	8012	8976	8937	8819	8894	8483	8112	8312
Australia/Australie-NZ	347	382	416	451	388	375	398	452	505	515	592	654	737	689
OECD/OCDE Europe	11643	11828	11466	11769	12172	12033	11847	11844	12238	11583	10722	10807	12112	12062
EU/UE-15	7288	7360	7670	7533	7600	7651	7686	7629	7962	7711	7080	7219	7530	7228
OECD/OCDE	28614	29611	29373	30208	31961	31444	32234	33129	33646	32091	30563	29246	29463	29190
World/Monde	72127	74627	76817	77497	83851	86335	92754	94298	98890	100115	97432	97402	98785	101418

Notes:
a)   Fish catches in inland and marine waters, including freshwater fish, diadromous fish, marine fish, crustaceans, and molluscs.

Notes:
a)   Captures de poisson dans les eaux intérieures et marines, comprenant les poissons d'eau douces, les poissons diadromes, les poissons marins, les crustacés et les mollusques.

Source: FAO

FISH PRODUCTION (a), OECD countries, 1980, 1985, 1990, 1992
PRODUCTION DE POISSON (a), pays de l'OCDE, 1980, 1985, 1990, 1992

	Weight type/ Type de poids (b)				Food/Alimentation (1000 tonnes)				Industrial/Industriel (1000 tonnes)				Total quantity/ Quantité totale (1000 tonnes)				Total value/ Valeur totale (million US$/$ EU) (c)			
	1980	1985	1990	1992 (d)	1980	1985	1990	1992 (d)	1980	1985	1990	1992 (d)	1980	1985	1990	1992 (d)	1980	1985	1990	1992 (d)
Canada *	A	A	A	A	1244	1322	1423	1389	96	89	127	121	1340	1411	1551	1510	617	763	1191	1256
Mexico/Mexique	A	A	A	A	1221	1216	1374	1184	37	40	63	63	1257	1256	1447	1246	..	..	..	1516
USA/Etats-Unis	A	A	A	A	1657	1518	3202	3602	1283	1321	1063	769	2940	2839	4265	4371	2237	2326	3522	3691
Japan/Japon	C	..	A	A	..	..	1081	9606	..	..	..	..	1112	..	1081	9606	..	..	..	..
Australia/lie	A	A	A	A	..	151	179	99	..	28	19	32	133	179	198	131	344	416	667	544
N.Zeal./N.Zél. *	B	A	A	A	..	166	186	250	..	--	--	..	106	166	186	250	67	..	..	..
Austria/Autriche	..	..	..	..	..	..	..	..	..	..	..	..	..	..	..	..	..	..	..	..
Belgium/Belgique	A	A	A	A	43	45	31	26	2	..	--	0	46	..	31	26	49	70	89	80
Denmark/Danemark *	B	A	A	A	429	483	408	452	1573	1224	1044	1478	2003	1707	1453	1930	370	426	546	552
Finland/Finlande	A	A	A	A	60	60	27	46	44	58	47	32	104	118	74	78	44	48	11	..
France *	B	B	B	..	695	659	560	..	39	62	--	..	734	721	560	..	739	765	1181	..
w.Germany/All.occ.	B	B	A	A	245	173	151	209	19	9	3	3	265	182	154	212	123	126	145	157
Greece/Grèce	..	C	C	..	..	130	147	..	..	--	--	..	..	130	147	..	..	183	629	..
Iceland/Islande	C	C	C	C	736	686	699	662	765	994	667	868	1501	1680	1366	1530	245	..	669	671
Ireland/Irlande *	B	B	A	A	129	167	211	34	15	26	10	21	144	193	221	54	54	39	149	191
Italy/Italie	B	B	B	..	369	396	..	..	49	..	..	..	418	..	337	..	511	1123	1596	..
Luxembourg	..	..	..	..	..	..	..	..	..	..	..	..	..	..	..	..	..	..	..	..
Netherl./Pays-Bas	B	A	A	A	300	479	538	462	5	..	--	--	305	..	538	462	190	295	590	604
Norway/Norvège	A	A	A	A	784	869	915	947	1617	1203	761	1290	2400	2071	1479	2238	583	605	669	..
Portugal *	B	B	B	..	233	376	..	..	60	13	..	..	292	389	331	..	225	213	..	..
Spain/Espagne	B	B	B	B	1119	1459	888	1006	15	325	74	70	1134	1784	962	1076	1341	1244	2371	2435
Sweden/Suède	B	B	B	B	183	157	138	106	42	41	58	32	225	198	196	138	102	92	103	..
Switzerl./Suisse	..	..	..	..	..	..	..	..	..	..	..	..	..	..	..	..	..	..	..	..
Turkey/Turquie	C	..	..	..	..	..	..	..	..	..	..	..	430	..	..	..	..	..	..	..
UK/Royaume-Uni	B	B	B	B	661	673	544	489	99	88	66	151	760	762	610	640	431	475	698	744

Notes:
a) Fish, crustaceans, molluscs, meal, etc.
b) A= live weight
   B= landed weight
   C= not specified
c) At current price levels and exchange rates.
d) 1992 or most recent year.
CAN) 1990 data refer to 1989.
NZL) 1985 data refer to 1984.
DNK) Greenland and Faroes not included.
FRA) Including aquaculture.
IRE) 1990 data refer to 1989.
PRT) 1990 data refer to 1989.

Notes:
a) Poissons, crustacés, mollusques, farine, etc.
b) A= poids vif
   B= poids débarqué
   C= non spécifié
c) Aux niveaux de prix et taux de change courants.
d) 1992 ou l'année la plus récente.
CAN) Les données 1990 sont de 1989.
NZL) Les données 1985 sont de 1984.
DNK) Le Groenland et les Iles Feroe ne sont pas inclus.
FRA) Y compris l'aquaculture.
IRE) Les données 1990 sont de 1989.
PRT) Les données 1990 sont de 1989.

Source: OECD/OCDE

The following table contains data about numbers of biosphere reserves and their total size in selected countries. The concept of the biosphere reserve combines nature conservation with scientific research, environmental monitoring, environmental training and education, and local participation.

For further details concerning protected areas in general and national parks in particular, the reader is referred to the section on land.

Le tableau suivant contient des données sur le nombre de réserves de la biosphère et leur superficie dans des pays sélectionnés. Le concept de réserve de la biosphère comprend : la conservation de la nature, la recherche scientifique, la surveillance de l'environnement, la formation et l'éducation à l'environnement et la participation de la population locale.

Pour plus de détails sur les zones protégées en général et les parcs nationaux en particulier, le lecteur est prié de consulter la section sur le sol.

BIOSPHERE RESERVES, 1993
RÉSERVES DE LA BIOSPHÈRE, 1993

	Number of sites / Nombre de zones	Total size/ Superficie totale (km²)
Canada	6	10 500
Mexico/Mexique	6	12 885
USA/Etats-Unis	47	270 291
Japan/Japon	4	1 160
Australia/Australie	12	47 432
Austria/Autriche	4	276
Denmark/Danemark *	1	700 000
Finland	1	3 500
France	8	6 466
Germany/Allemagne	12	11 588
Greece/Grèce	2	88
Ireland/Irlande	2	88
Italy/Italie	3	38
Netherlands/Pays-Bas	1	2 600
Norway/Norvège *	1	15 550
Portugal	1	4
Spain/Espagne	11	7 163
Sweden/Suède	1	960
Switzerland/Suisse	1	169
UK/Royaume-Uni	13	443
Czech Rep./Rép. Tchèque	5	3 627
Slovak Rep./Rép. Slovaque	4	2 025
Hungary/Hongrie	5	1 289
Poland/Pologne	7	1 638
OECD/OCDE	137	1 091 201

Notes:
DNK) Data refer to Northeast Greenland National Park (700 000 km²).
NOR) Data refer to the Northeast Svalbard Nature Reserve.

Notes:
DNK) Les données se rapportent au parc national nord-est du Groenland (700 000 km²).
NOR) Les données se rapportent à la réserve naturelle nord-est de Svalbard.

Source: IUCN, OECD/UICN, OCDE

This table provides further information on the types of protected areas. The classifications used have been developed by the IUCN in an effort to standardise the nomenclature for protected areas. The complete definition of protected area types can be found in: "Categories, Objectives and Criteria for Protected Areas", IUCN, 1978.

See also the other tables on protected areas in this section as well as in the land section.

Ce tableau fournit des informations complémentaires concernant les types de zones protégées. Les classifications utilisées ont été développées par l'UICN dans un effort de standardisation de la nomenclature des zones protégées. La définition complète de ces types de zones protégées peut être trouvée dans : "Catégories, Objectifs et Critères des zones protégées", UICN, 1978.

Voir également les autres tableaux sur les zones protégées dans cette section et dans la section sur le sol.

MAJOR PROTECTED AREAS, by type (a), 1993
PRINCIPALES ZONES PROTÉGÉES, par type (a), 1993

		I. Scientific reserves/ Réserves scientifiques	II. National parks/ Parcs nationaux	III. Natural monuments/ Monuments naturels	IV. Nature reserves/ Réserves naturelles	V. Protected landscapes/ Paysages protégés	Total
Canada		100	251	2	176	111	640
Mexico/Mexique	*	6	33	3	12	11	65
USA/Etats-Unis	*	451	176	70	394	389	1480
Japan/Japon		22	15	-	30	13	80
Australia/Australie	*	80	415	71	294	32	892
N.Zealand/N.Zélande		102	30	7	66	-	205
Austria/Autriche		-	1	-	47	122	170
Belgium/Belgique		-	-	-	1	2	3
Denmark/Danemark	*	10	1	2	61	41	115
Finland/Finlande	*	15	22	-	45	-	82
France	*	7	8	-	58	37	110
Germany/Allemagne		-	1	-	88	415	504
Greece/Grèce		-	8	2	6	8	24
Iceland/Islande		1	3	5	5	8	22
Ireland/Irlande	*	-	5	-	7	-	12
Italy/Italie		-	11	1	86	74	172
Luxembourg		-	-	-	-	1	1
Netherlands/Pays-Bas	*	3	6	23	47	-	79
Norway/Norvège	*	54	20	-	8	31	113
Portugal	*	2	1	1	10	11	25
Spain/Espagne	*	-	10	-	86	119	215
Sweden/Suède		38	15	-	135	26	214
Switzerland/Suisse		1	-	-	48	60	109
Turkey/Turquie	*	4	19	-	14	7	44
UK/Royaume-Uni		1	-	-	45	100	146
Czech Rep./ Rép. Tchèque		4	2	-	4	24	34
Slovak. Rep./ Rép. Slovaque		1	5	1	15	18	40
Hungary/Hongrie		-	5	-	6	42	53
Poland/Pologne		1	15	-	21	74	111
OECD/OCDE		897	1051	187	1769	1618	5522
World/Monde		1460	2041	250	3808	2273	9832

Notes:
a)   Includes only areas greater than 10 km² except for islands.
MEX)   There are 82 national protected areas under the National System of Natural Protected Areas (SINAP).
USA)   Including Alaska, American Samoa, Minor Outlying Islands, Puerto Rico and Virgin Islands.
AUS)   Includes the Great Barrier Reef Marine Park (cat. V).
DNK)   Including Greenland (1 national park and 1 scientific reserve).
FIN)   According to national classification there are 14 scientific reserves, 23 national parks, 94 nature reserves and 4 protected landscapes.
FRA)   Including non metropolitan areas (2 scientific reserves, 3 national parks, 17 nature reserves and 5 protected landscapes).
IRE)   According to national classification there are 1 356 scientific reserves, four national parks and 66 nature reserves.
NLD)   Including the Netherlands Antilles (2 national parks).
NOR)   Including Svalbard, Jan Mayen and Bouvet islands.
PRT)   Includes Azores and Madeira Islands.
ESP)   Includes Baleares and Canary Islands.
TUR)   According to national classification there are 27 natural parks, 33 national monuments, 31 nature reserves and 12 protected landscapes.

Source: IUCN, OECD/UICN, OCDE

Notes:
a)   Zones dont la superficie est supérieure à 10 km², à l'exception des îles.
MEX)   Il y a 82 zones protégées selon le système national des sites naturels protégés.
USA)   Y compris l'Alaska, les Samoa, Les îles Mineures, Puerto Rico et les îles Vierges américaines.
AUS)   Inclut le Parc marin du Récif de la Grande-Barrière (cat.V).
DNK)   Y compris le Groenland (un parc national et une réserve scientifique).
FIN)   Selon la classification nationale, il y a 14 réserves scientifiques, 23 parcs nationaux, 94 réserves naturelles et 4 paysages protégés.
FRA)   Comprend les zones non métropolitaines. (2 réserves scientifiques, 3 parcs nationaux, 17 réserves naturelles et 5 paysages protégés).
IRE)   Selon la classification nationale, il y a 1 356 réserves scientifiques, quatre parcs nationaux et 66 réserves naturelles.
NLD)   Comprend les Antilles Néerlandaises (2 parcs nationaux).
NOR)   Y compris les îles Svalbard, Jan Mayen et Bouvet.
PRT)   Inclut les îles des Açores et de Madère.
ESP)   Inclut les îles Baléares et Canaries.
TUR)   Selon la classification nationale, il y a 27 parcs nationaux, 33 monuments naturels, 31 réserves naturelles et 12 paysages protégés.

The following table presents the number and the total area of wetlands designated by the contracting parties of the 1971 Ramsar Convention on Wetlands of International Importance Especially as Waterfowl Habitat.

The term "wetlands" in this context refers to all inland and coastal wetlands (marshes, estuaries, lakes, ponds, lagoons, etc.). Such areas are of particular importance because of their ecological richness and diversity as well as that of the wildlife they support.

For more details the reader is referred to the table on the state and changes of wetlands presented in the land section.

Le tableau suivant présente le nombre et la superficie totale des zones humides désignées par les parties contractantes de la convention de Ramsar (1971) relative aux zones humides d'importance internationale, particulièrement comme habitat de la sauvagine.

Le terme de "zones humides" se réfère ici à toute zone humide, qu'elle soit intérieure ou côtière (marais, estuaires, lacs, étangs, lagunes...). Leur intérêt réside dans la diversité et la richesse de l'écosystème qu'elles constituent et de la faune et flore qu'elles abritent.

Pour plus de détails le lecteur peut consulter le tableau sur l'état et l'évolution des zones humides présenté dans la section sur les sols.

WETLANDS OF INTERNATIONAL IMPORTANCE (a), 1993
ZONES HUMIDES D'IMPORTANCE INTERNATIONALE (a), 1993

	Number of sites/ Nombre de sites	Total area/ Superficie totale km^2
Canada	31	130202
Mexico/Mexique	1	478
USA/Etats-Unis	12	11940
Japan/Japon	9	835
Australia/Australie	40	45105
New Zealand/N. Zélande	5	381
Austria/Autriche	7	1025
Belgium/Belgique	6	79
Denmark/Danemark *	27	7345
Finland/Finlande	11	1013
France	8	4256
Germany/Allemagne	31	6729
Greece/Grèce	11	1074
Iceland/Islande	2	575
Ireland/Irlande	21	130
Italy/Italie	46	570
Netherlands/Pays-Bas *	15	3129
Norway/Norvège *	14	163
Portugal	2	306
Spain/Espagne	26	1224
Sweden/Suède	30	3828
Switzerland/Suisse	8	70
UK/Royaume-Uni	63	2749
Czech republic /Républ. Tchèque	4	181
Slovak Republic/Républ. Slovaque	7	255
Hungary/Hongrie	13	1149
Poland/Pologne	5	71
OECD/OCDE	426	223206

Notes:
a) Wetlands designated by the contracting parties of the Ramsar Convention on Wetlands of International Importance especially as a Waterfowl Habitat.
DNK) Excluding Greenland: 11 sites with a total area of 10 985 km^2.
NLD) Excluding the Netherlands Antilles: 6 sites with a total area of 20 km^2.
NOR) Including Spitzbergen.

Source: IUCN/UICN

Notes :
a) Zones humides désignées par les parties contractantes de la Convention Ramsar relative aux zones humides d'importance internationale particulièrement comme habitats de la sauvagine.
DNK) Ne comprend pas le Groenland: 11 sites d'une superficie totale de 10 985 km^2.
NLD) Ne comprend pas les Antilles Néerlandaises: 6 sites d'une superficie totale de 20 km^2.
NOR) Y compris le Spitzbergen.

7. WASTE

7. DÉCHETS

INTRODUCTION

This section of the Compendium refers to material falling under waste regulations, which for some countries can include liquid sludge. It includes information on municipal and industrial waste, as well as on nuclear waste.

The tables presented in this section give information concerning:

a) the production and composition of waste:

- ▸ waste generated by sector or by source;

- ▸ municipal waste;

- ▸ industrial and hazardous waste;

- ▸ nuclear waste (i.e. spent fuel);

b) the management of waste:

- ▸ disposal of municipal waste;

- ▸ population served by municipal waste disposal;

- ▸ recovery of selected products;

- ▸ treatment and disposal installations.

It should be noted that some important topics are not well covered, or are not covered at all, by these data: they refer mainly to industrial and hazardous waste, and particularly to their disposal, and the problems of their accumulation over time.

Data presented in these tables come mainly from OECD sources. When reading these tables, it should be borne in mind that the definitions employed by Member countries may vary considerably.

INTRODUCTION

Cette section du compendium est relative aux matières qui sont prises en compte par les réglementations concernant les déchets et qui, pour certains pays, incluent les boues liquides. Elle concerne les déchets municipaux et les déchets industriels, de même que les déchets nucléaires.

Les tableaux présentés dans cette section fournissent des informations sur :

a) la production des déchets et leur composition :

   ▸ déchets produits par secteur ou par source ;

   ▸ déchets municipaux ;

   ▸ déchets industriels et dangereux ;

   ▸ déchets nucléaires (combustible irradié) ;

b) la gestion des déchets :

   ▸ l'élimination des déchets municipaux ;

   ▸ les populations desservies par un service d'élimination des déchets municipaux ;

   ▸ la récupération de certains produits ;

   ▸ les installations de traitement et d'élimination des déchets.

On doit noter que certains thèmes importants ne sont pas ou mal couverts par les données existantes : ceci concerne principalement les déchets industriels et dangereux et en particulier leur élimination, et les problèmes d'accumulation dans le temps.

Les données présentées dans ces tableaux proviennent principalement de source OCDE. Lorsqu'il lira ces tableaux, le lecteur devra garder à l'esprit que des différences importantes existent entre les pays quant aux définitions employées.

The following tables show total amounts of waste generated by sector and by type. They include waste from manufacturing industry, energy production, agriculture and mining, as well as selected waste streams such as demolition waste, dredge spoil and sewage sludge. The disaggregation of waste by sector follows the major divisions of International Standard Industrial Classification (ISIC) revision 3.

Waste is generated at various stages of human activities, and its composition and amount largely depend on consumption patterns and on industrial and economic structures. Its impact on the environment and on quality of life is mainly related to air, water and soil contamination, but also includes space consumption, odours and esthetic prejudice.

When interpreting these tables it should be borne in mind that the definitions and surveying methods employed by Member countries for each category of waste may vary considerably.

Les tableaux suivants présentent les quantités totales de déchets produits par secteur et par type. Ils incluent les déchets de l'industrie manufacturière, les déchets liés à la production d'énergie, les déchets agricoles, les déchets miniers, ainsi que quelques flux de déchets tels que les déchets de démolition, les résidus de dragage, les boues de stations d'épuration et d'autres. La ventilation des déchets par secteur d'activité suit les grandes catégories de la Classification Internationale Type par Industrie (CITI) révision 3.

Les déchets sont produits aux divers stades de l'activité humaine et leur composition et les quantités produites varient en fonction des modes de consommation et des structures industrielles et économiques. Leur impact sur l'environnement et sur la qualité de vie est principalement lié à la contamination de l'air, de l'eau et des sols, mais comprend aussi la consommation d'espace, la production d'odeurs et le préjudice esthétique.

Lors de l'interprétation de ces tableaux, on doit garder à l'esprit que les définitions et les méthodes d'enquête employées par les pays Membres pour les différentes catégories de déchets peuvent varier de façon considérable.

AMOUNTS OF WASTE GENERATED BY SECTOR, 1985-1993
QUANTITÉS DE DÉCHETS PRODUITS PAR SECTEUR, 1985-1993

1000 tonnes

		Agriculture, etc. (ISIC/CITI 01-02)			Mining & quarrying/ Mines et carrières (ISIC/CITI 10-14)			Manufacturing industry/ Industries manufacturières (ISIC/CITI 15-37)			Energy production/ Production d'énergie (ISIC/CITI 40)		
		1985	1990	1993	1985	1990	1993	1985	1990	1993	1985	1990	1993
Canada	*	13000	14000	..	910213	1052990	..	..	..	..	12400	..	..
Mexico/Mexique		..	11498	..	..	123187	..	..	29565	..	..	..	..
USA/Etats-Unis	*	165821	..	..	1541850	..	..	760000	..	..	1093039	..	..
Japan/Japon	*	62690	77390	72495	26017	34000	34802	132324	150388	143711	27748	54983	57289
Australia/Australie	*	..	..	562	..	..	..	..	..	37043	..	..	11000
Austria/Autriche	*	..	880	..	..	21	..	..	5577	..	..	1150	..
Belgium/Belgique	*	..	..	..	..	..	..	..	27000	..	..	..	..
Denmark/Danemark	*	..	..	..	..	..	..	2304	..	1817	1532	..	1395
Finland/Finlande	*	..	23000	..	21650	..	35500	10160	..	15450	950	..	1350
France	*	399400	400000	420000	75000	75000	75000	50000	50000	50000	..	..	..
Germany/Allem.		..	..	..	..	17787	..	..	79834	..	..	29858	..
w.Germany/All.occ.	*	..	..	..	8381	13721	..	61959	66757	..	10685	12935	..
Greece/Grèce		90	90	90	3900	3900	3900	4316	4304	..	..	7680	7000
Iceland/Islande	*	..	..	..	..	..	..	..	..	40	..	..	..
Ireland/Irlande	*	22000	..	..	1930	..	..	1580	..	..	130	..	..
Italy/Italie	*	29830	..	..	..	..	..	..	39978	33270	..	..	1330
Luxembourg	*	..	..	..	..	..	..	..	1440	..	..	..	..
Netherl./Pays-Bas	*	..	19210	14500	225	391	227	6417	7760	8049	698	1553	1273
Norway/Norvège	*	18000	18000	..	9000	9000	7600	..	2000	3290	..	..	..
Portugal	*	..	..	..	202	..	..	634	..	..	..	165	..
Spain/Espagne		107472	112102	114000	..	70000	70000	10000	13800	..	..	..	..
Sweden/Suède	*	21000	21000	..	28000	28000	..	..	13000	..	550	625	..
Switzerl./Suisse	*	..	..	..	..	..	..	..	1000	1300	..	..	..
Turkey/Turquie	*	..	..	..	..	..	..	..	..	25044	..	..	12250
UK/Royaume-Uni	*	..	80000	..	..	108000	92000	..	56000	..	..	13000	..
Former CSFR/Ex-RFTS	*	1123	..	..	538975	..	..	62206	..	..	28902	..	..
Czech Rep./R.Tchèque		451	..	..	533373	..	..	39604	..	..	25774	..	..
Slovak Rep./R.Slov.		942	..	..	4276	..	..	22602	..	..	3128	..	..
Hungary/Hongrie	*	59200	53000	46000	..	..	..	41600	42000	34000	..	..	..
Poland/Pologne	*	..	..	..	110135	91111	80392	37313	32846	21378	21092	17845	17417

Notes: see page 157 / voir page 157.

Source: OECD/OCDE

AMOUNTS OF WASTE GENERATED BY SELECTED WASTE STREAMS, latest year available
QUANTITÉS DE DÉCHETS PRODUITS PAR FLUX SÉLECTIONNÉS, dernière année disponible

1000 tonnes

		Year/ année	Construction-demolition waste/ déchets de constr.-démolition	Dredge spoils/ déblais de dragage	Sewage sludge (dry weight)/ boues d'épur. (poids sec)	Scrapped motor vehicles/ carcasses de véhic. à moteur	Rubber waste/ déchets de caoutchouc	Packaging waste/ déchets d'emballage			
								Total	- paper/ papiers	- plastics/ plastiques	-glass/ verre
Canada	*	1992	11000	7450	500	1000	254	10500	3680	1620	1950
Mexico/Mexique	*	1994	..	..	..	..	223	7174	4146	1290	1738
USA/Etats-Unis	*	1986	34692	..	11454	..	..	64000	..	..	..
Japan/Japon		1991	58431	..	169693	..	192	..	..	..	..
Australia/lie	*	1992	1568.5	..	60000	270.6	103	914	..	..	..
Austria/Autriche	*	1992	19800	111	180	250	16	482	248	60	175
Belgium/Belgique	*	1992	2100	721	18	..	..	..	..	..	..
Denmark/Danemark	*	1993	2374	..	192	..	..	..	..	..	157
Finland/Finlande	*	1991	7000	3000	150	120	29	420	84	99	52
France	*	1992	25000	..	865	..	..	6900	1200	2000	2500
w.Germany/All.occ.	*	1992	121892	..	2630	..	263	8000	..	..	..
Greece/Grèce	*	1993	..	..	..	20	30	..	..	..	..
Ireland/Irlande		1984	240	..	570	..	..	..	..	..	..
Italy/Italie	*	1991	34374	..	3428	1400	..	..	..	..	..
Luxembourg	*	1992	11900	..	10	..	6	..	..	..	..
Netherl./Pays-Bas	*	1992	12390	17500	583	300	..	2708	1461	531	500
Norway/Norvège	*	1992	2000	..	100	82	34	..	..	..	..
Portugal	*	1992	..	..	8	..	..	..	0.26	0.63	0.49
Spain/Espagne		1990	22000	..	10000	..	..	..	..	..	..
Sweden/Suède	*	1990	2900	..	220	100	50	..	..	..	..
Switzerl./Suisse	*	1993	3000	..	270	210	41	920	130	500	290
UK/Royaume-Uni	*	1993	30000	30000	1024	15	..	..	..	..	..
Former CSFR/Ex-RFTS		1987	8654	23071	3791	..	..	..	..	..	..
Czech Rep./R.Tchèque		1987	2677	23071	2750	..	..	..	..	..	..
Slovak Rep./R.Slov.		1987	5977	..	1041	..	..	..	..	..	..
Hungary/Hongrie	*	1992	..	..	30000	..	100	500	..	..	..

Notes: see next page / voir page suivante.

Source: OECD/OCDE

Notes (Table 7.1A):
CAN) Agriculture: animal manure only (dry matter). Mining 1990: 1989 data.
USA) Manufacturing ind.: 1985 data refer to 1986.
JPN) 1993 data refer to 1991.
AUS) Data refer to Queensland only.
AUT) 1990 data refer to 1991. Energy: including radioactive waste.
BEL) Manufact. 1990: composite total Brussels (1986), Flanders (1987), Wallonia (1990).
DNK) Energy: 1993 data refer to 1992.
FIN) Agriculture: excluding forestry waste; mining, manufacturing and energy 1985: 1987 data; mostly dry matter. 1993: 1992 data; wet weight.
FRA) 1993 data refer to 1992.
w.DEU) 1985 data refer to 1984.
ISL) Manufacturing ind.: mostly waste from fish processing industry.
IRL) 1985 data refer to 1984.
ITA) 1990 data refer to 1989. 1993 data refer to 1991. Manufacturing ind.: including mining & quarrying waste.
LUX) Manufacturing ind.: special industrial waste, mainly liquid waste assimilated in industrial waste water.
NLD) 1985 and 1993: 1986 and 1992 data. Agriculture: manure from intensive husbandry; part dumped at sea only.
NOR) Manufacturing ind. 1990: estimates based on expert opinion. Manufact. 1993: including 320 000 tonnes hazardous waste.
PRT) Hazardous waste only. Mining, manufacturing: 1985 data refer to 1987.
SWE) Rough estimates. Agriculture: most of this waste (i.e. 17 million tonnes) is recycled. Manufacturing ind.: waste 1990 data. Sector specific waste.
CHE) Manufacturing ind.: recycled waste only; but internal recycling is excluded.
TUR) Data refer to 1992.
UKD) Agriculture: manure from housed livestock only; wet weight. Mining: china clay extraction, deep coal mines, slate quarrying and primary aggregate extraction; excludes opencast coal mining. Manufact.: broad estimate valid for any 12 month period in the late 1980s.
CFSR) 1985 data refer to 1987.
HUN) 1993: 1992 data. Manufacturing: including mining & quarrying, and energy.
POL) Break in time series: until 1990, Polish classification; for 1993, ISIC classification. Mining: excluding overlay in surface mining.

Source: OECD/OCDE

Notes (tableau 7.1A):
CAN) Agriculture : fumier seulement (matière sèche). Mines 1990 : données 1989.
USA) Ind. manufact. 1985 : données 1986.
JPN) 1993 : données 1991.
AUS) Données relatives au Queensland uniquement.
AUT) 1990 : données 1991. Énergie : inclut les déchets radioactifs.
BEL) Ind. manuf. 1990 : total composé - Bruxelles (1986), Flandres (1987), Wallonie (1990).
DNK) Énergie 1993 : données 1992.
FIN) Agriculture : exclut les déchets forestiers ; mines, ind. manuf. et énergie 1985 : données 1987 (principalement matière sèche). 1993 : données 1992 en poids humide.
FRA) 1993: données 1992.
w.DEU) 1985 : données 1984.
ISL) Ind. manuf. : la plupart de ces déchets proviennent de l'industrie du poisson.
IRE) 1985 : données 1984.
ITA) 1990 : données 1989. 1993 : données 1991. Ind. manuf. : inclut mines & carrières.
LUX) Ind. manuf. : déchets industriels spéciaux essentiellement composés de déchets liquides assimilés aux eaux usées industrielles.
NLD) 1985 : données 1986. 1993 : données 1992. Agriculture : fumier de l'élevage intensif ; le montant se réfère aux rejets en mer.
NOR) Ind. manuf. 1990: données estimées fondées sur un avis d'expert. Ind. manuf. 1993 : inclut 320 000 tonnes de déchets dangereux.
PRT) Déchets dangereux seulement. Mines, Ind. manuf. 1985 : données 1987.
SWE) Estimations grossières. Agricult. : dont 17 mio de t. de quantités recyclées. Ind. manuf. : déchets spécifiques aux secteurs concernés.
CHE) Ind. manuf. : déchets recyclés uniquement (exclut le recyclage interne).
TUR) Données 1992.
UKD) Agriculture : fumier de ferme uniquement (poids humide). Mines : extraction de kaolin, exploitation souterraine de charbon, carrières d'ardoises et extractions primaires ; exclut les déchets mines de charbon à ciel ouvert. Ind. manuf. : estimation grossière pour une période de 12 mois de la fin des années 80.
CFSR) 1985 : données 1987.
HUN) 1993 : données 1992. Ind. manuf. : inclut les mines & carrières et l'énergie.
POL) Rupture de série : jusqu'en 1990, classification polonaise ; 1993, classification CITI. Mines : exclut les mines à ciel ouvert.

Notes (Table 7.1B):
CAN) Contruction/demolition w. includes road and bridge contruction and repair, and land clearing waste. Dredge spoils: data refer to 1988. Rubber waste: used tyres only. Packaging waste: includes large amounts that are recycled and reused.
MEX) Municipal waste only. Rubber waste: used tyres only.
USA) Packaging w.: municipal packaging waste for 1993.
AUS) Construction/demolition w.: partial total. Sewage sludge: Queensland only. Scrapped motor vehicles: data based on vehicle numbers (conversion factor = 1 t./veh.). Rubber waste: estimate for whole country is based on partial data from Northern Territory, Western Australia, Victoria and Queensland. Packaging waste: Queensland only.
AUT) Dredge spoils: 1990 data. Sewage sludge 1992: sludge treated by municipalities only. Rubber waste: 1990 data. Packaging waste 1992: waste from private households only. Plastics: including textiles and metals.
BEL) Wallonia only. Sewage sludge: 1993 data.
DNK) Excludes glass from refillable bottles recovered for reuse. Sewage sludge and packaging glass: 1992 data.
FIN) Rubber waste: used tyres only.
FRA) Packaging waste: household waste only.
wDEU) Construction/demolition w.: 1990 data. Sewage sludge and packaging: 1991 data. Rubber waste: used tyres only.
GRC) Scrapped vehicles: data based on vehicle numbers (1 t./veh.). Rubber waste: used tyres disposed in landfills only.
ITA) Construction/demolition w.: 1989 data Sewage sludge: 1990 data. May include liquid waste.
LUX) Construction/demolition w.: 1990 data.
NLD) Construction/demolition and dredge spoils: 1990 data. Packaging w.: 1993 provisional data.
NOR) Construction/demolition w.: estimate based on expert opinion and on earlier data. Scrapped vehicles: calculated from the number of cars entering the car wreckage system. Rubber waste: used tyres only, based on a specific study.
PRT) Sewage sludge: 1991 data.
SWE) Construction/demolition w.: including excavated material, primarily soil. Rubber waste: 1992 data.
CHE) Construction/demolition w.: data refer to waste, that is directly landfilled. Rubber waste: 1992 data. Packaging w.: estimates based on composition of municipal waste.
UKD) Contruction/demolition w.: hard materials from construction sites, e.g bricks and concrete, and road planings; 1990 data. Dredge spoils: wet weight; amounts diposed of in all UK waters (i.e. external and internal waters). Scrapped motor vehicles: Scotland only; 1990 data.
HUN) Sewage sludge: 1987 data.

Source: OECD/OCDE

Notes (tableau 7.1B):
CAN) Contruction/démolition: inclut les déchets de construction, de réparation des ponts et routes, et des opérations de déblaiement. Déblais de dragage : données 1988. Caoutchouc : pneus usés uniquement. Emballages : inclut de grandes quantités recyclées ou réutilisées.
MEX) Déchets municipaux seulement. Caoutchouc : pneus usés seulement.
USA) Déchets d'emballage : déchets municipaux pour 1993.
AUS) Construction/démolition: total partiel. Boues d'épuration: Queensland uniquement. Carcasses de voitures: données fondées sur le nombre de véhicules (facteur de conversion = 1 t./véh.). Caoutchouc: estimation fondée sur des données partielles des Territoires du Nord, de l'Australie de l'ouest, de Victoria et du Queensland. Emballages : Queensland uniquement.
AUT) Déblais de dragage : données 1990. Boues d'épuration 1992 : boues traitées par les municipalités seulement. Caoutchouc : données 1990. Emballages 1992 : déchets des ménages privés seulement. Plastiques : inclut les textiles et métaux.
BEL) Wallonie uniquement. Boues d'épuration : données 1993.
DNK) Verre : exclut les bouteilles récupérées pour réutilisation. Boues d'épuration et déchets d'emballage en verre: données 1992.
FIN) Caoutchouc : pneus usés seulement.
FRA) Emballages : déchets des ménages uniquement.
wDEU) Construction/démolition : 1990. Boues d'épuration et déchets d'emballage : 1991.
GRC) Carcasses de voitures : données fondées sur le nombre de véhicules (1 t./véh.). Caoutchouc : pneus usés mis en décharge uniquement.
ITA) Construction/démolition : données 1989. Boues d'épuration : données 1990. Peut inclure des déchets liquides.
LUX) Construction/démolition : données 1990.
NLD) Construction/démolition et déblais de dragage : 1990. Déchets d'emballage : données provisoire 1993.
NOR) Construction/démolition: estimation fondée sur un avis d'expert et sur des données plus anciennes. Carcassses de véhicules : fondé sur le nombre d'épaves entrant dans le système. Caoutchouc : pneus usés seulement (étude spécifique).
PRT) Boues d'épuration : données 1991.
SWE) Construction/démolition : inclut les matériaux d'excavation (terre principalement). Caoutchouc : 1992.
CHE) Construction/démolition : déchets de construction et des industries directement mis en décharge. Caoutchouc : 1992. Déchets d'emballage : estimation fondée sur la composition des déchets municipaux.
UKD) Contruction/démolition : matériaux durs provenant des sites de construction (p.ex.: briques, béton), et des travaux de voirie. Données 1990. Déblais de dragage : poids humide ; quantités rejetées dans les eaux du Royaume-Uni (i.e. eaux externes et internes). Carcasses de véhicules : Ecosse seulement ; données 1990.
HUN) Boues d'épuration : 1987.

The next two tables present trends in amounts of municipal and household waste, as well as their average composition expressed as the percentage contribution of various materials to total weight. In general, municipal waste is that which is collected and treated by or for municipalities: household waste and bulky waste as well as comparable waste from small commercial or industrial enterprises; and market and garden residue.

The amount and composition of waste generated in each country are related to the rate of urbanisation, the types and patterns of consumption, household revenue and lifestyles, and influence existing waste management policies.

When interpreting these tables it should be borne in mind that the definition of municipal waste and the surveying methods used vary from country to country.

Les deux tableaux suivants présentent les tendances concernant les quantités de déchets municipaux et des ménages, ainsi que leur composition moyenne exprimée en pourcentage du poids des divers materiaux. Les déchets municipaux sont en général les déchets qui sont collectés et traités par ou pour les municipalités : les déchets des ménages et les déchets encombrants, ainsi que des déchets similaires provenant des petites entreprises commerciales ou industrielles et les résidus des marchés et des jardins.

Les quantités de déchets générées dans chaque pays et leur composition sont liées au degré d'urbanisation, aux types et structures de consommation, au niveau des revenus et au style de vie des ménages, et influencent les politiques de gestion des déchets existantes.

Ces données doivent être interprétées en se rappelant que la définition des déchets municipaux et les méthodes d'enquête utilisées varient d'un pays à l'autre.

GENERATION OF MUNICIPAL WASTE (a), 1980-1992
PRODUCTION DE DÉCHETS MUNICIPAUX (a), 1980-1992

		Total amounts generated / Quantités totales produites (1000 tonnes)								Amounts per capita / Quantités par habitant (kg/capita / kg/habitant)							
		Municipal waste / Déchets municipaux				of which : Household waste / dont : Déchets des ménages				Municipal waste / Déchets municipaux				Household waste / Déchets des ménages			
		1980	1985	1990	1992 (b)	1980	1985	1990	1992	1980	1985	1990	1992	1980	1985	1990	1992
Canada	*	12600	..	18000	18800	..	..	10151	..	510	..	670	660	..	..	360	..
Mexico/Mexique	*	..	..	21062	28090	..	..	16850	22472	..	..	240	310	..	..	190	250
USA/Etats-Unis		137350	149144	177539	187790	..	..	..	..	600	620	710	730	..	..	..	..
Japan/Japon		43950	41530	50441	50767	..	..	..	..	380	340	410	410	..	..	..	..
Australia/lie	*	10000	..	..	12000	..	..	..	7000	700	..	..	690	..	..	..	400
Austria/Autriche	*	..	..	3283	..	1673	1727	2506	..	..	..	430	..	220	230	320	..
Belgium/Belgique	*	3082	..	3500	4000	..	..	..	..	310	..	350	400	..	..	..	..
Denmark/Danemark		2046	2430	..	2377	..	..	..	1753	400	480	..	460	..	..	..	340
Finland/Finlande		..	2500	3100	..	..	..	1200	..	..	510	620	..	..	..	240	..
France	*	..	..	26220	27000	16930	18700	20420	20500	..	..	460	470	310	340	360	360
Germany/Allem.	*	..	..	28401	..	..	..	..	..	..	..	360	..	..	..	..	..
w.Germany/All.occ.	*	21417	19387	21615	..	..	..	..	..	350	320	340	..	..	..	..	..
e.Germany/All.or.		..	..	6786	..	..	..	..	..	..	..	420	..	..	..	..	..
Greece/Grèce	*	2500	3023	3000	3200	..	..	..	..	260	300	300	310	..	..	..	..
Iceland/Islande		..	..	..	145	..	..	..	80	..	..	..	560	..	..	..	310
Ireland/Irlande	*	640	1100	..	..	..	..	..	..	190	310	..	..	..	..	..	..
Italy/Italie		14041	15000	20000	20033	..	..	..	..	250	260	350	350	..	..	..	..
Luxembourg		128	131	170	190	..	..	..	98	350	360	450	490	..	..	..	250
Netherl./Pays-Bas		7050	6357	7430	7602	5565	5177	6190	6570	500	440	500	500	390	360	410	440
Norway/Norvège	*	1700	1900	2000	2220	700	800	850	1100	420	460	470	510	170	190	200	260
Portugal		1980	2350	3000	3270	..	..	..	..	200	230	300	330	..	..	..	..
Spain/Espagne		10100	10014	12546	14256	..	..	..	..	270	260	320	360	..	..	..	..
Sweden/Suède		2510	2650	3200	..	..	..	..	..	300	320	370	..	..	..	..	..
Switzerl./Suisse	*	2290	2610	2930	2820	..	..	..	..	360	400	440	400	..	..	..	..
Turkey/Turquie	*	12000	18000	19500	22315	..	..	..	..	270	360	350	390	..	..	..	..
UK/Royaume-Uni	*	..	..	..	..	15500	17000	20000	..	..	..	..	..	310	340	350	..
Former CSFR/Ex-RFTS		..	4501	..	..	..	..	..	..	..	290	..	..	..	..	..	..
Czech Rep./R.Tchèque		..	2600	..	..	..	..	..	..	..	250	..	..	..	..	..	..
Slovak Rep./R.Slov.		..	1901	..	..	..	..	..	..	..	360	..	..	..	..	..	..
Hungary/Hongrie	*	..	4500	4900	4000	..	2100	2300	2000	..	430	470	390	..	200	220	190
Poland/Pologne		9489	10661	12806	13000	..	..	8324	8400	270	290	340	340	..	..	220	220
N.America/Amér.N.	*	150000	164000	217000	235000	..	..	..	..	590	620	600	630	..	..	..	..
OECD/OCDE Eur.	*	128000	136000	168000	174000	..	..	..	..	330	340	390	400	..	..	..	..
EU/UE-15	*	112000	117000	143000	147000	..	..	..	..	340	350	390	400	..	..	..	..
OECD/OCDE	*	334000	355000	449000	474000	..	..	..	..	430	440	480	500	..	..	..	..

Notes: see next page/voir page suivante.

Source: OECD/OCDE

COMPOSITION OF MUNICIPAL WASTE, 1980-1993
COMPOSITION DES DÉCHETS MUNICIPAUX, 1980-1993

(%)

		Paper and paperboard/ Papiers et cartons				Food & garden waste, etc./ Déchets alim.+jardin, etc.				Plastics/ Matières plastiques				Glass/ Verre				Metals/ Métaux				Textiles and other/ Textiles et autres			
		80	85	90	93	80	85	90	93	80	85	90	93	80	85	90	93	80	85	90	93	80	85	90	93
Canada	*	37	37	40	28	..	..	25	34	5	5	11	11	7	7	7	7	7	7	9	8	46	46	20	13
Mexico/Mexique		..	..	14	14	..	..	52	52	..	..	4	4	..	..	6	6	..	..	3	3	..	..	20	20
USA/Etats-Unis	*	36	37	37	38	27	26	25	23	5	7	8	9	10	8	7	7	10	9	8	8	12	13	15	16
Japan/Japon	*	26	33	38	46	..	34	32	26	12	12	11	9	8	8	7	7	4	6	6	8	45	7	7	12
Australia/lie	*	26	..	..	22	..	..	..	50	6	..	..	7	15	..	..	9	7	..	..	5	46	..	..	8
N.Zeal./N.Zél.		34	..	..	..	..	..	..	..	3	..	..	..	3	..	..	..	8	..	..	..	53	..	..	..
Austria/Autriche	*	20	34	27	..	..	25	26	..	4	7	9	..	7	10	8	..	5	4	7	..	64	20	23	..
Belgium/Belgique	*	35	..	30	..	..	..	45	..	6	..	8	..	8	..	8	..	5	..	4	..	46	..	5	..
Denmark/Danem.	*	34	22	..	30	..	55	..	37	7	4	..	7	6	5	..	6	5	3	..	3	47	11	..	17
Finland/Finlande	*	..	35	37	26	..	..	40	32	..	7	5	..	..	4	2	6	..	3	3	3	..	40	13	35
France	*	22	25	30	30	38	37	25	25	6	9	10	10	12	12	12	12	9	7	6	6	13	10	17	17
Germany/Allem.		..	..	..	..	..	..	..	..	..	..	..	..	..	..	..	..	..	..	..	..	..	..	..	..
w.Germ./All.occ.	*	20	18	..	..	..	..	..	..	6	5	..	..	12	9	..	..	4	3	..	..	59	64	..	..
e.Germ./All.or.		..	..	..	..	..	..	..	..	..	..	..	..	..	..	..	..	..	..	..	..	..	..	..	..
Greece/Grèce	*	20	19	22	20	..	59	49	49	7	7	11	9	3	3	4	5	4	4	4	5	67	9	11	13
Iceland/Islande	*	..	..	34	..	..	..	24	..	..	..	10	..	..	..	9	..	..	..	13	..	..	..	11	..
Ireland/Irlande	*	35	25	..	..	..	..	..	..	11	14	..	..	8	8	..	..	3	3	..	..	43	51	..	..
Italy/Italie	*	22	22	..	..	43	43	..	..	7	7	..	..	7	6	..	..	3	3	..	..	18	19	..	..
Luxembourg	*	..	17	..	20	..	..	..	44	..	6	..	8	..	7	..	7	..	3	..	3	..	67	..	17
Netherl./Pays-Bas	*	21	23	25	27	53	54	52	43	7	7	8	9	12	7	5	4	3	3	4	5	3	4	5	8
Norway/Norvège	*	31	31	31	31	..	..	18	18	4	4	6	6	3	3	4	4	7	7	5	5	56	56	36	36
Portugal	*	19	19	25	23	..	..	..	35	3	3	9	12	3	3	3	5	4	4	3	3	71	71	59	22
Spain/Espagne		15	15	20	21	..	53	49	44	6	7	7	11	6	7	9	7	3	3	4	4	..	15	11	13
Sweden/Suède	*	43	..	44	..	26	..	30	..	10	..	7	..	5	..	8	..	6	..	2	..	10	..	9	..
Switzerl./Suisse	*	30	..	..	28	30	..	..	27	13	..	..	15	9	..	..	3	6	..	..	3	12	..	..	24
Turkey/Turquie	*	..	..	..	6	..	..	..	64	..	..	..	3	..	..	..	2	..	..	..	1	..	..	..	24
UK/Roy.-Uni	*	29	..	37	..	..	..	19	..	7	..	10	..	10	..	9	..	8	..	7	..	46	..	18	..
Hungary/Hongrie	*	17	16	20	..	29	30	32	..	4	5	5	..	4	4	5	..	4	5	6	..	42	40	32	..
Poland/Pologne		..	..	10	..	..	..	38	..	..	..	10	..	..	..	12	..	..	..	8	..	..	..	23	..

Notes: see next page / voir page suivante.

Source: OECD/OCDE

Notes (Table 7.2A)

a) Municipal waste is waste collected by or on the order of municipalities. It includes waste originating from households, commercial activities, office buildings, institutions such as schools and government buildings, and small businesses that dispose of waste at the same facilities used for municipally collected waste. Household waste is waste generated by the domestic activity of households. It includes garbage, bulky waste and separately collected waste. National definitions may differ.

b) Or latest available year.

CAN) Municipal w.: all w. disposed of, except construction and demolition w., even if not collected by municipalities. Includes flows diverted for recycling or composting. 1980 data include some light industrial, commercial and institutional w. 1990 data refer to 1988.

MEX) 1990 data refer to 1991.

AUS) Municipal w.: 1980 data refer to 1978. 1992 data: Secretariat estimate based on composite total from State/Territory data; may include significant amounts of commercial and industrial waste.

NZL) 1980 data refer to 1982.

AUT) Municipal w.: Includes household w., similar w. from small industries and the commercial sector, and street cleaning w. Household w.: w. from households and similar sources, including bulky w. and separately collected w. 1980 and 1985 data refer to 1979 and 1984.

BEL) Municipal w.: Secretariat estimates based on figures from different years for Brussels, Flanders and Wallonia. Exclude bulky w. and separately collected waste.

FRA) Municipal w.: Includes household w. and similar w. from other activities, bulky w. (3 million tonnes in 1992), separately collected w. for recovery operations and w. from green space maintenance. Household w.: excludes bulky w.

DEU) Municipal w.: Includes household and similar w. from commercial activities, market and street w. and bulky w.; 1985: 1984 data.

GRC) Traditional waste collection only.

IRL) 1985 data refer to 1984.

NOR) Municipal w.: Before 1992, excludes similar w. from areas not served by municipal w. service. Excludes glass bottles which do not enter the w. stream. 1990 figure is rough estimate.

CHE) Municipal w.: w. from households and other similarly composed w. Excludes separately collected w. for recycling.

TUR) Municipal w. 1990 and 1992: 1989 and 1991 data based on daily amounts of w. collected in 1 974 municipalities out of a total of 2 033. 1980 and 1985: Secretariat estimates.

UKD) Household w.: The 1990 estimate is for the UK and is broadly representative of the annual tonnage in the late 1980s. Figures up to 1985 refer to England & Wales only and are less reliable than the 1990 estimate.

HUN) Municipal w.: w. from households, offices, firms and services.

TOT) North America: 1980 and 1985 data do not include Mexico. OECD Europe, European Union: 1980 and 1985 data do not include eastern Germany. OECD 1980, 1985: do not include Mexico and eastern Germany.

Source: OECD/OCDE

Notes (tableau 7.2A)

a) Les déchets municipaux sont ceux collectés par ou pour les municipalités. Ils comprennent les déchets produits par les ménages, les activités commerciales, les bureaux, les institutions telles que les écoles et les bâtiments administratifs et les petites entreprises dont les déchets sont traités dans les mêmes installations que ceux collectés par les municipalités. Les déchets des ménages sont ceux produits par l'activité domestique des ménages. Ils comprennent les ordures ménagères, les déchets encombrants et la collecte sélective. Les définitions nationales peuvent être différentes.

b) Ou dernière année disponible.

CAN) D. municipaux: tous les d. éliminés, même ceux qui ne sont pas collectés par les municipalités, excepté les d. de construction et de démolition. Inclut les flux extraits pour recyclage ou compostage ; 1980: inclut quelques d. industriels, commerciaux et institutionnels. 1990: données 1988.

MEX) 1990: données 1991.

AUS) D. municipaux: 1980 données sont de 1978. 1992: estimations du Secrétariat fondées sur un total composé de données des États ou Territoires ; peut inclure des quantités importantes de d. commerciaux et industriels.

NZL) 1980: données 1982.

AUT) D. municipaux: d. des ménages et d. similaires des petites entreprises, des commerces et du nettoyage des rues. D. des ménages: d. provenant des ménages et de sources similaires, y compris les d. encombrants et la collecte sélective. 1980 et 1985: données 1979 et 1984.

BEL) D. municipaux: estimations du Secrétariat fondées sur des chiffres d'années différentes pour Bruxelles, la Flandre et la Wallonie. Les données excluent les d. encombrants et la collecte sélective.

FRA) D. municipaux: d. des ménages et d. similaires d'autres activités, d. encombrants (3 millions de tonnes en 1992), collecte sélective et d. de l'entretien des espaces verts. D. des ménages: exclut les d. encombrants.

DEU) D. municipaux: d. des ménages et d. similaires des activités commerciales, d. de marché et d'entretien des rues, ainsi que les d. encombrants. 1985: données 1984.

GRC) Collecte traditionnelle des d. uniquement.

IRL) 1985: données 1984.

NOR) D. municipaux: avant 1992 exclut les d. similaires des zones non desservies par un service municipal des d. Exclut les bouteilles en verre qui n'entrent pas dans le flux des d. 1990: estimation grossière.

CHE) D. municipaux: d. des ménages et d. similaires. Exclut les d. collectés en vue du recyclage.

TUR) D. municipaux 1990 et 1992: données 1989 et 1991 fondées sur les quantités quotidiennes collectées dans 1 974 municipalités sur un total de 2 033. 1980 et 1985: estimations du Secrétariat.

UKD) D. des ménages: le chiffre 1990 est une estimation pour le Royaume-Uni qui est grossièrement représentative des tonnages annuels à la fin des années 1980. Jusqu'en 1985: Angleterre et Pays de Galle uniquement ; chiffres moins fiables que l'estimation 1990.

HUN) D. municipaux: d. des ménages, bureaux, entreprises et services.

TOT) Amérique du Nord 1980 et 1985: ne comprend pas le Mexique. OCDE Europe, Union Européenne 1980 et 1985: ne comprend pas l'Allemagne orientale. OCDE 1980 et 1985: ne comprend pas le Mexique et l'Allemagne orientale.

Notes (Table 7.2B)

CAN) 1980-90: Household waste only. Plastics: 1990 data refer to 1988.

USA) Food: Includes food waste and yard trimmings. Other: Includes rubber, leather, wood, and miscellaneous inorganic waste.

JPN) 1993: 1991 data. 1985, 1990, 1993: Tokyo metropolitan area only. 1980: average of 4 cities. Other: rubber, ceramics.

AUS) Composite results from State surveys (SA, NSW, Tasmania, ACT, Victoria, WA, Queensland). Data refer to various years of the early 1990s. Other 1980: includes textiles, food and garden waste.

AUT) Food: includes all organic waste.

BEL) Household waste only. Data include estimates.

DNK) Household waste only. 1980: 1979 data. Other: Institutional waste.

FIN) Household waste only. 1993 data refer to 1992.

FRA) Household waste only.

wDEU) Household waste only.

GRC) Other: 1980 includes food and garden waste and 1990 and 1992 data include inert and other waste not mentioned.

ISL) Household waste only.

IRL) 1980 data refer to 1979.

ITA) 1985 data refer to 1986. Glass: 1986 figure is a Secretariat estimate.

LUX) Household w. only. Other: Composite mater., baby nappies, haz. waste...

NLD) Household w. only (separate collection excluded); data based on the content of waste bags in four selected residential areas in three Dutch cities.

NOR) 1980 data refer to 1979/81 surveys. Data extrapolated from restricted areas. Other 1980, 85: includes textiles, food and garden waste, etc.

PRT) 1990 data refer to 1989.

ESP) Other: batteries, rubber and wood.

SWE) 1980: Estimates for the period 1975-1980. Paper: Includes fraction separated at source. Includes paper laminated with plastics. Textiles: Includes also leather and rubber. Food: putrescent wastes.

CHE) Other 1993: includes composit packaging and items, minerals and a fraction smaller than eight mm.

TUR) Data refer to household waste composition in 58 urban municipalities with a population > 20 000. Other: includes ash, slag, etc.

UKD) 1990: Household waste only. Composition based on a limited sample exercise. Not compatible with previous data. Other: fines and miscellaneous.

HUN) Data based on volumetric information. Other: Includes ash, slag and soil.

Source: OECD/OCDE

Notes (Table 7.2B)

CAN) 1980-90: D. des ménages seulement. Plastiques: 1990: données 1988.

USA) D.alim.: d. alim. et tontes de gazon. Autres: caoutchouc, cuir, bois et divers déchets non organiques.

JPN) 1993: données 1991. 1985, 1990 et 1993: zone métropolitaine de Tokyo uniquement. 1980: moyenne de 4 villes. Autres: caoutchouc, céramiques.

AUS) Résultats composites d'enquêtes de divers États (SA, NSW, Tasmanie, ACT, Victoria, WA, Queensland). Les données correspondent à diverses années du début des années 90. Autres 1980: comprend les textiles, les d. alim. et de jardin.

AUT) D.alim.: tous déchets organiques.

BEL) D. des ménages uniquement. Les données comprennent des estimations.

DNK) D. des ménages uniquement. 1980: données 1979. Autres: déchets des institutions.

FIN) D. des ménages uniquement. 1993: données 1992.

FRA) D. des ménages uniquement.

wDEU) D. des ménages uniquement.

GRC) Autres: 1980: inclut les d. alim. et de jardin ; 1990 et 1992: déchets inertes et autres déchets non mentionnés.

ISL) D. des ménages uniquement.

IRL) 1980: données 1979.

ITA) 1985: données 1986. Verre 1986: estimation du Secrétariat.

LUX) D. des ménages uniquement. Autres: matér. composites, couches, d. dangereux.

NLD) D. des ménages uniquement (collecte sélective exclue) ; données fondées sur le contenu des sacs poubelle dans 4 zones résidentielles dans 3 villes.

NOR) 1980: enquête 1979/81. Données extrapolées à partir de zones restreintes. Autres: 1980-85: textiles, déchets alim. et des jardins, etc.

PRT) 1990: données 1989.

ESP) Autres: piles, caoutchouc et bois.

SWE) 1980: estimation représentative de la période 1975-1980. Papier: inclut le tri à la source. Inclut le papier laminé de plastiques. Textiles: inclut également le cuir, le caoutchouc. D. alim.: déchets putrescibles.

CHE) Autres 1993: comprend les articles et emballages composites, les éléments minéraux et la fraction inférieure à 8 mm.

TUR) Composition des déchets ménagers dans 58 municipalités urbaines d'une population > 20 000. Autres: cendres, scories, etc.

UKD) 1990: d. des ménages uniquement. Composition fondée sur un échantillon limité non compatible avec les données précédentes. Autres: déchets fins et divers.

HUN) Données fondées sur des informations volumétriques. Autres: cendres, scories, terre.

Source: OECD/OCDE

The following table concerns the disposal of municipal waste. Because of recycling, and because treatment methods are not always mutually exclusive, the amounts collected and the sums of the treatment methods are not necessarily the same.

The following methods of disposal are presented: landfill, adequately managed or not; incineration; composting; recycling; and other, non-specified methods. Mechanical sorting is presented here not as a treatment method in itself, but rather as an operation prior to treatment and disposal.

When interpreting this table, the reader should bear in mind the notes regarding definitions and years of reference.

Le tableau suivant concerne l'élimination des déchets municipaux. En raison du recyclage et des méthodes de traitement qui ne sont pas toujours mutuellement exclusives, les quantités collectées et les sommes des types de traitement ne sont pas nécessairement les mêmes.

Les méthodes de traitement prises en compte sont la mise en décharge correctement gérée ou non, l'incinération, le compostage, ainsi que le recyclage et d'autres méthodes non spécifiées. Le triage mécanique est présenté ici non pas comme une méthode de traitement en soi mais comme une opération préalable au traitement et à l'élimination.

Lors de l'interprétation de ce tableau, il faut garder à l'esprit les notes en bas de page relatives aux définitions et aux années de référence.

DISPOSAL OF MUNICIPAL WASTE, latest year available
ÉLIMINATION DES DÉCHETS MUNICIPAUX, dernière année disponible

1 000 tonnes

		Year/ Année	Total amounts/ Quantités totales (a)	Mechanical Sorting/ Triage mécanique	Composting/ Compostage	Incineration / Incinération		Landfill/ Mise en décharge	Recycling/ Recyclage	Other/ Autres
						Total	% with energy recovery/ % avec récuperation d'énergie			
Canada		1992	18800	..	218	1101	81.3	14070	3400	..
Mexico/Mexique	*	1993	28089	..	..	..	..	7768	192	20321
USA/Etats-Unis	*	1993	187790	..	5821	29938	7.6	117028	34929	..
Japan/Japon		1991	50767	1503	57	36169	..	19379	1688	742
Austria/Autriche	*	1990	2506	450	85	310	100.0	1700	400	11
Belgium/Belgique	*	1994	1160	-	96	565	-	499	-	-
Denmark/Danemark		1993	2377	..	206	1500	100.0	468	203	-
Finland/Finlande		1990	3100	..	50	50	100.0	2400	600	-
France	*	1992	20500	..	1300	7600	72.4	9500	740	1360
w.Germany/Allemagne occ.		1990	21615	..	369	6039	..	14219	-	988
Greece/Grèce		1992	3200	4	-	1	..	2970	226	-
Iceland/Islande		1992	145	..	-	25	-	105	15	-
Ireland/Irlande		1984	1100	-	-	-	-	1100	-	-
Italy/Italie	*	1991	26600	..	-	2100	..	22800	1700	-
Luxembourg	*	1993	190	-	5	135	100.0	66	73	..
Netherlands/Pays-Bas		1991	7602	425	475	2500	93.0	3610	578	20
Norway/Norvège	*	1992	2223	80	15	416	96.4	1678	175	10
Portugal		1992	3270	..	444	-	-	2826	-	-
Spain/Espagne		1993	14256	12061	1560	635	78.1	12061	-	-
Sweden/Suède		1990	3200	..	100	1300	..	1400	400	-
Switzerland/Suisse	*	1992	2820	..	..	2140	93.5	650	1370	..
UK/Royaume-Uni	*	1989	20000	2500	..	2500	50.0	14000	1000	-
Former CSFR/Ex-RFTS		1987	4501	..	124	217	36.9	4160	-	-
Czech Rep./Rép.Tchèque		1987	2600	-	60	104	76.9	2436	-	-
Slovak Rep./Rép.Slovaque		1987	1901	..	64	113	..	1724	-	-
Hungary/Hongrie	*	1992	4000	25	25	310	100.0	3580	110	-
Poland/Pologne		1992	13000	..	89	..	..	11711	..	..

Notes:
a) Total amounts refer to total waste generated. This figure may be lower than the total of all disposals, because residues of some treatments (incineration, composting) are landfilled.
MEX) Data for other treatment include some illegal dumping.
USA) Data for landfill exclude residues from composting, recycling and incineration. Energy recovery refers to 1990.
AUT) Household waste only.
BEL) Wallonia only; separate collection and bulky waste excluded.
FRA) Household waste only.
ITA) Data include 3.2 million tonnes of special waste disposable as municipal and 3.4 million tonnes of sewage sludge (wet weight).
LUX) Total amounts: 1992 data, excluding recycled amounts.
NOR) Mechanical sorting refers to 1990.
CHE) Data for total amounts exclude recycled material, which is collected separately.
UKD) Household waste only. Data for landfill refer to direct landfill only. Incineration, landfill, and recycling include some industrial and commercial waste disposed of by municipal waste disposal authorities.
HUN) Mechanical sorting and composting: 1989 data.

Notes:
a) Les quantités totales se rapportent aux déchets produits. Elles peuvent être inférieures à la somme des quantités éliminées lorsque les résidus de certains traitements (incinération, compostage) sont ensuite mis en décharge.
MEX) Mise en décharge: sites d'enfouissement. "Autres": inclut des décharges illégales.
USA) Les données sur la mise en décharge excluent les résidus issus du recyclage, du compostage et de l'incinération. Récupération d'énergie : données 1990.
AUT) Ordures ménagères uniquement.
BEL) Wallonie uniquement ; collecte sélective et déchets encombrants exclus.
FRA) Ordures ménagères uniquement.
ITA) Comprend 3.2 millions de tonnes de déchets spéciaux éliminés avec les déchets municipaux et 3.4 millions de tonnes de boues d'épuration (poids humide).
LUX) Quantités totales : données 1992 ; les quantités recyclées sont exclues.
NOR) Triage mécanique : se réfère à 1990.
CHE) Quantités totales excluent les déchets collectés en vue du recyclage.
UKD) Ordures ménagères uniquement. Mise en décharge: mise en décharge directe uniquement. Incinération, mise en décharge et recyclage : comprennent des déchets industriels et commerciaux traités par les autorités municipales.
HUN) Triage mécanique et compostage : données 1989.

Source: OECD/OCDE

The following table provides information on trends in the percentage of population served by a municipal waste disposal service. Municipal waste services refer to regular collection of waste (including bulky waste), waste treatment and waste disposal. It can also include waste sorting and recycling.

For the various components of the municipal waste disposal system see the tables on the disposal and recycling of waste.

Le tableau suivant fournit des informations sur les tendances concernant le pourcentage de la population desservie par un service de ramassage des déchets municipaux. Les services municipaux des déchets incluent la collecte régulière des déchets, y compris des déchets encombrants, le traitement de ces déchets et leur élimination. Ils peuvent également inclure le triage et le recyclage.

Pour les différents types d'élimination des déchets municipaux, voir les tableaux relatifs à l'élimination et au recyclage des déchets.

PERCENTAGE OF POPULATION SERVED BY MUNICIPAL WASTE SERVICES, 1980 - early 1990s
POURCENTAGE DE LA POPULATION DESSERVIE PAR UN SERVICE DES DÉCHETS MUNICIPAUX, 1980 - début des années 90

		1980	1985	1990	early 1990s/ début des années 90
Canada		99.0	99.0	100.0	100.0
Mexico/Mexique		..	..	70.0	70.0
USA/Etats-Unis		100.0	100.0	100.0	100.0
Japan/Japon	*	94.6	99.6	99.9	99.9
Australia/Australie		..	..	..	..
N. Zealand/N. Zélande	*	91.0	..	..	..
Austria/Autriche		96.0	99.0	99.0	99.0
Belgium/Belgique	*	100.0	100.0	100.0	100.0
Denmark/Danemark		..	..	..	100.0
Finland/Finlande	*	..	75.0	75.0	..
France	*	98.0	98.0	99.0	99.5
Germany/Allemagne		..	..	..	99.8
w.Germany/Allemagne occ.	*	100.0	100.0	..	100.0
e.Germany/Allemagne or.		..	..	..	99.0
Greece/Grèce	*	69.0	..	100.0	100.0
Iceland/Islande		..	..	..	95.0
Ireland/Irlande	*	75.0	77.0	..	..
Italy/Italie		..	..	..	..
Luxembourg		100.0	100.0	100.0	100.0
Netherlands/Pays-Bas	*	99.0	99.0	>99.0	100.0
Norway/Norvège		76.0	80.0	85.0	97.0
Portugal	*	64.0	75.0	87.6	89.0
Spain/Espagne		..	85.0	..	90.0
Sweden/Suède		82.0	94.0	100.0	100.0
Switzerland/Suisse		96.0	98.0	99.0	99.0
Turkey/Turquie		..	..	..	..
UK/Royaume-Uni	*	100.0	100.0	100.0	100.0
Former CSFR/ex-RFTS	*	..	65.0	..	..
Czech Rep./Rép.Tchèque	*	..	70.0	..	..
Slovak Rep./Rép.Slovaque	*	..	55.0	..	..
Hungary/Hongrie	*	..	60.4	62.7	63.1
Poland/Pologne		..	..	55.0	55.0

Notes:
JPN) 1990 data refer to 1989.
NZL) 1980 data refer to 1982.
BEL) Flanders region only.
FIN) 1985 and 1990 data refer to 1983 and 1987 respectively. National percentage of waste collected by local authorities including rural areas. Towns/cities are at 100% collection.
IRL) National percentage of waste collected by local authorities including rural areas. Towns/cities are at 100% collection.
FRA) 1985 and 1989/90 data refer to 1984 and 1988 respectively.
wDEU) 1985 data refer to 1984.
GRC) 1980 data refer to 1979.
NLD) 1990 and 1992 data refer to 1989 and 1991 respectively.
PRT) 1985 data are Secretariat estimates. 1990 data refer to 1989.
UKD) Data exclude certain types of waste that municipal authorities are not obliged to collect.
CSF) 1985 data refer to 1987.
CZE) 1985 data refer to 1987.
SLO) 1985 data refer to 1987.
HUN) 1990 data refer to 1989.

Notes :
JPN) Les données 1990 sont de 1989.
NZL) Les données 1980 sont de 1982.
BEL) La Flandre seulement.
FIN) Les données 1985 et 1990 sont de 1983 et 1987 respectivement. Pourcentage national de déchets collectés par les autorités locales y compris les zones rurales. Villes : 100% desservies.
IRL) Pourcentage national de déchets collectés par les autorités locales y compris les zones rurales. Villes : 100% desservies.
FRA) Les données 1985 et 1990 sont de 1984 et 1988 respectivement.
wDEU) Les données 1985 sont de 1984.
GRC) Les données 1980 sont de 1979.
NLD) Les données 1990 et 1992 sont de 1989 et 1991 respectivement.
PRT) 1985: estimations du Secrétariat. 1990: données 1989.
UKD) Exclut certains types de déchets que les autorités municipales ne sont pas obligées de collecter.
CSF) Les données 1985 sont de 1987.
CZE) Les données 1985 sont de 1987.
SLO) Les données 1985 sont de 1987.
HUN) Les données 1990 sont de 1989.

Source: OECD/OCDE

The following table presents amounts of selected groups of industrial and/or hazardous waste generated in selected countries.

It provides information regarding the relative contribution of various sources to the amount of industrial waste generated.

When reading this table it should be borne in mind that the data do not represent all industrial and/or hazardous waste, nor its potential toxicity, and that the definitions for different groups of waste vary by country.

Le tableau suivant présente les quantités de divers groupes de déchets industriels et/ou dangereux produits dans certains pays.

Il fournit des informations sur la contribution relative des diverses sources aux quantités de déchets industriels produits.

Lors de l'interprétation des données, on doit se rappeler qu'elles ne représentent pas tous les déchets industriels et/ou dangereux ni leur toxicité potentielle, et que les définitions des différents groupes de déchets varient selon les pays.

GENERATION OF SELECTED GROUPS OF INDUSTRIAL WASTE (a), selected countries, latest year available
PRODUCTION DE DÉCHETS INDUSTRIELS SÉLECTIONNÉS (a), pays sélectionnés, dernière année disponible

tonnes

| | Year/ Année | Waste from / Déchets de | | Waste oil / Huiles usées | Waste containing PCBs / Déchets contenant des diphényles polychlorés | Clinical and pharmaceutical waste / Déchets cliniques et pharmaceutiques | Waste from the production and use of / Déchets issus de la production et de l'utilisation de | | | |
		surface treatment of metals and plastics/ la finition des métaux et des plastiques	biocide production / production de biocides				photographic materials/ matériaux photographiques	organic solvents/ solvants organiques	paints and pigments/ peintures et pigments	resins and latex / résines et latex
Canada *	1991	2 926 601	4 088	622 491	141 952	..	..	290 715	32 492	..
Mexico/Mexique	1992	..	..	560 000	..	..	..	..	..	..
USA/États-Unis *	1990	1 982 379	13 216	4 960 000	5 015 060	2 800 000	..	70 000 000	693 833	41 000 000
Japan/Japon *	1985	..	..	3 672 000	..	..	..	..	..	2 894 000
Australia/Australie *	1992	4 257	549	74 438	15 351	15 743	..	10 061	29 823	..
N.Zeal./N.Zélande	1990	3 030	..	18 151	4	2 770	451	3 690	29 381	12 892
Austria/Autriche	1990	14 731	450	60 300	81	8 254	1 400	27 253	15 000	..
Denmark/Danemark	1992	..	..	..	..	..	..	..	..	..
Finland/Finlande	1992	9 000	200	30 600	80	380	520	11 300	11 300	12 400
France *	1990	..	..	409 000	17 000	..	..	285 000	..	..
w.Germany/All.occ.	1987	219 527	..	859 456	10 537	..	..	454 489	225 525	867 015
Greece/Grèce	1992	..	..	60 000	1 600	15 000	..	21 000	6 000	150
Iceland/Islande	1992	..	..	5 000	1	700	..	..	..	..
Ireland/Irlande *	1991	7 000	5	1 000	..	..	..	12 500	..	45 000
Italy/Italie	1991	..	..	..	..	141 200	..	..	..	..
Luxembourg	1993	..	..	11 327	462	32	207	284	292	..
Netherl./Pays-Bas *	1992	29 200	1 200	288 000	500	5 400	18 000	73 500	31 600	19 200
Norway/Norvège *	1993	..	..	56 000	100	..	..	5 000	5 500	5 000
Portugal	1989	..	..	16 473	703	..	..	..	..	..
Spain/Espagne	1990	..	..	320 000	2 200	..	..	5 400	..	..
Switzerland	1993	15 000	190	175 070	550	2 950	5 950	91 560	12 250	..
Turkey/Turquie	1992	..	..	..	..	..	..	..	..	..
UK/Royaume-Uni	1990	..	..	..	..	144 000	..	..	..	..
Hungary/Hongrie	1992	5 514	7 390	507 790	130	56 520	4 930	27 150	9 040	7 260
Poland/Pologne	1992	..	..	32 340	..	..	..	..	144 853	..

Notes:
a) These categories are based on the classification of hazardous waste in the Basel Convention (Annex 4). The specific materials included in each column may differ, depending upon national classifications.
CAN) Waste containing PCBs: data refer to total amount in storage awaiting disposal and not to annual generation. Waste from surface treatment also includes wastes from heat treatment and operations containing cyanides. Waste from paints and pigments also includes resins and latex.
USA) Data refer to the late 1980s. Waste containing PCBs: based on a 1985 survey of hazardous waste generators; does not reflect the total volume for the United States. Waste from the production and use of organic solvents: includes all industrial organic chemicals. Resins and latex: includes plastics and rubber.
JPN) The figure for waste oil includes waste solvents. Data for waste from the surface treatment of metals refer to total waste metals. Data for resins and latex refer to waste plastics and rubber.
AUS) Data refer to Victoria, New South Wales and South Australia except for oils and pigments, which also include data from Tasmania; and for clinical waste, which only refer to Victoria. Waste from surface treatment also includes waste from heat treatment and operations containing cyanides.
FRA) Waste containing PCBs, and waste from the production and use of organic solvents: 1989 data.
IRL) Waste from the production and use of organic solvents: includes miscellaneous chemical waste. Waste oil: includes only lubricating oil.
LUX) Data for clinical waste refer only to exported waste. Data for organic solvents refer to 1990.
NLD) Data for clinical and pharmaceutical waste refer only to pharmaceutical waste. Waste from the production and use of resins and latex also includes waste from the production and use of plastics.
NOR) Waste containing PCBs: 1987 data. Waste from the production and use of paints and pigments also include resins and latex. Data are based on expert estimates.
CSFR) Secretariat estimates.

Source: OECD/OCDE

Notes:
a) Ces catégories sont fondées sur la classification des déchets dangereux de la Convention de Bâle (Annexe 4). Les matériaux spécifiques inclus dans chaque colonne peuvent être différents à cause des classifications nationales.
CAN) Déchets contenant des PCB: quantité stockées en attente d'élimination et non pas quantités produites annuellement. Déchets de finition des métaux et plastiques: incluent des déchets cyanurés de traitements thermiques et d'opérations de trempe. Déchets des peintures et pigments: incluent des résines et du latex.
USA) Les données sont de la fin des années 80. Les données sur les déchets contenant des PCB proviennent d'une enquête de 1985 auprès des producteurs de déchets dangereux; ils ne représentent donc pas le volume total des États-Unis. Les déchets issus de la production et de l'utilisation de solvants organiques incluent tous les déchets industriels organiques. Les résines et le latex incluent les plastiques et le caoutchouc.
JPN) Huiles usées: inclut les solvants usés. Déchets de finition des métaux concernent tous les déchets de métaux. Résines et latex: incluent les plastiques et le caoutchouc.
AUS) Les données concernent: Victoria, la Nouvelle-Galles du Sud et l'Australie-Méridionale; déchets des huiles usées et pigments: incluent aussi la Tasmanie; déchets cliniques: Victoria uniquement. Déchets de finition des métaux et plastiques: incluent des déchets cyanurés de traitements thermiques et d'opérations de trempe.
FRA) Déchets contenant des PCB et déchets issus de la production et de l'utilisation de solvants organiques: données 1989.
IRL) Les données sur les déchets issus de la production et de l'utilisation des solvants organiques comprennent des déchets chimiques divers. Les données sur les huiles usées ne comprennent que les huiles de graissage.
LUX) Les déchets cliniques se réfèrent aux déchets exportés uniquement. Déchets des solvants organiques: 1990.
NLD) Déchets cliniques et pharmaceutiques: déchets pharmaceutiques uniquement. Déchets des résines et latex: incluent les déchets de la production et de l'utilisation des plastiques.
NOR) Déchets contenant des PCB: 1987. Déchets des peintures et pigments: incluent les déchets des résines et latex. Données fondées sur des estimations d'experts.
CSFR) Estimations du Secrétariat.

The next table concerns the national production, movement and disposal of hazardous waste for selected countries.

It shows the importance of transfrontier movements of hazardous waste, and of the various disposal methods.

In reading this table one should bear in mind that definitions and methods of estimation vary from country to country.

Le tableau suivant est relatif à la production nationale, aux mouvements et au traitement de déchets dangereux dans divers pays.

Il montre l'importance des mouvements transfrontières des déchets dangereux, et des différentes méthodes d'élimination mises en oeuvre.

La lecture de ce tableau doit tenir compte des différences de définitions et de méthodes d'estimation entre les pays concernés.

GENERATION, MOVEMENT AND DISPOSAL OF HAZARDOUS WASTE (a), latest year available
PRODUCTION, MOUVEMENTS ET ÉLIMINATION DE DÉCHETS DANGEREUX (a), dernière année disponible

1000 tonnes

| | | Year / Année | Generation/ production | Movements/mouvements | | Thermal Treatment/ Traitement thermique | Other Treatment/ Autres traitements (c) | Recovery operations / Opérations de récupération | Landfill/ Mise en décharge (d) |
				Imports/ Importations (b)	Exports/ Exportations (b)				
Canada	*	1991	7 786	124	175	225	155	276	288
Mexico/Mexique		1992	7 700	..	32	..	..	..	197
USA/Etats-Unis	*	1991	276 000	..	143	3 036	209 760	6 072	24 840
Australia/Australie	*	1992	426	-	3	22	96	85	175
N.Zealand/N.Zélande		1990	110	-	10	..	..	..	..
Austria/Autriche		1990	668	28	84	123	154	15	354
Belgium/Belgique	*	1994	27 529	287	103	..	..	..	..
Denmark/Danemark	*	1993	91	100	16	..	85	3	3
Finland/Finlande	*	1992	560	5	21	44	448	20	24
France	*	1991	4 000	637	21	1 040	377	..	1 943
w.Germany/Allem.occ.	*	1990	6 633	76	569	..	..	..	..
Greece/Grèce	*	1992	450	-	0.1	..	..	88	..
Iceland/Islande	*	1992	6	-	-	6	..	..	-
Ireland/Irlande		..	66	..	14	..	..	..	..
Italy/Italie	*	1991	3 387	-	19	..	3 090	..	284
Luxembourg		1992	86	..	12	..	..	..	20
Netherlands/Pays-Bas	*	1992	1 430	243	173	160	161	36	438
Norway/Norvège	*	1992	151	15	17	3	2	40	7
Portugal	*	1992	1 365	7	0.8	10	-	46	960
Spain/Espagne		1987	1 708	63	14	..	..	..	..
Sweden/Suède		1985	500	60	10	..	..	..	..
Switzerland/Suisse	*	1993	837	8	126	266	247	112	212
Turkey/Turquie		1989	300	-	-	..	..	..	..
UK/Royaume-Uni	*	1993	1 957	67		224	668	195	936
Former CSFR/Ex-RFTS		1987	11 021	..	..	100	248	..	2 139
Czech R./R.Tchèque		1987	8 317	..	..	..	..	..	..
Slovak R./R.Slovaque		1987	2 704	..	..	..	..	..	..
Hungary/Hongrie	*	1992	795	1	4	..	..	..	..
Poland/Pologne		1992	3 444	..	..	..	..	..	..

Notes:
a) Hazardous waste refers to waste streams controlled according to the Basel Convention on Transboundary Movements of Hazardous wastes and their Disposal (see Annex IV of the convention for complete definition and methods of treatment, movement and disposal). National definitions often differ, and caution should be exercised when using these figures.
b) Imports, exports: should refer to actual amounts moved, but may in some cases refer to total authorisations (notifications) granted.
c) Physico-chemical and biological treatment.
d) Including land treatment, deep injection, surface impoundment and specially engineered landfill.
CAN) Treatment and disposal: Ontario only (approx. 32% of total generation). Movements: 1992 data.
USA) Exports: 1993 data. Movements: written notice and consent required for exports only. Other treatment: includes incineration with energy recovery.
AUS) Victoria only.
NZL) Movements: 1993 data; exports for recovery only.
AUT) Movements: 1993 data.
BEL) Wallonia region only.
DNK) Imports, exports: 1992 data.
FIN) Imports, exports: 1993 data.
FRA) Excludes internal thermal treatment by private enterprises.
DEU) Movements: waste going to final disposal only; imports: 1992; exports: 1993.
GRC) Exports: PCB waste only.
ISL) Excludes haz. waste from households and small enterprises.
ITA) Movements: 1993 data. Other treatment: includes thermal treatment.
NLD) Amount generated: all waste defined as special waste in Dutch legislation. Imports: includes 211 kt of contaminated soil.
NOR) Amount generated: all waste defined as special waste in Norwegian regulations. Data are based on expert estimates. Imports and exports: 1993 data. Thermal and other treatment: 1990 data.
PRT) Movements: 1993 data. Treatment and disposal: 1987 data.
CHE) Amount generated: all waste defined as special waste in Swiss legislation. Amount generated according to Basel Convention: 327 kt.
UKD) Data refer to fiscal year. England and Wales only. Only waste going to final disposal must be notified (under 1988 transfrontier shipments of hazardous waste regulations). Total generated in UK: 2 077 kt in 1993/94.
HUN) Under Hungarian law, hazardous waste amounts to 4 217 kt (in 1992).

Notes :
a) Voir L'annexe IV de la convention de Bâle pour une définition complète des déchets dangereux, de leurs mouvements et élimination, ainsi que des méthodes de traitement. Les définitions nationales peuvent être différentes; les chiffres sont à interpréter avec précaution.
b) Importations, exportations : quantités effectivement transportées ; dans certains cas les données se réfèrent aux quantitées autorisées (notifiées).
c) Traitements physico-chimiques et biologiques.
d) Y compris le traitement en milieu terrestre, l'injection en profondeur, le lagunage, la mise en décharge spécialement aménagée.
CAN) Traitements et élimination: Ontario uniquement (approx. 32% de la production totale). Mouvements: données 1992.
USA) Exportations : données 1993; mouvements: notification écrite et autorisation sont nécessaires aux exportations. Autres traitements: comprend l'incinération avec récupération d'énergie.
AUS) Victoria uniquement.
NZL) Mouvements: données 1993; exportations pour récupération seulement.
AUT) Mouvements: données 1993.
BEL) Wallonie uniquement.
DNK) Importations, exportations : données 1992.
FIN) Importations, exportations : données 1993.
FRA) Les traitements thermiques réalisés en interne par les entreprises sont exclus.
DEU) Mouvements: déchets destinés à l'élimination finale uniquement; importations: 1992; exportations: 1993.
GRC) Exportations : déchets contenant des diphényles polychlorés uniquement.
ISL) Les déchets dangereux des ménages et petites entreprises sont exclus.
ITA) Autres traitements: comprend le traitement thermique. Mouvements: données 1993.
NLD) La quantité totale produite correspond aux déchets spéciaux tels qu'ils sont définis par la législation hollandaise. Importations : incluent 211 kt de terre contaminée.
NOR) La quantité totale produite correspond aux déchets spéciaux tels qu'ils sont définis par la législation norvégienne ; données fondées sur des estimations d'experts ; mouvements : 1993 ; traitements thermiques et autres : 1990.
PRT) Mouvements: 1993. Traitement et élimination: 1987.
CHE) Quantité totale produite : déchets spéciaux tels qu'ils sont définis par la législation suisse. Selon la convention de Bâle cette quantité s'élèverait à 327 kt.
UKD) Année fiscale ; Angleterre et Pays de Galles uniquement ; selon la loi de 1988 sur les mouvements transfrontières, seuls les déchets destinés à l'élimination finale doivent être notifiés. Production totale du Royaume- Uni : 2 077 kt en 1993/94.
HUN) Selon la loi hongroise, la production de déchets dangereux s'élevait en 1992 à 4 217kt.

Source: OECD/OCDE

The following table concerns waste recycling in selected countries. It shows recycling rates for two materials: paper and glass. This table refers to municipal waste, waste handled by the scrapping industry and other waste; it excludes recycling <u>within</u> industrial establishments. Recycling is defined as any reuse of material that diverts it from the waste stream, except reuse as fuel.

"Recycling rates" refer to material reutilised in production processes relative to apparent consumption (economic notion of domestic production of the respective product + imports - exports).

It should, however, be noted that definitions may vary from one country to another. In particular, total amounts of waste produced rather than apparent consumption may be used in some areas to derive recycling rates.

Le tableau suivant concerne les activités de recyclage dans certains pays et présente les taux de recyclage pour deux types de matériaux qui sont le papier et le verre. Ce tableau concerne les déchets municipaux, les déchets traités par l'industrie de récupération et les autres déchets, en excluant le recyclage <u>interne</u> aux établissements industriels. Le recyclage est défini comme toute réutilisation de matériel qui le dévie du flux de déchets, à l'exception de la réutilisation comme combustible.

"Le taux de recyclage" fait référence aux matériaux réutilisés dans les processus de production par rapport à la consommation apparente (notion économique de la production nationale du produit concerné + les importations - les exportations).

Il faut cependant noter que les définitions peuvent varier d'un pays à l'autre. Le taux de recyclage peut ainsi dans certains cas se rapporter aux quantités de déchets produits et non à la consommation apparente.

WASTE RECYCLING RATES (a), 1980-1994
TAUX DE RECYCLAGE DES DÉCHETS (a), 1980-1994

(% of apparent consumption/% de la consommation apparente)

		Paper and Cardboard/Papiers et cartons										Glass/Verre										
		1980	1985	1986	1987	1988	1989	1990	1991	1992	1993	1980	1985	1986	1987	1988	1989	1990	1991	1992	1993	1994
Canada	*	20	23	..	..	..	..	28	..	32	..	..	..	..	..	..	..	69	..	75	..	..
Mexico/Mexique	*	..	..	..	..	..	..	..	2	2	2	..	..	..	..	..	..	..	4	4	4	..
USA/Etats-Unis	*	22	..	..	..	..	..	29	..	..	34	5	..	..	..	..	..	20	..	..	22	..
Japan/Japon	*	48	50	50	49	48	49	50	51	51	..	35	47	55	54	49	48	48	52	56	..	..
Australia/Australie	*	..	36	..	..	..	..	51	50	..	..	..	..	..	..	..	..	..	..	36	..	..
N.Zealand/N.Zélande		..	..	..	..	..	..	..	..	..	..	..	..	..	..	..	..	..	..	..	..	..
Austria/Autriche		..	37	..	..	..	..	78	..	..	..	..	38	39	44	..	..	..	60	64	68	76
Belgium/Belgique	*	..	14	14	14	..	..	..	..	..	11	..	42	44	39	..	..	..	55	54	55	67
Denmark/Danemark	*	26	31	..	..	..	30	35	35	36	..	..	19	32	32	..	..	..	35	48	62	67
Finland/Finlande		35	39	..	..	..	40	43	..	45	..	10	21	..	25	..	..	36	31	44	46	50
France		30	34	33	34	35	37	37	38	39	42	..	26	28	26	..	29	29	41	44	46	48
Germany/Allemagne	*	33	40	38	39	39	40	40	40	43	46	23	44	45	49	49	54	54	63	65	70	75
Greece/Grèce		22	25	..	..	..	..	28	29	30	30	15	15	..	..	..	..	15	17	20	20	29
Iceland/Islande		..	..	..	..	..	..	10	30	..	..	..	..	..	..	..	..	70	75	75	..	..
Ireland/Irlande		..	10	6	11	..	..	..	3	..	..	8	7	8	8	..	..	23	23	27	29	31
Italy/Italie		..	38	38	35	..	..	..	47	..	..	20	25	26	38	..	..	48	53	53	52	54
Luxembourg		..	..	..	..	..	..	..	..	..	..	..	..	..	..	..	..	..	..	..	..	..
Netherlands/Pays-Bas	*	46	50	..	..	..	..	50	53	..	..	17	49	49	50	52	55	67	70	73	76	77
Norway/Norvège	*	22	23	21	23	21	24	26	26	31	32	..	..	..	..	..	..	..	22	44	67	72
Portugal		..	37	..	..	..	39	45	..	41	..	..	10	13	14	14	24	27	30	30	29	32
Spain/Espagne		..	57	55	54	..	..	51	..	..	78	..	13	20	22	..	..	27	27	27	29	31
Sweden/Suède		34	43	41	44	..	..	43	46	..	50	..	20	..	..	22	22	..	44	58	59	56
Switzerland/Suisse		35	39	37	37	..	..	49	51	54	54	..	46	46	47	..	55	65	71	72	78	84
Turkey/Turquie		..	..	..	..	30	31	34	30	39	..	..	33	25	27	27	33	31	28	40	23	22
UK/Royaume-Uni	*	30	28	27	27	27	27	32	34	34	32	5	12	14	14	14	17	21	21	26	29	28

Notes:
a) Recycling is defined as reuse of material that diverts it from the waste stream, except for recycling within industrial plants and the reuse of material as fuel. The recycling rate is the ratio of the quantity recycled to the apparent consumption (domestic production + imports - exports).
CAN) Glass: data include the reuse of refillable money-back bottles.
MEX) Recycling rates are based on amounts of waste generated.
USA) Data refer to the material diverted from the municipal waste stream. Recycling rates are based on amounts of waste generated.
JPN) Glass: returnable bottles are excluded. Data refer to reuse of glass as cullet compared to national production of glass bottles.
AUS) Paper: data refer to newsprint, cardboard, and paper packaging; definitions of recycling vary according to the material collected (e.g. may include amounts incinerated to divert them from landfill).
BEL) Paper: 1993 data refer to 1994 and Wallonia only.
DNK) Glass: excluding refillable bottles recovered for reuse (400 million bottles in 1993).
DEU) Glass: recycling rate is based on total sales and western Germany only. Paper: until 1989 western Germany only.
NLD) Paper: data refer to reuse in the paper industry. Glass: glass collected in bottle banks.
NOR) Glass: excludes considerable amounts of glass recovered before entering the waste stream (deposit/reuse of bottles).
UKD) Glass: Great Britain only; glass collected in bottle banks and from industrial sources (bottlers and packers) and flat glass. Includes imports; excludes exports.

Source: OECD/OCDE, FEVE

Notes :
a) Le recyclage est défini comme toute réutilisation de matériau qui le dévie du flux des déchets, à l'exception du recyclage des matériaux sur place dans l'installation industrielle et de la réutilisation comme combustible. Le taux de recyclage est la proportion de la quantité recyclée par rapport à la consommation apparente (production intérieure + importations - exportations).
CAN) Verre : y compris la réutilisation de bouteilles consignées.
MEX) Taux de recyclage fondé sur les quantités de déchets produits.
USA) Données concernant les matériaux soustraits au flux de déchets municipaux. Taux de recyclage fondés sur les quantités de déchets produits.
JPN) Verre : exclut les bouteilles consignées; comprend le verre réutilisé comme calcin rapporté à la production nationale de bouteilles en verre.
AUS) Papiers : données concernant le papier journal, les cartons et les papiers d'emballage; les définitions du recyclage varient selon le matériau collecté (p.ex. peut inclure des quantités incinérées pour diminuer les mises en décharge).
BEL) Papier : les données 1993 sont de 1994 et concernent la Wallonie uniquement.
DNK) Verre : exclut la réutilisation des bout. consignées (400 millions de bouteilles en 1993).
DEU) Verre : taux de recyclage fondés sur les ventes totales et l'Allemagne occidentale uniquement. Papiers : jusqu'en 1989, l'Allemagne occidentale uniquement.
NLD) Papiers : réutilisation dans l'industrie du papier uniquement. Verre : provenant des conteneurs à bouteilles.
NOR) Verre : exclut des quantités importantes récupérées avant d'entrer dans le flux des déchets (réutilisation des bouteilles consignées).
UKD) Verre : Grande-Bretagne uniquement ; verre provenant des conteneurs à bouteilles et de sources industrielles (embouteilleurs et emballeurs) ; comprend aussi le verre plat. Inclut les importations ; exclut les exportations.

The following table presents the number and capacity of waste treatment and disposal installations. It shows landfill sites, incineration plants and other treatment plants (including physical, chemical and biological treatment).

It should be noted that these data do not represent all waste treatment and disposal facilities, and that the specific services and activities may vary from country to country.

Le tableau suivant présente le nombre et la capacité des installations de traitement et d'élimination des déchets. Il présente les décharges, les usines d'incinération et les autres centres de traitement (traitement physique, chimique et biologique).

Il faut noter que des données ne représentent pas tous les sites de traitement et d'élimination, et que les services et les activitiés spécifiques peuvent varier selon les pays.

WASTE TREATMENT AND DISPOSAL INSTALLATIONS, selected countries, latest year available
INSTALLATIONS DE TRAITEMENT ET D'ÉLIMINATION DES DÉCHETS, pays sélectionnés, dernière année disponible

		Year/ Année	Landfill Sites / Décharges		Incineration Plants / Usines d'incineration				Treatment Plants/ Centres de traitement (a)	
			total number/ nombre total	total capacity/ capacité totale (1 000 t)	total number/ nombre total	total capacity/ capacité totale (1 000 t)	% with energy reclamation/ % avec récupération d'énergie number/ nombre	capacity/ capacité	total number/ nombre total	total capacity/ capacité totale (1 000 t)
Canada	*	1992	10 000	..	18	1 600	44.4	81.3	..	..
Mexico/Mexique	*	1993	85	28 089	..	..	..	..	..	..
USA/Etats-Unis	*	1990	16 416	..	..	..	..	..	..	..
Japan/Japon	*	1991	2 205	156 830	1 841	64 816	..	..	617	8 848
Australia/Australie	*	1992	1 129	190 399	..	..	..	..	..	..
Austria/Autriche		1990	160	3 216	4	370	100.0	100.0	23	150
Belgium/ Belgique	*	1994	46	..	4	..	..	..	18	..
Denmark/Danemark	*	1992	170	45	38	2 150	97.4	97.7	..	..
Finland/Finlande		1990	750	25 000	2	150	100.0	100.0	1	25
France	*	1992	495	17 943	329	9 740	30.4	71.3	89	1 937
Germany/Allemagne		1990	8 594	..	161	..	..	..	221	..
Greece/Grèce		1992	4 850	2 971	1	..	..	..	..	4
Iceland/Islande		1992	6	140	3	25	..	..	-	-
Italy/Italie	*	1991	1 463	33 681	204	1 912	..	..	230	6 317
Luxembourg	*	1992	4	150	1	150	100.0	100.0	3	5
Netherl./Pays-Bas	*	1992	72	..	9	2 850	66.7	93.9	7	..
Norway/Norvège	*	1992	208	..	23	..	34.8	..	..	..
Portugal		1990	303	821	..	..	..	..	2	303
Spain/Espagne	*	1993	118	7 799	18	635	22.2	78.1	24	1 560
Sweden/Suède		1990	282	7 300	23	1 800	100.0	100.0	..	..
Switzerl./Suisse		1992	50	..	30	2 275	83.3	93.6	..	..
UK/Royaume-Uni	*	1993	3 435	..	214	..	..	..	328	..
Hungary/Hongrie	*	1992	2 683	..	2	330	100.0	100.0	..	..
Poland/Pologne	*	1993	1 334	56 811	..	5	..	..	..	502

Notes:
a) Includes physical, chemical and biological treatment, and solidification.
CAN) Landfill sites: 1990 data.
MEX) Installations for municipal waste only. Capacity of landfill sites includes open and illegal sites.
USA) Facilities for the disposal of hazardous solid waste are not included.
JPN) Installations for municipal waste only. Landfill capacity is in 1 000 m3.
AUS) Queensland and Northern Territory are not included. Definition of landfill varies from state to state. Figure for capacity refers to 1989.
BEL) Wallonia region only.
DNK) Landfill capacity is for 130 sites. Number of incineration plants: 1989 figure.
FRA) Treatment plants: biological treatment facilities only. Figures for capacity refer to the quantity disposed of per year.
ITA) Treatment includes recycling and recovery. Figures for capacity refer to the quantity disposed of per year.
LUX) The total number of landfill sites excludes facilities for inert material.
NLD) Landfill sites include only sites in active exploitation.
NOR) Excludes data from sites receiving less than 50 tonnes per year, dumps exclusively for bulky matter and private installations for industrial waste.
ESP) Includes only controlled landfill sites. The number of uncontrolled sites is estimated to be 5 800.
UKD) Data based on site licences issued. Great Britain only.
HUN) Landfill capacity is in 1 000 m³.
POL) Data for landfill sites include only facilities for industrial and municipal waste. The capacity of treatment plants is based on the amount of industrial and municipal waste that was actually treated.

Notes :
a) Comprend les procédés de traitement et de solidification physiques, chimiques et biologiques.
CAN) Décharges : données 1990.
MEX) Installations pour déchets municipaux uniquement. Décharges : le nombre se réfère aux sites d'enfouissement ; la capacité comprend les sites illégaux et les sites à ciel ouvert.
USA) Exclut les installations d'élimination des déchets dangereux.
JPN) Déchets municipaux uniquement. Capacité des décharges exprimée en 1000 m3.
AUS) Queensland et Territoire-du-Nord exclus ; les définitions des décharges varient d'un état à l'autre. Capacité totale des décharges : chiffre 1989.
BEL) Wallonie seulement.
DNK) Capacité des décharges: concerne 130 sites. Nombre d'usines d'incinération: chiffre 1989.
FRA) Centres de traitement : installations de traitement biologique uniquement. Les chiffres sur la capacité se réfèrent à la quantité effectivement eliminée chaque année.
ITA) Les données sur le traitement comprennent le recyclage et la récupération. Les chiffres sur la capacité totale se réfèrent à la quantité effectivement éliminée chaque année.
LUX) Le nombre total de décharges exclut les décharges pour déchets inertes.
NLD) Décharges : uniquement les sites en activité.
NOR) Exclut les sites recevant moins de 50 tonnes par an, les décharges pour déchets encombrants et les installations privées destinées aux déchets industriels.
ESP) Décharges contrôlées uniquement. Le nombre de sites sauvages est estimé à 5 800.
UKD) Les données sont fondées sur le nombre de permis délivré. Grande-Bretagne uniquement.
HUN) La capacité des décharges est exprimée en 1 000 m3.
POL) Les données sur les décharges ne comprennent que les installations d'élimination de déchets industriels et municipaux. La capacité des centres de traitement est fondée sur la quantité de déchets industriels et municipaux réellement traitée.

Source: OECD/OCDE

The following table refers to nuclear waste: it presents annual spent fuel arisings in nuclear power plants of OECD countries. The data are expressed in tonnes of heavy metal, and include projections and estimates up to the year 2010.

Spent fuel arisings are one part of the radioactive waste generated at various stages of the nuclear fuel cycle (uranium mining and milling, fuel enrichment, reactor operation, spent fuel reprocessing). Radioactive waste also arises from decontamination and decommissioning of nuclear facilities, and from other activities using isotopes, such as scientific research and medical activities.

The impact of nuclear waste on humans and the environment depends on the level of the radioactivity and on the conditions under which the waste is handled, treated, stored and disposed of.

While reading this table it should be noted that these data do not represent all radioactive waste generated, and that spent fuel arisings depend on the importance of nuclear electricity in the energy supply and on the nuclear plant technologies adopted.

Le tableau suivant porte sur les déchets nucléaires et présente les quantités de combustible irradié produites annuellement dans les centrales nucléaires des pays de l'OCDE. Les données sont exprimées en tonnes de métal lourd, et comprennent des projections et des estimations jusqu'en l'an 2010.

Le combustible irradié représente une partie des déchets radioactifs produits au cours du cycle du combustible nucléaire (extraction et traitement de l'uranium, enrichissement du combustible, fonctionnement des réacteurs, retraitement du combustible irradié). D'autres déchets radiocatifs sont issus des processus de décontamination et de déclassement des sites nucléaires et d'autres activités impliquant l'utilisation d'isotopes (recherche scientifique, secteur médical, etc.).

L'impact de ces déchets sur l'homme et sur l'environnement est lié au niveau de leur radioactivité et aux conditions dans lesquelles ils sont manipulés, traités, stockés et éliminés.

Lors de la lecture de ce tableau il faut se rappeler que ces données ne représentent pas l'ensemble des déchets radioactifs produits et que la quantité de combustible irradié dépend de l'importance de l'énergie nucléaire dans l'approvisionnement en énergie et des technologies appliquées dans les centrales nucléaires.

NUCLEAR WASTE: SPENT FUEL ARISINGS (a), 1982-2010
DÉCHETS NUCLÉAIRES: COMBUSTIBLE IRRADIÉ PRODUIT (a), 1982-2010

tonnes of HM/tonnes de ML

		1982	1983	1984	1985	1986	1987	1988	1989	1990	1991	1992	1993	1995	2000	2005	2010(b)
Canada		856	830	1 070	1 420	1 400	1 500	1 500	1 300	1 213	1 383	1 690	1 690	1 690	1 782	1 798	1 798
USA/Etats-Unis		1 100	1 116	1 200	1 300	1 600	1 621	1 700	2 000	2 200	2 100	2 300	2 400	2 400	2 100	2 000	1 800
Japan/Japon	*	510	530	630	625	660	1 060	830	790	688	995	869	876	1 023	1 115	1 265	1 457
Australia/Australie		-	-	-	-	-	-	-	-	-	-	-	-	-	-	-	-
N.Zealand/N.Zélande		-	-	-	-	-	-	-	-	-	-	-	-	-	-	-	-
Austria/Autriche		-	-	-	-	-	-	-	-	-	-	-	-	-	-	-	-
Belgium/Belgique		44	37	85	97	140	140	135	122	120	120	102	84	120	120	120	120
Denmark/Danemark		-	-	-	-	-	-	-	-	-	-	-	-	-	-	-	-
Finland/Finlande		62	62	64	65	72	76	73	73	74	63	60	68	65	64	64	64
France		375	200	200	300	640	750	900	1 000	1 120	1 200	1 050	1 250	1 205	1 200	1 250	1 300
w. Germany/Allemagne occ.		270	300	300	350	430	380	320	360	490	510	500	490	470	430	430	430
Greece/Grèce		-	-	-	-	-	-	-	-	-	-	-	-	-	-	-	-
Iceland/Islande		-	-	-	-	-	-	-	-	-	-	-	-	-	-	-	-
Ireland/Irlande		-	-	-	-	-	-	-	-	-	-	-	-	-	-	-	-
Italy/Italie	*	38	26	26	38	58	13	0	0	0	0	0	0	0	0	0	..
Luxembourg		-	-	-	-	-	-	-	-	-	-	-	-	-	-	-	-
Netherlands/Pays-Bas	*	16	16	12	12	14	14	14	15	17	15	15	15	14	13	15	30
Norway/Norvège		-	-	-	-	-	-	-	-	-	-	-	-	-	-	-	-
Portugal		-	-	-	-	-	-	-	-	-	-	-	-	-	-	-	-
Spain/Espagne		60	110	120	160	203	206	235	191	187	160	168	156	166	156	160	140
Sweden/Suède		100	100	245	238	296	236	250	190	230	250	250	230	250	250	250	0
Switzerland/Suisse		60	60	60	85	85	80	85	85	85	85	85	85	85	85	85	85
Turkey/Turquie	*	-	-	-	-	-	-	-	-	-	-	-	-	-	0	29	58
UK/Royaume-Uni	*	900	820	775	775	843	919	884	910	1 022	1 022	997	1 080	874	474	274	244
North America/Amérique N.*		1 956	1 946	2 270	2 720	3 000	3 121	3 200	3 300	3 413	3 483	3 990	4 090	4 090	3 882	3 798	3 598
OECD/OCDE Europe*		1 925	1 731	1 887	2 120	2 781	2 814	2 896	2 946	3 345	3 425	3 227	3 458	3 249	2 792	2 677	2 471
EU/UE-15*		1 865	1 671	1 827	2 035	2 696	2 734	2 811	2 861	3 260	3 340	3 142	3 373	3 164	2 707	2 563	2 328
OECD/OCDE* **		4 391	4 207	4 787	5 465	6 441	6 995	6 926	7 036	7 446	7 903	8 086	8 424	8 362	7 789	7 740	7 526

Notes:
a) Spent Fuel Arisings expressed in tonnes of Heavy Metal.
b) OECD estimates.
JPN) For fiscal year.
UK) OECD estimates.

Source: OECD/OCDE

Notes :
a) Quantités de combustible irradié produites, exprimées en tonnes de métal lourd.
b) Estimations de l'OCDE.
JPN) Pour l'exercice financier.
UK) estimations de l'OCDE.

8. ENERGY

8. ÉNERGIE

INTRODUCTION

This section refers to energy production, exchange and use, activities that generate pressures on the environment. These pressures include pollution of air, water and land; consumption of natural resources, such as land and materials; negative effects on wildlife and natural areas; and risks of contamination from nuclear activities and of spills from oil production and transport.

These pressures are due to:

- ▸ mining of energy sources and the production of energy;

- ▸ transport of energy carriers;

- ▸ use of energy;

- ▸ the nuclear fuel cycle.

The data presented come mainly from the OECD (IEA). In general, these data offer a reasonably good level of comparability.

Apart from some tables concerning electricity generation, all data are expressed using a common unit for energy: the tonne of oil equivalent. Coal and gas data are expressed in terms of the quantity of oil that gives the same amount of heat. Hydro and other non-thermal sources (e.g. wind, tide, photovoltaic) are converted to oil equivalent based on the energy content of the electricity generated assuming efficiency of 100 per cent. Nuclear power is converted based on the average efficiency of a modern nuclear power plant, i.e. 33 per cent, while geothermal heat assumes efficiency of 10 per cent. Further information concerning conversion factors can be found in the IEA publication "Energy Balances of OECD Countries", OECD, Paris.

Data on energy-related emissions of air pollutants and on energy reclamation from municipal waste are presented in the air and waste sections, respectively. Data on nuclear waste (spent fuel) are presented in the waste section.

INTRODUCTION

Cette section a trait aux secteurs de la production, des échanges et de l'utilisation de l'énergie qui exercent des pressions sur l'environnement. Ces pressions sont à l'origine de la pollution de l'air, de l'eau et des sols ; de la consommation de ressources naturelles telles que les sols ou les matériaux ; d'effets négatifs sur la faune, la flore et les zones naturelles ; des risques de contamination dus aux activités nucléaires, et de rejets de pétrole liés aux activités d'extraction ou de transport.

Ces pressions sont liées :

  ▸ à l'exploitation minière de minerais et à la production d'énergie ;

  ▸ au transport de l'énergie ;

  ▸ à l'utilisation de l'énergie ;

  ▸ au cycle du combustible nucléaire.

Les données présentées proviennent pour la plupart de l'OCDE (AIE). En règle générale ces données bénéficient d'un niveau assez élevé de comparabilité.

Toutes les données sont exprimées dans une unité commune, la tonne équivalent pétrole, sauf pour certains tableaux concernant la production d'énergie électrique. Les données concernant le gaz et le charbon ont été exprimées en quantité de pétrole fournissant la même quantité de chaleur. Les sources d'énergie hydraulique et non-thermique (p. ex. énergie éolienne, marémotrice, photovoltaïque, etc.) sont converties en prenant l'équivalent en énergie primaire de l'électricité produite par les centrales, sur la base d'un rendement moyen de 100 pour cent. L'énergie nucléaire est convertie sur la base d'un rendement moyen d'une centrale nucléaire moderne (33 pour cent), alors que la chaleur géothermique est convertie sur la base d'un rendement moyen de 10 pour cent. On pourra obtenir des renseignements complémentaires sur les facteurs de conversion dans la publication de l'AIE, "Bilans énergétiques des pays de l'OCDE", OCDE, Paris.

Les données concernant l'émission de polluants atmosphériques due à l'utilisation de l'énergie et la récupération d'énergie se trouvent respectivement dans les sections sur l'air et les déchets solides. Les données sur les déchets nucléaires (combustible irradié) se trouvent dans la section sur les déchets.

The following table shows indigenous production of primary energy, i.e. hard coal and lignite and other solid fuels, crude oil together with natural gas liquids and feedstocks, natural gas, nuclear power, hydroelectricity, geothermal power, solar electricity and heat extracted from ambient air by heat pumps.

Le tableau suivant présente la production nationale d'énergie primaire, c'est-à-dire la houille, le lignite et les autres combustibles solides, le pétrole brut ainsi que les condensats de gaz naturel et les produits d'alimentation des raffineries, le gaz naturel et l'électricité d'origine nucléaire, hydraulique, géothermique et solaire, la chaleur extraite du milieu ambiant par les pompes à chaleur.

INDIGENOUS ENERGY PRODUCTION, 1980-1993
PRODUCTION NATIONALE D'ÉNERGIE, 1980-1993

Mtoe/Mtep

	1980	1981	1982	1983	1984	1985	1986	1987	1988	1989	1990	1991	1992	1993
Canada	207.36	200.62	202.74	207.13	228.62	241.07	239.62	252.65	272.77	274.00	274.14	285.21	293.45	315.09
Mexico/Mexique	145.00	168.57	193.56	189.86	194.11	191.92	179.94	187.88	187.73	189.85	194.96	203.00	203.56	203.63
USA/Etats-Unis	1547.78	1542.28	1524.09	1462.87	1583.09	1564.89	1551.75	1583.92	1611.60	1617.11	1650.69	1664.23	1648.35	1616.70
Japan/Japon	43.25	44.58	47.97	50.83	54.75	62.21	63.95	66.65	64.40	64.91	68.90	72.70	76.06	83.87
Australia/Australie	86.10	95.15	99.30	103.78	112.10	125.29	135.21	145.07	138.03	145.09	157.43	162.97	170.07	173.20
N.Zealand/N.Zélande	5.59	5.79	6.69	7.12	7.91	8.89	9.80	9.67	10.46	11.52	12.15	12.67	12.82	13.16
Austria/Autriche	7.65	7.34	7.41	7.22	7.30	7.47	7.56	8.79	9.10	9.00	8.82	8.86	9.18	9.10
Belgium/Belgique	7.98	8.08	9.06	10.95	12.02	13.95	14.69	14.48	13.44	12.76	12.60	12.49	12.23	11.74
Denmark/Danemark	0.65	1.15	2.13	2.68	3.13	4.56	6.17	7.90	8.13	9.38	9.93	11.79	12.78	13.74
Finland/Finlande	6.89	8.93	10.07	10.15	10.51	10.36	11.32	10.69	11.21	11.65	11.34	10.73	11.50	11.96
France	47.00	58.81	58.38	66.99	78.98	86.11	92.99	96.33	97.78	102.53	104.76	109.71	111.59	118.54
Germany/Allemagne	184.24	190.89	191.49	188.21	196.11	207.90	199.49	198.96	201.61	199.83	184.84	166.27	160.72	149.36
w.Germany/All.occ.	123.45	127.49	127.23	122.92	128.15	136.50	130.68	131.06	132.48	132.37	130.17	..	..	..
Greece/Grèce	3.70	4.42	5.53	5.97	6.45	6.95	7.25	8.07	8.27	8.86	8.81	8.71	8.61	8.61
Iceland/Islande	0.80	0.95	1.02	1.13	1.15	1.16	1.19	1.23	1.29	1.31	1.33	1.30	1.30	1.32
Ireland/Irlande	1.89	2.49	3.03	3.21	3.63	2.85	2.63	3.01	2.87	3.76	3.36	3.18	2.99	3.37
Italy/Italie	20.03	20.94	22.71	21.64	22.81	22.94	25.00	24.47	25.82	25.39	25.48	26.22	27.45	28.55
Luxembourg	0.03	0.03	0.03	0.03	0.03	0.03	0.03	0.03	0.04	0.04	0.03	0.03	0.03	0.03
Netherlands/Pays-Bas	71.83	66.76	57.46	61.81	62.94	66.34	62.33	61.96	55.11	59.37	59.81	66.65	66.78	67.88
Norway/Norvège	55.74	56.04	56.14	64.00	69.76	72.88	77.31	86.66	94.26	115.02	120.12	130.88	146.25	153.24
Portugal	1.48	1.25	1.45	1.60	1.74	1.94	1.85	1.95	2.22	1.73	2.05	2.03	1.56	1.91
Spain/Espagne	15.78	17.72	19.67	21.96	25.09	26.49	28.33	27.91	30.27	31.48	31.15	31.24	30.92	30.14
Sweden/Suède	16.13	19.26	19.10	20.87	24.29	26.86	29.07	29.41	29.85	28.98	29.75	31.51	29.45	29.27
Switzerland/Suisse	7.03	7.64	7.72	7.80	8.10	9.41	9.55	9.81	9.86	9.36	9.58	9.65	9.82	10.17
Turkey/Turquie	17.19	18.12	18.95	19.21	20.11	21.67	23.28	27.72	24.51	25.40	26.35	26.39	26.92	26.70
UK/Royaume-Uni	197.77	206.57	221.07	233.22	205.09	236.78	246.08	240.92	232.77	208.72	207.85	213.67	210.88	219.65
Former CSFR/Ex-RFTS	48.92	48.46	49.02	48.94	49.35	49.78	52.01	53.28	50.94	49.31	45.17	42.08	39.05	..
Hungary/Hongrie	14.34	13.94	14.45	14.78	15.30	16.73	16.39	17.11	16.49	15.87	14.34	14.12	13.67	..
Poland/Pologne	120.72	103.92	118.04	120.00	122.21	124.25	126.11	128.08	124.52	115.07	97.27	93.80	88.48	..
North America/Amérique N.	1900.14	1911.47	1920.39	1859.86	2005.82	1997.88	1971.31	2024.45	2072.10	2080.96	2119.79	2152.44	2145.36	2135.42
Australia/Australie-NZ	91.69	100.94	105.99	110.90	120.01	134.18	145.01	154.74	148.49	156.61	169.58	175.64	182.89	186.36
OECD/OCDE Europe	663.81	697.39	712.42	748.65	759.24	826.65	846.12	860.30	858.41	864.57	857.96	871.31	880.96	895.28
EU/UE-15	583.05	614.64	628.59	656.51	660.12	721.53	734.79	734.88	728.49	713.48	700.58	703.09	696.67	703.85
OECD/OCDE	2698.89	2754.38	2786.77	2770.24	2939.82	3020.92	3026.39	3106.14	3143.40	3167.05	3216.23	3272.09	3285.27	3300.93
World/Monde	6646.12	6529.34	6478.61	6501.40	6853.07	7014.27	7271.72	7460.23	7735.10	7909.85	8010.53	8020.47	8040.10	..

Source: OECD-IEA/OCDE-AIE

The following table shows the structure of the production of primary energy in the OECD and the change of this structure over time (see the preceding table for a definition of indigenous energy production).

This table provides aggregated data for the OECD; it should be borne in mind that considerable differences exist among OECD countries as to the structure of their indigenous energy production by source.

Le tableau suivant montre la structure de la production d'énergie primaire pour l'ensemble de l'OCDE et l'évolution de cette structure dans le temps (voir le tableau précédent pour la définition de la production nationale d'énergie).

Ce tableau fournit des chiffres globaux pour l'OCDE ; on doit cependant garder à l'esprit que des différences considérables existent entre les pays de l'OCDE quant à leur production nationale d'énergie par source.

INDIGENOUS ENERGY PRODUCTION BY SOURCE, OECD, 1980-1993
PRODUCTION NATIONALE D'ÉNERGIE PAR SOURCE, OCDE, 1980-1993

Mtoe/Mtep

Source of Primary Energy/ Source d'énergie primaire		1980	1981	1982	1983	1984	1985	1986	1987	1988	1989	1990	1991	1992	1993
Coal/Charbon		792.1	802.6	815.7	779.4	812.5	841.4	853.8	877.5	874.2	901.1	913.9	880.7	865.3	813.8
Combustible Renewables and Waste/ Énergies renouvelables combustibles et déchets	a)	102.6	104.2	105.0	110.6	119.3	119.2	121.4	129.7	130.2	134.7	127.9	154.8	144.6	151.2
Crude Oil, Natural Gas Liquids/ Pétrole brut, condensats de gaz naturel		830.7	850.2	891.7	914.9	957.2	970.1	951.7	953.2	947.2	908.1	910.4	930.5	945.3	948.8
Gas/Gaz		710.7	703.7	664.3	626.2	665.9	655.1	636.4	661.0	675.5	693.1	712.5	728.0	745.0	777.9
Nuclear Power/ Énergie nucléaire		160.2	189.0	202.8	226.3	270.1	319.7	345.6	367.4	397.7	409.8	426.1	449.4	455.6	472.8
Hydroelectricity/ Énergie hydroélectrique	b)	92.5	94.0	96.7	100.9	101.3	100.1	99.5	97.9	99.1	96.5	99.6	102.4	101.5	107.5
Geothermal and Solar Energy/ Énergie géothermique et solaire		10.1	10.8	10.6	12.0	13.6	15.4	17.9	19.5	19.5	23.8	25.8	26.3	27.8	28.6
Heat/Chaleur	c)	-	-	-	-	-	-	-	-	-	-	-	-	0.3	0.3
TOTAL		2698.9	2754.4	2786.8	2770.2	2939.8	3020.9	3026.4	3106.2	3143.4	3167.0	3216.2	3272.1	3285.3	3300.9

Notes:
a) Solid biomass and animal products, gas/liquids from biomass, industrial and municipal waste.
b) Excludes electricity output from pumped storage plants.
c) Heat extracted from ambient air by heat pumps.

Source: OECD-IEA/OCDE-AIE

Notes:
a) Biomasse solide et produits d'origine animale, gaz/liquides tirés de la biomasse, déchets industriels et urbains.
b) Exclut la production d'électricité des centrales à accumulation par pompage.
c) Chaleur extraite de l'air ambiant par les pompes à chaleur.

The next table presents net imports of crude oil, natural gas liquids, refinery feedstocks and petroleum products (liquefied petroleum gas, refinery gas, aviation gasoline, motor gasoline, gas/diesel oil, residual fuel oil, etc.). Net oil imports equal imports minus exports (bunkers not deducted). Imports and exports are amounts having crossed the national territorial boundaries of the country, whether or not customs clearance has taken place.

Le tableau suivant présente les importations nettes de pétrole brut, de produits d'alimentation des raffineries, de condensats de gaz naturels et de produits pétroliers (gaz de pétrole liquéfié, gaz de raffinerie, essence aviation, essence auto, gazole/carburant diesel, fuel résiduel, etc.). Les importations nettes de pétrole sont égales aux importations moins les exportations, les soutages n'étant pas déduits. Les importations et exportations représentent les quantités ayant traversé les frontières politiques du pays, que le dédouanement ait été effectué ou non.

NET OIL IMPORTS (a), 1980-1993
IMPORTATIONS NETTES DE PÉTROLE (a), 1980-1993

Mtoe/Mtep

	1980	1981	1982	1983	1984	1985	1986	1987	1988	1989	1990	1991	1992	1993
Canada	8.6	9.1	-1.1	-10.1	-11.7	-17.7	-14.4	-14.0	-21.0	-13.5	-15.1	-21.1	-25.1	-26.8
Mexico/Mexique	-44.5	-61.0	-84.0	-85.4	-84.2	-79.0	-71.3	-72.4	-71.2	-65.6	-67.5	-70.5	-70.3	-71.0
USA/Etats-Unis	334.9	286.1	231.4	230.0	250.4	230.1	285.3	309.1	341.3	369.9	369.2	345.6	367.6	401.6
Japan/Japon	252.3	227.6	213.6	214.7	224.8	212.5	217.1	219.2	233.1	249.7	259.5	260.9	265.6	263.7
Australia/Australie	11.2	10.5	10.5	9.2	4.6	0.6	-0.3	1.9	1.8	6.5	5.3	2.7	4.1	7.5
N.Zealand/N.Zélande	4.2	3.5	3.2	3.3	3.3	3.0	2.0	2.8	2.1	2.4	2.4	2.4	2.6	2.7
Austria/Autriche	11.4	9.9	8.8	8.4	8.9	8.7	9.5	9.7	9.0	9.3	10.0	10.4	10.3	10.2
Belgium/Belgique	26.3	21.6	22.3	20.3	19.0	19.5	23.4	22.7	23.1	23.2	22.5	25.2	25.8	25.0
Denmark/Danemark	13.4	10.7	9.9	8.8	8.5	8.6	7.8	6.3	5.5	4.0	3.2	2.4	1.6	1.2
Finland/Finlande	13.9	11.8	10.6	11.0	9.3	10.9	11.8	12.7	10.5	11.6	10.5	10.3	9.5	9.3
France	115.0	96.0	90.0	84.8	85.9	82.5	83.1	86.5	86.2	87.7	87.9	92.9	88.9	87.7
Germany/Allemagne	149.5	126.6	118.5	116.3	117.7	121.1	132.0	127.6	127.7	119.5	122.9	131.7	135.4	134.0
w.Germany/All.occ.	133.6	111.4	105.8	104.3	106.3	108.3	119.0	113.7	113.9	105.7	110.1	..	..	..
Greece/Grèce	13.5	12.4	10.5	10.1	10.1	10.7	12.5	11.7	13.0	13.7	14.6	15.0	16.6	16.6
Iceland/Islande	0.6	0.6	0.5	0.5	0.5	0.6	0.6	0.6	0.6	0.7	0.8	0.6	0.8	0.7
Ireland/Irlande	5.9	5.1	4.6	4.2	4.3	4.2	5.1	4.6	4.0	4.2	5.1	5.0	4.9	5.3
Italy/Italie	99.6	94.8	91.8	85.0	86.2	83.9	84.6	89.9	86.1	91.9	91.5	88.5	92.5	88.9
Luxembourg	1.1	1.1	1.1	1.0	1.0	1.1	1.2	1.4	1.3	1.5	1.7	1.9	2.0	1.9
Netherlands/Pays-Bas	38.0	31.6	28.0	26.2	25.8	24.9	30.0	26.6	31.1	30.8	31.3	33.3	34.3	33.0
Norway/Norvège	-15.1	-15.8	-16.2	-23.4	-27.6	-31.0	-33.8	-41.0	-49.2	-67.3	-73.4	-87.0	-100.6	-107.6
Portugal	9.5	8.6	9.7	9.6	10.0	8.7	9.8	9.8	9.8	12.4	12.4	12.6	13.8	13.1
Spain/Espagne	50.1	48.8	43.3	43.1	39.6	40.0	39.5	42.4	46.7	49.0	49.9	50.7	53.5	51.2
Sweden/Suède	26.3	21.6	20.0	18.2	15.3	17.4	19.8	15.8	16.2	15.1	15.5	15.1	15.2	15.7
Switzerland/Suisse	13.5	12.2	11.5	12.8	12.4	12.4	13.8	12.4	12.7	12.5	13.4	13.3	13.5	12.2
Turkey/Turquie	13.5	13.6	14.1	15.3	15.2	15.3	17.1	20.0	19.5	18.9	20.9	17.8	20.1	24.4
UK/Royaume-Uni	1.9	-18.6	-29.0	-44.4	-39.8	-51.0	-51.4	-49.5	-36.8	-9.9	-10.9	-7.9	-10.8	-16.8
Former CSFR/Ex-RFTS	18.5	18.1	16.8	16.2	17.2	17.0	15.7	16.1	15.3	15.1	13.1	10.9	10.3	..
Hungary/Hongrie	8.4	7.9	7.9	8.3	7.9	7.1	6.9	6.6	6.1	6.0	6.4	4.6	5.8	..
Poland/Pologne	18.9	16.7	16.0	16.0	16.8	16.9	17.4	17.1	17.6	17.1	14.5	12.9	14.6	..
North America/Amérique N.	299.1	234.2	146.3	134.6	154.5	133.4	199.6	222.8	249.2	290.8	286.6	254.0	272.1	303.8
Australia/Australie-NZ	15.3	14.0	13.7	12.4	7.9	3.6	1.7	4.7	3.9	8.9	7.7	5.1	6.7	10.2
OECD/OCDE Europe	587.8	492.5	450.0	407.7	402.4	388.4	416.3	409.9	417.1	428.7	429.9	431.6	427.1	406.0
EU/UE-15	575.3	482.0	440.0	402.5	401.9	391.1	418.5	418.0	433.4	463.9	468.3	486.9	493.4	476.3
OECD/OCDE	1154.5	968.4	823.6	769.4	789.6	738.0	834.6	856.6	903.3	978.1	983.7	951.5	971.5	983.7

Notes:
a) A negative number shows net exports.

Notes:
a) Un chiffre négatif correspond à des exportations nettes.

Source: OECD-IEA/OCDE-AIE

This table shows total primary energy supply, which is made up of indigenous production + imports - exports - international marine bunkers and ± stock changes. Primary energy comprises hard coal, lignite and other solid fuels, crude oil and natural gas liquids, natural gas, and nuclear, hydro, geothermal and solar electricity.

———————————————————————

Ce tableau présente l'approvisionnement total en énergie primaire qui est égal à la somme de la production nationale + les importations - les exportations - les soutages maritimes internationaux et ± les variations de stocks. L'énergie primaire comprend la houille, le lignite et les autres combustibles solides, le pétrole brut et les condensats de gaz naturel, le gaz naturel et l'éléctricité d'origine nucléaire, hydraulique, géothermique et solaire.

TOTAL PRIMARY ENERGY SUPPLY, 1980-1993
APPROVISIONNEMENTS TOTAUX EN ÉNERGIE PRIMAIRE, 1980-1993

Mtoe/Mtep

	1980	1981	1982	1983	1984	1985	1986	1987	1988	1989	1990	1991	1992	1993
Canada	193.2	188.3	181.5	180.0	189.3	193.4	197.0	203.6	212.2	218.3	210.2	209.7	214.0	220.7
Mexico/Mexique	97.4	103.8	107.0	102.0	108.4	112.6	108.6	114.5	115.5	122.7	127.1	133.4	136.1	134.6
USA/Etats-Unis	1801.0	1751.3	1677.8	1679.7	1752.3	1771.2	1771.6	1847.1	1920.1	1956.4	1920.6	1959.4	1973.6	2028.6
Japan/Japon	347.1	338.0	331.6	334.9	361.4	362.0	366.3	368.7	397.5	410.7	432.6	443.0	453.1	457.4
Australia/Australie	70.4	70.8	74.0	71.0	73.2	74.0	75.2	78.5	79.9	85.5	88.1	87.3	88.0	92.6
N.Zealand/N.Zélande	9.2	9.0	9.6	9.9	10.6	11.4	11.4	11.8	12.3	13.3	14.0	14.2	14.8	14.9
Austria/Autriche	23.5	22.3	21.6	21.7	22.7	23.2	23.5	25.1	24.7	25.0	26.1	27.6	26.4	26.2
Belgium/Belgique	46.1	43.0	41.9	41.3	42.5	44.7	46.3	47.3	47.9	48.2	48.3	51.3	51.9	50.7
Denmark/Danemark	19.5	17.5	17.7	16.7	17.4	19.7	19.8	20.2	19.2	18.1	18.3	20.2	19.4	19.8
Finland/Finlande	25.0	24.0	23.5	23.8	24.3	26.2	27.3	29.9	28.1	29.1	28.5	28.9	27.6	28.9
France	190.7	186.2	181.4	185.6	192.9	200.7	204.1	209.3	208.2	218.3	221.2	232.5	228.8	233.8
Germany/Allemagne	359.2	347.0	335.3	335.4	348.2	359.8	360.5	363.4	365.8	359.9	355.1	347.3	340.7	337.2
w.Germany/All.occ.	272.9	260.1	251.3	251.8	262.6	270.0	271.6	272.7	276.5	271.6	278.2	..	..	..
Greece/Grèce	16.0	15.6	16.1	16.7	17.3	18.6	17.6	18.9	20.1	22.0	22.1	22.4	22.9	22.7
Iceland/Islande	1.4	1.6	1.6	1.7	1.8	1.8	1.8	1.9	2.0	2.1	2.1	2.0	2.0	2.1
Ireland/Irlande	8.5	8.5	8.5	8.4	8.5	8.9	9.4	9.6	9.5	9.7	10.5	10.5	10.3	10.7
Italy/Italie	139.2	136.2	132.3	132.1	134.9	136.5	138.7	144.0	147.4	153.4	154.6	158.7	159.0	156.5
Luxembourg	3.6	3.2	3.0	2.8	3.1	3.2	3.1	3.1	3.2	3.4	3.6	3.8	3.8	3.9
Netherlands/Pays-Bas	65.1	61.4	54.8	57.1	60.3	61.3	63.6	65.0	64.2	64.7	66.0	69.5	68.9	69.7
Norway/Norvège	18.9	18.6	18.0	18.7	19.7	20.4	21.8	21.6	20.6	21.9	21.5	22.1	21.9	22.3
Portugal	10.3	10.2	11.4	11.4	11.4	11.4	12.6	12.9	13.9	16.1	16.4	16.6	17.9	17.6
Spain/Espagne	68.7	69.8	68.1	69.3	70.7	71.9	73.4	75.3	81.4	86.4	88.0	91.9	94.2	91.0
Sweden/Suède	41.0	42.9	41.0	41.5	43.9	47.6	49.6	48.8	49.9	48.0	47.8	49.3	47.0	47.1
Switzerland/Suisse	20.8	20.4	19.8	21.2	21.7	23.0	24.0	23.4	23.7	23.3	24.8	25.0	25.2	24.7
Turkey/Turquie	31.3	31.5	33.7	35.5	36.6	38.9	41.9	49.2	46.7	48.8	53.2	54.2	55.5	59.2
UK/Royaume-Uni	201.2	193.9	193.3	193.1	192.7	203.0	206.5	209.0	210.6	210.8	212.2	217.8	214.4	217.0
Former CSFR/Ex-RFTS	73.7	72.7	72.8	72.2	74.3	74.5	77.0	78.1	74.0	72.3	70.3	63.5	58.0	..
Hungary/Hongrie	28.3	27.5	27.8	28.8	29.7	30.2	30.1	31.2	30.8	29.7	28.6	27.1	25.6	..
Poland/Pologne	124.5	114.2	114.2	116.0	122.8	126.5	128.5	132.9	124.9	119.4	97.9	96.3	93.4	..
North America/Amérique N.	2091.6	2043.4	1966.2	1961.7	2050.0	2077.3	2077.1	2165.2	2247.8	2297.3	2257.9	2302.4	2323.7	2383.9
Australia/Australie-NZ	79.6	79.9	83.6	80.9	83.8	85.3	86.6	90.3	92.2	98.8	102.1	101.5	102.8	107.5
OECD/OCDE Europe	1289.9	1253.8	1223.0	1233.9	1270.4	1320.6	1345.4	1377.9	1387.2	1409.3	1420.0	1451.5	1437.8	1440.8
EU/UE-15	1217.5	1181.7	1149.9	1156.9	1190.7	1236.6	1255.9	1281.7	1294.2	1313.3	1318.4	1348.2	1333.2	1332.6
OECD/OCDE	3808.2	3715.0	3604.5	3611.3	3765.5	3845.2	3875.4	4002.1	4124.8	4216.1	4212.5	4298.4	4317.4	4389.6
World/Monde	6465.4	6403.3	6365.8	6468.0	6757.3	6969.2	7124.6	7407.9	7651.8	7807.3	7821.3	7922.5	7932.5	..

Source: OECD-IEA/OCDE-AIE

This table shows changes in the structure of primary energy supply by type of energy: solid fuels, oil, gas and nuclear power, as well as hydro, geothermal and solar energy.

Country totals in this table may not add up to the corresponding figures of the preceding table because electricity trade and heat extracted from ambient air by heat pumps are not included in the present table.

Ce tableau présente les changements structurels dans les approvisionnements en énergie primaire par type d'énergie : combustibles solides, pétrole, gaz, énergie nucléaire ainsi que énergie hydraulique, géothermique et solaire.

Les totaux par pays dans ce tableau-ci peuvent être légèrement différents des chiffres du tableau précédent en raison du commerce d'électricité et de la chaleur extraite de l'air ambiant par les pompes à chaleur non inclus dans le présent tableau.

ENERGY SUPPLY BY SOURCE, 1970, 1980, 1993
APPROVISIONNEMENT EN ÉNERGIE PAR SOURCE, 1970, 1980, 1993

Mtoe/Mtep

		Solid fuels/ Combustibles solides (a)			Oil/Pétrole			Gas/Gaz			Nuclear Power/ Énergie nucléaire			Hydro, Geothermal and Solar Energy/ Énergie hydroélectrique, géothermique et solaire		
		1970	1980	1993	1970	1980	1993	1970	1980	1993	1970	1980	1993	1970	1980	1993
Canada		24.6	28.8	32.8	72.1	89.2	76.4	29.2	45.6	61.2	0.3	10.4	24.9	13.6	21.6	27.8
Mexico/Mexique	*	9.6	11.0	13.2	24.8	62.9	87.6	9.8	21.3	25.2	-	-	1.3	1.23	2.2	7.3
USA/Etats-Unis		327.4	432.2	558.7	691.1	791.7	769.6	499.0	476.8	489.4	6.1	69.4	168.6	22.0	28.6	39.9
Japan/Japon		61.6	59.6	79.0	185.4	236.2	255.9	3.1	21.5	47.7	1.2	21.5	65.0	6.5	8.4	9.9
Australia/Australie		24.9	30.9	42.1	24.4	30.9	34.2	1.2	7.5	14.9	-	-	-	0.8	1.1	1.4
N.Zealand/N.Zélande		1.2	1.6	2.2	3.7	4.1	4.5	0.1	0.9	4.4	-	-	-	2.1	2.7	3.9
Austria/Autriche		5.3	4.8	6.0	9.2	12.3	11.5	2.5	4.2	5.7	-	-	-	1.8	2.5	3.2
Belgium/Belgique		12.3	10.5	9.2	24.5	23.6	20.9	3.4	8.9	9.4	-	3.3	10.9	-	-	-
Denmark/Danemark		2.4	6.2	8.5	18.1	13.4	8.7	-	-	2.4	-	-	-	-	-	0.1
Finland/Finlande		6.5	8.4	10.0	10.7	13.0	9.4	-	0.8	2.6	-	1.8	5.2	0.8	0.9	1.2
France		39.0	35.9	19.2	93.7	110.9	89.5	8.2	21.6	29.0	1.5	16.0	96.0	4.9	6.0	5.5
Germany/Allemagne		150.3	143.9	100.4	138.1	147.3	135.5	12.3	51.2	59.7	1.7	14.5	40.0	1.5	1.6	1.5
w.Germany/All.occ.		91.0	84.3	..	128.0	131.2	..	11.8	44.0	..	1.6	11.4	..	1.4	1.5	..
Greece/Grèce		1.8	3.7	8.7	6.1	11.9	13.6	-	-	0.1	-	-	-	0.2	0.3	0.2
Iceland/Islande		-	-	-	0.5	0.6	0.7	-	-	-	-	-	-	0.4	0.8	1.3
Ireland/Irlande		2.1	1.9	3.4	4.1	5.8	5.1	-	0.7	2.2	-	-	-	0.1	0.1	0.1
Italy/Italie		10.8	12.6	11.7	82.3	96.6	92.7	10.6	22.7	41.9	0.8	0.6	-	5.8	6.2	6.8
Luxembourg		2.7	1.9	1.1	1.3	1.1	2.0	-	0.4	0.5	-	-	-	-	-	-
Netherlands/Pays-Bas		4.7	4.0	8.2	29.1	29.6	25.2	15.4	30.4	34.3	0.1	1.1	1.0	-	-	-
Norway/Norvège		1.1	1.6	1.9	7.9	9.2	8.3	-	0.9	2.5	-	-	-	5.0	7.2	10.2
Portugal		1.5	1.1	4.3	4.0	8.3	12.6	-	-	-	-	-	-	0.5	0.7	0.7
Spain/Espagne		9.0	12.7	19.8	26.8	50.8	48.6	0.1	1.5	5.7	0.2	1.4	14.6	2.4	2.5	2.1
Sweden/Suède		4.8	5.8	8.9	29.2	23.1	14.8	-	-	0.7	-	6.9	16.0	3.6	5.1	6.4
Switzerland/Suisse		0.8	0.8	1.2	13.0	13.3	13.0	-	0.9	2.0	0.5	3.7	6.1	2.7	2.8	3.1
Turkey/Turquie		4.2	14.7	24.2	7.7	15.6	27.7	-	-	4.2	-	-	-	0.3	1.0	3.0
UK/Royaume-Uni		89.0	68.8	50.8	101.3	82.1	83.2	10.2	40.3	57.9	6.8	9.7	23.3	0.4	0.3	0.4
Former CSFR/Ex-RFTS	*	43.3	46.1	32.1	11.6	18.5	10.7	2.0	7.3	8.60	-	1.2	6.32	0.2	0.4	0.3
Hungary/Hongrie	*	9.2	9.2	5.4	7.0	11.3	8.4	2.9	7.2	7.84	-	-	3.64	-	-	-
Poland/Pologne	*	67.9	97.6	71.3	8.8	17.9	14.4	4.9	8.8	7.76	-	-	-	0.2	0.3	0.3
N.America/Amér.N.		361.7	472.0	604.8	788.0	943.8	933.6	538.0	543.6	575.8	6.4	79.8	194.8	36.9	52.4	75.0
Australia/Ilie-NZ		26.1	32.5	44.2	28.1	35.0	38.7	1.3	8.4	19.3	-	-	-	2.8	3.8	5.3
OECD/OCDE Europe		348.4	339.5	297.4	607.7	668.5	622.8	62.7	184.5	260.7	11.6	58.9	213.1	30.3	37.9	45.8
EU/UE-15		342.3	322.4	270.1	578.5	629.8	573.1	62.7	182.8	251.9	11.1	55.1	207.0	22.0	26.2	28.1
OECD/OCDE		797.8	903.5	1025.4	1609.2	1883.4	1850.9	605.0	757.9	903.5	19.1	160.2	472.8	76.4	102.5	136.1
World/Monde	*	1501.7	1887.4	2293.2	2328.2	2990.1	3110.3	896.0	1237.6	1744.6	29.0	185.9	554.1	110.3	164.5	229.1

Notes:		Notes:	
a)	Coal, combustible renewables and waste.	a)	Charbon, énergies renouvelables combustibles et déchets.
MEX)	1970 data refer to 1971.	MEX)	Les données 1970 sont de 1971.
CSFR)	1970 and 1993 data refer to 1971 and 1992.	RFTS)	Les données 1970 et 1993 sont de 1971 et 1992.
HUN)	1970 and 1993 data refer to 1971 and 1992.	HUN)	Les données 1970 et 1993 sont de 1971 et 1992.
POL)	1970 and 1993 data refer to 1971 and 1992.	POL)	Les données 1970 et 1993 sont de 1971 et 1992.
World)	1970 and 1993 data refer to 1971 and 1992.	Monde)	Les données 1970 et 1993 sont de 1971 et 1992.

Source: OECD-IEA/OCDE-AIE

The following table shows changes in total primary energy supply per unit of GDP since 1980, and the value of this ratio for 1991. Calculations are based on GDP at 1991 price levels, and 1991 purchasing power parties are used for conversions to US$.

See preceding tables for definitions of total primary energy supply and the general data section for data on GDP and related notes.

Le tableau suivant montre l'évolution des approvisionnements totaux en énergie primaire par unité de PIB depuis 1980, et la valeur de ce ratio pour 1991. Les calculs sont basés sur la valeur du PIB aux prix de 1991. Les parités de pouvoir d'achat de 1991 ont été employées pour les conversions en $EU.

Voir les tableaux précédents pour les définitions concernant les approvisionnements totaux en énergie primaire et la section sur les données générales pour les données et les notes sur le PIB.

TOTAL ENERGY SUPPLY PER UNIT OF GDP, OECD countries, 1980-1993
APPROVISIONNEMENTS TOTAUX EN ÉNERGIE PAR UNITÉ DE PIB, pays de l'OCDE, 1980-1993

	Index 1991 = 100														Toe/1 000 $US Tep/1 000 $EU
	1980	1981	1982	1983	1984	1985	1986	1987	1988	1989	1990	1991	1992	1993	1991
Canada	120	113	113	108	107	105	103	102	102	102	98	100	101	102	0.40
Mexico/Mexique	89	87	91	90	93	94	94	97	97	100	99	100	100	98	0.30
USA/Etats-Unis	118	113	111	107	105	103	100	101	101	100	97	100	98	98	0.34
Japan/Japon	122	115	109	107	111	106	105	101	103	101	102	100	101	102	0.19
Australia/Australie	109	106	111	106	102	98	98	98	95	98	99	100	99	100	0.31
N.Zealand/N.Zélande	78	73	76	76	75	79	79	82	82	90	95	100	103	99	0.31
Austria/Autriche	108	103	99	97	100	100	100	105	100	97	97	100	94	93	0.20
Belgium/Belgique	111	104	100	98	99	103	106	106	102	99	96	100	99	99	0.30
Denmark/Danemark	120	108	106	98	98	106	103	104	98	92	92	100	95	96	0.22
Finland/Finlande	110	104	98	96	95	100	101	107	96	94	92	100	99	106	0.37
France	104	101	96	97	100	102	101	101	96	97	96	100	97	101	0.22
Germany/Allemagne	..	..	..	..	..	..	..	..	..	..	..	100	96	96	0.26
Greece/Grèce	86	84	86	89	89	93	87	94	95	100	102	100	102	101	0.23
Iceland/Islande	94	97	96	105	106	102	100	97	99	104	108	100	104	106	0.45
Ireland/Irlande	119	116	113	112	109	111	118	114	109	103	103	100	94	93	0.25
Italy/Italie	110	107	104	103	102	101	100	100	99	100	99	100	99	99	0.16
Luxembourg	140	123	115	105	107	107	101	97	95	95	97	100	98	98	0.47
Netherlands/Pays-Bas	117	111	100	103	106	105	106	107	103	99	97	100	98	99	0.28
Norway/Norvège	111	108	104	104	103	102	104	101	97	102	99	100	96	95	0.31
Portugal	86	84	91	92	94	91	96	93	95	103	101	100	107	106	0.16
Spain/Espagne	103	105	100	100	101	100	99	96	98	100	98	100	102	99	0.19
Sweden/Suède	100	105	100	99	100	107	109	104	104	98	96	100	97	100	0.34
Switzerland/Suisse	102	99	97	103	103	105	107	102	101	95	99	100	101	100	0.17
Turkey/Turquie	97	93	96	96	93	95	96	103	95	99	99	100	97	96	0.20
UK/Royaume-Uni	118	115	113	109	106	108	105	101	97	95	95	100	99	98	0.24
North America/Amérique N.	117	111	110	106	104	102	100	101	101	101	98	100	99	99	0.34
Australia/Australie-NZ	104	101	106	101	97	95	95	95	93	97	99	100	99	100	0.31
OECD/OCDE Europe	..	..	..	..	..	..	..	..	..	..	..	100	98	98	0.23
EU/UE-15	..	..	..	..	..	..	..	..	..	..	..	100	98	98	0.23
OECD/OCDE	..	..	..	..	..	..	..	..	..	..	..	100	99	99	0.27

Source: OECD-IEA/OCDE-AIE

The following table shows changes in total primary energy supply per capita since 1980, and the value of this ratio for 1991.

See preceding tables for the definition of total energy supply, and the general data section for population data and related comments.

Le tableau suivant présente l'évolution des approvisionnements totaux en énergie primaire par habitant depuis 1980 et la valeur de ce ratio pour 1991.

Voir les tableaux précédents pour les définitions relatives aux approvisionnements totaux en énergie primaire, et la section sur les données générales pour les chiffres et commentaires relatifs à la population.

TOTAL ENERGY SUPPLY PER CAPITA, 1980-1993
APPROVISIONNEMENTS TOTAUX EN ÉNERGIE PAR HABITANT, 1980-1993

	Index 1991=100														Toe/capita Tep/habitant
	1980	1981	1982	1983	1984	1985	1986	1987	1988	1989	1990	1991	1992	1993	1991
Canada	105	101	97	95	99	100	101	103	106	107	101	100	101	103	7.46
Mexico/Mexique	92	96	97	90	94	95	90	93	92	96	97	100	100	97	1.52
USA/Etats-Unis	102	98	93	92	95	95	94	97	100	101	99	100	100	101	7.77
Japan/Japon	83	80	78	79	84	84	84	84	91	93	98	100	102	103	3.57
Australia/Australie	95	94	96	91	93	93	93	96	96	101	102	100	100	104	5.05
N.Zealand/N.Zélande	70	68	73	74	78	83	83	85	89	96	100	100	103	103	4.17
Austria/Autriche	88	83	81	81	85	87	88	94	92	93	96	100	95	93	3.53
Belgium/Belgique	91	85	83	82	84	89	92	93	94	95	94	100	101	98	5.12
Denmark/Danemark	97	87	88	84	87	98	98	100	96	90	91	100	96	97	3.92
Finland/Finlande	91	87	85	85	87	93	97	106	99	102	99	100	96	100	5.74
France	87	84	82	83	86	89	90	92	91	95	96	100	98	100	4.07
Germany/Allemagne	106	102	98	99	103	107	107	108	108	105	103	100	97	96	4.35
Greece/Grèce	75	73	75	77	80	85	81	86	91	100	100	100	101	100	2.19
Iceland/Islande	81	86	86	90	94	93	97	101	101	104	108	100	100	102	7.79
Ireland/Irlande	84	83	82	81	81	85	89	91	90	93	100	100	98	101	2.98
Italy/Italie	88	86	84	83	85	86	88	91	93	97	97	100	100	98	2.80
Luxembourg	101	88	83	78	84	87	85	83	86	91	94	100	99	99	9.90
Netherlands/Pays-Bas	100	93	83	86	91	92	95	96	94	94	96	100	98	99	4.61
Norway/Norvège	89	88	85	88	92	95	101	100	95	100	98	100	99	100	5.18
Portugal	62	62	68	68	68	68	75	77	83	96	99	100	108	106	1.68
Spain/Espagne	78	78	76	77	78	79	80	82	89	94	96	100	102	99	2.36
Sweden/Suède	86	90	86	87	92	100	104	102	104	99	98	100	95	95	5.72
Switzerland/Suisse	89	86	83	89	91	96	99	96	97	95	101	100	100	97	3.68
Turkey/Turquie	74	73	76	78	78	81	86	99	92	93	99	100	101	105	0.95
UK/Royaume-Uni	95	91	91	91	91	95	97	97	98	98	98	100	98	99	3.77
Former CSFR/Ex-RFTS	118	116	116	115	118	118	122	124	117	114	111	100	91	..	4.08
Hungary/Hongrie	101	98	99	103	107	109	109	114	113	109	105	100	95	..	2.62
Poland/Pologne	139	126	125	126	132	135	136	140	131	125	102	100	97	..	2.52
North America/Amérique N.	104	100	95	94	97	97	96	98	101	102	99	100	100	101	6.25
Australia/Australie-NZ	91	90	93	89	91	91	91	94	95	100	102	100	100	104	4.91
OECD/OCDE Europe	94	91	88	89	91	94	95	97	97	98	98	100	98	98	3.34
EU/UE-15	93	90	87	88	90	94	95	97	97	98	98	100	98	98	3.68
OECD/OCDE	97	94	90	89	93	94	94	96	98	100	99	100	100	100	4.54

Source: OECD-IEA/OCDE-AIE

The following table shows total electricity generated by all power plants (public utilities and autoproducers), excluding pump storage production. Data are expressed in terawatt hours (TWh). One TWh equals 10^{12} Wh.

Le tableau suivant présente l'électricité totale produite par toutes les centrales d'énergie, (secteur public et autoproducteurs), à l'exclusion des centrales à accumulation par pompage. Les données sont exprimés en térawattheures (TWh). Un TWh représente 10^{12} Wh.

ELECTRICITY GENERATED, 1980-1993
ÉLECTRICITÉ PRODUITE, 1980-1993

TWh

	1980	1981	1982	1983	1984	1985	1986	1987	1988	1989	1990	1991	1992	1993
Canada	373.3	390.5	387.4	407.9	437.0	459.0	468.5	496.3	505.9	499.4	481.9	507.8	520.8	527.3
Mexico/Mexique	61.9	67.9	73.2	74.8	79.5	85.4	89.4	96.3	101.9	110.1	114.3	118.4	121.7	126.6
USA/Etats-Unis	2427.3	2437.0	2376.6	2449.0	2562.8	2621.9	2639.7	2717.2	2858.0	3127.5	3181.5	3252.2	3271.4	3389.9
Japan/Japon	572.5	580.3	578.9	614.7	645.4	666.9	671.1	713.0	748.1	792.7	850.7	880.0	888.2	899.1
Australia/Australie	95.2	102.2	104.4	105.5	111.5	119.7	125.4	131.5	138.3	147.1	154.3	156.6	159.2	163.3
N.Zealand/N.Zélande	22.3	23.1	24.6	26.1	27.1	27.3	28.2	28.7	29.5	31.0	31.6	32.7	31.3	33.6
Austria/Autriche	41.6	42.3	42.3	42.1	41.8	43.9	44.1	49.8	48.3	49.3	49.4	50.2	49.9	51.4
Belgium/Belgique	53.1	50.1	50.0	51.9	53.7	56.3	57.6	62.3	64.5	66.8	70.2	71.2	71.4	70.1
Denmark/Danemark	26.8	19.8	23.7	22.2	22.6	29.1	30.7	29.5	28.0	22.3	25.8	36.3	30.9	33.7
Finland/Finlande	40.8	40.9	41.2	42.2	45.3	49.7	49.3	53.4	53.9	53.8	54.4	58.0	57.7	61.2
France	256.9	274.7	277.4	294.3	321.8	341.7	359.8	375.4	388.6	402.9	416.2	450.1	458.2	467.8
Germany/Allemagne	466.3	467.7	468.1	476.8	503.2	520.6	521.8	530.5	547.1	557.4	547.5	535.6	533.3	521.9
w.Germany/All.occ.	367.5	367.0	365.2	371.9	393.1	406.7	406.5	416.3	428.8	438.4	447.1	..	..	..
Greece/Grèce	22.7	23.4	23.3	24.0	24.8	27.7	28.1	30.1	33.2	34.2	34.8	35.7	37.2	38.1
Iceland/Islande	3.2	3.3	3.6	3.8	4.0	3.9	4.1	4.2	4.5	4.5	4.5	4.5	4.6	4.7
Ireland/Irlande	10.6	10.5	10.5	10.8	11.2	11.7	12.3	12.6	12.9	13.5	14.2	14.9	15.8	16.2
Italy/Italie	183.5	179.0	181.8	180.1	179.6	182.2	188.9	198.3	200.7	207.3	213.4	218.7	222.7	219.7
Luxembourg	0.9	0.7	0.5	0.5	0.5	0.5	0.6	0.6	0.6	0.6	0.6	0.7	0.7	0.7
Netherlands/Pays-Bas	64.8	64.1	60.3	59.7	62.8	63.0	67.2	68.4	69.6	73.1	71.9	74.3	77.2	77.0
Norway/Norvège	83.8	93.0	92.8	106.0	106.2	102.7	96.7	103.8	109.3	118.9	121.6	110.6	117.1	119.6
Portugal	15.2	13.8	15.4	18.1	19.2	18.8	20.3	20.1	22.4	25.6	28.4	29.7	29.7	31.0
Spain/Espagne	109.2	110.0	113.5	115.4	118.1	125.6	128.2	132.6	138.6	147.1	151.0	154.7	156.5	155.1
Sweden/Suède	96.3	102.9	99.5	108.9	123.3	136.5	138.1	146.0	145.6	142.9	146.0	147.0	145.9	145.2
Switzerland/Suisse	48.2	51.8	52.5	52.2	49.6	55.5	56.5	58.8	59.7	53.8	54.6	56.5	57.8	60.2
Turkey/Turquie	23.1	24.6	26.6	27.4	30.6	34.2	39.7	44.4	48.1	52.0	57.5	60.3	67.3	73.8
UK/Royaume-Uni	284.1	276.7	271.7	275.6	280.4	294.7	299.4	301.6	306.7	312.7	317.7	321.3	319.3	321.6
Former CSFR/Ex-RFTS	72.7	73.5	74.8	76.3	78.4	80.6	84.8	85.8	87.4	89.2	86.6	83.4	81.6	..
Hungary/Hongrie	23.9	24.2	24.8	25.8	26.3	26.8	28.1	29.8	29.2	29.6	28.4	30.0	31.6	..
Poland/Pologne	121.9	115.0	117.6	125.8	134.8	137.7	140.3	145.8	144.4	145.5	136.3	134.7	132.8	..
North America/Amérique N.	2862.5	2895.4	2837.3	2931.8	3079.3	3166.3	3197.6	3309.8	3465.8	3737.0	3777.6	3878.3	3913.8	4043.8
Australia/Australie-NZ	117.5	125.3	129.0	131.7	138.6	147.0	153.5	160.2	167.8	178.0	186.0	189.3	190.5	197.0
OECD/OCDE Europe	1830.9	1849.2	1854.7	1911.7	1998.7	2098.4	2143.4	2222.4	2282.2	2338.8	2379.6	2430.1	2453.1	2469.1
EU/UE-15	1672.7	1676.5	1679.2	1722.3	1808.4	1902.0	1946.4	2011.2	2060.6	2109.6	2141.4	2198.4	2206.3	2210.7
OECD/OCDE	5383.4	5450.2	5399.9	5589.8	5862.0	6078.6	6165.7	6405.3	6663.9	7046.5	7194.0	7377.7	7445.6	7608.8
World/Monde	8298.1	8458.1	8552.2	8913.4	9410.4	9808.2	10107.7	10574.0	11035.8	11576.0	11831.7	12109.1	12225.9	..

Source: OECD-IEA/OCDE-AIE

The next table shows the changes in the primary sources of electricity generation in OECD countries: coal, oil, natural gas, nuclear, hydro and other. For total electricity generated, see the preceding table.

It must be kept in mind that the structure of primary sources of electricity production may differ widely among countries.

Le tableau suivant montre les évolutions des sources d'énergie primaire pour la production d'électricité dans les pays de l'OCDE : charbon, pétrole, énergie d'origine nucléaire, gaz naturel, hydraulique ou autre. Pour le volume total d'électricité produite, voir le tableau précédent.

On doit garder à l'esprit que la structure des sources d'énergie primaires pour produire de l'électricité varie considérablement entre les pays.

ELECTRICITY GENERATED BY SOURCE, OECD, 1980-1993
ÉLECTRICITÉ PRODUITE PAR SOURCE, OCDE, 1980-1993

Per cent/Pour cent

Source of Primary Energy/ Source d'énergie primaire	1980	1981	1982	1983	1984	1985	1986	1987	1988	1989	1990	1991	1992	1993
Coal/Charbon	39.7	40.2	41.1	41.6	40.7	41.5	41.0	41.4	41.1	40.1	39.7	39.2	39.1	38.7
Combustible Renewables and a) Waste/ Énergies renouvelables combustibles et déchets	0.2	0.2	0.2	0.2	0.2	0.2	0.3	0.3	0.3	1.0	1.2	1.0	1.3	1.4
Crude Oil, Natural Gas Liquids/ Pétrole brut, condensats de gaz naturel	17.3	15.2	13.2	12.0	10.9	9.0	9.3	8.9	9.3	10.1	9.5	9.3	8.7	7.6
Gas/Gaz	11.3	10.7	10.1	9.5	10.2	9.7	8.9	9.3	8.7	10.2	10.4	10.5	11.1	11.5
Nuclear Power/ Énergie nucléaire	11.4	13.3	14.3	15.5	17.6	20.1	21.5	22.0	22.9	22.3	22.7	23.4	23.5	23.8
Hydro, Geothermal and Solar Energy/ Énergie hydroélectrique, géothermique et solaire	20.2	20.3	21.0	21.2	20.4	19.4	19.1	18.1	17.6	16.4	16.6	16.6	16.3	16.9
TOTAL	100.0	100.0	100.0	100.0	100.0	100.0	100.0	100.0	100.0	100.0	100.0	100.0	100.0	100.0

Notes:
a) Solid biomass and animal products, gas/liquids from biomass, industrial and municipal waste.

Notes:
a) Biomasse solide et produits d'origine animale, gaz/liquides tirés de la biomasse, déchets industriels et urbains.

Source: OECD-IEA/OCDE-AIE

The following table relates to the total final consumption of energy by the different end-use sectors (i.e. industry, transport, agriculture, commerce, public services and residential uses, as well as non-energy uses of gas, coal, oil and oil products). It includes consumption of solid fuels (mainly coal), oil, gas, electricity and heat.

Le tableau suivant présente la consommation finale totale d'énergie par les différents secteurs d'utilisation finale (*i.e.* industries, transports, agriculture, commerces, services publics et usages résidentiels, ainsi que les usages non énergétiques de gaz, de charbon, de pétrole et de produits dérivés du pétrole). Ceci comprend la consommation de combustibles solides (principalement le charbon), de pétrole, de gaz, d'électricité et de chaleur.

TOTAL FINAL CONSUMPTION OF ENERGY, 1980-1993
CONSOMMATION FINALE TOTALE D'ÉNERGIE, 1980-1993

Mtoe/Mtep

	1980	1981	1982	1983	1984	1985	1986	1987	1988	1989	1990	1991	1992	1993
Canada	157.6	153.0	144.7	143.1	149.0	153.0	153.5	156.0	163.2	166.8	162.4	160.6	164.5	169.1
Mexico/Mexique	72.6	80.7	82.6	80.9	81.8	85.5	82.7	86.1	85.8	92.6	94.6	99.5	101.2	101.4
USA/Etats-Unis	1333.5	1311.6	1245.2	1229.2	1300.7	1289.0	1289.8	1336.7	1395.0	1406.9	1388.6	1379.5	1372.4	1406.7
Japan/Japon	248.9	242.5	239.6	243.1	257.3	256.4	257.5	266.6	284.1	293.6	304.4	311.9	316.9	316.4
Australia/Australie	47.3	47.4	47.8	46.2	48.2	50.3	53.0	54.0	56.3	58.7	60.9	60.5	60.8	62.6
N.Zealand/N.Zélande	7.1	7.2	7.4	7.6	8.4	7.9	8.1	8.5	9.0	9.3	9.8	10.3	10.5	10.7
Austria/Autriche	19.8	18.8	18.5	18.8	19.6	20.0	20.3	21.4	21.2	21.3	22.1	23.3	22.8	22.6
Belgium/Belgique	34.7	32.3	31.0	29.8	31.0	32.7	33.6	33.8	34.3	34.3	34.4	36.5	37.0	36.4
Denmark/Danemark	15.2	13.8	12.6	12.2	12.8	13.7	14.0	14.1	13.8	13.4	14.3	15.0	14.8	15.0
Finland/Finlande	19.4	19.1	18.8	19.1	19.5	19.6	20.5	22.0	22.1	22.8	22.9	22.8	23.2	23.2
France	143.8	135.4	132.1	133.5	134.8	136.8	138.7	140.5	141.1	142.8	144.2	152.9	154.3	152.2
Germany/Allemagne	260.3	250.4	240.3	242.7	251.3	258.8	261.1	261.9	261.5	254.4	251.2	247.6	242.8	243.2
w.Germany/All.occ.	198.8	189.2	181.0	183.2	190.4	193.8	197.2	196.4	197.6	191.4	196.7	..	..	..
Greece/Grèce	11.7	11.3	11.7	12.0	12.5	12.9	12.6	13.4	14.1	14.8	15.1	15.3	15.3	15.5
Iceland/Islande	1.3	1.4	1.4	1.5	1.5	1.5	1.5	1.6	1.7	1.7	1.8	1.7	1.8	1.8
Ireland/Irlande	6.6	6.7	6.5	6.5	6.5	6.7	7.2	7.4	7.2	7.5	7.8	7.9	7.7	7.9
Italy/Italie	106.3	103.1	100.6	100.9	104.7	105.2	106.3	111.5	114.6	118.2	119.3	122.0	122.7	121.6
Luxembourg	3.3	3.0	2.9	2.7	2.9	3.0	3.0	2.9	3.0	3.2	3.4	3.6	3.6	3.7
Netherlands/Pays-Bas	52.0	49.0	45.4	47.3	49.3	50.5	51.4	52.8	51.1	50.9	52.3	55.8	54.7	55.1
Norway/Norvège	16.5	16.3	15.9	16.3	17.4	18.0	18.1	19.1	18.4	18.1	18.1	18.0	17.9	18.3
Portugal	8.4	8.4	9.1	8.8	9.2	9.5	10.1	10.6	11.6	12.2	12.7	12.8	13.4	13.4
Spain/Espagne	50.7	49.0	48.1	49.2	49.6	50.1	50.3	51.9	57.5	59.0	60.4	63.6	64.8	63.0
Sweden/Suède	35.5	34.4	32.4	31.7	31.6	33.4	34.3	34.2	34.1	33.1	32.7	32.6	34.0	34.3
Switzerland/Suisse	17.5	16.9	16.4	17.6	17.6	18.9	19.0	19.2	19.2	19.6	19.7	20.4	20.7	20.2
Turkey/Turquie	27.0	27.0	28.8	30.3	30.9	31.7	33.4	38.1	38.9	39.4	42.0	42.8	44.0	47.5
UK/Royaume-Uni	136.9	133.8	132.7	132.7	133.1	138.9	143.4	145.8	148.6	147.0	147.5	152.9	150.4	151.9
Former CSFR/Ex-RFTS	48.4	46.1	45.8	45.4	47.3	47.4	57.0	59.3	48.8	48.7	47.6	42.5	37.6	..
Hungary/Hongrie	22.5	23.4	23.5	22.4	23.1	23.3	23.1	23.3	23.0	23.7	21.6	19.4	17.8	..
Poland/Pologne	86.1	80.2	80.6	79.1	80.9	82.9	85.6	88.9	84.5	81.4	65.6	63.6	62.7	..
North America/Amérique N.	1563.8	1545.3	1472.5	1453.2	1531.6	1527.5	1526.0	1578.8	1643.9	1666.2	1645.6	1639.6	1638.1	1677.2
Australia/Australie-NZ	54.4	54.6	55.2	53.8	56.6	58.2	61.1	62.5	65.3	68.1	70.7	70.8	71.2	73.3
OECD/OCDE Europe	966.8	929.9	905.0	913.8	935.5	961.9	978.8	1002.0	1013.9	1013.6	1021.8	1047.5	1045.8	1046.7
EU/UE-15	904.4	868.3	842.6	848.1	868.1	891.8	906.7	924.1	935.7	934.7	940.2	964.6	961.5	959.0
OECD/OCDE	2833.9	2772.3	2672.3	2663.8	2781.0	2803.9	2823.4	2910.0	3007.2	3041.5	3042.5	3069.8	3072.1	3113.7
World/Monde	4801.8	4750.9	4687.7	4733.3	4929.0	5035.6	5156.4	5324.3	5494.8	5570.5	5555.5	5581.6	5594.9	..

Source: OECD-IEA/OCDE-AIE

The following table shows the shares of the different types of energy in the total final consumption of energy in the OECD. This distribution varies widely among OECD countries.

Le tableau suivant montre la répartition des divers types d'énergie dans la consommation finale totale d'énergie dans l'ensemble des pays de l'OCDE. Cette répartition varie dans de grandes proportions entre les pays de l'OCDE.

TOTAL FINAL CONSUMPTION OF ENERGY BY TYPE, OECD, 1980-1993
CONSOMMATION FINALE TOTALE D'ÉNERGIE PAR TYPE, OCDE, 1980-1993

Per cent/Pour cent

Type of Energy/ Type d'énergie		1980	1981	1982	1983	1984	1985	1986	1987	1988	1989	1990	1991	1992	1993
Coal/Charbon		8.10	8.47	8.08	8.09	8.31	8.49	7.89	7.72	7.63	7.39	7.14	6.30	5.21	4.81
Combustible Renewables and Waste/ Énergies renouvelables combustibles et déchets	a)	3.49	3.61	3.78	4.00	4.13	4.08	4.13	4.28	4.13	3.99	3.72	3.57	3.03	3.09
Oil/Pétrole		54.65	53.25	53.44	52.90	52.06	51.78	52.81	52.42	52.28	51.73	51.90	51.47	52.59	52.19
Gas/Gaz		19.53	19.86	19.47	19.14	19.45	19.21	18.54	18.75	19.05	19.62	19.50	20.27	20.61	21.20
Electricity/Électricité		13.76	14.32	14.68	15.25	15.45	15.83	16.01	16.21	16.35	16.71	17.16	17.64	17.73	17.88
Heat/Chaleur	b)	0.46	0.48	0.53	0.59	0.57	0.59	0.60	0.60	0.54	0.54	0.55	0.73	0.80	0.81
TOTAL		100.00	100.00	100.00	100.00	100.00	100.00	100.00	100.00	100.00	100.00	100.00	100.00	100.00	100.00

Notes:
a) Solid biomass and animal products, gas/liquids from biomass, industrial and municipal waste.
b) Includes heat production from combined heat and power plants, heat plants, and heat extracted from ambient air by heat pumps.

Notes:
a) Biomasse solide et produits d'origine animale, gaz/liquides tirés de la biomasse, déchets industriels et urbains.
b) Comprend la chaleur produite par les centrales de cogénération chaleur/électricité et les centrales calogènes, ainsi que la chaleur extraite de l'air ambiant par les pompes à chaleur.

Source: OECD-IEA/OCDE-AIE

The next table shows the structure of final consumption of energy by sector: industry, transport and others (agriculture, commercial, residential, public services, etc.).

Le tableau suivant montre la structure de la consommation finale d'énergie par secteur : industrie, transports, et autres (agriculture, commerce, résidentiel, services publics, etc.).

TOTAL FINAL CONSUMPTION OF ENERGY BY SECTOR, OECD, 1980-1993
CONSOMMATION FINALE TOTALE D'ÉNERGIE PAR SECTEUR, OCDE, 1980-1993

Per cent/Pour cent

Final Consumption Sector/ Secteur de consommation finale		1980	1981	1982	1983	1984	1985	1986	1987	1988	1989	1990	1991	1992	1993
Industry/Industrie	a)	36.8	36.4	34.9	34.5	35.1	34.5	33.5	33.8	33.8	33.9	33.7	33.1	32.4	31.9
Transportation/Transports	b)	27.8	28.3	29.1	29.4	29.1	29.2	29.9	30.1	30.6	31.1	31.5	31.2	32.2	32.3
Others/Autres	c)	31.8	31.7	32.6	32.7	32.4	32.9	33.0	32.5	32.0	31.5	31.1	32.1	31.8	32.1
Non-energy use/ Utilisation non énergétique	d)	3.7	3.6	3.4	3.4	3.4	3.5	3.6	3.6	3.6	3.5	3.7	3.7	3.7	3.6
TOTAL		100.0	100.0	100.0	100.0	100.0	100.0	100.0	100.0	100.0	100.0	100.0	100.0	100.0	100.0

Notes:
a) Includes feedstocks from petrochemical industry; does not cover non-energy use of oil products, or energy used in transport in the industry sector.
b) Excludes international marine bunkers.
c) Agriculture, residential, commercial, public services.
d) Includes exclusively non-energy use of oil products (such as white spirit, paraffin waxes, lubricants, bitumen) and coal by all sectors.

Source: OECD-IEA/OCDE-AIE

Notes:
a) Inclut les produits d'alimentations de l'industrie pétrochimique; exclut l'utilisation non énergétique des produits pétroliers, et l'énergie utilisée pour le transport par l'industrie.
b) Exclut les soutages maritimes internationaux.
c) Agriculture, commerces, secteurs publique et résidentiel.
d) Inclut l'utilisation strictement non-énergétique des produits pétroliers (tels que white spirit, paraffines, lubrifiants, bitume) et du charbon par l'ensemble des secteurs.

This table shows changes in total final consumption of energy per unit of GDP since 1980, and the value of this ratio for 1991. Calculations are based on GDP at 1991 price levels, and 1991 purchasing power parties are used for conversions to US$.

See preceding tables for total final consumption of energy, and the table on GDP in the general data section.

Ce tableau montre l'évolution de la consommation finale totale d'énergie par unité de PIB depuis 1980 et la valeur de ce ratio pour 1991. Les calculs sont basés sur la valeur du PIB aux prix de 1991. Les parités de pouvoir d'achat de 1991 ont été employées pour les conversions en $EU.

Voir les tableaux précédents pour la consommation finale totale d'énergie et le tableau sur le PIB dans la section sur les données générales.

TOTAL FINAL CONSUMPTION OF ENERGY PER UNIT OF GDP, 1980-1993
CONSOMMATION FINALE TOTALE D'ÉNERGIE PAR UNITÉ DE PIB, 1980-1993

	Index 1991=100														Toe/1 000 $US Tep/1 000 $EU
	1980	1981	1982	1983	1984	1985	1986	1987	1988	1989	1990	1991	1992	1993	1991
Canada	128	120	117	112	110	108	105	102	102	102	99	100	102	102	0.31
Mexico/Mexique	89	91	94	96	94	95	96	98	96	101	99	100	100	99	0.23
USA/Etats-Unis	125	120	117	111	111	106	103	104	104	103	100	100	97	97	0.24
Japan/Japon	124	117	112	111	112	107	104	104	104	103	102	100	100	101	0.13
Australia/Australie	106	103	104	100	97	96	99	97	97	97	99	100	98	98	0.22
N.Zealand/N.Zélande	84	82	81	81	82	76	77	82	83	88	92	100	101	99	0.22
Austria/Autriche	108	103	100	100	103	103	102	106	101	98	97	100	96	95	0.17
Belgium/Belgique	117	110	104	100	101	106	108	106	103	99	96	100	100	100	0.21
Denmark/Danemark	125	115	102	97	97	99	98	99	95	92	97	100	98	98	0.17
Finland/Finlande	107	105	99	98	97	94	96	99	95	93	93	100	105	107	0.29
France	120	111	106	106	106	106	104	103	99	96	95	100	100	100	0.15
Germany/Allemagne	..	..	..	..	..	..	..	..	..	..	..	100	96	97	0.18
Greece/Grèce	91	88	91	93	95	95	91	97	98	99	102	100	99	101	0.16
Iceland/Islande	99	100	99	108	107	102	99	92	99	103	104	100	106	107	0.38
Ireland/Irlande	124	122	116	115	110	110	121	117	109	106	101	100	93	92	0.19
Italy/Italie	110	106	103	102	103	101	99	101	100	100	99	100	100	100	0.13
Luxembourg	135	121	115	106	107	107	101	97	95	96	97	100	99	99	0.45
Netherlands/Pays-Bas	116	111	104	107	108	108	107	108	102	97	96	100	97	97	0.23
Norway/Norvège	119	116	113	111	112	110	106	110	106	104	103	100	96	96	0.25
Portugal	90	88	94	91	97	97	99	98	102	101	101	100	103	105	0.13
Spain/Espagne	110	106	103	103	102	100	98	95	100	98	97	100	101	100	0.13
Sweden/Suède	132	127	119	114	109	113	114	110	107	102	99	100	106	109	0.22
Switzerland/Suisse	105	100	98	104	102	106	104	102	100	98	96	100	101	100	0.14
Turkey/Turquie	106	101	104	104	100	98	97	100	101	102	99	100	97	97	0.16
UK/Royaume-Uni	114	113	110	106	104	105	104	101	98	95	95	100	99	98	0.17
N.America/Amérique N.	123	118	115	110	110	106	103	103	104	103	100	100	98	97	0.25
Australia/Australie-NZ	102	99	100	97	94	93	96	95	95	96	98	100	99	98	0.22
OECD/OCDE Europe	..	..	..	..	..	..	..	..	..	..	..	100	99	99	0.16
EU/UE-15	..	..	..	..	..	..	..	..	..	..	..	100	99	99	0.16
OECD/OCDE	..	..	..	..	..	..	..	..	..	..	..	100	98	99	0.19

Source: OECD-IEA/OCDE-AIE

9. TRANSPORT

9. TRANSPORTS

INTRODUCTION

This section covers road transport activity, which generates pressures on the environment through the restructuring of the environment and the consumption of natural resources, such as land, materials and energy; pollution and nuisances, such as air pollution and noise; and detrimental effects on the quality of life due to congestion and accidents.

These pressures are due to:

▸ the stock of infrastructure and its changes over time;

▸ the stock of vehicles in use and its changes over time;

▸ the use of infrastructure and vehicles or, in other terms, traffic volume and its changes over time;

▸ the consumption of energy by the transport sector.

The data come from various international sources, such as IRF, MVMA, Eurostat, UNECE, ECMT and OECD-IEA, and have been supplemented as necessary by data from national sources. In general, these data offer a reasonably good level of comparability.

The reader may also refer to the section on air, which presents data on air pollution. Hazardous waste movements are covered in the waste section.

INTRODUCTION

Cette section concerne les transports routiers, qui exercent des pressions sur l'environnement. Ces pressions comprennent la restructuration de l'environnement et la consommation de ressources naturelles telles que les sols, les matières premières et l'énergie ; la génération de pollution et de nuisances telles que la pollution de l'air et le bruit ; et les effets néfastes sur la qualité de la vie dus à la congestion routière et aux accidents.

Ces pressions sont déterminées par :

▸ le stock des infrastructures et son évolution dans le temps ;

▸ le parc des véhicules en circulation et son évolution dans le temps ;

▸ l'utilisation des infrastructures et des véhicules ou, en d'autres termes, le volume de la circulation routière et son évolution dans le temps ;

▸ la consommation d'énergie par le secteur des transports.

Les données proviennent de sources internationales telles que la FRI, la MVMA, Eurostat, la CEE de l'ONU, la CEMT, l'OCDE-AIE, et elles ont été complétées par des données provenant de sources nationales. En général, ces données bénéficient d'un assez bon niveau de comparabilité.

Le lecteur peut également consulter la section sur l'air où il trouvera des données concernant la pollution de l'air. Les mouvements de déchets dangereux sont traités dans la section sur les déchets.

The following shows the total length of road networks by country, and changes over time. Roads refer to motorways, main or national highways, secondary or regional roads, and others. In principle the data refer to all public roads, streets and paths in urban and rural areas, but not private roads, and describe the situation on 31 December of each year.

The extension of road networks is part of transport activity and affects the environment by physically restructuring it.

In interpreting this table the reader should take into account some differences in the detailed definition of roads according to countries (see footnotes). This table should be read in connection with the following one on motorway networks.

Le tableau suivant présente la longueur des réseaux routiers par pays et leur évolution dans le temps. Le réseau routier inclut les autoroutes, les routes principales ou nationales, les routes secondaires ou régionales et d'autres routes. En principe les données se réfèrent à la voirie publique (routes, rues et chemins) en zones urbaines et rurales et non pas aux routes privées. La situation décrite correspond au 31 décembre de chaque année.

L'extension du réseau routier fait partie des activités de transport et agit sur l'environnement par un processus de restructuration physique.

L'interprétation de ce tableau doit tenir compte de certaines différences qui existent entre pays concernant les définitions détaillées du réseau routier (voir les notes). Ce tableau doit être lu en relation avec le tableau suivant concernant les réseaux autoroutiers.

ROAD NETWORK LENGTH: ALL ROADS (a), 1980-1993
LONGUEUR DU RÉSEAU ROUTIER : TOUTES LES ROUTES (a), 1980-1993

1 000 km

		1980	1981	1982	1983	1984	1985	1986	1987	1988	1989	1990	1991	1992	1993 (b)
Canada		914	928	930	930	930	930	930	930	930	930	930	930	930	930
Mexico/Mexique		213	213	214	218	223	227	231	233	235	237	239	242	244	245
USA/Etats-Unis		6232	6235	6240	6242	6242	6242	6242	6242	6243	6243	6243	6258	6278	6287
Japan/Japon		1113	1118	1123	1123	1125	1128	1127	1099	1104	1110	1115	1116	1125	1131
Australia/Australie	*	811	812	818	820	820	853	853	853	853	853	853	853	853	853
N.Zealand/N.Zélande		93	93	93	93	93	93	93	93	92	93	93	93	93	92
Austria/Autriche		106	107	107	107	104	105	105	107	107	107	107	109	110	111
Belgium/Belgique		127	127	127	128	128	128	136	137	138	138	141	142	143	144
Denmark/Danemark		69	69	70	70	70	70	70	70	71	71	71	71	71	71
Finland/Finlande		75	75	75	76	76	76	76	76	77	77	76	77	77	78
France		803	803	804	804	805	805	805	805	805	805	806	810	811	812
Germany/Allemagne		..	..	..	..	..	..	..	..	..	..	626	636	641	646
w.Germany/Allem.occ.		486	485	486	487	490	491	492	494	497	499	501	512	516	521
Greece/Grèce	*	37	37	37	37	37	37	38	38	38	41	41	41	41	41
Iceland/Islande		12	12	12	12	12	12	11	11	11	11	11	11	11	11
Ireland/Irlande		92	92	92	92	92	92	92	92	92	92	92	92	92	92
Italy/Italie		297	297	299	300	301	302	302	302	302	304	304	305	306	307
Luxembourg		5	5	5	5	5	5	5	5	5	5	5	5	5	5
Netherlands/Pays-Bas	*	93	93	98	103	112	113	114	115	115	116	117	118	119	120
Norway/Norvège		82	82	83	84	85	86	86	87	88	88	89	89	90	91
Portugal		52	52	52	52	52	52	57	63	64	74	83	85	91	100
Spain/Espagne	*	151	151	151	150	150	152	152	151	151	153	156	162	167	171
Sweden/Suède		129	129	130	130	130	131	131	131	131	134	135	136	136	136
Switzerland/Suisse		64	65	67	69	71	71	71	71	71	71	71	71	71	71
Turkey/Turquie	*	60	60	60	59	59	59	59	59	59	59	59	60	61	61
UK/Royaume-Uni	*	339	342	343	344	347	348	350	352	352	354	357	360	362	365
Former CSFR/ex-RFTS		74	74	74	74	74	74	73	73	73	73	73	73	74	74
Hungary/Hongrie		88	87	88	88	89	91	91	95	105	105	106	106	159	179
Poland/Pologne		299	299	299	300	300	301	301	340	361	361	363	365	367	368
N. America/Amérique N.		7359	7377	7384	7391	7395	7399	7403	7406	7408	7410	7412	7430	7452	7462
Australia/Australie-NZ		904	905	911	913	913	946	946	946	945	946	946	946	946	945
OECD/OCDE - Europe		3199	3205	3217	3229	3247	3258	3278	3291	3299	3324	3346	3380	3406	3433
EU/UE-15		2982	2986	2996	3006	3020	3031	3050	3063	3070	3094	3115	3149	3173	3199
OECD/OCDE		12576	12605	12636	12656	12679	12731	12754	12742	12757	12790	12819	12872	12929	12971

Notes:
a)   Data include Secretariat estimates.
b)   Includes provisional data.
AUS) The types of road taken into account changed in 1984 and in 1985.
FIN) Urban streets are excluded.
FRA) Excludes certain rural roads (700,000 km in 1987).
GRC) Figures are based on motorways, main or national roads, and secondary or regional roads.
NLD) Unsurfaced roads are excluded.
ESP) Motorways, national roads and secondary roads only. Other roads include rural paths and unsurfaced forest trails (167,185 in 1987).
TUR) National and provincial roads only. Village roads are excluded (308,000 in 1991).
UKD) Great Britain only.

Notes:
a)   Les données comprennent des estimations du Secrétariat.
b)   Inclut des données provisoires.
AUS) Les types de routes pris en compte ont changé en 1984 et 1985.
FIN) La voirie urbaine est exclue.
FRA) Certaines routes rurales sont exclues (700,000 Km en 1987).
GRC) Les chiffres sont basés sur les autoroutes, les routes principales ou nationales, et les routes secondaires ou régionales.
NLD) Les routes non revêtues sont exclues.
ESP) Autoroutes, routes nationales et routes secondaires seulement. Les autres routes (167,185 Km en 1987) comprennent des chemins ruraux et des sentiers forestiers non revêtus.
TUR) Routes nationales et provinciales seulement. Les routes rurales (308,000 Km en1991) sont exclues.
UKD) Grande-Bretagne seulement.

Source: IRF, OECD, national statistical yearbooks / FRI, OCDE, annuaires statistiques nationaux

The following shows the length of motorway networks by country, and changes over time. Motorways are a class of roads differing from main or national, secondary or regional, and other roads. For most countries the data describe the situation as of 31 December of each year.

The extension of the motorway network is part of transport activity and affects the environment by physically restructuring it.

This table should exhibit a reasonably good level of comparability among countries and over time, with a few exceptions (see footnotes). It should be read in connection with the preceding table on total road networks.

Le tableau suivant présente la longueur des réseaux autoroutiers par pays et leur évolution dans le temps. Les autoroutes se distinguent des routes principales ou nationales, des routes secondaires ou régionales et d'autres routes. Pour la plupart des pays, les données se réfèrent à la situation au 31 décembre de chaque année.

L'extension du réseau autoroutier fait partie des activités de transport et agit sur l'environnement par un processus de restructuration physique.

Ce tableau devrait bénéficier d'un assez bon niveau de comparabilité entre les pays et dans le temps, avec quelques exceptions (voir les notes). Ce tableau doit être lu en relation avec le tableau précédent concernant les réseaux routiers dans leur totalité.

ROAD NETWORK LENGTH: MOTORWAYS (a), 1980-1993
LONGUEUR DU RÉSEAU ROUTIER : AUTOROUTES (a), 1980-1993

km

	1980	1981	1982	1983	1984	1985	1986	1987	1988	1989	1990	1991	1992	1993 (b)
Canada	4718	4939	5244	5548	6387	7225	7445	7445	7445	7445	7686	7782	7852	7937
Mexico/Mexique	1091	1149	1178	1191	1198	1201	1208	1211	1218	1231	1761	3166	3470	4286
USA/Etats-Unis	71189	74303	77416	80530	81105	81678	82279	83214	83964	84361	84865	85267	86818	87558
Japan/Japon	2579	2860	3010	3232	3435	3555	3721	3910	4280	4407	4661	4869	5054	5410
Australia/Australie	1086	1092	1100	1100	1100	1100	1100	1100	1100	1197	1197	1197	1197	1197
N.Zealand/N.Zélande	119	123	126	130	134	140	140	140	140	140	141	141	141	144
Austria/Autriche	938	956	1047	1109	1137	1261	1289	1376	1405	1407	1470	1499	1554	1554
Belgium/Belgique	1192	1246	1317	1375	1375	1456	1549	1567	1613	1631	1631	1649	1667	1686
Denmark/Danemark	516	525	526	518	539	593	593	599	599	601	653	653	706	747
Finland/Finlande	204	205	205	204	204	204	204	204	214	215	225	249	318	334
France *	5264	5715	5905	5845	6005	6150	6265	6440	6570	6950	7100	7450	7700	8100
Germany/Allemagne	..	..	..	..	..	..	..	..	..	..	10809	10955	11093	11221
w.Germany/Allem.occ.	7538	7784	7919	8080	8198	8350	8437	8618	8721	8822	8959	9105	9244	9373
Greece/Grèce	91	91	91	92	92	92	92	91	91	120	190	225	280	355
Iceland/Islande	-	-	-	-	-	-	-	-	-	-	-	-	-	-
Ireland/Irlande	-	-	-	8	8	8	8	8	8	8	8	8	32	32	50
Italy/Italie	5900	5900	5900	5901	5941	5955	5979	6612	6695	6767	6852	6896	6940	7008
Luxembourg	44	46	58	58	58	58	58	64	75	79	79	84	95	100
Netherlands/Pays-Bas	1773	1831	1858	1884	1971	1975	2054	2056	2059	2061	2092	2105	2118	2150
Norway/Norvège	56	68	71	74	74	74	74	74	74	74	75	75	75	82
Portugal	127	127	154	181	183	183	183	221	221	256	318	453	519	519
Spain/Espagne *	1842	1877	1882	1927	1977	1977	1977	2142	2142	1863	2368	2700	2850	3042
Sweden/Suède *	850	854	868	881	892	897	999	999	999	1010	1016	1027	1033	1044
Switzerland/Suisse	876	957	986	1006	1030	1054	1075	1451	1486	1495	1495	1502	1514	1530
Turkey/Turquie	24	24	24	24	73	73	84	104	125	141	256	352	707	1030
UK/Royaume-Uni *	2585	2641	2666	2775	2793	2838	2843	2980	2981	2993	2903	3100	3147	3183
Former CSFR/ex-RFTS	373	428	428	482	482	482	489	489	518	527	548	560	564	580
Hungary/Hongrie	209	209	228	246	285	324	324	324	311	311	349	351	441	471
Poland/Pologne	139	139	168	168	168	204	213	213	220	243	257	257	257	257
N. America/Amérique N.	76998	80391	83838	87269	88690	90104	90932	91870	92627	93037	94312	96215	98140	99781
Australia/Australie-NZ	1205	1215	1226	1230	1234	1240	1240	1240	1240	1337	1338	1338	1338	1341
OECD/OCDE - Europe	31507	32567	33295	33760	34400	35048	35618	37461	37933	38343	39539	41006	42347	43734
EU/UE-15	30551	31518	32214	32656	33223	33847	34385	35832	36248	36633	37713	39077	40051	41092
OECD/OCDE	112289	117032	121369	125491	127759	129947	131511	134481	136080	137124	139850	143428	146879	150266

Notes:
a)   Data include Secretariat estimates.
b)   Includes provisional data.
FRA) Of which 1 150 km are urban motorways.
ESP) Two-lane motor traffic roads are included.
SWE) Excludes access and exit ramps.
UKD) Great Britain only. Slip roads are not included.

Notes:
a)   Les données comprennent des estimations du Secretariat.
b)   Inclut des données provisoires.
FRA) Dont 1 150 km d'atuoroutes urbaines.
ESP) Y compris les semi-autoroutes à deux voies.
SWE) Exclut les rampes d'accès et de sortie.
UKD) Grande-Bretagne seulement. Les bretelles d'accès sont exclues.

Source: IRF, OECD, national statistical yearbooks / FRI, OCDE, annuaires statistiques nationaux

The following gives the total number of motor vehicles in use by country, and changes over time. Motor vehicles include passenger cars, goods vehicles, buses and coaches. In principle the data refer to autonomous road vehicles with four or more wheels, excluding caravans and trailers, military vehicles, special vehicles (for emergency services, construction machinery, etc.) and agricultural tractors; and they describe the situation as of 31 December of each year.

The growth in the stock of motor vehicles in use is a major factor in explaining the impact of transport on the environment.

This table should exhibit a reasonably good level of comparability among countries and over time, with a few exceptions (see footnotes). It should be read in connection with the following tables on passenger cars in use and goods vehicles in use.

Le tableau suivant donne le nombre total de véhicules à moteur en service par pays et son évolution dans le temps. Les véhicules à moteur comprennent les voitures particulières, les véhicules de marchandises de même que les autobus et les autocars. En principe, les données se réfèrent aux véhicules routiers autonomes de quatre roues ou plus, à l'exception des caravanes et remorques, des véhicules militaires, des véhicules spéciaux (pour les services d'urgence, machines de chantier, etc.), et des tracteurs agricoles. La situation décrite correspond au 31 décembre de chaque année.

La croissance du parc de véhicules à moteur en service est un facteur explicatif majeur de l'impact des activités de transport sur l'environnement.

Ce tableau devrait bénéficier d'un assez bon niveau de comparabilité entre les pays et dans le temps, avec quelques exceptions (voir les notes). Ce tableau doit être lu en relation avec les tableaux suivants concernant le parc de voitures particulières et de véhicules de marchandises en service.

ROAD VEHICLE STOCKS: MOTOR VEHICLES (a), 1980-1993
PARCS DE VÉHICULES ROUTIERS : VÉHICULES À MOTEUR (a), 1980-1993

1 000

		1980	1981	1982	1983	1984	1985	1986	1987	1988	1989	1990	1991	1992	1993 (b)
Canada		13211	13392	13824	14094	13880	14267	14798	15263	15852	16270	16553	16805	16986	17190
Mexico/Mexique		5828	6545	6876	6919	7196	7476	7499	7786	8330	9015	9882	10399	11351	11897
USA/Etats-Unis		155796	158286	159643	163749	166249	171654	176191	179044	184397	187261	188655	188372	190362	194063
Japan/Japon	*	37856	39621	41336	42932	44524	46157	47972	49902	52450	55093	57698	59915	61658	63263
Australia/Australie		7264	7566	7969	8188	8434	8730	8916	9023	9222	9489	9776	9649	9954	10140
N.Zealand/N.Zélande		1568	1605	1647	1688	1757	1802	1809	1822	1829	1835	1849	1855	1866	1900
Austria/Autriche		2810	2890	2947	3012	3080	3153	3244	3336	3458	3596	3692	3812	3977	4114
Belgium/Belgique	*	3478	3510	3535	3600	3611	3662	3738	3842	3972	4114	4260	4385	4457	4566
Denmark/Danemark		1650	1617	1602	1635	1693	1768	1841	1882	1898	1900	1893	1900	1917	1939
Finland/Finlande		1393	1453	1533	1598	1668	1747	1829	1920	2034	2181	2233	2218	2231	2156
France		21705	22466	23190	23830	24110	25070	25700	26340	27090	27758	28460	28827	29054	29450
Germany/Allemagne		..	..	..	..	..	..	..	..	..	..	37226	38685	40075	41089
w.Germany/Allem.occ.		24572	25022	25357	26011	26698	27426	28564	29659	30563	31563	32148	32854	33908	34382
Greece/Grèce		1265	1371	1511	1624	1744	1883	2005	2107	2216	2358	2523	2592	2650	2807
Iceland/Islande		96	101	107	108	113	117	125	133	141	136	138	137	136	132
Ireland/Irlande		803	849	882	897	906	914	922	959	981	1019	1052	1102	1122	1146
Italy/Italie		19115	20151	21258	22153	22681	24405	25504	26389	27481	28578	29910	31033	32161	32346
Luxembourg		138	143	148	151	156	161	166	173	179	188	195	204	214	223
Netherlands/Pays-Bas	*	4835	4922	4960	5061	5168	5277	5359	5568	5731	5868	6028	6108	6235	6367
Norway/Norvège		1398	1450	1518	1578	1644	1764	1875	1926	1936	1935	1943	1949	1961	1986
Portugal	*	1205	1288	1371	1433	1482	1541	1605	1684	1849	1908	2198	2448	2716	2969
Spain/Espagne		8937	9383	9859	10287	10360	10845	11364	12083	12807	13675	14374	15079	15799	16223
Sweden/Suède		3077	3093	3143	3222	3305	3383	3497	3626	3764	3887	3925	3943	3906	3882
Switzerland/Suisse	*	2427	2573	2663	2722	2756	2827	2897	2961	3001	3178	3297	3377	3409	3424
Turkey/Turquie		1170	1221	1276	1345	1440	1537	1678	1812	1954	2102	2360	2621	2915	3524
UK/Royaume-Uni	*	17330	17516	17930	18457	19083	19559	20190	20731	21923	22859	23393	23350	24136	24335
Former CSFR/ex-RFTS		2540	2658	2728	2799	2934	3026	2947	3035	3316	3450	3576	3686	3862	4028
Hungary/Hongrie		1176	1281	1361	1441	1535	1628	1728	1862	1995	2055	2195	2252	2310	2412
Poland/Pologne		3067	3343	3572	3910	4238	4534	4877	5185	5528	5914	6397	7442	7849	8132
N. America/Amérique N.		174835	178223	180343	184762	187325	193397	198488	202093	208579	212546	215090	215576	218699	223150
Australia/Australie-NZ		8832	9171	9616	9876	10191	10532	10725	10845	11051	11324	11625	11504	11820	12040
OECD/OCDE - Europe		120331	124084	127955	131984	135091	140581	145800	150971	156968	162958	169101	173771	179069	182677
EU/UE-15		115241	118739	122392	126230	129137	134337	139225	144138	149935	155607	161362	165687	170649	173611
OECD/OCDE		341855	351100	359251	369554	377131	390667	402986	413811	429048	441921	453513	460766	471246	481130
World/Monde		410982	427204	439053	455920	473030	487507	499786	515206	539790	556932	582982	595307	613530	617087

Notes:
a)   Data include Secretariat estimates.
b)   Includes provisional data.
JPN) Three-wheeled vehicles are included.
BEL) Figures are reported on 1st August of the reference year.
NLD) Figures are reported on 31st July of the reference year.
PRT) The definition of commercial vehicles changed in 1990.
CHE) Figures are reported on 30th September of the reference year.
UKD) Includes electric vehicles.

Notes
a)   Les données comprennent des estimations du Secretariat.
b)   Inclut des données provisoires.
JPN) Les véhicules à trois roues sont inclus.
BEL) Les chiffres sont établis chaque année à la date du 1er août.
NLD) Les chiffres sont établis chaque année à la date du 31er juillet.
PRT) La définition de véhicules de marchandises a été changée en 1990.
CHE) Les chiffres sont établis chaque année à la date du 30 septembre.
UKD) Inclut les véhicules électriques.

Source: OECD, MVMA, IRF / OCDE, MVMA, FRI

The following gives the total number of passenger cars in use by country, and changes over time. In principle the data refer to passenger cars seating not more than nine persons (including the driver), including rental cars, taxis, jeeps, estate cars/station wagons and similar light, dual-purpose vehicles; and describe the situation as of 31 December of each year.

The growth in the stock of passenger cars in use is a major factor in explaining the impact of transport on the environment.

This table should exhibit a good level of comparability among countries and over time, with a few exceptions (see footnotes). It should be read in connection with the preceding and following tables on the total stock of motor vehicles and of goods vehicles in use.

Le tableau suivant donne le nombre total de voitures particulières en service par pays et son évolution dans le temps. En principe, les données se réfèrent aux voitures de tourisme n'ayant pas plus de neuf places (celle du chauffeur incluse), y compris les voitures de location, les taxis, les jeeps, les breaks et autres véhicules légers de transport mixte. La situation décrite correspond au 31 décembre de chaque année.

La croissance du parc de voitures particulières en service est un facteur explicatif majeur de l'impact des activités de transport sur l'environnement.

Ce tableau devrait bénéficier d'un bon niveau de comparabilité entre les pays et dans le temps, avec quelques exceptions (voir les notes). Ce tableau doit être lu en relation avec les tableaux précédent et suivant concernant le parc total de véhicules à moteur et de véhicules de marchandises en service.

ROAD VEHICLE STOCKS: PASSENGER CARS IN USE (a), 1980-1993
PARCS DE VÉHICULES ROUTIERS : VOITURES PARTICULIÈRES EN SERVICE (a), 1980-1993

1 000

	1980	1981	1982	1983	1984	1985	1986	1987	1988	1989	1990	1991	1992	1993 (b)
Canada	10256	10199	10530	10732	10781	11118	11586	11686	12086	12380	12622	13061	13298	13478
Mexico/Mexique	4255	4745	4958	4870	5029	5282	5203	5403	5807	6219	6819	7053	7750	8100
USA/Etats-Unis	121601	123098	123702	126444	128158	131864	135431	137324	141252	143081	143550	142956	144213	146314
Japan/Japon	23660	24612	25539	26385	27144	27845	28654	29478	30776	32621	34924	37076	38964	40772
Australia/Australie *	5801	6021	6308	6470	6636	6843	6985	7073	7244	7442	7672	7734	7913	8050
N.Zealand/N.Zélande	1307	1332	1367	1401	1471	1500	1506	1518	1524	1530	1542	1548	1551	1572
Austria/Autriche	2247	2313	2361	2414	2468	2531	2609	2685	2785	2903	2991	3100	3245	3368
Belgium/Belgique *	3159	3206	3231	3263	3300	3343	3409	3498	3614	3736	3864	3970	4022	4110
Denmark/Danemark *	1390	1367	1358	1390	1440	1501	1558	1588	1596	1597	1591	1594	1605	1618
Finland/Finlande	1226	1279	1352	1410	1474	1546	1620	1699	1796	1909	1939	1923	1936	1873
France	19130	19750	20300	20600	20800	21090	21500	21970	22520	23010	23550	23810	24020	24385
Germany/Allemagne	..	..	..	..	..	..	..	..	..	..	35512	36859	38136	38882
w.Germany/Allem.occ.	23236	23681	24036	24689	25378	26099	27224	28304	29190	30152	30695	31309	32286	32732
Greece/Grèce	859	912	996	1069	1155	1263	1359	1433	1508	1609	1730	1777	1829	1959
Iceland/Islande	86	90	95	97	100	103	113	120	129	124	120	121	120	116
Ireland/Irlande	734	775	709	719	711	710	711	737	749	773	796	837	859	891
Italy/Italie	17686	18603	19616	20389	20888	22495	23495	24320	25290	26267	27416	28435	29450	29600
Luxembourg	129	133	138	141	146	152	156	162	168	177	183	192	201	209
Netherlands/Pays-Bas	4515	4594	4630	4728	4818	4901	4950	5118	5251	5371	5509	5569	5658	5755
Norway/Norvège	1234	1279	1338	1383	1430	1514	1592	1623	1622	1613	1613	1615	1619	1633
Portugal	941	990	1040	1092	1136	1185	1236	1290	1427	1474	1605	1800	2020	2210
Spain/Espagne	7557	7943	8354	8714	8874	9274	9643	10219	10787	11468	11996	12537	13102	13441
Sweden/Suède	2883	2893	2936	3007	3081	3151	3254	3367	3483	3578	3601	3619	3587	3566
Switzerland/Suisse *	2247	2395	2473	2521	2552	2617	2679	2733	2761	2917	3012	3085	3119	3138
Turkey/Turquie	742	776	811	856	920	983	1087	1193	1310	1435	1650	1864	2111	2620
UK/Royaume-Uni *	14660	14867	15264	15543	16055	16454	16981	17421	18432	19266	19742	19737	20116	20344
Former CSFR/ex-RFTS	2274	2373	2441	2511	2640	2726	2639	2724	3000	3122	3242	3342	3506	3689
Hungary/Hongrie	1013	1105	1182	1258	1347	1436	1539	1660	1790	1848	1944	2015	2058	2149
Poland/Pologne	2383	2634	2882	3179	3426	3671	3964	4232	4519	4846	5261	6112	6505	6771
N. America/Amérique N.	136112	138042	139190	142046	143968	148264	152220	154413	159145	161680	162991	163070	165261	167892
Australia/Australie-NZ	7108	7353	7675	7870	8107	8343	8491	8591	8768	8972	9214	9282	9464	9622
OECD/OCDE - Europe	107339	110658	113960	117044	119884	124218	128638	133080	138162	143278	148419	152444	156755	159716
EU/UE-15	103030	106118	109243	112188	114881	119001	123167	127410	132340	137189	142025	145759	149786	152209
OECD/OCDE	274218	280665	286364	293345	299103	308670	318003	325562	336851	346551	355549	361872	370444	378002
World/Monde	320390	330799	340266	352031	365105	374483	386350	394030	412907	424366	444900	456033	469943	469460

Notes:
a) Data include Secretariat estimates.
b) Includes provisional data.
AUS) Includes utility vehicles.
BEL) Figures are reported on 1st August of the reference year.
DNK) Passenger cars includes vans under 2 tonnes.
CHE) Figures are reported on 30th September of the reference year.
UKD) Excludes taxis and electric cars.

Notes:
a) Les données comprennent des estimations du Secrétariat.
b) Inclut des données provisoires.
AUS) Inclut des véhicules utilitaires.
BEL) Les chiffres son établis chaque année à la date du 1er août.
DNK) Les voitures particulières incluent des véhicules de livraison ayant une charge utile inférieure à 2 tonnes.
CHE) Les chiffres son établis chaque année à la date du 30 septembre.
UKD) Exclut les taxis et les voitures électriques.

Source: OECD, MVMA, IRF / OCDE, MVMA, FRI

The following gives the total number of goods vehicles in use by country, and changes over time. In principle the data refer to vans, lorries (trucks) and road tractors. They do not include caravans, trailers and semi-trailers, military or special vehicles, or agricultural tractors. They describe the situation as of 31 December of each year.

The growth in the stock of goods vehicles in use is a major factor in explaining the impact of transport on the environment.

The interpretation of this table should take into account some differences in the detailed definition of goods vehicles, especially road tractors, according to countries (see footnotes). This table should be read in connection with the preceding tables on total stocks of motor vehicles and of passenger cars in use.

Le tableau suivant donne le nombre total de véhicules de marchandises en service par pays et son évolution dans le temps. En principe les données se réfèrent aux fourgonnettes, camions et tracteurs routiers. Elles ne comprennent pas de caravanes, de remorques et de semi-remorques, ni de véhicules militaires ou spéciaux, ni de tracteurs agricoles. La situation décrite correspond au 31 décembre de chaque année.

La croissance du parc de véhicules de marchandises en service est un facteur explicatif majeur de l'impact des activités de transport sur l'environnement.

L'interprétation de ce tableau doit tenir compte de certaines différences entre pays concernant la définition des véhicules de marchandises, surtout des tracteurs routiers (voir les notes). Ce tableau doit être lu en relation avec les tableaux précédents concernant le parc total de véhicules à moteurs et de voitures particulières en service.

ROAD VEHICLE STOCKS: GOODS VEHICLES IN USE (a), 1980-1993
PARCS DE VÉHICULES ROUTIERS : VÉHICULES DE MARCHANDISES EN SERVICE (a), 1980-1993

1 000

	1980	1981	1982	1983	1984	1985	1986	1987	1988	1989	1990	1991	1992	1993 (b)
Canada	2903	3138	3239	3308	3047	3095	3156	3517	3706	3827	3867	3680	3624	3648
Mexico/Mexique	1489	1719	1822	1969	2098	2115	2213	2299	2436	2704	2969	3248	3506	3700
USA/Etats-Unis	33667	34644	35382	36723	37507	39196	40166	41119	42529	43554	44479	44785	45504	47095
Japan/Japon *	13177	13956	14717	15437	16241	17140	18109	19162	20350	21085	21321	21323	21132	20881
Australia/Australie *	1463	1545	1661	1718	1798	1887	1931	1950	1978	2047	2104	1915	2041	2090
N.Zealand/N.Zélande	256	270	276	284	281	297	297	298	298	298	299	299	307	320
Austria/Autriche	184	190	193	197	203	207	212	221	235	247	253	259	269	276
Belgium/Belgique *	283	285	285	289	294	302	312	328	343	362	380	399	419	440
Denmark/Danemark	253	243	236	237	245	259	275	286	294	295	294	299	305	313
Finland/Finlande	149	155	162	168	174	180	187	198	214	244	264	264	263	253
France	2516	2655	2829	3168	3248	3916	4135	4305	4505	4680	4840	4941	4959	4989
Germany/Allemagne	..	..	..	..	..	..	..	..	..	..	1628	1739	1851	2119
w.Germany/Allem.occ.	1265	1270	1250	1251	1251	1257	1271	1286	1303	1340	1383	1475	1551	1579
Greece/Grèce	389	441	497	537	571	601	627	656	689	729	772	793	798	826
Iceland/Islande	9	10	11	11	12	12	12	12	12	12	13	15	15	14
Ireland/Irlande	65	67	68	70	84	93	101	111	119	130	143	148	145	135
Italy/Italie	1371	1485	1575	1693	1720	1834	1930	1995	2115	2234	2417	2520	2632	2668
Luxembourg	9	9	9	9	9	9	9	9	10	10	11	11	12	13	14
Netherlands/Pays-Bas	309	316	319	321	338	364	398	438	468	485	507	527	565	600
Norway/Norvège	153	159	166	179	198	233	265	284	294	300	308	311	315	323
Portugal *	264	298	331	341	346	356	369	394	422	434	593	648	696	759
Spain/Espagne	1338	1397	1462	1529	1445	1529	1679	1822	1976	2162	2333	2495	2650	2735
Sweden/Suède	182	186	193	202	210	218	230	246	267	295	310	310	305	302
Switzerland/Suisse *	169	168	178	190	193	201	207	218	228	248	272	277	276	272
Turkey/Turquie	331	345	360	377	396	418	442	459	475	490	521	554	586	660
UK/Royaume-Uni *	2148	2112	2101	2180	2242	2290	2364	2437	2598	2704	2729	2664	3070	3220
Former CSFR/ex-RFTS	246	253	255	254	260	264	271	274	278	288	293	301	317	302
Hungary/Hongrie	124	130	144	159	163	167	163	175	179	181	225	227	229	242
Poland/Pologne	618	641	616	655	732	780	827	866	919	977	1045	1243	1257	1276
N. America/Amérique N.	38059	39501	40443	42000	42652	44406	45535	46935	48671	50085	51315	51713	52634	54443
Australia/Australie-NZ	1718	1815	1937	2002	2080	2184	2228	2248	2276	2345	2403	2214	2348	2410
OECD/OCDE - Europe	11621	12028	12453	13172	13398	14499	15244	15928	16797	17642	18588	19175	20132	20919
EU/UE-15	10959	11347	11738	12415	12600	13636	14318	14956	15787	16592	17474	18018	18940	19649
OECD/OCDE	64575	67300	69550	72610	74370	78229	81116	84273	88094	91157	93627	94424	96246	98653
World/Monde	90592	96405	98787	103888	107925	113024	113436	121176	126882	132566	138082	139274	143587	147627

Notes:
a)   Data include Secretariat estimates.
b)   Includes provisional data.
JPN) Three-wheel vehicles are included.
AUS) Includes buses and coaches.
BEL) Figures refer to 1st August of the reference year.
PRT) Definitions change in 1990.
CHE) Figures refer to 30th September of the reference year.
UKD) Exclude electric goods vehicles.

Source: OECD, MVMA, IRF / OCDE, MVMA, FRI

Notes:
a)   Les données comprennent des estimations du Secrétariat.
b)   Inclut des données provisoires.
JPN) Les véhicules à trois roues sont inclues.
AUS) Y compris autobus es autocars.
BEL) Les chiffres sont établis chaque année à la date du 1er août.
PRT) Les définitions ont été changées en 1990.
CHE) Les chiffres sont établis chaque année à la date du 30 septembre.
UKD) Exclut les véhicules de marchandises électriques.

The following shows total traffic volumes of road vehicles. Traffic volumes are expressed in billions of kilometres travelled by road vehicles. They are usually estimates: the average number of kilometres travelled each year by road vehicles is multiplied by the number of motor vehicles in use. In principle the data refer to total kilometres travelled on all roads on national territory by national vehicles, with the exception of two- and three-wheeled vehicles, caravans and trailers.

Changes in traffic volumes are a major factor in explaining the impact of transport on the environment.

The interpretation of this table should take into account differences in the definition of traffic volumes: e.g. inclusion or exclusion of kilometres travelled on national territory by foreign vehicles, variations in the method of estimation. This table should be read in connection with the tables on passenger car traffic and goods vehicle traffic.

Le tableau suivant indique les volumes totaux de circulation routière. Le volume de circulation routière est exprimé en milliards de kilomètres parcourus par les véhicules routiers. D'habitude ce sont des estimations : le parcours annuel moyen des véhicules routiers en kilomètres est multiplié par le nombre de véhicules en service. En principe les données se réfèrent à l'ensemble des kilomètres parcourus sur tous les réseaux routiers sur le territoire national par des véhicules nationaux à l'exception des véhicules à deux ou trois roues et des remorques.

L'évolution du volume de la circulation routière est un facteur explicatif majeur de l'impact des activités de transport sur l'environnement.

L'interprétation de ce tableau doit tenir compte des différences dans la définition du volume de la circulation routière : p. ex. incorporation ou exclusion des kilomètres parcourus sur le territoire national par des véhicules étrangers, variations dans la méthode d'estimation. Ce tableau doit être lu en relation avec les tableaux concernant le volume de circulation des voitures particulières et des véhicules de marchandises.

ROAD TRAFFIC VOLUMES: MOTOR VEHICLES (a), 1980-1993
VOLUMES DE LA CIRCULATION ROUTIÈRE: VÉHICULES À MOTEUR (a), 1980-1993

billion / milliards veh.-km

		1980	1981	1982	1983	1984	1985	1986	1987	1988	1989	1990	1991	1992	1993
Canada		206	202	204	204	202	201	207	217	221	225	230	236	243	248
Mexico/Mexique		..	..	..	..	..	..	..	49	50	51	55	53	54	54
USA/Etats-Unis	*	2419	2425	2475	2634	2745	2840	2937	3078	3244	3357	3435	3480	3589	3701
Japan/Japon	*	389	395	432	465	478	517	540	549	576	600	629	657	678	708
Australia/Australie		115	119	125	129	133	138	140	144	152	148	142	139	140	141
N.Zealand/N.Zélande		17	17	18	19	18	19	19	20	21	22	22	23	24	25
Austria/Autriche		35	36	36	36	38	38	39	44	46	49	52	55	56	59
Belgium/Belgique		46	46	47	46	47	47	48	50	53	55	57	57	58	60
Denmark/Danemark		26	27	26	27	28	30	32	33	35	36	36	37	38	39
Finland/Finlande		27	27	28	29	30	31	32	34	37	39	40	39	42	43
France	*	296	305	308	315	324	328	344	357	374	382	394	411	426	441
Germany/Allemagne		..	..	..	..	..	..	..	..	..	..	511	526	551	578
w.Germany/Allem.occ.	*	328	331	335	341	351	351	375	396	417	427	446	454	472	489
Greece/Grèce	*	20	22	23	25	27	29	30	32	34	36	38	41	43	46
Iceland/Islande	*	1	1	1	1	1	1	2	2	2	2	2	2	2	2
Ireland/Irlande		19	19	18	18	18	19	19	20	21	23	24	25	26	27
Italy/Italie	*	227	235	249	240	248	258	265	279	294	310	345	363	386	412
Luxembourg		2	2	2	2	3	3	3	3	3	3	3	4	4	4
Netherlands/Pays-Bas	*	70	70	69	72	74	74	78	82	87	90	90	91	93	98
Norway/Norvège		17	17	17	18	18	20	21	22	24	25	26	26	26	26
Portugal		21	23	25	26	28	28	29	30	32	33	34	35	39	41
Spain/Espagne	*	71	72	73	74	76	75	83	86	93	95	100	102	101	104
Sweden/Suède	*	44	44	45	46	47	48	51	53	59	61	64	67	71	75
Switzerland/Suisse		37	38	40	41	41	42	43	44	45	48	49	50	52	53
Turkey/Turquie	*	15	15	16	17	19	19	19	21	22	27	27	26	29	31
UK/Royaume-Uni	*	242	245	252	258	268	274	285	311	328	357	399	406	444	444
Former CSFR/Ex-RFTS	*	..	..	..	..	..	..	3	2	2	2	2	2	2	2
Hungary/Hongrie		19	19	20	20	20	21	21	21	22	22	23	23	25	26
Poland/Pologne		45	40	35	37	42	44	46	49	55	59	60	91	111	111
N.America/Amérique N.	*	2624	2627	2679	2838	2948	3041	3144	3344	3514	3633	3720	3769	3885	4004
Australia/Australie-NZ		131	135	143	148	151	156	159	165	173	170	164	162	164	166
OECD/OCDE - Europe		1579	1614	1647	1669	1724	1755	1841	1944	2052	2147	2292	2363	2486	2583
EU/UE-15		1510	1542	1572	1593	1644	1673	1756	1854	1960	2046	2188	2259	2378	2470
OECD/OCDE	*	4724	4771	4901	5120	5300	5469	5685	6001	6315	6549	6805	6951	7213	7460

Notes:
a) Data include Secretariat estimates.
b) Includes provisional data.
USA) Traffic by local and urban buses is excluded.
JPN) Traffic by light vehicles is excluded.
FRA) Traffic by buses of the Régie Autonome des Transports Parisiens is excluded.
wGER) Except for caravans and large trailers hauled by passenger-carrying vehicles, traffic by special vehicles is included.
GRC) Data refer to inter-city traffic only.
ISL) Traffic by local and urban buses is excluded.
ITA) Traffic by three-wheel goods vehicles is included.
NLD) Traffic by trams and subways is included.
ESP) Data refer only to traffic on motorways and national roads.
SWE) Data include traffic by Swedish passenger cars abroad. Traffic by goods vehicles with a load capacity under 2 tonnes is excluded. Up to 1988, only the public network is included; after 1989, the total network is taken into account.
TUR) Data refer only to traffic on motorways and national roads.
UKD) Data refer to Great Britain only.
CSFR) Data refer to traffic by buses and goods vehicles only.
TOT) From 1987, data include Mexico.

Notes:
a) Les données comprennent des estimations du Secrétariat.
b) Inclut des données provisoires.
USA) Le trafic des autobus locaux ou urbains est exclu.
JPN) Le trafic des véhicules légers est exclu.
FRA) Le trafic des autobus de la Régie Autonome des Transports Parisiens est exclu.
wGER) Le trafic des véhicules spéciaux est exclu, excepté les caravanes et les grandes remorques tirées par des véhicules pour le transport de passagers.
GRC) Les données comprennent la circulation inter-urbaine seulement.
ISL) Le trafic des autobus locaux ou urbains est exclu.
ITA) Le trafic des véhicules de marchandises à trois roues est inclu.
NLD) Le trafic des systèmes de tramway et de métro est inclu.
ESP) Les données comprennent la circulation sur les réseaux autoroutier et national seulement.
SWE) Les données comprennent le trafic des voitures particulières suédoises à l'étranger. Le trafic des véhicules de marchandises ayant une charge utile inférieure à 2 tonnes est exclu. Jusqu'à 1988, les données ne comprennent que le réseau public; depuis 1989, le réseau total est pris en compte.
TUR) Les données comprennent la circulation sur les réseaux autoroutier et national seulement.
UKD) Grande-Bretagne seulement.
RFTS) Les données comprennent uniquement le trafic des autobus et véhicules de marchandises.
TOT) Depuis 1987 les données comprennent le Mexique.

Source: OECD, IRF, national statistical yearbooks / OCDE, FRI, annuaires nationaux statistique

The following table shows passenger car traffic volumes and changes over time. Traffic volumes are expressed in billions of kilometres travelled by the stock of passenger cars in use. In principle the data refer to total kilometres travelled on all roads by national passenger cars on national territory.

Changes in traffic volumes are a major factor in explaining the impact of transport on the environment.

The interpretation of this table should take into account differences in the definition of traffic volumes: e.g. inclusion or exclusion of kilometres travelled on national territory by foreign vehicles, variations in the method of estimation. This table should be read in connection with the tables on total road vehicle traffic and goods vehicle traffic.

Le tableau suivant indique les volumes de circulation des voitures particulières et leur évolution dans le temps. Les volumes de circulation sont exprimés en millards de kilomètres parcourus par le parc de voitures particulières en service. En principe les données se réfèrent à l'ensemble des kilomètres parcourus sur tous les réseaux routiers sur le territoire national par des voitures particulières nationales.

L'évolution des volumes de circulation routière est un facteur explicatif majeur de l'impact des activités de transport sur l'environnement.

L'interprétation de ce tableau doit tenir compte des différences dans la définition des volumes de circulation routière : p. ex. incorporation ou exclusion des kilomètres parcourus sur le territoire national par des véhicules étrangers, variations dans la méthode d'estimation. Ce tableau doit être lu en relation avec les tableaux concernant le volume total de circulation routière et de véhicules de marchandises.

ROAD TRAFFIC VOLUMES: PASSENGER CARS (a), 1980-1993
VOLUMES DE LA CIRCULATION ROUTIÈRE : VOITURES PARTICULIÈRES (a), 1980-1993

billion / milliards veh.-km

		1980	1981	1982	1983	1984	1985	1986	1987	1988	1989	1990	1991	1992	1993 (b)
Canada		152	146	148	148	145	143	148	151	153	156	158	162	165	168
Mexico/Mexique		..	..	..	..	..	..	..	34	35	35	38	37	37	38
USA/Etats-Unis		1789	1793	1824	1966	2020	2028	2094	2181	2300	2378	2435	2467	2567	2652
Japan/Japon	*	241	247	256	260	265	291	301	308	321	341	366	387	406	429
Australia/Australie		87	90	93	96	100	103	106	109	117	116	115	114	116	117
N.Zealand/N.Zélande		13	13	13	15	14	14	15	15	16	16	17	17	18	18
Austria/Autriche		26	26	26	26	27	28	28	32	34	37	40	41	43	45
Belgium/Belgique		41	42	42	42	42	42	43	44	47	49	50	52	53	55
Denmark/Danemark		22	22	21	22	23	24	25	27	28	29	30	30	31	32
Finland/Finlande		22	23	23	24	25	26	27	29	31	33	33	33	36	39
France		245	253	253	258	265	267	280	288	300	303	311	325	332	343
Germany/Allemagne		..	..	..	..	..	..	..	..	..	..	453	463	476	494
w.Germany/Allem.occ.	*	297	283	294	304	314	313	336	357	377	386	402	406	411	425
Greece/Grèce	*	11	11	12	13	15	16	17	18	20	21	22	24	25	27
Iceland/Islande		1	1	1	1	1	1	1	1	1	1	1	1	2	2
Ireland/Irlande		15	15	14	14	14	15	16	16	17	18	19	20	21	22
Italy/Italie		191	198	209	199	205	214	219	231	245	260	292	309	331	356
Luxembourg		2	2	2	2	2	2	2	3	3	3	3	3	3	3
Netherlands/Pays-Bas		61	61	60	63	65	65	68	71	76	77	77	78	80	81
Norway/Norvège		14	15	15	15	16	17	18	19	20	22	23	22	22	22
Portugal		17	18	19	20	21	23	23	24	24	25	26	27	30	33
Spain/Espagne	*	53	54	55	56	57	56	62	64	70	71	74	76	78	81
Sweden/Suède	*	41	42	42	43	44	45	47	49	53	56	56	58	61	63
Switzerland/Suisse		32	33	34	35	35	36	37	38	39	39	40	41	42	43
Turkey/Turquie	*	8	8	8	9	9	8	8	9	10	13	14	13	15	17
UK/Royaume-Uni	*	197	201	209	213	222	228	236	257	270	294	330	335	335	334
Former CSFR/ex-RFTS		..	..	..	..	..	..	..	..	..	..	..	..	..	..
Hungary/Hongrie		12	12	12	12	12	12	12	13	15	16	17	18	19	21
Poland/Pologne		20	18	16	17	19	20	22	23	27	29	34	61	73	73
N. America/Amérique N.	*	1941	1939	1972	2114	2165	2171	2241	2366	2488	2569	2631	2666	2769	2858
Australia/Australie-NZ		99	103	107	111	114	117	121	125	132	132	131	131	133	135
OECD/OCDE - Europe		1322	1334	1368	1390	1434	1459	1530	1615	1704	1779	1894	1953	2015	2089
EU/UE-15		1267	1277	1310	1330	1373	1397	1466	1548	1633	1704	1816	1874	1934	2006
OECD/OCDE	*	3604	3622	3703	3875	3978	4039	4193	4414	4646	4822	5023	5137	5323	5511

Notes:
a) Data include Secretariat estimates.
b) Includes provisional data.
JPN) Traffic by light vehicles is excluded.
wGER) Except for caravans and large trailers hauled by passenger-carrying vehicles, traffic by special vehicles is included.
GRC) Data refer to inter-city traffic only.
ESP) Data refer only to traffic on motorways and national roads.
SWE) Up to 1988, only the public network is included; after 1989, the total network is taken into account.
TUR) Data refer only to traffic on motorways and national roads.
UKD) Data refer to Great Britain only. 1992-1993 data exclude taxis.
TOT) From 1987, data include Mexico.

Notes:
a) Les données comprennent des estimations du Secrétariat.
b) Inclut des données provisoires.
JPN) Le trafic des véhicules légers est exclu.
wGER) Sauf les caravanes et les grandes remorques tirées par des véhicules pour le transport de passagers, le trafic des véhicules spéciaux est inclu.
GRC) Circulation inter-urbaine seulement.
ESP) Circulation sur les réseaux autoroutier et national seulement.
SWE) Jusqu'à 1988, les données ne comprennent que le réseau public; depuis 1989, le réseau total est pris en compte.
TUR) Circulation sur les réseaux autoroutier et national seulement.
UKD) Grande-Bretagne seulement. Les données 1992, 1993 excluent les taxis.
TOT) Depuis 1987 les données comprennent le Mexique.

Source: OECD, IRF, selected national reports / OCDE, FRI, annuaires nationaux sélectionnés

The following shows road traffic volumes of goods vehicles and changes over time. Traffic volumes are expressed in billions of kilometres travelled by the stock of goods vehicles in use. In principle the data refer to total kilometres travelled on all roads by national goods vehicles on national territory.

Changes in traffic volumes are a major factor in explaining the impact of transport on the environment.

The interpretation of this table should take into account differences in the definition of traffic volumes: e.g. inclusion or exclusion of kilometres travelled on national territory by foreign vehicles, variations in the method of estimation. This table should be read in connection with the tables on total road vehicle traffic and passenger car traffic.

Le tableau suivant indique les volumes de circulation des véhicules de marchandises et leur évolution dans le temps. Les volumes de circulation sont exprimés en milliards de kilomètres parcourus par le parc de véhicules de marchandises en service. En principe les données se réfèrent à l'ensemble des kilomètres parcourus sur tous les réseaux routiers sur le territoire national par des véhicules de marchandises nationaux.

L'évolution des volumes de circulation routière est un facteur explicatif majeur de l'impact des activités de transport sur l'environnement.

L'interprétation de ce tableau doit tenir compte des différences dans la définition des volumes de circulation routière : p. ex. incorporation ou exclusion des kilomètres parcourus sur le territoire national par des véhicules étrangers, variations dans la méthode d'estimation. Ce tableau doit être lu en se référant aux tableaux concernant le volume total de circulation routière et de voitures particulières.

ROAD TRAFFIC VOLUMES: GOODS VEHICLES (a), 1980-1993
VOLUMES DE LA CIRCULATION ROUTIÈRE : VÉHICULES DE MARCHANDISES (a), 1980-1993

billion / milliards veh.-km

		1980	1981	1982	1983	1984	1985	1986	1987	1988	1989	1990	1991	1992	1993 (b)
Canada		53	55	56	56	56	57	58	65	66	68	71	74	77	80
Mexico/Mexique		..	..	..	..	..	..	..	15	15	15	16	16	16	16
USA/Etats-Unis		619	622	640	657	715	804	835	889	935	970	991	1003	1012	1039
Japan/Japon	*	142	141	170	199	207	217	230	234	247	252	256	263	265	272
Australia/Australie		26	27	28	29	30	31	33	33	34	31	26	23	23	23
N.Zealand/N.Zélande		4	4	4	4	4	4	4	5	5	5	5	5	6	6
Austria/Autriche		9	10	10	10	10	10	11	11	11	11	12	13	13	14
Belgium/Belgique		5	4	4	4	4	5	5	5	6	6	5	5	5	5
Denmark/Danemark		4	5	5	5	5	5	6	6	6	6	6	6	6	7
Finland/Finlande		4	4	4	4	4	5	5	5	5	5	6	5	6	4
France	*	49	51	53	55	57	59	63	67	72	77	81	84	89	94
Germany/Allemagne		..	..	..	..	..	..	..	..	..	..	54	60	54	55
w.Germany/Allem.occ.	*	32	34	34	34	34	34	36	36	37	38	41	43	47	46
Greece/Grèce	*	9	9	10	10	10	11	11	12	13	14	14	15	16	17
Iceland/Islande		0.2	0.2	0.2	0.2	0.2	0.2	0.2	0.2	0.2	0.2	0.2	0.2	0.3	0.3
Ireland/Irlande		4	4	4	4	4	4	4	4	4	4	5	5	5	5
Italy/Italie	*	33	35	37	37	39	41	42	43	45	46	48	49	51	52
Luxembourg		0.2	0.2	0.2	0.2	0.2	0.3	0.3	0.3	0.3	0.3	0.4	0.6	0.6	0.6
Netherlands/Pays-Bas		8	8	8	8	8	9	10	10	11	12	13	13	12	16
Norway/Norvège		2	2	2	2	2	2	3	3	3	3	3	3	3	4
Portugal		4	5	5	6	6	5	5	5	6	5	6	6	6	6
Spain/Espagne	*	16	17	17	17	18	18	19	20	22	21	21	20	20	20
Sweden/Suède	*	2	2	2	2	2	2	2	3	3	3	3	3	3	4
Switzerland/Suisse		5	5	5	6	6	6	6	6	7	7	7	8	8	8
Turkey/Turquie	*	6	6	6	7	7	7	9	10	10	11	11	10	11	12
UK/Royaume-Uni	*	41	41	41	42	43	43	46	50	54	58	65	66	65	64
Former CSFR/ex-RFTS		..	..	..	..	..	..	1.9	1.2	1.2	1.2	1.1	0.8	0.7	0.6
Hungary/Hongrie		5	6	6	6	6	7	7	6	6	5	5	5	4	4
Poland/Pologne		20	18	15	15	18	19	20	21	23	24	21	25	33	33
N. America/Amérique N.	*	671	677	695	713	771	861	894	968	1016	1053	1078	1093	1105	1135
Australia/Australie-NZ		29	31	32	33	34	35	37	38	38	36	31	28	29	29
OECD/OCDE - Europe		244	249	250	255	267	273	289	305	321	337	361	373	375	386
EU/UE-15		231	236	237	241	252	257	271	286	302	315	339	352	352	362
OECD/OCDE	*	1086	1098	1148	1200	1279	1386	1449	1545	1623	1678	1725	1757	1774	1823

Notes:
a)   Data include Secretariat estimates.
b)   Includes provisional data.
JPN) Excludes light vehicles.
FRA) Excludes goods vehicles over 15 years old, with a load capacity >= 3 tonnes.
wGER) Data refer to semi-trailer tractors only.
GRC) Data refer to inter-city traffic only.
ITA) Includes three-wheeled vehicles.
ESP) Data refer only to traffic on motorways and national roads.
SWE) Excludes goods vehicles with a load capacity < 2 tonnes.
TUR) Data refer only to traffic on motorways and national roads.
UKD) Great Britain only.
TOT) From 1987, data include Mexico.

Notes:
a)   Les données comprennent des estimations du Secrétariat.
b)   Inclut des données provisoires.
JPN) Exclut les véhicules légers.
FRA) Exclut les véhicules de marchandises de plus de 15 ans ayant une charge utile de >= 3 tonnes.
wGER) Les données comprennent les tracteurs semi-remorque seulement.
GRC) Les données comprennent la circulation inter-urbaine seulement.
ITA) Y compris les véhicules à trois roues.
ESP) Les données comprennent la circulation sur les réseaux autoroutier et national seulement.
SWE) Exclut les véhicules de marchandises ayant une charge utile inférieure à 2 tonnes.
TUR) Les données comprennent la circulation sur les réseaux autoroutier et national seulement.
UKD) Grande-Bretagne uniquement.
TOT) Depuis 1987 les données comprennent le Mexique.

Source: OECD, IRF, national statistical yearbooks / OCDE, FRI, annuaires nationaux statistiques

The following shows trends in total final energy consumption by the transport sector as a whole, and by major transport modes: air, road, rail.

Energy consumption by the transport sector is a major concern for the environment because of the sector's high dependence on oil and because of the resulting air pollutant emissions.

This table should display a good level of comparability.

———————————————————

Le tableau suivant montre l'évolution de la consommation totale finale d'énergie par le secteur des transports et par principal mode : air, route, rail.

La consommation d'énergie par les transports n'est pas sans poser d'importants problèmes pour l'environnement, ce secteur étant largement tributaire du pétrole et émettant de ce fait de larges quantités de polluants atmosphériques.

Ce tableau devrait bénéficier d'un bon niveau de comparabilité.

TOTAL FINAL ENERGY CONSUMPTION BY THE TRANSPORT SECTOR, 1980, 1985, 1993
CONSOMMATION TOTALE FINALE D'ÉNERGIE PAR LES TRANSPORTS, 1980, 1985, 1993

Mtoe/Mtep

	Air transport/ Transports aériens			Road transport/ Transports routiers			Rail transport/ Transports ferroviaires			Total (a)		
	1980	1985	1993	1980	1985	1993	1980	1985	1993	1980	1985	1993
Canada	4.0	3.8	3.9	35.0	30.6	33.5	2.2	2.0	2.1	44.9	39.8	45.6
Mexico/Mexique	1.4	1.5	2.2	22.4	23.9	33.3	-	0.1	0.1	23.8	25.4	35.6
USA/Etats-Unis	55.9	63.3	74.0	346.6	359.4	407.3	14.5	10.8	11.3	432.9	449.9	513.6
Japan/Japon	3.8	5.1	8.3	43.6	46.2	66.3	2.6	2.2	2.3	55.5	57.7	84.2
Australia/Australie	1.8	2.0	3.2	14.1	16.1	19.0	0.7	0.8	0.7	17.7	19.6	23.4
N.Zealand/N.Zélande	0.3	0.4	0.7	1.7	1.8	2.2	-	-	-	2.5	2.7	3.8
Austria/Autriche	0.1	0.2	0.4	4.1	4.1	5.4	0.3	0.3	0.3	4.6	4.6	6.2
Belgium/Belgique	0.5	0.6	1.0	5.1	5.2	7.1	0.2	0.2	0.2	5.9	6.2	8.5
Denmark/Danemark	0.8	0.7	0.8	2.4	2.9	3.4	0.1	0.1	0.1	3.6	4.2	4.5
Finland/Finlande	0.3	0.3	0.4	2.6	3.0	3.5	0.1	0.1	0.1	3.0	3.4	4.1
France	2.6	2.8	4.6	28.2	30.0	39.0	1.2	1.0	1.1	32.8	34.6	45.5
Germany/Allemagne	3.6	4.3	5.8	40.4	41.6	55.1	2.9	2.5	2.1	47.8	49.1	63.8
w.Germany/All.occ.	3.0	3.7	..	35.9	37.1	..	1.7	1.5	..	41.5	43.0	..
Greece/Grèce	1.2	1.2	1.5	2.3	3.1	4.5	0.1	0.1	0.1	4.0	4.8	6.6
Iceland/Islande	0.1	0.1	0.1	0.1	0.2	0.2	..	..	..	0.2	0.3	0.3
Ireland/Irlande	0.2	0.2	0.5	1.5	1.5	1.8	-	0.1	0.1	1.8	1.7	2.3
Italy/Italie	2.0	2.0	2.6	22.3	25.0	34.0	0.6	0.5	0.6	25.4	28.3	37.8
Luxembourg	0.1	0.1	0.1	0.4	0.5	1.2	-	-	-	0.5	0.6	1.3
Netherlands/Pays-Bas	1.0	1.3	2.2	7.0	6.9	8.8	0.1	0.1	0.1	8.8	9.0	11.8
Norway/Norvège	0.4	0.5	0.5	1.9	2.3	2.9	0.1	0.1	0.1	3.2	3.5	4.7
Portugal	0.6	0.5	0.6	1.9	2.1	3.8	0.1	0.1	0.1	2.6	2.7	4.6
Spain/Espagne	2.1	2.1	2.8	10.7	12.1	19.9	0.4	0.4	0.4	16.3	16.1	25.1
Sweden/Suède	0.6	0.6	0.9	5.2	5.5	6.3	0.2	0.3	0.2	6.1	6.6	7.5
Switzerland/Suisse	0.8	0.9	1.3	3.5	3.9	4.8	0.2	0.2	0.2	4.5	5.1	6.3
Turkey/Turquie	0.1	0.2	0.7	4.9	5.9	10.0	0.4	0.3	0.3	5.6	6.6	11.2
UK/Royaume-Uni	5.0	5.4	7.6	26.5	29.2	37.7	1.2	1.0	1.2	34.0	36.8	47.7
Former CSFR/ex-RFTS	0.6	0.5	..	4.7	4.7	..	0.3	0.3	..	5.6	5.4	..
Hungary/Hongrie *	-	0.2	0.1	2.9	2.8	3.2	0.6	0.4	0.2	3.6	3.5	3.5
Poland/Pologne *	-	-	0.3	7.2	7.0	7.6	0.6	0.6	0.9	10.1	9.0	8.9
North America/Amérique	61.3	68.5	80.0	404.1	413.9	474.1	16.7	12.9	13.5	501.7	515.1	594.8
Australia/Australie-NZ	2.2	2.4	3.9	15.7	17.9	21.1	0.7	0.8	0.7	20.2	22.4	27.2
OECD/OCDE Europe	22.0	23.9	34.2	170.9	184.9	249.3	8.2	7.4	7.1	210.6	224.3	299.9
EU/UE-15	20.6	22.2	31.7	160.5	172.6	231.4	7.5	6.8	6.6	197.2	208.9	277.4
OECD/OCDE	89.3	99.9	126.5	634.2	662.9	810.8	28.2	23.2	23.6	788.0	819.4	1006.2

Notes:
a)   The sum of the categories does not necessarily add up to the total because of pipeline transport, internal navigation and "non-specified" use.
HUN)   1993: 1992 data.
POL)   1993: 1992 data.

Notes:
a)   La somme des catégories ne correspond pas nécessairement au total en raison des catégories: transport par pipeline, navigation intérieure et "non spécifié".
HUN)   1993 : données 1992.
POL)   1993 : données 1992.

Source: OECD-IEA/OCDE-AIE

The following tables show the consumption of fuels for road transport as well as prices and taxes for diesel oil, leaded gasoline and unleaded gasoline.

Road fuel consumption is a major concern because of the resulting local and regional air pollution and its effects on human health and the environment.

This table should be read in connection with the tables on road traffic volumes.

Les tableaux suivants montrent la consommation de carburants pour les transports routiers, de même que les prix et taxes pour le diesel, l'essence avec plomb et l'essence sans plomb.

Les carburants routiers jouent un rôle important dans la pollution de l'air locale et régionale qui affecte la santé humaine et l'environnement.

Ces tableaux devraient être lus en relation avec les tableaux sur les volumes de la circulation routière.

CONSUMPTION OF ROAD FUELS (a), 1980, 1985, 1993 (b)
CONSOMMATION DE CARBURANTS ROUTIERS (a), 1980, 1985, 1993 (b)

Mtoe/Mtep

	Gas Oil or Diesel/ Diesel			Motor Gasoline/ Essence moteur			Others/Autres (c)			Total		
	1980	1985	1993	1980	1985	1993	1980	1985	1993	1980	1985	1993
Canada	4.77	4.60	5.93	30.26	25.74	26.76	0.01	0.22	0.78	35.04	30.56	33.47
Mexico/Mexique	7.47	7.33	8.97	14.79	15.45	23.92	0.15	1.07	0.42	22.41	23.85	33.31
USA/Etats-Unis	47.35	58.57	72.96	298.80	299.86	333.96	0.49	1.00	0.39	346.64	359.43	407.31
Japan/Japon	14.63	15.40	26.93	27.21	28.76	37.61	1.72	2.07	1.76	43.56	46.23	66.30
Australia/Australie	2.29	3.50	4.66	11.68	12.35	13.43	0.09	0.23	0.87	14.06	16.08	18.96
N.Zealand/N.Zélande	-	-	-	1.64	1.64	2.01	0.01	0.19	0.14	1.65	1.83	2.15
Austria/Autriche	1.49	1.51	2.66	2.61	2.57	2.75	0.03	0.02	0.01	4.13	4.10	5.42
Belgium/Belgique	1.86	2.47	3.97	3.15	2.68	3.04	0.04	0.08	0.05	5.05	5.23	7.06
Denmark/Danemark	0.71	1.19	1.45	1.59	1.59	1.95	0.07	0.08	0.01	2.37	2.86	3.41
Finland/Finlande	1.14	1.34	1.55	1.41	1.61	1.99	0.01	-	-	2.56	2.95	3.54
France	9.42	10.89	20.96	18.71	19.02	17.99	0.03	0.07	0.04	28.16	29.98	38.99
Germany/Allemagne	12.25	13.72	21.64	28.12	27.81	33.50	-	0.01	-	40.37	41.54	55.14
w.Germany/All. occ.	10.23	12.05	..	25.63	25.07	..	-	0.01	..	35.86	37.13	..
Greece/Grèce	0.92	1.24	1.64	1.42	1.86	2.78	-	0.02	0.05	2.34	3.12	4.47
Iceland/Islande	0.03	0.04	0.05	0.10	0.11	0.14	-	-	-	0.13	0.15	0.19
Ireland/Irlande	0.39	0.53	0.75	1.09	0.90	1.02	0.01	0.03	0.01	1.49	1.46	1.78
Italy/Italie	8.80	11.79	15.38	12.41	11.88	16.90	1.08	1.36	1.68	22.29	25.03	33.96
Luxembourg	0.12	0.19	0.60	0.30	0.32	0.56	-	0.01	-	0.42	0.52	1.16
Netherlands/Pays-Bas	2.06	2.38	3.79	4.12	3.63	4.05	0.79	0.91	0.93	6.97	6.92	8.77
Norway/Norvège	0.46	0.62	1.15	1.46	1.68	1.78	-	-	-	1.92	2.30	2.93
Portugal	1.14	1.18	1.92	0.80	0.91	1.92	-	-	-	1.94	2.09	3.84
Spain/Espagne	4.72	5.69	10.33	5.80	6.31	9.47	0.13	0.08	0.07	10.65	12.08	19.87
Sweden/Suède	1.44	1.46	1.87	3.76	4.01	4.41	0.01	0.01	-	5.21	5.48	6.28
Switzerland/Suisse	0.55	0.69	0.87	2.90	3.24	3.92	-	-	-	3.45	3.93	4.79
Turkey/Turquie	2.84	3.93	5.79	2.04	2.01	4.21	-	-	-	4.88	5.94	10.00
UK/Royaume-Uni	6.06	7.35	12.22	20.49	21.83	25.43	-	-	-	26.55	29.18	37.65
Former CSFR/ex-RFTS	2.95	2.62	..	1.74	2.03	1.64	-	-	-	4.69	4.65	..
Hungary/Hongrie	0.45	0.52	0.85	2.41	2.29	2.32	-	-	-	2.86	2.81	3.17
Poland/Pologne	3.34	3.64	2.84	3.84	3.33	4.56	-	-	-	7.18	6.97	7.40
North America/Amérique N.	59.6	70.5	87.9	343.9	341.1	384.6	0.7	2.3	1.6	404.1	413.8	474.1
Australia/Australie-NZ	2.3	3.5	4.7	13.3	14.0	15.4	0.1	0.4	1.0	15.7	17.9	21.1
OECD/OCDE Europe	56.4	68.2	108.6	112.3	114.0	137.8	2.2	2.7	2.9	170.9	184.9	249.3
EU/UE-15	52.5	62.9	100.7	105.8	106.9	127.8	2.2	2.7	2.9	160.5	172.5	231.3
OECD/OCDE	132.9	157.6	228.0	496.7	497.8	575.5	4.7	7.5	7.2	634.2	662.8	810.8

Notes:
a)   All fuels used in road vehicles (including military) as well as agricultural and industrial highway use; excludes motor gasoline used in stationary engines, and diesel oil in tractors that are not for highway use.
b)   For Non OECD member countries 1993 data refer to 1992.
c)   Natural gas, liquefied petroleum gases, kerosene, heavy fuel oil and other petroleum products.

Notes:
a)   Totalité des carburants utilisés dans les véhicules routiers (militaires compris) ainsi que le carburant consommé par les transports agricoles et industriels sur route ; exclut l'essence moteur utilisée dans les moteurs fixes, et le gazole employé par les tracteurs ailleurs que sur route.
b)   Pour les pays non membres de l'OCDE les données 1993 sont de 1992.
c)   Gaz naturel, gaz de pétrole liquéfiés, kérosène, fioul lourd et autres produits pétroliers.

Source: OECD-IEA/OCDE-AIE

ROAD FUEL PRICES AND TAXES (a), 1980-1993
PRIX ET TAXES DES CARBURANTS ROUTIERS (a), 1980-1993

		Diesel fuel/Diesel						Leaded petrol/Essence au plomb						Unleaded petrol/Essence sans plomb (b)					
		Price/Prix US$/litre (c)			Taxation % of price/% du prix			Price/Prix US$/litre (c)			Taxation % of price/% du prix			Price/Prix US$/litre (c)			Taxation % of price/% du prix		
		1980	1985	1993	1980	1985	1993	1980	1985	1993	1980	1985	1993	1980	1985	1993	1980	1985	1993
Canada	*	0.32	0.37	0.41	..	24.0	40.5	..	..	..	..	..	..	..	0.43	0.49	..	28.3	44.9
Mexico/Mexique	*	0.04	0.23	0.43	0.0	0.0	0.0	0.13	0.41	0.65	9.1	13.0	9.1	0.33	0.52	0.70	9.1	13.0	9.1
USA/Etats-Unis	*	0.27	0.32	0.30	14.8	27.3	35.6	0.34	..	..	..	..	..	0.39	0.35	0.34	..	23.5	26.2
Japan/Japon	*	0.40	0.46	0.40	23.5	24.0	36.5	..	..	..	..	..	..	0.57	0.64	0.67	36.7	38.6	46.7
Australia/Australie		0.28	0.41	0.49	20.9	26.5	50.3	0.29	0.44	0.49	18.7	23.4	49.1	..	..	0.53	..	..	45.6
N.Zeal./N.Zél.	*	0.41	0.59	0.32	2.3	10.4	11.8	0.52	0.75	0.66	27.6	20.9	46.5	..	..	0.63	..	..	45.6
Austria/Autriche	*	0.53	0.62	0.49	32.5	38.2	48.2	0.58	0.82	..	41.6	49.2	..	..	0.61	0.70	..	56.8	60.5
Belgium/Belgique		0.32	0.50	0.55	33.5	25.9	54.9	0.58	0.84	0.89	53.3	53.1	71.8	..	..	0.79	..	..	68.8
Denmark/Danemark	*	0.22	0.30	0.36	0.0	0.0	40.2	0.54	0.66	0.64	58.8	55.5	64.6	..	..	0.63	..	..	60.4
Finland/Finlande		0.39	0.48	0.52	32.1	29.3	54.9	0.58	0.67	0.88	36.1	35.1	71.8	..	..	0.77	..	..	69.7
France	*	0.43	0.60	0.47	47.4	41.7	59.9	0.61	0.85	0.83	58.0	62.3	78.6	..	..	0.80	..	..	74.2
Germany/Allemagne	*	0.41	0.54	0.44	41.4	37.5	59.0	0.48	0.66	0.72	48.7	48.7	73.5	..	0.48	0.66	..	55.8	72.0
Greece/Grèce		0.36	0.45	0.62	12.6	22.0	58.5	0.85	0.86	1.09	41.8	38.0	74.8	..	..	1.02	..	..	70.9
Iceland/Islande		..	..	1.06	..	..	20.3	..	..	1.01	..	..	68.5	..	..	0.97	..	..	68.8
Ireland/Irlande		0.41	0.63	0.82	28.0	40.9	41.8	0.57	0.92	0.92	48.1	56.5	65.0	..	..	0.87	..	..	63.5
Italy/Italie		0.34	0.50	0.67	7.6	19.1	64.0	0.86	1.09	1.05	61.4	64.4	74.6	..	..	1.00	..	..	72.0
Luxembourg		0.32	0.50	0.42	17.3	22.7	51.9	0.50	0.72	0.66	43.8	43.6	66.0	..	..	0.57	..	..	61.4
Netherl./Pays-Bas		0.30	0.43	0.51	22.7	18.7	54.2	0.53	0.78	0.93	52.3	53.2	72.5	..	0.76	0.85	..	54.4	70.2
Norway/Norvège		0.19	0.25	0.38	1.3	1.1	31.0	0.45	0.54	0.96	51.7	50.8	72.0	..	..	0.86	..	..	69.2
Portugal	*	0.51	1.00	0.84	7.2	33.7	59.2	1.35	1.64	1.29	61.4	51.9	73.2	..	1.39	1.21	..	67.6	70.1
Spain/Espagne		0.39	0.68	0.60	24.7	19.4	54.6	0.78	1.02	0.89	34.6	39.3	68.2	..	..	0.87	..	..	65.0
Sweden/Suède		0.21	0.39	0.43	8.4	17.2	31.8	0.43	0.59	..	49.3	50.0	..	..	..	0.78	..	..	70.6
Switzerl./Suisse		0.53	0.61	0.56	50.6	46.9	67.7	0.51	0.58	0.57	51.1	48.2	68.8	..	0.56	0.53	..	..	66.8
Turkey/Turquie		0.55	0.83	0.84	..	..	57.0	0.94	1.27	1.19	..	..	64.5	..	..	1.20	..	..	62.7
UK/Royaume-Uni		0.48	0.67	0.66	39.5	41.1	59.2	0.55	0.79	0.85	46.3	54.3	70.6	..	..	0.78	..	..	65.4

Notes:
a)   Includes taxes that have to be paid by the consumer as part of the transaction and are not refundable.
b)   Unleaded petrol: unleaded premium (95 RON) except as noted.
c)   Expressed in US$ at current prices and purchasing power parities.
CAN)   1980 data refer to 1981. Unleaded petrol: unleaded premium (97 RON).
MEX)   1980 data refer to 1981. Unleaded petrol: unleaded regular (92 RON). Unleaded petrol was introduced in September 1990.
USA)   Unleaded petrol: 1980 data refer to 1981.
JPN)   Unleaded petrol: unleaded regular (91 RON).
NLZ)   Unleaded petrol: unleaded regular (91 RON).
AUT)   Leaded petrol: since November 1993 leaded premium has been prohibited. Unleaded petrol: 1985 data refer to 1987.
DNK)   Unleaded petrol: unleaded premium (98 RON).
FRA)   Up to February 1985 prices were kept within a set range. Figures before 1985 refer to maximum price for Paris. Figures after 1985 refer to average price for all of France. Unleaded petrol: unleaded premium (98 RON).
DEU)   1980 and 1985 data refer to western Germany only. Unleaded petrol: 1985 data refer to 1986.
PRT)   Unleaded petrol: 1985 data refer to 1987.

Source: IEA-OECD/AIE-OCDE

Notes:
a)   Inclut les taxes effectivement payées par le consommateur (non récupérables).
b)   Essence sans plomb: concerne le super sans plomb (95 RON).
c)   Prix donnés en $EU aux prix et parités de pouvoir d'achat courants.
CAN)   Données 1980: 1981. Essence sans plomb: super sans plomb (97 RON).
MEX)   Données 1980: 1981. Essence sans plomb: ordinaire sans plomb (92 RON). L'essence sans plomb fut introduite en septembre 1990.
USA)   Essence sans plomb: les données 1980 sont de 1981.
JPN)   Essence sans plomb: ordinaire sans plomb (91 RON).
NLZ)   Essence sans plomb: ordinaire sans plomb (91 RON).
AUT)   Essence au plomb: depuis novembre 1993 le super sans plomb est interdit. Essence sans plomb: les données 1985 sont de 1987.
DNK)   Essence sans plomb: super sans plomb (98 RON).
FRA)   Jusqu'en 1985 une fourchette de prix était imposée par la loi. Avant 1985 les données se réfèrent au prix maxímum à Paris. Après 1985, elles représentent une moyenne sur l'ensemble de la France. Essence sans plomb: super sans plomb (98 RON).
DEU)   Les données 1980 et 1985 concernent l'Allemagne occidentale seulement. Essence sans plomb: les données 1985 sont de 1986.
PRT)   Essence sans plomb: les données 1985 sont de 1987.

10. INDUSTRY

10. INDUSTRIE

INTRODUCTION

This section refers to industrial activities that generate pressures on the environment. These include direct pressures, such as emission of air and water pollutants, production of hazardous wastes, emission of noise and consumption of natural resources in production processes, as well as indirect pressures through the consumption and use of industrial products.

The section provides data on:

- ► total industrial production;

- ► changes in industrial structure;

- ► production by environmentally significant industries;

- ► business sector investment.

In addition, this section presents data on tourism, a service industry that also exerts pressures on the environment.

Data presented in this section come mainly from OECD sources. They evince a good level of comparability. Readers are referred to the section on waste for data on industrial and hazardous waste.

INTRODUCTION

Cette section concerne les activités industrielles qui sont à l'origine des pressions sur l'environnement. Ces pressions peuvent être directes telles que les émissions de polluants de l'air et de l'eau, la production de déchets dangereux, les émissions sonores et la consommation de ressources naturelles pour les processus de production; ou bien indirectes à travers la consommation et l'utilisation de produits industriels.

Les données présentées concernent :

- ► la production industrielle totale ;

- ► l'évolution de la structure industrielle ;

- ► la production des industries ayant une signification pour l'environnement ;

- ► l'investissement du secteur privé.

Cette section fournit en outre des données sur le tourisme, une activité qui exerce également des pressions sur l'environnement.

Les données présentées dans cette section proviennent principalement de l'OCDE. Elles ont un bon niveau de comparabilité. Le lecteur pourra consulter la section sur les déchets pour les données sur les déchets industriels et dangereux.

The following table shows the evolution of total industrial production expressed as volume indices (1991=100). Total industry comprises mining and quarrying (ISIC 2), manufacturing (ISIC 3) and gas, electricity and water (ISIC 4).

Le tableau suivant montre l'évolution de la production industrielle totale exprimée en indices de volume (1991=100). L'ensemble de l'industrie comprend les industries extractives (CITI 2), les industries manufacturières (CITI 3), ainsi que l'électricité, le gaz et l'eau (CITI 4).

INDUSTRIAL PRODUCTION (a), OECD countries, 1980-1995
PRODUCTION INDUSTRIELLE (a), pays de l'OCDE, 1980-1995

Production indices/Indices de production (1991=100)

		1980	1985	1986	1987	1988	1989	1990	1991	1992	1993	1994	1995 (b)
Canada		85	97	98	103	108	108	104	100	101	105	112	118
USA/Etats-Unis		81	91	91	96	100	102	102	100	103	107	113	116
Japan/Japon	*	64	78	78	81	88	93	98	100	94	90	91	93
Australia/Australie		78	87	87	92	98	100	102	100	101	106	114	116
Austria/Autriche		75	81	82	82	86	91	98	100	99	97	101	104
Belgium/Belgique	*	84	87	88	90	95	98	102	100	100	95	97	109
Denmark/Danemark	*	76	93	99	95	97	99	100	100	104	101	111	116
Finland/Finlande		83	97	98	103	107	110	110	100	101	106	118	126
France		89	88	88	90	94	98	100	100	99	95	99	108
w.Germany/Allemagne occ.		79	83	84	85	88	93	97	100	98	91	94	98
Greece/Grèce		92	99	98	97	102	104	101	100	99	96	97	93
Ireland/Irlande		52	67	69	75	83	92	96	100	109	115	128	145
Italy/Italie		89	87	90	93	99	103	102	100	98	96	98	106
Luxembourg		69	84	86	85	93	100	100	100	99	96	102	115
Netherlands/Pays-Bas		84	89	89	90	90	94	98	100	100	98	101	107
Norway/Norvège		62	78	80	85	88	96	98	100	106	110	119	128
Portugal	*	65	74	79	83	86	92	100	100	98	95	95	96
Spain/Espagne		84	87	89	94	96	101	101	100	97	93	99	108
Sweden/Suède	*	87	97	97	100	101	105	106	100	96	99	110	122
Switzerland/Suisse	*	81	84	87	88	95	97	99	100	99	99	107	110
Turkey/Turquie		..	68	76	85	86	89	97	100	105	114	109	103
UK/Royaume-Uni		85	92	94	98	102	104	104	100	100	102	108	113
North America/Amérique N.	*	81	91	92	96	101	102	102	100	103	107	113	116
EU/UE-15	*	84	87	89	90	94	98	100	100	99	96	100	..
OECD/OCDE Europe	*	83	86	88	90	94	98	100	100	99	97	100	..
OECD/OCDE	*	79	86	87	90	95	99	100	100	99	99	103	..

Notes:
a)   Industrial production includes mining and quarrying (ISIC 2), manufacturing (ISIC 3) and gas, electricity and water (ISIC 4).
b)   First quarter.
JPN)   Excluding printing, publishing and allied industries.
BEL)   Excluding metal ore mining, printing, publishing and allied industries, manufacture of watches and clocks and "other manufacturing industries".
DNK)   Mining and manufacturing only.
PRT)   Excluding manufacture of furniture and fixtures (except primarily of metal), printing, publishing and allied industries.
SWE)   Mining and manufacturing only.
CHE)   Excluding mining and quarrying.
TOT)   Only include countries and data presented in the table.

Source: OECD/OCDE

Notes:
a)   La production industrielle comprend les industries extractives (CITI 2) et manufacturières (CITI 3), ainsi que l'électricité, le gaz et l'eau (CITI 4).
b)   Premier trimestre.
JPN)   Non compris l'imprimerie, l'édition et industries annexes.
BEL)   Non compris l'extraction des minerais métalliques, l'imprimerie, l'édition et industries annexes , la fabrication des montres et horloges et les "autres industries manufacturières".
DNK)   Industries extractives et manufacturières uniquement.
PRT)   Non compris la fabrication de meubles et d'accessoires (sauf ceux faits essentiellement en métal), l'imprimerie, l'édition et industries annexes.
SWE)   Industries extractives et manufacturières uniquement.
CHE)   Non compris les industries extractives.
TOT)   Incluent uniquement les données et pays présentés dans le tableau.

The following tables show changes in industrial structure for selected OECD countries. Data refer to production indices (1991=100) for the major divisions and groups of the manufacturing industry, according to the International Standard Industrial Classification (ISIC).

The first table shows changes in the structure of the manufacturing industry as a whole.

The second shows selected environmentally significant industries; it presents six industries given as examples of "traditional industries" and "new industries", as well as examples of industries that imply pressures on the environment through their production process or the use of their products.

The environmental impact of industrial activities may vary considerably with structural change: the decline in the OECD countries of the so-called traditional industries, such as iron and steel, has typically reduced quantitative pressures on the environment; the growth of the so-called new industries can create qualitative pressures, such as soil and groundwater contamination by trace toxic chemicals.

Les tableaux suivants montrent les changements structurels dans l'industrie de pays sélectionnés de l'OCDE. Les données représentent des indices de production (1991=100) pour les divisions et groupes principaux des industries manufacturières selon la Classification Internationale Type par Industries (CITI).

Le premier tableau montre les changements structurels de l'industrie manufacturière.

Le second tableau présente des données sur des industries sélectionnées ayant une signification pour l'environnement. Il présente six industries choisies comme exemples d'industries "traditionnelles" et d'industries "nouvelles" qui exercent des pressions sur l'environnement par le biais de leurs processus de production et l'utilisation de leurs produits.

Les impacts sur l'environnement des activités industrielles peuvent varier considérablement selon les changements structurels : le déclin dans les pays de l'OCDE des industries dites "traditionnelles" telles que la sidérurgie, a entraîné une réduction significative des pressions quantitatives sur l'environnement ; le développement des industries appelées "nouvelles" peut créer des pressions qualitatives telles que contamination du sol et des eaux par des composés chimiques toxiques.

INDUSTRIAL STRUCTURE, selected countries, 1980-1995 (a)
STRUCTURE INDUSTRIELLE, pays sélectionnés, 1980-1995 (a)

Production indices/Indices de production (1991=100)

	3100 b) Food/ Alimentaires	3200 c) Textile/ Textiles	3300 d) Wood/ Bois	3400 e) Paper/ Papier	3500 f) Chemical/ Chemiques	3600 g) Non-metal/ Non Métalliques	3700 h) Basic metal/ Métallurgique	3800 i) Machinery/ Machines		3100 b) Food/ Alimentaires	3200 c) Textile/ Textiles	3300 d) Wood/ Bois	3400 e) Paper/ Papier	3500 f) Chemical/ Chemiques	3600 g) Non-metal/ Non Métalliques	3700 h) Basic metal/ Métallurgique	3800 i) Machinery/ Machines
				Canada									**Austria/Autriche** *				
1980	99	108	92	100	75	117	91	79	**1980**	83	110	67	59	81	81	95	63
1985	105	110	110	101	91	116	98	94	**1985**	87	103	67	71	84	84	102	72
1990	103	108	114	107	107	118	100	109	**1990**	98	102	94	96	98	100	106	100
1991	100	100	100	100	100	100	100	100	**1991**	100	100	100	100	100	100	100	100
1992	102	98	104	97	103	96	102	101	**1992**	101	95	102	102	101	101	96	98
1993	103	102	108	98	108	97	112	109	**1993**	102	83	100	103	99	100	93	95
1994	107	107	112	100	113	103	114	123	**1994**	104	80	104	111	104	106	102	100
1995	100	113	114	98	119	83	120	136	**1995**	98	81	101	118	108	91	115	106
				USA/Etats-Unis *									**Belgium/Belgique** *				
1980	83	101	84	75	76	99	112	69	**1980**	72	95	73	70	71	112	101	80
1985	91	99	96	89	83	101	103	86	**1985**	84	96	70	79	80	83	95	85
1990	99	100	107	102	101	108	108	102	**1990**	97	108	94	102	103	107	103	102
1991	100	100	100	100	100	100	100	100	**1991**	100	100	100	100	100	100	100	100
1992	102	105	106	101	104	103	103	106	**1992**	101	100	94	104	104	104	86	95
1993	103	105	111	104	109	107	108	114	**1993**	98	100	92	96	96	104	87	91
1994	107	107	118	107	114	113	116	125	**1994**	96	100	92	100	99	110	95	95
1995	105	105	118	106	116	112	123	131	**1995**	97	114	102	127	113	133	110	114
				Japan/Japon *									**Denmark/Danemark** *				
1980	92	115	125	65	68	87	86	49	**1980**	78	99	71	76	70	107	107	69
1985	94	113	99	73	77	83	86	72	**1985**	90	116	99	92	87	102	105	92
1990	99	102	103	97	98	99	98	97	**1990**	97	97	101	98	100	104	104	102
1991	100	100	100	100	100	100	100	100	**1991**	100	100	100	100	100	100	100	100
1992	100	96	95	98	99	93	92	91	**1992**	102	96	104	102	108	97	100	105
1993	99	86	91	96	97	90	90	86	**1993**	103	91	101	99	107	92	84	99
1994	99	81	88	98	100	92	89	87	**1994**	110	96	117	105	118	105	85	112
1995	86	76	85	98	103	92	93	92	**1995**	99	108	135	113	131	100	..	121
				Australia/Australie *									**Finland/Finlande** *				
1980	87	105	107	82	80	102	77	85	**1980**	83	204	124	78	77	89	73	74
1985	86	110	115	95	88	104	84	94	**1985**	92	197	114	92	87	99	88	99
1990	100	107	110	102	100	111	101	106	**1990**	102	124	125	106	105	117	103	120
1991	100	100	100	100	100	100	100	100	**1991**	100	100	100	100	100	100	100	100
1992	105	95	95	94	97	105	98	101	**1992**	101	91	100	99	102	87	111	106
1993	110	93	95	97	101	122	102	113	**1993**	105	88	109	104	104	81	119	116
1994	119	87	108	121	110	142	109	130	**1994**	107	96	122	110	115	84	130	140
1995	120	89	108	135	111	150	106	132	**1995**	101	96	126	116	122	79	147	158

Notes: see page 240 / voir page 240.

... / ...

INDUSTRIAL STRUCTURE, selected countries, 1980-1995 (a)
STRUCTURE INDUSTRIELLE, pays sélectionnés, 1980-1995 (a)

Production indices/Indices de production (1991=100)

	3100 b) Food/ Alimentaires	3200 c) Textile/ Textiles	3300 d) Wood/ Bois	3400 e) Paper/ Papier	3500 f) Chemical/ Chemiques	3600 g) Non-metal/ Non Métalliques	3700 h) Basic metal/ Métallurgique	3800 i) Machinery/ Machines		3100 b) Food/ Alimentaires	3200 c) Textile/ Textiles	3300 d) Wood/ Bois	3400 e) Paper/ Papier	3500 f) Chemical/ Chemiques	3600 g) Non-metal/ Non Métalliques	3700 h) Basic metal/ Métallurgique	3800 i) Machinery/ Machines
	France *									**Italy/Italie**							
1980	83	141	106	71	78	109	117	93	**1980**	82	104	93	69	84	96	94	90
1985	88	126	86	78	82	92	97	86	**1985**	87	100	78	75	86	84	88	87
1990	98	106	101	101	99	104	103	103	**1990**	99	102	97	98	101	102	99	107
1991	100	100	100	100	100	100	100	100	**1991**	100	100	100	100	100	100	100	100
1992	100	96	96	102	104	95	98	97	**1992**	101	100	102	103	98	97	99	95
1993	101	89	91	99	104	88	90	90	**1993**	101	94	102	119	95	90	95	90
1994	102	90	94	103	110	95	99	94	**1994**	97	98	106	140	97	92	102	88
1995	101	101	98	109	121	104	108	102	**1995**	95	119	109	161	105	94	116	91
	w.Germany/Allemagne occ. *									**Luxembourg ***							
1980	72	125	97	72	81	99	99	72	**1980**	64	43	84	65	58	41	99	53
1985	76	109	76	76	86	82	98	79	**1985**	90	47	90	75	74	58	105	79
1990	93	101	93	95	98	96	102	97	**1990**	95	97	104	97	100	100	103	97
1991	100	100	100	100	100	100	100	100	**1991**	100	100	100	100	100	100	100	100
1992	99	90	100	99	102	102	95	97	**1992**	101	105	90	103	109	108	94	94
1993	98	80	96	96	99	99	86	86	**1993**	94	95	97	105	103	101	95	90
1994	98	72	98	96	104	105	94	90	**1994**	101	101	111	110	115	121	95	97
1995	92	76	105	101	110	106	111	94	**1995**	104	121	77	123	152	142	102	106
	Greece/Grèce *									**Netherlands/Pays-Bas**							
1980	79	122	133	83	..	113	98	115	**1980**	77	109	111	80	62	94	78	84
1985	96	113	90	105	92	102	92	98	**1985**	81	105	84	82	84	91	85	91
1990	94	107	100	100	106	113	97	97	**1990**	96	104	100	99	102	104	97	100
1991	100	100	100	100	100	100	100	100	**1991**	100	100	100	100	100	100	100	100
1992	105	93	95	100	98	96	97	104	**1992**	99	93	101	100	99	101	100	100
1993	105	89	89	94	99	96	91	94	**1993**	97	92	101	98	99	97	100	95
1994	108	86	85	97	104	99	95	90	**1994**	98	94	105	101	103	107	108	99
1995	78	89	86	98	109	89	102	89	**1995**	102	105	107	101	108	106	109	100
	Ireland/Irlande									**Norway/Norvège**							
1980	66	112	96	70	37	98	71	30	**1980**	106	182	142	82	53	133	68	101
1985	75	100	85	66	58	91	92	54	**1985**	98	143	124	96	92	120	88	102
1990	96	105	100	92	85	106	112	103	**1990**	97	101	108	100	105	114	101	102
1991	100	100	100	100	100	100	100	100	**1991**	100	100	100	100	100	100	100	100
1992	107	102	102	109	115	104	90	112	**1992**	101	96	99	99	99	104	100	105
1993	113	99	104	117	125	100	95	118	**1993**	101	94	98	101	104	103	101	108
1994	120	102	114	119	148	111	91	137	**1994**	110	103	107	106	108	118	111	114
1995	135	103	116	128	181	90	80	159	**1995**	108	118	117	115	117	131	117	123

Notes: see page 240 / voir page 240

... / ...

INDUSTRIAL STRUCTURE, selected countries, 1980-1995 (a)
STRUCTURE INDUSTRIELLE, pays sélectionnés, 1980-1995 (a)

Production indices/Indices de production (1991=100)

	3100 b) Food/ Alimentaires	3200 c) Textile/ Textiles	3300 d) Wood/ Bois	3400 e) Paper/ Papier	3500 f) Chemical/ Chemiques	3600 g) Non-metal/ Non Métalliques	3700 h) Basic metal/ Métallurgique	3800 i) Machinery/ Machines		3100 b) Food/ Alimentaires	3200 c) Textile/ Textiles	3300 d) Wood/ Bois	3400 e) Paper/ Papier	3500 f) Chemical/ Chemiques	3600 g) Non-metal/ Non Métalliques	3700 h) Basic metal/ Métallurgique	3800 i) Machinery/ Machines
	Portugal *									**Switzerland/Suisse ***							
1980	68	75	89	..	78	59	89	81	**1980**	88	118	90	68	60	124	91	88
1985	72	88	95	..	90	68	92	78	**1985**	90	113	85	85	73	117	92	79
1990	99	102	92	..	115	101	113	101	**1990**	98	101	105	102	100	114	107	95
1991	100	100	100	..	100	100	100	100	**1991**	100	100	100	100	100	100	100	100
1992	93	94	104	..	93	103	110	97	**1992**	100	93	99	99	103	93	100	98
1993	97	90	105	..	91	108	109	92	**1993**	101	89	94	97	110	91	95	93
1994	95	90	90	..	95	110	113	93	**1994**	103	93	103	106	124	100	104	96
1995	85	90	63	..	105	107	126	100	**1995**	105	104	108	111	146	89	103	88
	Spain/Espagne *									**Turkey/Turquie**							
1980	74	112	96	78	86	88	97	75	**1981**	64	66	69	60	56	50	38	36
1985	87	107	80	82	90	75	103	72	**1985**	75	83	78	77	73	63	69	61
1990	98	106	102	96	100	100	100	103	**1990**	92	109	107	106	101	96	108	89
1991	100	100	100	100	100	100	100	100	**1991**	100	100	100	100	100	100	100	100
1992	96	93	93	101	101	93	95	97	**1992**	96	104	101	110	103	112	106	108
1993	98	83	84	100	97	88	94	88	**1993**	102	109	100	114	109	114	118	130
1994	101	91	86	104	108	96	103	98	**1994**	105	103	84	109	107	113	118	98
1995	99	99	94	108	118	102	114	115	**1995**	99	106	73	108	113	98	113	81
	Sweden/Suède *									**UK/Royaume-Uni**							
1980	94	147	102	89	81	118	100	75	**1980**	93	113	96	79	74	99	107	87
1985	98	129	94	98	91	105	110	92	**1985**	95	115	97	79	84	96	99	89
1990	102	108	108	105	101	114	104	108	**1990**	100	111	115	105	97	111	112	108
1991	100	100	100	100	100	100	100	100	**1991**	100	100	100	100	100	100	100	100
1992	96	87	88	97	101	86	102	97	**1992**	101	100	99	101	100	96	95	98
1993	99	76	87	98	106	83	106	100	**1993**	102	100	100	104	103	99	96	98
1994	103	79	94	100	114	85	113	118	**1994**	104	101	105	107	108	102	97	104
1995	103	85	105	105	125	83	124	136	**1995**	98	95	101	107	116	104	104	108
	OECD/OCDE Europe *									**OECD/OCDE ***							
1980	80	113	96	75	78	98	101	80	**1980**	83	110	97	75	75	95	98	68
1985	85	106	82	80	83	85	95	82	**1985**	89	106	91	84	82	89	94	81
1990	..	104	100	100	99	102	103	100	**1990**	..	103	103	101	100	103	102	101
1991	100	100	100	100	100	100	100	100	**1991**	100	100	100	100	100	100	100	100
1992	100	97	99	101	101	98	97	97	**1992**	101	98	101	100	102	98	97	98
1993	100	91	97	103	101	95	94	91	**1993**	101	94	101	102	103	97	96	97
1994	101	..	..	108	107	100	101	95	**1994**	103	94	104	107	108	101	101	103
1995	..	..	..	..	..	..	..	..	**1995**	..	..	..	..	..	..	..	..

Notes: see next page / voir page suivante

Notes:

a)   1995: first quarter.
b)   Manufacture of food, beverages and tobacco products.
c)   Textile, wearing apparel and leather industries.
d)   Manufacture of wood and wood products, including furniture.
e)   Manufacture of paper and paper products; printing and publishing.
f)   Manufacture of chemicals and of chemical, petroleum, coal, rubber and plastic products.
g)   Manufacture of non-metallic mineral products, except oil and coal products.
h)   Basic metal industries.
i)   Manufacture of fabricated metal products, machinery and equipment.
USA)   ISIC 3500: excludes ISIC 354.
JPN)   ISIC 3400: excludes ISIC 342.
AUS)   ISIC 3800: excludes ISIC 381.
AUT)   ISIC 3200: excludes ISIC 324.
BEL)   ISIC 3400: excludes ISIC 342.
DNK)   ISIC 3800: includes ISIC 37.
FIN)   ISIC 3200: excludes ISIC 324.
FRA)   ISIC 3300: excludes ISIC 332.
w.DEU) ISIC 3700: includes agricultural and craft tools, steel wire-drawing, surface treatment and hardening.
GRC)   ISIC 3400: excl. ISIC 3412 and 3419; ISIC 3800: excl. ISIC 385.
LUX)   ISIC 3200: ISIC 322, 3212, 3219 only; ISIC 3400: excl. ISIC 3411 and 3419.
PRT)   ISIC 3300: excludes ISIC 332 .
SPA)   ISIC 3300: excludes ISIC 332 ; ISIC 3800: excludes ISIC 3841.
SWE)   ISIC 3800: excludes ISIC 3841.
CHE)   ISIC 3200: excludes ISIC 323; ISIC 3300: incl. ISIC 3903 and parts of ISIC 3849 and 3909; ISIC 3500: excl. coal products, includes ISIC 323; ISIC 3800: excl. ISIC 381, incl. ISIC 3901 and 3902.
TOT)   Only include countries and data presented in the table.

Source: OECD/OCDE

Notes:

a)   1995: premier trimestre.
b)   Fabrication de produits alimentaires, boissons et tabac.
c)   Industries des textiles, de l'habillement et du cuir.
d)   Industrie du bois et fabrication d'ouvrages en bois, y compris les meubles.
e)   Fabrication de papier et d'articles en papier; imprimerie et édition.
f)   Industrie chimique et fabrication de produits chimiques, de dérivés du pétrole et du charbon et d'ouvrages en caoutchouc et en matière plastique.
g)   Fabrication de produits minéraux non métalliques, à l'exclusion des dérivés du pétrole et du charbon.
h)   Industrie métallurgique de base.
i)   Fabrication d'ouvrages en métaux, de machines et de matériel.
USA)   CITI 3500: CITI 354 exclue.
JPN)   CITI 3400: CITI 342 exclue.
AUS)   CITI 3800: CITI 381 exclue.
AUT)   CITI 3200: CITI 324 exclue.
BEL)   CITI 3400: CITI 342 exclue.
DNK)   CITI 3800: CITI 37 inclue.
FIN)   CITI 3200: CITI 324 exclue.
FRA)   CITI 3300: CITI 332 exclue.
w.DEU) CITI 3700: y compris les instruments aratoires et industriels, le tréfilage, le polissage et le trempage.
GRC)   CITI 3400: CITI 3412 et 3419 exclues; CITI 3800: CITI 385 exclue.
LUX)   CITI 3200: CITI 322, 3212, 3219 uniquement; CITI 3400: CITI 3411 et 3419 exclues.
PRT)   CITI 3300: CITI 332 exclue.
SPA)   CITI 3300: CITI 332 exclue; CITI 3800: CITI 3841 exclue.
SWE)   CITI 3800: CITI 3841 exclue.
CHE)   CITI 3200: CITI 323 exclue; CITI 3300: y compris la CITI 3903 et une partie des CITI 3849 et 3909; CITI 3500: dérivés du charbon exclus, CITI 323 inclue; CITI 3800: CITI 381 exclue, CITI 3901 et 3902 inclues.
TOT)   Incluent uniquement les données et pays présentés dans le tableau.

SELECTED ENVIRONMENTALLY SIGNIFICANT INDUSTRIES, 1980-1995 (a)
INDUSTRIES SÉLECTIONNÉES AYANT UNE SIGNIFICATION POUR L'ENVIRONNEMENT, 1980-1995 (a)

Production Indices/Indices de production (1991=100)

	3411 b) Pulp,paper, paperboard/ Pâte à papier, papier,carton	3510 c) Chemical products/ Industrie chimique	3530 d) Petroleum refineries/ Raffineries de pétrole	3710 e) Iron and steel/ Fer et acier	3830 f) Electrical Machinery/ Machines électriques	3843 g) Motor vehicles/ Véhicules automobiles		3411 b) Pulp,paper, paperboard/ Pâte à papier, papier,carton	3510 c) Chemical products/ Industrie chimique	3530 d) Petroleum refineries/ Raffineries de pétrole	3710 e) Iron and steel/ Fer et acier	3830 f) Electrical Machinery/ Machines électriques	3843 g) Motor vehicles/ Véhicules automobiles
	Canada *							**Belgium/Belgique**					
1980	105	68	96	119	77	..	1980	70	75	112	104	94	64
1985	99	80	89	114	87	..	1985	75	86	57	97	89	82
1990	103	109	103	107	107	..	1990	97	100	90	99	102	103
1991	100	100	100	100	100	..	1991	100	100	100	100	100	100
1992	99	100	98	101	104	..	1992	104	112	104	85	94	95
1993	103	102	101	113	106	..	1993	93	108	97	76	93	99
1994	11	104	103	117	113	..	1994	93	109	98	84	92	103
1995	..	116	109	126	120	..	1995	..	..	..	..	..	..
	USA/Etats-Unis							**Denmark/Danemark** *					
1980	78	79	98	125	65	71	1980	69	76	102	..	71	..
1985	87	82	90	104	82	105	1985	87	94	103	..	94	..
1990	99	101	100	111	98	107	1990	96	100	96	..	105	..
1991	100	100	100	100	100	100	1991	100	100	100	..	100	..
1992	102	103	101	105	107	114	1992	100	109	104	..	108	..
1993	107	107	103	111	123	128	1993	86	109	104	..	109	..
1994	110	112	103	118	141	146	1994	97	121	110	..	123	..
1995	115	112	99	126	152	157	1995	..	138	111	..	129	..
	Japan/Japon							**Finland/Finlande** *					
1980	..	74	101	90	30	68	1980	78	77	82	74	50	..
1985	..	78	84	91	63	76	1985	88	88	79	87	67	..
1990	..	98	94	99	93	99	1990	103	106	96	97	111	125
1991	..	100	100	100	100	100	1991	100	100	100	100	100	100
1992	..	100	105	90	90	97	1992	104	101	104	114	128	101
1993	..	98	108	88	90	90	1993	113	103	100	124	165	74
1994	..	103	112	87	97	86	1994	122	111	119	134	214	103
1995	..	110	120	91	104	91	1995	131	123	115	152	248	115
	Austria/Autriche							**France**					
1980	59	..	116	97	50	..	1980	72	69	145	128	81	81
1985	71	..	88	102	67	..	1985	75	81	98	102	90	76
1990	96	..	96	104	94	..	1990	96	98	96	104	102	103
1991	100	..	100	100	100	..	1991	100	100	100	100	100	100
1992	102	..	102	94	98	..	1992	105	106	97	96	97	103
1993	103	..	103	94	98	..	1993	108	107	102	87	94	90
1994	111	..	102	102	105	..	1994	118	115	100	97	94	103
1995	..	..	..	..	..	..	1995	128	..	97	104	99	..

Notes: see page 243 / voir page 243.

... / ...

SELECTED ENVIRONMENTALLY SIGNIFICANT INDUSTRIES, 1980-1995 (a)
INDUSTRIES SÉLECTIONNÉES AYANT UNE SIGNIFICATION POUR L'ENVIRONNEMENT, 1980-1995 (a)

Production Indices/Indices de production (1991=100)

	3411 b) Pulp,paper, paperboard/ Pâte à papier, papier,carton	3510 c) Chemical products/ Industrie chimique	3530 d) Petroleum refineries/ Raffineries de pétrole	3710 e) Iron and steel/ Fer et acier	3830 f) Electrical Machinery/ Machines électriques	3843 g) Motor vehicles/ Véhicules automobiles		3411 b) Pulp,paper, paperboard/ Pâte à papier, papier,carton	3510 c) Chemical products/ Industrie chimique	3530 d) Petroleum refineries/ Raffineries de pétrole	3710 e) Iron and steel/ Fer et acier	3830 f) Electrical Machinery/ Machines électriques	3843 g) Motor vehicles/ Véhicules automobiles
	w.Germany/Allemagne occ. *							**Luxembourg** *					
1980	63	81	125	109	63	67	1980	..	33	..	103	41	..
1985	77	88	98	103	76	80	1985	..	48	..	105	73	..
1990	98	99	99	101	96	97	1990	..	93	..	104	93	..
1991	100	100	100	100	100	100	1991	..	100	..	100	100	..
1992	100	101	109	94	98	101	1992	..	142	..	94	100	..
1993	100	100	114	85	93	82	1993	..	166	..	93	99	..
1994	108	106	117	94	98	90	1994	..	184	..	95	106	..
1995	..	..	..	..	..	..	1995	..	..	..	..	..	..
	Greece/Grèce							**Netherlands/Pays-Bas** *					
1980	62	79	85	120	105	..	1980	71	62	90	..	84	..
1985	84	96	84	100	110	144	1985	82	88	79	..	101	..
1990	93	105	115	100	89	106	1990	101	103	101	..	101	..
1991	100	100	100	100	100	100	1991	100	100	100	..	100	..
1992	102	97	116	90	102	156	1992	102	99	100	..	99	..
1993	95	100	101	82	111	96	1993	100	97	110	..	98	..
1994	101	102	118	74	109	130	1994	105	102	111	..	102	..
1995	107	116	123	89	105	142	1995	109	105	103	..	..	..
	Ireland/Irlande *							**Norway/Norvège** *					
1980	107	33	97	..	20	225	1980	71	47	..	78	72	..
1985	91	55	84	..	40	97	1985	97	92	..	117	92	..
1990	98	82	98	..	93	120	1990	101	105	..	105	106	..
1991	100	100	100	..	100	100	1991	100	100	..	100	100	..
1992	102	117	103	..	112	92	1992	98	96	..	103	102	..
1993	101	129	105	..	124	87	1993	105	105	..	96	108	..
1994	105	153	121	..	158	92	1994	114	107	..	115	115	..
1995	..	191	97	..	184	..	1995	125	116	..	126	125	..
	Italy/Italie							**Portugal** *					
1980	84	80	108	102	77	91	1980	48	81	69	92	44	76
1985	82	88	84	94	84	83	1985	73	98	73	92	69	62
1990	98	103	100	102	101	111	1990	90	120	112	113	97	101
1991	100	100	100	100	100	100	1991	100	100	100	100	100	100
1992	102	98	104	98	94	88	1992	96	90	113	112	102	109
1993	104	94	106	95	93	70	1993	90	87	104	110	100	90
1994	..	..	..	..	..	..	1994	96	88	126	111	102	90
1995	..	..	..	..	..	..	1995	..	..	..	..	..	..

Notes: see page 243 / voir page 243.

... / ...

SELECTED ENVIRONMENTALLY SIGNIFICANT INDUSTRIES, 1980-1995 (a)
INDUSTRIES SÉLECTIONNÉES AYANT UNE SIGNIFICATION POUR L'ENVIRONNEMENT, 1980-1995 (a)

Production Indices/Indices de production (1991=100)

	3411 b) Pulp,paper, paperboard/ Pâte à papier, papier,carton	3510 c) Chemical products/ Industrie chimique	3530 d) Petroleum refineries/ Raffineries de pétrole	3710 e) Iron and steel/ Fer et acier	3830 f) Electrical Machinery/ Machines électriques	3843 g) Motor vehicles/ Véhicules automobiles		3411 b) Pulp,paper, paperboard/ Pâte à papier, papier,carton	3510 c) Chemical products/ Industrie chimique	3530 d) Petroleum refineries/ Raffineries de pétrole	3710 e) Iron and steel/ Fer et acier	3830 f) Electrical Machinery/ Machines électriques	3843 g) Motor vehicles/ Véhicules automobiles
	Spain/Espagne							**Turkey/Turquie**					
1980	81	86	87	100	76	57	1980	..	..	..	..	..	...
1985	85	91	85	107	70	68	1985	66	69	83	62	55	..
1990	98	100	100	99	106	100	1990	104	105	102	106	83	..
1991	100	100	100	100	100	100	1991	100	100	100	100	100	..
1992	100	100	106	92	94	101	1992	121	102	104	108	98	..
1993	102	98	101	89	99	83	1993	121	100	115	124	116	..
1994	112	112	104	96	113	102	1994	120	100	112	124	102	..
1995	124	122	97	107	126	127	1995	..	..	..	..	..	..
	Sweden/Suède							**UK/Royaume-Uni**					
1980	86	75	77	99	52	..	1980	75	69	85	66	126	115
1985	93	85	72	110	70	..	1985	74	83	85	102	145	101
1990	100	95	112	102	98	..	1990	98	96	96	113	107	109
1991	100	100	100	100	100	..	1991	100	100	100	100	100	100
1992	102	102	95	102	104	..	1992	102	103	101	96	97	101
1993	106	109	98	107	121	..	1993	106	105	105	97	101	102
1994	110	118	92	116	146	..	1994	116	110	103	100	108	111
1995	..	..	..	..	..	..	1995	128	120	99	105	115	129

Notes:
a) First quarter.
b) Manufacture of pulp, paper and paperbord.
c) Manufacture of industrial chemicals.
d) Petroleum refineries.
e) Iron and steel basic industries.
f) Manufacture of electrical machinery.
g) Manufacture of motor vehicles.
CAN) ISIC 3411: ISIC 3410, i.e. manufacture of paper and paper products only; ISIC 3530: includes ISIC 3540.
DNK) ISIC 3411: ISIC 3410, i.e. manufacture of paper and paper products only; ISIC 3530: includes ISIC 3540; ISIC 3830: includes ISIC 3850.
FIN) ISIC 3411: ISIC 3410, i.e. manufacture of paper and paper products only.
w.DEU) ISIC 3530: includes ISIC 3540.
IRL) ISIC 3411: ISIC 3410, i.e. manufacture of paper and paper products only; ISIC 3530: includes ISIC 3540.
LUX) ISIC 3510: incl. ISIC 3540; ISIC 3830: incl. ISIC 3825 and ISIC 3850.
NLD) ISIC 3530: includes ISIC 3540.
NOR) ISIC 3411: ISIC 3410, i.e. manufacture of paper and paper products only.
PRT) ISIC 3530: includes ISIC 3540.

Source: OECD/OCDE

Notes:
a) Premier trimestre.
b) Fabrication de la pâte à papier, du papier et du carton.
c) Industrie chimique.
d) Raffineries de pétrole.
e) Sidérurgie et première transformation de la fonte, du fer et de l'acier.
f) Fabrication de machines électriques.
g) Construction de véhicules automobiles.
CAN) CITI 3411: CITI 3410, soit la fabrication de papier et d'articles en papier uniquement; CITI 3530: inclut CITI 3540.
DNK) CITI 3411: CITI 3410, soit la fabrication de papier et d'articles en papier uniquement; CITI 3530: inclut CITI 3540; CITI 3830: inclut CITI 3850.
FIN) CITI 3411: CITI 3410, soit la fabrication de papier et d'articles en papier uniquement.
w.DEU) CITI 3530: inclut CITI 3540.
IRL) CITI 3411: CITI 3410, soit la fabrication de papier et d'articles en papier uniquement; CITI 3530: inclut CITI 3540.
LUX) CITI 3510: inclut CITI 3540; CITI 3830: inclut CITI 3825 et CITI 3850.
NLD) CITI 3530: inclut CITI 3540.
NOR) CITI 3411: CITI 3410, soit la fabrication de papier et d'articles en papier uniquement.
PRT) CITI 3530: inclut CITI 3540.

The next table shows trends in business sector investment expressed as indices (1991=100). Indices reflect gross fixed capital formation (GFCF) at constant prices for total business sector including private services.

Le tableau suivant présente l'évolution de l'investissement du secteur privé exprimée en indices (1985=100). Les indices reflètent la formation brute de capital fixe (FBCF) à prix constants pour l'ensemble du secteur privé, y compris les services.

BUSINESS SECTOR INVESTMENT (a), OECD countries, 1980-1994
INVESTISSEMENT DU SECTEUR PRIVÉ (a), pays de l'OCDE, 1980-1994

Index (1991=100)

		1980	1981	1982	1983	1984	1985	1986	1987	1988	1989	1990	1991	1992	1993	1994
Canada		68	79	70	65	66	72	75	82	95	101	99	100	92	93	100
Mexico/Mexique		80	90	70	48	53	61	51	55	66	70	85	100	115	114	123
USA/États-Unis		85	88	84	82	95	101	97	97	103	105	106	100	102	115	130
Japan/Japon		42	44	44	45	50	57	59	63	72	84	94	100	95	86	79
Australia/Australie		80	93	95	85	90	102	100	106	112	126	116	100	97	96	110
N.Zealand/N.Zélande		69	78	85	79	102	104	99	111	113	126	118	100	111	138	173
Austria/Autriche		70	68	61	61	63	69	71	75	81	88	95	100	97	91	97
Belgium/Belgique		61	58	59	57	60	62	66	70	81	92	103	100	95	87	86
Denmark/Danemark		67	56	68	69	78	93	110	104	96	102	105	100	89	86	88
Finland/Finlande		83	87	90	96	94	100	104	109	118	141	132	100	79	62	69
France		74	72	72	69	68	71	75	80	88	95	100	100	95	89	88
Germany/Allemagne		..	..	..	..	..	..	..	..	..	..	..	100	101	92	92
w.Germany/Allemagne occ.		69	66	63	66	66	69	72	75	79	85	93	100	..	..	..
Greece/Grèce		96	99	101	90	88	96	80	74	86	96	107	100	103	104	109
Iceland/Islande		77	79	80	71	82	99	106	128	117	92	100	100	86	61	61
Ireland/Irlande		96	111	107	95	92	80	78	81	87	99	114	100	94	90	99
Italy/Italie		80	74	68	65	70	70	74	80	90	95	100	100	99	81	80
Netherlands/Pays-Bas		73	64	62	66	69	78	87	87	89	96	98	100	99	97	97
Norway/Norvège		107	135	115	123	142	115	148	140	143	141	95	100	107	132	137
Spain/Espagne		64	61	59	59	53	53	60	73	83	94	98	100	99	84	87
Sweden/Suède		75	70	71	73	78	88	90	98	104	119	118	100	85	72	85
Switzerland/Suisse		59	61	59	61	63	70	79	88	95	100	104	100	91	86	94
UK/Royaume-Uni		59	56	60	60	68	77	78	91	107	114	111	100	95	94	95
North America/Amérique N.		82	87	81	77	88	95	91	92	99	101	104	100	102	113	128
EU/UE-15	*	70	66	66	65	67	71	74	81	89	96	101	100	..	..	..
OECD/OCDE Europe	*	71	68	67	67	69	72	76	82	90	97	101	100	..	..	..
OECD/OCDE	*	69	70	68	67	73	78	79	83	91	97	101	100	..	..	..

Notes:
a)   Business investment in volume, refering to industrial and service sectors, excluding public sector.
TOT) Includes western Germany only.

Notes :
a)   Investissement en volume des entreprises, des secteurs de l'industrie et des services, à l'exclusion du secteur public.
TOT) Inclut l'Allemagne occidentale uniquement.

Source: OECD/OCDE

The following table presents trends in international tourist receipts in OECD countries. Data refer to receipts in real terms, expressed as indices (1991=100). The last column presents the amount of these receipts in 1994 expressed in US$ at 1991 price levels and exchange rates.

Tourism activity can exert pressures on the environment because it often implies major concentrations of people in environmentally sensitive areas (e.g. coastal and mountain areas) within a relatively short period.

Le tableau suivant présente les tendances concernant les recettes de l'activité touristique internationale dans les pays de l'OCDE. Les données concernent les recettes en termes réels exprimées sous forme d'indices (1991=100). La dernière colonne présente la valeur de ces recettes en 1994 exprimée en $EU aux prix et aux taux de change 1991.

L'activité touristique peut exercer des pressions sur l'environnement en raison des grandes concentrations de population qu'elle entraîne souvent sur des périodes relativement courtes et dans des zones sensibles du point de vue de l'environnement (par exemple : zones côtières, montagnes).

INTERNATIONAL TOURIST RECEIPTS (a), 1980-1994
RECETTES DU TOURISME INTERNATIONAL (a), 1980-1994

	Index (1991=100)											million US$/ millions de $EU b)
	1980	1985	1986	1987	1988	1989	1990	1991	1992	1993	1994	1994
Canada	74	84	101	95	98	98	103	100	101	109	121	7 088
Mexico/Mexique	..	..	..	..	98	101	103	100	92	89	91	3 424
USA/Etats-Unis	34	46	52	58	71	82	93	100	108	113	112	54 216
Japan/Japon	39	64	58	71	87	100	116	100	97	83	75	2 565
Australia/Australie	35	44	50	73	94	82	90	100	110	115	143	5 966
N.Zealand/N.Zélande	22	50	64	61	99	94	100	100	104	80	90	1 360
Austria/Autriche	76	75	75	78	85	94	98	100	95	91	86	11 874
Belgium/Belgique *	68	91	90	101	112	105	103	100	103	108	128	4 648
Denmark/Danemark	62	79	77	80	81	80	95	100	101	82	87	3 029
Finland/Finlande	105	86	82	93	100	99	96	100	118	134	126	1 510
France	54	71	65	67	75	92	94	100	108	105	107	22 772
Germany/Allemagne	..	..	..	..	..	..	..	100	96	92	87	8 974
Greece/Grèce	121	130	137	137	140	116	121	100	131	137	145	3 203
Iceland/Islande	27	59	66	76	87	94	108	100	89	103	109	148
Ireland/Irlande	63	67	64	68	77	86	96	100	98	110	113	1 710
Italy/Italie	82	98	85	87	85	81	110	100	110	138	147	27 019
Netherlands/Pays-Bas	54	74	74	74	76	86	86	100	109	102	100	4 284
Norway/Norvège	77	85	95	95	100	92	93	100	111	117	135	2 234
Portugal	57	68	72	87	92	99	104	100	84	105	96	3 606
Spain/Espagne	65	100	112	116	118	109	100	100	108	112	122	23 424
Sweden/Suède	58	92	96	107	113	121	115	100	107	117	125	3 370
Switzerland/Suisse	77	92	90	93	96	101	99	100	101	95	98	6 907
Turkey/Turquie	19	103	82	105	140	133	131	100	135	138	200	5 318
UK/Royaume-Uni	80	104	103	111	106	109	111	100	103	113	118	15 374
North America/Amérique N.	..	..	..	..	75	85	94	100	106	111	112	64728
EU/UE-15	..	..	..	..	..	..	..	100	104	110	113	134797
OECD/OCDE Europe	..	..	..	..	..	..	..	100	105	110	115	149405
OECD/OCDE	..	..	..	..	..	..	..	100	105	109	113	224024

Notes:
a)   Real term international tourism receipts.
b)   At 1991 price levels and exchange rates.
BEL) Belgium-Luxembourg Economic Union.

Source: OECD/OCDE

Notes:
a)   Recettes de l'activité touristique internationale en termes réels.
b)   Aux niveaux de prix et taux de change de 1991.
BEL) Union économique belgo-luxembourgeoise.

11. AGRICULTURE

11. AGRICULTURE

INTRODUCTION

This section refers to agricultural activities that generate pressures on the environment, such as land degradation by erosion, compaction or pollution; water resource degradation through perturbation related to irrigation or drainage; pollution by nitrogenous and phosphate fertilizers, manure and slurry as well as pesticides; and landscape and wildlife deterioration through loss of diversity and habitat alteration.

The section provides data on major factor inputs to agricultural activities with significance for the environment:

- ▸ land;

- ▸ water for irrigation;

- ▸ labour;

- ▸ machines;

- ▸ energy;

- ▸ fertilizers;

- ▸ pesticides;

- ▸ livestock.

The data presented in this section mainly come from the FAO; they have been supplemented by data from other international and national sources. In general, these data exhibit a good level of comparability, although special care is required in the interpretation of land use and pesticide data.

The reader may also refer to the sections on inland waters, land, forest and wildlife to supplement this section.

INTRODUCTION

Cette section concerne les activités agricoles qui exercent des pressions sur l'environnement. Ces pressions sont à l'origine : de la dégradation des sols par l'érosion, le compactage et la pollution ; de la dégradation des ressources en eau liée à l'irrigation ou au drainage ; de la pollution par les engrais azotés ou phosphatés, les engrais naturels et les pesticides ; de la détérioration des paysages et de la faune et flore sauvages par perte de diversité et altération des habitats.

Cette section fournit des données sur les facteurs de production agricole qui ont des répercussions sur l'environnement :

- ▸ les sols ;

- ▸ l'eau d'irrigation ;

- ▸ le travail ;

- ▸ les machines ;

- ▸ l'énergie ;

- ▸ les engrais ;

- ▸ les pesticides ;

- ▸ les cheptels d'animaux d'élevage.

Les données présentées dans cette section proviennent principalement de la FAO ; elles ont été complétées par des données provenant d'autres sources internationales et nationales. En général, ces données bénéficient d'un bon niveau de comparabilité bien que l'interprétation des données sur l'occupation des sols et sur les pesticides demande une attention particulière.

Le lecteur pourra se référer aux sections concernant les eaux intérieures, le sol, la forêt et la faune et la flore pour compléter cette section.

The following table concerns land used for agriculture, specifically arable and permanent crop land:

▸ Arable land refers to land under temporary crops (double-cropped areas are counted only once), temporary meadows for mowing or pasture, land under market and kitchen gardens (including cultivation under glass) and land temporarily fallow or lying idle.

▸ Permanent crop land refers to land cultivated with crops that occupy the land for long periods and need not be replanted after each harvest, such as cocoa, coffee and rubber; it includes land under shrubs, fruit trees, nut trees and vines, but excludes land under trees grown for wood or timber.

The data refer, in principle, to the situation at the end of the year indicated.

The restructuring of the natural environment and associated farming practices have important consequences for soil resources, wildlife and the quality of air and water over extensive areas.

When interpreting this table it should be borne in mind that the land use definitions employed by Member countries may vary considerably.

Le tableau suivant concerne les sols utilisés par l'agriculture, notamment les terres arables et les cultures permanentes:

▸ Les terres arables sont les terres affectées aux cultures temporaires (les superficies récoltées deux fois n'étant comptées qu'une fois), aux prairies temporaires à faucher ou à pâturer, aux jardins maraîchers ou potagers (y compris les cultures sous-serre) et aux terres temporairement en jachères ou non cultivées.

▸ Les cultures permanentes sont les terres consacrées à des cultures qui occupent le terrain pendant de longues périodes et ne doivent pas être replantées après chaque récolte, comme le cacao, le café et le caoutchouc. Cette rubrique comprend les superficies couvertes d'arbres et d'arbustes à fleur, d'arbres fruitiers et de vignes, mais non les terres plantées en arbres destinés à la production de bois ou de grumes.

En principe, les données se rapportent à la situation à la fin de l'année indiquée.

La restructuration de l'environnement naturel et les pratiques agricoles associées ont des conséquences importantes sur les ressources en sols, la flore et la faune, et la qualité de l'air et de l'eau.

Ce tableau doit tenir compte du fait que les définitions d'utilisation des sols employées par les pays Membres peuvent varier de façon considérable.

ARABLE AND PERMANENT CROP LAND (a), 1980-1993
TERRES ARABLES ET CULTURES PERMANENTES (a), 1980-1993

km^2

		1980	1981	1982	1983	1984	1985	1986	1987	1988	1989	1990	1991	1992	1993
Canada		386500	406680	406680	406680	406680	406680	416800	416800	416800	416800	416800	414290	414290	414290
Mexico/Mexique		245300	246880	246880	246880	246880	247000	247050	247050	247100	247100	247100	247200	247300	247300
USA/Etats-Unis		1906240	1906240	1897990	1897990	1897990	1897990	1897990	1877760	1877760	1877760	1877760	1877760	1877760	1877760
Japan/Japon		48810	48530	48290	48060	47800	47580	47320	47080	46810	46370	45960	45550	45150	44630
Australia/Australie	*	451000	431710	465310	449750	472390	482000	482000	482000	482000	482000	479000	457000	472000	464860
N. Zealand/N. Zélande		4530	4560	4700	4820	4950	5110	5080	4470	4200	4250	4120	4120	4100	4100
Austria/Autriche		16350	16480	16340	15160	15220	15250	15130	15130	15320	15330	15050	15240	15060	14980
Belgium/Belgique		7730	7690	7550	7540	7580	7570	7590	7610	7630	7650	7240	7190	7170	7170
Denmark/Danemark	*	26530	26510	26230	26100	26260	26140	26050	25890	25700	25550	25710	25580	25480	25420
Finland/Finlande		25630	25400	25170	24670	24390	24100	23920	24110	24410	24530	25440	25790	25800	25800
France		188720	189160	190230	190330	191450	192420	193090	194590	190510	191270	192110	192340	192510	194390
Germany/Allemagne	*	125280	124980	124640	124500	124280	124260	124200	124090	123900	123910	124150	118070	117070	117070
w.Germany/Allemagne occ.		74940	74830	74620	74490	74370	74530	74630	74750	74660	74780	74920	75190	75340	75340
Greece/Grèce		39250	39510	39510	39450	39520	39400	39410	39420	39250	39100	39050	35150	35100	34940
Iceland/Islande		1330	1340	1340	1350	1350	1360	1370	1380	1380	1390	1400	1400	1400	1400
Ireland/Irlande		11100	10850	10600	10200	10440	10320	10100	9830	9630	9530	9430	9330	9230	9230
Italy/Italie		124360	124240	124150	122680	122320	121140	120980	120700	119810	119670	119720	119750	119090	118600
Luxembourg		590	580	570	570	580	560	560	570	570	570	570	570	670	670
Netherlands/Pays-Bas		8720	8770	8810	8850	8900	9160	9260	9370	9480	9590	9530	9470	9550	9550
Norway/Norvège		8300	8280	8410	8490	8550	8590	8690	8690	8740	8820	8820	8930	8830	8900
Portugal	*	31410	31440	31470	31500	31530	31560	31590	31630	31670	31670	31730	31730	31730	31600
Spain/Espagne		204990	204880	204870	205080	205120	204160	204200	203900	203680	203240	201720	200890	199460	196560
Sweden/Suède	*	29790	29600	29500	29410	29330	29220	29080	28900	29560	29560	29560	29560	29880	29880
Switzerland/Suisse		4930	4930	4930	4930	4930	4940	4940	4940	4940	4940	4940	4940	4940	4670
Turkey/Turquie		284790	285130	270910	266180	274130	275300	274830	279270	277630	278970	278560	276540	275750	275750
UK/Royaume-Uni	*	69960	69820	69860	69700	69900	70610	70110	70040	69240	67360	66570	66050	65950	65950
Former CSFR/Ex RFTS		51690	51700	51710	51700	51650	51530	51450	51340	51190	51080	50950	50500	50270	49060
Czech Rep./R.Tchèque		..	..	..	..	..	..	..	..	..	..	..	..	..	32930
Slovak Rep./R. Slovaque		..	..	..	..	..	..	..	..	..	..	..	..	..	16130
Hungary/Hongrie		53330	53170	52990	52920	52890	52930	52890	52890	52870	52870	52880	52870	49720	49730
Poland/Pologne		149610	148580	148210	147990	148630	148450	148190	148170	147800	147590	147330	147150	146990	146680
N. America/Amér. N.		2538040	2559800	2551550	2551550	2551550	2551670	2561840	2541610	2541660	2541660	2541660	2539250	2539350	2539350
Australia/Australie-NZ		455530	436270	470010	454570	477340	487110	487080	486470	486200	486250	483120	461120	476100	468960
OECD/OCDE Europe		1209770	1209580	1195080	1186690	1195790	1196050	1195100	1200070	1193050	1192650	1191300	1178520	1174670	1172530
EU/UE-15		910410	909900	909490	905740	906820	905860	905270	905790	900360	898530	897580	886710	883750	881810
OECD/OCDE		4252150	4254170	4264930	4240870	4272480	4282400	4291340	4275230	4267720	4266940	4262050	4224430	4235270	4225460
World/Monde		14269290	14303580	14348310	14327350	14389810	14427950	14467470	14513210	14539100	14550720	14524010	14462140	14587780	14475090

Notes:
a)   Include Secretariat estimates. Figures rounded to the nearest 10 km^2.
AUS) Includes crops and about 300 000 km^2 of cultivated grassland.
DNK) 1980-81: data based on holdings with agricultural land of 0.5 hectare and over; from 1982: based on holdings with agricultural land of at least 5 hectares and less than 5 hectares whose production exceeds a fixed minimum.
DEU) Includes land on holdings of 1 hectare and above, and on holdings of less than 1 hectare whose production market value exceeds a fixed minimum.
PRT) Includes about 8 000 km^2 of temporary crops grown in association with permanent crops and forests.
SWE) Holdings of 2 hectares and above.
UKD) Includes fallow land.

Notes :
a)   Inclut des estimations du Secrétariat. Tous les chiffres sont arrondis à 10 km^2 pres.
AUS) Y compris 300 000 km^2 d'herbages cultivés.
DNK) 1980-81: les données se rapportent aux terres des exploitations de 0.5 hectares et plus. Depuis 1982: exploitations d'au moins 5 hectares et exploitations de moins de 5 hectares dont la production dépasse un minimum fixé.
DEU) Terres des exploitations d'au moins 1 hectare, et des exploitations de moins de 1 hectare dont la production a une valeur marchande qui dépasse un minimum donné.
PRT) Y compris environ 8 000 km^2 de cultures temporaires associées à des cultures permanentes et à des forêts.
SWE) Exploitations de 2 hectares et plus.
UKD) Inclut les terres en jachère.

Source: FAO, OECD, national statistical yearbooks/ FAO, OCDE, annuaires statistiques nationaux

The following table concerns land used by agriculture, in this case land considered as permanent grassland. Permanent grassland refers to meadows and pastures used for five years or more for herbaceous forage crops, either cultivated or growing wild (wild prairie or grazing land). Together with arable and permanent crop land these areas make up the total land area devoted to agriculture. The data refer, in principle, to the situation at the end of the year indicated.

The restructuring of the natural environment into meadows and pastures, and the intensity of grazing on these lands, have important consequences for vegetation cover, soil resources and water quality.

When interpreting this table it should be borne in mind that the land use definitions employed by reporting countries may vary considerably and items classified under the same category can therefore relate to very different kinds of land. Comparability of data is particularly unsatisfactory in the case of permanent grassland; readers are also referred to related tables in this section and in the section concerning land.

Le tableau suivant concerne les sols utilisés par l'agriculture, notamment la superficie considérée comme étant toujours en herbe : cette superficie comprend les prairies et pâturages consacrés de façon permanente (cinq ans au minimum) aux herbacées fourragères, cultivées ou sauvages (prairies sauvages ou pâturages). Ajoutée à celle des terres arables et des cultures permanentes, elles donnent la superficie totale des terres consacrées à l'agriculture. En principe, les données se rapportent à la situation à la fin de l'année indiquée.

La restructuration de l'environnement naturel en prairies et pâturages et l'intensité de l'élevage pratiqué sur ces terres ont des conséquences importantes sur la végétation, les ressources en sols et la qualité de l'eau.

L'interprétation de ce tableau doit tenir compte du fait que les définitions d'utilisation des sols employées par les pays Membres peuvent varier de façon considérable et que certaines informations dans la même catégorie peuvent donc se rapporter à des types de sols qui ont des caractéristiques très différentes. La comparabilité des données est particulièrement insatisfaisante en ce qui concerne les prairies et pâturages permanents. Ce tableau est à lire en liaison avec les autres tableaux sur ce thème qui se trouvent dans la présente section et dans la section sur les sols.

PERMANENT GRASSLAND (a), 1980-1993
PRAIRIES ET PÂTURAGES PERMANENTS (a), 1980-1993

km²

	1980	1981	1982	1983	1984	1985	1986	1987	1988	1989	1990	1991	1992	1993
Canada	300120	252210	252210	252210	252210	252210	261730	261730	261730	261730	261730	263250	263250	263250
Mexico/Mexique	744990	744990	744990	744990	744990	744990	744990	744990	744990	744990	744990	744990	744990	744990
USA/Etats-Unis	2375390	2375390	2416000	2416000	2416000	2416000	2416000	2391720	2391720	2391720	2391720	2391720	2391720	2391720
Japan/Japon	5800	5890	5970	6050	6160	6210	6260	6320	6360	6420	6470	6490	6570	6610
Australia/Australie *	4506000	4484400	4462800	4441200	4419600	4398000	4348870	4299730	4250600	4192000	4187000	4171000	4188000	4138000
N.Zealand/N.Zélande	141560	147350	141500	141090	139780	138810	138810	138100	137700	136770	134900	135050	135200	135200
Austria/Autriche	20400	20410	20410	19860	19860	19860	19860	19860	20000	20150	19950	19950	19860	19540
Belgium/Belgique	6260	6190	6560	6520	6430	6410	6320	6250	6190	6130	6130	6300	6050	6050
Denmark/Danemark *	2520	2460	2390	2360	2280	2210	2140	2110	2170	2190	2170	2120	2080	1970
Finland/Finlande	1640	1610	1600	1360	1330	1320	1320	1270	1250	1230	1220	1230	1200	1060
France	128500	127710	126230	125380	123630	122000	120930	118940	117790	115650	113800	112100	110960	107640
Germany/Allemagne *	59890	59630	59320	58800	58560	58180	57880	57350	57070	56650	56180	53300	52430	52430
w.Germany/Allemagne occ.	47540	47140	46750	46300	46070	45660	45370	44810	44490	44070	43150	43260	42940	42940
Greece/Grèce	52550	52550	52550	52550	52550	52550	52550	52550	52550	52550	52550	52550	52550	52500
Iceland/Islande	17670	17660	17660	17650	17650	17640	17630	17620	17620	17610	17600	17600	17600	17600
Ireland/Irlande	46170	46470	46670	46840	46520	46730	46840	46860	46880	46900	46920	46940	46900	46900
Italy/Italie	51260	51270	51210	49920	50120	49810	49440	49420	48580	48830	48680	48780	48780	48780
Luxembourg	710	700	700	710	710	700	700	700	690	690	690	690	820	820
Netherlands/Pays-Bas	11600	11520	11430	11430	11410	11270	11080	10900	10810	10670	10620	10440	10300	10510
Norway/Norvège	1230	1080	1010	960	990	990	1000	1010	1020	1090	1090	1180	1200	1230
Portugal	8380	8380	8380	8380	8380	8380	8380	8380	8380	8380	8380	8380	8380	8400
Spain/Espagne	107390	107180	107040	102830	101160	102960	101900	102110	102100	103770	103000	102820	102600	103000
Sweden/Suède	5840	5840	5840	5720	5720	5720	5680	5650	5650	5680	5680	5720	5760	5760
Switzerl./Suisse	12730	12730	12730	12730	12730	12610	12610	12610	12610	12610	12610	12610	12610	11140
Turkey/Turquie	97000	96000	94000	92000	90000	89000	88000	87000	86000	86000	85190	85190	85190	85190
UK/Royaume-Uni *	107440	106800	106160	105530	104890	104260	104700	105150	105600	106040	106490	106590	106860	106860
Former CSFR/Ex-RFTS	16820	16730	16690	16650	16610	16410	16410	16440	16460	16410	16410	16730	17030	17080
Czech Rep./R. Tchèque	..	..	..	..	..	..	..	..	..	..	..	..	..	8730
Slovak Rep./R. Slov.	..	..	..	..	..	..	..	..	..	..	..	..	..	8350
Hungary/Hongrie	12940	12840	12830	12790	12650	12470	12340	12220	12100	11970	11860	11730	11640	11570
Poland/Pologne	40460	40520	40700	40800	40760	40690	40600	40520	40400	40480	40600	40380	40440	40470
N.America/Amér.N.	3420500	3372590	3413200	3413200	3413200	3413200	3422720	3398440	3398440	3398440	3398440	3399960	3399960	3399960
Australia/Australie-NZ	4647560	4631750	4604300	582290	4559380	4536810	4487680	4437830	4388300	4328770	4321900	4306050	4323200	4273200
OECD/OCDE Europe	739180	736190	731890	721530	714920	712600	708960	705730	702950	702820	698950	694470	692110	687370
EU/UE-15	610550	608720	606490	598190	593560	592360	589730	587490	585710	585510	582460	577900	575510	572210
OECD/OCDE	8813040	8746420	8755370	4723080	8693670	8668820	8625620	8548320	8496050	8436440	8425760	8406970	8421840	8367140
World/Monde	32342550	32404750	32475450	32529240	32659390	32828010	33008370	33133740	33338850	33468410	33502660	33502070	33816700	33617330

Notes:
a)   Data include Secretariat estimates. All figures are rounded to the nearest km².
AUS) Data refer to native pasture and include fallow and unused land.
DNK) 1980-81: based on holdings with agricultural land of 0.5 hectare and over; from 1982: based on holdings with agricultural land of at least 5 hectares and less than 5 hectares whose production exceeds a fixed minimum.
DEU) Includes land on holdings of 1 hectare and above, and on holdings of less than 1 hectare whose production market value exceeds a fixed minimum.
UKD) Includes set-aside land from 1990 onwards.

Notes :
a)   Inclut des estimations du Secrétariat. Tous les chiffres sont arrondis à 10 km² pres.
AUS) Pâturages indigènes ainsi que les jachères et les terres non utilisées.
DNK) 1980-81: terres des exploitations de 0.5 hectares et plus; depuis 1982: exploitations d'au moins 5 hectares et exploitations de moins de 5 hectares dont la production dépasse un minimum fixe.
DEU) Terres des exploitations d'au moins 1 hectare, et des exploitations de moins de 1 hectare dont la production a une valeur marchande qui dépasse un minimum donné.
UKD) A partir de 1990 les données incluent les terres en friche.

Source: FAO, OECD, national statistical yearbooks/ FAO, OCDE, annuaires statistiques nationaux

The next table concerns land irrigated for agricultural purposes. The data on irrigation relate to areas purposely provided with water, including land flooded by river water for crop production or pasture improvement (controlled flooding), whether this area is irrigated several times or only once during the year stated. The data refer, in principle, to the situation at the end of the year stated.

Water is indispensable to agriculture and the investment in irrigation emphasises this fact. Irrigation is also important because of its impact on the soil-water and overall ecological balance (e.g. leaching of fertilizers).

When interpreting this table allowance must be made for the differences in the definition of irrigated land among countries. Readers are referred to related tables concerning land use in this section and in the section on land.

Le tableau suivant concerne les terres agricoles irriguées. Les données sur l'irrigation se réfèrent aux superficies irriguées volontairement, y compris les terres couvertes par les crues à des fins de culture ou pour améliorer les pâturages (submersion côntrolée), qu'elles aient été irriguées plusieurs fois ou une seule fois dans l'année indiquée. En principe, les données se rapportent à la situation à la fin de l'année indiquée.

L'eau est indispensable à l'agriculture et les investissements dans des travaux d'irrigation mettent l'accent sur ce fait. L'irrigation est également importante en raison de ses impacts sur les grands équilibres sol-eau et écologiques (e.g. lessivage des engrais dans le sol).

L'interprétation de ce tableau doit tenir compte des différences de définition des terres irriguées entre les pays. Ce tableau est à lire en liaison avec les autres tableaux sur le thème occupation des sols qui se trouvent dans cette section et dans la section sur les sols.

IRRIGATED AREA, 1980-1993
SUPERFICIE IRRIGUÉE, 1980-1993

km²

	1980	1981	1982	1983	1984	1985	1986	1987	1988	1989	1990	1991	1992	1993
Canada	5960	6250	6550	6850	7150	7480	7420	7380	7320	7260	7180	7100	7100	7100
Mexico/Mexique	49800	50200	50530	48450	48820	52850	51760	50840	52000	54000	56000	58000	61000	61000
USA/Etats-Unis	205820	205820	198310	198310	198310	198310	198310	187710	187710	187710	193000	198000	203000	207000
Japan/Japon *	30550	30310	30100	29710	29520	29520	29310	29100	28890	28680	28460	28250	28020	27820
Australia/Australie	15000	16540	16450	16380	16250	17000	17700	18360	18350	18330	18320	20120	20690	21070
N.Zealand/N.Zél.	1830	2000	2180	2300	2400	2560	2650	2680	2750	2800	2800	2830	2850	2850
Austria/Autriche	40	40	40	40	40	40	40	40	40	40	40	40	40	40
Belgium/Belgique *	10	10	10	10	10	10	10	10	10	10	10	10	10	10
Denmark/Danemark *	3910	3880	3900	4000	4050	4100	4150	4190	4250	4300	4300	4350	4350	4350
Finland/Finlande *	600	600	600	600	600	620	620	620	620	620	640	640	640	640
France *	8700	9300	9600	9900	10200	10500	10800	11100	11470	11470	14850	14850	14850	14850
Germany/Allemagne	4600	4600	4660	4680	4700	4700	4720	4750	4770	4800	4820	4820	4750	4750
w.Germany/Allem.occ.	3150	3150	3160	3180	3200	3200	3220	3250	3270	3300	3320	..	..	..
Greece/Grèce	9610	9620	9680	10190	10300	10990	11260	11690	11870	12040	11950	11900	12600	13140
Iceland/Islande	-	-	-	-	-	-	-	-	-	-	-	-	-	-
Ireland/Irlande	-	-	-	-	-	-	-	-	-	-	-	-	-	-
Italy/Italie	24000	24000	24250	24250	24250	24250	24250	24250	24250	24250	27110	27100	27100	27100
Netherl./Pays-Bas	4800	4900	5000	5090	5200	5300	5350	5400	5450	5500	5550	5570	5600	5600
Norway/Norvège	740	770	790	820	860	900	920	930	940	960	970	970	970	970
Portugal	6300	6300	6300	6300	6300	6300	6300	6300	6300	6310	6300	6300	6300	6300
Spain/Espagne	30290	30580	31230	31330	32150	32170	32610	33160	33450	33710	34020	33880	34030	34530
Sweden/Suède	700	750	800	850	900	990	1050	1080	1100	1120	1140	1160	1150	1150
Switzerland/Suisse	250	250	250	250	250	250	250	250	250	250	250	250	250	250
Turkey/Turquie *	27000	29000	29000	30000	31000	32000	33000	33000	35000	36000	36000	36740	36740	36740
UK/Royaume-Uni *	1400	1450	1520	1520	1520	1520	1550	1550	1550	1570	1640	1360	1080	1080
Former CSFR/Ex-RFTS	1230	1500	1890	1850	1930	1870	2570	2270	3100	2810	2820	1700	1350	1040
Hungary/Hongrie	1340	1840	1550	1750	2340	1380	1630	1430	1670	1900	2040	2100	2240	2060
Poland/Pologne	1000	1000	1000	1000	1000	1000	1000	1000	1000	1000	1000	1000	1000	1000
N.America/Amér.N.	261580	262270	255390	253610	254280	258640	257490	245930	247030	248970	256180	263100	271100	275100
Australia/Iie-NZ	16830	18540	18630	18680	18650	19560	20350	21040	21100	21130	21120	22950	23540	23920
OECD/OCDE Europe	122950	126050	127630	129830	132330	134640	136880	138320	141320	142950	149590	149940	150460	151500
EU/UE-15	94960	96030	97590	98760	100220	101490	102710	104140	105130	105740	112370	111980	112500	113540
OECD/OCDE	431910	437170	431750	431830	434780	442360	444030	434390	438340	441730	455350	464240	473120	478340
World/Monde	2097010	2130270	2150010	2182700	2217660	2238280	2263900	2281260	2304450	2357590	2415480	2443880	2465690	2481250

Notes:
a) All figures are rounded to the nearest 10km2.
JPN) Rice irrigation only.
BEL) Data include Luxembourg.
DNK) Land provided with irrigation facilities only.
FIN) Land provided with irrigation facilities only.
FRA) Land provided with irrigation facilities only.
TUR) Includes about 10 percent of meadows and pastures.
UKD) England and Wales only.

Source: FAO, OECD/ OCDE

Notes:
a) Tous les chiffres sont arondis à 10km2 près.
JPN) Irrigation des champs de riz uniquement.
BEL) Les données incluent le Luxembourg.
DNK) Terres avec installations d'irrigation uniquement.
FIN) Terres avec installations d'irrigation uniquement.
FRA) Terres avec installations d'irrigation uniquement.
TUR) Y compris environ 10 pourcent de prairies et de pâturages.
UKD) Angleterre et Pays de Galles uniquement.

The following table concerns the economically active population in the primary sector, comprising persons engaged principally in agriculture, forestry, hunting or fishing. The data refer, in principle, to the situation at the end of the year indicated and to the latest estimation method.

Changes in the size of the agricultural labour force indicate the profound changes in the structural organisation of the sector and the application of modern technology and farming practices that have occurred in recent decades.

When interpreting this table, differences among countries' statistical treatment of, for example, unpaid family workers, particularly housewives, must be borne in mind. The reader is also referred to the next two tables, on farm machinery in use and final consumption of energy.

Le tableau suivant concerne la population active du secteur primaire qui comprend l'ensemble des personnes occupées économiquement et de manière principale dans l'agriculture, la sylviculture, la chasse et la pêche. Les données se rapportent en principe à la fin de l'année indiquée et à la méthode d'estimation la plus récente.

Des changements dans l'importance de la main-d'oeuvre agricole indiquent des changements profonds dans l'organisation structurelle de ce secteur et dans l'application de technologies et de techniques agricoles modernes durant ces dernières décennies.

L'interprétation de ce tableau doit tenir compte des différences entre les pays concernant les méthodologies statistiques employées, par exemple pour les aides familiaux non rémunérés et surtout pour les femmes au foyer. Il est conseillé de lire le présent tableau en liaison avec les tableaux suivants sur les machines agricoles en service et sur la consommation finale d'énergie.

ECONOMICALLY ACTIVE POPULATION IN THE PRIMARY SECTOR (a), 1980-1993
POPULATION ÉCONOMIQUEMENT ACTIVE DANS LE SECTEUR PRIMAIRE (a), 1980-1993

1 000

		1980	1981	1982	1983	1984	1985	1986	1987	1988	1989	1990	1991	1992	1993
Canada		583	600	561	590	588	575	570	566	556	536	531	554	533	550
Mexico/Mexique		7913	8032	8129	8210	8287	8367	8453	8544	8635	8721	8796	8860	8915	8964
USA/Etats-Unis		3529	3519	3570	3541	3469	3338	3350	3400	3326	3378	3355	3390	3383	3257
Japan/Japon		5770	5570	5480	5310	5120	5090	4950	4890	4740	4630	4510	4270	4110	3830
Australia/Australie	*	408	415	412	416	403	412	426	412	431	426	437	420	402	406
N.Zealand/N.Zélande	*	138	143	146	142	143	148	167	164	157	152	157	157	159	158
Austria/Autriche	*	323	317	320	313	304	291	284	285	269	266	269	256	250	249
Belgium/Belgique		116	113	111	111	110	109	107	105	102	101	100	98	95	..
Denmark/Danemark		175	174	177	177	165	169	154	151	153	148	147	149	136	132
Finland/Finlande		314	305	312	302	294	280	266	251	237	218	207	198	187	174
France		1854	1791	1732	1677	1627	1582	1534	1479	1425	1368	1248	1196	1150	1101
w.Germany/Allem. occ.		1403	1367	1321	1278	1238	1195	1176	1124	1076	1025	990	957	909	854
Greece/Grèce		1016	1083	1011	1060	1044	1037	1026	971	972	930	889	807	807	794
Iceland/Islande	*	14	14	14	14	13	14	14	14	14	13	13	14	14	13
Ireland/Irlande		209	196	193	189	182	168	168	164	166	163	167	154	..	..
Italy/Italie	*	2899	2732	2522	2526	2426	2296	2242	2169	2053	1946	1863	1823	1749	1504
Luxembourg		8	8	8	7	7	7	7	7	6	6	6	6	..	..
Netherlands/Pays-Bas	*	244	247	249	247	247	248	249	281	284	286	289	293	261	255
Norway/Norvège		159	159	154	148	143	147	151	139	134	132	129	116	110	111
Portugal	*	1074	1017	991	957	969	969	891	926	885	830	833	836	505	505
Spain/Espagne		2228	2108	2062	2069	1988	1950	1758	1723	1695	1598	1486	1345	1253	1198
Sweden/Suède	*	237	237	236	229	218	208	179	171	168	159	153	147	140	136
Switzerland/Suisse		218	213	210	208	204	203	202	202	199	197	198	197	194	191
Turkey/Turquie	*	8360	8353	8326	8300	8272	8246	8223	8197	8192	8562	8731	8713	8168	8397
UK/Royaume-Uni		654	639	632	622	615	616	603	591	580	566	567	607	576	547
Former CSFR/Ex-RFTS		1061	1033	1002	970	937	906	877	849	822	797	772	749	727	706
Hungary/Hongrie		949	907	866	827	789	752	716	681	648	617	590	565	541	517
Poland/Pologne		5282	5144	5019	4906	4796	4676	4550	4417	4286	4151	4031	3918	3813	3713
North America/Amérique N.		12025	12151	12260	12341	12344	12280	12373	12510	12517	12635	12682	12804	12831	12771
Australia/Australie-NZ		546	558	558	558	546	560	593	576	588	578	594	577	561	564
OECD/OCDE Europe*	*	21505	21073	20581	20434	20066	19735	19234	18950	18610	18514	18285	17912	16660	16420
EU/UE-15*	*	12754	12334	11877	11764	11434	11125	10644	10398	10071	9610	9214	8872	8180	7700
OECD/OCDE*	*	39846	39352	38879	38643	38076	37665	37150	36926	36455	36357	36071	35563	34170	33580
World/Monde		992334	1004929	1017372	1029528	1041291	1052566	1063391	1073747	1083444	1092284	1100204	1107300	1113773	1120085

Notes:
a)   Agriculture, hunting, fishing and forestry.
AUS)   Break in time series in 1989.
NZL)   Break in time series in 1986.
AUT)   Breaks in time series in 1982, 1984.
ISL)   Break in time series in 1991.
ITA)   Break in time series in 1993.
NLD)   Breaks in time series in 1987, 1993.
PRT)   Breaks in time series in 1983, 1992.
SWE)   Breaks in time series in 1986, 1987.
TUR)   Break in time series in 1988.
TOT)   Includes western Germany only. 1992 and 1993: include Secretariat estimates.

Source: OECD/OCDE, FAO

Notes :
a)   Agriculture, chasse, pêche et sylviculture.
AUS)   Rupture de série en 1989.
NZL)   Rupture de série en 1986.
AUT)   Ruptures de série en 1982, 1984.
ISL)   Rupture de série en 1991.
ITA)   Rupture de série en 1993.
NLD)   Ruptures de série en 1987, 1993.
PRT)   Ruptures de série en 1983 et 1992.
SWE)   Ruptures de série en 1986, 1987.
TUR)   Rupture de série en 1988.
TOT)   Inclut l'Allemagne occidentale uniquement. 1992 et 1993: inclut des estimations du Secrétariat.

This table concerns the mechanisation of agriculture, notably the use of tractors and combined harvester-threshers. The data for tractors refer to both wheel and crawler tractors used in agriculture (excluding garden tractors). Wheel tractors are generally limited to those having three or four wheels and engines of over 8 HP. Crawler or track-layer type tractors are also generally limited to those over 8 HP. The data for combined harvester-threshers are generally limited to machines that reap and thresh in one operation. In principle the data refer to the number of units in use at the end of the year indicated or during the first quarter of the following year.

The growth in the stock of tractors and other machinery in use is an important aspect of farming practices and a factor in explaining the impact of farming activities on the environment.

This table should display a reasonably good level of comparability among countries and over time. The reader is also referred to the tables concerning the agricultural labour force and energy consumption by the sector.

Ce tableau concerne la mécanisation de l'agriculture, notamment l'utilisation de tracteurs et de moissonneuses-batteuses. Les données relatives aux tracteurs se rapportent aux tracteurs à roues et à chenilles utilisés dans l'agriculture (à l'exclusion des motoculteurs). Par tracteurs à roues, on n'entend en général que les tracteurs à trois ou quatre roues d'une puissance supérieure à 8 ch. De même, par tracteurs à chenilles, on n'entend en général que ceux dont la puissance dépasse 8 ch. Les données présentées pour les moissonneuses-batteuses se limitent en général aux machines qui coupent et battent en une seule opération. En principe, les données se rapportent au nombre d'unités en service à la fin de l'année indiquée ou pendant le premier trimestre de l'année suivante.

La croissance du parc de tracteurs et d'autres équipements agricoles en service est un aspect important des pratiques agricoles et contribue à expliquer l'impact des activités agricoles sur l'environnement.

Ce tableau devrait bénéficier d'un assez bon niveau de comparabilité entre les pays et dans le temps. Il est conseillé de lire ce tableau en liaison avec les tableaux sur la main-d'oeuvre agricole et sur la consommation d'énergie par ce secteur.

TRACTORS AND COMBINED HARVESTER-THRESHERS IN USE, 1980-1993
TRACTEURS AGRICOLES ET MOISSONNEUSES-BATTEUSES EN SERVICE, 1980-1993

1 000

		1980	1981	1982	1983	1984	1985	1986	1987	1988	1989	1990	1991	1992	1993
Canada		819.0	818.7	832.5	846.0	859.0	872.6	886.0	899.5	913.0	926.5	905.5	889.1	895.0	895.0
Mexico/Mexique		130.1	158.7	162.1	168.8	172.0	174.3	177.8	181.0	183.2	186.5	188.8	191.0	191.5	191.5
USA/Etats-Unis		5398.9	5369.0	5340.2	5341.3	5345.4	5338.6	5397.7	5456.1	5456.0	5465.0	5464.0	5463.0	5462.0	5462.0
Japan/Japon	*	2355.3	2329.2	2500.2	2596.2	2692.1	2963.1	2983.9	3105.2	3228.2	3307.2	3357.1	3135.0	3161.0	3199.0
Australia/Australie		384.7	383.6	382.5	381.4	380.3	379.2	378.1	377.0	375.9	374.8	373.7	372.6	371.5	371.5
N.Zealand/N.Zélande		96.7	100.2	104.5	89.8	88.1	86.4	84.8	83.1	81.5	80.1	79.0	78.0	79.1	79.1
Austria/Autriche		351.8	353.7	356.0	356.4	356.4	356.4	356.4	356.4	378.5	378.5	378.5	378.5	378.5	362.3
Belgium/Belgique	*	126.1	126.7	126.7	126.3	126.6	127.0	126.7	126.2	126.2	125.7	124.5	124.2	121.0	122.9
Denmark/Danemark	*	228.2	219.7	222.7	212.5	205.2	200.9	202.6	198.8	202.7	198.9	196.1	192.9	186.5	187.8
Finland/Finlande		257.0	264.0	273.0	280.0	284.0	287.0	287.0	286.0	290.0	285.0	285.0	283.0	273.0	270.0
France		1616.0	1629.1	1640.6	1643.2	1640.6	1640.5	1635.4	1632.5	1627.4	1622.5	1618.0	1613.5	1614.0	1614.0
Germany/Allemagne		1792.1	1795.6	1802.0	1816.5	1809.4	1813.5	1812.0	1797.6	1775.4	1749.8	1722.5	1641.2	1461.9	1435.8
w. Germany/Allem. occ.		1634.0	1634.1	1638.0	1647.9	1637.5	1638.6	1633.0	1615.0	1589.5	1560.9	1534.6	..	..	..
Greece/Grèce		146.4	158.6	166.0	175.1	185.3	190.0	199.7	209.6	214.0	218.8	222.0	222.0	222.0	222.0
Iceland/Islande		13.2	13.5	13.8	14.0	14.0	13.2	13.2	13.0	12.0	11.4	11.5	11.2	10.9	10.8
Ireland/Irlande		150.4	153.3	155.3	157.2	160.2	163.2	165.2	167.2	169.1	170.1	171.1	172.1	172.6	172.6
Italy/Italie		1107.4	1143.0	1177.0	1208.7	1238.0	1267.8	1311.1	1359.1	1408.3	1445.7	1476.7	1503.5	1479.8	1478.5
Netherlands/Pays-Bas	*	184.0	183.9	185.9	188.8	189.0	189.1	188.8	188.6	188.2	188.1	187.8	187.6	187.6	187.6
Norway/Norvège		147.0	152.9	156.6	161.9	163.3	167.9	172.4	169.2	171.8	171.4	171.5	172.3	172.0	172.0
Portugal		89.5	94.9	100.2	105.8	111.5	117.1	122.8	128.5	134.0	139.8	139.6	139.4	139.0	139.0
Spain/Espagne		565.5	590.4	613.9	636.0	656.1	678.3	704.9	726.2	751.8	771.7	789.1	804.6	815.1	824.3
Sweden/Suède	*	232.0	238.6	237.1	235.5	234.1	232.5	230.9	225.8	221.6	217.4	213.2	208.3	205.0	205.0
Switzerland/Suisse		99.8	103.1	107.5	111.2	108.2	109.9	110.5	112.3	113.2	114.1	117.2	118.0	118.0	118.0
Turkey/Turquie		449.0	470.5	503.3	525.9	568.7	595.9	622.5	647.3	664.2	681.9	701.4	712.0	737.0	757.7
UK/Royaume-Uni		569.8	572.8	577.6	586.2	578.7	580.1	575.0	571.5	566.0	559.8	554.0	548.0	547.0	547.0
Former CSFR/Ex-RFTS		154.4	151.8	150.1	152.5	154.2	156.6	159.3	161.3	162.7	161.5	160.0	152.6	133.9	132.0
Hungary		69.5	68.0	68.0	67.9	67.6	67.3	65.4	64.7	63.1	61.2	59.4	54.7	49.4	47.5
Poland		658.7	712.3	755.7	805.8	858.5	980.8	1050.4	1110.9	1172.9	1230.1	1265.0	1261.8	1256.1	1239.6
North America/Amérique N.		6348.0	6346.4	6334.8	6356.1	6376.4	6385.5	6461.5	6536.6	6552.2	6578.0	6558.3	6543.1	6548.5	6548.5
Australia/Australie-NZ		481.4	483.8	487.0	471.2	468.4	465.6	462.9	460.1	457.4	454.9	452.7	450.6	450.6	450.6
OECD/OCDE Europe		8125.1	8264.3	8415.0	8541.2	8629.4	8730.2	8837.2	8915.6	9014.5	9050.5	9079.7	9032.3	8840.9	8827.2
EU/UE-15		7416.1	7524.3	7633.9	7728.2	7775.1	7843.4	7918.6	7973.8	8053.3	8071.8	8078.2	8018.8	7802.9	7768.7
OECD/OCDE		17309.8	17423.7	17737.0	17964.7	18166.2	18544.4	18745.5	19017.5	19252.3	19390.6	19447.8	19161.0	19001.0	19025.3
World/Monde		25492.0	25979.3	26664.9	27267.5	27870.5	28662.6	29147.3	29601.9	30049.0	30360.9	30406.1	29924.4	29826.9	29551.9

Notes:
JPN)　Data are not fully comparable with those of other countries.
BEL)　Data include Luxembourg.
DNK)　Data include garden tractors.
NLD)　Data include garden tractors.
SWE)　Data include tractors used in forestry.

Source: FAO

Notes:
JPN)　Les données ne sont pas entièrement comparables à celles des autres pays.
BEL)　Les données incluent le Luxembourg.
DNK)　Les données incluent des motoculteurs.
NLD)　Les données incluent des motoculteurs.
SWE)　Les données incluent des tracteurs utilisés pour les travaux en forêt.

The following table concerns the total final consumption of commercial energy sources by the agricultural sector. The data do not include "non-commercial" sources of energy (e.g. peat and wood), nor do they include final energy consumption by the food processing, beverage and tobacco industry. (See the section on energy for definitions.)

The substitution of manpower and animal power by commercial energy sources is a marked feature of modern agricultural practices and has important consequences for the environment.

When interpreting this table it should be borne in mind that in certain countries administrations find it impossible to separate energy consumption by agriculture from that by the residential sector. In these cases, the residential sector will also include energy consumption in agriculture and/or commercial and/or public services. The reader is also referred to the preceding tables concerning agricultural manpower and machinery in use.

Le tableau suivant concerne la consommation finale totale en énergie commerciale par le secteur agricole. Ces données ne prennent en compte ni les sources d'énergie non commerciales (e.g. la tourbe, le bois) ni la consommation finale d'énergie de l'industrie alimentaire, des boissons et des tabacs. (Voir la section sur l'énergie pour les définitions.)

La substitution de la main-d'oeuvre et des animaux de trait par des sources d'énergie commerciales est une caractéristique marquante des pratiques agricoles modernes et a des conséquences importantes sur l'environnement.

L'interprétation de ce tableau doit tenir compte du fait que dans certains pays il est impossible pour les administrations de distinguer la consommation d'énergie du secteur agricole de celle du secteur résidentiel. Dans ce cas, le secteur résidentiel englobe également la consommation d'énergie par l'agriculture, et/ou par le secteur commercial et/ou par les services publics. Il est conseillé de lire ce tableau en liaison avec les tableaux précédents qui concernent la main d'oeuvre agricole et la mécanisation de l'agriculture.

TOTAL ENERGY CONSUMPTION BY AGRICULTURE, 1980-1993
CONSOMMATION TOTALE D'ÉNERGIE PAR L'AGRICULTURE, 1980-1993

Mtoe/Mtep

	1980	1981	1982	1983	1984	1985	1986	1987	1988	1989	1990	1991	1992	1993
Canada	2.46	2.48	2.43	3.90	2.72	2.79	2.81	2.73	2.95	3.28	3.41	3.37	4.19	3.72
Mexico/Mexique	2.29	2.35	2.50	2.16	2.15	2.20	2.19	2.39	2.44	2.33	2.26	2.30	2.24	2.28
USA/Etats-Unis	13.77	13.05	12.14	11.88	13.22	17.27	16.73	16.04	16.42	15.67	14.59	14.38	15.88	16.15
Japan/Japon	3.51	3.05	2.71	2.87	3.83	3.87	4.31	4.78	5.66	5.68	6.62	7.02	7.00	7.23
Australia/Australie	1.07	1.11	1.22	1.13	1.26	1.24	1.23	1.28	1.26	1.33	1.32	1.34	1.36	1.40
N.Zealand/N.Zélande	0.27	0.27	0.30	0.29	0.30	0.29	0.26	0.25	0.25	0.24	0.27	0.28	0.27	0.28
Austria/Autriche	0.09	0.10	0.10	0.10	0.10	0.11	0.11	0.11	0.11	0.11	0.11	0.12	0.12	0.13
Belgium/Belgique	0.51	0.44	0.44	0.40	0.37	0.37	0.46	0.44	0.58	0.56	0.50	0.55	0.72	0.79
Denmark/Danemark	1.26	1.18	1.05	1.03	0.96	0.70	0.78	0.84	0.83	0.87	0.73	0.75	1.17	1.00
Finland/Finlande	0.79	0.78	0.80	0.76	0.79	0.83	0.83	0.85	0.90	0.93	0.94	0.82	0.85	0.85
France	3.25	3.11	3.11	3.05	3.08	3.06	3.04	3.05	3.08	3.08	3.12	3.27	3.25	2.95
Germany/Allemagne	3.05	3.11	3.09	3.10	3.26	3.32	3.60	3.22	3.19	3.21	3.16	3.70	3.50	2.99
w.Germany/All.occ.	2.05	2.06	2.18	2.18	2.32	2.37	2.33	2.30	2.20	2.23	2.26	..	..	..
Greece/Grèce	0.76	0.70	0.74	0.84	0.92	0.96	0.86	0.95	1.03	1.03	1.04	1.11	1.07	1.08
Iceland/Islande	0.18	0.19	0.20	0.22	0.21	0.20	0.22	0.24	0.25	0.26	0.27	0.29	0.30	0.31
Ireland/Irlande	0.03	0.02	0.02	0.01	0.01	0.01	0.21	0.20	0.20	0.20	0.22	0.22	0.23	0.23
Italy/Italie	2.23	2.17	2.17	2.20	2.20	2.36	2.37	2.57	2.75	3.10	3.16	2.96	3.04	3.29
Luxembourg	0.02	0.01	0.02	0.01	0.01	0.01	0.01	0.01	0.01	0.01	0.01	0.01	0.01	0.01
Netherlands/Pays-Bas	0.56	0.41	0.51	0.45	2.38	2.54	2.87	2.99	3.01	3.07	3.37	3.75	3.69	3.92
Norway/Norvège	0.27	0.27	0.27	0.26	0.26	0.27	0.28	0.28	0.30	0.29	0.27	0.26	0.26	0.25
Portugal	0.33	0.33	0.35	0.39	0.39	0.41	0.41	0.41	0.43	0.45	0.47	0.47	0.47	0.47
Spain/Espagne	2.36	2.22	2.39	2.43	2.47	2.62	2.55	2.69	2.41	1.62	1.72	1.82	1.94	1.98
Sweden/Suède	0.68	0.61	0.56	0.51	0.53	0.58	0.70	0.67	0.63	0.58	0.56	0.56	0.54	0.50
Switzerland/Suisse	0.15	0.16	0.16	0.33	0.15	0.16	0.16	0.16	0.16	0.16	0.18	0.18	0.22	0.23
Turkey/Turquie	0.94	0.98	1.22	1.33	1.37	1.51	1.48	1.81	1.83	1.77	1.98	1.98	2.03	2.45
UK/Royaume-Uni	1.44	1.35	1.35	1.34	1.34	1.37	1.37	1.32	1.29	1.21	1.22	1.24	1.24	1.24
Former CSFR/Ex-RFTS	0.44	0.41	0.46	0.48	0.59	0.64	0.66	0.60	2.38	3.87	2.17	..	..	..
Hungary/Hongrie	1.77	1.60	1.65	1.43	1.55	1.69	1.66	1.74	1.67	1.31	1.17	0.84	0.73	..
Poland/Pologne	2.66	2.64	2.66	2.65	2.29	2.47	2.42	2.01	3.18	3.29	3.18	2.91	2.75	..
North America/Amérique N.	18.52	17.88	17.07	17.94	18.09	22.26	21.73	21.16	21.81	21.28	20.26	20.05	22.31	22.15
Australia/Australie-NZ	1.34	1.38	1.52	1.42	1.56	1.53	1.49	1.53	1.51	1.57	1.59	1.62	1.63	1.68
OECD/OCDE Europe	18.90	18.14	18.55	18.76	20.80	21.39	22.31	22.81	22.99	22.51	23.03	24.06	24.65	24.67
EU/UE-15	17.36	16.54	16.70	16.62	18.81	19.25	20.17	20.32	20.45	20.03	20.33	21.35	21.84	21.43
OECD/OCDE	42.27	40.45	39.85	40.99	44.28	49.05	49.84	50.28	51.97	51.04	51.50	52.75	55.59	55.73

Source: OECD-IEA/OCDE-AIE

The following table concerns consumption of commercial nitrogenous fertilizers by agriculture. The data refer to the nitrogen (N) content of commercial inorganic fertilizers, and relate to apparent consumption during the fertilizer year (generally 1 July to 30 June) except as noted. Data for 1980, for instance, refer to apparent consumption during the 12-month period from 1 July 1980 to 30 June 1981.

Nitrogen is one of the major plant nutrients and its application in the form of synthetic chemical fertilizers has important consequences for water quality.

This table should exhibit fairly good comparability of data between countries and over time. Readers are also referred to the next two tables, concerning phosphate fertilizer and total commercial fertilizer consumption.

Le tableau suivant concerne la consommation d'engrais azotés commerciaux par l'agriculture. Les données se rapportent au contenu en azote (N) des engrais commerciaux inorganiques et à la consommation apparente pendant des périodes de douze mois (genéralement du 1er juillet au 30 juin) sauf exceptions (voir les notes). Ainsi, les chiffres pour 1980 se réfèrent à la consommation apparente pendant une période de douze mois allant du 1er juillet 1980 au 30 juin 1981.

L'azote est un des principaux éléments nutritifs des plantes et son application sous forme d'engrais chimiques synthétiques a des conséquences importantes sur la qualité de l'eau.

Ce tableau devrait bénéficier d'un bon niveau de comparabilité entre les pays et dans le temps. Il est conseillé de lire ce tableau en liaison avec les tableaux suivants concernant la consommation d'engrais phosphatés et d'engrais commerciaux.

APPARENT CONSUMPTION OF NITROGENOUS FERTILIZERS, 1980-1993
CONSOMMATION APPARENTE D'ENGRAIS AZOTÉS, 1980-1993

1 000 tonnes

		1980	1981	1982	1983	1984	1985	1986	1987	1988	1989	1990	1991	1992 (a)	1993 (a)
Canada		938	966	1002	1157	1255	1225	1145	1160	1160	1197	1158	1253	1317	1784
Mexico/Mexique		904	1112	1255	1088	1193	1263	1325	1378	1270	1293	1346	1130	1230	1276
USA/Etats-Unis	*	10817	9964	8280	10063	10426	9457	9262	9536	9609	10048	10239	10384	10304	11469
Japan/Japon		614	643	683	701	697	680	693	669	640	641	612	574	572	600
Australia/Australie		238	245	273	269	330	340	360	372	394	440	439	462	488	518
N.Zealand/N.Zélande		20	22	28	31	40	32	27	37	40	37	46	64	90	103
Austria/Autriche		160	162	146	153	161	165	138	146	141	136	135	132	124	125
Belgium/Belgique	*	194	195	197	199	199	195	199	199	196	191	186	182	173	169
Denmark/Danemark	*	374	376	391	419	398	382	381	367	377	400	395	370	333	326
Finland/Finlande		197	184	216	205	196	202	218	215	199	232	207	166	174	171
France		2147	2193	2196	2320	2337	2408	2568	2557	2605	2660	2492	2569	2154	2222
Germany/Allemagne		2303	2073	2072	2072	2149	2286	2287	2375	2413	2254	1788	1720	1680	1612
w.Germany/Allemagne occ.		1551	1323	1465	1378	1452	1516	1578	1601	1540	1487	1180	..	..	..
Greece/Grèce	*	333	373	384	418	428	450	432	384	409	426	427	408	393	337
Iceland/Islande	*	15	15	14	15	14	13	13	11	11	10	12	12	14	13
Ireland/Irlande		275	275	296	331	330	314	343	340	349	379	370	358	353	401
Italy/Italie		1006	988	968	996	1026	1055	1011	1047	924	827	879	907	906	873
Netherlands/Pays-Bas		483	477	457	478	505	500	504	458	456	412	390	392	390	374
Norway/Norvège		110	107	114	110	113	107	110	114	110	110	111	111	109	108
Portugal		137	145	139	126	123	137	150	153	157	145	150	135	127	130
Spain/Espagne		902	818	799	808	917	962	1063	1148	1168	1109	1063	999	818	937
Sweden/Suède	*	244	248	249	258	253	246	241	241	240	221	212	185	211	226
Switzerland/Suisse		66	63	60	67	71	72	71	73	72	70	63	63	64	63
Turkey/Turquie	*	807	799	863	1021	955	916	952	1142	1082	1140	1200	1100	1206	1335
UK/Royaume-Uni	*	1240	1386	1560	1601	1580	1568	1671	1525	1462	1582	1525	1365	1219	1268
Former CSFR/Ex-RFTS	*	675	615	646	682	692	671	646	589	642	705	588	289	300	..
Czech Rep./R.Tchèque		..	..	..	..	..	..	..	..	..	..	..	..	..	220
Slovak Rep./R.Slovaque		..	..	..	..	..	..	..	..	..	..	..	..	..	65
Hungary/Hongrie	*	537	563	647	625	626	558	593	614	646	583	358	159	144	152
Poland/Pologne	*	1312	1344	1213	1245	1322	1239	1337	1388	1335	1521	1274	735	683	758
North America/Amérique N.		12659	12041	10536	12308	12874	11944	11731	12074	12039	12538	12743	12767	12851	14529
Australia/Australie-NZ		259	267	301	300	370	372	387	409	434	477	485	527	578	621
OECD/OCDE Europe		10992	10877	11122	11598	11755	11977	12351	12494	12371	12305	11604	11173	10448	10690
EU/UE-15		9994	9894	10070	10384	10603	10869	11206	11155	11097	10974	10218	9887	9054	9171
OECD/OCDE		24524	23828	22642	24907	25696	24974	25163	25646	25484	25961	25444	25041	24449	26440
World/Monde		60776	60452	61192	67665	70647	69830	71492	75600	79606	79142	77245	75491	74520	72761

Notes:
a)   Data include estimates. 1993: provisional data.
USA)   Includes data for Puerto Rico.
BEL)   Data include Luxembourg.
DNK) Fertiliser year: August-July.
GRC) Fertiliser year: calendar year.
ISL)   Fertiliser year: calendar year.
LUX) Data for Belgium include Luxembourg.
SWE) Data include forest fertilisation. Fertiliser year: June-May.
TUR) Fertiliser year: calendar year.
UKD) Fertiliser year: June-May.
CSFR) Fertiliser year: calendar year.
HUN) Fertiliser year: calendar year.
POL)   Fertiliser year: calendar year.

Notes:
a)   Les données comprennent des estimations. 1993: données provisoires.
USA)   Y compris les données de Porto Rico.
BEL)   Les données incluent le Luxembourg.
DNK) Périodes de 12 mois: août-juillet.
GRC) Périodes de 12 mois: année civile.
ISL)   Périodes de 12 mois: année civile.
LUX) Les données de la Belgique incluent celles du Luxembourg.
SWE) Y compris la fertilisation des forêts. Périodes de 12 mois: juin-mai.
TUR) Périodes de 12 mois: année civile.
UKD) Périodes de 12 mois: juin-mai.
CSFR) Périodes de 12 mois: année civile.
HUN) Périodes de 12 mois: année civile.
POL)   Périodes de 12 mois: année civile.

Source: FAO, IFA

This table concerns consumption of commercial phosphate fertilizers by agriculture. The data refer to commercial phosphoric acid (P_2O_5) and cover the P_2O_5 content of superphosphates, ammonium phosphate and basic slag. The data relate to apparent consumption during the fertilizer year, generally a 12-month period (1 July to 30 June) except as noted.

Phosphate is a major plant nutrient and its application both in the form of synthetic chemical fertilizers and as manure has important consequences for water quality.

This table should exhibit a fairly good comparability of data between countries and over time. Readers are referred to related tables concerning apparent consumption of nitrogenous and all commercial fertilizers.

Ce tableau concerne la consommation d'engrais phosphatés commerciaux par l'agriculture. Les données se rapportent à l'acide phosphorique commercial (P_2O_5) et englobent le contenu en P_2O_5 des superphosphates, du phosphate d'ammonium et des scories de déphosphoration. Les données se rapportent à la consommation apparente pendant des périodes de douze mois (en général du 1er juillet au 30 juin) sauf exceptions (voir les notes).

Le phosphate est un des principaux éléments nutritifs des plantes et son application sous forme d'engrais chimiques synthétiques et de déchets animaliers a des conséquences importantes sur la qualité de l'eau.

Ce tableau devrait bénéficier d'un bon niveau de comparabilité entre les pays et dans le temps. Il est conseillé de consulter ce tableau en liaison avec les tableaux concernant la consommation d'engrais azotés et d'engrais commerciaux.

APPARENT CONSUMPTION OF PHOSPHATE FERTILIZERS (a), 1980-1993
CONSOMMATION APPARENTE D'ENGRAIS PHOSPHATÉS (a), 1980-1993

1 000 tonnes

		1980	1981	1982	1983	1984	1985	1986	1987	1988	1989	1990	1991	1992 (b)	1993 (b)
Canada		635	636	652	713	728	703	626	635	614	609	578	592	616	637
Mexico/Mexique		255	384	487	331	382	383	410	404	395	354	374	380	298	352
USA/Etats-Unis	*	4930	4367	3753	4446	4225	3790	3636	3745	3735	3941	3811	3826	4024	4102
Japan/Japon		690	701	721	765	777	741	753	766	726	728	690	695	699	728
Australia/Australie		797	754	730	773	764	685	758	831	836	791	579	640	782	810
N.Zealand/N.Zélande		338	327	330	375	332	300	246	258	179	253	220	269	318	356
Austria/Autriche		99	93	83	95	95	91	76	80	78	74	74	72	65	61
Belgium/Belgique	*	102	93	94	98	94	91	89	87	87	87	78	65	55	51
Denmark/Danemark	*	111	105	113	119	111	106	107	96	92	95	89	76	64	54
Finland/Finlande		150	142	160	163	158	155	159	156	141	143	117	76	82	82
France	*	1773	1677	1631	1679	1580	1466	1425	1405	1460	1494	1349	1253	1029	1014
Germany/Allemagne		1226	1127	1044	1078	1051	1055	1036	1003	992	951	609	519	490	415
w.Germany/Allemagne occ.		837	753	740	745	732	737	683	679	644	594	381	..	..	..
Greece/Grèce	*	158	166	164	175	181	180	182	170	176	189	187	176	178	133
Iceland/Islande	*	8	8	9	8	7	7	7	7	6	5	6	6	5	4
Ireland/Irlande		145	142	145	152	151	133	150	142	148	146	139	136	137	136
Italy/Italie		748	706	657	682	694	692	667	786	715	608	645	663	613	536
Netherlands/Pays-Bas		83	81	77	87	89	81	88	80	86	76	74	75	70	67
Norway/Norvège		63	62	66	60	56	54	53	45	40	37	35	34	31	32
Portugal		81	85	81	67	61	70	79	84	89	81	80	75	77	72
Spain/Espagne		476	340	422	398	436	462	494	537	542	559	534	502	423	497
Sweden/Suède	*	123	122	115	112	101	86	79	76	69	70	58	46	46	53
Switzerland/Suisse		47	42	44	43	44	42	39	40	40	39	38	37	36	31
Turkey/Turquie	*	619	489	565	618	555	477	520	585	490	600	625	620	658	787
UK/Royaume-Uni	*	404	445	464	474	469	439	446	435	433	428	380	371	360	366
Former CSFR/Ex-FRTS	*	495	494	479	529	524	537	523	452	480	437	359	75	77	..
Czech Rep./Rép. Tchèque		..	..	..	..	..	..	..	..	..	..	..	..	..	47
Slovak Rep./Rép. Slovaque		..	..	..	..	..	..	..	..	..	..	..	..	..	17
Hungary/Hongrie	*	390	399	392	410	431	336	355	332	322	266	127	24	14	12
Poland/Pologne	*	885	817	826	900	885	908	961	837	944	752	411	223	232	243
North America/Amérique N.		5820	5388	4892	5490	5335	4876	4672	4784	4744	4905	4763	4799	4938	5090
Australia/Australie-NZ		1135	1081	1060	1147	1096	985	1004	1089	1015	1044	799	909	1100	1166
OECD/OCDE Europe		6416	5925	5934	6106	5935	5685	5694	5814	5686	5681	5116	4802	4420	4391
EU/UE-15		5680	5324	5250	5378	5272	5106	5076	5137	5110	5000	4412	4105	3690	3537
OECD/OCDE		14061	13094	12607	13508	13143	12287	12124	12453	12170	12358	11368	11204	11157	11375
World/Monde		31700	30946	30864	33084	34022	33224	34658	36685	37989	37393	36279	35293	30909	28813

Notes:
a)   Includes ground rock phosphates.
b)   Data include estimates.
USA) Includes data for Puerto rico.
BEL) Exclude other citrate soluble phosphates. Data include Luxembourg.
DNK) Fertiliser year: August-July.
FRA) Fertiliser year: May-April.
GRC) Fertiliser year: calendar year.
ISL) Fertiliser year: calendar year.
SWE) Fertiliser year: June-May.
TUR) Fertiliser year: calendar year.
UKD) Fertiliser year: June-May.
CSFR) Fertiliser year: calendar year.
HUN) Fertiliser year: calendar year.
POL) Fertiliser year: calendar year.

Notes:
a)   Y compris les phosphates naturels broyés.
b)   Les données comprennent des estimations.
USA) Y compris les données de Porto Rico.
BEL) Les données excluent les autres phosphates solubles dans le citrate. Les données incluent le Luxembourg.
DNK) Périodes de 12 mois: août-juillet.
FRA) Périodes de 12 mois: mai-avril.
GRC) Périodes de 12 mois: année civile.
ISL) Périodes de 12 mois: année civile.
SWE) Périodes de 12 mois: juin-mai.
TUR) Périodes de 12 mois: année civile.
UKD) Périodes de 12 mois: juin-mai.
CSFR) Périodes de 12 mois: année civile.
HUN) Périodes de 12 mois: année civile.
POL) Périodes de 12 mois: année civile.

Source: FAO, IFA

The following table concerns consumption of all commercial fertilizers by agriculture. The data refer to the nitrogen (N) and phosphoric acid (P_2O_5) contents of nitrogenous and phosphate fertilizers, and to the K_2O content of commercial potash, muriate, nitrate and sulphate of potash, manure salts, kainit and nitrate of soda potash. The data relate to apparent consumption during the fertilizer year, generally a 12-month period (1 July to 30 June) except as noted.

The growing application of the three major plant nutrients (N,P,K) as synthetic chemical fertilizers has important consequences for water quality and the environment in general and reflects the growing specialisation and intensification of cropping practices.

This table should have a fairly good comparability of data between countries and over time. Readers are referred to the preceding tables concerning apparent consumption of nitrogenous and phosphate fertilizers.

Le tableau suivant concerne la consommation de l'ensemble des engrais commerciaux par l'agriculture. Les données se rapportent au contenu en azote (N) et en acide phosphorique (P_2O_5) des engrais azotés et phosphatés respectivement (comme définis précédemment) et au contenu en K_2O des engrais potassiques commerciaux suivants : muriate, nitrate et sulfate de potasse, sels d'engrais, kainite et nitrate de soude potassique. Les données se rapportent à la consommation apparente pendant des périodes de douze mois (en général du 1er juillet au 30 juin) sauf exceptions (voir les notes).

L'application croissante des trois principaux éléments nutritifs des plantes (N,P,K) sous forme d'engrais chimiques synthétiques a des conséquences importantes sur la qualité de l'eau et de l'environnement dans son ensemble. Elle reflète la spécialisation et l'intensification croissantes des techniques de culture.

Ce tableau devrait bénéficier d'un assez bon niveau de comparabilité entre les pays et dans le temps. Il est conseillé de lire ce tableau en liaison avec les tableaux précédents concernant la consommation d'engrais azotés et phosphatés.

APPARENT CONSUMPTION OF COMMERCIAL FERTILIZERS (NPK), 1980-1993
CONSOMMATION APPARENTE D'ENGRAIS COMMERCIAUX (NPK), 1980-1993

1 000 tonnes

		1980	1981	1982	1983	1984	1985	1986	1987	1988	1989	1990	1991	1992 (a)	1993 (a)
Canada		1939	1946	1996	2241	2379	2325	2160	2200	2131	2166	2074	2156	2261	2737
Mexico/Mexique		1238	1561	1825	1486	1661	1714	1826	1862	1743	1740	1799	1583	1616	1753
USA/Etats-Unis	*	21480	19439	16416	19768	19688	17831	17286	17792	17733	18709	18587	18784	18991	20350
Japan/Japon		1816	1879	1985	2098	2105	2034	2053	2037	1943	1938	1839	1763	1784	1817
Australia/Australie		1162	1144	1126	1178	1230	1155	1254	1349	1387	1393	1164	1244	1420	1488
N.Zealand/N.Zélande		464	463	478	534	516	427	352	370	316	376	362	432	533	587
Austria/Autriche		407	395	353	382	390	388	316	334	322	308	303	297	267	262
Belgium/Belgique	*	447	416	424	445	417	421	425	417	415	408	384	362	332	320
Denmark/Danemark	*	627	618	653	694	659	634	642	606	614	651	633	580	506	485
Finland/Finlande		489	459	529	523	508	507	529	522	473	516	443	331	346	341
France	*	5609	5570	5571	5833	5780	5695	5872	5818	6000	6103	5683	5563	4531	4611
Germany/Allemagne		5169	4856	4654	4587	4738	4823	4835	4810	4876	4591	3351	2968	2843	2672
w.Germany/Allemagne occ.		2733	2557	2389	2453	2417	2439	2324	2318	2404	2152	1609	..	..	..
Greece/Grèce	*	527	580	591	640	661	685	675	607	648	688	685	652	624	518
Iceland/Islande	*	29	30	30	29	27	25	25	23	22	20	22	23	23	21
Ireland/Irlande		601	592	616	678	678	620	691	670	691	706	692	672	665	710
Italy/Italie		2111	2057	2004	2064	2091	2102	2061	2303	2092	1813	1948	1986	1916	1750
Netherlands/Pays-Bas		679	664	636	682	720	701	696	636	647	587	559	561	542	523
Norway/Norvège		259	252	268	253	252	238	232	232	218	213	201	208	201	204
Portugal		259	275	259	225	217	241	269	283	295	274	278	251	240	237
Spain/Espagne		1662	1377	1485	1456	1639	1734	1855	2021	2094	2052	1976	1882	1571	1826
Sweden/Suède	*	484	485	479	481	456	419	406	401	382	363	328	292	308	333
Switzerland/Suisse		181	169	170	177	180	180	173	177	178	177	168	159	158	150
Turkey/Turquie	*	1456	1297	1460	1664	1541	1427	1519	1778	1614	1798	1888	1767	1928	2207
UK/Royaume-Uni	*	2054	2301	2545	2617	2590	2524	2666	2484	2416	2535	2370	2177	1999	2071
Former CSFR/Ex-FRTS	*	1730	1720	1742	1776	1749	1734	1703	1556	1606	1602	1303	429	440	..
Czech Rep./Rép. Tchèque		..	..	..	..	..	..	..	..	..	..	..	..	..	267
Slovak Rep./Rép. Slovaque		..	..	..	..	..	..	..	..	..	..	..	..	..	81
Hungary/Hongrie	*	1399	1485	1528	1586	1524	1338	1383	1373	1418	1221	679	221	179	197
Poland/Pologne	*	3468	3476	3150	3347	3363	3315	3532	3329	3440	3275	2291	1251	1193	1282
North America/Amérique N.		24656	22946	20236	23494	23728	21869	21271	21855	21607	22615	22459	22523	22868	24839
Australia/Australie-NZ		1627	1607	1604	1712	1746	1582	1606	1719	1703	1769	1526	1676	1953	2075
OECD/OCDE Europe		23052	22393	22726	23434	23543	23365	23888	24122	23994	23802	21912	20730	18999	19241
EU/UE-15		21126	20644	20798	21310	21544	21495	21939	21912	21964	21594	19634	18574	16689	16659
OECD/OCDE		51151	48825	46551	50737	51122	48850	48818	49733	49247	50124	47736	46692	45604	47973
World/Monde		116720	115147	115041	126292	130565	128613	132254	139589	145637	143420	138047	134352	126114	120672

Notes:
a) Includes estimates.
USA) Includes data for Puerto rico.
BEL) Data include Luxembourg.
DNK) Fertiliser year: August-July.
FRA) Fertiliser year: May-April.
GRC) Fertiliser year: calendar year.
ISL) Fertiliser year: calendar year.
SWE) Fertiliser year: June-May.
TUR) Fertiliser year: calendar year.
UKD) Fertiliser year: June-May.
CSFR) Fertiliser year: calendar year.
HUN) Fertiliser year: calendar year.
POL) Fertiliser year: calendar year.

Notes:
a) Y compris des estimations.
USA) Y compris les données de Porto Rico.
BEL) Les données incluent le Luxembourg.
DNK) Périodes de 12 mois: août-juillet.
FRA) Périodes de 12 mois: mai-avril.
GRC) Périodes de 12 mois: année civile.
ISL) Périodes de 12 mois: année civile.
SWE) Périodes de 12 mois: juin-mai.
TUR) Périodes de 12 mois: année civile.
UKD) Périodes de 12 mois: juin-mai.
CSFR) Périodes de 12 mois: année civile.
HUN) Périodes de 12 mois: année civile.
POL) Périodes de 12 mois: année civile.

Source: FAO, IFA

The next tables show, for selected countries, the state and trends in the consumption of agricultural pesticides. They concern total pesticides, insecticides, fungicides and herbicides.

State data are given for amounts of active ingredients, except for some countries where figures give the formulation weight including diluents and adjuvants. "Active ingredients" are the substances in a commercial pesticide that cause the desired effects on agriculturally harmful fungi, plants or animals. There are additional data for "other pesticides", which include fumigants, rodenticides and anti-coagulants.

Trend data refer to pesticide consumption relative to a base year.

The application of certain pesticides may affect the quality of soil and water and have undesirable effects on flora and fauna. Moreover, residues of pesticides sometimes remain on crops after harvesting.

When interpreting these tables, the reader should be extremely careful in making comparisons among countries and over time.

Les tableaux suivants montrent l'état et l'évolution de la consommation de pesticides par l'agriculture dans des pays sélectionnés. Ils présentent les pesticides totaux, les insecticides, les fongicides et les herbicides.

Les données sur l'état sont exprimées en équivalent d'éléments actifs sauf pour certains pays où elles se rapportent au poids du produit préparé (comprenant également les diluants et les adjuvants). Le terme "éléments actifs" signifie les substances des pesticides commerciaux qui provoquent les effets desirés sur les champignons, plantes ou animaux nuisibles à l'agriculture. Il y a des données additionelles sur les "autres" pesticides qui comprennent les fumigants, les produits contre les rongeurs et les anticoagulants.

Les données sur l'évolution représentent la consommation relative de pesticides par rapport à une année de référence.

L'application de certains pesticides peut avoir des incidences sur la qualité du sol et de l'eau et peut avoir des effets indésirables sur la faune et la flore. De plus, des résidus de pesticides persistent quelquefois dans les cultures après la récolte.

En interprétant ces tableaux le lecteur devra être extrêmement prudent dans la comparaison entre les différents pays et dans le temps.

CONSUMPTION OF PESTICIDES, selected countries, latest year available
CONSOMMATION DE PESTICIDES, pays sélectionnés, dernière année disponible

tonnes (active ingredients/éléments actifs)

		Year/ Année	Total pesticides	Insecticides	Fungicides/ Fongicides	Herbicides	Other pesticides/ Autres pesticides
Canada	*	1990	33716	2262	2512	26414	2528
USA/Etats-Unis	*	1991	370918	79450	66738	224730	-
Japan/Japon		1985	83056	45018	18622	19416	-
Australia/Australie		1992	4688	690	1618	2380	-
Austria/Autriche		1992	3565	143	1483	1859	80
Belgium/Belgique	*	1993	9885	1118	2781	5587	399
Denmark/Danemark		1993	4103	107	1033	2632	331
Finland/Finlande	*	1993	1279	146	210	892	31
France	*	1992	84709	6110	44786	27281	6532
Germany/Allemagne		1993	28930	4327	7660	12688	4255
Greece/Grèce		1993	8583	2362	2474	2305	1442
Ireland/Irlande		1991	1915	162	535	1097	121
Italy/Italie		1990	91671	10943	58473	10267	11989
Netherlands/Pays-Bas	*	1993	11551	463	4014	2784	4290
Norway/Norvège		1993	750	17	164	512	58
Portugal	*	1988	21570	2700	12870	5000	1000
Spain/Espagne	*	1993	80760	21150	20560	17620	21430
Sweden/Suède	*	1993	1464	15	318	1093	38
Switzerland/Suisse	*	1993	1936	238	982	676	40
Turkey/Turquie	*	1991	28220	10412	5599	7191	5018
UK/Royaume-Uni	*	1992	27748	625	6105	18370	2648
Former CSFR/Ex-RFTS		1985	16862	1298	1442	12450	1671
Hungary/Hongrie		1992	11383	1063	4181	6087	52
Poland/Pologne	*	1989	20620	1065	7206	11875	474

Notes:
CAN) "Other pesticides" include growth regulators, animal repellents, rodenticides and fumigants.
USA) Agricultural pesticides only.
BEL) Data include Luxembourg.
FIN) The definition of "pesticides" includes forest pesticides, insect repellents, growth regulators and other pesticides.
FRA) The figure for total pesticides represents the principal materials used, which account for 80 percent of all pesticides applied. Data for fungicides include copper and sulphur compounds but not elemental sulphur.
NLD) Data are provisional.
PRT) Formulation weight.
ESP) Data include estimates based on the formulation weight.
SWE) A special sales tax has been applied to pesticides since 1987.
CHE) Data refer to sales and include Liechtenstein.
TUR) Formulation weight. Excludes powdered sulphur and copper sulphate.
UKD) Great Britain only.
POL) "Other pesticides" include growth regulators, rodenticides, animal repellents and other pesticides.

Notes:
CAN) Les "autres pesticides" comprennent les régulateurs de croissance, les répulseurs d'animaux, les rodenticides et les fumigants.
USA) Uniquement les pesticides agricoles.
BEL) Les données incluent le Luxembourg.
FIN) La définition de "pesticides" inclut les pesticides forestiers, les produits répulseurs d'insectes, les régulateurs de croissance et d'autres insecticides.
FRA) Le total présenté ici comprend les principaux produits qui assurent plus de 80 pour cent du tonnage total utilisé. Le chiffre sur les fongicides comprend les composés à base de cuivre et de soufre mais non le soufre en l'état.
NLD) Les données sont provisoires.
PRT) Les données se rapportent au poids total du produit préparé.
ESP) Les données comprennent des estimations qui sont basées sur le poids total du produit préparé.
SWE) Depuis 1987, une taxe spéciale est appliquée aux ventes de pesticides.
CHE) Les données se réfèrent aux ventes et incluent le Liechtenstein.
TUR) Les données se rapportent au poids total du produit préparé. Le soufre en poudre et les sulphates de cuivre sont exclus.
UKD) Grande Bretagne seulement.
POL) Les "autres pesticides" comprennent les régulateurs de croissance de plantes, les rodenticides, les répulseurs et les autres pesticides.

Source: FAO, national statistical yearbooks, UNECE, UNEP / FAO, annuaires statistiques nationaux, CEE de l'ONU, PNUE

TRENDS IN THE CONSUMPTION OF PESTICIDES, 1980-1993
ÉVOLUTION DE LA CONSOMMATION DE PESTICIDES, 1980-1993

		Tonnes base year/ année de référence (a)		Index 1985 = 100 (a)									
				1980	1985	1986	1987	1988	1989	1990	1991	1992	1993
Canada	Insecticides	3172		..	100	..	..	86	..	71	..	..	..
	Fungicides/Fongicides	2823		..	100	..	..	92	..	89	..	..	..
	Herbicides	30181		..	100	..	..	92	..	88	..	..	..
	Total pesticides	39259		..	100	..	..	90	..	86	..	..	..
USA/Etats-Unis	Insecticides	102150		136	100	93	80	82	67	77	78	..	..
	Fungicides/Fongicides	50394		86	100	117	135	135	122	131	132	..	..
	Herbicides	238350		87	100	95	96	97	99	98	94	..	..
	Total pesticides	390894		99	100	95	95	98	94	97	95	..	..
Japan/Japon *	Insecticides	45018		100	100	..	..	..	..	..	..	..	..
	Fungicides/Fongicides	18622		103	100	..	..	..	..	..	..	..	..
	Herbicides	19416		133	100	..	..	..	..	..	..	..	..
	Total pesticides	83056		108	100	95	92	84	83	82	79	78	..
Austria/Autriche	Insecticides	428		80	100	117	..	..	..	..	37	33	..
	Fungicides/Fongicides	2072		81	100	117	..	..	..	..	89	72	..
	Herbicides	2648		83	100	115	..	..	..	..	82	70	..
	Total pesticides	5270		82	100	115	..	..	..	..	80	68	..
Belgium/Belgique *	Insecticides	1669		94	100	91	82	83	82	77	70	76	67
	Fungicides/Fongicides	2123		51	100	103	105	122	124	129	134	155	131
	Herbicides	4617		99	100	100	105	112	114	113	110	111	121
	Total pesticides	8748		85	100	100	102	109	113	114	110	115	113
Denmark/Danemark	Insecticides	262		..	100	89	60	57	86	99	56	49	41
	Fungicides/Fongicides	2199		..	100	76	51	49	58	63	65	61	47
	Herbicides	4079		..	100	93	96	92	97	77	70	69	65
	Total pesticides	6863		..	100	89	80	77	84	82	67	67	60
Finland/Finlande *	Insecticides	165		102	100	54	53	112	119	61	42	71	89
	Fungicides/Fongicides	110		87	100	101	91	131	162	148	133	176	191
	Herbicides	1641		120	100	93	97	87	105	96	84	65	54
	Total pesticides	1980		117	100	94	97	95	113	104	88	72	65
France *	Insecticides	5483		87	100	132	119	120	131	141	129	111	..
	Fungicides/Fongicides	53941		73	100	93	84	92	85	77	103	83	..
	Herbicides	32827		99	100	108	104	110	116	114	103	83	..
	Total pesticides	92251		83	100	101	93	100	99	94	104	85	..
Germany/Allemagne	Insecticides	3901	(1991)	..	..	..	..	..	..	..	100	105	111
	Fungicides/Fongicides	9760	(1991)	..	..	..	..	..	..	..	100	96	78
	Herbicides	18992	(1991)	..	..	..	..	..	..	..	100	82	67
	Total pesticides	36937	(1991)	..	..	..	..	..	..	..	100	91	78
w.Germany/Allem.occ.	Insecticides	1566		149	100	93	86	82	85	97	..	..	..
	Fungicides/Fongicides	8491		77	100	102	110	135	127	129	..	..	..
	Herbicides	17390		120	100	107	97	99	109	98	..	..	..
	Total pesticides	30053		110	100	105	100	108	115	110	..	..	..
Greece/Grèce	Insecticides	2762	(1986)	..	..	100	86	99	103	..	..	83	86
	Fungicides/Fongicides	2056	(1986)	..	..	100	94	80	94	..	..	133	120
	Herbicides	2158	(1986)	..	..	100	85	103	140	..	..	99	107
	Total pesticides	7346	(1986)	..	..	100	89	92	111	..	..	117	117
Ireland/Irlande	Insecticides	107	(1983)	172	..	..	..	..	..	139	151	..	..
	Fungicides/Fongicides	497	(1983)	42	..	..	..	..	..	93	108	..	..
	Herbicides	1647	(1983)	64	..	..	..	..	..	60	67	..	..
	Total pesticides	2250	(1983)	65	..	..	..	..	..	78	85	..	..
Italy/Italie *	Insecticides	34401		95	100	97	29	33	31	32	..	..	..
	Fungicides/Fongicides	85126		187	100	110	81	77	67	69	..	..	..
	Herbicides	28525		78	100	104	37	38	37	36	..	..	..
	Total pesticides	166839		139	100	108	59	60	55	55	..	..	..
Netherlands/Pays-Bas *	Insecticides	634		..	100	88	79	91	118	115	94	93	73
	Fungicides/Fongicides	4363		..	100	82	93	95	93	95	98	96	92
	Herbicides	3977		..	100	95	98	92	84	87	81	75	70
	Total pesticides	21002		..	100	103	86	86	91	90	82	76	55
Norway/Norvège	Insecticides	39		93	100	122	83	98	71	49	48	69	43
	Fungicides/Fongicides	138		69	100	104	80	78	86	111	96	96	118
	Herbicides	1236		97	100	96	86	74	69	78	46	45	41
	Total pesticides	1529		90	100	99	87	78	68	77	50	50	49

Notes: see next page / voir page suivante

... / ...

TRENDS IN THE CONSUMPTION OF PESTICIDES, 1980-1993
ÉVOLUTION DE LA CONSOMMATION DE PESTICIDES, 1980-1993

		Tonnes base year/ année de référence (a)		Index 1985 = 100 (a)									
				1980	1985	1986	1987	1988	1989	1990	1991	1992	1993
Portugal	* Insecticides	2412		75	100	81	96	112	..	..	..	..	..
	Fungicides/Fongicides	15118		130	100	76	79	85	..	..	..	..	..
	Herbicides	4284		65	100	107	112	117	..	..	..	..	..
	Total pesticides	22596		109	100	83	88	95	106	..	..	..	..
Spain/Espagne	* Insecticides	56539	(1987)	..	..	..	100	94	93	57	60	46	37
	Fungicides/Fongicides	23502	(1987)	..	..	..	100	117	123	112	106	94	87
	Herbicides	16450	(1987)	..	..	..	100	116	124	134	134	116	107
	Total pesticides	121050	(1987)	..	..	..	100	106	111	92	92	75	67
Sweden/Suède	* Insecticides	140		122	100	108	37	74	28	19	14	21	11
	Fungicides/Fongicides	639		78	100	156	80	106	78	101	113	81	50
	Herbicides	2752		136	100	152	64	73	67	59	38	34	40
	Total pesticides	3660		121	100	153	66	78	66	64	50	41	40
Switzerland/Suisse	* Insecticides	385	(1988)	31	..	..	..	100	93	101	75	70	62
	Fungicides/Fongicides	1120	(1988)	100	..	..	..	100	99	88	81	85	88
	Herbicides	885	(1988)	93	..	..	..	100	105	93	88	85	76
	Total pesticides	2455	(1988)	84	..	..	..	100	100	93	84	82	79
Turkey/Turquie	* Insecticides	20336		67	100	113	73	74	92	87	51	..	..
	Fungicides/Fongicides	5804		76	100	102	105	110	101	95	96	..	..
	Herbicides	6839		62	100	87	109	115	90	93	105	..	..
	Total pesticides	36662		73	100	107	90	93	95	93	77	81	..
UK/Royaume-Uni	* Insecticides	655	(1988)	226	..	..	..	100	..	110	..	95	..
	Fungicides/Fongicides	8488	(1988)	56	..	..	..	100	..	63	..	72	..
	Herbicides	16295	(1988)	173	..	..	..	100	..	100	..	113	..
	Total pesticides	27217	(1988)	148	..	..	..	100	..	91	..	102	..
Hungary/Hongrie	* Insecticides	4343	(1986)	..	..	100	67	65	77	52	36	24	..
	Fungicides/Fongicides	13657	(1986)	..	..	100	80	83	120	86	38	31	..
	Herbicides	12872	(1986)	..	..	100	92	81	113	85	70	47	..
	Total pesticides	31065	(1986)	..	..	100	84	80	111	81	51	37	..
Poland/Pologne	* Insecticides	1305	(1986)	..	..	100	97	97	82	..	..	..	..
	Fungicides/Fongicides	3622	(1986)	..	..	100	147	190	199	..	..	..	..
	Herbicides	9035	(1986)	..	..	100	126	154	131	..	..	..	..
	Total pesticides	14408	(1986)	..	..	100	127	161	143	..	..	..	..

Notes:
a) Unless otherwise specified, data refer to active ingredients and the reference year is 1985. Insecticides: acaricides, molluscicides and nematocides. Fungicides: bactericides and seed treatments. Herbicides: defoliants and dessicants. Total pesticides may include other pesticides such as plant growth regulators and rodenticides.
JPN) Data refer to national production of pesticides.
BEL) Data include Luxembourg.
FIN) Data include forest pesticides.
FRA) Data are based on the principal materials used, which represent 80 per cent of the total tonnage applied. Fungicides include copper and sulphur compounds but not elemental sulphur.
ITA) From 1981, data include only agricultural pesticides. Until 1986 figures are based on formulation weight.
NLD) Data include soil disinfectants which correspond, for the years presented, about the half of the total consumption.
PRT) Formulation weight. 1980: 1981 data.
ESP) Formulation weight. Data include estimates.
SWE) A special sales tax has been applied to pesticides since 1987.
CHE) Data refer to sales and include Liechtenstein.
TUR) Excl. powdered sulphur and copper sulphate. Formulation weight.
UKD) Great Britain only. 1980: early 1980s.
HUN) Total: represents the principal materials used, which account for 80 per cent of the total tonnage applied. From 1979, fungicides include copper and sulphur compounds but not elemental sulphur.
POL) Total: represents the principal materials used, which account for 80 per cent of the total tonnage applied. From 1979, fungicides include copper and sulphur compounds but not elemental sulphur.

Notes:
a) Les données se rapportent aux éléments actifs et l'année de référence est 1985 sauf en cas d'indication contraire. Insecticides: acaricides, mollusquicides et nematocides. Fongicides: bactericides et traitements de semences. Herbicides: défoliants et déssicants. Le total des pesticides peut inclure d'autres pesticides tels que les régulateurs de croissance des plantes et les rodenticides.
JPN) Les données sont fondées sur la production nationale de pesticides.
BEL) Les données incluent le Luxembourg.
FIN) Les données incluent les pesticides forestiers.
FRA) Les totaux représentent les principaux produits qui assurent plus de 80 pour cent du tonnage total utilisé. Les fongicides comprennent les composés à base de cuivre et de soufre mais non le soufre en l'état.
ITA) Depuis 1981, les données ne comprennent que les pesticides agricoles. Jusqu'en 1986 les données se rapportent au poids total de produit préparé.
NLD) Les données incluent les désinfectants qui correspondent environ, pour les années considérées, à la moitié de la consommation totale.
PRT) Poids total de produit préparé. 1980: données 1981.
ESP) Poids total de produit préparé. Les données comprennent des estimations.
SWE) Depuis 1987, une taxe spéciale est appliquée aux ventes de pesticides.
CHE) Les données se réfèrent aux ventes et incluent le Liechtenstein.
TUR) Exclut le soufre en poudre et le sulphate de cuivre. Poids total de produit préparé.
UKD) Grande Bretagne seulement. 1980: données du début des années 80.
HUN) Total: comprend les principaux produits qui assurent plus de 80 % du tonnage total utilisé. Fongicides: à partir de 1979, comprend les spécialités à base de cuivre et de soufre mais non le soufre en l'état.
POL) Total: comprend les principaux produits qui assurent plus de 80 % du tonnage total utilisé. Fongicides: à partir de 1979, comprend les spécialités à base de cuivre et de soufre mais non le soufre en l'état.

SOURCE: FAO, national statistical yearbooks, UNECE, UNEP/FAO, annuaires statistiques nationaux, CEE de l'ONU, PNUE

The following table presents numbers of selected domestic animals: cattle; sheep and goats; horses, mules and asses; and pigs.

Domestic animals exert various types of pressures on the environment (e.g. water and soil pollution, contribution to the greenhouse effect). Herbivores, particularly ruminants, contribute to emissions of methane through their digestive process and the production of manure. In sensitive areas, overgrazing can lead to erosion and desertification.

Le tableau suivant présente le nombre d'animaux dans des cheptels d'élevage sélectionnés : bovins ; ovins et caprins ; chevaux, mules et ânes ; et porcins.

Les animaux d'élevage exercent divers types de pressions sur l'environnement (p.ex. pollution de l'eau et des sols, contribution à l'effet de serre). Les herbivores et particulièrement les ruminants, contribuent aux émissions de méthane par leur processus de digestion et par la production de fumier et de lisier. Dans des zones sensibles le surpâturage peut provoquer des phénomènes d'érosion et de désertification.

LIVESTOCK, 1980-1994
CHEPTELS D'ANIMAUX D'ÉLEVAGE, 1980-1994

1 000 head/têtes

		Cattle/Bovins			Sheeps and Goats/ Ovins et Caprins			Horses, Mules and Asses/ Chevaux, Mules et Anes			Pigs/ Porcins		
		1980	1985	1994	1980	1985	1994	1980	1985	1994	1980	1985	1994
Canada	*	12126	11330	12306	507	539	719	374	394	429	10091	10573	11200
Mexico/Mexique		27742	31489	30702	16120	17354	16355	12555	12448	12611	16890	17233	18000
USA/Etats-Unis		111242	109582	100988	14099	12266	11609	5107	5255	3944	67318	54073	57904
Japan/Japon	*	4248	4698	4989	79	75	56	23	23	28	9998	10718	10621
Australia/Australie	*	26203	22738	24732	136166	150203	132850	499	421	274	2518	2512	2740
N.Zealand/N.Zélande	*	8131	7921	8550	68825	68281	50619	70	99	80	434	454	430
Austria/Autriche	*	2548	2669	2430	230	250	364	43	41	65	4004	4027	3800
Belgium/Belgique	*	3111	3210	3289	115	157	169	38	29	21	5067	5340	6948
Denmark/Danemark	*	2961	2623	2082	56	52	82	50	32	17	9957	9104	10864
Finland/Finlande	*	1753	1592	1230	108	71	85	33	38	49	1451	1256	1300
France		23919	23481	20112	13036	13782	11507	403	329	370	11446	10975	13383
Germany/Allemagne	*	20646	21536	15891	3186	3895	2448	446	471	530	34505	36808	26044
Greece/Grèce		932	725	608	12575	13074	15161	472	351	200	948	1061	1143
Iceland/Islande	*	57	73	77	797	709	500	50	54	82	11	14	22
Ireland/Irlande		6171	5861	6308	2369	3091	6000	98	77	68	1120	1020	1487
Italy/Italie		8719	9106	7683	10088	12187	11716	500	401	388	8807	9041	8200
Netherlands/Pays-Bas	*	5226	5248	4629	888	848	2211	67	62	66	10138	12383	13991
Norway/Norvège	*	985	970	1003	2077	2512	2405	18	16	22	664	692	745
Portugal		1324	1297	1322	5293	5695	6827	305	288	275	3500	3127	1487
Spain/Espagne		4679	5007	5000	16647	20155	26577	643	547	412	10714	11390	18188
Sweden/Suède	*	1935	1837	1830	392	426	483	57	57	86	2714	2589	2168
Switzerland/Suisse		2031	1926	1700	434	437	477	47	48	57	2205	1988	1680
Turkey/Turquie		15567	12410	11910	64801	53491	47674	2453	2062	1463	13	12	9
UK/Royaume-Uni	*	13363	12985	11735	21609	23946	29300	155	175	184	7813	7793	7910
Former CSFR/Ex-RFTS	*	4915	5150	3029	938	1122	650	47	46	30	7588	6743	6250
Hungary/Hongrie		1925	1901	1002	2942	2848	1316	130	106	76	8355	9237	5002
Poland/Pologne	*	12649	11055	7696	4207	4837	870	1780	1404	721	21326	17614	19466
North America/Amérique N.	*	151110	152401	143996	30726	30159	28683	18036	18097	16984	94299	81879	87104
Australia/Australie-NZ	*	34334	30659	33282	204991	218484	183469	569	520	354	2952	2966	3170
OECD/OCDE Europe	*	115927	112556	98839	154701	154778	163986	5878	5078	4355	115077	118620	119369
EU/UE-15	*	97287	97177	84149	86592	97629	112930	3310	2898	2731	112184	115914	116913
OECD/OCDE	*	305619	300314	281106	390497	403496	376194	24506	23718	21721	222326	214183	220264
World/Monde	*	1216464	1260066	1288124	1549696	1602156	1696149	110500	114524	116882	795400	791252	875407

Notes:
CAN)	Horses and mules only.
JPN)	Horses only.
AUS)	Horses and asses only.
NZL)	Horses only.
AUT)	Horses only.
BEL)	Data include Luxembourg; horses and mules only.
DNK)	Sheep only; horses only.
FIN)	Horses only.
DEU)	Horses only.
ISL)	Sheep only; horses only.
NLD)	Horses only.
NOR)	Horses only.
SWE)	Sheep only; horses only.
UKD)	Sheep only; horses and asses only.
CSFR)	Horses only.
POL)	Sheep only; horses only.
TOT)	Includes restrictions in the preceding notes.

Notes:
CAN)	Chevaux et mules uniquement.
JPN)	Chevaux uniquement.
AUS)	Chevaux et ânes uniquement.
NZL)	Chevaux uniquement.
AUT)	Chevaux uniquement.
BEL)	Les données incluent le Luxembourg; chevaux et mules uniquement.
DNK)	Ovins uniquement; chevaux uniquement.
FIN)	Chevaux uniquement.
DEU)	Chevaux uniquement.
ISL)	Ovins uniquement; chevaux uniquement.
NLD)	Chevaux uniquement.
NOR)	Chevaux uniquement.
SWE)	Ovins uniquement; chevaux uniquement.
UKD)	Ovins uniquement; chevaux et ânes uniquement.
RFTS)	Chevaux uniquement.
POL)	Ovins uniquement; chevaux uniquement.
TOT)	Restreints selon les notes précédentes.

Source: FAO

The following table presents trends in agricultural production. Data refer to indices showing the volume of aggregate agricultural production in comparison with the base year 1991. Production indices are based on price-weighted quantities of agricultural commodities produced after deduction of quantities used as seed and feed.

The development of agricultural production through specialisation and intensification of land use may give rise to environmental effects such as physical and chemical soil degradation or degradation of water resources.

Le tableau suivant présente l'évolution de la production agricole. Les données sont des indices indiquant le volume global de la production agricole par rapport à l'année de référence 1991. Les indices de production sont fondés sur la production des divers produits agricoles, pondérée par les prix, déduction faite des quantités utilisées comme semences ou pour l'alimentation animale.

Le développement de la production agricole par la spécialisation et l'intensification des modes d'exploitation peut avoir des effets sur l'environnement tels que la dégradation physique et chimique des sols ou la dégradation de la qualité des ressources en eau.

AGRICULTURAL PRODUCTION (a), 1980-1994
PRODUCTION AGRICOLE (a), 1980-1994

Index 1991=100

	1980	1981	1982	1983	1984	1985	1986	1987	1988	1989	1990	1991	1992	1993	1994
Canada	78	85	91	86	85	89	96	90	80	88	100	100	97	96	100
Mexico/Mexique	85	88	88	92	92	95	95	95	95	88	97	100	98	105	106
USA/Etats-Unis	91	101	99	84	97	102	95	95	90	97	100	100	109	99	115
Japan/Japon	105	108	112	111	117	118	117	112	107	109	108	100	106	90	110
Australia/Australie	82	89	80	98	95	96	98	95	101	97	102	100	109	114	99
N.Zealand/N.Zélande	94	98	98	100	101	108	104	102	104	102	96	100	102	100	102
Austria/Autriche	92	87	99	94	97	96	97	96	102	98	99	100	97	98	100
Belgium/Belgique *	74	80	75	70	78	78	84	81	87	89	84	100	107	111	111
Denmark/Danemark	73	74	81	76	92	90	87	84	89	93	100	100	89	98	96
Finland/Finlande	94	85	96	106	106	103	102	90	94	105	111	100	91	97	98
France	96	93	99	96	104	101	100	104	101	99	101	100	106	98	96
Germany/Allemagne	87	88	92	90	97	97	102	99	102	101	101	100	93	95	91
Greece/Grèce	91	91	93	88	91	97	93	90	97	100	85	100	98	98	98
Iceland/Islande	114	115	117	115	119	121	117	113	98	96	95	100	102	91	93
Ireland/Irlande	86	73	78	80	88	90	91	92	89	86	97	100	102	102	98
Italy/Italie	96	95	93	100	94	96	94	97	94	96	92	100	100	97	95
Netherlands/Pays-Bas	82	91	92	91	93	92	100	97	94	101	96	100	103	110	106
Norway/Norvège	88	90	95	90	97	94	90	94	93	93	104	100	93	104	102
Portugal	71	62	75	67	74	76	75	84	68	92	98	100	86	74	79
Spain/Espagne	89	80	89	82	97	93	92	103	100	100	105	100	102	96	91
Sweden/Suède	107	111	114	112	124	117	114	100	99	110	117	100	93	104	96
Switzerland/Suisse	89	88	97	93	96	96	98	95	95	103	99	100	100	97	96
Turkey/Turquie	74	77	80	78	87	86	96	93	98	94	100	100	100	100	99
UK/Royaume-Uni	90	88	90	92	101	96	96	96	93	95	97	100	98	90	90

Notes:
a)   Data refer to agricultural disposable production for any use except as seed and feed.
BEL) Data for Belgium include Luxembourg.

Notes:
a)   Les données représentent la production agricole disponible pour toute autre utilisation que les semences, les pâturages et le fourrage.
BEL) Les données incluent le Luxembourg.

Source: OECD/OCDE,FAO

12. GENERAL DATA

12. DONNÉES GÉNÉRALES

INTRODUCTION

This section contains general quantitative information concerning population, area, gross domestic product and private final consumption expenditure in OECD countries. These data provide background information, as well as inputs for the calculation of derived figures (e.g. per capita figures). It also includes a list of multilateral conventions on the environment.

INTRODUCTION

Cette section contient des renseignements quantitatifs généraux concernant la population, la superficie, le produit intérieur brut et la consommation finale privée dans les pays de l'OCDE. Les tableaux qui y sont présentés fournissent des renseignements de base ainsi que les éléments pour le calcul de chiffres dérivés (e.g. données par habitant). Elle inclut aussi une liste des conventions multilatérales concernant l'environnement.

Population, shown in the following table, is defined as all nationals present in or temporarily absent from a country, and aliens permanently settled in the country.

La population est définie comme l'ensemble des nationaux présents ou temporairement absents du pays, et des étrangers établis en permanence dans le pays.

NATIONAL POPULATIONS (a), 1980-1994
POPULATIONS NATIONALES (a), 1980-1994

1000

		1980	1985	1986	1987	1988	1989	1990	1991	1992	1993	1994
Canada		24593	25942	26204	26550	26895	27379	27791	28118	28436	28753	29100
Mexico/Mexique		69655	77938	79570	81200	82840	84490	86150	87840	89540	91210	93010
USA/Etats-Unis	*	227757	239279	241625	243942	246307	248781	249924	252137	255078	257908	260730
Japan/Japon	*	116800	120750	121490	122090	122610	123120	123540	123920	124320	124670	124960
Australia/Australie	*	14695	15788	16018	16264	16518	16803	17045	17284	17489	17657	17840
N.Zealand/N.Zélande	*	3144	3272	3277	3304	3317	3330	3363	3406	3443	3480	3520
Austria/Autriche		7549	7558	7566	7575	7595	7624	7718	7823	7884	7991	8031
Belgium/Belgique		9847	9858	9862	9870	9921	9938	9967	10005	10045	10084	10124
Denmark/Danemark	*	5125	5114	5121	5127	5130	5133	5141	5154	5171	5189	5200
Finland/Finlande		4780	4902	4918	4932	4946	4964	4986	5029	5042	5066	5090
France		53880	55284	55547	55824	56118	56423	56735	57055	57374	57667	57960
Germany/Allemagne		78275	77619	77634	77718	78116	78677	79565	79884	80595	81190	81410
w.Germany/Allemagne occ.		61538	60975	61010	61077	61450	62063	63254	64074	64865	65532	..
Greece/Grèce	*	9642	9934	9964	9984	10005	10038	10089	10200	10314	10368	10430
Iceland/Islande		228	241	243	246	250	253	255	258	260	262	265
Ireland/Irlande		3401	3540	3541	3542	3538	3515	3503	3524	3547	3560	3570
Italy/Italie		56434	56674	56675	56674	56688	56705	56737	56760	56859	57070	57190
Luxembourg		365	367	370	372	375	378	382	385	390	395	398
Netherlands/Pays-Bas		14150	14491	14572	14665	14760	14849	14951	15070	15184	15300	15400
Norway/Norvège		4087	4153	4169	4187	4209	4227	4241	4262	4287	4312	4337
Portugal	*	9819	10014	10007	9981	9955	9920	9873	9860	9865	9887	9900
Spain/Espagne	*	37386	38505	38668	38716	38809	38888	38959	38916	39006	39083	39140
Sweden/Suède		8311	8350	8370	8398	8436	8493	8566	8617	8668	8718	8770
Switzerland/Suisse	*	6385	6533	6573	6619	6672	6647	6712	6800	6875	6938	6990
Turkey/Turquie		44737	50664	51630	52747	53970	55255	56570	57306	58400	59490	60580
UK/Royaume-Uni		56314	56618	56763	56930	57065	57236	57411	57808	58007	58191	58375
Former CSFR/Ex-RFTS		15260	15445	15470	15496	15520	15543	15562	15579	15594	15609	15628
Hungary/Hongrie		10707	10579	10534	10486	10442	10385	10365	10348	10327	10293	10210
Poland/Pologne		35574	37203	37456	37664	37862	37963	38119	38245	38365	38460	38362
North America/Amérique N.		322005	343159	347399	351692	356042	360650	363865	368095	373054	377871	382840
Australia/Australie-NZ		17839	19060	19295	19568	19835	20133	20408	20690	20932	21137	21360
OECD/OCDE Europe		410715	420419	422193	424107	426558	429163	432361	434716	437773	440761	443160
EU/UE-15		355278	358828	359578	360308	361457	362781	364583	366090	367951	369759	370988
OECD/OCDE		867359	903388	910377	917457	925045	933066	940174	947421	956079	964439	972320
World/Monde		4444331	4845962	4916419	4996989	5114979	5204120	5284808	5294252	5458981	5544612	5630240

Notes:
a)   Resident population.
USA)   Includes armed forces overseas; break in time series in 1991.
JPN)   Excludes allied military and civilian personnel and their dependants.
AUS)   Excludes national armed forces stationed abroad.
NZL)   Excludes national armed forces stationed abroad.
DNK)   Excludes Faroe Islands and Greenland.
GRC)   Excludes national armed forces stationed abroad.
PRT)   Includes Azores and Madera Islands.
ESP)   Includes Baleares and Canary Islands; break in time series in 1991.
CHE)   Excludes seasonal foreign workers.

Notes:
a)   Population résidente.
USA)   Inclut les forces armées stationnées outre-mer; rupture de série en 1991.
JPN)   Exclut les militaires et les civils alliés ainsi que les personnes à leur charge.
AUS)   Exclut les militaires stationnés hors du pays.
NZL)   Exclut les militaires stationnés hors du pays.
DNK)   Exclut le Groenland et les îles Feroé.
GRC)   Exclut les militaires stationnés hors du pays.
PRT)   Inclut les îles des Açores et de Madère.
ESP)   Inclut les îles Baléares et Canaries; rupture de série en 1991.
CHE)   Exclut les travailleurs étrangers saisonniers.

Source: OECD/OCDE, FAO

Data for total areas provided in the next table include agricultural land, forest land and other areas, such as built-up land. They also include inland waters (rivers, lakes, artificial waters, impoundments, coastal lagoons) but exclude "internal" waters such as estuaries and waters lying on the landward side of what is considered the normal baseline along the coast.

Les données sur les superficies totales des pays dans le tableau suivant comprennent les sols agricoles, les forêts, et les autres sols tels que les sols bâtis. Ces données incluent également les eaux intérieures (rivières, lacs, canaux et réservoirs artificiels, lagunes et plans d'eaux côtiers situés à l'intérieur des terres), mais excluent les eaux littorales telles que les estuaires et les eaux situées du côté de la terre par rapport à la ligne considerée comme ligne de base normale le long de la côte.

TOTAL AREA, 1993
SUPERFICIE TOTALE, 1993

	Area/Superficie 1000 km^2
Canada	9976.1
Mexico/Mexique	1958.2
USA/Etats-Unis	9809.4
Japan/Japon	377.8
Australia/Australie	7713.4
New Zealand/Nouvelle Zélande	270.0
Austria/Autriche	83.9
Belgium/Belgique	30.5
Denmark/Danemark	43.1
Finland/Finlande	338.1
France	551.5
Germany/Allemagne	356.9
w.Germany/Allemagne occ.	248.6
Greece/Grèce	132.0
Iceland/Islande	104.0
Ireland/Irlande	70.3
Italy/Italie	301.3
Luxembourg	2.6
Netherlands/Pays-Bas	37.3
Norway/Norvège	323.9
Portugal	92.0
Spain/Espagne	504.8
Sweden/Suède	450.0
Switzerland/Suisse	41.3
Turkey/Turquie	779.5
UK/Royaume-Uni	244.9
CSFR/RFTS	127.9
Hungary/Hongrie	93.0
Poland/Pologne	312.7
North America/Amérique N.	21743.8
Australia/Australie-NZ	7983.4
OECD/OCDE Europe	4487.7
EU/UE-15	3239.1
OECD/OCDE	34592.6
World/Monde	134223.6

Notes:
NLD) Excluding Lake IJssel (1 708 km^2) and internal waters
(Wadden Sea and North Sea: 2 473 km^2).
SWE) Including internal waters.

Notes:
NLD) A l'exclusion du Lac IJssel (1 708 km^2) et des eaux littorales
(mer des Wadden et mer du Nord : 2 473 km^2).
SWE) Inclut les eaux littorales.

Source: OECD/OCDE, FAO

The following table presents population density calculated using the value of total land area including inland waters (lakes, rivers, etc.). See the two preceding tables for the definition of national population and total area.

Le tableau suivant présente la densité de population calculée par rapport à la superficie totale des terres comprenant les eaux intérieures (lacs, rivières, etc.). Voir les deux tableaux précédents pour les définitions des populations nationales et des superficies totales des pays.

POPULATION DENSITY, 1980-1993
DENSITÉ DE POPULATION, 1980-1993

inhabitants per km²/habitants par km²

	1980	1981	1982	1983	1984	1985	1986	1987	1988	1989	1990	1991	1992	1993
Canada	2.5	2.5	2.5	2.6	2.6	2.6	2.6	2.7	2.7	2.7	2.8	2.8	2.9	2.9
Mexico/Mexique	35.6	36.4	37.3	38.1	39.0	39.8	40.6	41.5	42.3	43.1	44.0	44.9	45.7	46.6
USA/Etats-Unis	23.2	23.5	23.7	23.9	24.2	24.4	24.6	24.9	25.1	25.4	25.5	25.7	26.0	26.3
Japan/Japon	309.2	311.4	313.5	315.7	317.7	319.6	321.6	323.2	324.5	325.9	327.0	328.0	329.1	330.0
Australia/Australie	1.9	1.9	2.0	2.0	2.0	2.0	2.1	2.1	2.1	2.2	2.2	2.2	2.3	2.3
N.Zealand/N.Zélande	11.6	11.7	11.8	11.9	12.1	12.1	12.1	12.2	12.3	12.3	12.5	12.6	12.8	12.9
Austria/Autriche	90.0	90.2	90.3	90.1	90.1	90.1	90.2	90.3	90.6	90.9	92.0	93.3	94.0	95.3
Belgium/Belgique	322.7	322.9	323.0	323.0	323.0	323.1	323.2	323.5	325.1	325.7	326.6	327.9	329.2	330.5
Denmark/Danemark	119.0	118.9	118.8	118.7	118.7	118.7	118.9	119.0	119.1	119.1	119.3	119.6	120.0	120.4
Finland/Finlande	14.1	14.2	14.3	14.4	14.4	14.5	14.5	14.6	14.6	14.7	14.7	14.9	14.9	15.0
France	97.7	98.2	98.8	99.3	99.8	100.2	100.7	101.2	101.8	102.3	102.9	103.5	104.0	104.6
Germany/Allemagne	219.3	219.7	219.4	218.7	218.0	217.5	217.5	217.8	218.9	220.4	222.9	223.8	225.8	227.5
w.Germany/Allemagne occ.	247.6	248.1	247.8	246.9	245.9	245.3	245.4	245.7	247.2	249.7	254.5	257.8	260.9	263.6
Greece/Grèce	73.1	73.7	74.2	74.6	75.0	75.3	75.5	75.6	75.8	76.1	76.4	77.3	78.1	78.6
Iceland/Islande	2.2	2.2	2.3	2.3	2.3	2.3	2.3	2.4	2.4	2.4	2.5	2.5	2.5	2.5
Ireland/Irlande	48.4	49.0	49.5	49.9	50.2	50.4	50.4	50.4	50.3	50.0	49.8	50.1	50.5	50.7
Italy/Italie	187.3	187.6	187.8	188.0	188.0	188.1	188.1	188.1	188.2	188.2	188.3	188.4	188.7	189.4
Luxembourg	141.1	141.5	141.5	141.5	141.5	141.9	143.1	143.9	145.0	146.2	147.7	148.9	150.8	152.7
Netherlands/Pays-Bas	379.3	381.9	383.6	385.3	386.8	388.2	390.4	392.8	395.4	397.8	400.5	403.7	406.8	409.9
Norway/Norvège	12.6	12.7	12.7	12.7	12.8	12.8	12.9	12.9	13.0	13.1	13.1	13.2	13.2	13.3
Portugal	106.7	107.4	108.0	108.4	108.8	108.9	108.8	108.5	108.2	107.8	107.3	107.2	107.2	107.5
Spain/Espagne	74.1	74.8	75.2	75.6	76.0	76.3	76.6	76.7	76.9	77.0	77.2	77.1	77.3	77.4
Sweden/Suède	18.5	18.5	18.5	18.5	18.5	18.6	18.6	18.7	18.7	18.9	19.0	19.2	19.3	19.4
Switzerland/Suisse	154.7	155.7	156.6	157.0	157.6	158.2	159.2	160.3	161.6	161.0	162.6	164.7	166.5	168.1
Turkey/Turquie	57.4	58.8	60.3	61.8	63.4	65.0	66.2	67.7	69.2	70.9	72.6	73.5	74.9	76.3
UK/Royaume-Uni	230.0	230.2	230.1	230.2	230.7	231.2	231.8	232.5	233.0	233.7	234.4	236.1	236.9	237.6
Former CSFR/Ex-RFTS	119.3	119.8	120.2	120.4	120.6	120.8	121.0	121.2	121.4	121.6	121.7	121.8	122.0	122.1
Hungary/Hongrie	115.1	115.0	114.8	114.5	114.2	113.7	113.2	112.7	112.2	111.6	111.4	111.2	111.0	110.6
Poland/Pologne	113.8	114.8	115.8	116.9	118.0	119.0	119.8	120.5	121.1	121.4	121.9	122.3	122.7	123.0
North America/Amérique N.	14.8	15.0	15.2	15.4	15.6	15.8	16.0	16.2	16.4	16.6	16.7	16.9	17.2	17.4
Australia/Australie-NZ	2.2	2.3	2.3	2.3	2.4	2.4	2.4	2.5	2.5	2.5	2.6	2.6	2.6	2.6
OECD/OCDE Europe	91.5	92.1	92.5	92.9	93.3	93.7	94.1	94.5	95.1	95.6	96.3	96.9	97.6	98.2
EU/UE-15	109.7	110.1	110.3	110.5	110.6	110.8	111.0	111.2	111.6	112.0	112.6	113.0	113.6	114.2
OECD/OCDE	25.1	25.3	25.5	25.7	25.9	26.1	26.3	26.5	26.7	27.0	27.2	27.4	27.6	27.9
World/Monde	33.1	33.6	34.2	34.8	35.4	36.1	36.6	37.2	38.1	38.7	39.3	39.4	40.7	41.3

Notes:
See notes of preceding tables.

Notes:
Voir les notes des tableaux précédents.

Source: OECD/OCDE, FAO

The next table shows the changes in volume of gross domestic product (GDP) since 1980 and its value in 1991.

Data are expressed as indices (1991=100) calculated from the value of GDP at constant prices. The last column provides the 1991 GDP value expressed in US$ at 1991 price levels and purchasing power parities.

Le tableau suivant montre l'évolution en volume du produit intérieur brut (PIB) depuis 1980 et sa valeur en 1991.

Les données sont exprimées en indices (1991=100) calculés à partir des valeurs du PIB aux prix constants. La dernière colonne donne la valeur en 1991 du PIB exprimée en $EU aux niveaux de prix et parités de pouvoir d'achat de 1991.

TRENDS IN GROSS DOMESTIC PRODUCT (a), 1980-1995
ÉVOLUTION DU PRODUIT INTÉRIEUR BRUT (a), 1980-1995

	Index (1991=100)																billion US$/ milliards de $EU
	1980	1981	1982	1983	1984	1985	1986	1987	1988	1989	1990	1991	1992	1993	1994	1995b)	1991
Canada	76.5	79.3	76.8	79.2	84.2	88.2	91.2	95.0	99.7	102.1	101.9	100.0	100.6	102.8	107.5	111.6	522.9
Mexico/Mexique	81.8	89.0	88.4	84.6	87.6	90.1	86.7	88.3	89.4	92.4	96.5	100.0	102.1	102.9	106.6	103.4	438.7
USA/Etats-Unis	77.6	79.0	77.3	80.3	85.2	87.9	90.5	93.3	96.9	99.4	100.6	100.0	102.3	105.5	109.8	113.3	5724.8
Japan/Japon	64.1	66.4	68.5	70.4	73.4	77.0	79.0	82.3	87.4	91.5	95.9	100.0	101.1	100.9	101.5	102.8	2348.4
Australia/Australie	73.8	76.3	76.2	76.7	82.4	86.3	88.1	92.2	95.9	100.1	101.5	100.0	102.0	106.0	111.7	116.0	277.9
N.Zealand/N.Zélande	82.5	86.3	89.2	91.4	99.3	100.8	102.1	101.0	105.3	103.7	103.8	100.0	100.8	106.0	110.0	114.2	46.1
Austria/Autriche	78.5	78.3	79.2	80.7	81.8	83.8	84.8	86.2	89.7	93.2	97.1	100.0	101.8	101.8	104.6	107.5	135.7
Belgium/Belgique	81.1	80.3	81.5	81.9	83.7	84.4	85.6	87.3	91.5	94.7	97.8	100.0	101.9	100.1	102.4	105.2	171.7
Denmark/Danemark	80.7	80.0	82.4	84.5	88.2	92.0	95.3	95.6	96.7	97.3	98.7	100.0	100.8	102.3	106.8	110.5	89.9
Finland/Finlande	78.9	80.2	83.0	85.5	88.1	91.1	93.2	97.1	101.8	107.6	107.6	100.0	96.4	94.9	98.6	103.3	77.8
France	78.6	79.5	81.5	82.1	83.2	84.8	86.9	88.9	92.8	96.8	99.2	100.0	101.3	99.9	102.5	105.6	1037.7
Germany/Allemagne	..	..	..	..	..	..	..	..	..	..	..	100.0	102.2	101.1	103.9	107.0	1359.0
w.Germany/Allem.occ.	76.6	76.7	75.9	77.3	79.5	81.1	83.0	84.2	87.3	90.5	95.7	100.0	101.6	99.4	..	..	1257.8
Greece/Grèce	83.4	83.4	83.7	84.1	86.4	89.1	90.5	90.1	94.1	97.9	96.9	100.0	100.8	100.2	101.7	103.6	98.3
Iceland/Islande	75.9	79.2	80.5	78.9	82.2	85.2	90.7	98.6	98.3	98.5	99.0	100.0	96.8	98.0	100.9	103.4	4.5
Ireland/Irlande	67.6	69.9	71.5	71.3	74.4	76.7	75.6	79.9	83.4	89.5	97.2	100.0	105.0	109.3	115.8	122.6	42.2
Italy/Italie	79.4	79.8	80.0	80.8	82.9	85.1	87.6	90.3	94.0	96.7	98.8	100.0	100.7	99.5	101.7	104.7	974.3
Luxembourg	68.3	67.9	68.7	70.8	75.1	77.3	81.0	83.4	88.2	94.0	97.0	100.0	101.9	103.6	106.4	109.7	8.1
Netherl./Pays-Bas	80.1	79.5	78.4	79.5	82.0	84.1	86.4	87.4	89.7	93.9	97.8	100.0	101.3	101.6	104.2	107.5	247.5
Norway/Norvège	77.2	77.9	78.2	81.8	86.5	91.1	94.9	96.8	96.3	96.8	98.4	100.0	103.4	105.8	111.2	116.4	71.5
Portugal	72.5	73.7	75.2	75.1	73.7	75.8	79.5	83.9	88.8	93.9	97.9	100.0	101.1	99.9	101.2	104.1	102.6
Spain/Espagne	72.8	72.6	73.8	75.4	76.5	78.5	81.0	85.6	90.0	94.3	97.8	100.0	100.7	99.6	101.6	104.7	495.8
Sweden/Suède	82.9	82.9	83.7	85.2	88.6	90.3	92.4	95.3	97.5	99.8	101.1	100.0	98.6	96.0	98.1	100.6	145.1
Switzerland/Suisse	81.4	82.5	81.8	82.6	84.1	87.2	89.7	91.5	94.1	97.8	100.0	100.0	99.7	98.8	101.0	102.7	148.0
Turkey/Turquie	59.6	62.5	64.7	68.0	72.5	75.6	80.9	88.6	90.5	90.7	99.1	100.0	106.0	113.9	107.8	110.8	275.1
UK/Royaume-Uni	78.4	77.4	78.7	81.6	83.5	86.5	90.3	94.7	99.4	101.6	102.0	100.0	99.5	101.7	105.5	109.1	903.3
N. America/Amérique N.	77.8	79.6	77.9	80.5	85.3	88.1	90.3	93.1	96.7	99.1	100.4	100.0	102.1	105.1	109.4	112.5	6686.4
Australia/Australie-NZ	75.0	77.7	78.0	78.8	84.8	88.4	90.1	93.4	97.3	100.6	101.8	100.0	101.8	106.0	111.5	115.7	324.0
OECD/OCDE Europe *	77.2	77.4	78.1	79.6	81.5	83.7	86.2	88.9	92.5	95.7	98.7	100.0	101.1	100.7	..	..	6286.7
EU/UE-15 *	77.9	78.0	78.7	80.0	81.8	83.9	86.3	88.8	92.6	95.8	98.6	100.0	100.8	100.1	..	..	5787.7
OECD/OCDE *	75.4	76.7	76.6	78.5	82.0	84.7	87.0	89.8	93.6	96.6	99.1	100.0	101.5	102.7	..	..	15645.5

Notes:
a)   GDP at 1991 price levels and purchasing power parities.
b)   Estimates.
TOT) Includes western Germany only.

Notes:
a)   PIB aux niveaux de prix et parités de pouvoir d'achat de 1991.
b)   Données estimées.
TOT) Incluent l'Allemagne occidentale uniquement.

Source: OECD/OCDE

The following table shows the structure of GDP by main economic sector, and changes since 1974. Data represent the value added by economic sector, thus showing sectoral contributions to GDP. They are expressed as a percentage of GDP.

Le tableau suivant montre la structure du PIB, selon les principaux secteurs de l'économie, et son évolution depuis 1974. Les données représentent la valeur ajoutée par secteur économique et donc la contribution de chacun de ces secteurs à la création du PIB. Elles sont exprimées en pourcentage du PIB.

STRUCTURE OF GROSS DOMESTIC PRODUCT, OECD countries, 1974-1992
STRUCTURE DU PRODUIT INTÉRIEUR BRUT, pays de l'OCDE, 1974-1992

Value added as % of GDP/
Valeur ajoutée en % du PIB

		Agriculture (a)				Industry/Industrie (b)				Services (c)			
		1974	1980	1985	1992 (d)	1974	1980	1985	1992 (d)	1974	1980	1985	1992 (d)
Canada		4.6	3.8	2.8	2.1	32.9	32.9	31.4	26.3	62.5	63.3	65.8	71.6
Mexico/Mexique		..	8.2	9.1	7.0	..	32.8	33.4	29.6	..	59.0	57.6	63.4
USA/Etats-Unis		3.6	2.5	2.1	2.0	33.5	33.5	31.1	27.0	62.9	64.0	66.8	71.0
Japan/Japon		5.6	3.7	3.2	2.2	44.7	42.0	41.0	41.1	49.7	54.3	55.8	56.7
Australia/Australie		5.8	5.3	3.9	3.2	36.6	36.5	34.4	29.4	57.6	58.2	61.7	67.4
N.Zealand/N.Zélande		8.7	10.8	8.7	7.3	34.0	31.3	31.2	25.9	57.3	57.9	60.0	66.8
Austria/Autriche		5.3	4.5	3.3	2.4	42.8	39.5	36.9	35.1	51.9	56.0	59.8	62.5
Belgium/Belgique		3.0	2.1	2.2	1.6	41.1	34.1	31.5	29.0	55.9	63.8	66.3	69.4
Denmark/Danemark		5.9	4.8	4.9	3.2	27.8	25.0	24.2	23.7	66.3	70.2	70.9	73.1
Finland/Finlande		9.3	8.8	7.3	4.5	38.9	35.6	32.7	27.5	51.8	55.6	59.9	68.0
France		5.7	4.2	3.9	2.8	37.7	33.7	30.5	28.5	56.6	62.1	65.6	68.7
w.Germany/Allemagne occ.		2.7	2.1	1.8	1.2	46.2	42.5	40.7	36.6	51.1	55.4	57.5	62.2
Greece/Grèce		17.8	15.8	15.5	12.5	27.5	27.7	26.2	22.2	54.7	56.5	58.3	65.3
Iceland/Islande		10.6	9.7	9.5	9.6	25.5	26.3	26.7	22.1	63.9	64.0	63.8	68.3
Ireland/Irlande		14.0	10.6	9.6	7.2	34.6	34.0	34.4	35.5	51.4	55.4	56.0	57.3
Italy/Italie		6.9	5.8	4.5	3.1	41.1	39.0	35.2	32.1	52.0	55.2	60.3	64.8
Luxembourg		3.0	2.6	2.6	1.4	52.2	38.7	37.9	33.7	44.8	58.7	59.5	64.9
Netherlands/Pays-Bas		4.1	3.5	3.9	3.6	36.6	32.8	32.4	27.8	59.3	63.7	63.7	68.6
Norway/Norvège		5.0	3.8	3.0	2.9	32.9	39.6	41.3	34.7	62.1	56.6	55.7	62.4
Portugal		14.0	10.3	8.0	5.8	42.0	40.2	39.6	37.8	44.0	49.5	52.4	56.4
Spain/Espagne		9.5	7.1	5.9	4.1	38.3	38.6	37.3	34.4	52.2	54.3	56.8	61.5
Sweden/Suède		4.5	3.3	3.3	2.1	37.6	30.5	30.5	27.4	57.9	66.1	66.3	70.5
Switzerland/Suisse		..	..	3.6	3.0	..	..	35.5	33.5	..	..	60.9	63.5
Turkey/Turquie		26.3	21.7	17.8	15.0	27.1	31.0	35.6	32.4	46.6	47.3	46.6	52.6
UK/Royaume-Uni		2.4	1.8	1.6	1.6	36.9	36.6	34.7	27.8	60.7	61.6	63.7	70.6
OECD/OCDE Europe	*	5.9	4.8	4.2	3.3	39.4	37.1	35.1	31.5	54.7	58.1	60.7	65.2
EU/UE-15	*	5.2	4.2	3.6	2.7	39.9	37.3	34.9	31.4	54.9	58.6	61.4	65.9
OECD/OCDE	*	4.9	3.9	3.4	2.7	37.4	36.0	34.2	31.0	57.7	60.1	62.5	66.3

Notes:
a)   Also includes hunting, forestry and fishing.
b)   ISIC: groups 2 through 5.
c)   Includes import duties and other adjustments; excludes imputed bank service charge.
d)   Or latest year available.
TOT) Includes western Germany only; 1974: excludes Mexico; 1974 and 1980: excludes Switzerland.

Notes:
a)   Inclut également la chasse, la sylviculture et la pêche.
b)   Catégories 1 à 5 de la CITI.
c)   Inclut les droits et les taxes sur les importations et les autres ajustements ; exclut la production imputée de services bancaires.
d)   Ou dernière année disponible.
TOT) Inclut l'Allemagne occidentale uniquement; 1974: Mexique non compris; 1974 et 1980: Suisse non comprise.

Source: OECD/OCDE

The following table shows the changes in volume of private final consumption expenditure since 1980 and its value in 1991.

Data are expressed as indices (1991=100) calculated from the value of private final consumption expenditure at constant prices. The last column provides the 1991 value expressed in US$ at 1991 price levels and purchasing power parities.

Ce tableau suivant montre l'évolution en volume de la consommation finale privée depuis 1980 et sa valeur en 1991.

Les données sont exprimées en indices (1991=100) calculés à partir des valeurs de la consommation finale privée aux prix constants. La dernière colonne donne la valeur en 1991 exprimée en $EU aux niveaux de prix et parités de pouvoir d'achat de 1991.

TRENDS IN PRIVATE FINAL CONSUMPTION EXPENDITURE (a), OECD countries, 1980-1993
ÉVOLUTION DE LA CONSOMMATION FINALE PRIVÉE (a), pays de l'OCDE, 1980-1993

	Index (1991=100)														billion US$/ milliards de $EU
	1980	1981	1982	1983	1984	1985	1986	1987	1988	1989	1990	1991	1992	1993	1991
Canada	75.5	77.3	75.2	77.8	81.5	85.7	89.4	93.3	97.4	100.6	101.5	100.0	101.4	103.1	298.7
Mexico/Mexique	80.4	86.3	84.2	79.7	82.3	85.2	82.8	82.7	84.2	89.9	95.3	100.0	103.9	104.1	312.8
USA/Etats-Unis	74.6	75.6	76.3	79.7	83.6	87.3	90.6	93.2	96.7	98.7	100.2	100.0	103.0	106.6	3776.5
Japan/Japon	68.3	69.4	72.5	75.0	77.0	79.6	82.3	85.8	90.3	94.2	97.9	100.0	101.7	102.7	1248.8
Australia/Australie	75.2	78.4	79.7	80.4	83.0	86.8	87.4	90.3	94.3	98.6	98.7	100.0	102.5	105.1	168.1
N.Zealand/N.Zélande	85.7	87.5	86.3	88.9	92.4	93.6	97.8	99.4	101.3	101.8	101.6	100.0	100.3	103.4	28.2
Austria/Autriche	76.4	76.7	77.6	81.5	81.4	83.3	84.8	87.5	90.6	93.8	97.1	100.0	101.9	102.1	75.2
Belgium/Belgique	82.7	81.8	82.9	81.6	82.6	84.2	86.1	88.7	91.2	94.7	97.0	100.0	102.8	102.6	105.4
Denmark/Danemark	87.2	85.2	86.4	88.7	91.7	96.2	101.7	100.2	99.2	98.8	98.8	100.0	101.1	103.5	44.5
Finland/Finlande	73.8	74.8	78.5	80.9	83.4	86.5	90.0	94.7	99.5	103.8	103.7	100.0	95.1	91.4	39.3
France	78.0	79.4	82.0	82.7	83.4	85.3	88.4	90.8	93.5	96.2	98.6	100.0	101.3	101.7	614.4
w.Germany/Allem.occ.	77.0	76.6	75.5	76.7	78.0	79.4	82.1	84.9	87.3	89.7	94.6	100.0	101.4	100.9	709.3
Greece/Grèce	77.4	79.0	82.1	82.3	83.7	87.0	87.5	88.6	91.8	95.8	97.8	100.0	101.8	102.0	56.4
Iceland/Islande	73.4	78.0	81.8	77.2	80.1	83.5	89.2	103.7	99.7	95.6	96.0	100.0	95.6	91.3	2.7
Ireland/Irlande	79.7	81.1	75.3	76.0	77.5	81.1	82.7	85.4	89.2	96.3	97.5	100.0	102.9	104.1	24.4
Italy/Italie	73.7	75.0	75.7	76.1	77.8	80.2	83.7	87.4	91.4	94.7	97.5	100.0	101.7	98.7	621.6
Luxembourg	72.2	73.5	73.7	74.1	75.2	77.2	79.3	83.3	86.0	89.1	93.4	100.0	104.5	..	5.0
Netherlands/Pays-Bas	84.1	82.0	81.1	81.8	82.6	84.6	86.8	89.2	89.9	93.1	97.0	100.0	102.6	103.3	150.8
Norway/Norvège	83.5	84.5	86.0	87.3	89.6	98.5	104.0	103.0	100.1	97.3	100.0	100.0	101.8	100.9	32.6
Portugal	71.7	73.8	75.5	74.5	72.3	72.8	76.8	81.5	86.1	89.2	95.4	100.0	103.7	104.1	63.5
Spain/Espagne	75.8	74.8	74.7	75.0	74.8	77.4	80.0	84.6	88.8	93.8	97.2	100.0	102.1	100.1	299.4
Sweden/Suède	85.1	84.7	85.2	83.2	84.4	86.6	90.8	95.2	97.7	99.1	98.9	100.0	98.6	95.0	74.8
Switzerland/Suisse	84.1	84.6	84.6	86.0	87.3	88.6	91.1	93.0	95.0	97.1	98.6	100.0	99.8	99.0	84.3
Turkey/Turquie	72.5	67.0	71.6	76.4	82.6	82.1	86.9	86.6	87.7	86.7	98.1	100.0	103.3	110.6	178.4
UK/Royaume-Uni	72.7	72.8	73.5	76.9	78.4	81.4	87.0	91.6	98.5	101.7	102.3	100.0	100.0	102.6	576.9
N.America/Amérique N.	75.1	76.4	76.8	79.5	83.4	87.0	89.9	92.4	95.9	98.2	100.0	100.0	102.9	106.2	4388.0
Australia/Australie-NZ	76.7	79.7	80.6	81.6	84.3	87.7	88.9	91.6	95.3	99.0	99.1	100.0	102.2	104.9	196.3
OECD/OCDE Europe *	76.5	76.5	77.3	78.5	79.9	82.0	85.4	88.5	91.9	94.8	97.9	100.0	101.4	..	3759.0
EU/UE-15 *	76.5	76.7	77.3	78.4	79.5	81.7	85.1	88.4	92.0	95.1	97.9	100.0	101.3	..	3461.0
OECD/OCDE *	74.8	75.6	76.5	78.6	81.2	84.1	87.2	90.0	93.6	96.4	98.9	100.0	102.1	..	9592.1

Notes:
a)   Private final consumption expenditure at 1991 price levels and purchasing power parities.
TOT) Includes western Germany only.

Source: OECD/OCDE

Notes:
a)   Consommation finale privée exprimée aux niveaux de prix et parité de pouvoir d'achat de 1991.
TOT) Inclut l'Allemagne occidentale uniquement.

The following table lists multilateral conventions concerning the environment over the past 60 years. It includes conventions on sea pollution, nuclear activities, fauna and flora, global and regional air pollution, the Rhine River and other topics. The number of OECD and other country signatures and ratifications, and the date of entry into force, are given. Only multilateral conventions signed or ratified by at least one OECD country are included.

Efforts to improve the environment have been made at the international level. The international dimensions of environmental problems (regional problems, transboundary problems, global problems, trade problems) are increasingly recognised.

Le tableau suivant présente la liste des conventions multilatérales des soixante dernières années concernant l'environnement. Il comprend des conventions sur la pollution de la mer, les activités nucléaires, la faune et la flore, la pollution mondiale et régionale de l'air, le Rhin et divers autres sujets. Le nombre de signatures et de ratifications des pays de l'OCDE et des autres pays ainsi que la date d'entrée en vigueur sont donnés. La liste ne contient que les conventions multilatérales signées ou ratifiées par au moins un pays de l'OCDE.

Des efforts pour améliorer l'environnement ont été faits au niveau international. Les dimensions internationales des problèmes environnementaux (problèmes régionaux, problèmes transfrontaliers, problèmes globaux, problèmes commerciaux) sont de plus en plus reconnues.

MULTILATERAL CONVENTIONS ON THE ENVIRONMENT (a)

No.	Subject		Place and date	Number of parties OECD Signed	Number of parties OECD Ratified	Number of parties Total Signed	Number of parties Total Ratified	Entry into Force

GENERAL

No.		Subject	Place and date	OECD Signed	OECD Ratified	Total Signed	Total Ratified	Entry into Force
1.01	Treaty-	Antarctic	Washington, 1959	19	19	42	42	23.06.1961
1.01.1		Protocol (environmental protection)	Madrid, 1991	19	5	37	8	pending
1.02	Conv. -	Nordic environmental protection	Stockholm, 1974	4	4	4	4	05.10.1976
1.03	Conv. -	Transfrontier co-operation between territorial communities or authorities	Madrid, 1980	15	15	19	19	22.12.1981
1.04	Conv. -	Control of transboundary movements of hazardous wastes and their disposal	Basel, 1989	24 +EC	22 +EC	90	81	05.05.1992
1.05	Conv. -	Environmental impact assessment in a transboundary context	Espoo, 1991	19 +EC	6	31	8	pending
1.06	Conv. -	Protection of Alps	Salzburg, 1991	5 +EC	2	8	3	06.03.1995
1.07	Conv. -	Transboundary effects of industrial accidents	Helsinki, 1992	18 +EC	2	28	7	pending
1.08	Conv. -	Civil liability for damage resulting from activities dangerous to the environment	Lugano, 1993	6	-	8	-	pending
1.09		North American agreement on environmental co-operation	1993	3	3	3	3	01.01.1994
1.10	Conv. -	Prevention of major industrial accidents (ILO 174)	Geneva, 1993	1	1	..	..	pending
1.11	Conv. -	South Pacific hazardous waste	Waigani, 1995	4	..	..	..	..

ATMOSPHERIC POLLUTION

No.		Subject	Place and date	OECD Signed	OECD Ratified	Total Signed	Total Ratified	Entry into Force
2.01	Agr.-	Adoption of unif. cond. of approv. and recipr. recogn. of approv. for motor veh. equip. and parts	Geneva, 1958	15	15	23	23	20.06.1959
2.02	Conv. -	Protection against hazards of poisoning arising from benzene (ILO 136)	Geneva, 1971	7	7	34	34	27.07.1973
2.03	Conv. -	Prev. and control of occup. hazards caused by carcinog. subst. and agents (ILO 139)	Geneva, 1974	11	11	31	31	10.06.1976
2.04	Conv. -	Protec. of workers against occup. hazards in the working env. due to air poll., noise and vibrat. (ILO 148)	Geneva, 1977	11	11	37	37	11.07.1979
2.05	Conv. -	Long-range transboundary air pollution	Geneva, 1979	21 +EC	21 +EC	41	39	16.03.1983
2.05.1		Protocol (financing of EMEP)	Geneva, 1984	20 +EC	20 +EC	35	35	28.01.1988
2.05.2		Protocol (reduction of sulphur emissions or their transboundary fluxes by at least 30 %)	Helsinki, 1985	13	13	21	21	02.09.1987
2.05.3		Protocol (control of emissions of nitrogen oxides or their transboundary fluxes)	Sofia, 1988	18 +EC	16 +EC	28	25	14.02.1991
2.05.4		Protocol (control of emissions of volatile organic compounds or their transboundary fluxes)	Geneva, 1991	18 +EC	10	23	11	pending
2.05.5		Protocol (sulphur emission ceilings and percentage emission reduction)	Oslo, 1994	17 +EC	..	28	..	..
2.06	Conv. -	Protection of the ozone layer	Vienna, 1985	25 +EC	25 +EC	152	151	22.09.1988
2.06.1		Protocol (substances that deplete the ozone layer)	Montreal, 1987	25 +EC	25 +EC	150	149	01.01.1989
2.06.2		Amendment to protocol	London, 1990	24 +EC	24 +EC	102	102	10.08.1992
2.06.3		Amendment to protocol	Copenhagen, 1992	17	17	45	45	14.06.1994
2.07	Conv. -	Framework convention on climate change	New York, 1992	24 +EC	23 +EC	174	128	21.03.1994

INLAND WATER POLLUTION

No.		Subject	Place and date	OECD Signed	OECD Ratified	Total Signed	Total Ratified	Entry into Force
3.01	Agr. -	Protection of Lake Constance against pollution	Steckborn, 1960	3	3	3	3	10.11.1960
3.01.1		Regulation (water withdrawal)	Bern, 1966	3	3	3	3	25.11.1967
3.02	Prot. -	Constitution of an int'l commission for the protection of the Mosel against pollution	Paris, 1961	3	3	3	3	01.07.1962
3.02.1		Complementary protocol (int'l commi. for the protection of Mosel and Sarre)	Brussels, 1990	3	3	3	3	01.01.1993
3.02.2		2nd compl.prot. (to int'l comm. prot. of Mosel & Sarre, and to first compl. prot.)	Maria Laach, 1992	3	3	3	3	pending
3.03	Agr. -	International commission for the protection of the Rhine against pollution	Bern, 1963	5 +EC	5 +EC	6	6	01.05.1965
3.03.1		Supplementary agreement	Bonn, 1976	5 +EC	5 +EC	6	6	01.02.1979
3.03.2	Conv. -	Protection of the Rhine against chemical pollution	Bonn, 1976	5 +EC	5 +EC	6	6	01.02.1979
3.03.3	Conv. -	Protection of the Rhine from pollution by chlorides (modified by exchanges of letters)	Bonn, 1976	5	5	5	5	05.07.1985
3.03.3.1		Protocol	Brussels, 1991	5	5	5	5	pending
3.04	Agr. -	Restriction of the use of certain detergents in washing and cleaning products	Strasbourg, 1968	10	10	10	10	16.02.1971
3.04.1		Protocol	Strasbourg, 1983	7	5	7	5	01.11.1984
3.05	Conv. -	Protection and use of transboundary water courses and international lakes	Helsinki, 1992	16 +EC	6	27	10	pending
3.06	Conv. -	Co-operation for the protection and sust. use of the Danube river	Sofia, 1994	2	-	9	-	pending

SEA POLLUTION

No.		Subject	Place and date	OECD Signed	OECD Ratified	Total Signed	Total Ratified	Entry into Force
4.01	Conv. -	Limitation of the liability of owners of sea-going ships	Brussels, 1957	7	5	51	45	31.05.1968
4.01.1		Protocol	Brussels, 1979	8	6	13	8	06.10.1984
4.02	Conv. -	International council for the exploration of the sea	Copenhagen, 1964	15	15	17	17	22.07.1968
4.02.1		Protocol	Copenhagen, 1970	15	15	17	17	12.11.1975
4.03	Conv. -	Intervention on the high seas in cases of oil pollution casualties (INTERVENTION)	Brussels, 1969	21	20	69	63	06.05.1975
4.03.1		Protocol (pollution by substances other than oil)	London, 1973	17	16	33	32	30.03.1983
4.04	Conv. -	Civil liability for oil pollution damage (CLC)	Brussels, 1969	23	22	92	89	19.06.1975
4.04.1		Protocol	London, 1976	21	21	49	49	08.04.1981
4.04.2		Protocol	London, 1992	10	5	14	6	pending
4.05	Conv. -	International fund for compensation for oil pollution damage (FUND)	Brussels, 1971	21	19	67	64	16.10.1978
4.05.1		Protocol	London, 1976	17	17	29	29	22.11.1994
4.05.2		Protocol	London, 1992	10	5	14	6	pending
4.06	Agr. -	Co-operation in taking measures against pollution of the sea by oil	Copenhagen, 1971	4	4	4	4	16.10.1971

Notes: see page 297 / voir page 297

... / ...

MULTILATERAL CONVENTIONS ON THE ENVIRONMENT (a)

No.	Subject		Place and date	OECD Signed	OECD Ratified	Total Signed	Total Ratified	Entry into Force
4.07	Conv. -	Prevention of marine pollution by dumping of wastes and other matter (LC)	London, Mexico, Moscow, Washington, 1972	23	23	73	73	30.08.1975
4.07.1		Amendments to Annexes (incineration at sea)	1978	21	21	71	71	11.03.1979
4.07.2		Amendments to convention (settlement of disputes)	1978	16	16	19	19	pending
4.07.3		Amendments (annexes)	1980	21	21	71	71	11.03.1981
4.08	Conv. -	Prevention of marine pollution by dumping from ships and aircraft	Oslo, 1972	13	13	13	13	07.04.1974
4.08.1		Protocol	1983	13	13	13	13	01.09.1989
4.09	Conv. -	Prevention of pollution from ships (MARPOL)	London, 1973	14	6	36	25	..
4.09.1		Amendment (segregated ballast)	London, 1978	23	23	92	92	02.10.1983
4.09.1.1		Annex IIi	London, 1978	20	20	71	71	02.10.1983
4.09.1.2		Annex IV	London, 1978	12	12	58	58	02.10.1983
4.09.1.3		Annex V	London, 1978	21	21	73	73	02.10.1983
4.10	Conv. -	Prevention of marine pollution from land-based sources	Paris, 1974	13 +EC	12 +EC	14	13	06.05.1978
4.10.1		Protocol	Paris, 1986	12 +EC	12 +EC	13	13	01.09.1989
4.10.2	Conv. -	Protection of North-East Atlantic marine env. (ex Oslo-1972 and Paris-1974)	Paris, 1992	15 +EC	6	16	3	pending
4.11	Conv. -	Protection of the marine environment of the Baltic Sea area	Helsinki, 1974	4 +EC	4 +EC	10	10	03.05.1980
4.11.1	Conv. -	Protection of the marine environment of the Baltic Sea area (amendment)	Helsinki, 1992	4 +EC	2 +EC	10	4	pending
4.12	Conv. -	Protection of the Mediterranean Sea against pollution	Barcelona, 1976	5 +EC	5 +EC	22	22	12.02.1978
4.12.1		Protocol (dumping from ships and aircraft)	Barcelona, 1976	5 +EC	5 +EC	22	22	12.02.1978
4.12.2		Protocol (pollution by oil and other harmful substances in cases of emergency)	Barcelona, 1976	5 +EC	5 +EC	22	22	12.02.1978
4.12.3		Protocol (pollution from land-based sources)	Athens, 1980	5 +EC	5 +EC	22	21	17.06.1983
4.12.4		Protocol (specially protected areas)	Geneva, 1982	5 +EC	5 +EC	21	21	23.03.1986
4.12.5		Protocol (pollution from exploitation of continental shelf, seabed and subsoil)	Madrid, 1994	3	-	9	-	pending
4.13	Conv. -	Limitation of liability for maritime claims (LLMC)	London, 1976	16	16	26	26	01.12.1986
4.14	Conv. -	Law of the sea	Montego Bay, 1982	22 +EC	5	164	74	16.11.1994
4.14.1		Agreem. - relating to the implementation of part XI of the convention	New York, 1994	22 +EC	3	71	13	16.11.1994
4.15		Memorandum of understanding on port state control	Paris, 1982	14	14	14	14	01.07.1982
4.16	Agr. -	Co-operation in dealing with pollution of the North Sea by oil and other harmful subst.	Bonn, 1983	8 +EC	8 +EC	9	9	01.09.1989
4.16.1		Amendment	Bonn, 1989	8 +EC	8 +EC	9	9	01.04.1994
4.17	Conv. -	Protection and development of the marine environment of the wider Caribbean region	Cartagena, 1983	5 +EC	5	22	19	11.10.1986
4.17.1		Protocol (oil spills)	Cartagena, 1983	5	5	21	19	11.10.1986
4.17.2		Protocol (specially protected areas and wildlife)	Kingston, 1990	5	1	16	3	pending
4.18	Conv. -	Protection of the natural resources and environment of the South Pacific region (SPREP)	Noumea, 1986	5	4	15	11	22.08.1990
4.18.1		Protocol (prevention of pollution by dumping)	Noumea, 1986	5	3	15	10	22.08.1990
4.18.2		Protocol (co-operation in combating pollution emergencies)	Noumea, 1986	5	4	15	11	22.08.1990
4.18.3	Agr. -	South Pacific Regional Environment Programme (SPREP)	Apia, 1993	4	2	15	9	pending
4.19	Conv. -	Salvage	London, 1989	14	5	23	12	pending
4.20	Conv. -	Oil pollution preparedness, response and co-operation (OPPRC)	London, 1990	15	11	35	19	13.05.1995
4.21	Agr. -	Co-op. for the protection of the coasts and waters of the North-East Atlantic	Lisbon, 1990	3 +EC	2 +EC	5	3	pending
4.22	Conv. -	Protection of the Black Sea against pollution	Bucharest, 1992	1	1	6	6	15.01.1994
4.23		Memorandum of understanding on port state control in the Asia-Pacific region	Tokyo, 1993	4	4	..	..	in force
FLORA AND FAUNA								
5.01	Conv. -	Preservation of fauna and flora in their natural state	London, 1933	6	4	11	9	14.01.1936
5.02	Conv. -	Nature protection and wild life preservation in the Western Hemisphere	Washington, 1940	2	2	22	19	01.05.1942
5.03	Conv. -	Regulation of whaling	Washington, 1946	18	18	48	48	10.11.1948
5.03.1		Protocol	Washington, 1956	17	17	43	43	04.05.1959
5.04	Conv. -	Protection of birds	Paris, 1950	13	9	16	10	17.01.1963
5.05	Agr. -	Plant protection for the Asia and Pacific region	Rome, 1956	6	6	25	25	02.07.1956
5.06	Conv. -	Conservation of North Pacific fur seals	Washington, 1957	3	3	4	4	14.10.1957
5.06.1		Extension	Washington, 1969	3	3	..	..	in force
5.07	Agr. -	Measures for the Conservation of Antarctic Fauna and Flora	Brussels, 1964	9	9	17	17	in force
5.08	Conv. -	Wetlands of international importance especially as waterfowl habitat	Ramsar, 1971	25	24	94	91	21.12.1975
5.08.1		Protocol	Paris, 1982	24	23	84	82	01.10.1986
5.09	Conv. -	Conservation of Antarctic seals	London, 1972	11	10	17	16	11.03.1978
5.10	Conv. -	International trade in endangered species of wild fauna and flora (CITES)	Washington, 1973	23	22	134	129	01.07.1975
5.11	Agr. -	Conservation of polar bears	Oslo, 1973	4	4	5	5	26.05.1976
5.12	Conv. -	Conservation of nature in the South Pacific	Apia, 1976	3	3	7	7	28.06.1990
5.13	Conv. -	Conservation of migratory species of wild animals	Bonn, 1979	16 +EC	16 +EC	46	46	01.11.1983
5.14	Conv. -	Conservation of European wildlife and natural habitats	Bern, 1979	19 +EC	19 +EC	34	31	01.06.1982
5.15	Conv. -	Conservation of Antarctic marine living resources	Canberra, 1980	16 +EC	16 +EC	28	28	07.04.1982
5.16	Agr. -	Tropical timber	Geneva, 1983	22 +EC	22 +EC	52	52	01.04.1985
5.16.1		Revised agreement	New York, 1994	2	1	12	4	..
5.17	Conv. -	Biological diversity	Rio de Janeiro, 1992	25 +EC	21 +EC	176	117	29.12.1993
5.18	Agr. -	Conservation of small cetaceans of the Baltic and North Sea	New York, 1992	6 +EC	5	7	5	29.03.1994

Notes: see page 297 / voir page 297

... / ...

MULTILATERAL CONVENTIONS ON THE ENVIRONMENT (a)

No.		Subject	Place and date	Number of parties OECD Signed	Number of parties OECD Ratified	Number of parties Total Signed	Number of parties Total Ratified	Entry into Force
FISHERIES								
6.01	Conv. -	Regulation of the meshes of fishing nets and the size limits of fish	London, 1946	12	12	14	14	05.04.1953
6.01.1		Amendments	Dublin, 1958	12	12	14	14	30.01.1959
6.01.2		Amendments	London, 1960	12	12	14	14	06.05.1960
6.01.3		Amendments	Copenhagen, 1961	12	12	14	14	09.05.1961
6.01.4		Amendments	Hamburg, 1962	12	12	14	14	11.05.1962
6.01.5		Amendments	London, 1963	12	12	14	14	01.06.1963
6.02	Conv. -	Establishment of an inter-American tropical tuna commission	Washington, 1949	3	3	10	10	03.03.1950
6.03	Conv. -	High seas fisheries of the North Pacific Ocean	Tokyo, 1952	3	3	3	3	12.06.1953
6.03.1		Protocol	Tokyo, 1978	3	3	3	3	15.02.1979
6.03.2		Conv. - Conservation anadromous stocks (North Pacific Ocean)	Moscow, 1992	3	1	4	1	pending
6.04	Conv. -	Fishing and conservation of the living resources of the high seas	Geneva, 1958	16	12	57	36	20.03.1966
6.05	Agr. -	Protection of the salmon in the Baltic Sea	Stockholm, 1962	3	3	4	4	01.03.1966
6.05.1		Protocol	Stockholm, 1972	3	3	4	4	24.11.1976
6.06	Conv. -	Fisheries	London, 1964	12	11	13	12	15.03.1966
6.07	Conv. -	International convention for the conservation of Atlantic tunas (ICCAT)	Rio de Janeiro, 1966	6	6	24	23	21.03.1969
6.08	Conv. -	Conduct of fishing operations in the North Atlantic	London, 1967	15	12	17	13	26.09.1976
6.09	Conv. -	Conservation of the living resources of the Southeast Atlantic	Rome, 1969	5	5	17	17	24.10.1971
6.10	Conv. -	Fishing and conservation of the living resources in the Baltic Sea and the Belts	Gdansk, 1973	2 +EC	2 +EC	7	7	28.07.1974
6.10.1		Amendments	Warsaw, 1982	2 +EC	2 +EC	7	7	10.02.1984
6.11	Conv. -	Future multilateral co-operation in the Northwest Atlantic fisheries (NAFO)	Ottawa, 1978	5 +EC	5 +EC	17	17	01.01.1979
6.12	Conv. -	South Pacific Forum Fisheries Agency	Honiara, 1979	2		16	16	10.07.1979
6.13	Conv. -	Multilateral co-operation in North-East Atlantic fisheries	London, 1980	6 +EC	6 +EC	11	10	17.03.1982
6.14	Conv. -	Conservation of salmon in the North Atlantic Ocean	Reykjavik, 1982	7 +EC	7 +EC	9	9	01.10.1983
6.15	Treaty -	South Pacific fisheries	Port Moresby, 1987	3	3	13	13	..
6.16	Conv. -	Prohibition of fishing with long driftnets in the South Pacific	Wellington, 1989	4	3	15	7	17.05.1991
6.17	Conv. -	Conservation of Southern Pacific Bluefin Tuna	Canberra, 1993	3	3	3	3	in force
6.18	Conv. -	Conservation and management of pollock resources in the Central Bering Sea	Washington, 1994	2	-	6	-	pending
NUCLEAR								
7.01	Conv. -	Third party liability in the field of nuclear energy	Paris, 1960	17	14	17	14	01.04.1968
7.01.1		Supplementary convention	Brussels, 1963	14	11	14	11	04.12.1974
7.01.2		Additional protocol to the convention	Paris, 1964	17	14	17	14	01.04.1968
7.01.3		Additional protocol to the supplementary convention	Paris, 1964	14	11	14	11	04.12.1974
7.01.4		Protocol amending the convention	Brussels, 1982	17	14	17	14	07.10.1988
7.01.5		Protocol amending the supplementary convention	Brussels, 1982	14	11	14	11	01.08.1991
7.01.6		Joint protocol relating to the application of the Vienna Convention and the Paris Convention	Vienna, 1988	15	5	23	10	27.04.1992
7.02	Conv. -	Liability of operators of nuclear ships	Brussels, 1962	5	2	17	3	pending
7.03	Conv. -	Civil liability for nuclear damage	Vienna, 1963	3	1	28	24	12.11.1977
7.03.1		Joint protocol relating to the application of the Vienna Convention and the Paris Convention	Vienna, 1988	15	6	29	17	27.04.1992
7.04	Treaty -	Banning nuclear weapon tests in the atmosphere, in outer space and under water	Moscow, 1963	24	23	130	118	10.10.1963
7.05	Conv. -	Civil liability in maritime carriage of nuclear material	Brussels, 1971	12	10	18	14	15.07.1975
7.06	Conv. -	Prohib.emplacement of nuclear and mass destruct. weapons on sea-bed, ocean floor & subsoil	London, Moscow, Washington, 1971	24	24	108	86	18.05.1972
7.07	Conv. -	South Pacific nuclear free zone treaty	Rarotonga, 1985	2	2	11	11	11.12.1986
7.08	Conv. -	Early notification of a nuclear accident	Vienna, 1986	25	23	95	74	23.10.1987
7.09	Conv. -	Assistance in the case of a nuclear accident or radiological emergency	Vienna, 1986	24	19	94	70	26.02.1987
7.10	Conv. -	Nuclear safety	Vienna, 1994	22	1	54	1	pending
MISCELLANEOUS								
8.01	Conv. -	Road traffic	Geneva, 1949	23	22	91	90	26.03.1952
8.02	Agr. -	International carriage of dangerous goods by road (ADR)	Geneva, 1957	16	16	25	25	29.01.1968
8.02.1		Protocol	New York, 1975	15	15	18	18	19.04.1985
8.03	Conv. -	Protection of animals during international transport	Paris, 1968	19	19	22	22	20.02.1971
8.03.1		Protocol	Strasbourg, 1979	18	18	21	21	07.11.1989
8.04	Conv. -	Protection of the archaeological heritage	London, 1969	14	14	23	23	20.11.1970
8.05	Conv. -	Transport of goods by rail (CIM)	Bern, 1970	18	18	33	33	01.01.1975
8.06	Conv. -	Safe container (CSC)	Geneva, 1972	24	21	64	61	06.09.1977
8.07	Conv. -	International liability for damage caused by space objects	London, Moscow, Washington, 1972	23	21	101	74	01.09.1972
8.08	Conv. -	Protection of the world cultural and natural heritage	Paris, 1972	23	23	139	139	17.12.1975
8.09	Conv. -	Civil liab. for damage caused during carriage of dang. goods by road, rail, and inland navig. (CRTD)	Geneva, 1989	1	-	2	-	pending
8.10	Conv. -	Combat desertification in those countries experiencing to serious drought and/or desertification	Paris, 1994	21 +EC	..	101	..	..

Notes:
a) Ratifications: includes accessions, acceptances, approvals and successions.

Source: Bonn Agreement, UNECE, Council of Europe, IAEA, ILO, IMO, IUCN - Environmental Law Centre, OECD, UN, UNEP.

CONVENTIONS MULTILATÉRALES CONCERNANT L'ENVIRONNEMENT (a)

N°	Sujet		Lieu et date	Nombre de parties				Entrée en vigueur
				OCDE		Total		
				Signé	Ratifié	Signé	Ratifié	
GÉNÉRAL								
1.01	Traité -	Antarctique	Washington, 1959	19	19	42	42	23.06.1961
1.01.1		Protocole - (protection de l'environnement)	Madrid, 1991	19	5	37	8	en cours
1.02	Conv. -	Protection de l'environnement nordique	Stockholm, 1974	4	4	4	4	05.10.1976
1.03	Conv. -	Coopération transfrontalière des collectivés ou autorités territoriales	Madrid, 1980	15	15	19	19	22.12.1981
1.04	Conv. -	Contrôle des mouvements transfrontières de déchets dangereux et leur élimination	Bâle, 1989	24 +EC	22 +EC	90	81	05.05.1992
1.05	Conv. -	Évaluation de l'impact sur l'environnement dans un contexte transfrontière	Espoo, 1991	19 +EC	6	31	8	en cours
1.06	Conv. -	Protection des Alpes	Salzburg , 1991	5 +EC	2	8	3	06.03.1995
1.07	Conv. -	Effets transfrontières des accidents industriels	Helsinki, 1992	18 +EC	2	28	7	en cours
1.08	Conv. -	Responsabilité civile des dommages résultant d'activités dangereuses pour l'environnement	Lugano, 1993	6	-	8	-	en cours
1.09		Accord nord américain de coopération dans le domaine de l'environnement	1993	3	3	3	3	01.01.1994
1.10	Conv. -	Prévention des accidents industriels majeurs (OIT 174)	Genève, 1993	1	1	..	..	en cours
1.11	Conv. -	Déchets dangereux dans le Pacifique Sud	Waigani, 1995	4	..	..	..	..
POLLUTION ATMOSPHÉRIQUE								
2.01	Accord -	Adop. de cond. unif. d'homologation et reconnaiss. réciproque de l'homolog. des équip.et pièces des véh.	Genève, 1958	15	15	23	23	20.06.1959
2.02	Conv. -	Protection contre les risques d'intoxication dus au benzène (OIT 136)	Genève, 1971	7	7	34	34	27.07.1973
2.03	Conv. -	Prévention et contrôle des risques professionnels causés par les substances et agents cancérogènes (OIT 139)	Genève, 1974	11	11	31	31	10.06.1976
2.04	Conv. -	Protection des travailleurs contre les risques profess. dus à la pollution de l'air, au bruit et aux vibrations (OIT 148)	Genève, 1977	11	11	37	37	11.07.1979
2.05	Conv. -	Pollution atmosphérique transfrontière à longue distance	Genève, 1979	21 +EC	21 +EC	41	39	16.03.1983
2.05.1		Protocole (financement du programme EMEP)	Genève, 1984	20 +EC	20 +EC	35	35	28.01.1988
2.05.2		Protocole (réduction des émissions de soufre ou de leurs flux transfrontières d'au moins 30 pour cent)	Helsinki, 1985	13	13	21	21	02.09.1987
2.05.3		Protocole (lutte contre les émissions d'oxydes d'azote ou de leurs flux transfrontières)	Sofia, 1988	18 +EC	16 +EC	28	25	14.02.1991
2.05.4		Protocole (lutte contre les émissions des composés organiques volatils ou de leurs flux transfrontières)	Genève, 1991	18 +EC	10	23	11	en cours
2.05.5		Protocole (plafonds relatifs aux émissions de soufre et pourcentages de réduction)	Oslo, 1994	17 +EC	..	28	..	en cours
2.06	Conv. -	Protection de la couche d'ozone	Vienne, 1985	25 +EC	25 +EC	152	151	22.09.1988
2.06.1		Protocole (substances qui appauvrissent la couche d'ozone)	Montréal, 1987	25 +EC	25 +EC	150	149	01.01.1989
2.06.2		Amendement au protocole	Londres, 1990	24 +EC	24 +EC	102	102	10.08.1992
2.06.3		Amendement au protocole	Copenhague, 1992	17	17	45	45	14.06.1994
2.07	Conv. -	Convention-cadre sur les changements climatiques	New York, 1992	24 +EC	23 +EC	174	128	21.03.1994
POLLUTION DES EAUX INTÉRIEURES								
3.01	Accord -	Protection du lac de Constance contre la pollution	Steckborn, 1960	3	3	3	3	10.11.1960
3.01.1		Réglementation (prélèvements d'eau)	Berne, 1966	3	3	3	3	25.11.1967
3.02	Prot. -	Constitution d'une commission internationale pour la protection de la Moselle contre la pollution	Paris, 1961	3	3	3	3	01.07.1962
3.02.1		Protocole complémentaire (commission internat. pour la protection de la Moselle et de la Sarre)	Bruxelles, 1990	3	3	3	3	01.01.1993
3.02.2		Deuxième prot. complém. (à la comm. de protection de la Moselle et de la Sarre, et au premier prot. compl.)	Maria Laach, 1992	3	3	3	3	en cours
3.03	Accord -	Commission internationale pour la protection du Rhin contre la pollution	Berne, 1963	5 +EC	5 +EC	6	6	01.05.1965
3.03.1		Accord additionnel	Bonn, 1976	5 +EC	5 +EC	6	6	01.02.1979
3.03.2	Conv. -	Protection du Rhin contre la pollution chimique	Bonn, 1976	5 +EC	5 +EC	6	6	01.02.1979
3.03.3	Conv. -	Protection du Rhin contre la pollution par les chlorures (modifiée par échanges de lettres)	Bonn, 1976	5	5	5	5	05.07.1985
3.03.3.1		Protocole	Bruxelles, 1991	5	5	5	5	en cours
3.04	Accord -	Limitation de l'emploi de certains détergents dans les produits de lavage et de nettoyage	Strasbourg, 1968	10	10	10	10	16.02.1971
3.04.1		Protocole	Strasbourg, 1983	7	5	7	5	01.11.1984
3.05	Conv. -	Protection et utilisation des cours d'eau transfrontières et des lacs internationaux	Helsinki, 1992	16 +EC	6	27	10	en cours
3.06	Conv. -	Coopération pour la protection et l'utilisation durable du Danube	Sofia, 1994	2	-	9	-	en cours
POLLUTION MARINE								
4.01	Conv. -	Limitation de la responsabilité des propriétaires de navires de mer	Bruxelles, 1957	7	5	51	45	31.05.1968
4.01.1		Protocole	Bruxelles, 1979	8	6	13	8	06.10.1984
4.02	Conv. -	Conseil international pour l'exploration de la mer	Copenhague, 1964	15	15	17	17	22.07.1968
4.02.1		Protocole	Copenhague, 1970	15	15	17	17	12.11.1975

Notes: see page 301 / voir page 301

... / ...

CONVENTIONS MULTILATÉRALES CONCERNANT L'ENVIRONNEMENT (a)

N°	Sujet		Lieu et date	OCDE Signé	OCDE Ratifié	Total Signé	Total Ratifié	Entrée en vigueur
4.03	Conv. -	Interv. en haute mer en cas d'accident entraînant ou pouvant entr. poll. par les hydrocarbures (INTERVENTION)	Bruxelles, 1969	21	20	69	63	06.05.1975
4.03.1		Protocole (substances autres que les hydrocarbures)	Londres, 1973	17	16	33	32	30.03.1983
4.04	Conv. -	Responsabilité civile pour les dommages dus à la pollution par les hydrocarbures (CLC)	Bruxelles, 1969	23	22	92	89	19.06.1975
4.04.1		Protocole	Londres, 1976	21	21	49	49	08.04.1981
4.04.2		Protocole	Londres, 1992	10	5	14	6	en cours
4.05	Conv. -	Fonds international d'indemnisation pour les dommages dus à la poll. par les hydrocarbures (FUND)	Bruxelles, 1971	21	19	67	64	16.10.1978
4.05.1		Protocole	Londres, 1976	17	17	29	29	22.11.1994
4.05.2		Protocole	Londres, 1992	10	5	14	6	en cours
4.06	Accord-	Coopération concernant les mesures prises contre la pollution des eaux de mer par les hydrocarbures	Copenhague, 1971	4	4	4	4	16.10.1971
4.07	Conv. -	Prévention de la pollution des mers résultant de l'immersion de déchets (LC)	Londres,Mexico, Moscou, Washington, 1972	23	23	73	73	30.08.1975
4.07.1		Amendements aux annexes (incinération en mer)	1978	21	21	71	71	11.03.1979
4.07.2		Amendements à la convention (règlement des différends)	1978	16	16	19	19	en cours
4.07.3		Amendements aux annexes	1980	21	21	71	71	11.03.1981
4.08	Conv. -	Prévention de la pollution marine par les opérations d'immersion effectuées par les navires et aéronefs	Oslo, 1972	13	13	13	13	07.04.1974
4.08.1		Protocole	1983	13	13	13	13	01.09.1989
4.09	Conv. -	Prévention de la pollution par les navires (MARPOL)	Londres, 1973	14	6	36	25	..
4.09.1		Amendement (ballast séparé)	Londres, 1978	23	23	92	92	02.10.1983
4.09.1.1		Annexe III	Londres, 1978	20	20	71	71	02.10.1983
4.09.1.2		Annexe IV	Londres, 1978	12	12	58	58	02.10.1983
4.09.1.3		Annexe V	Londres, 1978	21	21	73	73	02.10.1983
4.10	Conv. -	Prévention de la pollution marine d'origine tellurique	Paris, 1974	13 +EC	12 +EC	14	13	06.05.1978
4.10.1		Protocole	Paris, 1986	12 +EC	12 +EC	13	13	01.09.1989
4.10.2	Conv. -	Prévention de la pollution marine de l'Atlantique nord-est (ex Oslo 1972 et Paris 1974)	Paris, 1992	15 +EC	6	16	3	en cours
4.11	Conv. -	Protection du milieu marin dans la zone de la mer Baltique	Helsinki, 1974	4 +EC	4 +EC	10	10	03.05.1980
4.11.1	Conv. -	Protection du milieu marin dans la zone de la mer Baltique (amendements)	Helsinki, 1992	4 +EC	2 +EC	10	4	en cours
4.12	Conv. -	Protection de la mer Méditerranée contre la pollution	Barcelone, 1976	5 +EC	5 +EC	22	22	12.02.1978
4.12.1		Protocole (immersion effectuées par les navires et aéronefs)	Barcelone, 1976	5 +EC	5 +EC	22	22	12.02.1978
4.12.2		Protocole (pollution par les hydrocarbures et autres substances nuisibles en cas de situation critique)	Barcelone, 1976	5 +EC	5 +EC	22	22	12.02.1978
4.12.3		Protocole (pollution d'origine tellurique)	Athènes, 1980	5 +EC	5 +EC	22	21	17.06.1983
4.12.4		Protocole (aires spécialement protégées)	Genève, 1982	5 +EC	5 +EC	21	21	23.03.1986
4.12.5		Protocole (pollution due à l'exploration et l'exploitation du plateau continental, du fond et du sous sol marin)	Madrid, 1994	3	-	9	-	en cours
4.13	Conv. -	Limitation de la responsabilité en matière de créances maritimes (LLMC)	Londres, 1976	16	16	26	26	01.12.1986
4.14	Conv. -	Droit de la mer	Montego Bay, 1982	22 +EC	5	164	74	16.11.1994
4.14.1		Accord - relatif à la mise en ouvre de la partie XI de la convention	New York, 1994	22 +EC	3	71	13	16.11.1994
4.15		Memorandum d'entente sur le contrôle par l'État du port	Paris, 1982	14	14	14	14	01.07.1982
4.16	Accord-	Coopération contre la pollution mer du Nord par les hydrocarbures et autres subst. dangereuses	Bonn, 1983	8 +EC	8 +EC	9	9	01.09.1989
4.16.1		Amendement	Bonn, 1989	8 +EC	8 +EC	9	9	01.04.1994
4.17	Conv. -	Protection et mise en valeur du milieu marin dans la région des Caraïbes	Cartagène, 1983	5 +EC	5	22	19	11.10.1986
4.17.1		Protocole (déversements d'hydrocarbures)	Cartagène, 1983	5	5	21	19	11.10.1986
4.17.2		Protocole (zones et vie sauvage spécialement protégées)	Kingston, 1990	5	1	16	3	en cours
4.18	Conv. -	Protection des ressources naturelles et de l'environnement de la région du Pacifique Sud (SPREP)	Nouméa, 1986	5	4	15	11	22.08.1990
4.18.1		Protocole (prévention de la pollution résultant de l'immersion des déchets)	Nouméa, 1986	5	3	15	10	22.08.1990
4.18.2		Protocole (coopération dans les interventions d'urgence contre les incidents générateurs de pollution)	Nouméa, 1986	5	4	15	11	22.08.1990
4.18.3	Accord-	Programme environnemental pour la région du Pacifique Sud	Apia, 1993	4	2	15	9	en cours
4.19	Conv. -	Assistance	Londres, 1989	14	5	23	12	en cours
4.20	Conv. -	Préparation, lutte et coopération en matière de pollution par les hydrocarbures (OPPRC)	Londres, 1990	15	11	35	19	13.05.1995
4.21	Accord -	Coopération pour la protection des côtes de l'Atlantique du Nord-Est contre la pollution	Lisbonne, 1990	3 +EC	2 +EC	5	3	en cours
4.22	Conv. -	Protection de la Mer Noire contre la pollution	Bucarest, 1992	1	1	6	6	15.01.1994
4.23		Memorandum d'entente sur le contrôle par l'État du port dans la région de l'Asie-Pacifique	Tokyo, 1993	4	4	..	..	en vigueur

Notes: see page 301 / voir page 301

... / ...

CONVENTIONS MULTILATÉRALES CONCERNANT L'ENVIRONNEMENT (a)

N°	Sujet		Lieu et date	OCDE Signé	OCDE Ratifié	Total Signé	Total Ratifié	Entrée en vigueur
FAUNE ET FLORE								
5.01	Conv. -	Conservation de la faune et de la flore à l'état naturel	Londres, 1933	6	4	11	9	14.01.1936
5.02	Conv. -	Protection de la flore, de la faune et des beautés panoramiques naturelles des pays de l'Amérique	Washington, 1940	2	2	22	19	01.05.1942
5.03	Conv. -	Réglementation de la chasse à la baleine	Washington, 1946	18	18	48	48	10.11.1948
5.03.1		Protocole	Washington, 1956	17	17	43	43	04.05.1959
5.04	Conv. -	Protection des oiseaux	Paris, 1950	13	9	16	10	17.01.1963
5.05	Accord-	Protection des végétaux dans la région de l'Asie et du Pacique	Rome, 1956	6	6	25	25	02.07.1956
5.06	Conv. -	Conservation des phoques à fourrure du Pacifique nord	Washington, 1957	3	3	4	4	14.10.1957
5.06.1		Prolongation	Washington, 1969	3	3	..	..	en vigueur
5.07	Accord-	Mesures convenues pour la conservation de la faune et de la flore de l'Antarctique	Bruxelles, 1964	9	9	17	17	en vigueur
5.08	Conv. -	Zones humides d'importance internationale particulièrement comme habitats des oiseaux d'eau	Ramsar, 1971	25	24	94	91	21.12.1975
5.08.1		Protocole	Paris, 1982	24	23	84	82	01.10.1986
5.09	Conv. -	Protection des phoques de l'Antarctique	Londres, 1972	11	10	17	16	11.03.1978
5.10	Conv. -	Commerce international des espèces de faune et de flore sauvages menacées d'extinction (CITES)	Washington, 1973	23	22	134	129	01.07.1975
5.11	Accord-	Protection des ours blancs	Oslo, 1973	4	4	5	5	26.05.1976
5.12	Conv. -	Protection de la nature dans le Pacifique Sud	Apia, 1976	3	3	7	7	28.06.1990
5.13	Conv. -	Conservation des espèces migratrices appartenant à la faune sauvage	Bonn, 1979	16 +EC	16 +EC	46	46	01.11.1983
5.14	Conv. -	Conservation de la vie sauvage et du milieu naturel de l'Europe	Berne, 1979	19 +EC	19 +EC	34	31	01.06.1982
5.15	Conv. -	Conservation de la faune et flore marines de l'Antarctique	Canberra, 1980	16 +EC	16 +EC	28	28	07.04.1982
5.16	Accord-	Bois tropicaux	Genève, 1983	22 +EC	22 +EC	52	52	01.04.1985
5.16.1		Accord revisé - bois tropicaux	New York, 1994	2	1	12	4	..
5.17	Conv. -	Diversité biologique	Rio de Janeiro, 1992	25 +EC	21 +EC	176	117	29.12.1993
5.18	Accord-	Conservation des petits cétacés de la mer Baltique et de la mer du Nord	New York, 1992	6 +EC	5	7	5	29.03.1994
PECHE								
6.01	Conv. -	Réglementation du maillage des filets de pêche et des tailles limites des poissons	Londres, 1946	12	12	14	14	05.04.1953
6.01.1		Modification	Dublin, 1958	12	12	14	14	30.01.1959
6.01.2		Modification	Londres, 1960	12	12	14	14	06.05.1960
6.01.3		Modification	Copenhague, 1961	12	12	14	14	09.05.1961
6.01.4		Modification	Hambourg, 1962	12	12	14	14	11.05.1962
6.01.5		Modification	Londres, 1963	12	12	14	14	01.06.1963
6.02	Conv. -	Création d'une commission interaméricaine du thon tropical	Washington, 1949	3	3	10	10	03.03.1950
6.03	Conv. -	Pêcheries hauturières de l'océan Pacifique nord	Tokyo, 1952	3	3	3	3	12.06.1953
6.03.1		Protocole	Tokyo, 1978	3	3	3	3	15.02.1979
6.03.2		Conv. - Conservation des ress. d'anadromes (océan Pacifique nord)	Moscou, 1992	3	1	4	1	en cours
6.04	Conv. -	Pêche et conservation des ressources biologiques de la haute mer	Genève, 1958	16	12	57	36	20.03.1966
6.05	Accord-	Protection du saumon dans la mer Baltique	Stockholm, 1962	3	3	4	4	01.03.1966
6.05.1		Protocole	Stockholm, 1972	3	3	4	4	24.11.1976
6.06	Conv. -	Pêche	Londres, 1964	12	11	13	12	15.03.1966
6.07	Conv. -	Convention internationale pour la conservation des thonidés de l'Atlantique (ICCAT)	Rio de Janeiro, 1966	6	6	24	23	21.03.1969
6.08	Conv. -	Exercice de la pêche dans l'Atlantique Nord	Londres, 1967	15	12	17	13	26.09.1976
6.09	Conv. -	Conservation des ressources biologiques de l'Atlantique Sud-Est	Rome, 1969	5	5	17	17	24.10.1971
6.10	Conv. -	Pêche et conservation des ressources vivantes dans la mer Baltique et les Belts	Gdansk, 1973	2 +EC	2 +EC	7	7	28.07.1974
6.10.1		Amendements	Varsovie, 1982	2 +EC	2 +EC	7	7	10.02.1984
6.11	Conv. -	Future coopération multilatérale dans les pêches de l'Atlantique du Nord-Ouest (NAFO)	Ottawa, 1978	5 +EC	5 +EC	17	17	01.01.1979
6.12	Conv. -	Agence arbitrale des pêches du Pacifique Sud	Honiara, 1979	2	2	16	16	10.07.1979
6.13	Conv. -	Future coopération multilatérale dans les pêches de l'Atlantique du Nord-Est	Londres, 1980	6 +EC	6 +EC	11	10	17.03.1982
6.14	Conv. -	Conservation du saumon dans l'Atlantique Nord	Reykjavik, 1982	7 +EC	7 +EC	9	9	01.10.1983
6.15	Traité -	Pêcheries du Pacifique Sud	Port Moresby, 1987	3	3	13	13	..
6.16	Conv. -	Interdiction de la pêche au filet maillant dérivant de grande dimension dans le Pacifique Sud	Wellington, 1989	4	3	15	7	17.05.1991
6.17	Conv. -	Protection du Thon Rouge du Pacifique Sud	Canberra, 1993	3	3	3	3	en vigueur
6.18	Conv. -	Conserv. et gestion des ressources de lieu jaune dans la mer de Béring	Washington, 1994	2	-	6	-	en cours

Notes: *see page 301 / voir page 301*

... / ...

CONVENTIONS MULTILATÉRALES CONCERNANT L'ENVIRONNEMENT (a)

N°	Sujet		Lieu et date	Nombre de parties				Entrée en vigueur
				OCDE		Total		
				Signé	Ratifié	Signé	Ratifié	
NUCLÉAIRE								
7.01	Conv. -	Responsabilité civile dans le domaine de l'énergie nucléaire	Paris, 1960	17	14	17	14	01.04.1968
7.01.1		Conv. complémentaire	Bruxelles, 1963	14	11	14	11	04.12.1974
7.01.2		Protocole additionnel à la convention	Paris, 1964	17	14	17	14	01.04.1968
7.01.3		Protocole additionnel à la convention complémentaire	Paris, 1964	14	11	14	11	04.12.1974
7.01.4		Protocole portant modification de la convention	Bruxelles, 1982	17	14	17	14	07.10.1988
7.01.5		Protocole portant modification de la convention complémentaire	Bruxelles, 1982	14	11	14	11	01.08.1991
7.01.6		Protocole commun relatif à l'application de la Conv. de Vienne et de la Conv. de Paris	Vienne, 1988	15	5	23	10	27.04.1992
7.02	Conv. -	Responsabilité des exploitants de navires nucléaires	Bruxelles, 1962	5	2	17	3	en cours
7.03	Conv. -	Responsabilité civile en matière de dommage nucléaire	Vienne, 1963	3	1	28	24	12.11.1977
7.03.1		Protocole commun relatif à l'application des Conventions de Vienne et de Paris	Vienne, 1988	15	6	29	17	27.04.1992
7.04	Traité. -	Interdisant les essais d'armes nucléaires dans l'atmosphère, dans l'espace extra-atmosphérique et sous l'eau	Moscou, 1963	24	23	130	118	10.10.1963
7.05	Conv. -	Responsabilité civile dans le domaine du transport maritime de matières nucléaires	Bruxelles, 1971	12	10	18	14	15.07.1975
7.06	Traité. -	Interdisant de placer des armes nucléaires et d'autres armes de destruction massive sur le fond des mers et des océans, ainsi que dans leur sous-sol	Londres, Moscou, Washington, 1971	24	24	108	86	18.05.1972
7.07	Conv. -	Sur une zone nucléaire libre dans le Pacifique Sud	Rarotonga, 1985	2	2	11	11	11.12.1986
7.08	Conv. -	Notification rapide d'un accident nucléaire	Vienne, 1986	25	23	95	74	23.10.1987
7.09	Conv. -	Assistance en cas d'accident nucléaire ou de situation d'urgence radiologique	Vienne, 1986	24	19	94	70	26.02.1987
7.10	Conv. -	Sûreté nucléaire	Vienne, 1994	22	1	54	1	en cours
DIVERS								
8.01	Conv. -	Circulation routière	Genève, 1949	23	22	91	90	26.03.1952
8.02	Accord-	Transport international des marchandises dangereuses par route (ADR)	Genève, 1957	16	16	25	25	29.01.1968
8.02.1		Protocole	New York, 1975	15	15	18	18	19.04.1985
8.03	Conv. -	Protection des animaux en transport international	Paris, 1968	19	19	22	22	20.02.1971
8.03.1		Protocole	Strasbourg, 1979	18	18	21	21	07.11.1989
8.04	Conv. -	Protection du patrimoine archéologique	Londres, 1969	14	14	23	23	20.11.1970
8.05	Conv. -	Transport des marchandises par chemins de fer (CIM)	Bern, 1970	18	18	33	33	01.01.1975
8.06	Conv. -	Sécurité des conteneurs (CSC)	Genève, 1972	24	21	64	61	06.09.1977
8.07	Conv. -	Responsabilité internationale pour les dommages causés par les objets spatiaux	Londres, Moscou, Washington, 1972	23	21	101	74	01.09.1972
8.08	Conv. -	Protection du patrimoine mondial, culturel et naturel	Paris, 1972	23	23	139	139	17.12.1975
8.09	Conv. -	Resp. civile pour dommages causés au cours du transp. de march. dangereuses par route, rail ou bateaux de navig. intérieure (CRTD)	Genève, 1989	1	-	2	-	en cours
8.10	Conv. -	Lutte contre la désertification dans les pays gravement touchés par la sécheresse et/ou la désertification	Paris, 1994	21 +EC	..	101	..	..

Notes:
a)   Ratifications: y compris les adhésions, les acceptations, les approbations et les successions.
Source: Accord de Bonn, CEE-NU, Conseil d'Europe, AIEA, BIT, OMI, UICN - Centre de droit d'environnement, OCDE, NU, PNUE.

REFERENCES
RÉFÉRENCES

Most of the data in this Compendium were provided to the Secretariat by Member countries by means of the OECD questionnaire. Further data are drawn from other sources quoted in the Compendium or below.

La plupart des données présentées dans ce compendium ont été fournies au Secrétariat par les pays Membres au moyen du questionnaire OCDE. Des données complémentaires proviennent d'autres sources citées dans ce compendium ou ci-dessous.

ECMT/CEMT*	Trends in Investment; infrastructure, rolling stock and traffic
EMEP-COC	Cooperative Programme for Monitoring and Evaluation of Long-Range Transmission of Air Pollutants in Europe, April 1984
FAO*	Yearbook of Forest Products, Rome, annual publication
FAO*	Production Yearbook, Rome, annual publication
FAO*	Fertilizer Yearbook, Rome, annual publication
FAO*	Yearbook of Fishery Statistics, Rome, annual publication
FEVE	Fédération Européenne du Verre d'Emballage, Bruxelles
IFA	World Fertilizer Consumption Statistics, Paris, annual publication
IMO/OMI	Secretariat of the International Maritime Organization, London
IRF/FRI*	World Road Statistics, Washington, D.C./Geneva, annual publication
IUCN/UICN*	United Nations List of National Parks and Protected Areas, periodic publication
OECD/OCDE*	Main Economic Indicators, Paris, monthly publication
OECD/OCDE*	National Accounts, volume 1, Main Aggregates, Paris, annual publication
IEA-OECD/OCDE-AIE*	Energy Balances of OECD Countries, International Energy Agency, Paris, annual publication
IEA-OECD/OCDE-AIE*	Energy Statistics and Balances in Non-OECD Countries, International Energy Agency, Paris, annual publication
OECD/OCDE*	Review of Fisheries in OECD Member Countries, Paris, annual publication
OECD/OCDE*	Tourism Policy and International Tourism in OECD Member Countries, Paris, annual publication
UNECE/CEENU*	Standard International Classification of Land Use, Geneva, 1989
UNECE/CEENU	Forest Fire Statistics, Geneva, periodic publication
UNECE/CEENU	The Environment in Europe and North America, Annotated Statistics, Geneva, 1992
UNEP/PNUE	Environmental Data Report, New York, biennial publication
UNO/ONU*	Statistics Yearbook, New York, annual publication
UNO/ONU*	Index to the International Standard Classification of All Economic Activities, New York
UNO/ONU	Population and Vital Statistics Report, New York, quarterly publication
USMVMA/ACVMEU	World Motor Vehicle Data, Detroit, annual publication
World Bank/Banque Mondiale*	World Development Report, Washington, D.C., annual publication
WRI	World Resources, New York

---

* publication also available in French / publication également disponible en français

General Abbreviations / Abréviations générales

BOD/DBO	- biochemical oxygen demand	/ demande biochimique en oxygène
Cap/hab	- capita	/ habitant
Cd	- cadmium	/ cadmium
CFC	- chlorofluorocarbons	/ hydrocarbures chlorofluorés
c.i.f./c.a.f.	- cost, insurance, freight	/ coût, assurance, fret
CO	- carbon monoxide	/ monoxyde de carbone
CO_2	- carbon dioxide	/ dioxyde de carbone
COD/DCO	- chemical oxygen demand	/ demande chimique en oxygène
Cr	- chromium	/ chrome
Cu	- copper	/ cuivre
dB(A)	- decibels A-weighted	/ décibel pondération A
DO/OD	- dissolved oxygen	/ oxygène dissous
Exp	- export	/ exportation
f.o.b.	- free on board	/ franco de bord
GDP/PIB	- gross domestic product	/ produit intérieur brut
HC	- hydrocarbons	/ hydrocarbures
Hg	- mercury	/ mercure
Imp	- import	/ importation
Inh/hab	- inhabitant	/ habitant
ISIC/CITI	- International Standard Industrial classification	/ Classification Internationale Type par Industrie
K	- potassium	/ potassium
Mtoe/Mtep	- million tonnes oil equivalent	/ millions de tonnes équivalent pétrole
NO_x	- nitrogen oxides	/ oxydes d'azote
NO_3^-	- nitrates	/ nitrates
PART	- particulate matter	/ particules
Pb	- lead	/ plomb
PCBs/PCB	- polychlorinated biphenyls	/ diphényles polychlorés
pH	- hydrogen power	/ pouvoir hydrogène
SO_x	- sulphur oxides	/ oxydes de soufre
SO_4^{--}	- sulphates	/ sulphates
Toe/Tep	- tonnes of oil equivalent	/ tonnes équivalent pétrole
TWh	- terawatt hour	/ terawatt heure
VOC/COV	- volatile organic compounds	/ composés organiques volatils
CH_4	- methane	/ méthane
PPP/PPA	- purchasing power parities	/ parités de pouvoir d'achat

Country Codes / Codes des pays

AUS	- Australia	/ Australie
AUT	- Austria	/ Autriche
BEL	- Belgium	/ Belgique
CAN	- Canada	/ Canada
DEN	- Denmark	/ Danemark
FIN	- Finland	/ Finlande
FRA	- France	/ France
DEU	- Germany	/ Allemagne
GRC	- Greece	/ Grèce
ICE	- Iceland	/ Islande
IRL	- Ireland	/ Irlande
ITA	- Italy	/ Italie
JAP	- Japan	/ Japon
LUX	- Luxembourg	/ Luxembourg
MEX	- Mexico	/ Mexico
NLD	- Netherlands	/ Pays-Bas
NOR	- Norway	/ Norvège
PRT	- Portugal	/ Portugal
ESP	- Spain	/ Espagne
SWE	- Sweden	/ Suède
CHE	- Switzerland	/ Suisse
TUR	- Turkey	/ Turquie
UKD	- United Kingdom	/ Royaume Uni
USA	- United States	/ Etats Uni

Signs / Signes

..	=	not available	/ non disponible
-	=	nil or negligible	/ nul ou négligeable
.	=	decimal point	/ point décimal
>	=	more than	/ plus que
<	=	less than	/ moins que
%	=	percentage	/ pourcentage
$	=	dollar	/ dollar

Units/Unités

µg	-	micrograms	/ microgrammes	$(1\ \mu g = 10^{-6}\ g)$
mg	-	milligrams	/ milligrammes	$(1\ mg = 10^{-3}\ g)$
g	-	grams	/ grammes	$(1\ g = 0.0353\ oz.)$
kg	-	kilograms	/ kilogrammes	$(1\ kg = 1\ 000\ g = 2.2046\ lb.)$
tonnes	-	metric tons	/ tonnes métriques	$(1\ tonne = 1\ 000\ kg = 0.9842\ tn.l. = 1.1023\ tn.sh)$
kt	-	kilotonne	/ kilotonne	$(1\ 000\ tonnes)$
km	-	kilometres	/ kilomètres	$(1\ km = 1\ 000\ m = 0.6214\ mi.)$
km²	-	square kilometres	/ kilomètres carrés	$(1\ km^2 = 0.3861\ mi.^2)$
ha	-	hectares	/ hectares	$(1\ ha = 0.01\ km^2)$
m³	-	cubic metres	/ mètres cubes	$(1\ m^3 = 1.3079\ cu.td.)$
TWh	-	terawatt hour	/ terawatt heure	$(1\ TWh = 10^{12}\ Wh = 859.8 \times 10^6\ kcal)$
Toe/Tep	-	tonnes of oil equivalent	/ tonnes équivalent pétrole	$(1\ Toe = 10^7\ kcal = 41.868.10^9\ J)$

Country Aggregations

EU (European Union)	Austria, Belgium, Denmark, Finland, France, Germany, Greece, Ireland, Italy, Luxembourg, Netherlands, Portugal, Spain, Sweden, United Kingdom
OECD Europe	All European Member countries of OECD, i.e. EU countries plus Iceland, Norway, Switzerland, Turkey
OECD	All Member countries of OECD, i.e. countries of OECD Europe plus Canada, Mexico, United States, Japan, Australia, New Zealand
North America	Canada, Mexico, United States

N.B.:
- ▸ In this publication "Germany" refers to the entire country, i.e. to the western plus the eastern part. The term "w. Germany" refers to western Germany; the term "e. Germany" refers to eastern Germany only. Country aggregations presented in this publication include Germany whenever possible. Country aggregations including western Germany only are marked with an asterisk.
- ▸ Country aggregations for North America and OECD total include Mexico whenever possible. Country aggregations including Canada and the United States only are marked with two asterisks.

Groupes de pays

UE (Union Européenne)	Autriche, Belgique, Danemark, Finlande, France, Allemagne, Grèce, Irlande, Italie, Luxembourg, Pays-Bas, Portugal, Espagne, Suède, Royaume-Uni
OCDE Europe	Ensemble des pays européens membres de l'OCDE, c.à.d. pays de l'UE CE plus Islande, Norvège, Suisse, Turquie
OCDE	Ensemble des pays membres de l'OCDE, c.à.d. pays de l'OCDE Europe plus Canada, Mexique, Etats-Unis, Japon, Australie et Nouvelle Zélande
Amérique de Nord	Canada, Mexique, Etats-Unis

N.B.:
- ▸ Dans cette publication l'utilisation du terme "Allemagne" se rapporte à l'ensemble du pays, c.à.d. la partie occidentale plus la partie orientale. Le terme "Allemagne occ." se rapporte à l'Allemagne occidentale uniquement ; le terme "Allemagne or." se rapporte à l'Allemagne orientale uniquement. Les groupes de pays présentés dans cette publication incluent l'Allemagne dans son ensemble à chaque fois que cela est possible. Les groupes de pays incluant l'Allemagne occidentale uniquement sont marqués d'un astérisque.
- ▸ Les totaux Amérique du Nord et OCDE incluent le Mexique à chaque fois que cela est possible. Les groupes de pays incluant le Canada et les États-Unis uniquement sont marqués de deux astérisques.

LIST OF THE MEMBERS OF THE GROUP ON THE STATE OF THE ENVIRONMENT
LISTE DES MEMBRES DU GROUPE SUR L'ÉTAT DE L'ENVIRONNEMENT
1995
PRESIDENT: MR. H. SALMI

AUSTRALIA AUSTRALIE	Mr. M. BOOTH Mr. T. FLEMING Mr. A. HAINES	LUXEMBOURG	M. Ch. ZIMMER
		MEXICO MEXIQUE	Ms. C. CORTINAS DE NAVA Mr. G. GONZALES-DAVILA Mr. F. GUILLEN MARTIN
AUSTRIA AUTRICHE	Mr. G. SIMHANDL		
		NETHERLANDS PAYS-BAS	Mr. P. KLEIN Mr. M. LOK
BELGIUM BELGIQUE	M. A. DONEUX M. A. DACHELET		
		NEW ZEALAND NOUVELLE-ZÉLANDE	Mr. J. SHEERIN Mr. R. TAYLOR
CANADA	Ms. A. KERR Mr. P. RUMP Mr. T. WILLIAMSON		
		NORWAY NORVÈGE	Mr. O. NESJE Mr. H.V. SAEBO
DENMARK DANEMARK	Mr. M. D. OLSEN		
		PORTUGAL	Mme. L. GOMES M. P. NUNES LIBERATO Mme. I. MARTINS
FINLAND FINLANDE	Mr. H. SALMI Mr. H. SISULA Mr. E. WAHLSTROM		
		SPAIN ESPAGNE	M. A. GARCIA ALVAREZ M. A. HERRERA PERREDA
FRANCE	M. D. DESAULTY Mme. F. NIRASCOU M. J.L. WEBER		
		SWEDEN SUÈDE	Ms. I. OHMAN Ms. M. NOTTER
GERMANY ALLEMAGNE	Ms. U. LAUBER Mr. W. RADERMACHER Mr. K. TIETMANN		
		SWITZERLAND SUISSE	M. P. RUCH Ms. R. SCHMID
GREECE GRÈCE	Ms. ZOGRAFOU	TURKEY TURQUIE	Ms. S. GUVEN Mr. H. KASNAKOGLU
ICELAND ISLANDE	Ms. E. HERMANNSDOTTIR	UNITED KINGDOM ROYAUME-UNI	Mr. A. BROWN Mr. S. HALL
IRELAND IRLANDE	Mr. L. GRIFFIN	UNITED STATES ÉTATS-UNIS	Mr. J. MORANT Mr. P. ROSS
ITALY ITALIE	M. C. CATTENA M. C. CONSTANTINO M. G. GUIDOTTI M. P. SOPRANO	CEC CCE	Mr. J. ALLEN Mr. J. JESINGHAUS Mr. J. PARKER Mr. T. VAN CRUCHTEN
JAPAN JAPON	Mr. Y. MORIGUCHI Mr. N. TSUKAMOTO		

OBSERVERS / OBSERVATEURS

CZECH Republic Rép. TCHÈQUE	Ms. M. BRCHANOVA	POLAND POLOGNE	Ms. L. DYGAS-CIOLKOWSKA Mr. M. GRZESIAK
HUNGARY HONGRIE	Ms. E. HORVATH Mr. E. SZABO	SLOVAK Republic Rép.SLOVAQUE	Mr. J. BREZAK Mr. B. BEZUCH

OECD SECRETARIAT / SECRÉTARIAT OCDE

Ms. M. LINSTER
Ms. F. ZEGEL

Consultants: Ms. C. BERTUZZI, Ms. P. HEINONEN, Ms. T. COSTA PEREIRA, Mr. A. YANEZ

MAIN SALES OUTLETS OF OECD PUBLICATIONS
PRINCIPAUX POINTS DE VENTE DES PUBLICATIONS DE L'OCDE

ARGENTINA – ARGENTINE
Carlos Hirsch S.R.L.
Galería Güemes, Florida 165, 4° Piso
1333 Buenos Aires   Tel. (1) 331.1787 y 331.2391
Telefax: (1) 331.1787

AUSTRALIA – AUSTRALIE
D.A. Information Services
648 Whitehorse Road, P.O.B 163
Mitcham, Victoria 3132   Tel. (03) 9873.4411
Telefax: (03) 9873.5679

AUSTRIA – AUTRICHE
Gerold & Co.
Graben 31
Wien I   Tel. (0222) 533.50.14
Telefax: (0222) 512.47.31.29

BELGIUM – BELGIQUE
Jean De Lannoy
Avenue du Roi 202 Koningslaan
B-1060 Bruxelles   Tel. (02) 538.51.69/538.08.41
Telefax: (02) 538.08.41

CANADA
Renouf Publishing Company Ltd.
1294 Algoma Road
Ottawa, ON K1B 3W8   Tel. (613) 741.4333
Telefax: (613) 741.5439
Stores:
61 Sparks Street
Ottawa, ON K1P 5R1   Tel. (613) 238.8985
211 Yonge Street
Toronto, ON M5B 1M4   Tel. (416) 363.3171
Telefax: (416)363.59.63

Les Éditions La Liberté Inc.
3020 Chemin Sainte-Foy
Sainte-Foy, PQ G1X 3V6   Tel. (418) 658.3763
Telefax: (418) 658.3763

Federal Publications Inc.
165 University Avenue, Suite 701
Toronto, ON M5H 3B8   Tel. (416) 860.1611
Telefax: (416) 860.1608

Les Publications Fédérales
1185 Université
Montréal, QC H3B 3A7   Tel. (514) 954.1633
Telefax: (514) 954.1635

CHINA – CHINE
China National Publications Import
Export Corporation (CNPIEC)
16 Gongti E. Road, Chaoyang District
P.O. Box 88 or 50
Beijing 100704 PR   Tel. (01) 506.6688
Telefax: (01) 506.3101

CHINESE TAIPEI – TAIPEI CHINOIS
Good Faith Worldwide Int'l. Co. Ltd.
9th Floor, No. 118, Sec. 2
Chung Hsiao E. Road
Taipei   Tel. (02) 391.7396/391.7397
Telefax: (02) 394.9176

**CZECH REPUBLIC – RÉPUBLIQUE
TCHÈQUE**
Artia Pegas Press Ltd.
Narodni Trida 25
POB 825
111 21 Praha 1   Tel. (2) 2 46 04
Telefax: (2) 2 78 72

DENMARK – DANEMARK
Munksgaard Book and Subscription Service
35, Nørre Søgade, P.O. Box 2148
DK-1016 København K   Tel. (33) 12.85.70
Telefax: (33) 12.93.87

EGYPT – ÉGYPTE
Middle East Observer
41 Sherif Street
Cairo   Tel. 392.6919
Telefax: 360-6804

FINLAND – FINLANDE
Akateeminen Kirjakauppa
Keskuskatu 1, P.O. Box 128
00100 Helsinki
Subscription Services/Agence d'abonnements :
P.O. Box 23
00371 Helsinki   Tel. (358 0) 121 4416
Telefax: (358 0) 121.4450

FRANCE
OECD/OCDE
Mail Orders/Commandes par correspondance:
2, rue André-Pascal
75775 Paris Cedex 16   Tel. (33-1) 45.24.82.00
Telefax: (33-1) 49.10.42.76
Telex: 640048 OCDE
Internet: Compte.PUBSINQ @ oecd.org
Orders via Minitel, France only/
Commandes par Minitel, France exclusivement :
36 15 OCDE
OECD Bookshop/Librairie de l'OCDE :
33, rue Octave-Feuillet
75016 Paris   Tel. (33-1) 45.24.81.81
(33-1) 45.24.81.67
Dawson
B.P. 40
91121 Palaiseau Cedex   Tel. 69.10.47.00
Telefax : 64.54.83.26
Documentation Française
29, quai Voltaire
75007 Paris   Tel. 40.15.70.00
Economica
49 rue Héricart
75015 Paris   Tel. 45.78.12.92
Telefax : 40.58.15.70
Gibert Jeune (Droit-Économie)
6, place Saint-Michel
75006 Paris   Tel. 43.25.91.19
Librairie du Commerce International
10, avenue d'Iéna
75016 Paris   Tel. 40.73.34.60
Librairie Dunod
Université Paris-Dauphine
Place du Maréchal de Lattre de Tassigny
75016 Paris   Tel. 44.05.40.13
Librairie Lavoisier
11, rue Lavoisier
75008 Paris   Tel. 42.65.39.95
Librairie des Sciences Politiques
30, rue Saint-Guillaume
75007 Paris   Tel. 45.48.36.02
P.U.F.
49, boulevard Saint-Michel
75005 Paris   Tel. 43.25.83.40
Librairie de l'Université
12a, rue Nazareth
13100 Aix-en-Provence   Tel. (16) 42.26.18.08
Documentation Française
165, rue Garibaldi
69003 Lyon   Tel. (16) 78.63.32.23
Librairie Decitre
29, place Bellecour
69002 Lyon   Tel. (16) 72.40.54.54
Librairie Sauramps
Le Triangle
34967 Montpellier Cedex 2   Tel. (16) 67.58.85.15
Tekefax: (16) 67.58.27.36
A la Sorbonne Actual
23 rue de l'Hôtel des Postes
06000 Nice   Tel. (16) 93.13.77.75
Telcfax: (16) 93.80.75.69

GERMANY – ALLEMAGNE
OECD Publications and Information Centre
August-Bebel-Allee 6
D-53175 Bonn   Tel. (0228) 959.120
Telefax: (0228) 959.12.17

GREECE – GRÈCE
Librairie Kauffmann
Mavrokordatou 9
106 78 Athens   Tel. (01) 32.55.321
Telefax: (01) 32.30.320

HONG-KONG
Swindon Book Co. Ltd.
Astoria Bldg. 3F
34 Ashley Road, Tsimshatsui
Kowloon, Hong Kong   Tel. 2376.2062
Telefax: 2376.0685

HUNGARY – HONGRIE
Euro Info Service
Margitsziget, Európa Ház
1138 Budapest   Tel. (1) 111.62.16
Telefax: (1) 111.60.61

ICELAND – ISLANDE
Mál Mog Menning
Laugavegi 18, Pósthólf 392
121 Reykjavik   Tel. (1) 552.4240
Telefax: (1) 562.3523

INDIA – INDE
Oxford Book and Stationery Co.
Scindia House
New Delhi 110001   Tel. (11) 331.5896/5308
Telefax: (11) 332.5993
17 Park Street
Calcutta 700016   Tel. 240832

INDONESIA – INDONÉSIE
Pdii-Lipi
P.O. Box 4298
Jakarta 12042   Tel. (21) 573.34.67
Telefax: (21) 573.34.67

IRELAND – IRLANDE
Government Supplies Agency
Publications Section
4/5 Harcourt Road
Dublin 2   Tel. 661.31.11
Telefax: 475.27.60

ISRAEL
Praedicta
5 Shatner Street
P.O. Box 34030
Jerusalem 91430   Tel. (2) 52.84.90/1/2
Telefax: (2) 52.84.93
R.O.Y. International
P.O. Box 13056
Tel Aviv 61130   Tel. (3) 546 1423
Telefax: (3) 546 1442
Palestinian Authority/Middle East:
INDEX Information Services
P.O.B. 19502
Jerusalem   Tel. (2) 27.12.19
Telefax: (2) 27.16.34

ITALY – ITALIE
Libreria Commissionaria Sansoni
Via Duca di Calabria 1/1
50125 Firenze   Tel. (055) 64.54.15
Telefax: (055) 64.12.57
Via Bartolini 29
20155 Milano   Tel. (02) 36.50.83
Editrice e Libreria Herder
Piazza Montecitorio 120
00186 Roma   Tel. 679.46.28
Telefax· 678 47 51

Libreria Hoepli
Via Hoepli 5
20121 Milano   Tel. (02) 86.54.46
                      Telefax: (02) 805.28.86
Libreria Scientifica
Dott. Lucio de Biasio 'Aeiou'
Via Coronelli, 6
20146 Milano   Tel. (02) 48.95.45.52
                      Telefax: (02) 48.95.45.48

JAPAN – JAPON
OECD Publications and Information Centre
Landic Akasaka Building
2-3-4 Akasaka, Minato-ku
Tokyo 107   Tel. (81.3) 3586.2016
                      Telefax: (81.3) 3584.7929

KOREA – CORÉE
Kyobo Book Centre Co. Ltd.
P.O. Box 1658, Kwang Hwa Moon
Seoul   Tel. 730.78.91
                      Telefax: 735.00.30

MALAYSIA – MALAISIE
University of Malaya Bookshop
University of Malaya
P.O. Box 1127, Jalan Pantai Baru
59700 Kuala Lumpur
Malaysia   Tel. 756.5000/756.5425
                      Telefax: 756.3246

MEXICO – MEXIQUE
OECD Publications and Information Centre
Edificio INFOTEC
Av. San Fernando no. 37
Col. Toriello Guerra
Tlalpan C.P. 14050
Mexico D.F.
                 Tel. (525) 606 00 11 Extension 100
                      Fax : (525) 606 13 07

Revistas y Periodicos Internacionales S.A. de C.V.
Florencia 57 - 1004
Mexico, D.F. 06600   Tel. 207.81.00
                      Telefax: 208.39.79

NETHERLANDS – PAYS-BAS
SDU Uitgeverij Plantijnstraat
Externe Fondsen
Postbus 20014
2500 EA's-Gravenhage Tel. (070) 37.89.880
Voor bestellingen: Telefax: (070) 34.75.778

NEW ZEALAND
NOUVELLE-ZÉLANDE
GPLegislation Services
P.O. Box 12418
Thorndon, Wellington Tel. (04) 496.5655
                      Telefax: (04) 496.5698

NORWAY – NORVÈGE
Narvesen Info Center – NIC
Bertrand Narvesens vei 2
P.O. Box 6125 Etterstad
0602 Oslo 6   Tel. (022) 57.33.00
                      Telefax: (022) 68.19.01

PAKISTAN
Mirza Book Agency
65 Shahrah Quaid-E-Azam
Lahore 54000   Tel. (42) 353.601
                      Telefax: (42) 231.730

PHILIPPINE – PHILIPPINES
International Booksource Center Inc.
Rm 179/920 Cityland 10 Condo Tower 2
HV dela Costa Ext cor Valero St.
Makati Metro Manila   Tel. (632) 817 9676
                      Telefax : (632) 817 1741

POLAND – POLOGNE
Ars Polona
00-950 Warszawa
Krakowskie Przedmieácie 7   Tel. (22) 264760
                      Telefax : (22) 268673

PORTUGAL
Livraria Portugal
Rua do Carmo 70-74
Apart. 2681
1200 Lisboa   Tel. (01) 347.49.82/5
                      Telefax: (01) 347.02.64

SINGAPORE – SINGAPOUR
Gower Asia Pacific Pte Ltd.
Golden Wheel Building
41, Kallang Pudding Road, No. 04-03
Singapore 1334   Tel. 741.5166
                      Telefax: 742.9356

SPAIN – ESPAGNE
Mundi-Prensa Libros S.A.
Castelló 37, Apartado 1223
Madrid 28001   Tel. (91) 431.33.99
                      Telefax: (91) 575.39.98

Mundi-Prensa Barcelona
Consell de Cent No. 391
08009 – Barcelona   Tel. (93) 488.34.92
                      Telefax: (93) 487.76.59

Llibreria de la Generalitat
Palau Moja
Rambla dels Estudis, 118
08002 – Barcelona
          (Subscripcions) Tel. (93) 318.80.12
          (Publicacions) Tel. (93) 302.67.23
                      Telefax: (93) 412.18.54

SRI LANKA
Centre for Policy Research
c/o Colombo Agencies Ltd.
No. 300-304, Galle Road
Colombo 3   Tel. (1) 574240, 573551-2
                      Telefax: (1) 575394, 510711

SWEDEN – SUÈDE
CE Fritzes AB
S–106 47 Stockholm   Tel. (08) 690.90.90
                      Telefax: (08) 20.50.21

Subscription Agency/Agence d'abonnements :
Wennergren-Williams Info AB
P.O. Box 1305
171 25 Solna   Tel. (08) 705.97.50
                      Telefax: (08) 27.00.71

SWITZERLAND – SUISSE
Maditec S.A. (Books and Periodicals - Livres
et périodiques)
Chemin des Palettes 4
Case postale 266
1020 Renens VD 1   Tel. (021) 635.08.65
                      Telefax: (021) 635.07.80

Librairie Payot S.A.
4, place Pépinet
CP 3212
1002 Lausanne   Tel. (021) 320.25.11
                      Telefax: (021) 320.25.14

Librairie Unilivres
6, rue de Candolle
1205 Genève   Tel. (022) 320.26.23
                      Telefax: (022) 329.73.18

Subscription Agency/Agence d'abonnements :
Dynapresse Marketing S.A.
38 avenue Vibert
1227 Carouge   Tel. (022) 308.07.89
                      Telefax: (022) 308.07.99
See also – Voir aussi :
OECD Publications and Information Centre
August-Bebel-Allee 6
D-53175 Bonn (Germany)   Tel. (0228) 959.120
                      Telefax: (0228) 959.12.17

THAILAND – THAÏLANDE
Suksit Siam Co. Ltd.
113, 115 Fuang Nakhon Rd.
Opp. Wat Rajbopith
Bangkok 10200   Tel. (662) 225.9531/2
                      Telefax: (662) 222.5188

TURKEY – TURQUIE
Kültür Yayinlari Is-Türk Ltd. Sti.
Atatürk Bulvari No. 191/Kat 13
Kavaklidere/Ankara   Tel. 428.11.40 Ext. 2458
Dolmabahce Cad. No. 29
Besiktas/Istanbul   Tel. (312) 260 7188
                      Telex: (312) 418 29 46

UNITED KINGDOM – ROYAUME-UNI
HMSO
Gen. enquiries   Tel. (171) 873 8496
Postal orders only:
P.O. Box 276, London SW8 5DT
Personal Callers HMSO Bookshop
49 High Holborn, London WC1V 6HB
                      Telefax: (171) 873 8416
Branches at: Belfast, Birmingham, Bristol,
Edinburgh, Manchester

UNITED STATES – ÉTATS-UNIS
OECD Publications and Information Center
2001 L Street N.W., Suite 650
Washington, D.C. 20036-4910 Tel. (202) 785.6323
                      Telefax: (202) 785.0350

VENEZUELA
Libreria del Este
Avda F. Miranda 52, Aptdo. 60337
Edificio Galipán
Caracas 106   Tel. 951.1705/951.2307/951.1297
                      Telegram: Libreste Caracas

Subscriptions to OECD periodicals may also be
placed through main subscription agencies.

Les abonnements aux publications périodiques de
l'OCDE peuvent être souscrits auprès des
principales agences d'abonnement.

Orders and inquiries from countries where Distribu-
tors have not yet been appointed should be sent to:
OECD Publications Service, 2 rue André-Pascal,
75775 Paris Cedex 16, France.

Les commandes provenant de pays où l'OCDE n'a
pas encore désigné de distributeur peuvent être
adressées à : OCDE, Service des Publications,
2, rue André-Pascal, 75775 Paris Cedex 16, France.

10-1995

OECD PUBLICATIONS, 2 rue André-Pascal, 75775 PARIS CEDEX 16
PRINTED IN FRANCE
(97 95 16 3) ISBN 92-64-04614-3 - No. 48216 1995